The Complete Peanuts

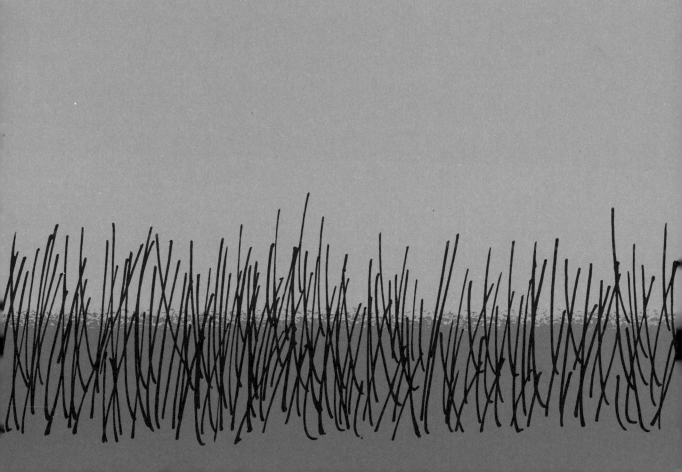

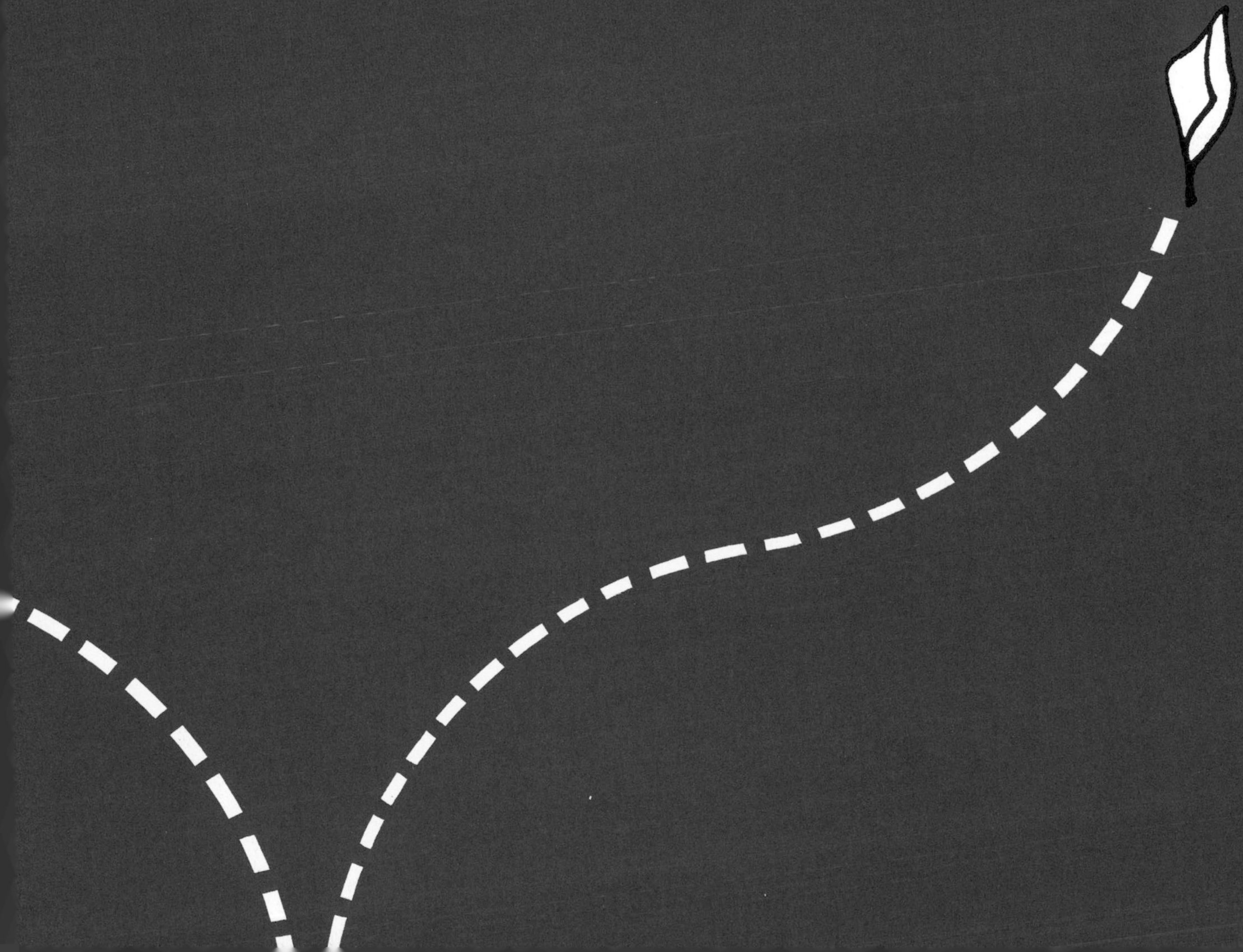

THE COMPLETE PEANUTS
by Charles M. Schulz
published by
Fantagraphics Books

Editor: Gary Groth
Designer: Seth
Production Manager: Kim Thompson
Production, assembly, and restoration: Paul Baresh
Archival and production assistance: Marcie Lee, Stephanie Hayes, and Stephanie Olczyk
Index compiled by Eric Buckler and Sam Schultz
Promotion: Eric Reynolds
Publishers: Gary Groth & Kim Thompson

Special thanks to Jeannie Schulz, without whom
this project would not have come to fruition.
Thanks also to the
Charles M. Schulz Creative Associates,
especially Paige Braddock and Kim Towner.
Thanks for special support from United Media.

Fantagraphics Books, 7563 Lake City Way, Seattle, WA 98115, USA. For a free full-color catalogue of comics,
call 1-800-657-1100. Our books may be viewed on our website at www.fantagraphics.com.

Distributed to the book trade by:

USA: W.W. Norton and Company, Inc.
500 Fifth Avenue, New York, NY 10010
212-354-5500
Order Department: 800-233-4830

CANADA: Diamond Comic Distributors, Inc.
1966 Greenspring Drive, Suite 300, Timonium. MD 21093
Order department: 416-516-0911

ISBN: 978-1-56097-827-5
First printing: July 2008   Printed in China

CHARLES M. SCHULZ

THE COMPLETE PEANUTS

1969 TO 1970

" EVEN MY WINTERS ARE SUMMERS! " pg.18

▫ FANTAGRAPHICS BOOKS ▫

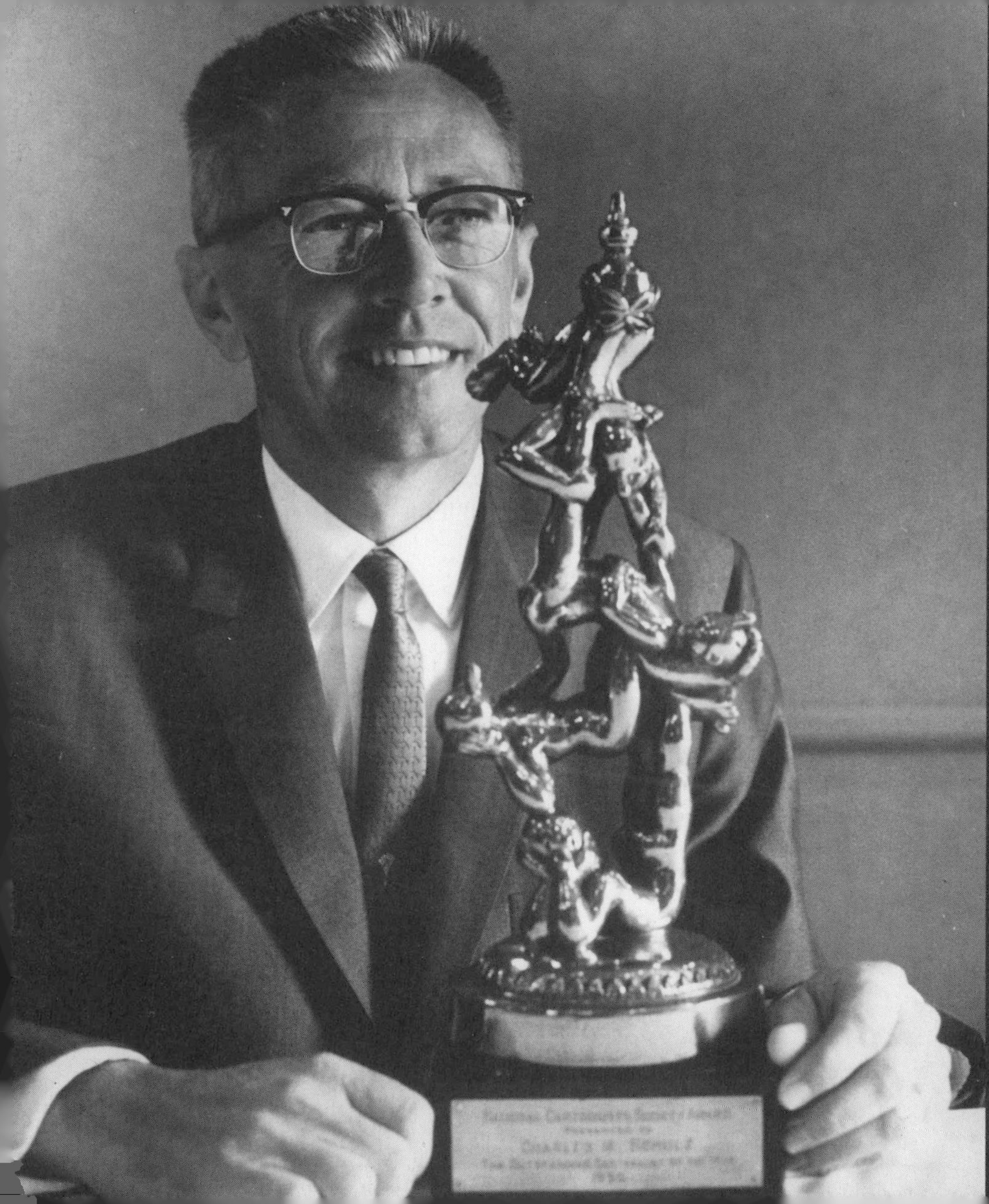

Charles Schulz with his second Reuben award, circa 1964.

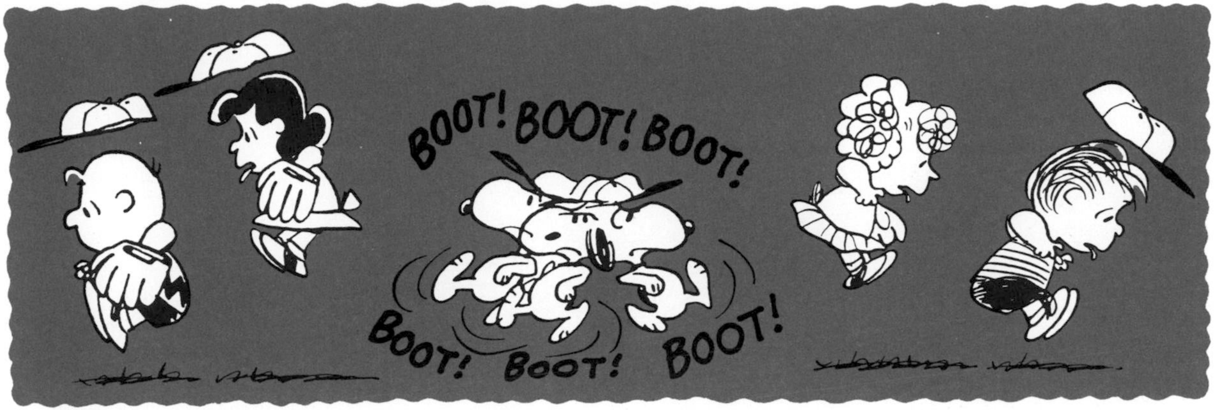
BOOT! BOOT! BOOT!
BOOT! BOOT! BOOT!

FOREWORD by MO WILLEMS

Perhaps this is the wrong venue for a confession, but here it is: I began my career by creating black-market pirated drawings of Snoopy and Charlie Brown.

The year was 1975, and I needed the work. You see, the second grade bully had a weakness for comics, so in return for an original daily *Peanuts* sketch he would pat down his proto-moustache and bully someone else during recess.

Everybody, even preternaturally hairy bullies, loved *Peanuts*.

And why not? Charles Schulz managed to take that one universal emotion, grief, and make it good. Good Grief.

Charlie Brown was the only major cartoon star who wasn't insanely merry. Charlie Brown frowned more than he smiled. Charlie Brown was real.

For me, an immigrants' kid recently plopped into the middle of a small school in the insular world of uptown New Orleans, Charlie Brown was the only one who understood how confused and unhappy I felt. Because he had it worse than me.

Amazingly, even though the real kids at school

didn't like me, they did like what I liked. They also thought Snoopy was cool, and fun to draw. Lucy, hilarious. Schroeder, a brooding genius. Linus, a mensch. *Peanuts* was common ground on the playground.

Like most everyone in my class, I fancied myself to be like one of Charlie Brown's neighbors. I suppose pretending to be Snoopy was the most popular, but I aspired to Linus-ness; to be wise and kind and highly skilled at making gigantic structures out of playing cards.

But that was fantasy. I knew, deep down, that I was Charlie Brown.

I suspect we all did. I suspect we all do.

The how and why of *Peanuts'* genius is a slippery question. But the answer certainly resides in, or more accurately flows through, this collection of strips. Lucy starts off on a strong note by declaring that this year is hers, we meet Woodstock at his dopiest, Snoopy discovers that absolute power is an absolute pain as Head Beagle, Sally vents her paranoid anger at the complexities of Kindergarten, the Little Red Haired Girl leaves town, and (in my favorite series) Lucy feeds Schroeder's toy piano to the kite eating tree!

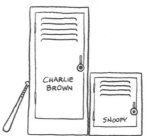

It's an amazingly confident slice of Schulz's career, one where the characters, gags, stories, and draftsmanship are all at their peak.

Linus's security blanket is nowhere to be found.

For me, re-reading the classic strips I grew up with is like going back to the school that nurtured every one of my own cartoon characters from the Pigeon to Sheep in the Big City to Elephant and Piggie. They are all a direct homage to Sparky's secure draftsmanship and insecure characters.

Besides the pacing and drawings and dialog and character, this volume embodies *Peanuts'* great lesson of comic-strip comedy: *never let your characters know they're funny.*

Take poor good old Charlie Brown. He's funny because he faces his obstacles with deadly seriousness. The more impossible, the more absurd, the more hilarious the situation becomes, the less funny it is for Charlie Brown.

It's fun to laugh at that round-headed kid from the safety of our chairs, but we also feel for the poor guy. Too bad he can't see beyond those four skinny daily panels. Too bad he doesn't realize his problems are just jokes in the funny pages, and not *real.*

Sometimes when I am in a deep funk and feel like my life is a constant uphill battle like that of Charles Sisyphus Brown's, I try to stop and imagine someone reading the comic strip of my frustrated life, and laughing.

And that is part of the magic of *Peanuts*; the ability to see-saw between heartfelt empathy for these funny little sketches and the heartless desire to see their lives get worse and worse so that we can laugh more.

It is a balance that very few cartoonists have achieved, and none so brightly, consistently, or charmingly.

Many have spent time arguing that comics in general and Sparky's strip in particular are works of Art. But to me, that misses the point. *Peanuts* isn't Art.

It's *better*.

Art is a single work, or maybe a small collection of pieces, finite and quickly consumed. It hangs in a guarded room, existing only in one place. Any reproductions are inherently inferior to the real thing.

But Sparky's comic strip transcends those petty limitations. Charlie Brown's adventures continue for half a century, and you don't have to make a pilgrimage to experience them. The strip comes to you, into your home, with reproductions that aren't inferior to the work: they *are* the work.

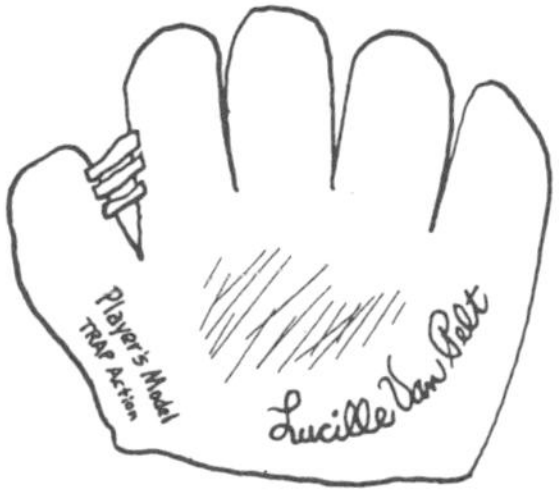
Player's Model
TRAP Action
Lucille Van Pelt

A few months back while touring for one of my books, I managed to sneak an afternoon in at the Charles M. Schulz Museum and Research Center in Santa Rosa, California. Karen Johnson, Jeannie Schulz, and the staff were as generous and affable as you could hope, and they let me spend some time in the vault to dig through their mountains of original *Peanuts* strips.

Yup, I got to hold the original comics that made me giggle every Sunday on my father's lap before I could read, the original comics I read and re-re-read as a kid in piles of dog-eared cheap paperbacks on my bed, the comics that became my creative touchstone as an animator and children's book maker.

And it was, uh, anti-climactic. The originals were too precious to really be enjoyed. I mean, there I was wobblingy holding onto big and floppy pieces of paper with little white gloves; afraid to laugh in case I'd get spittle on the drawings. They weren't comics, I'm sorry to say; they were merely works of Art.

The magic was missing.

It was missing because it's *in* this book. You have Sparky's magic in your hands right now.

Go on, read it. It's here for everyone.

Even second grade bullies.

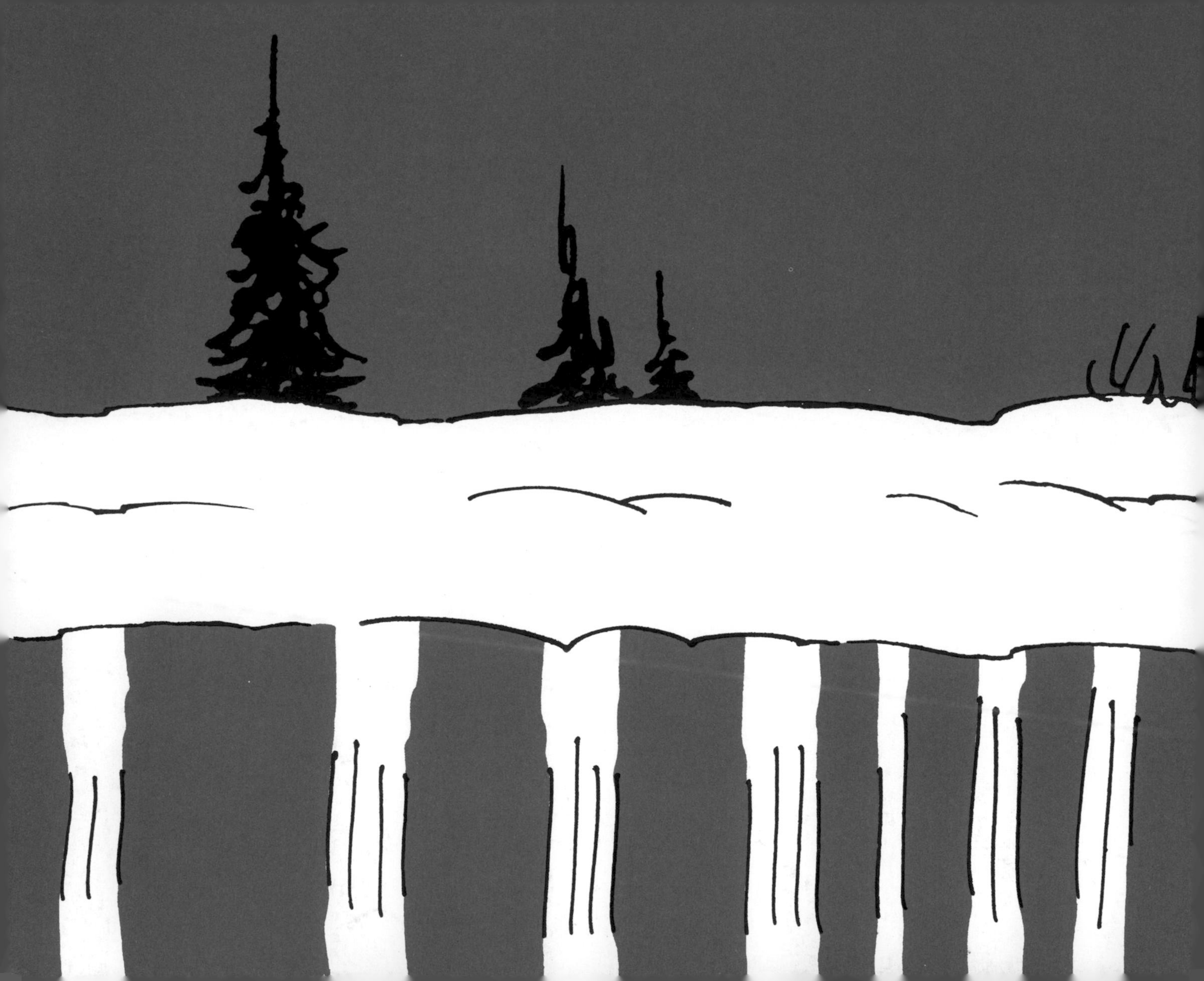

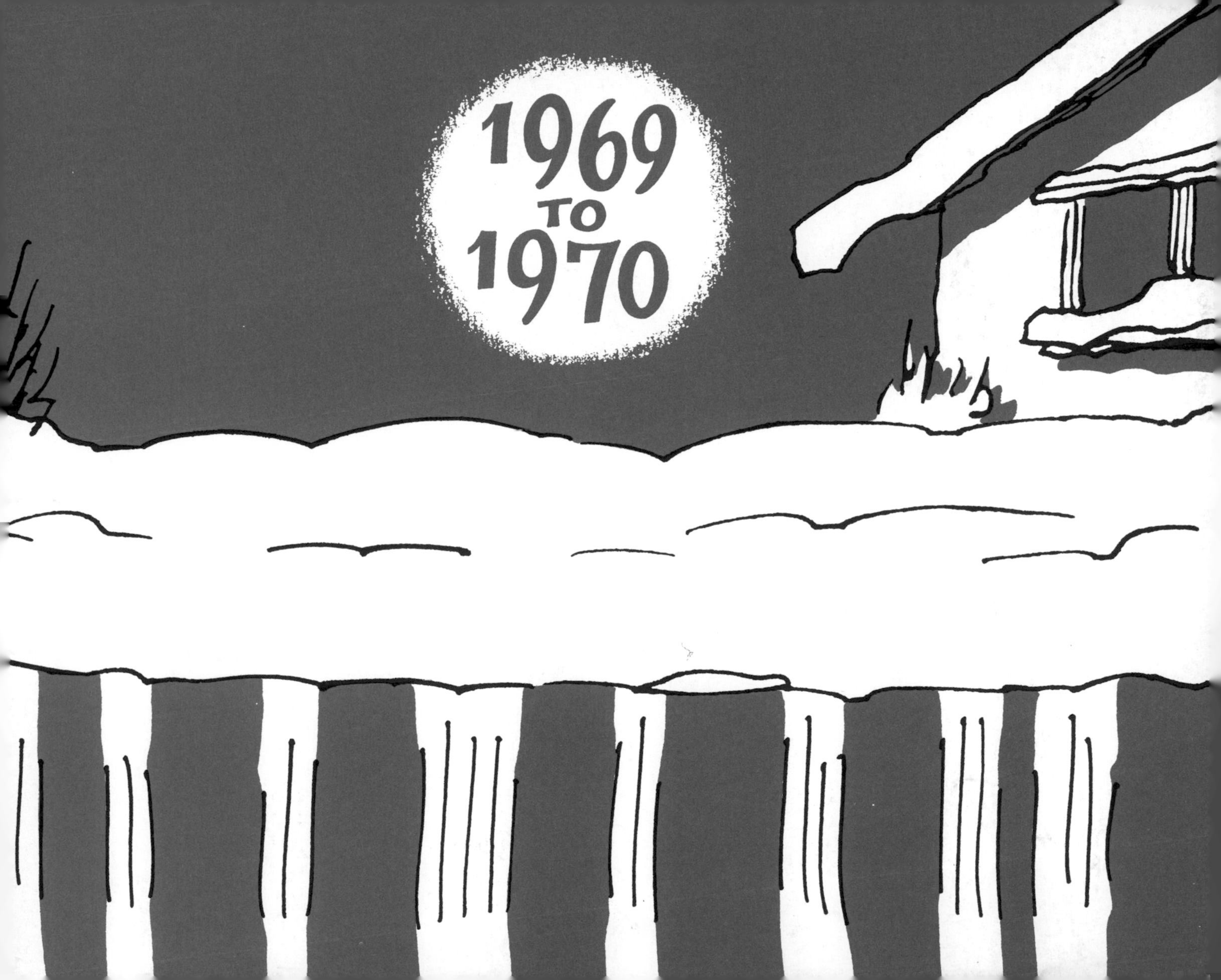
1969
TO
1970

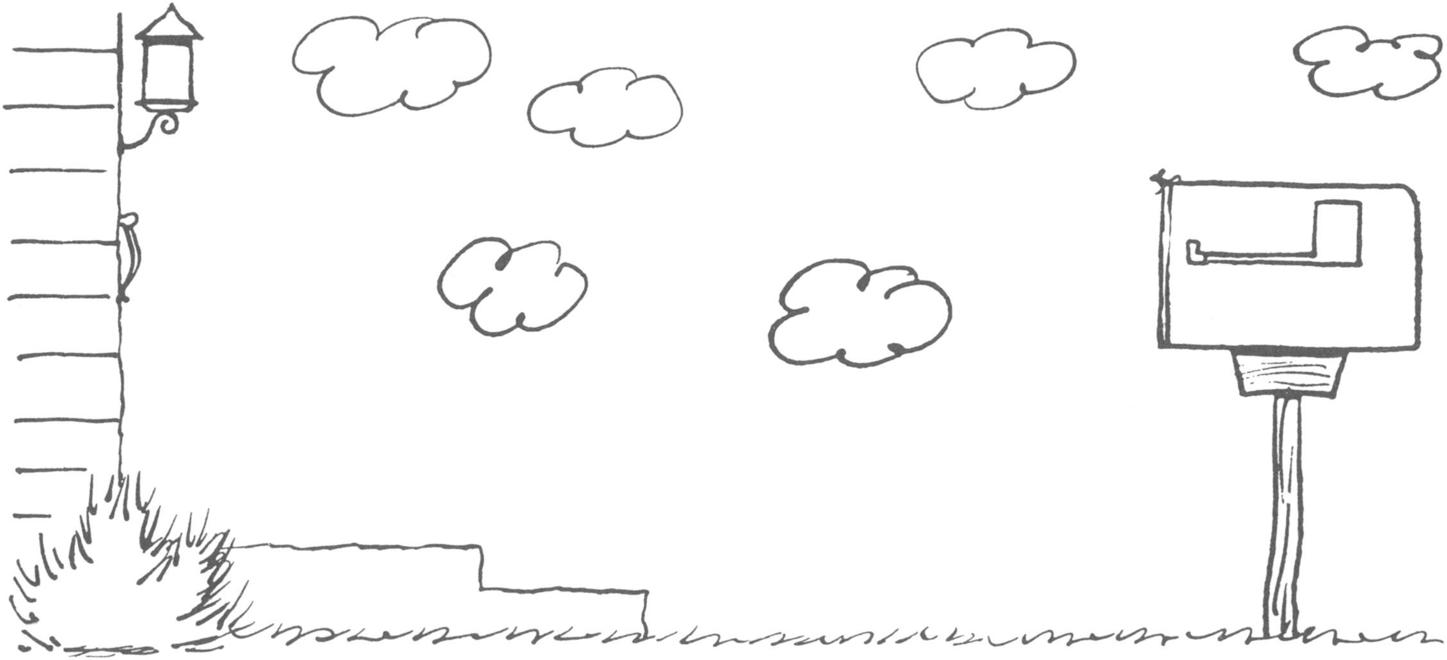

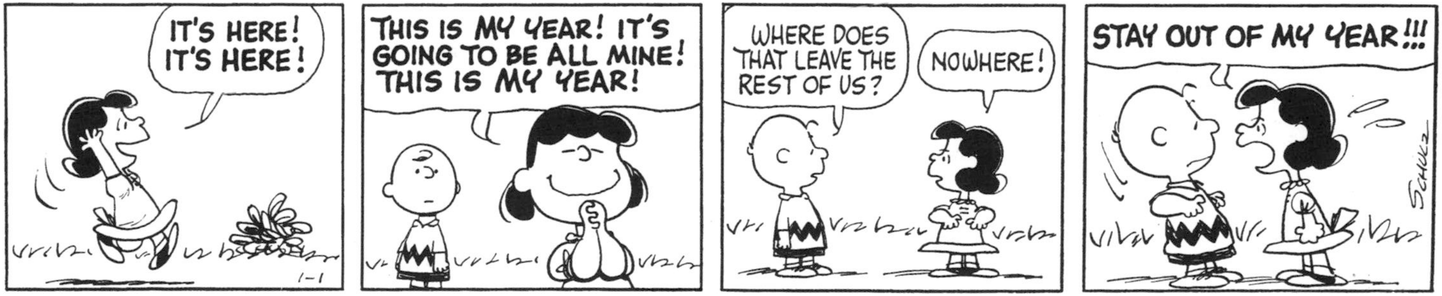
IT'S HERE! IT'S HERE!
1-1
THIS IS MY YEAR! IT'S GOING TO BE ALL MINE! THIS IS MY YEAR!
WHERE DOES THAT LEAVE THE REST OF US?
NOWHERE!
STAY OUT OF MY YEAR!!!
SCHULZ

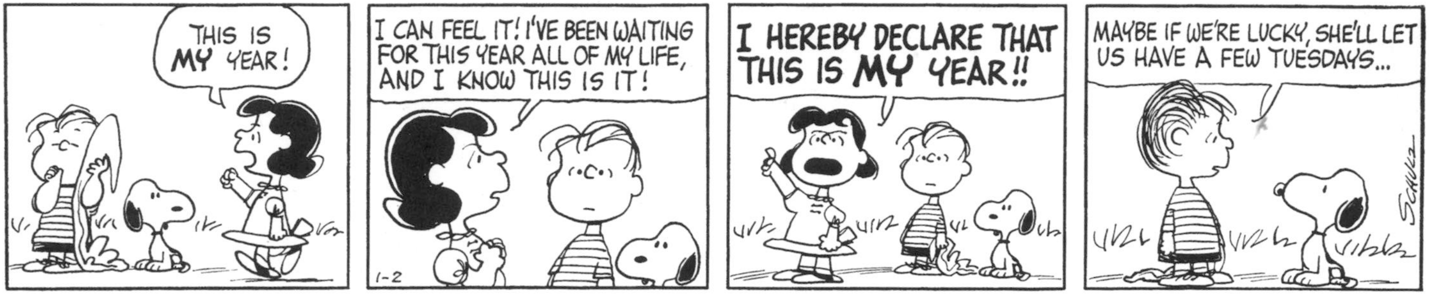
THIS IS MY YEAR!
I CAN FEEL IT! I'VE BEEN WAITING FOR THIS YEAR ALL OF MY LIFE, AND I KNOW THIS IS IT!
1-2
I HEREBY DECLARE THAT THIS IS MY YEAR!!
MAYBE IF WE'RE LUCKY, SHE'LL LET US HAVE A FEW TUESDAYS...
SCHULZ

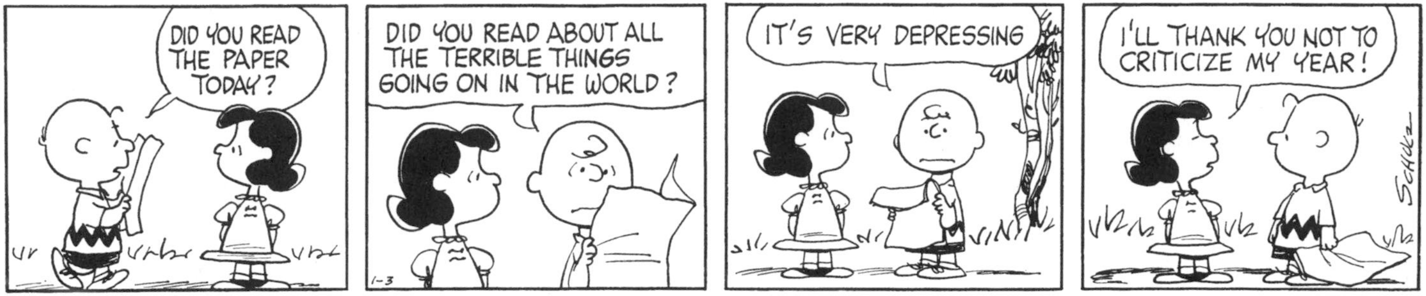
DID YOU READ THE PAPER TODAY?
DID YOU READ ABOUT ALL THE TERRIBLE THINGS GOING ON IN THE WORLD?
1-3
IT'S VERY DEPRESSING
I'LL THANK YOU NOT TO CRITICIZE MY YEAR!
SCHULZ

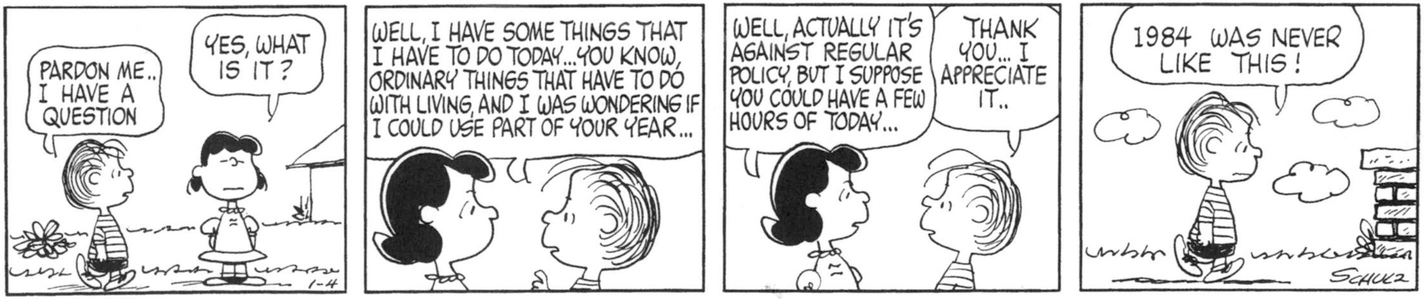
PARDON ME.. I HAVE A QUESTION
YES, WHAT IS IT?
1-4
WELL, I HAVE SOME THINGS THAT I HAVE TO DO TODAY...YOU KNOW, ORDINARY THINGS THAT HAVE TO DO WITH LIVING, AND I WAS WONDERING IF I COULD USE PART OF YOUR YEAR...
WELL, ACTUALLY IT'S AGAINST REGULAR POLICY, BUT I SUPPOSE YOU COULD HAVE A FEW HOURS OF TODAY...
THANK YOU... I APPRECIATE IT..
1984 WAS NEVER LIKE THIS!
SCHULZ

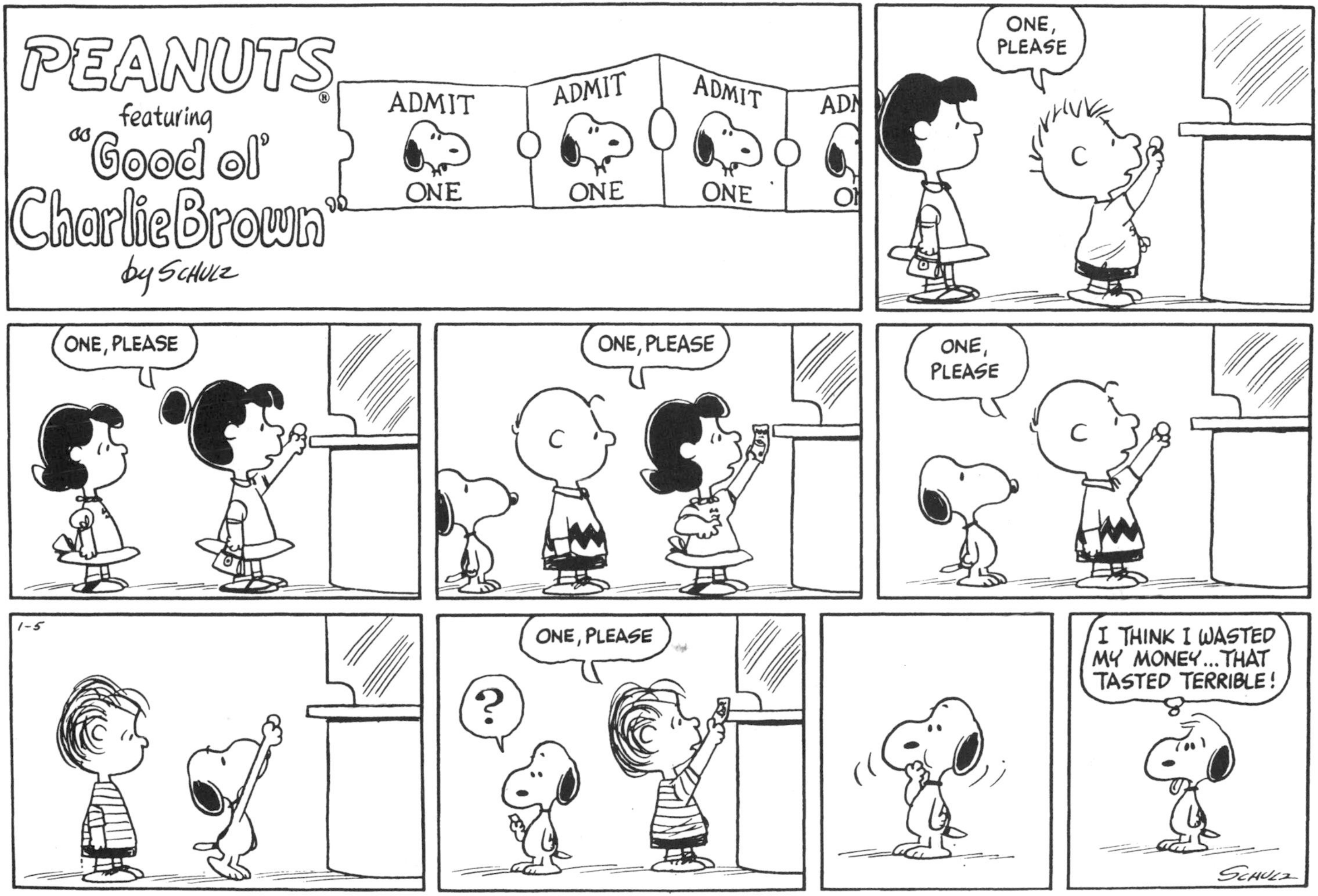
PEANUTS®
featuring "Good ol' Charlie Brown"
by SCHULZ
ADMIT ONE
ADMIT ONE
ADMIT ONE
ONE, PLEASE
ONE, PLEASE
ONE, PLEASE
ONE, PLEASE
1-5
ONE, PLEASE
?
I THINK I WASTED MY MONEY...THAT TASTED TERRIBLE!
SCHULZ

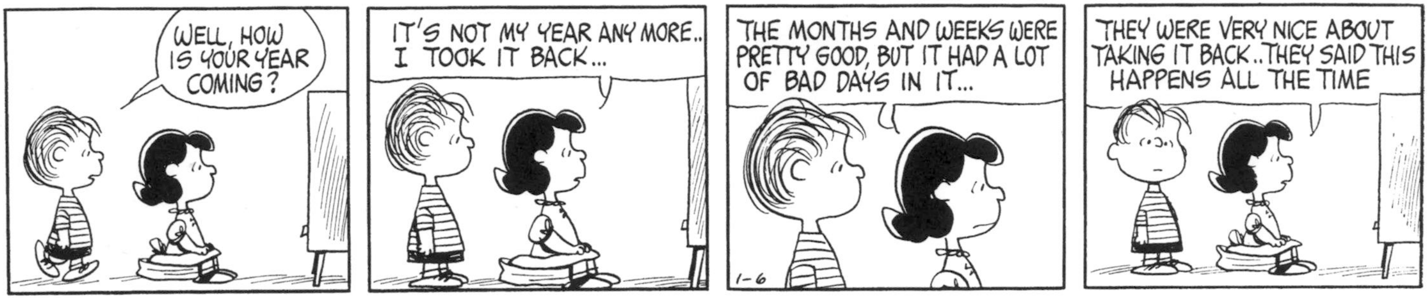
WELL, HOW IS YOUR YEAR COMING?
IT'S NOT MY YEAR ANY MORE.. I TOOK IT BACK...
THE MONTHS AND WEEKS WERE PRETTY GOOD, BUT IT HAD A LOT OF BAD DAYS IN IT...
THEY WERE VERY NICE ABOUT TAKING IT BACK..THEY SAID THIS HAPPENS ALL THE TIME

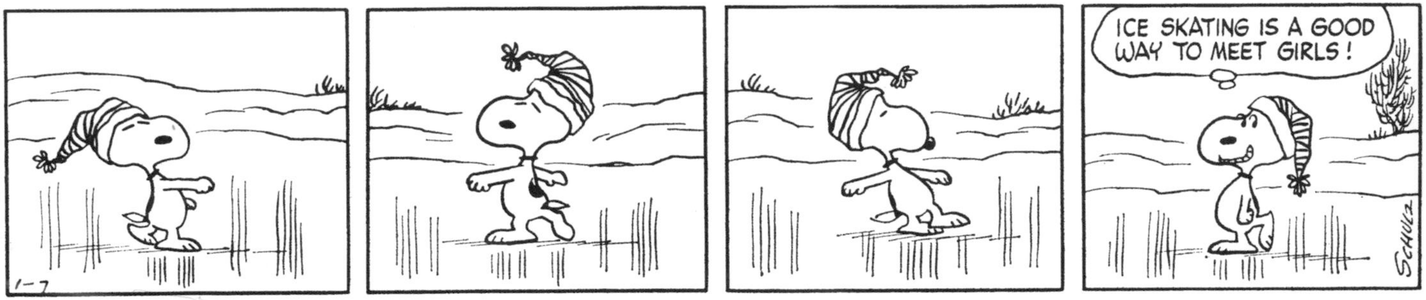
ICE SKATING IS A GOOD WAY TO MEET GIRLS!
SCHULZ

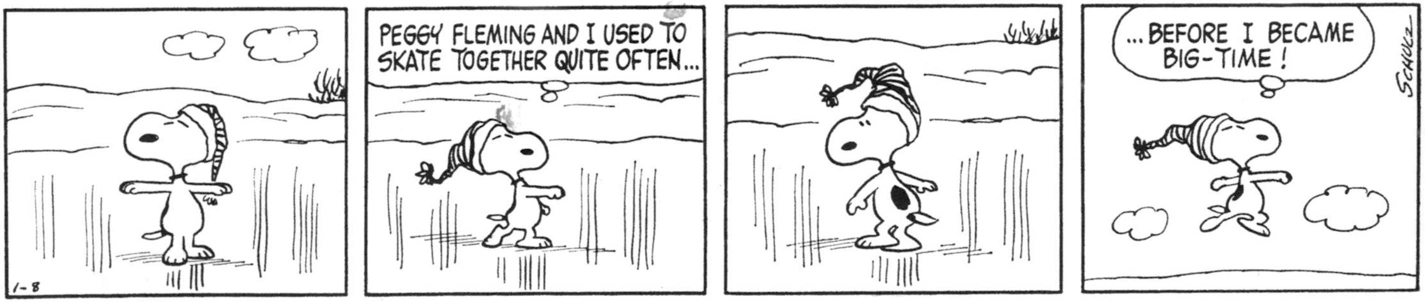
PEGGY FLEMING AND I USED TO SKATE TOGETHER QUITE OFTEN...
...BEFORE I BECAME BIG-TIME!
SCHULZ

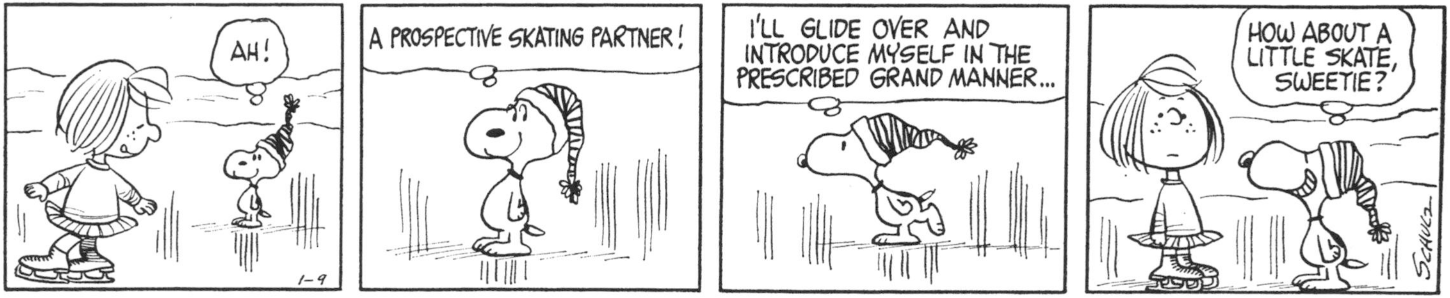
AH!
A PROSPECTIVE SKATING PARTNER!
I'LL GLIDE OVER AND INTRODUCE MYSELF IN THE PRESCRIBED GRAND MANNER...
HOW ABOUT A LITTLE SKATE, SWEETIE?
1-9
SCHULZ

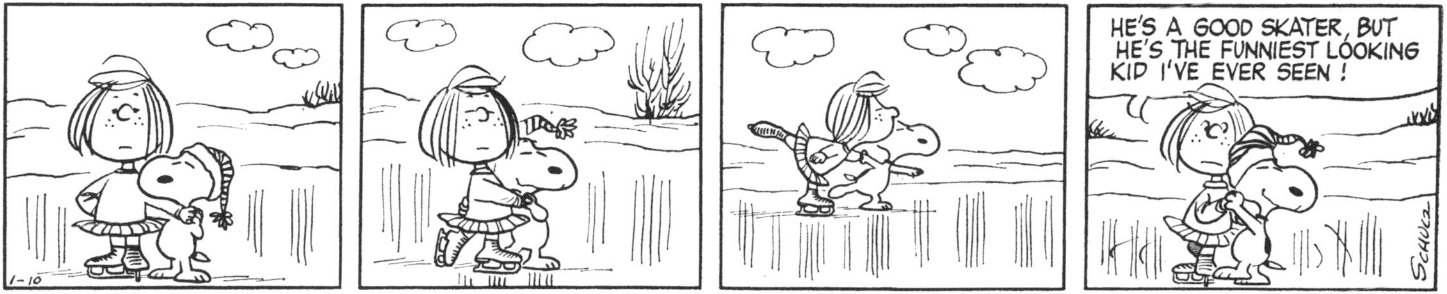
1-10
HE'S A GOOD SKATER, BUT HE'S THE FUNNIEST LOOKING KID I'VE EVER SEEN!
SCHULZ

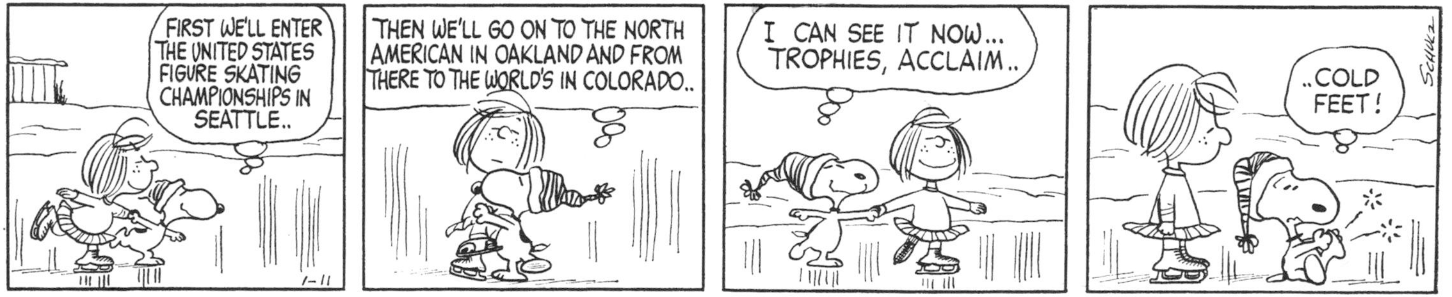
FIRST WE'LL ENTER THE UNITED STATES FIGURE SKATING CHAMPIONSHIPS IN SEATTLE..
1-11
THEN WE'LL GO ON TO THE NORTH AMERICAN IN OAKLAND AND FROM THERE TO THE WORLD'S IN COLORADO..
I CAN SEE IT NOW... TROPHIES, ACCLAIM..
..COLD FEET!
SCHULZ

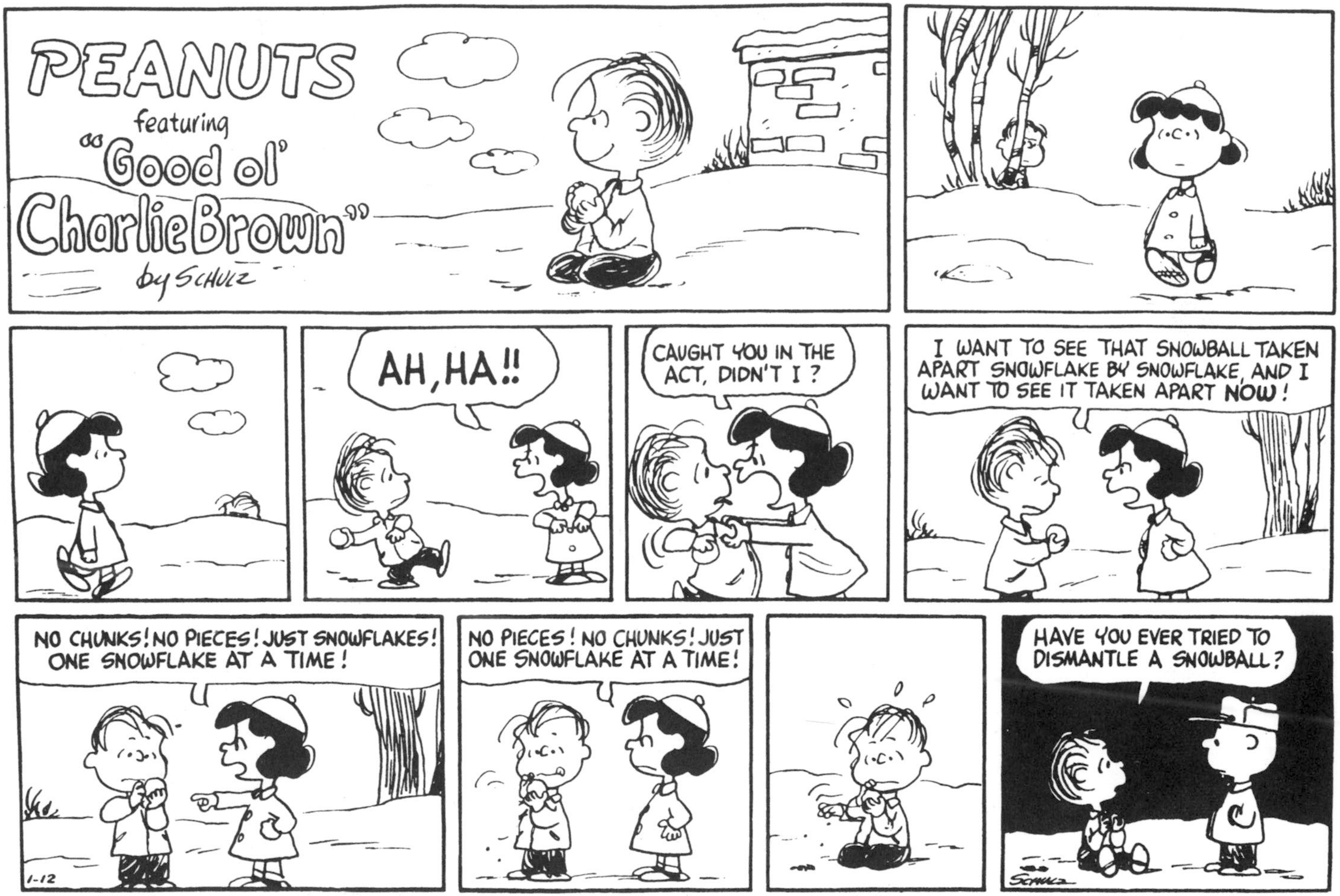
PEANUTS
featuring
"Good ol' Charlie Brown"
by SCHULZ
AH, HA!!
CAUGHT YOU IN THE ACT, DIDN'T I ?
I WANT TO SEE THAT SNOWBALL TAKEN APART SNOWFLAKE BY SNOWFLAKE, AND I WANT TO SEE IT TAKEN APART NOW !
NO CHUNKS! NO PIECES! JUST SNOWFLAKES! ONE SNOWFLAKE AT A TIME!
1-12
NO PIECES! NO CHUNKS! JUST ONE SNOWFLAKE AT A TIME!
HAVE YOU EVER TRIED TO DISMANTLE A SNOWBALL?
SCHULZ

Panel 1: WHEN ARE YOU LEAVING FOR OAKLAND?

Panel 2: OAKLAND?! WHO SAID ANYTHING ABOUT LEAVING FOR OAKLAND?

Panel 3: SNOOPY'S COUNTING ON YOU TO SKATE WITH HIM THERE IN THE NORTH AMERICAN CHAMPIONSHIPS... / HE IS?

1-13

Panel 4: GEE, CHUCK, I DON'T EVEN KNOW WHERE OAKLAND IS.. / I LOOKED IT UP. IT'S ABOUT FIFTY MILES FROM PETALUMA / PETALUMA?

Panel 5: LOOK, SNOOPY, LET'S FACE IT... I CAN'T GO TO OAKLAND..

Panel 6: I APPRECIATE YOUR WANTING ME TO SKATE WITH YOU IN THE CHAMPIONSHIPS, BUT I JUST CAN'T GO...I'M SORRY...LET'S JUST SAY IT WAS FUN, AND, "SO LONG"...OKAY?

1-14

Panel 8: SHE DIDN'T EVEN KISS ME ON THE NOSE!

Panel 9: I'M GOING TO HAVE TO FIND ANOTHER SKATING PARTNER..

1-15

Panel 10: AH! THAT DARK-HAIRED LASS LOOKS LIKE SHE MIGHT BE INTERESTING... I'LL APPROACH HER IN THE TIME-HONORED CUSTOM

Panel 11: HOW ABOUT A SKATE, SWEETIE? / GET AWAY FROM ME, YOU STUPID BEAGLE!!

Panel 12: I APPROACHED HER IN THE TIME-HONORED CUSTOM, AND I WAS TURNED AWAY IN THE TIME-HONORED CUSTOM...

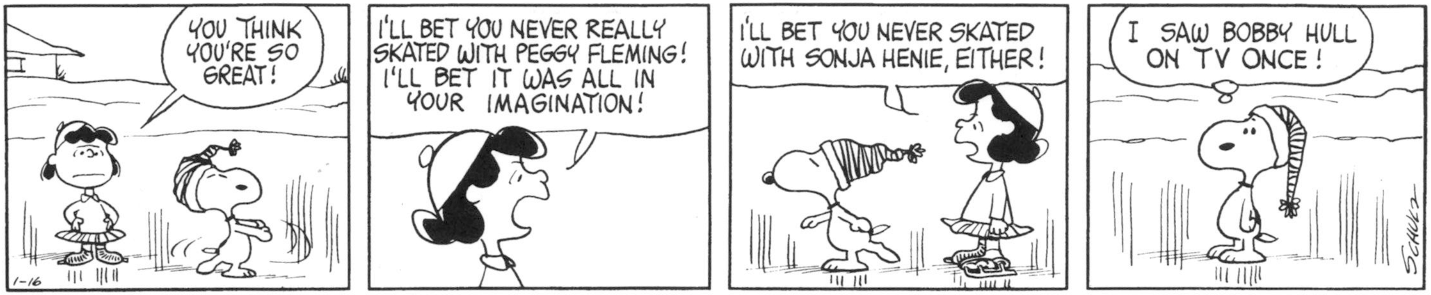
YOU THINK YOU'RE SO GREAT!
I'LL BET YOU NEVER REALLY SKATED WITH PEGGY FLEMING! I'LL BET IT WAS ALL IN YOUR IMAGINATION!
I'LL BET YOU NEVER SKATED WITH SONJA HENIE, EITHER!
I SAW BOBBY HULL ON TV ONCE!

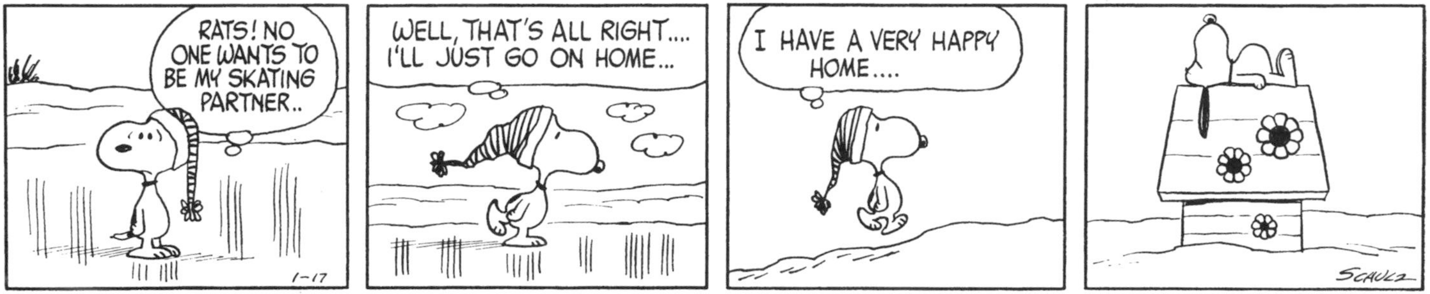
RATS! NO ONE WANTS TO BE MY SKATING PARTNER..
WELL, THAT'S ALL RIGHT.... I'LL JUST GO ON HOME...
I HAVE A VERY HAPPY HOME....

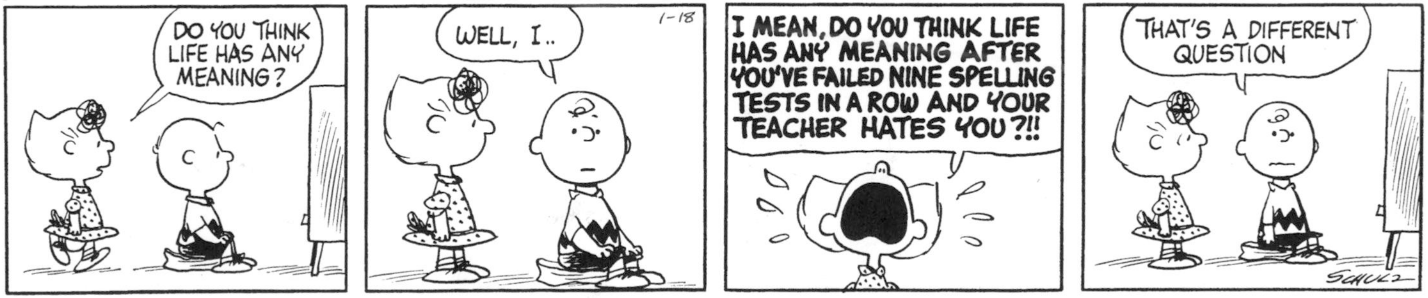
DO YOU THINK LIFE HAS ANY MEANING?
WELL, I..
I MEAN, DO YOU THINK LIFE HAS ANY MEANING AFTER YOU'VE FAILED NINE SPELLING TESTS IN A ROW AND YOUR TEACHER HATES YOU?!!
THAT'S A DIFFERENT QUESTION

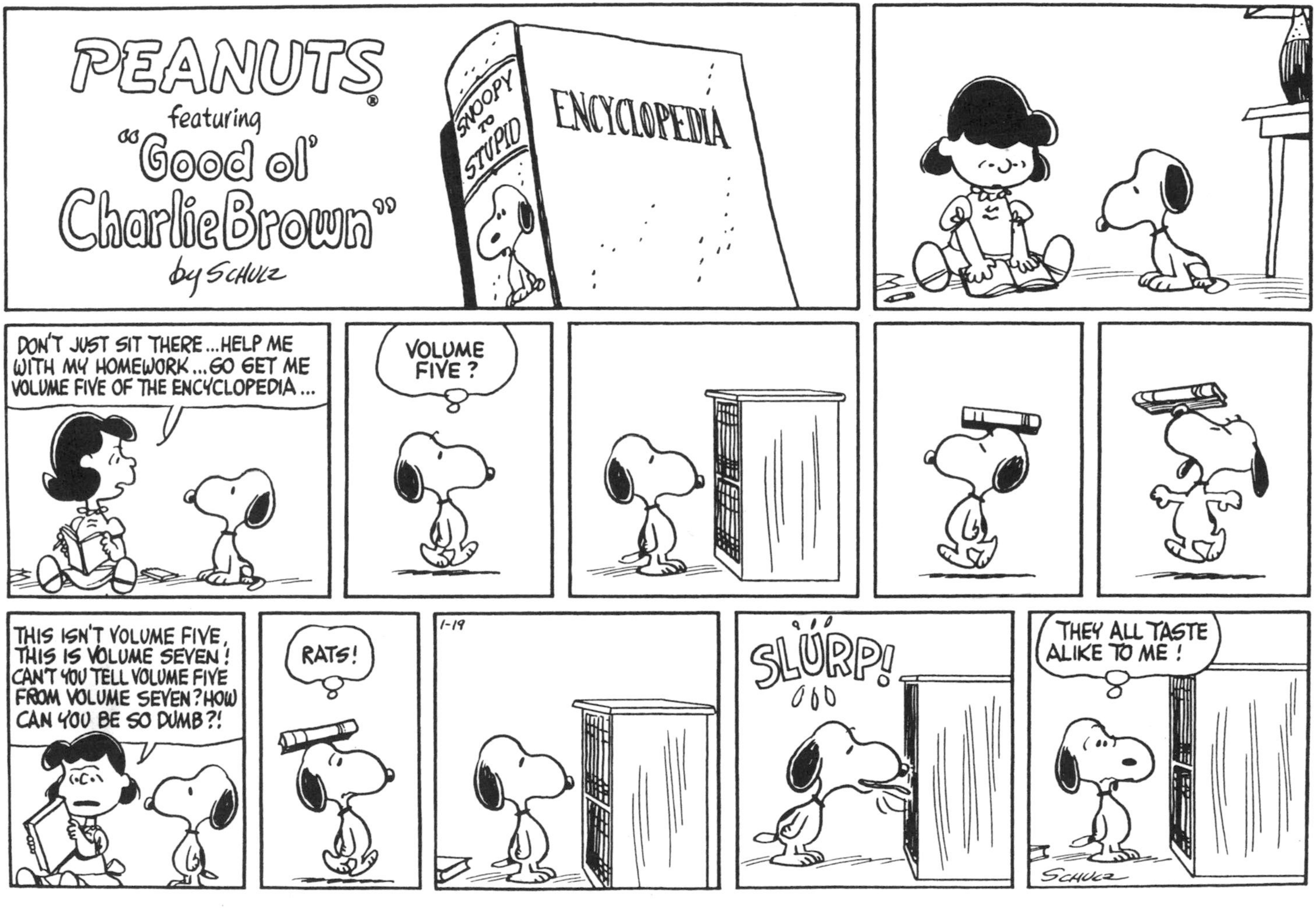
PEANUTS®
featuring
"Good ol' Charlie Brown"
by SCHULZ
SNOOPY TO STUPID
ENCYCLOPEDIA
DON'T JUST SIT THERE...HELP ME WITH MY HOMEWORK...GO GET ME VOLUME FIVE OF THE ENCYCLOPEDIA...
VOLUME FIVE ?
THIS ISN'T VOLUME FIVE, THIS IS VOLUME SEVEN! CAN'T YOU TELL VOLUME FIVE FROM VOLUME SEVEN? HOW CAN YOU BE SO DUMB?!
RATS!
1-19
SLURP!
THEY ALL TASTE ALIKE TO ME!
SCHULZ

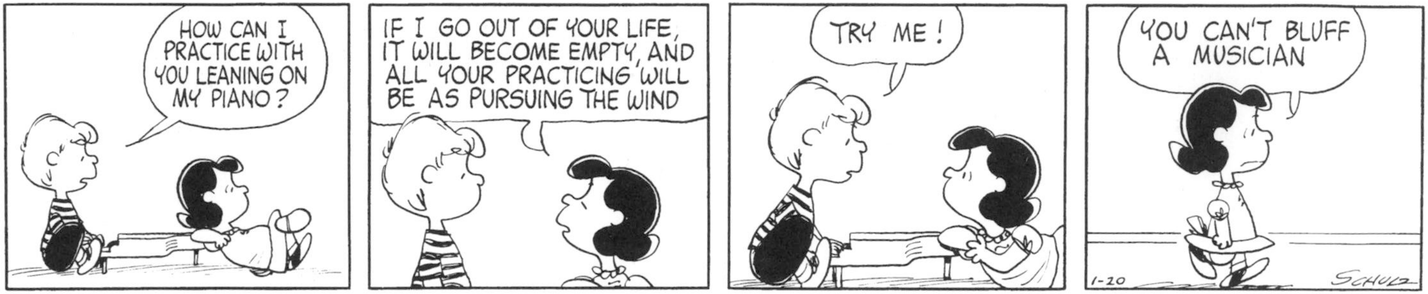
HOW CAN I PRACTICE WITH YOU LEANING ON MY PIANO?
IF I GO OUT OF YOUR LIFE, IT WILL BECOME EMPTY, AND ALL YOUR PRACTICING WILL BE AS PURSUING THE WIND
TRY ME!
YOU CAN'T BLUFF A MUSICIAN
1-20
SCHULZ

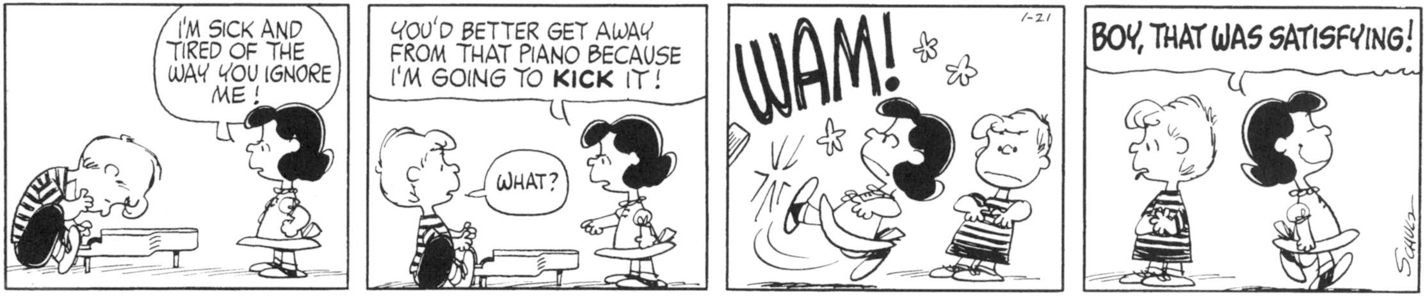
I'M SICK AND TIRED OF THE WAY YOU IGNORE ME!
YOU'D BETTER GET AWAY FROM THAT PIANO BECAUSE I'M GOING TO **KICK** IT!
WHAT?
1-21
WAM!
BOY, THAT WAS SATISFYING!
SCHULZ

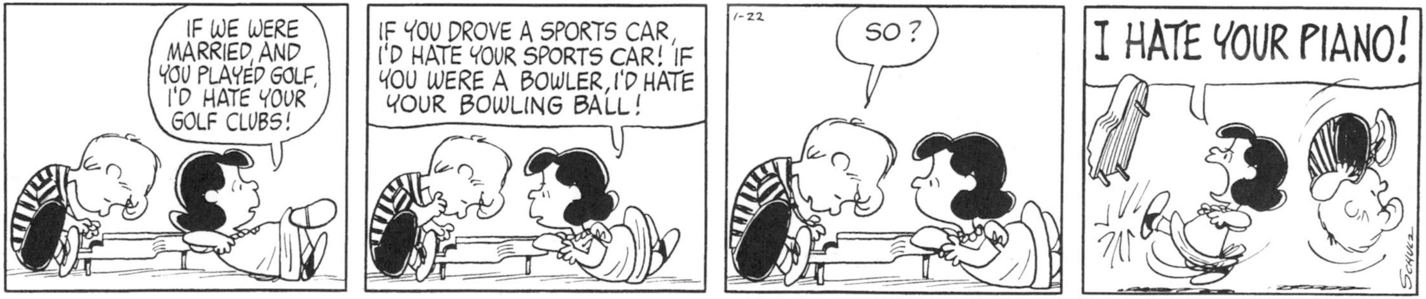
IF WE WERE MARRIED, AND YOU PLAYED GOLF, I'D HATE YOUR GOLF CLUBS!
IF YOU DROVE A SPORTS CAR, I'D HATE YOUR SPORTS CAR! IF YOU WERE A BOWLER, I'D HATE YOUR BOWLING BALL!
1-22
SO?
I HATE YOUR PIANO!
SCHULZ

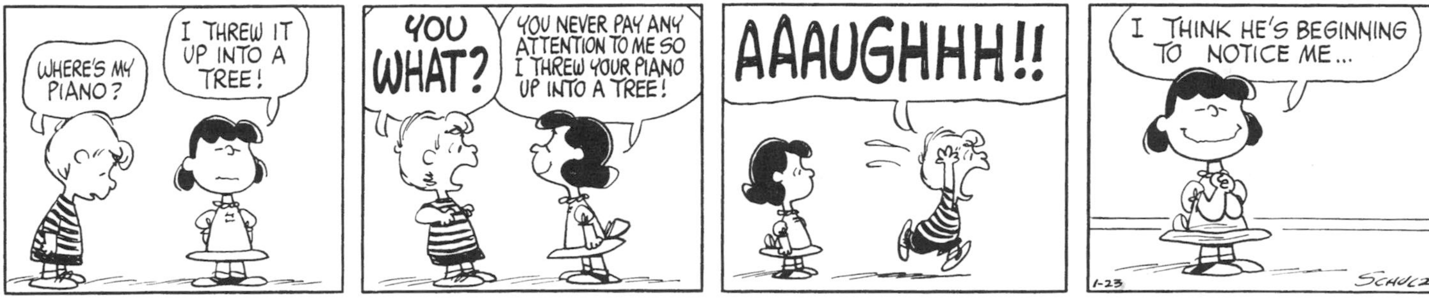
WHERE'S MY PIANO?
I THREW IT UP INTO A TREE!
YOU WHAT?
YOU NEVER PAY ANY ATTENTION TO ME SO I THREW YOUR PIANO UP INTO A TREE!
AAAUGHHH!!
I THINK HE'S BEGINNING TO NOTICE ME...
1-23
SCHULZ

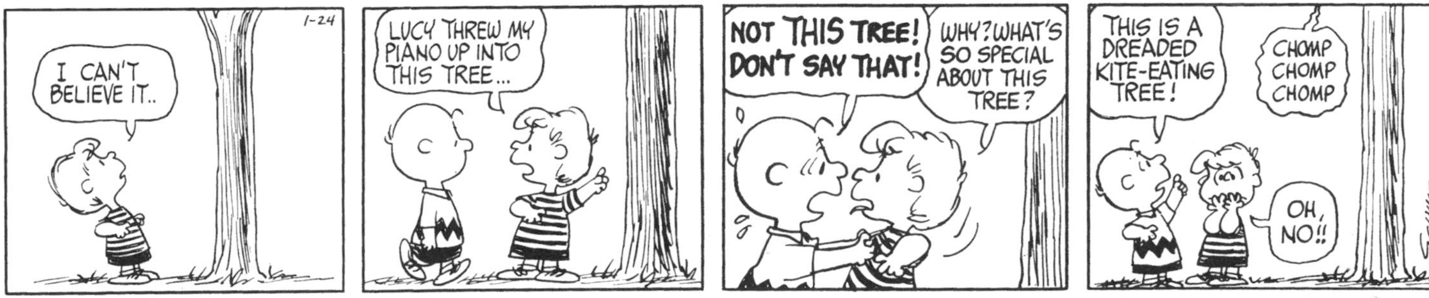
1-24
I CAN'T BELIEVE IT..
LUCY THREW MY PIANO UP INTO THIS TREE...
NOT THIS TREE! DON'T SAY THAT!
WHY? WHAT'S SO SPECIAL ABOUT THIS TREE?
THIS IS A DREADED KITE-EATING TREE!
CHOMP CHOMP CHOMP
OH, NO!!
SCHULZ

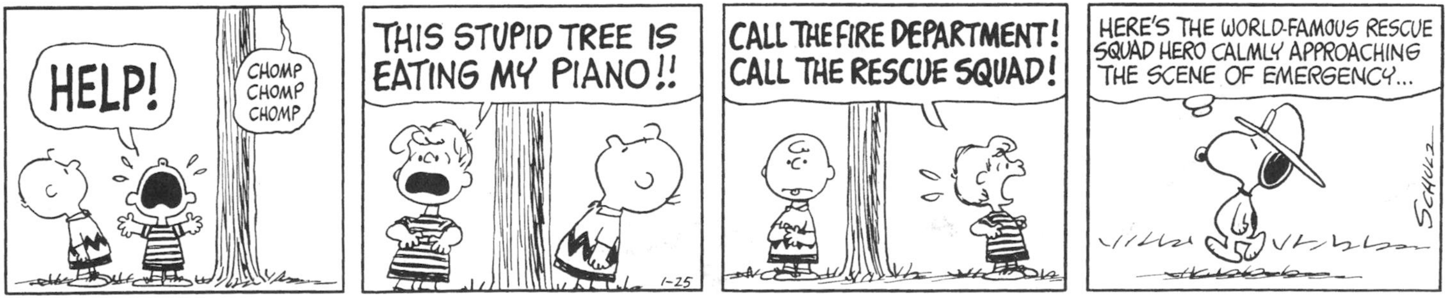
HELP!
CHOMP CHOMP CHOMP
THIS STUPID TREE IS EATING MY PIANO!!
1-25
CALL THE FIRE DEPARTMENT! CALL THE RESCUE SQUAD!
HERE'S THE WORLD-FAMOUS RESCUE SQUAD HERO CALMLY APPROACHING THE SCENE OF EMERGENCY...
SCHULZ

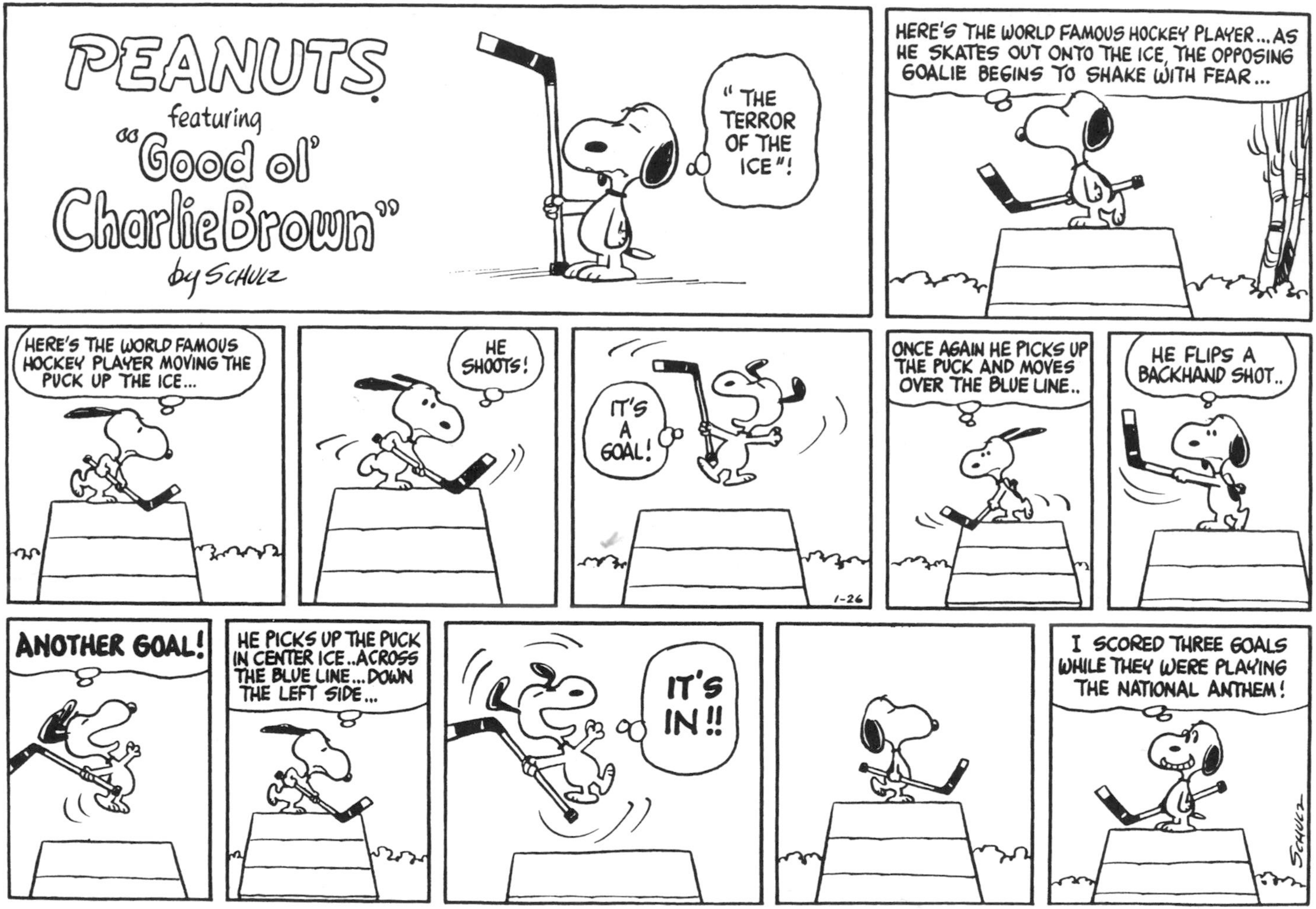
PEANUTS
featuring
"Good ol' Charlie Brown"
by SCHULZ
"THE TERROR OF THE ICE"!
HERE'S THE WORLD FAMOUS HOCKEY PLAYER...AS HE SKATES OUT ONTO THE ICE, THE OPPOSING GOALIE BEGINS TO SHAKE WITH FEAR...
HERE'S THE WORLD FAMOUS HOCKEY PLAYER MOVING THE PUCK UP THE ICE...
HE SHOOTS!
IT'S A GOAL!
1-26
ONCE AGAIN HE PICKS UP THE PUCK AND MOVES OVER THE BLUE LINE..
HE FLIPS A BACKHAND SHOT..
ANOTHER GOAL!
HE PICKS UP THE PUCK IN CENTER ICE..ACROSS THE BLUE LINE...DOWN THE LEFT SIDE...
IT'S IN!!
I SCORED THREE GOALS WHILE THEY WERE PLAYING THE NATIONAL ANTHEM!
SCHULZ

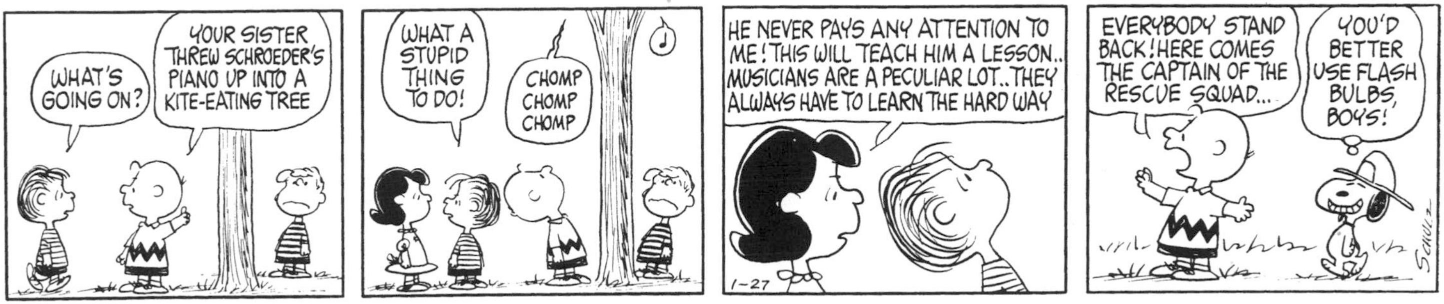
WHAT'S GOING ON?
YOUR SISTER THREW SCHROEDER'S PIANO UP INTO A KITE-EATING TREE
WHAT A STUPID THING TO DO!
CHOMP CHOMP CHOMP CHOMP
HE NEVER PAYS ANY ATTENTION TO ME! THIS WILL TEACH HIM A LESSON.. MUSICIANS ARE A PECULIAR LOT.. THEY ALWAYS HAVE TO LEARN THE HARD WAY
1-27
EVERYBODY STAND BACK! HERE COMES THE CAPTAIN OF THE RESCUE SQUAD...
YOU'D BETTER USE FLASH BULBS, BOYS!
SCHULZ

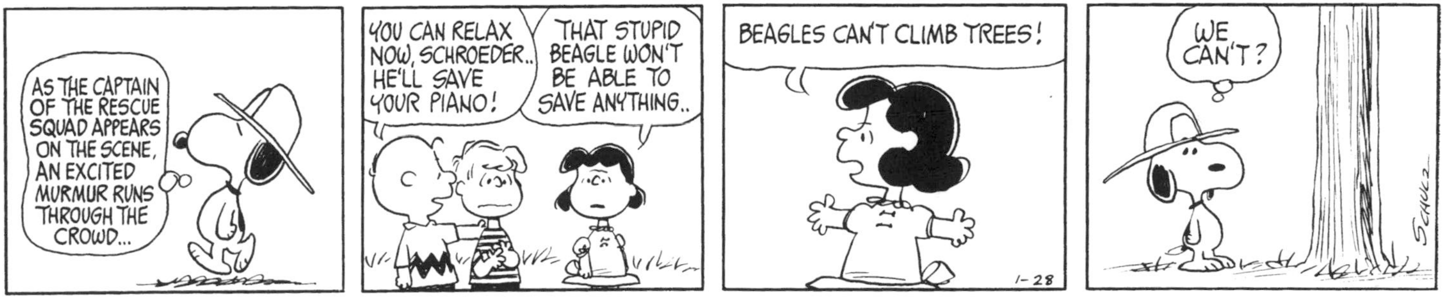
AS THE CAPTAIN OF THE RESCUE SQUAD APPEARS ON THE SCENE, AN EXCITED MURMUR RUNS THROUGH THE CROWD...
YOU CAN RELAX NOW, SCHROEDER.. HE'LL SAVE YOUR PIANO!
THAT STUPID BEAGLE WON'T BE ABLE TO SAVE ANYTHING..
BEAGLES CAN'T CLIMB TREES!
1-28
WE CAN'T?
SCHULZ

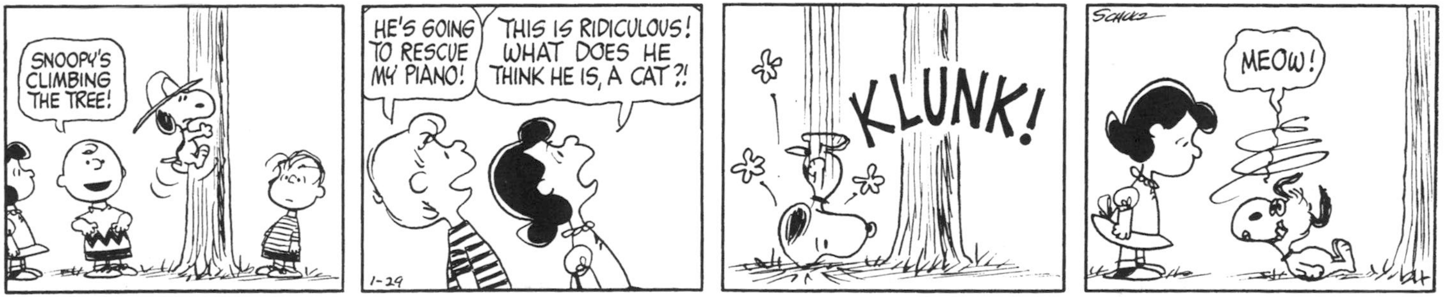
SNOOPY'S CLIMBING THE TREE!
HE'S GOING TO RESCUE MY PIANO!
THIS IS RIDICULOUS! WHAT DOES HE THINK HE IS, A CAT?!
1-29
KLUNK!
SCHULZ
MEOW!

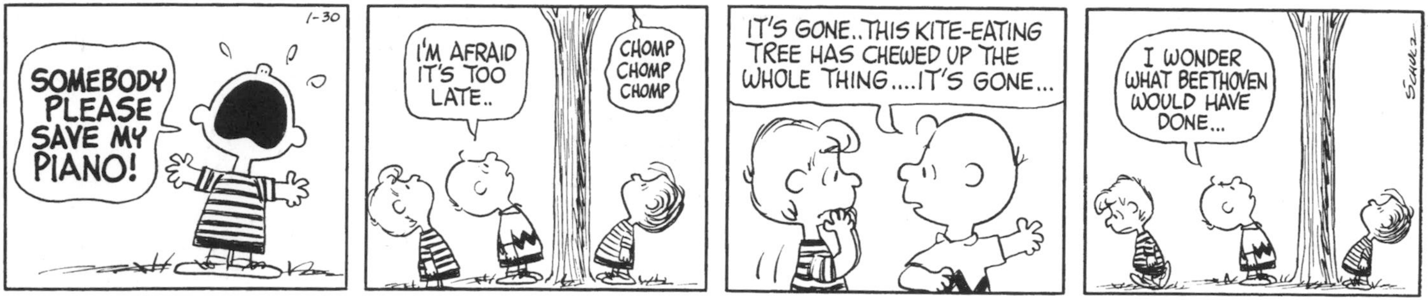
1-30
SOMEBODY PLEASE SAVE MY PIANO!
I'M AFRAID IT'S TOO LATE..
CHOMP CHOMP CHOMP
IT'S GONE..THIS KITE-EATING TREE HAS CHEWED UP THE WHOLE THING....IT'S GONE...
I WONDER WHAT BEETHOVEN WOULD HAVE DONE...

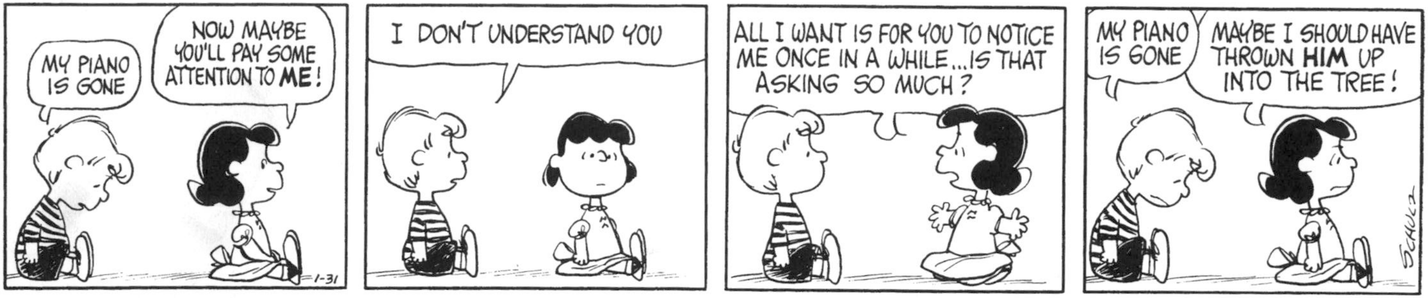
MY PIANO IS GONE
NOW MAYBE YOU'LL PAY SOME ATTENTION TO **ME**!
1-31
I DON'T UNDERSTAND YOU
ALL I WANT IS FOR YOU TO NOTICE ME ONCE IN A WHILE...IS THAT ASKING SO MUCH?
MY PIANO IS GONE
MAYBE I SHOULD HAVE THROWN **HIM** UP INTO THE TREE!

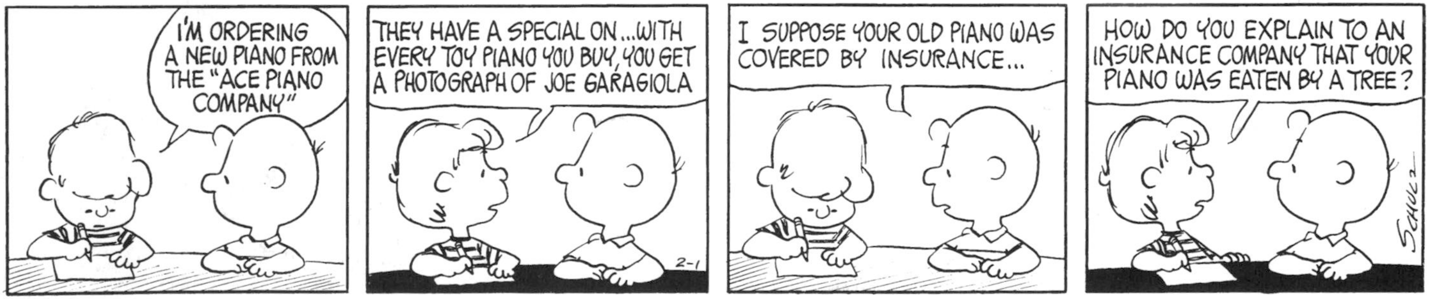
I'M ORDERING A NEW PIANO FROM THE "ACE PIANO COMPANY"
THEY HAVE A SPECIAL ON...WITH EVERY TOY PIANO YOU BUY, YOU GET A PHOTOGRAPH OF JOE GARAGIOLA
2-1
I SUPPOSE YOUR OLD PIANO WAS COVERED BY INSURANCE...
HOW DO YOU EXPLAIN TO AN INSURANCE COMPANY THAT YOUR PIANO WAS EATEN BY A TREE?

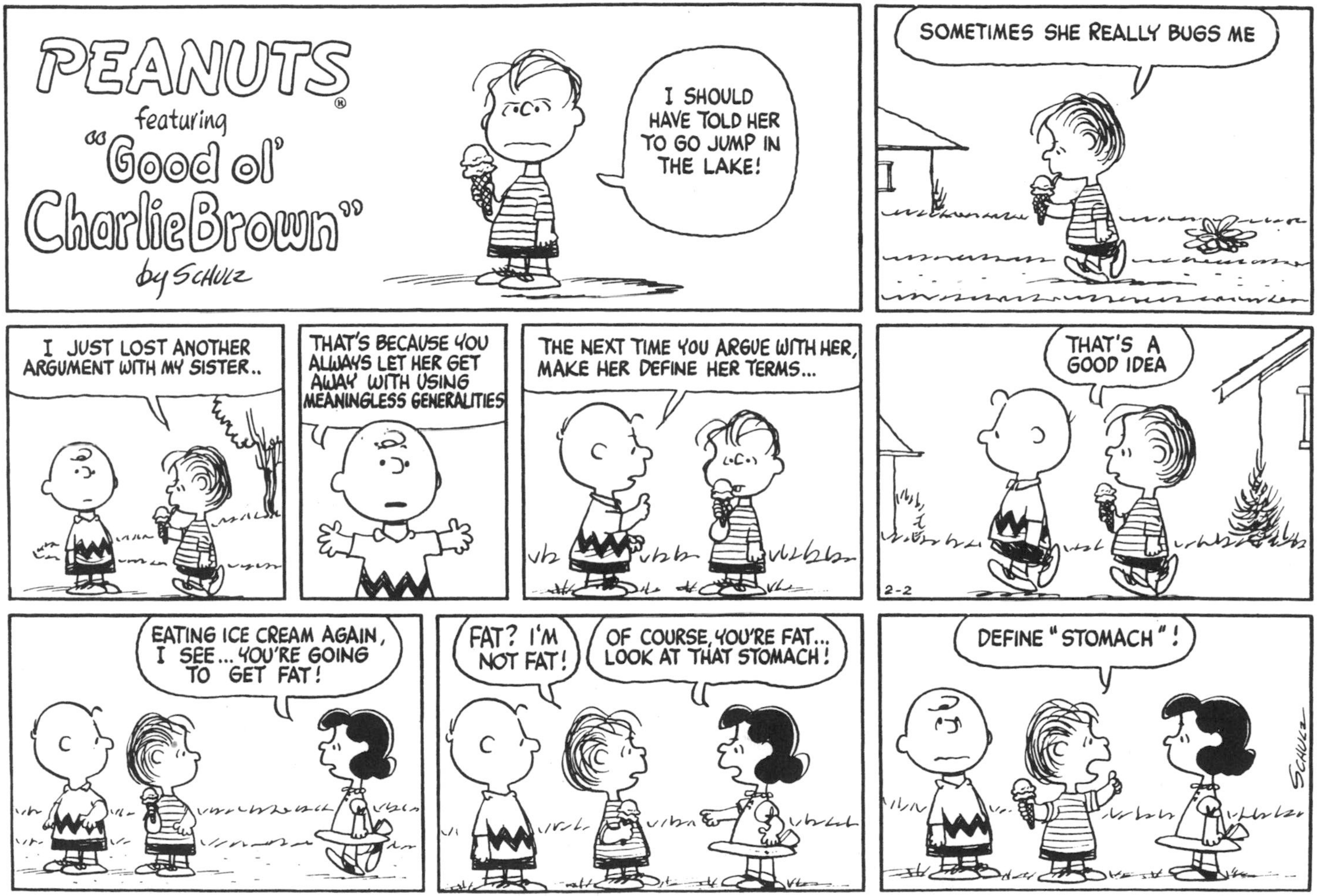
PEANUTS
featuring
"Good ol' CharlieBrown"
by SCHULZ
I SHOULD HAVE TOLD HER TO GO JUMP IN THE LAKE!
SOMETIMES SHE REALLY BUGS ME
I JUST LOST ANOTHER ARGUMENT WITH MY SISTER..
THAT'S BECAUSE YOU ALWAYS LET HER GET AWAY WITH USING MEANINGLESS GENERALITIES
THE NEXT TIME YOU ARGUE WITH HER, MAKE HER DEFINE HER TERMS...
THAT'S A GOOD IDEA
2-2
EATING ICE CREAM AGAIN, I SEE... YOU'RE GOING TO GET FAT!
FAT? I'M NOT FAT!
OF COURSE, YOU'RE FAT... LOOK AT THAT STOMACH!
DEFINE "STOMACH"!
SCHULZ

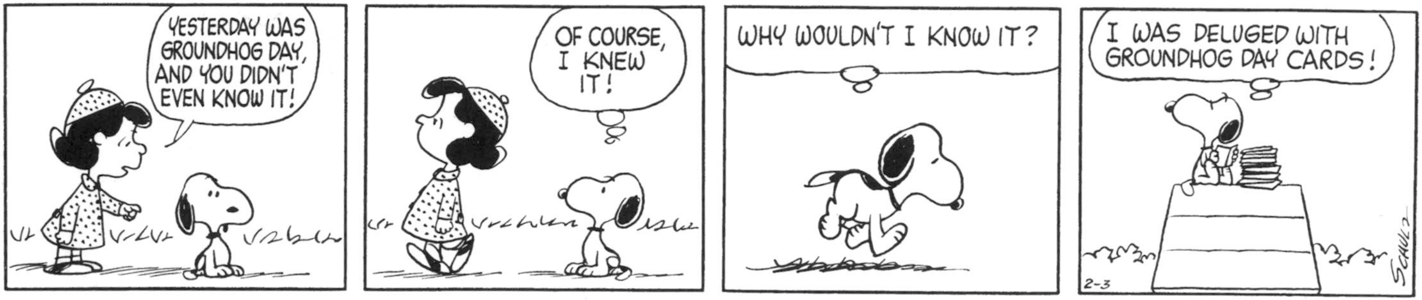
YESTERDAY WAS GROUNDHOG DAY, AND YOU DIDN'T EVEN KNOW IT!
OF COURSE, I KNEW IT!
WHY WOULDN'T I KNOW IT?
I WAS DELUGED WITH GROUNDHOG DAY CARDS!

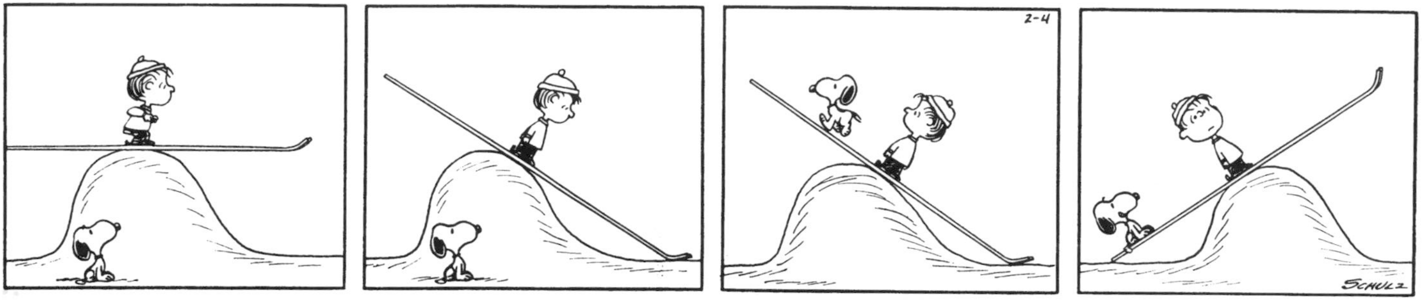

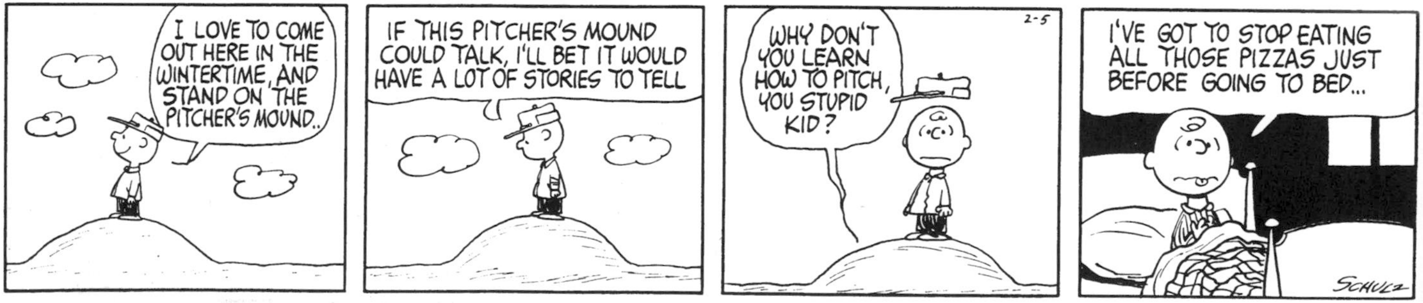
I LOVE TO COME OUT HERE IN THE WINTERTIME, AND STAND ON THE PITCHER'S MOUND..
IF THIS PITCHER'S MOUND COULD TALK, I'LL BET IT WOULD HAVE A LOT OF STORIES TO TELL
WHY DON'T YOU LEARN HOW TO PITCH, YOU STUPID KID?
I'VE GOT TO STOP EATING ALL THOSE PIZZAS JUST BEFORE GOING TO BED...

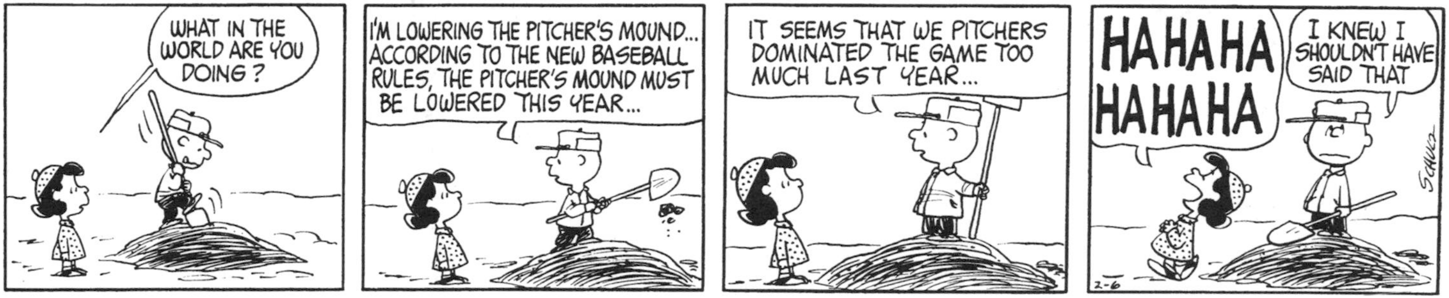
WHAT IN THE WORLD ARE YOU DOING ?
I'M LOWERING THE PITCHER'S MOUND... ACCORDING TO THE NEW BASEBALL RULES, THE PITCHER'S MOUND MUST BE LOWERED THIS YEAR...
IT SEEMS THAT WE PITCHERS DOMINATED THE GAME TOO MUCH LAST YEAR...
HAHAHA HAHAHA
I KNEW I SHOULDN'T HAVE SAID THAT
SCHULZ
2-6

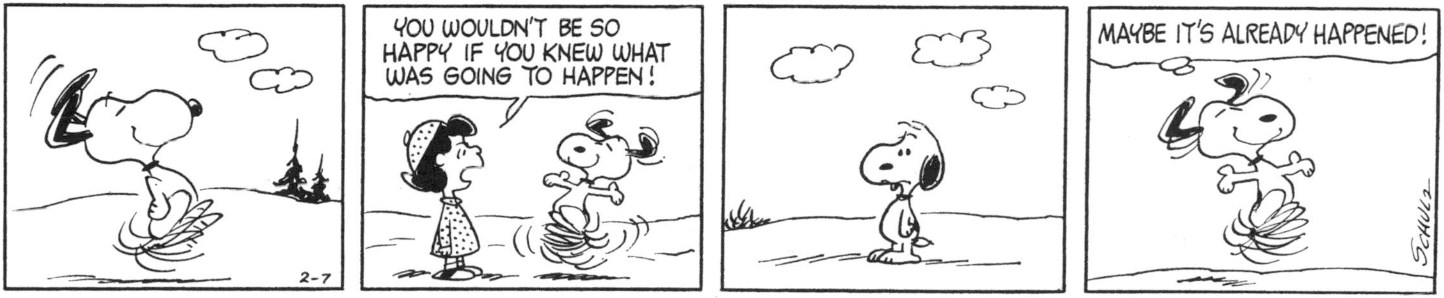
2-7
YOU WOULDN'T BE SO HAPPY IF YOU KNEW WHAT WAS GOING TO HAPPEN !
MAYBE IT'S ALREADY HAPPENED !
SCHULZ

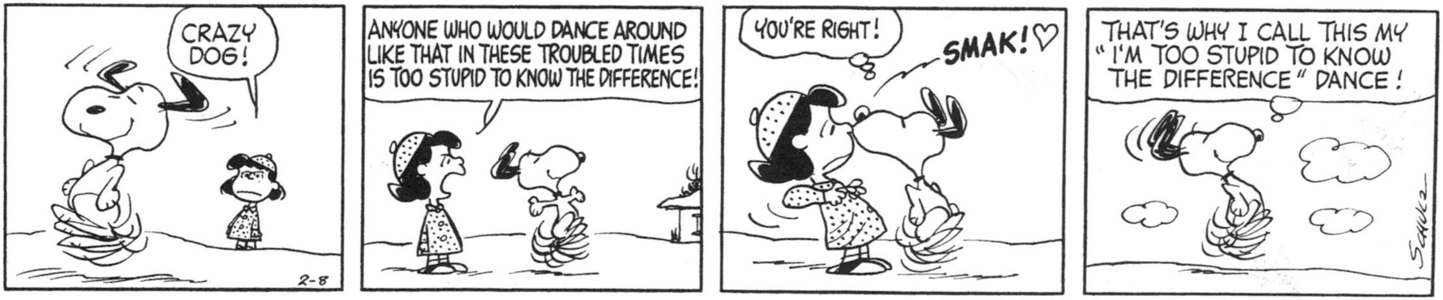
CRAZY DOG !
2-8
ANYONE WHO WOULD DANCE AROUND LIKE THAT IN THESE TROUBLED TIMES IS TOO STUPID TO KNOW THE DIFFERENCE !
YOU'RE RIGHT !
SMAK!
THAT'S WHY I CALL THIS MY "I'M TOO STUPID TO KNOW THE DIFFERENCE" DANCE !
SCHULZ

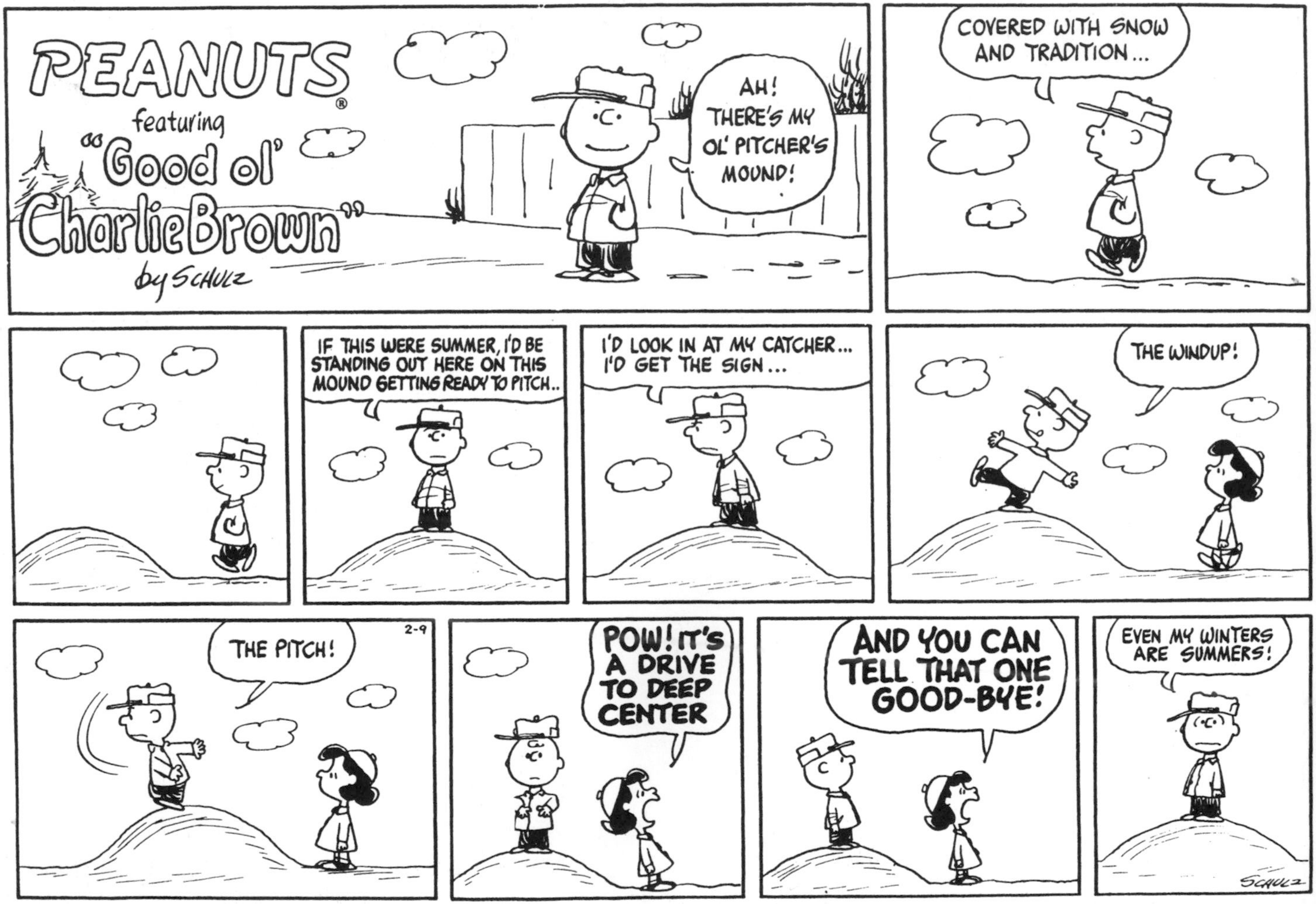
PEANUTS®
featuring "Good ol' CharlieBrown"
by SCHULZ
AH! THERE'S MY OL' PITCHER'S MOUND!
COVERED WITH SNOW AND TRADITION...
IF THIS WERE SUMMER, I'D BE STANDING OUT HERE ON THIS MOUND GETTING READY TO PITCH..
I'D LOOK IN AT MY CATCHER... I'D GET THE SIGN...
THE WINDUP!
THE PITCH!
2-9
POW! IT'S A DRIVE TO DEEP CENTER
AND YOU CAN TELL THAT ONE GOOD-BYE!
EVEN MY WINTERS ARE SUMMERS!
SCHULZ

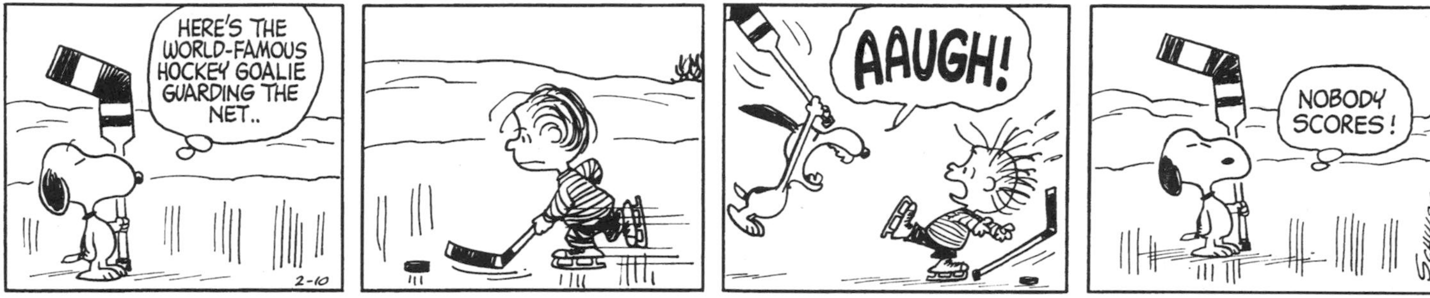
HERE'S THE WORLD-FAMOUS HOCKEY GOALIE GUARDING THE NET..
2-10
AAUGH!
NOBODY SCORES!
SCHULZ

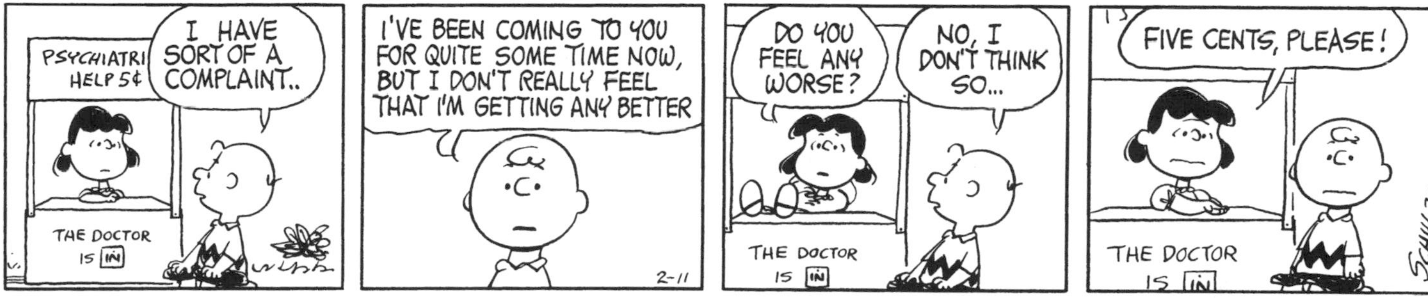
PSYCHIATRI HELP 5¢
THE DOCTOR IS IN
I HAVE SORT OF A COMPLAINT..
I'VE BEEN COMING TO YOU FOR QUITE SOME TIME NOW, BUT I DON'T REALLY FEEL THAT I'M GETTING ANY BETTER
2-11
DO YOU FEEL ANY WORSE?
NO, I DON'T THINK SO...
THE DOCTOR IS IN
FIVE CENTS, PLEASE!
THE DOCTOR IS IN
SCHULZ

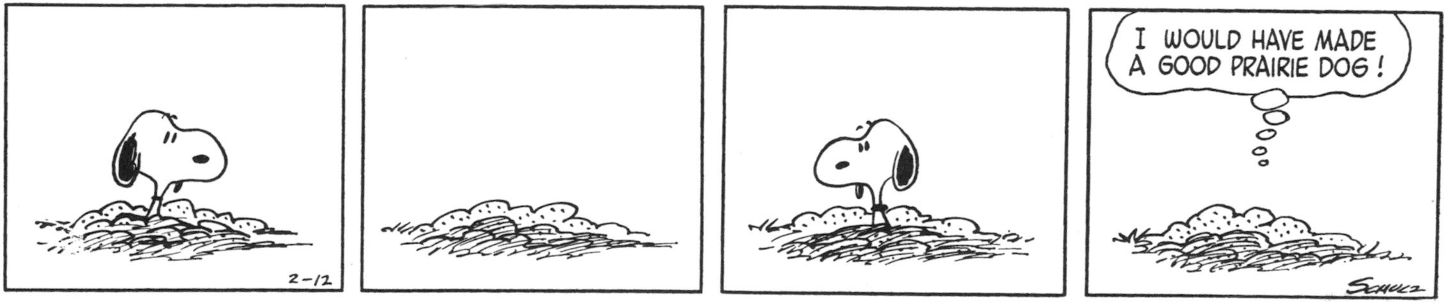
2-12
I WOULD HAVE MADE A GOOD PRAIRIE DOG!
SCHULZ

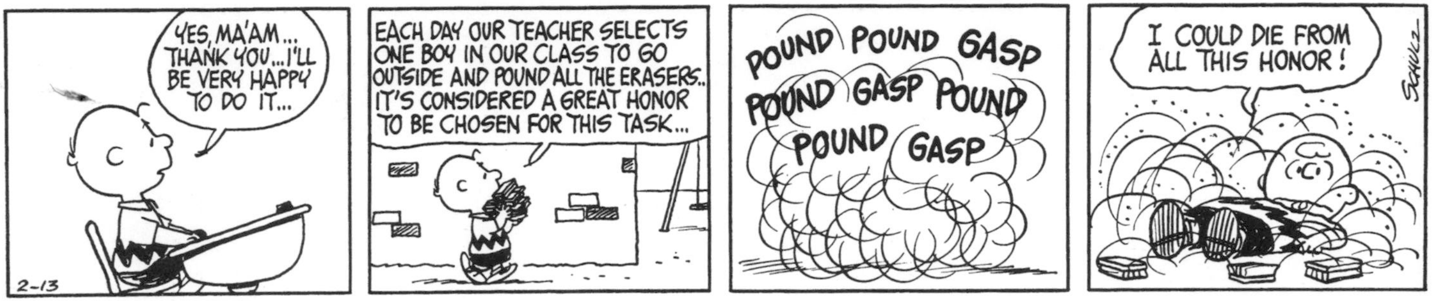
YES, MA'AM... THANK YOU... I'LL BE VERY HAPPY TO DO IT...
EACH DAY OUR TEACHER SELECTS ONE BOY IN OUR CLASS TO GO OUTSIDE AND POUND ALL THE ERASERS.. IT'S CONSIDERED A GREAT HONOR TO BE CHOSEN FOR THIS TASK...
POUND POUND GASP POUND GASP POUND POUND GASP
I COULD DIE FROM ALL THIS HONOR!

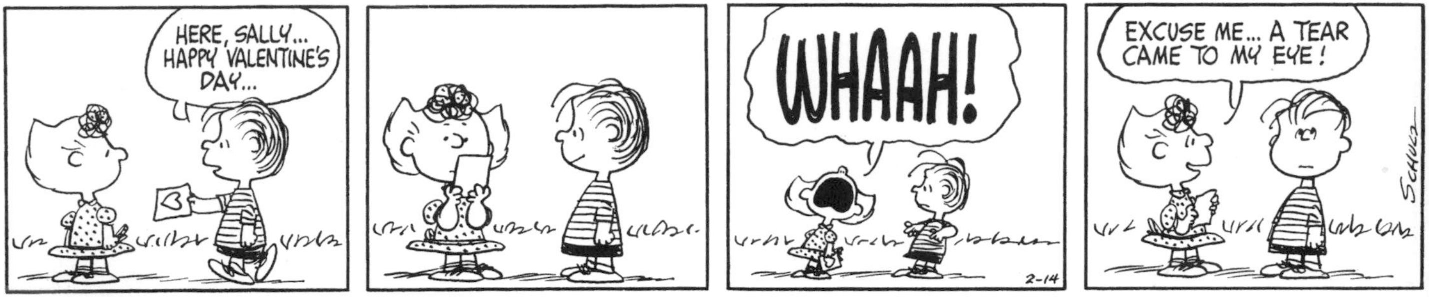
HERE, SALLY... HAPPY VALENTINE'S DAY...
WHAAH!
EXCUSE ME... A TEAR CAME TO MY EYE!

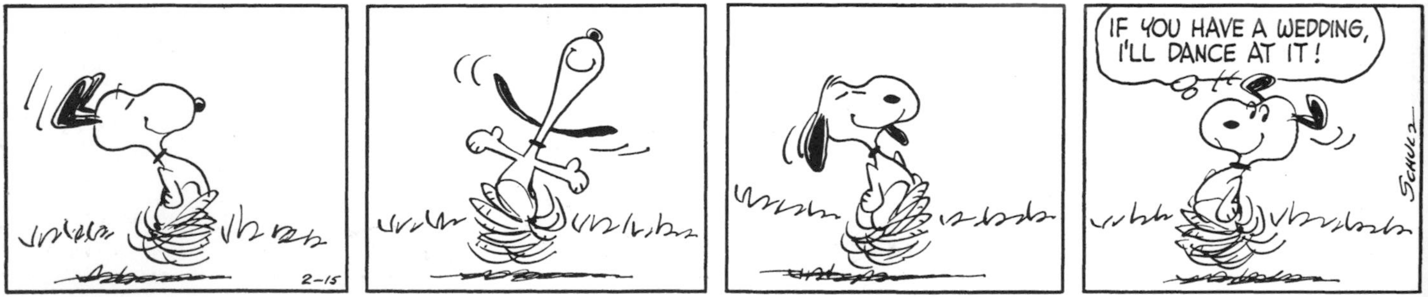
IF YOU HAVE A WEDDING, I'LL DANCE AT IT!

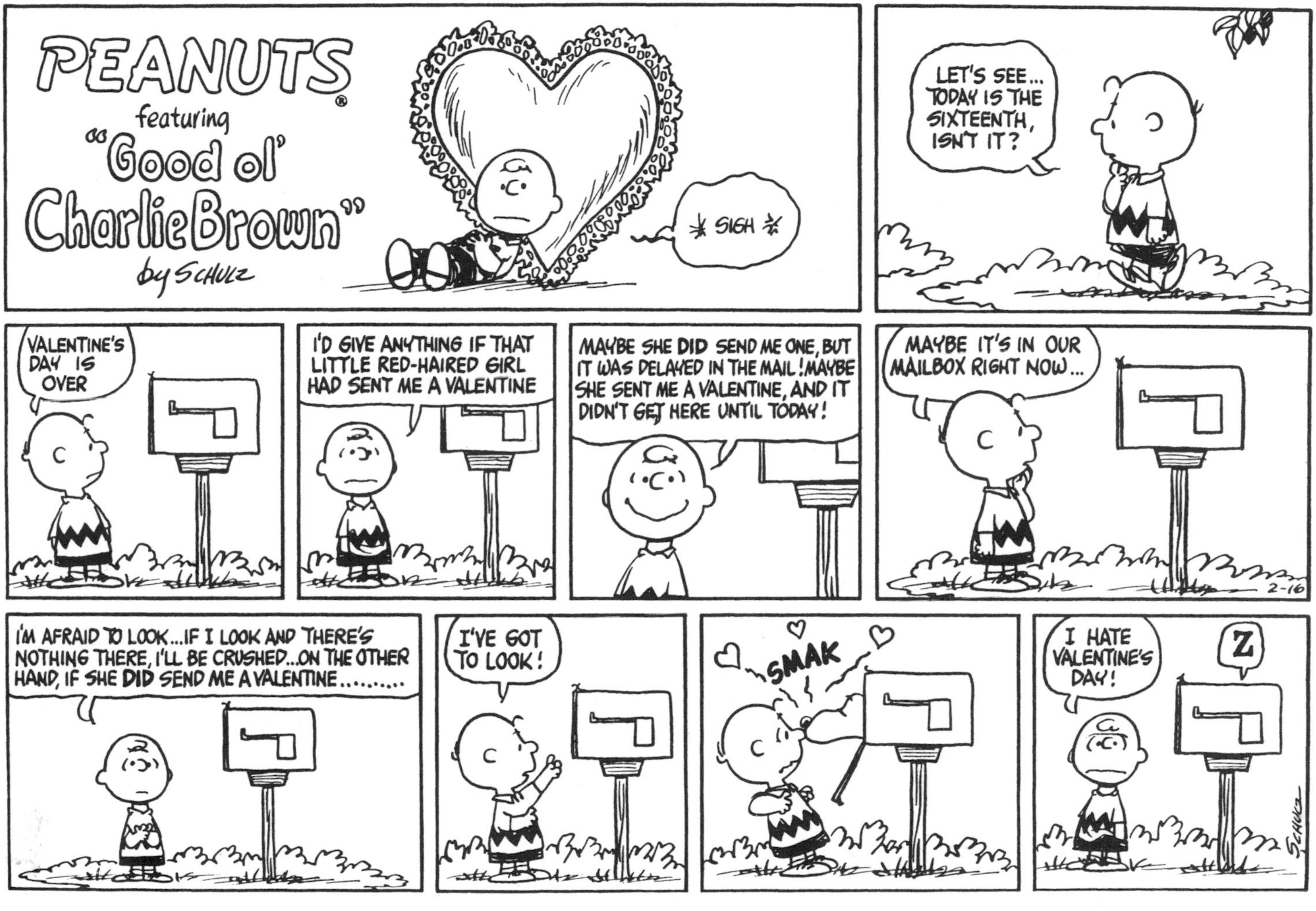
PEANUTS®
featuring
"Good ol' Charlie Brown"
by SCHULZ
SIGH
LET'S SEE... TODAY IS THE SIXTEENTH, ISN'T IT?
VALENTINE'S DAY IS OVER
I'D GIVE ANYTHING IF THAT LITTLE RED-HAIRED GIRL HAD SENT ME A VALENTINE
MAYBE SHE DID SEND ME ONE, BUT IT WAS DELAYED IN THE MAIL! MAYBE SHE SENT ME A VALENTINE, AND IT DIDN'T GET HERE UNTIL TODAY!
MAYBE IT'S IN OUR MAILBOX RIGHT NOW...
2-16
I'M AFRAID TO LOOK...IF I LOOK AND THERE'S NOTHING THERE, I'LL BE CRUSHED...ON THE OTHER HAND, IF SHE DID SEND ME A VALENTINE.........
I'VE GOT TO LOOK!
SMAK
I HATE VALENTINE'S DAY!
Z
SCHULZ

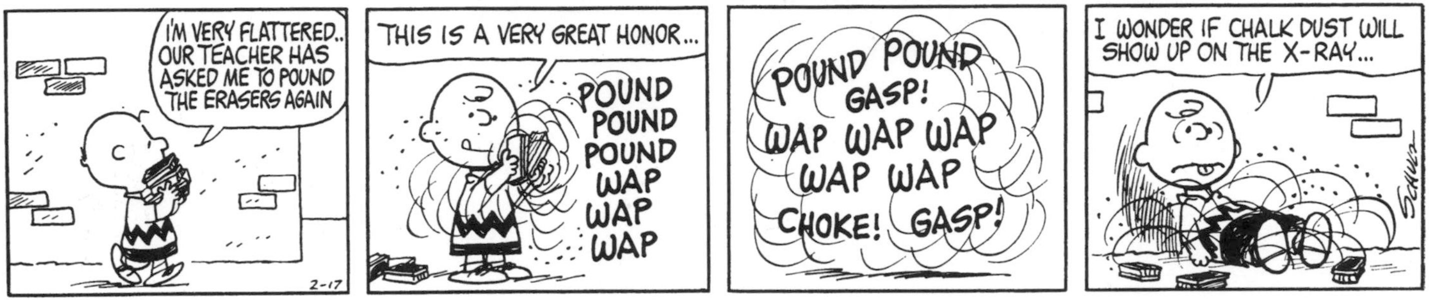
I'M VERY FLATTERED.. OUR TEACHER HAS ASKED ME TO POUND THE ERASERS AGAIN
2-17
THIS IS A VERY GREAT HONOR...
POUND POUND POUND WAP WAP WAP
POUND POUND GASP! WAP WAP WAP WAP WAP CHOKE! GASP!
I WONDER IF CHALK DUST WILL SHOW UP ON THE X-RAY...
SCHULZ

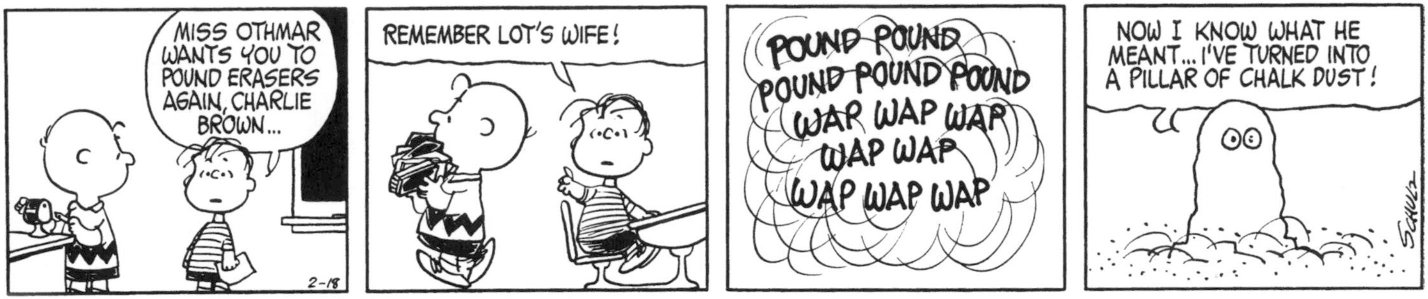
MISS OTHMAR WANTS YOU TO POUND ERASERS AGAIN, CHARLIE BROWN...
2-18
REMEMBER LOT'S WIFE!
POUND POUND POUND POUND POUND WAP WAP WAP WAP WAP WAP WAP WAP
NOW I KNOW WHAT HE MEANT... I'VE TURNED INTO A PILLAR OF CHALK DUST!
SCHULZ

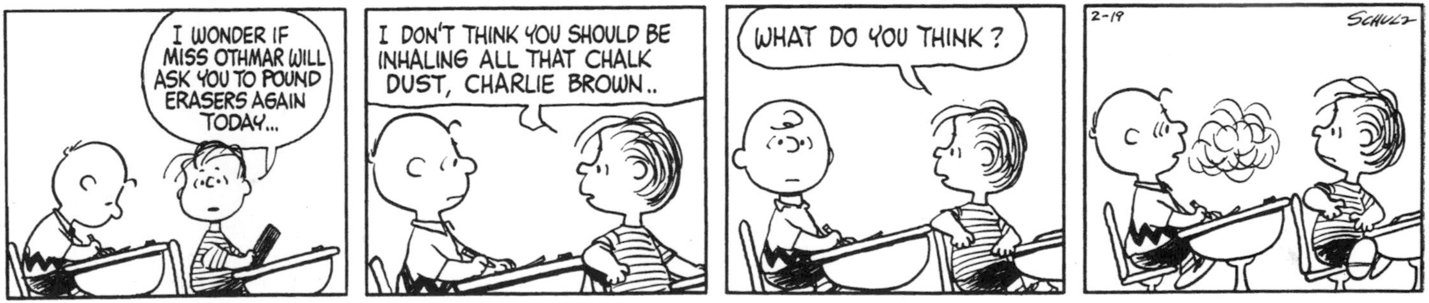
I WONDER IF MISS OTHMAR WILL ASK YOU TO POUND ERASERS AGAIN TODAY...
I DON'T THINK YOU SHOULD BE INHALING ALL THAT CHALK DUST, CHARLIE BROWN..
WHAT DO YOU THINK?
2-19
SCHULZ

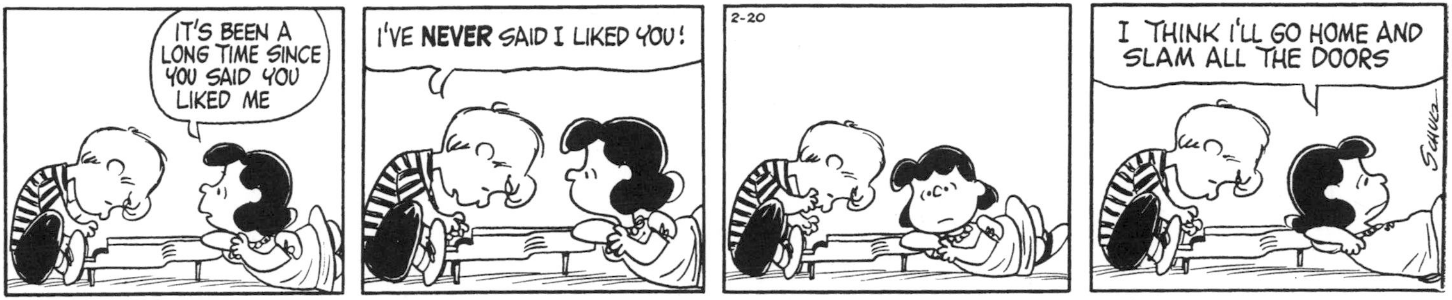
IT'S BEEN A LONG TIME SINCE YOU SAID YOU LIKED ME
I'VE NEVER SAID I LIKED YOU!
2-20
I THINK I'LL GO HOME AND SLAM ALL THE DOORS
SCHULZ

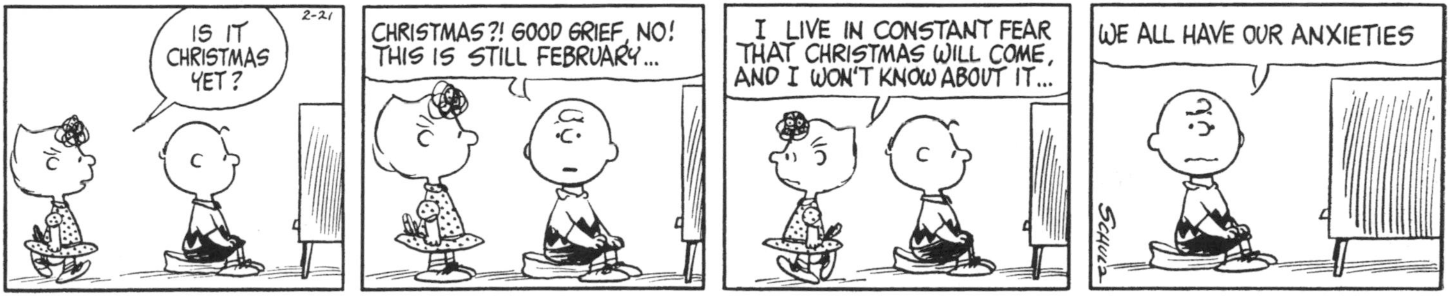
2-21
IS IT CHRISTMAS YET?
CHRISTMAS?! GOOD GRIEF, NO! THIS IS STILL FEBRUARY...
I LIVE IN CONSTANT FEAR THAT CHRISTMAS WILL COME, AND I WON'T KNOW ABOUT IT...
WE ALL HAVE OUR ANXIETIES
SCHULZ

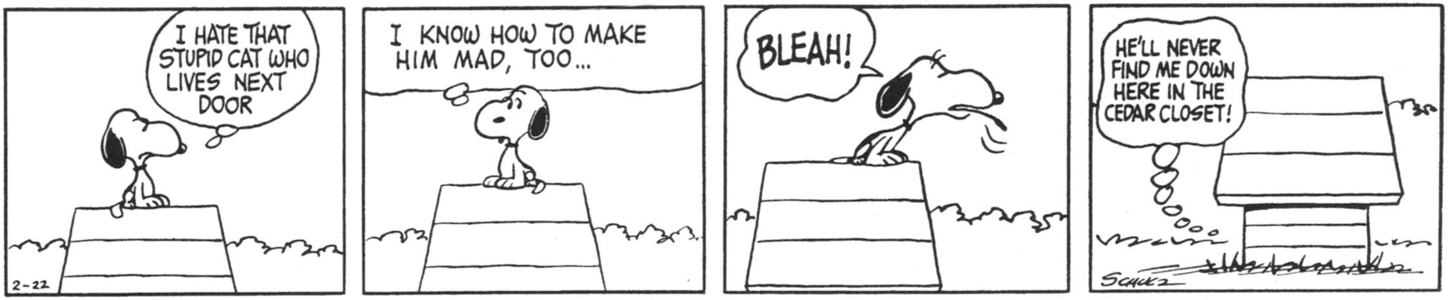
I HATE THAT STUPID CAT WHO LIVES NEXT DOOR
2-22
I KNOW HOW TO MAKE HIM MAD, TOO...
BLEAH!
HE'LL NEVER FIND ME DOWN HERE IN THE CEDAR CLOSET!
SCHULZ

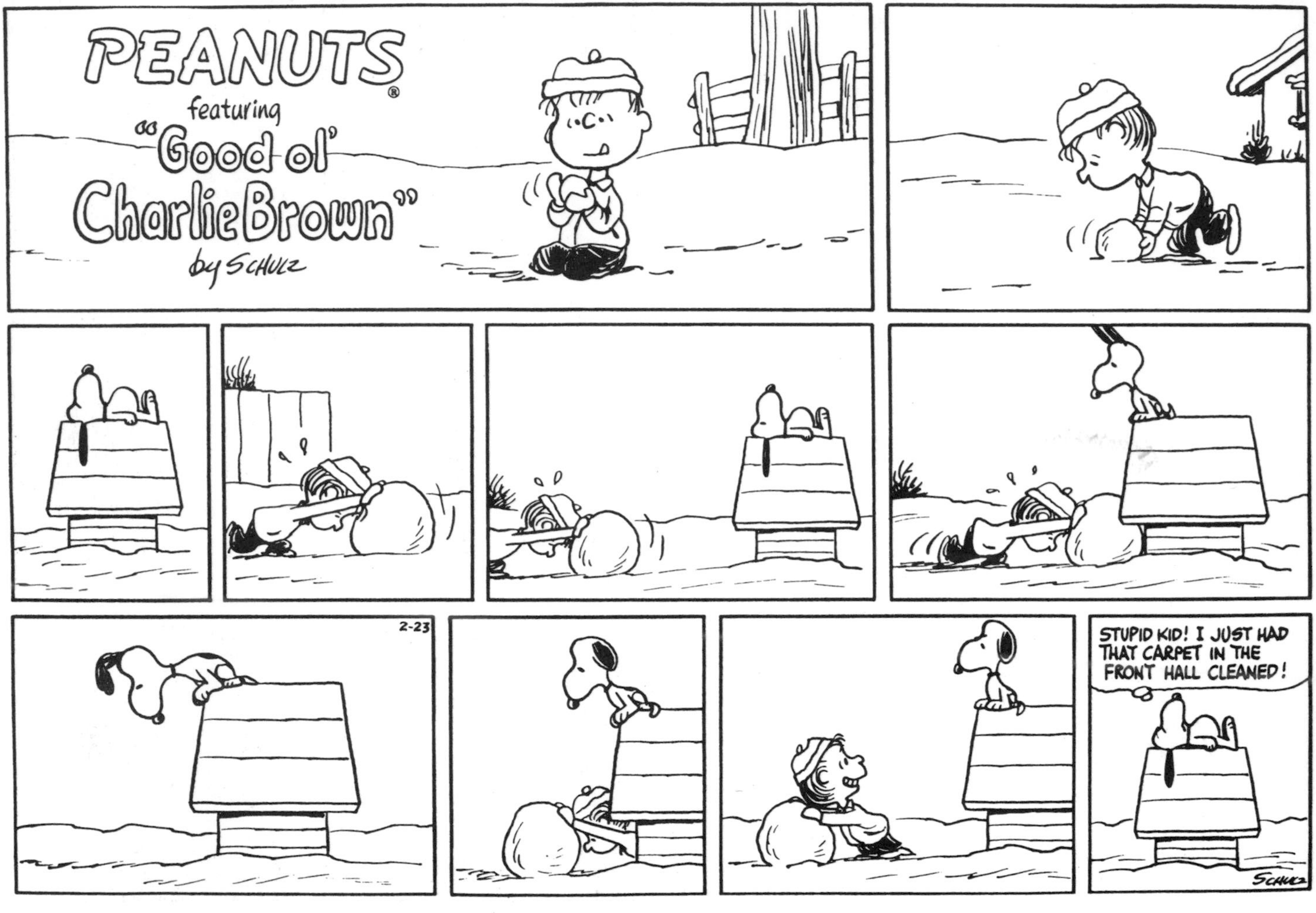
PEANUTS
featuring
"Good ol' Charlie Brown"
by SCHULZ
2-23
STUPID KID! I JUST HAD THAT CARPET IN THE FRONT HALL CLEANED!
SCHULZ

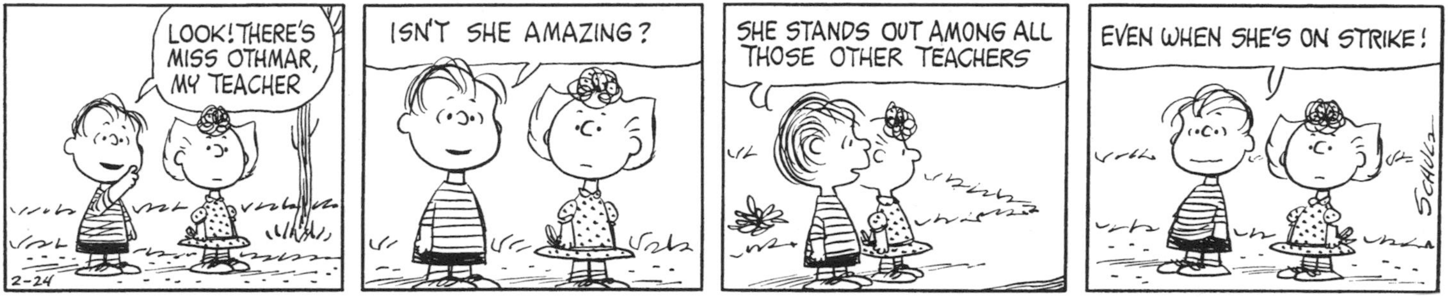
LOOK! THERE'S MISS OTHMAR, MY TEACHER
ISN'T SHE AMAZING?
SHE STANDS OUT AMONG ALL THOSE OTHER TEACHERS
EVEN WHEN SHE'S ON STRIKE!

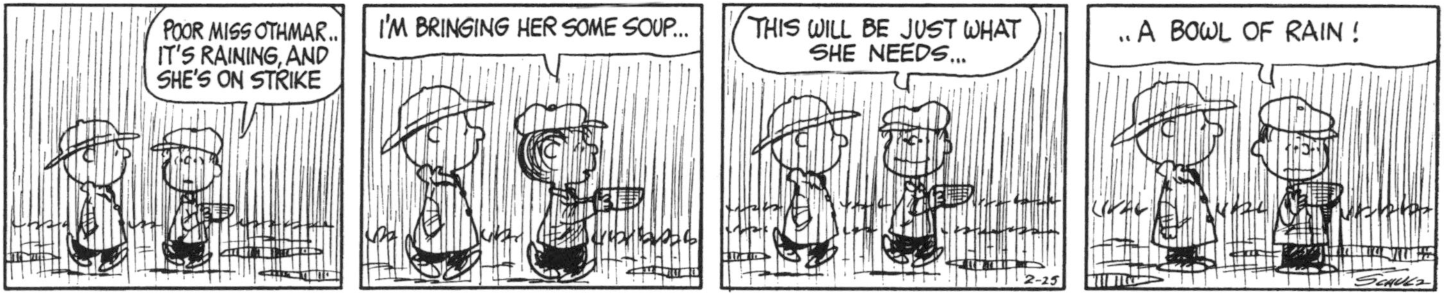
POOR MISS OTHMAR.. IT'S RAINING, AND SHE'S ON STRIKE
I'M BRINGING HER SOME SOUP...
THIS WILL BE JUST WHAT SHE NEEDS...
..A BOWL OF RAIN!

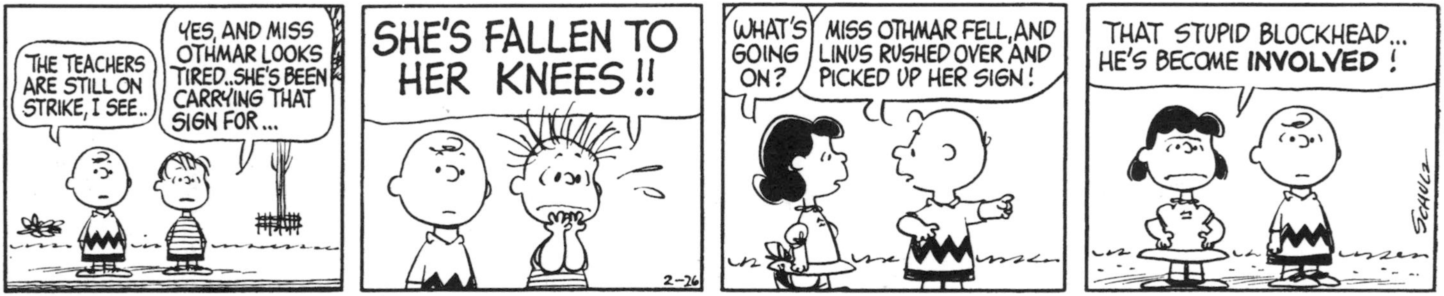
THE TEACHERS ARE STILL ON STRIKE, I SEE..
YES, AND MISS OTHMAR LOOKS TIRED..SHE'S BEEN CARRYING THAT SIGN FOR...
SHE'S FALLEN TO HER KNEES!!
WHAT'S GOING ON?
MISS OTHMAR FELL, AND LINUS RUSHED OVER AND PICKED UP HER SIGN!
THAT STUPID BLOCKHEAD... HE'S BECOME INVOLVED!

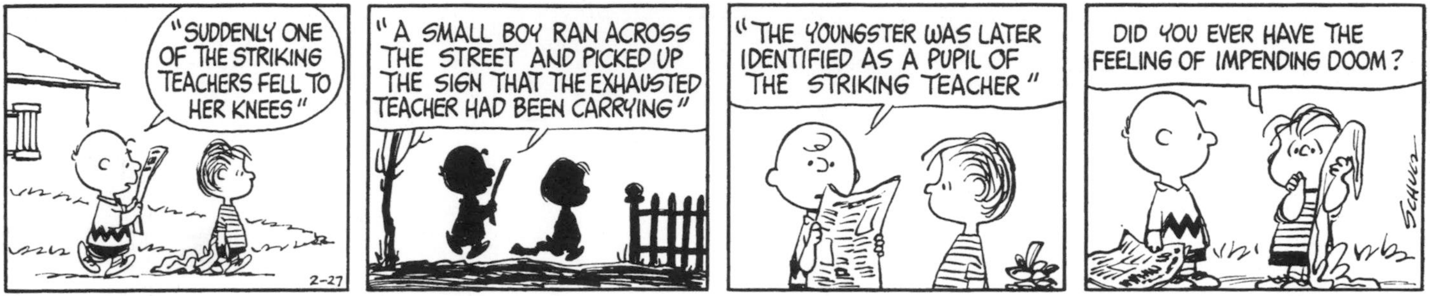
"SUDDENLY ONE OF THE STRIKING TEACHERS FELL TO HER KNEES"
"A SMALL BOY RAN ACROSS THE STREET AND PICKED UP THE SIGN THAT THE EXHAUSTED TEACHER HAD BEEN CARRYING"
"THE YOUNGSTER WAS LATER IDENTIFIED AS A PUPIL OF THE STRIKING TEACHER"
DID YOU EVER HAVE THE FEELING OF IMPENDING DOOM?

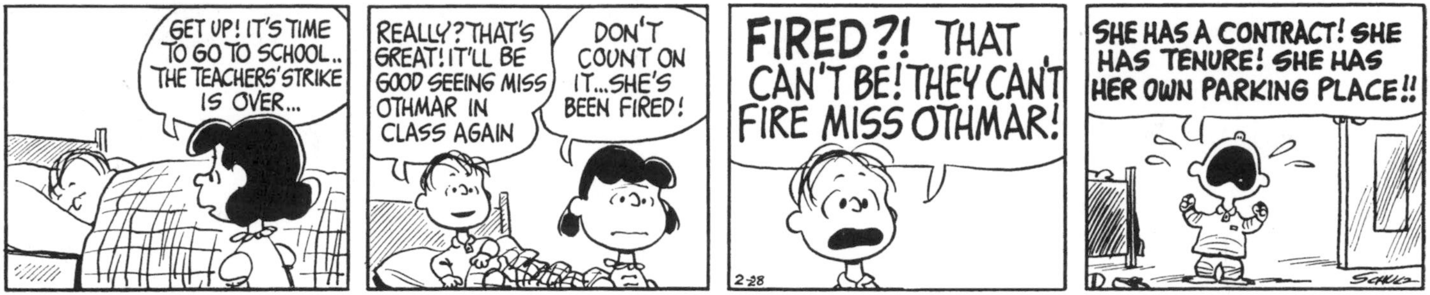
GET UP! IT'S TIME TO GO TO SCHOOL.. THE TEACHERS' STRIKE IS OVER...
REALLY? THAT'S GREAT! IT'LL BE GOOD SEEING MISS OTHMAR IN CLASS AGAIN
DON'T COUNT ON IT...SHE'S BEEN FIRED!
FIRED?! THAT CAN'T BE! THEY CAN'T FIRE MISS OTHMAR!
SHE HAS A CONTRACT! SHE HAS TENURE! SHE HAS HER OWN PARKING PLACE!!

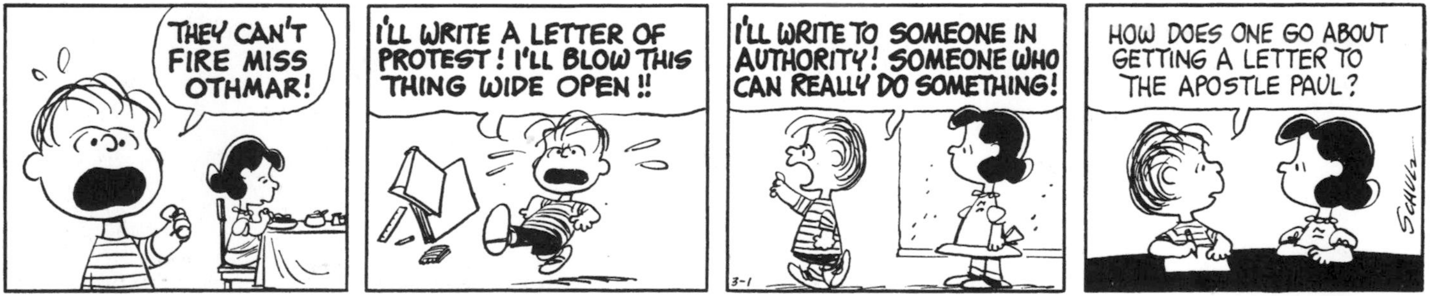
THEY CAN'T FIRE MISS OTHMAR!
I'LL WRITE A LETTER OF PROTEST! I'LL BLOW THIS THING WIDE OPEN!!
I'LL WRITE TO SOMEONE IN AUTHORITY! SOMEONE WHO CAN REALLY DO SOMETHING!
HOW DOES ONE GO ABOUT GETTING A LETTER TO THE APOSTLE PAUL?

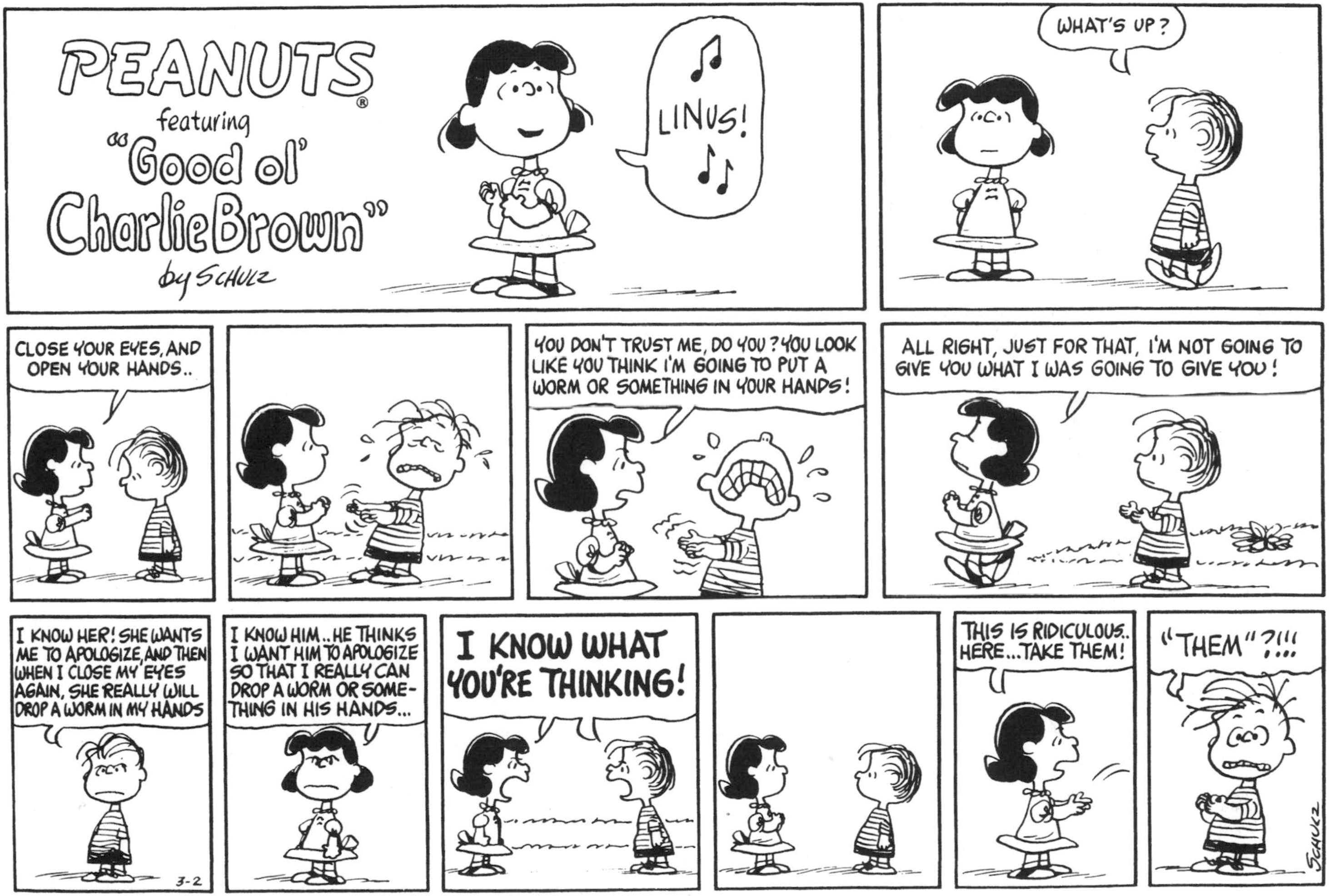

PEANUTS®
featuring "Good ol' Charlie Brown"
by SCHULZ
LINUS!
WHAT'S UP?
CLOSE YOUR EYES, AND OPEN YOUR HANDS..
YOU DON'T TRUST ME, DO YOU? YOU LOOK LIKE YOU THINK I'M GOING TO PUT A WORM OR SOMETHING IN YOUR HANDS!
ALL RIGHT, JUST FOR THAT, I'M NOT GOING TO GIVE YOU WHAT I WAS GOING TO GIVE YOU!
I KNOW HER! SHE WANTS ME TO APOLOGIZE, AND THEN WHEN I CLOSE MY EYES AGAIN, SHE REALLY WILL DROP A WORM IN MY HANDS
3-2
I KNOW HIM..HE THINKS I WANT HIM TO APOLOGIZE SO THAT I REALLY CAN DROP A WORM OR SOMETHING IN HIS HANDS...
I KNOW WHAT YOU'RE THINKING!
THIS IS RIDICULOUS.. HERE...TAKE THEM!
"THEM"?!!!
SCHULZ

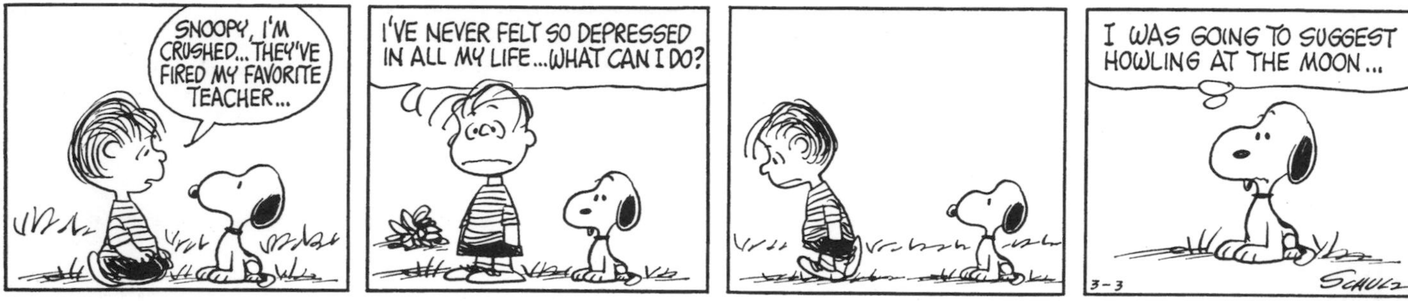
SNOOPY, I'M CRUSHED... THEY'VE FIRED MY FAVORITE TEACHER...
I'VE NEVER FELT SO DEPRESSED IN ALL MY LIFE... WHAT CAN I DO?
I WAS GOING TO SUGGEST HOWLING AT THE MOON...
3-3
SCHULZ

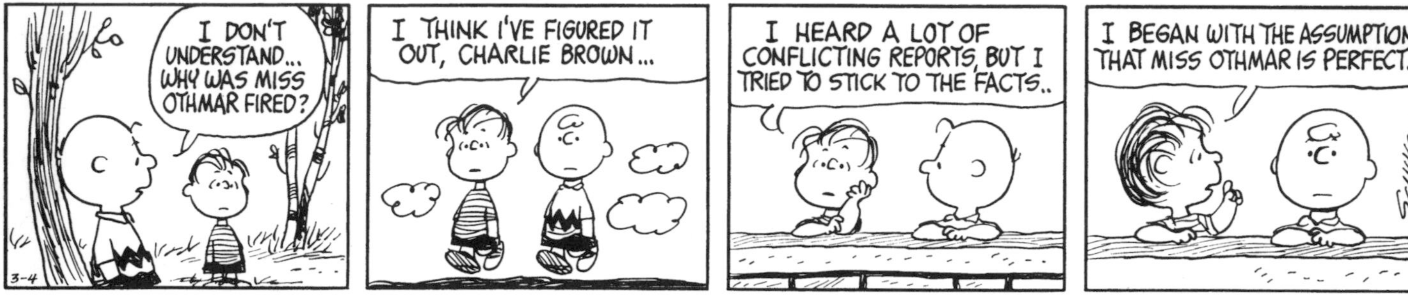
I DON'T UNDERSTAND... WHY WAS MISS OTHMAR FIRED?
3-4
I THINK I'VE FIGURED IT OUT, CHARLIE BROWN...
I HEARD A LOT OF CONFLICTING REPORTS, BUT I TRIED TO STICK TO THE FACTS..
I BEGAN WITH THE ASSUMPTION THAT MISS OTHMAR IS PERFECT..
SCHULZ

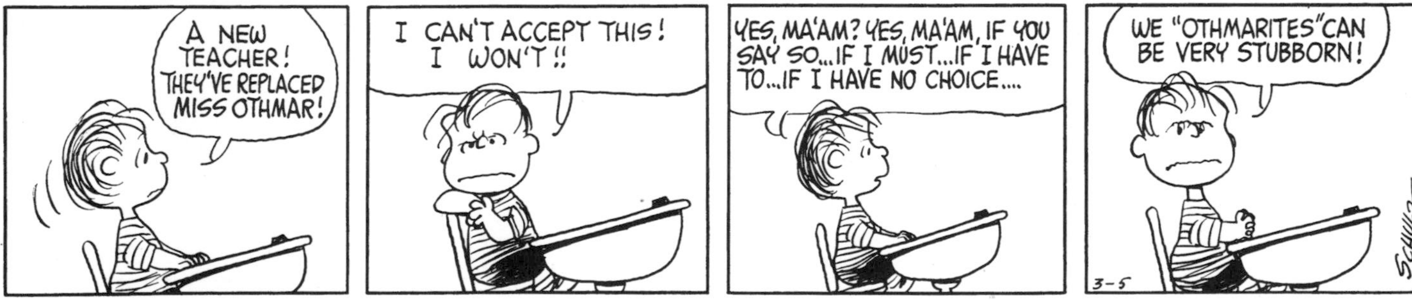
A NEW TEACHER! THEY'VE REPLACED MISS OTHMAR!
I CAN'T ACCEPT THIS! I WON'T!!
YES, MA'AM? YES, MA'AM, IF YOU SAY SO... IF I MUST... IF I HAVE TO... IF I HAVE NO CHOICE....
WE "OTHMARITES" CAN BE VERY STUBBORN!
3-5
SCHULZ

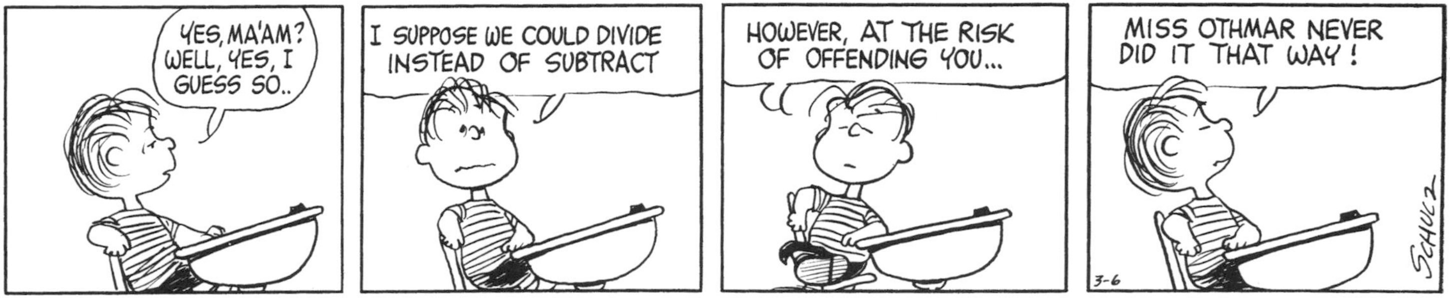
YES, MA'AM? WELL, YES, I GUESS SO..
I SUPPOSE WE COULD DIVIDE INSTEAD OF SUBTRACT
HOWEVER, AT THE RISK OF OFFENDING YOU...
MISS OTHMAR NEVER DID IT THAT WAY!

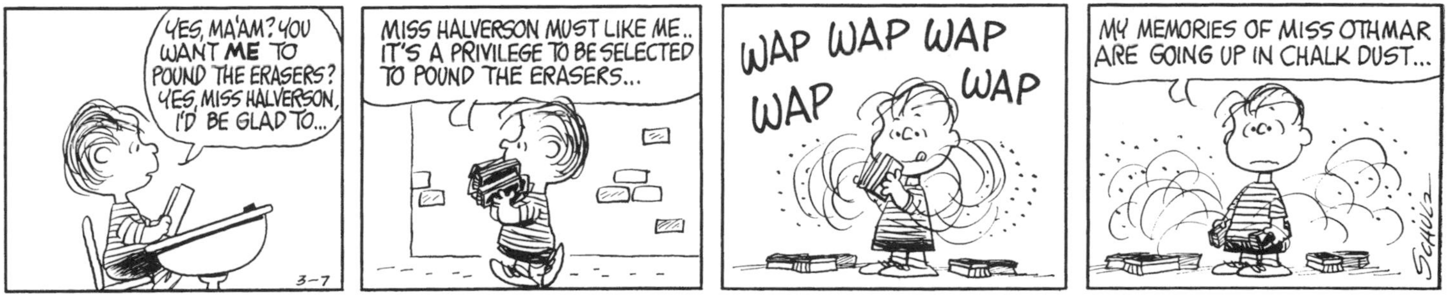
YES, MA'AM? YOU WANT **ME** TO POUND THE ERASERS? YES, MISS HALVERSON, I'D BE GLAD TO...
MISS HALVERSON MUST LIKE ME.. IT'S A PRIVILEGE TO BE SELECTED TO POUND THE ERASERS...
WAP WAP WAP
WAP
WAP
MY MEMORIES OF MISS OTHMAR ARE GOING UP IN CHALK DUST...

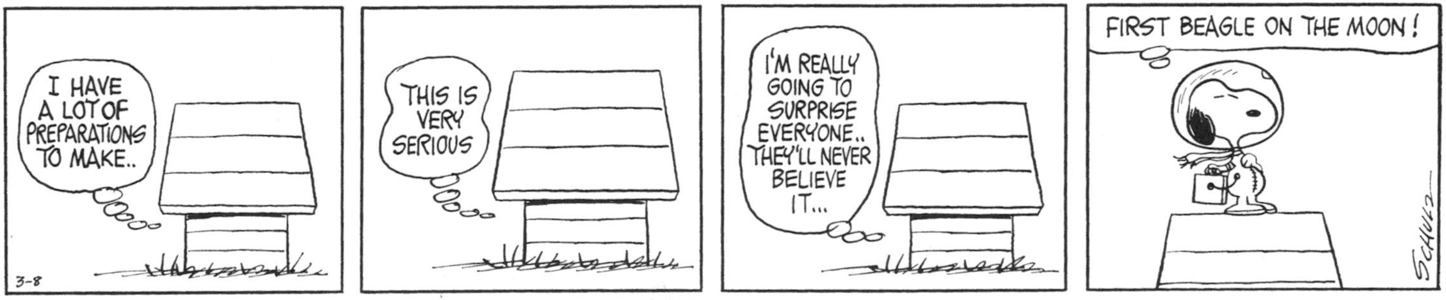
I HAVE A LOT OF PREPARATIONS TO MAKE..
THIS IS VERY SERIOUS
I'M REALLY GOING TO SURPRISE EVERYONE.. THEY'LL NEVER BELIEVE IT...
FIRST BEAGLE ON THE MOON!

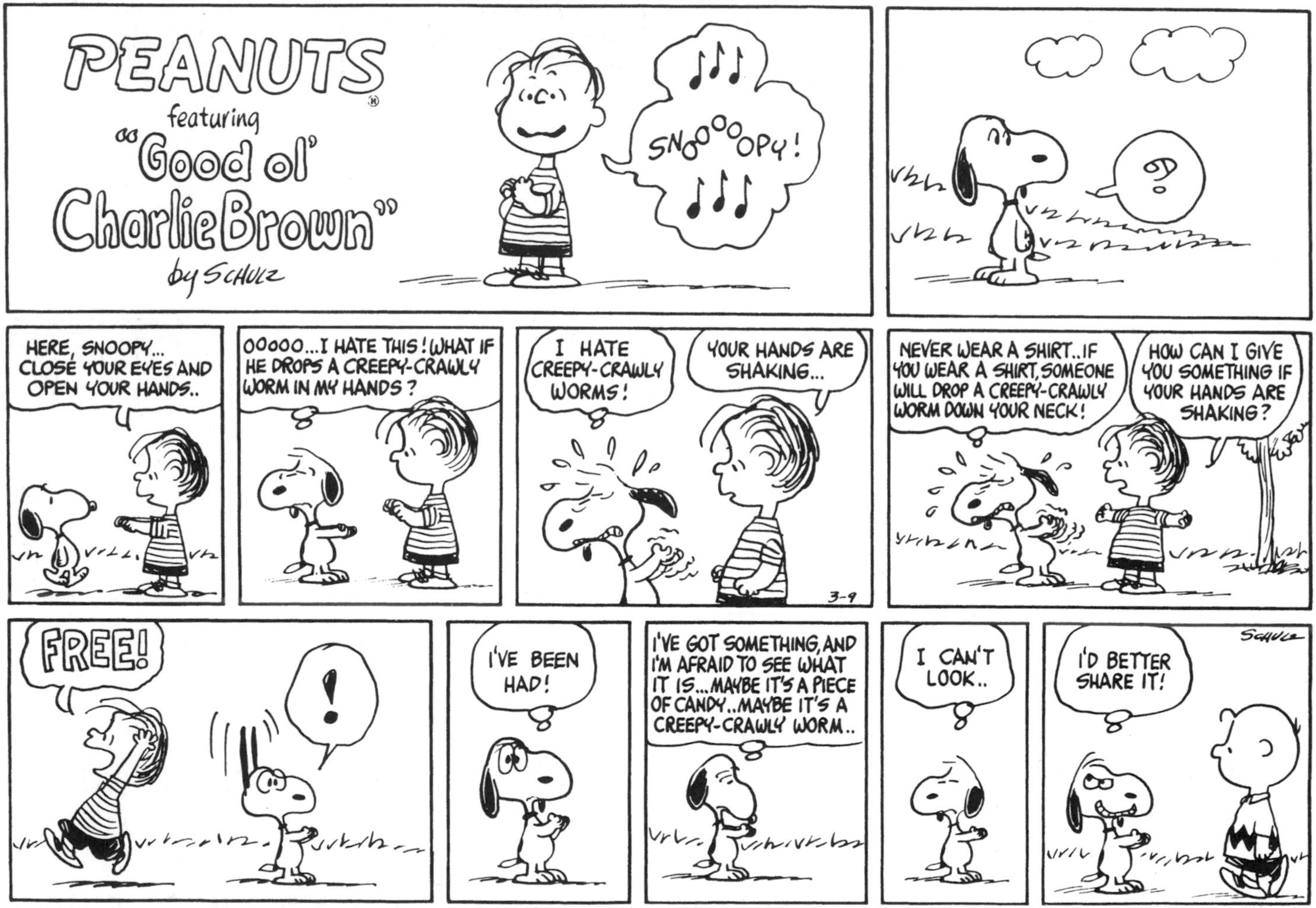
PEANUTS
featuring "Good ol' Charlie Brown"
by SCHULZ
SNOOOOOPY!
?
HERE, SNOOPY... CLOSE YOUR EYES AND OPEN YOUR HANDS..
OOOOO...I HATE THIS! WHAT IF HE DROPS A CREEPY-CRAWLY WORM IN MY HANDS?
I HATE CREEPY-CRAWLY WORMS!
YOUR HANDS ARE SHAKING...
3-9
NEVER WEAR A SHIRT..IF YOU WEAR A SHIRT, SOMEONE WILL DROP A CREEPY-CRAWLY WORM DOWN YOUR NECK!
HOW CAN I GIVE YOU SOMETHING IF YOUR HANDS ARE SHAKING?
FREE!
!
I'VE BEEN HAD!
I'VE GOT SOMETHING, AND I'M AFRAID TO SEE WHAT IT IS...MAYBE IT'S A PIECE OF CANDY..MAYBE IT'S A CREEPY-CRAWLY WORM..
I CAN'T LOOK..
SCHULZ
I'D BETTER SHARE IT!

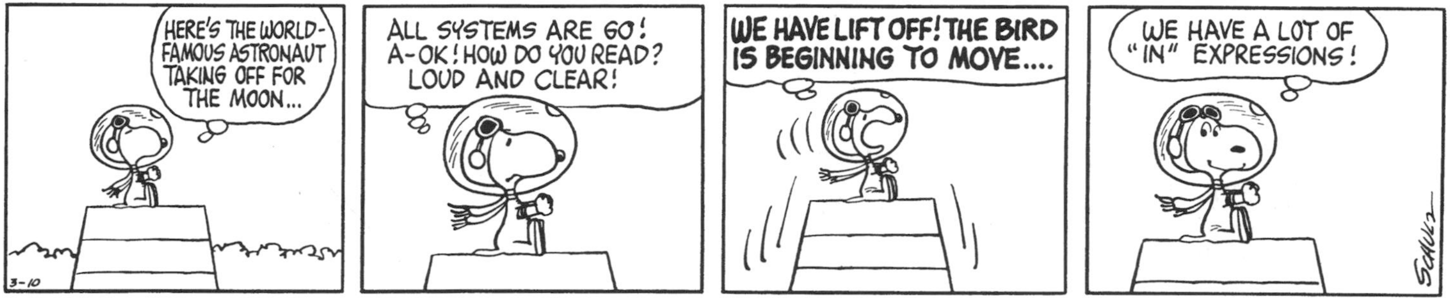
HERE'S THE WORLD-FAMOUS ASTRONAUT TAKING OFF FOR THE MOON...
ALL SYSTEMS ARE GO! A-OK! HOW DO YOU READ? LOUD AND CLEAR!
WE HAVE LIFT OFF! THE BIRD IS BEGINNING TO MOVE....
WE HAVE A LOT OF "IN" EXPRESSIONS!

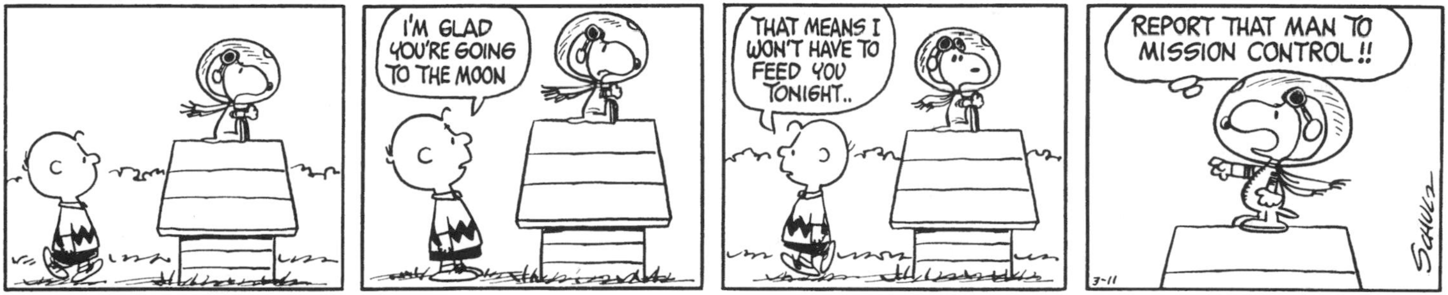
I'M GLAD YOU'RE GOING TO THE MOON
THAT MEANS I WON'T HAVE TO FEED YOU TONIGHT..
REPORT THAT MAN TO MISSION CONTROL!!

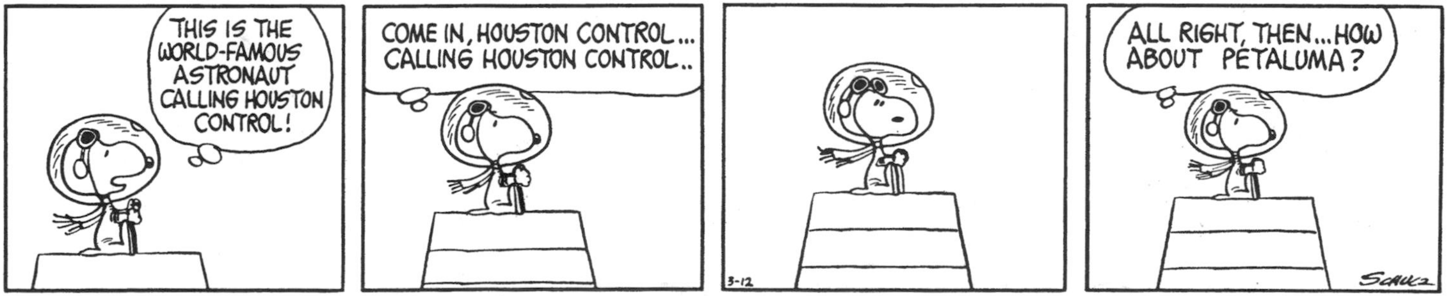
THIS IS THE WORLD-FAMOUS ASTRONAUT CALLING HOUSTON CONTROL!
COME IN, HOUSTON CONTROL... CALLING HOUSTON CONTROL..
ALL RIGHT, THEN...HOW ABOUT PETALUMA?

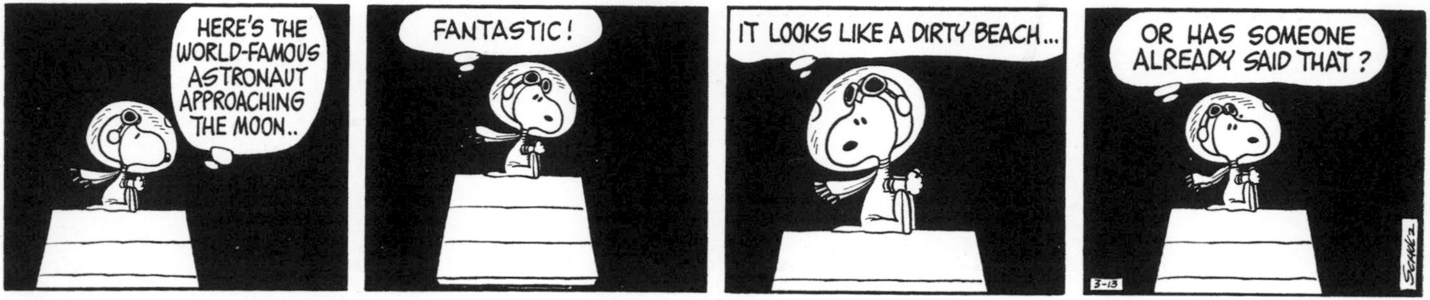
HERE'S THE WORLD-FAMOUS ASTRONAUT APPROACHING THE MOON..
FANTASTIC!
IT LOOKS LIKE A DIRTY BEACH...
OR HAS SOMEONE ALREADY SAID THAT?
3-13
SCHULZ

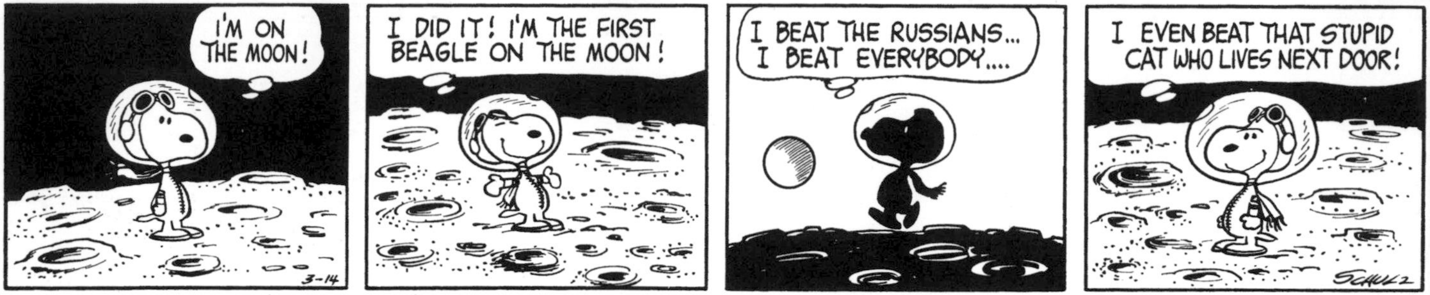
I'M ON THE MOON!
3-14
I DID IT! I'M THE FIRST BEAGLE ON THE MOON!
I BEAT THE RUSSIANS... I BEAT EVERYBODY....
I EVEN BEAT THAT STUPID CAT WHO LIVES NEXT DOOR!
SCHULZ

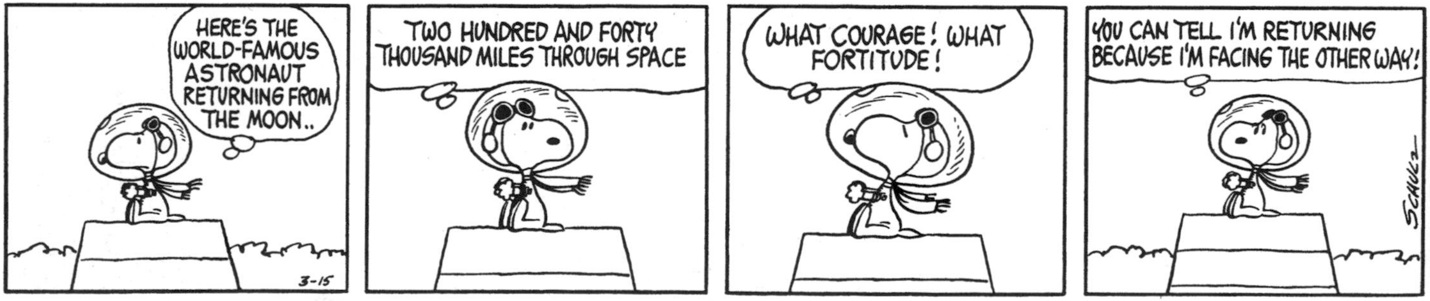
HERE'S THE WORLD-FAMOUS ASTRONAUT RETURNING FROM THE MOON..
3-15
TWO HUNDRED AND FORTY THOUSAND MILES THROUGH SPACE
WHAT COURAGE! WHAT FORTITUDE!
YOU CAN TELL I'M RETURNING BECAUSE I'M FACING THE OTHER WAY!
SCHULZ

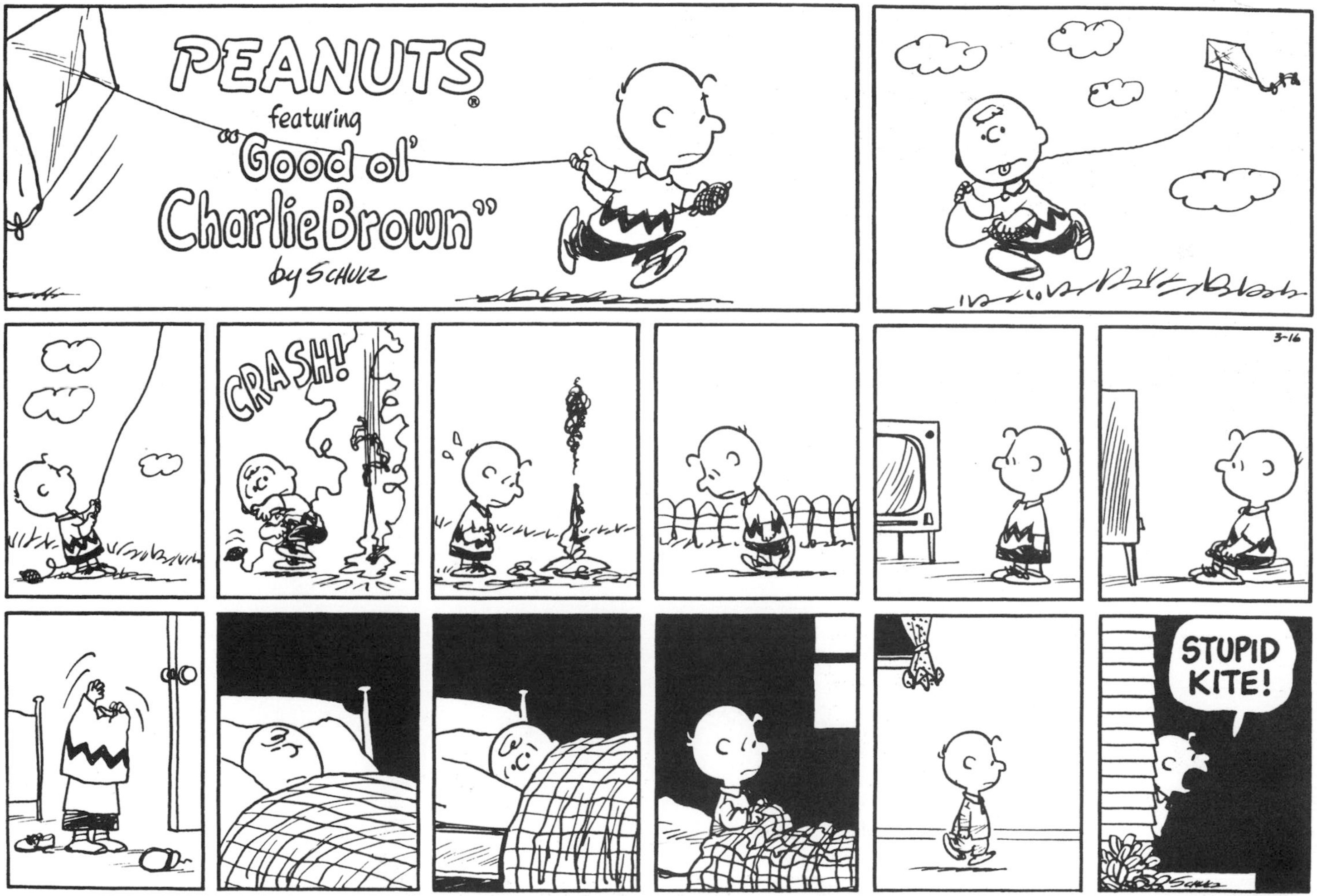
PEANUTS®
featuring
"Good ol' Charlie Brown"
by SCHULZ
CRASH!
3-16
STUPID KITE!

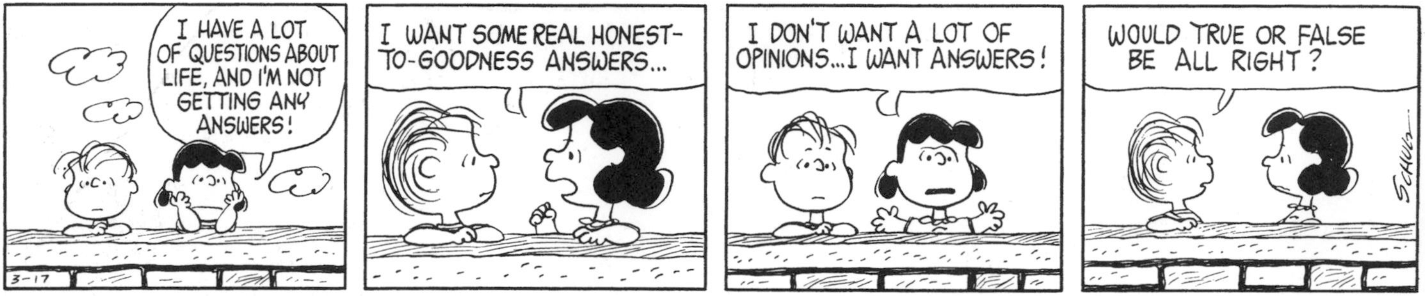
I HAVE A LOT OF QUESTIONS ABOUT LIFE, AND I'M NOT GETTING ANY ANSWERS!
I WANT SOME REAL HONEST-TO-GOODNESS ANSWERS...
I DON'T WANT A LOT OF OPINIONS...I WANT ANSWERS!
WOULD TRUE OR FALSE BE ALL RIGHT?
3-17
SCHULZ

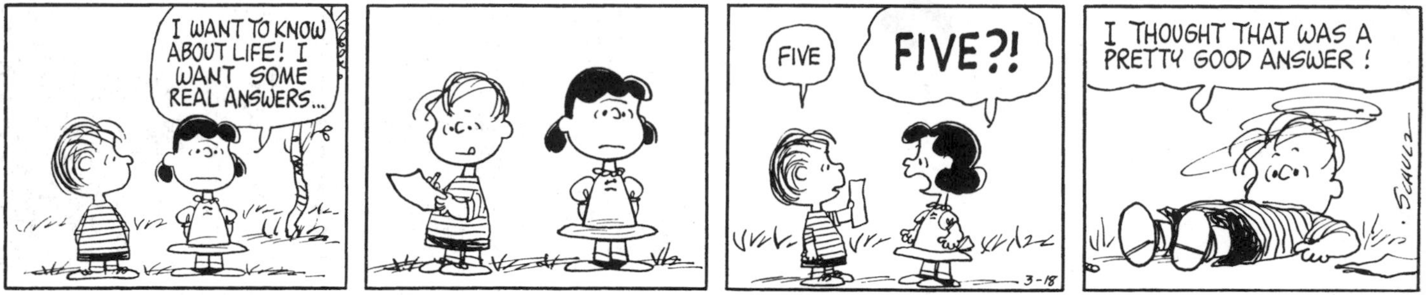
I WANT TO KNOW ABOUT LIFE! I WANT SOME REAL ANSWERS...
FIVE
FIVE?!
3-18
I THOUGHT THAT WAS A PRETTY GOOD ANSWER!
SCHULZ

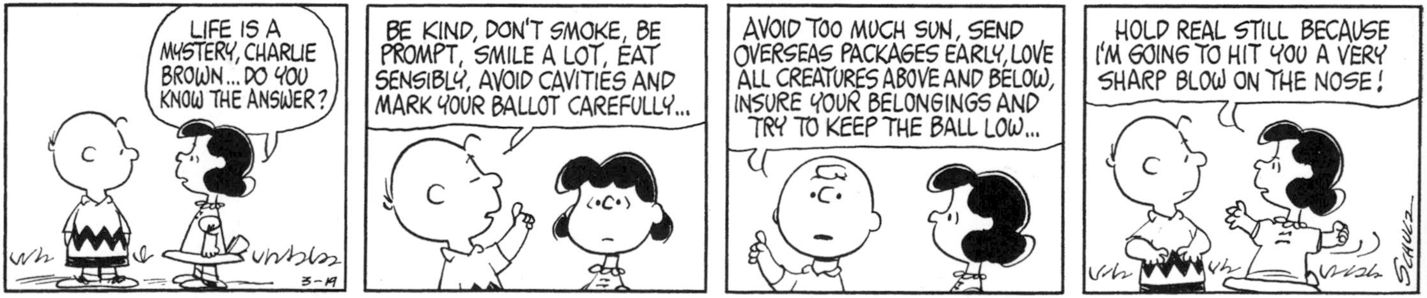
LIFE IS A MYSTERY, CHARLIE BROWN... DO YOU KNOW THE ANSWER?
3-19
BE KIND, DON'T SMOKE, BE PROMPT, SMILE A LOT, EAT SENSIBLY, AVOID CAVITIES AND MARK YOUR BALLOT CAREFULLY...
AVOID TOO MUCH SUN, SEND OVERSEAS PACKAGES EARLY, LOVE ALL CREATURES ABOVE AND BELOW, INSURE YOUR BELONGINGS AND TRY TO KEEP THE BALL LOW...
HOLD REAL STILL BECAUSE I'M GOING TO HIT YOU A VERY SHARP BLOW ON THE NOSE!
SCHULZ

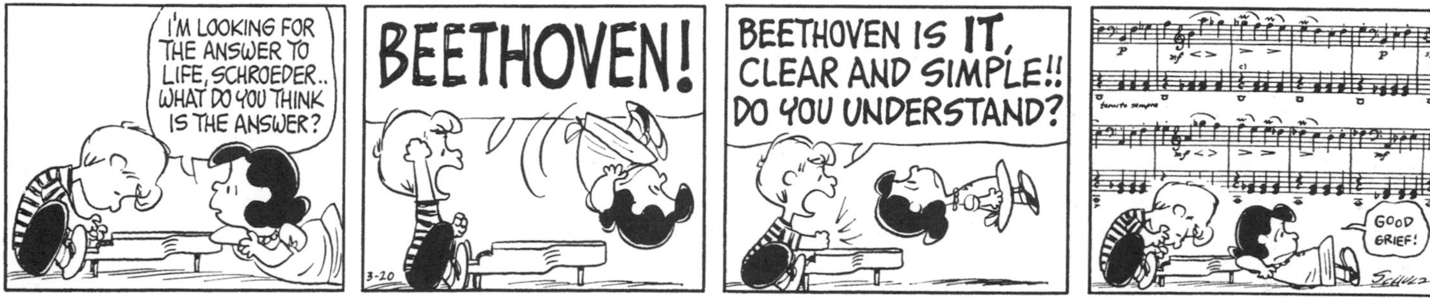
I'M LOOKING FOR THE ANSWER TO LIFE, SCHROEDER.. WHAT DO YOU THINK IS THE ANSWER?
BEETHOVEN!
BEETHOVEN IS IT, CLEAR AND SIMPLE!! DO YOU UNDERSTAND?
GOOD GRIEF!

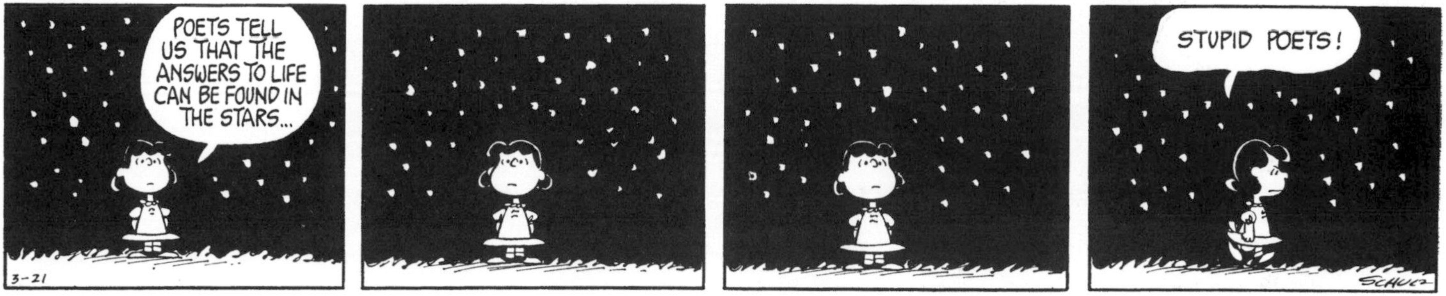
POETS TELL US THAT THE ANSWERS TO LIFE CAN BE FOUND IN THE STARS...
STUPID POETS!

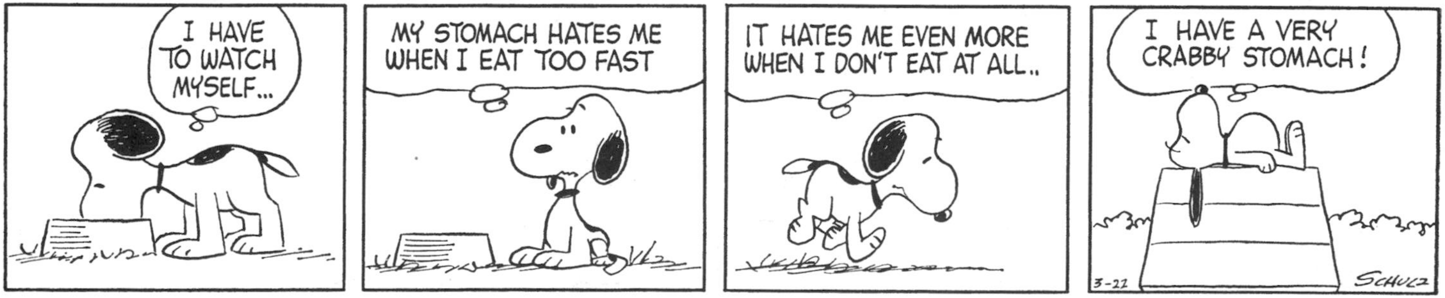
I HAVE TO WATCH MYSELF...
MY STOMACH HATES ME WHEN I EAT TOO FAST
IT HATES ME EVEN MORE WHEN I DON'T EAT AT ALL..
I HAVE A VERY CRABBY STOMACH!

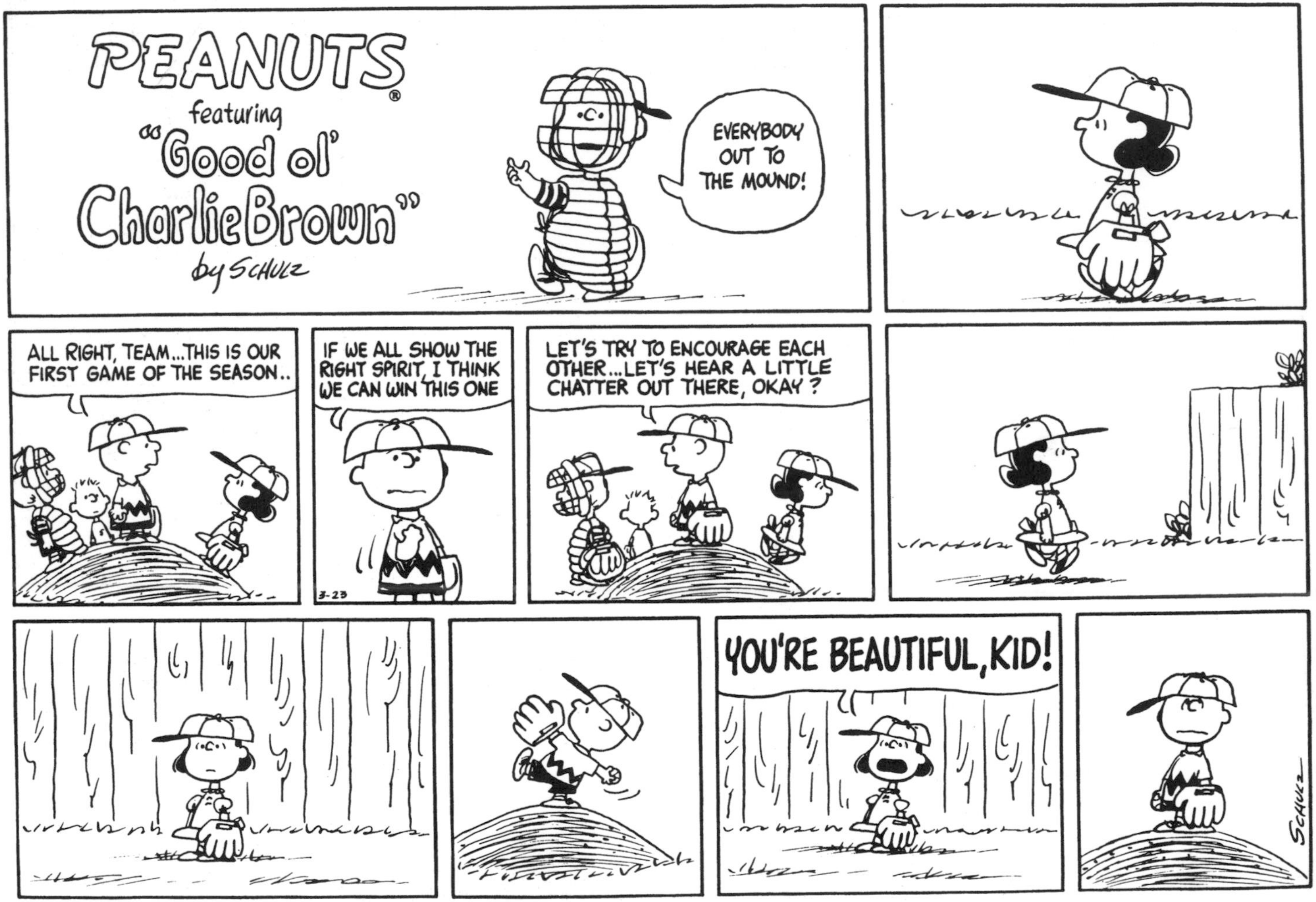
PEANUTS®
featuring
"Good ol' CharlieBrown"
by SCHULZ
EVERYBODY OUT TO THE MOUND!
ALL RIGHT, TEAM...THIS IS OUR FIRST GAME OF THE SEASON..
IF WE ALL SHOW THE RIGHT SPIRIT, I THINK WE CAN WIN THIS ONE
3-23
LET'S TRY TO ENCOURAGE EACH OTHER...LET'S HEAR A LITTLE CHATTER OUT THERE, OKAY ?
YOU'RE BEAUTIFUL, KID!
SCHULZ

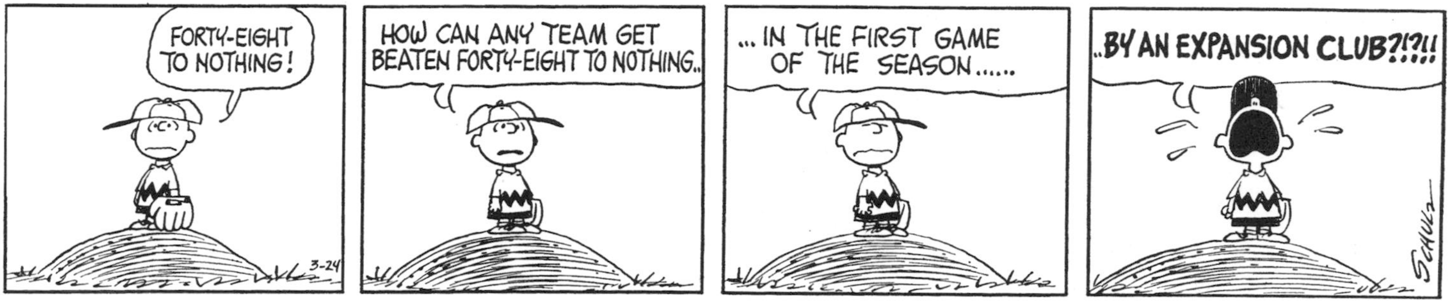
FORTY-EIGHT TO NOTHING!
3-24
HOW CAN ANY TEAM GET BEATEN FORTY-EIGHT TO NOTHING..
...IN THE FIRST GAME OF THE SEASON......
..BY AN EXPANSION CLUB?!?!!
SCHULZ

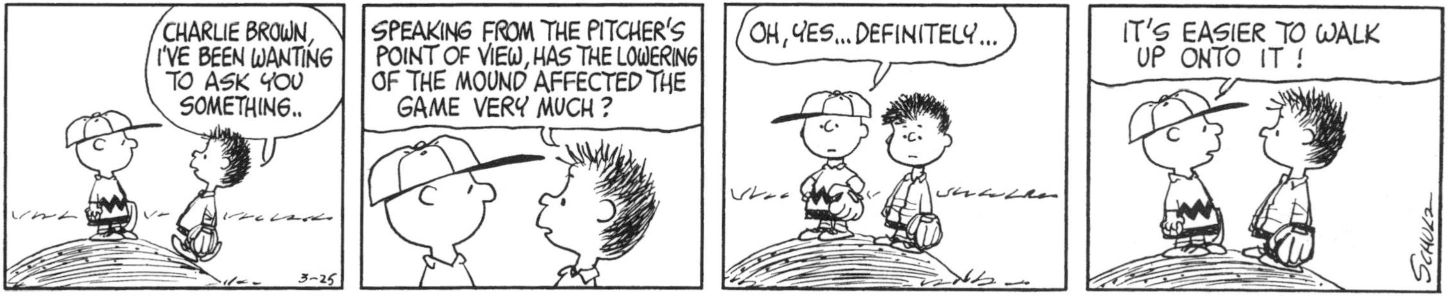
CHARLIE BROWN, I'VE BEEN WANTING TO ASK YOU SOMETHING..
3-25
SPEAKING FROM THE PITCHER'S POINT OF VIEW, HAS THE LOWERING OF THE MOUND AFFECTED THE GAME VERY MUCH?
OH, YES...DEFINITELY...
IT'S EASIER TO WALK UP ONTO IT!
SCHULZ

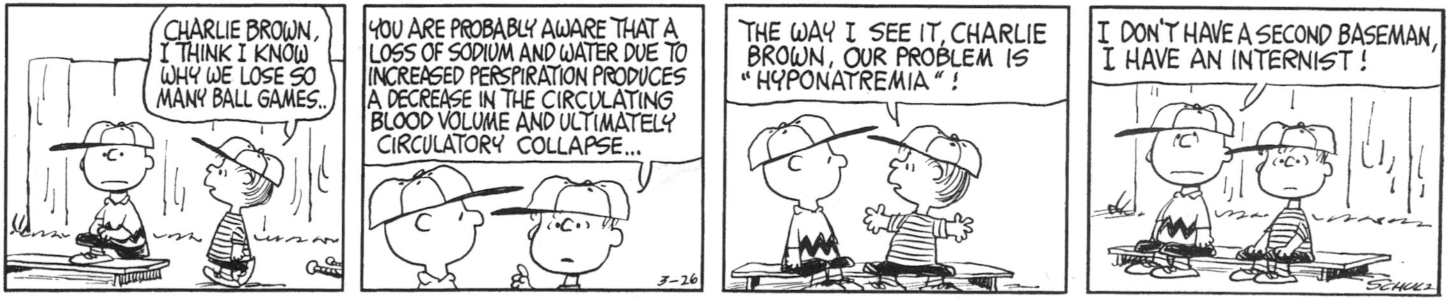
CHARLIE BROWN, I THINK I KNOW WHY WE LOSE SO MANY BALL GAMES..
YOU ARE PROBABLY AWARE THAT A LOSS OF SODIUM AND WATER DUE TO INCREASED PERSPIRATION PRODUCES A DECREASE IN THE CIRCULATING BLOOD VOLUME AND ULTIMATELY CIRCULATORY COLLAPSE...
3-26
THE WAY I SEE IT, CHARLIE BROWN, OUR PROBLEM IS "HYPONATREMIA"!
I DON'T HAVE A SECOND BASEMAN, I HAVE AN INTERNIST!
SCHULZ

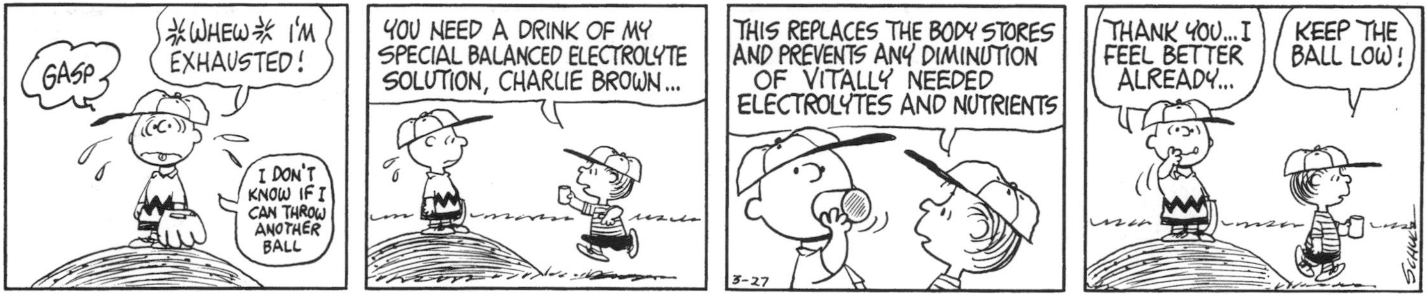
GASP
WHEW I'M EXHAUSTED!
I DON'T KNOW IF I CAN THROW ANOTHER BALL
YOU NEED A DRINK OF MY SPECIAL BALANCED ELECTROLYTE SOLUTION, CHARLIE BROWN...
THIS REPLACES THE BODY STORES AND PREVENTS ANY DIMINUTION OF VITALLY NEEDED ELECTROLYTES AND NUTRIENTS
3-27
THANK YOU... I FEEL BETTER ALREADY...
KEEP THE BALL LOW!
SCHULZ

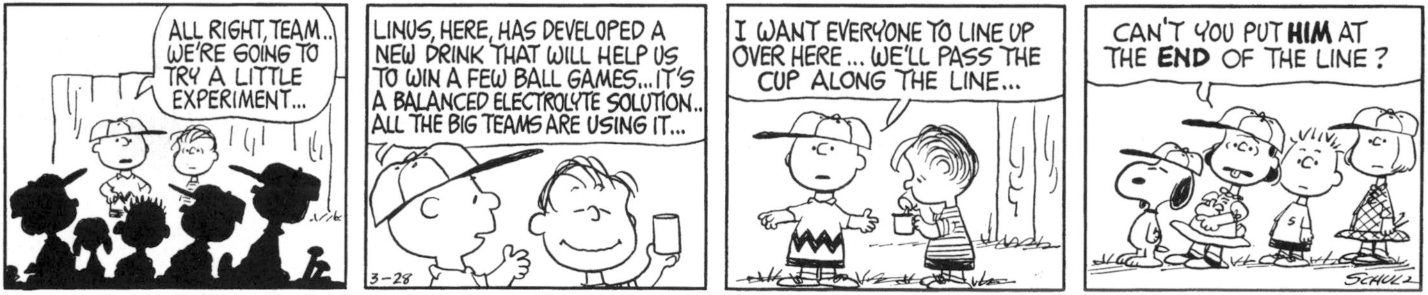
ALL RIGHT, TEAM.. WE'RE GOING TO TRY A LITTLE EXPERIMENT...
LINUS, HERE, HAS DEVELOPED A NEW DRINK THAT WILL HELP US TO WIN A FEW BALL GAMES...IT'S A BALANCED ELECTROLYTE SOLUTION.. ALL THE BIG TEAMS ARE USING IT...
3-28
I WANT EVERYONE TO LINE UP OVER HERE ... WE'LL PASS THE CUP ALONG THE LINE...
CAN'T YOU PUT **HIM** AT THE **END** OF THE LINE?
SCHULZ

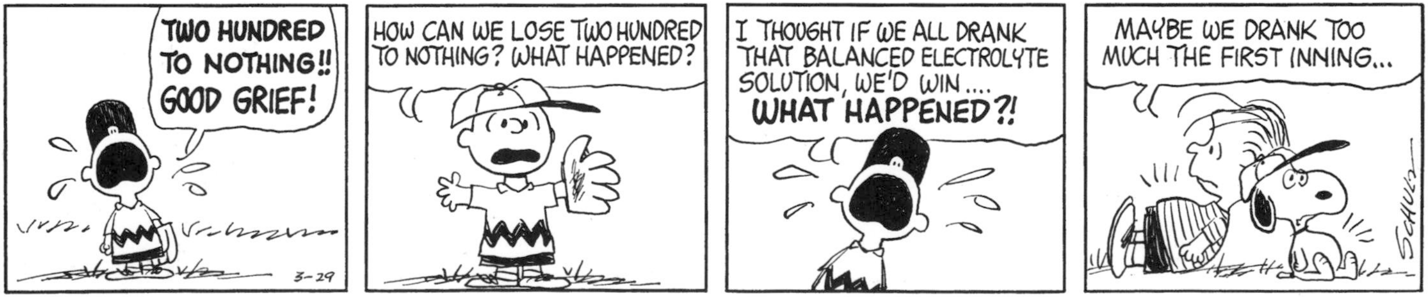
TWO HUNDRED TO NOTHING!! GOOD GRIEF!
3-29
HOW CAN WE LOSE TWO HUNDRED TO NOTHING? WHAT HAPPENED?
I THOUGHT IF WE ALL DRANK THAT BALANCED ELECTROLYTE SOLUTION, WE'D WIN.... **WHAT HAPPENED?!**
MAYBE WE DRANK TOO MUCH THE FIRST INNING...
SCHULZ

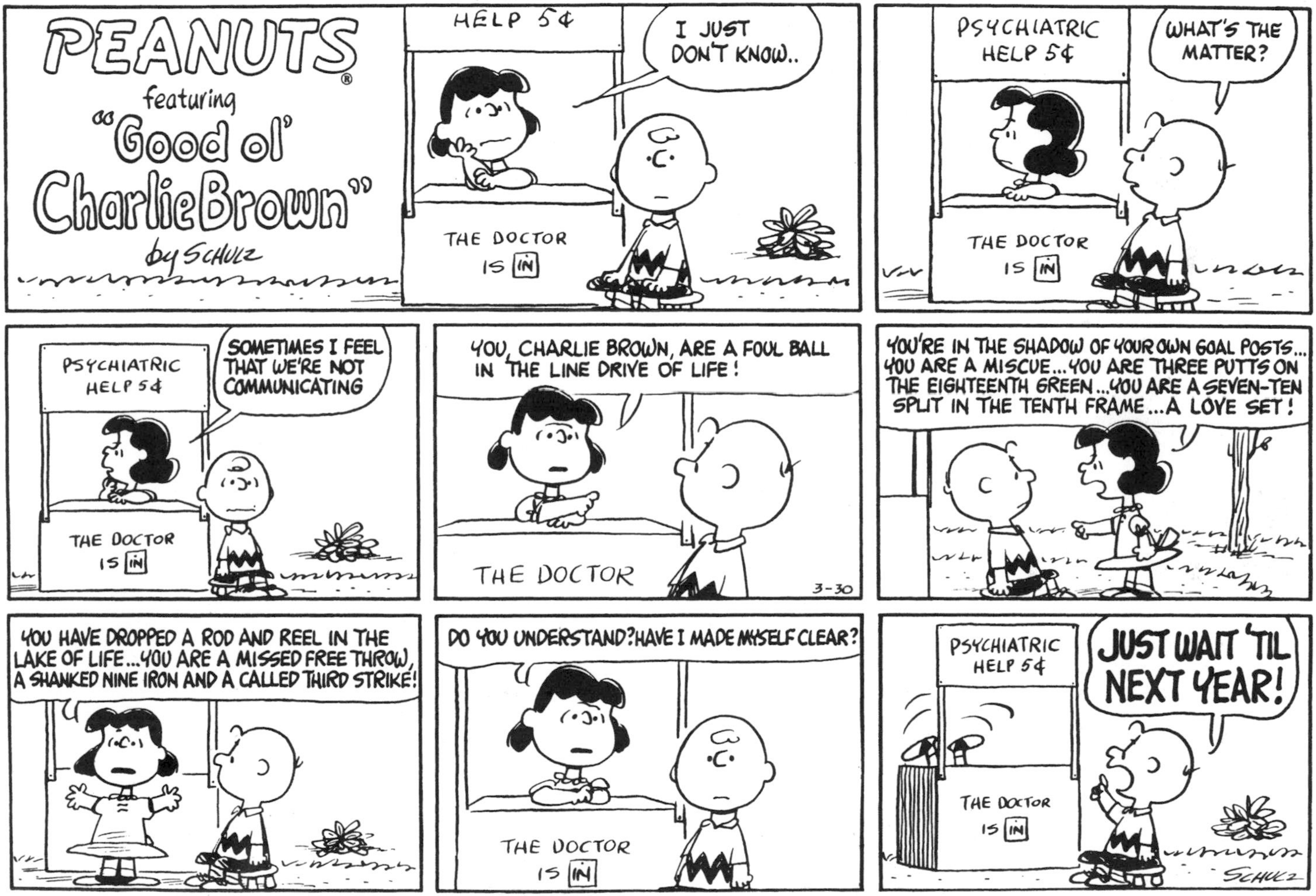
PEANUTS®
featuring "Good ol' Charlie Brown"
by SCHULZ
HELP 5¢
I JUST DON'T KNOW..
THE DOCTOR IS IN
PSYCHIATRIC HELP 5¢
WHAT'S THE MATTER?
THE DOCTOR IS IN
PSYCHIATRIC HELP 5¢
SOMETIMES I FEEL THAT WE'RE NOT COMMUNICATING
THE DOCTOR IS IN
YOU, CHARLIE BROWN, ARE A FOUL BALL IN THE LINE DRIVE OF LIFE!
THE DOCTOR
3-30
YOU'RE IN THE SHADOW OF YOUR OWN GOAL POSTS... YOU ARE A MISCUE... YOU ARE THREE PUTTS ON THE EIGHTEENTH GREEN... YOU ARE A SEVEN-TEN SPLIT IN THE TENTH FRAME... A LOVE SET!
YOU HAVE DROPPED A ROD AND REEL IN THE LAKE OF LIFE... YOU ARE A MISSED FREE THROW, A SHANKED NINE IRON AND A CALLED THIRD STRIKE!
DO YOU UNDERSTAND? HAVE I MADE MYSELF CLEAR?
THE DOCTOR IS IN
PSYCHIATRIC HELP 5¢
JUST WAIT 'TIL NEXT YEAR!
THE DOCTOR IS IN
SCHULZ

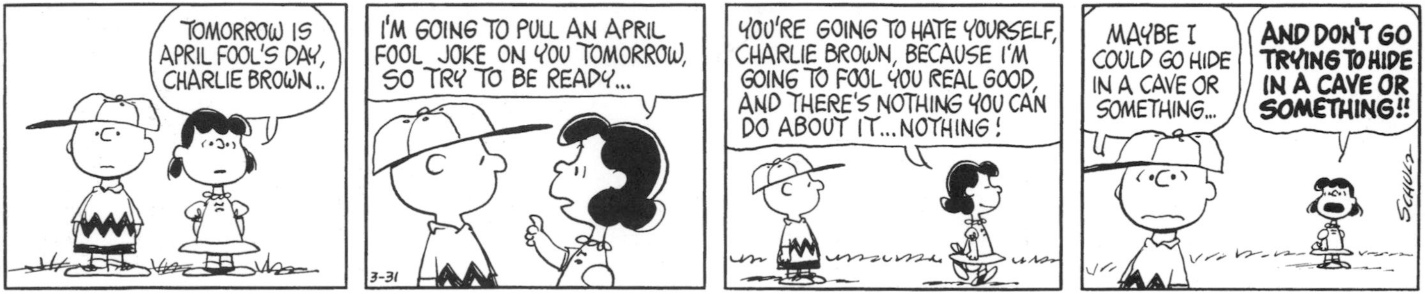
TOMORROW IS APRIL FOOL'S DAY, CHARLIE BROWN..
I'M GOING TO PULL AN APRIL FOOL JOKE ON YOU TOMORROW, SO TRY TO BE READY...
3-31
YOU'RE GOING TO HATE YOURSELF, CHARLIE BROWN, BECAUSE I'M GOING TO FOOL YOU REAL GOOD, AND THERE'S NOTHING YOU CAN DO ABOUT IT... NOTHING!
MAYBE I COULD GO HIDE IN A CAVE OR SOMETHING...
AND DON'T GO TRYING TO HIDE IN A CAVE OR SOMETHING!!
SCHULZ

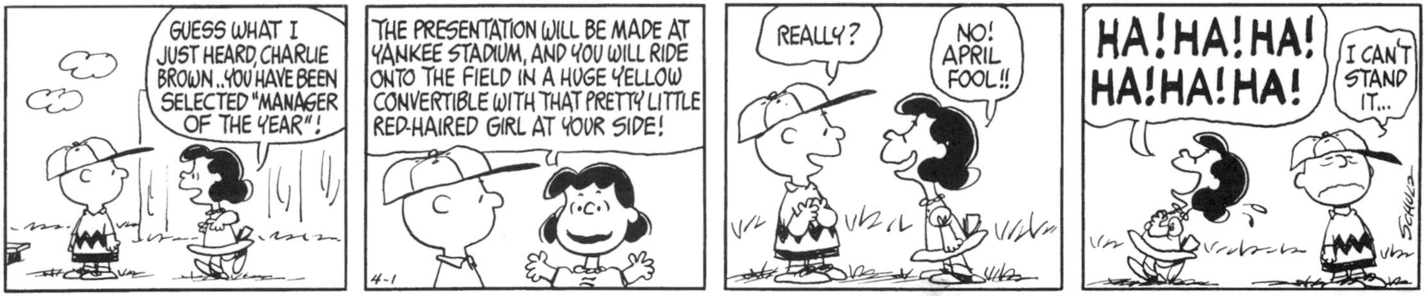
GUESS WHAT I JUST HEARD, CHARLIE BROWN.. YOU HAVE BEEN SELECTED "MANAGER OF THE YEAR"!
THE PRESENTATION WILL BE MADE AT YANKEE STADIUM, AND YOU WILL RIDE ONTO THE FIELD IN A HUGE YELLOW CONVERTIBLE WITH THAT PRETTY LITTLE RED-HAIRED GIRL AT YOUR SIDE!
4-1
REALLY?
NO! APRIL FOOL!!
HA! HA! HA! HA! HA! HA!
I CAN'T STAND IT...
SCHULZ

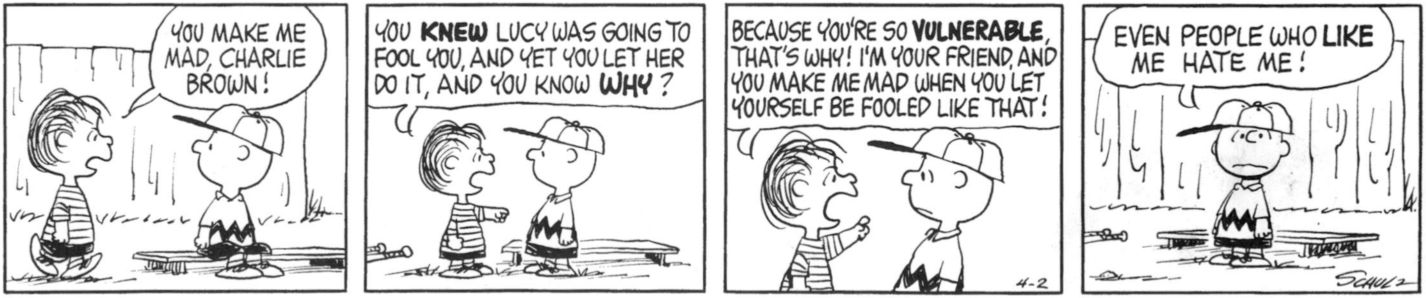
YOU MAKE ME MAD, CHARLIE BROWN!
YOU KNEW LUCY WAS GOING TO FOOL YOU, AND YET YOU LET HER DO IT, AND YOU KNOW WHY?
BECAUSE YOU'RE SO VULNERABLE, THAT'S WHY! I'M YOUR FRIEND, AND YOU MAKE ME MAD WHEN YOU LET YOURSELF BE FOOLED LIKE THAT!
4-2
EVEN PEOPLE WHO LIKE ME HATE ME!
SCHULZ

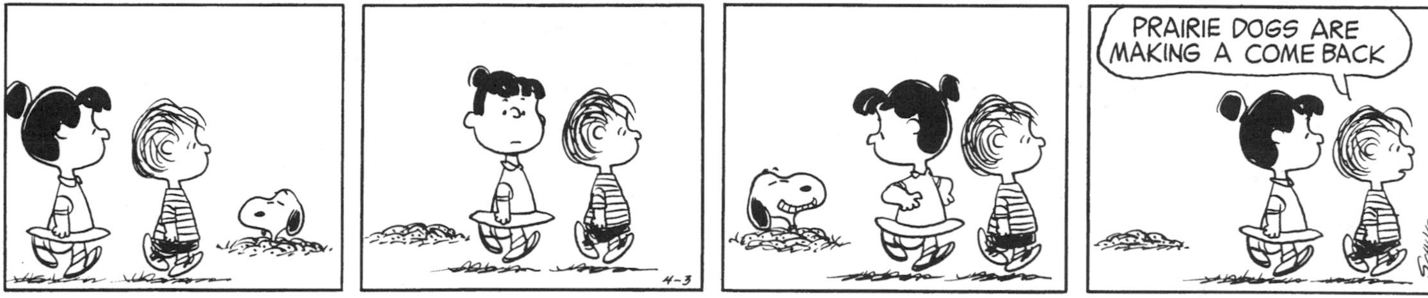
4-3
PRAIRIE DOGS ARE MAKING A COME BACK
SCHULZ

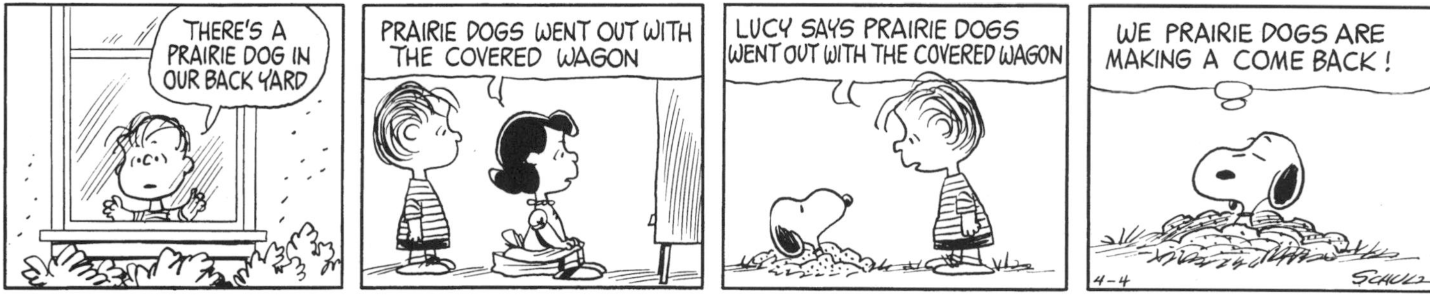
THERE'S A PRAIRIE DOG IN OUR BACK YARD
PRAIRIE DOGS WENT OUT WITH THE COVERED WAGON
LUCY SAYS PRAIRIE DOGS WENT OUT WITH THE COVERED WAGON
WE PRAIRIE DOGS ARE MAKING A COME BACK !
4-4
SCHULZ

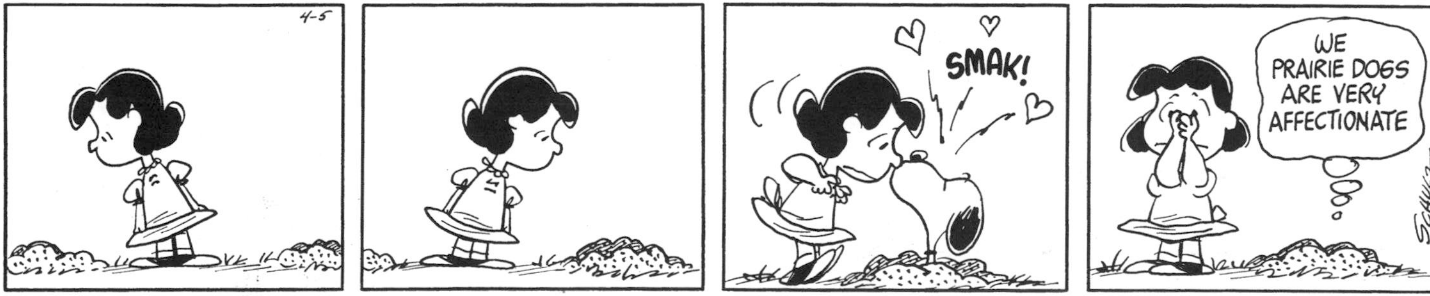
4-5
SMAK!
WE PRAIRIE DOGS ARE VERY AFFECTIONATE
SCHULZ

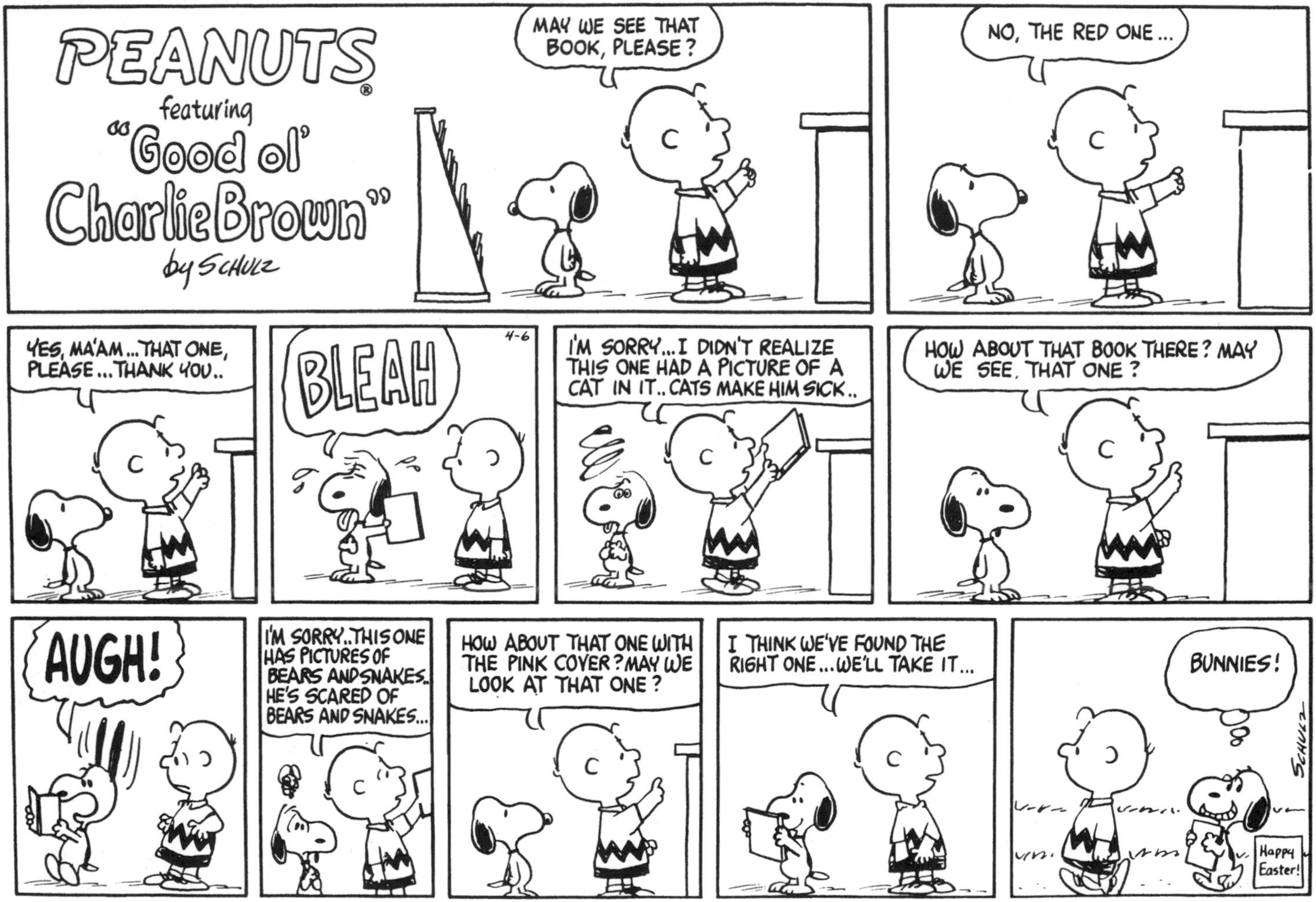
PEANUTS®
featuring "Good ol' Charlie Brown"
by SCHULZ
MAY WE SEE THAT BOOK, PLEASE?
NO, THE RED ONE...
YES, MA'AM...THAT ONE, PLEASE...THANK YOU..
4-6
BLEAH
I'M SORRY...I DIDN'T REALIZE THIS ONE HAD A PICTURE OF A CAT IN IT.. CATS MAKE HIM SICK..
HOW ABOUT THAT BOOK THERE? MAY WE SEE, THAT ONE?
AUGH!
I'M SORRY..THIS ONE HAS PICTURES OF BEARS AND SNAKES.. HE'S SCARED OF BEARS AND SNAKES...
HOW ABOUT THAT ONE WITH THE PINK COVER? MAY WE LOOK AT THAT ONE?
I THINK WE'VE FOUND THE RIGHT ONE...WE'LL TAKE IT...
BUNNIES!
SCHULZ
Happy Easter!

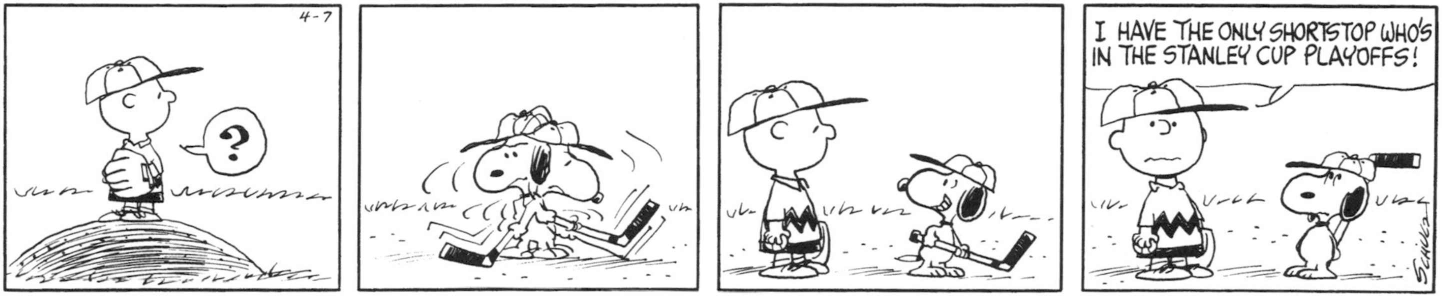
4-7
?
I HAVE THE ONLY SHORTSTOP WHO'S IN THE STANLEY CUP PLAYOFFS!
SCHULZ

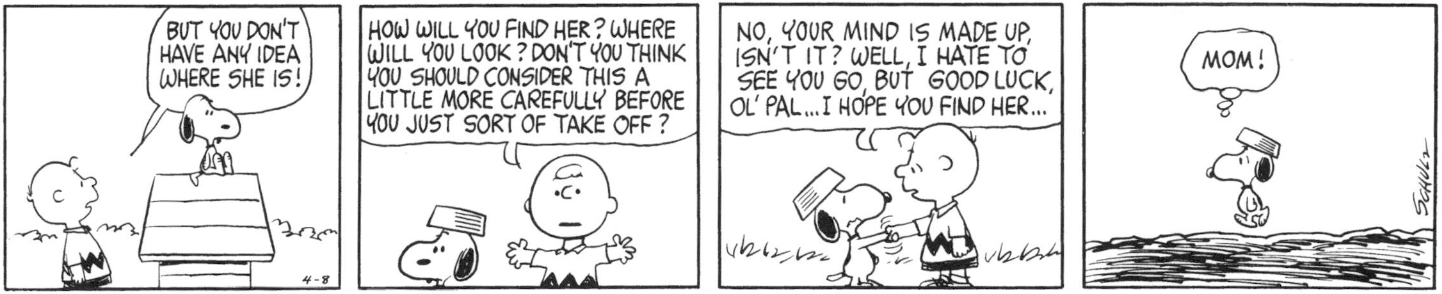
BUT YOU DON'T HAVE ANY IDEA WHERE SHE IS!
4-8
HOW WILL YOU FIND HER? WHERE WILL YOU LOOK? DON'T YOU THINK YOU SHOULD CONSIDER THIS A LITTLE MORE CAREFULLY BEFORE YOU JUST SORT OF TAKE OFF?
NO, YOUR MIND IS MADE UP, ISN'T IT? WELL, I HATE TO SEE YOU GO, BUT GOOD LUCK, OL' PAL...I HOPE YOU FIND HER...
MOM!
SCHULZ

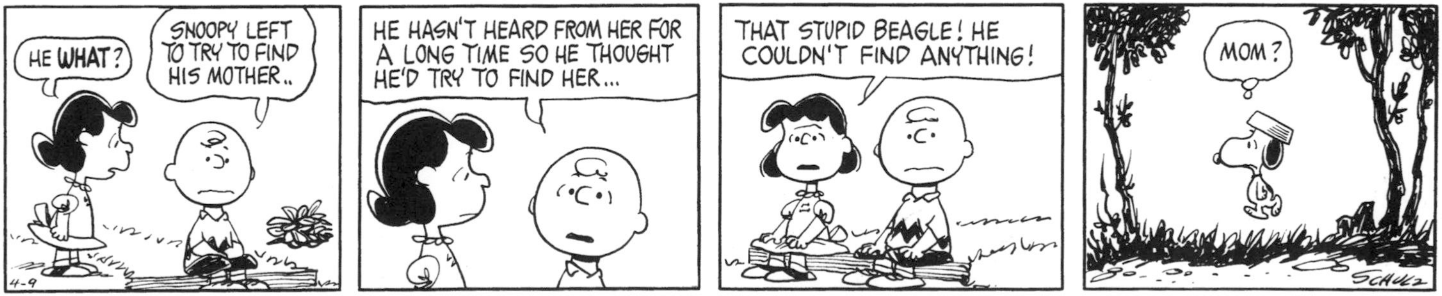
HE **WHAT**?
SNOOPY LEFT TO TRY TO FIND HIS MOTHER..
4-9
HE HASN'T HEARD FROM HER FOR A LONG TIME SO HE THOUGHT HE'D TRY TO FIND HER...
THAT STUPID BEAGLE! HE COULDN'T FIND ANYTHING!
MOM?
SCHULZ

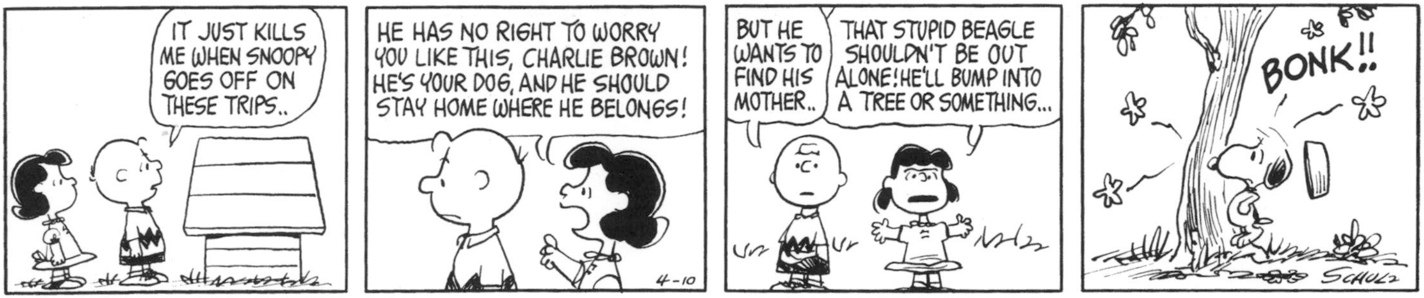
IT JUST KILLS ME WHEN SNOOPY GOES OFF ON THESE TRIPS..
HE HAS NO RIGHT TO WORRY YOU LIKE THIS, CHARLIE BROWN! HE'S YOUR DOG, AND HE SHOULD STAY HOME WHERE HE BELONGS!
4-10
BUT HE WANTS TO FIND HIS MOTHER..
THAT STUPID BEAGLE SHOULDN'T BE OUT ALONE! HE'LL BUMP INTO A TREE OR SOMETHING...
BONK!!
SCHULZ

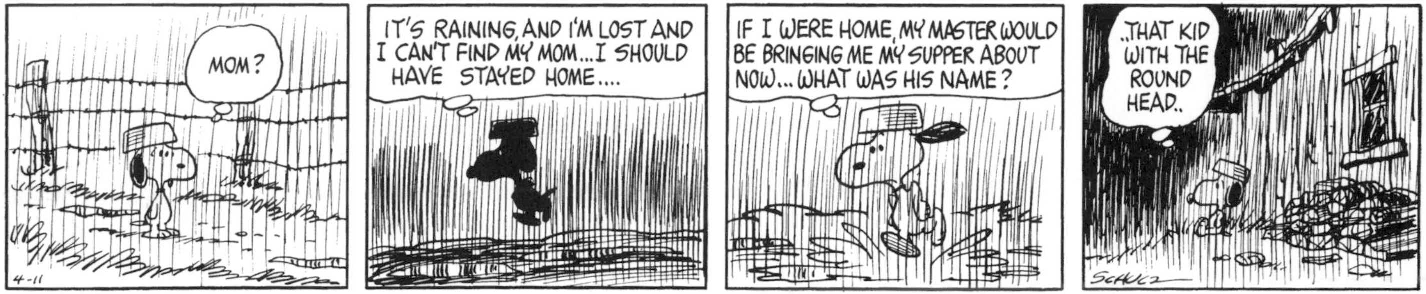
MOM?
4-11
IT'S RAINING, AND I'M LOST AND I CAN'T FIND MY MOM...I SHOULD HAVE STAYED HOME....
IF I WERE HOME, MY MASTER WOULD BE BRINGING ME MY SUPPER ABOUT NOW... WHAT WAS HIS NAME?
..THAT KID WITH THE ROUND HEAD..
SCHULZ

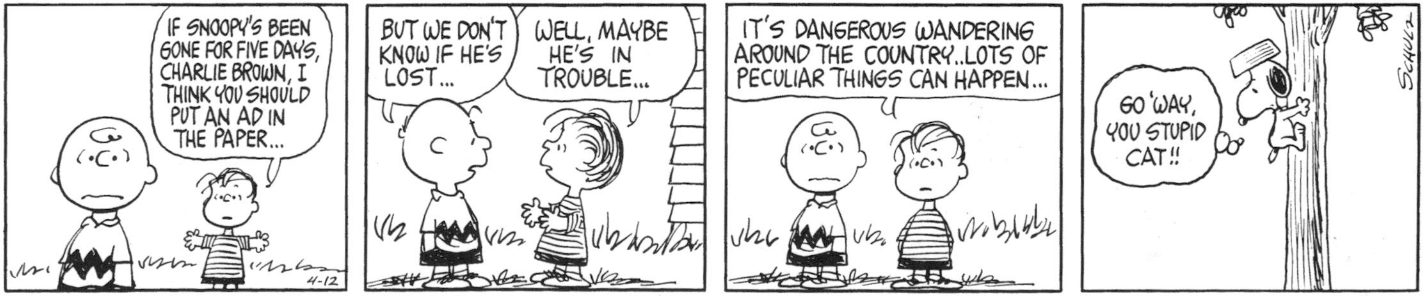
IF SNOOPY'S BEEN GONE FOR FIVE DAYS, CHARLIE BROWN, I THINK YOU SHOULD PUT AN AD IN THE PAPER...
4-12
BUT WE DON'T KNOW IF HE'S LOST...
WELL, MAYBE HE'S IN TROUBLE...
IT'S DANGEROUS WANDERING AROUND THE COUNTRY..LOTS OF PECULIAR THINGS CAN HAPPEN...
GO 'WAY, YOU STUPID CAT!!
SCHULZ

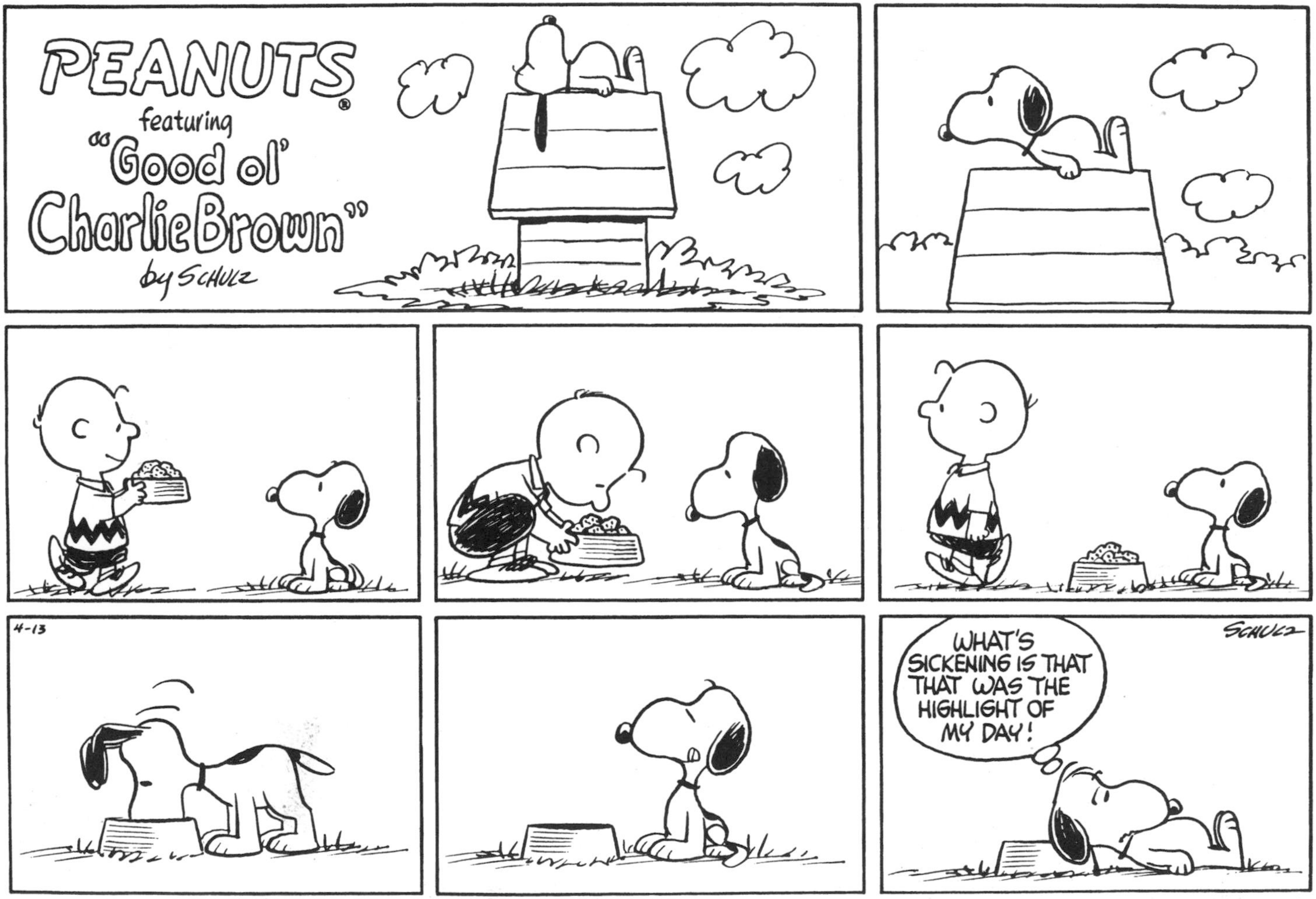
PEANUTS®
featuring
"Good ol' Charlie Brown"
by SCHULZ
4-13
SCHULZ
WHAT'S SICKENING IS THAT THAT WAS THE HIGHLIGHT OF MY DAY!

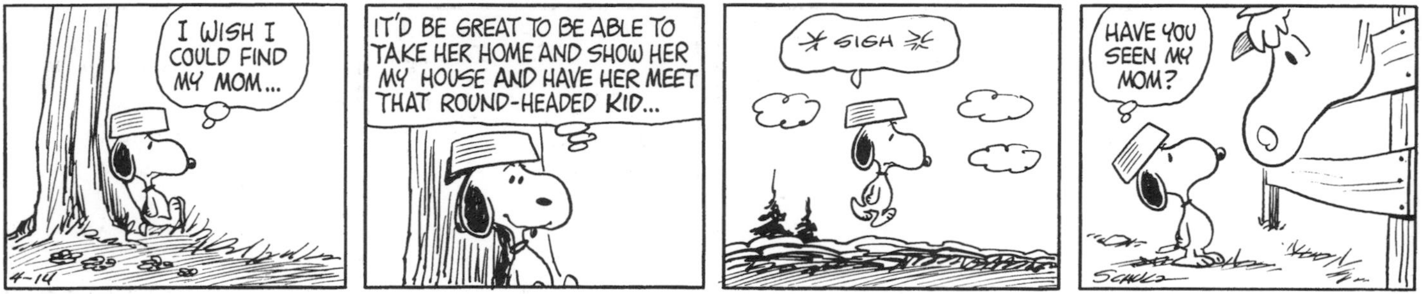

I WISH I COULD FIND MY MOM...
IT'D BE GREAT TO BE ABLE TO TAKE HER HOME AND SHOW HER MY HOUSE AND HAVE HER MEET THAT ROUND-HEADED KID...
SIGH
HAVE YOU SEEN MY MOM?
4-14

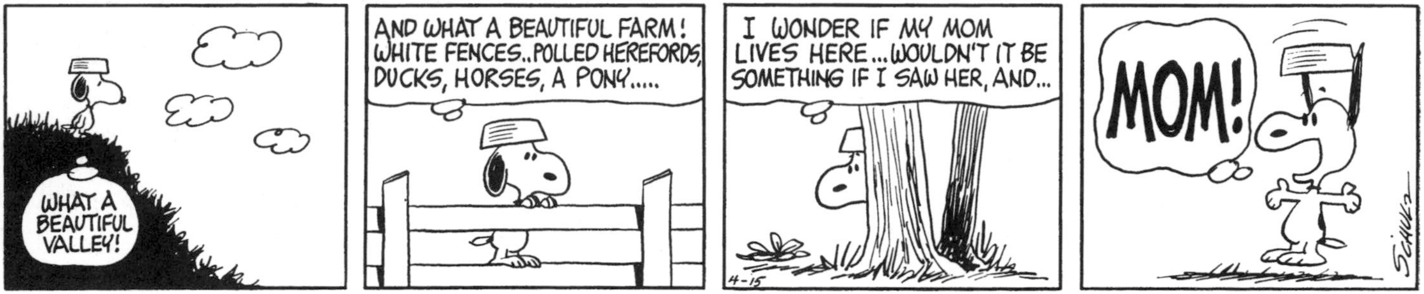

WHAT A BEAUTIFUL VALLEY!
AND WHAT A BEAUTIFUL FARM! WHITE FENCES..POLLED HEREFORDS, DUCKS, HORSES, A PONY.....
I WONDER IF MY MOM LIVES HERE...WOULDN'T IT BE SOMETHING IF I SAW HER, AND...
MOM!
4-15

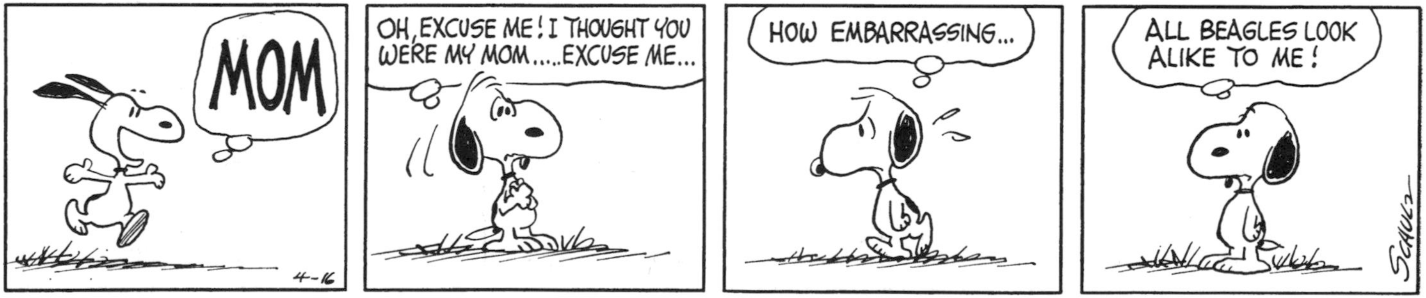

MOM
OH, EXCUSE ME! I THOUGHT YOU WERE MY MOM.....EXCUSE ME...
HOW EMBARRASSING...
ALL BEAGLES LOOK ALIKE TO ME!
4-16

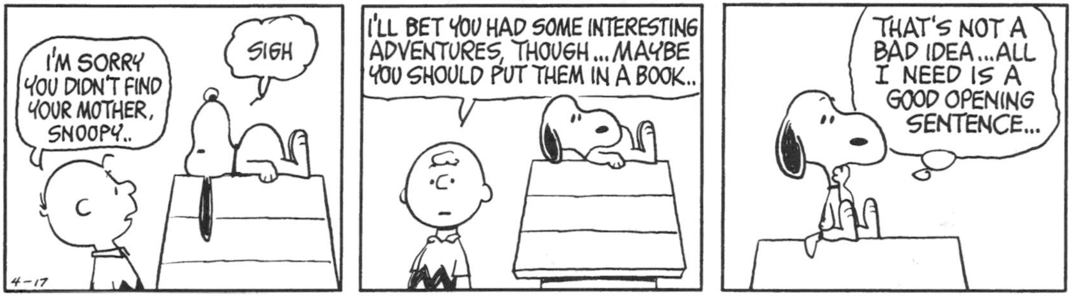
I'M SORRY YOU DIDN'T FIND YOUR MOTHER, SNOOPY..
SIGH
I'LL BET YOU HAD SOME INTERESTING ADVENTURES, THOUGH... MAYBE YOU SHOULD PUT THEM IN A BOOK..
THAT'S NOT A BAD IDEA...ALL I NEED IS A GOOD OPENING SENTENCE...
It was a dark and stormy night...

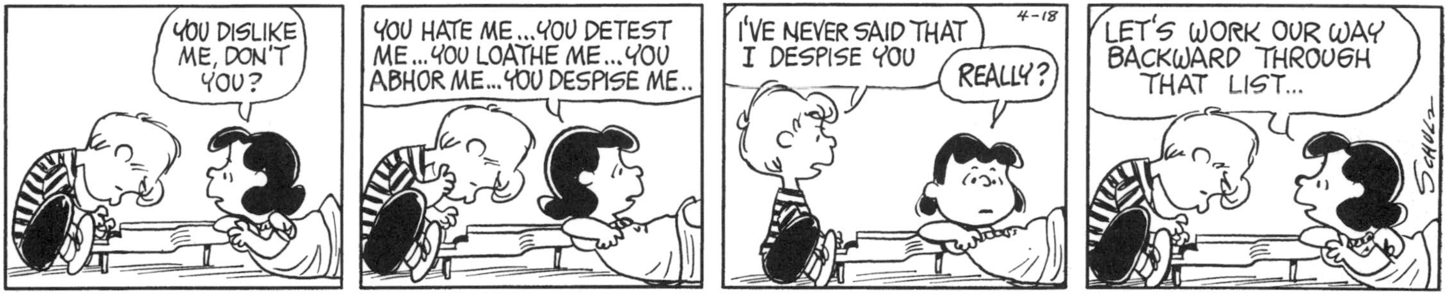
YOU DISLIKE ME, DON'T YOU?
YOU HATE ME...YOU DETEST ME...YOU LOATHE ME...YOU ABHOR ME...YOU DESPISE ME..
I'VE NEVER SAID THAT I DESPISE YOU
REALLY?
LET'S WORK OUR WAY BACKWARD THROUGH THAT LIST...

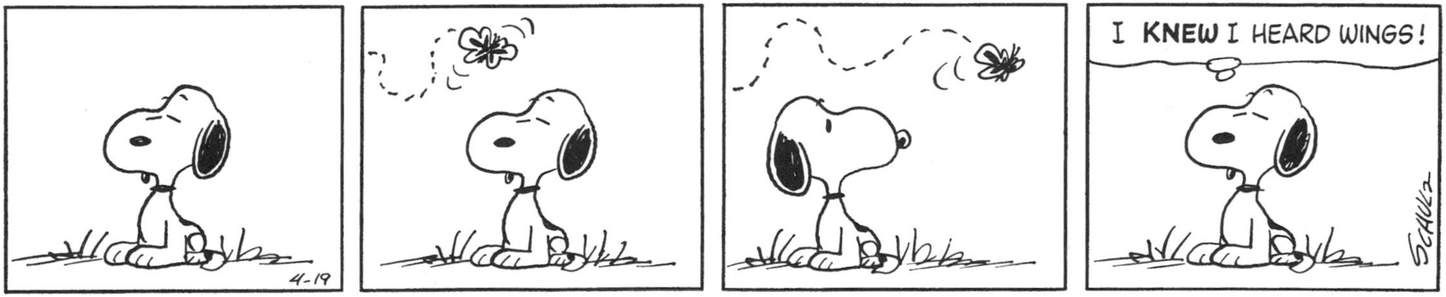
I **KNEW** I HEARD WINGS!

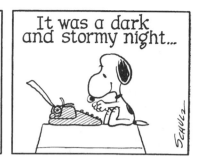

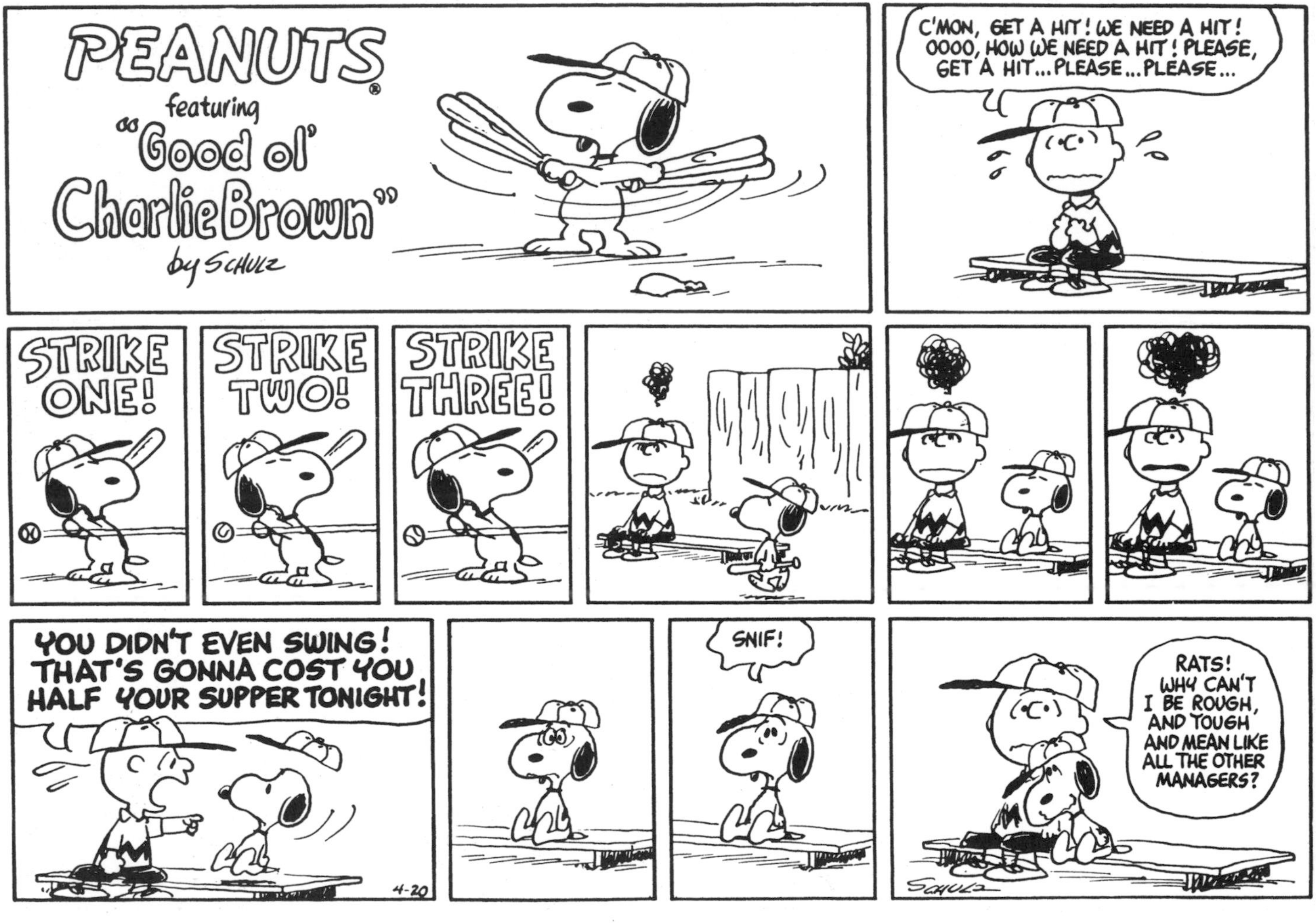
PEANUTS
featuring
"Good ol' CharlieBrown"
by SCHULZ
C'MON, GET A HIT! WE NEED A HIT! OOOO, HOW WE NEED A HIT! PLEASE, GET A HIT...PLEASE...PLEASE...
STRIKE ONE!
STRIKE TWO!
STRIKE THREE!
YOU DIDN'T EVEN SWING! THAT'S GONNA COST YOU HALF YOUR SUPPER TONIGHT!
4-20
SNIF!
RATS! WHY CAN'T I BE ROUGH, AND TOUGH AND MEAN LIKE ALL THE OTHER MANAGERS?
SCHULZ

I'M GOING OVER TO THE PENCIL SHARPENER..THIS LEAD BROKE...

ACTUALLY, IT ISN'T LEAD AT ALL.. IT'S A COMBINATION OF BAVARIAN CLAY AND MADAGASCAR GRAPHITE

4-21

YOU'RE THE ONLY PERSON I KNOW WHO CAN TAKE THE JOY OUT OF SHARPENING A PENCIL!

BAD NEWS, CHUCK...

MY TEAM CAN'T PLAY YOUR TEAM TODAY.. WE HAVE TOO MANY GUYS WHO AREN'T FEELING WELL...WE'RE GOING TO HAVE TO FORFEIT THE GAME

4-22

YOU WIN, CHUCK

ALL RIGHT, TEAM...I DON'T WANT ANY LETDOWN NOW.. WE'VE GOT A STREAK GOING!

HELLO, CHARLIE BROWN? THIS IS FRANKLIN..

WE WON'T BE ABLE TO PLAY YOUR TEAM TODAY...FIVE OF OUR GUYS CAN'T MAKE IT...

4-23

WE'LL JUST HAVE TO FORFEIT THE GAME....YOU WIN, CHARLIE BROWN..

I CAN'T BELIEVE IT....A TWO-GAME WINNING STREAK

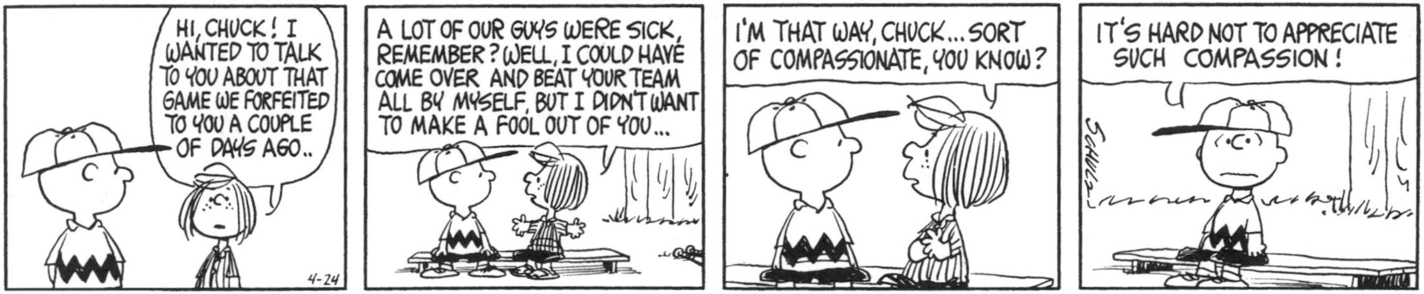
HI, CHUCK! I WANTED TO TALK TO YOU ABOUT THAT GAME WE FORFEITED TO YOU A COUPLE OF DAYS AGO..
A LOT OF OUR GUYS WERE SICK, REMEMBER? WELL, I COULD HAVE COME OVER AND BEAT YOUR TEAM ALL BY MYSELF, BUT I DIDN'T WANT TO MAKE A FOOL OUT OF YOU...
I'M THAT WAY, CHUCK... SORT OF COMPASSIONATE, YOU KNOW?
IT'S HARD NOT TO APPRECIATE SUCH COMPASSION!

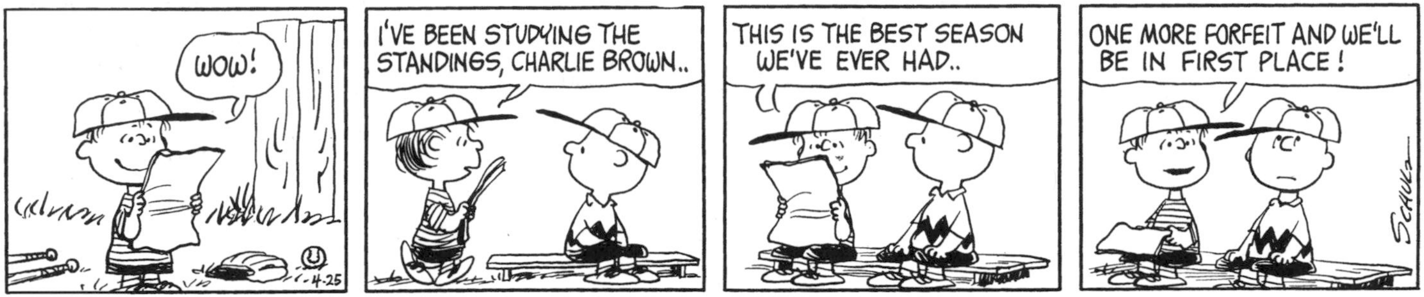
WOW!
I'VE BEEN STUDYING THE STANDINGS, CHARLIE BROWN..
THIS IS THE BEST SEASON WE'VE EVER HAD..
ONE MORE FORFEIT AND WE'LL BE IN FIRST PLACE!

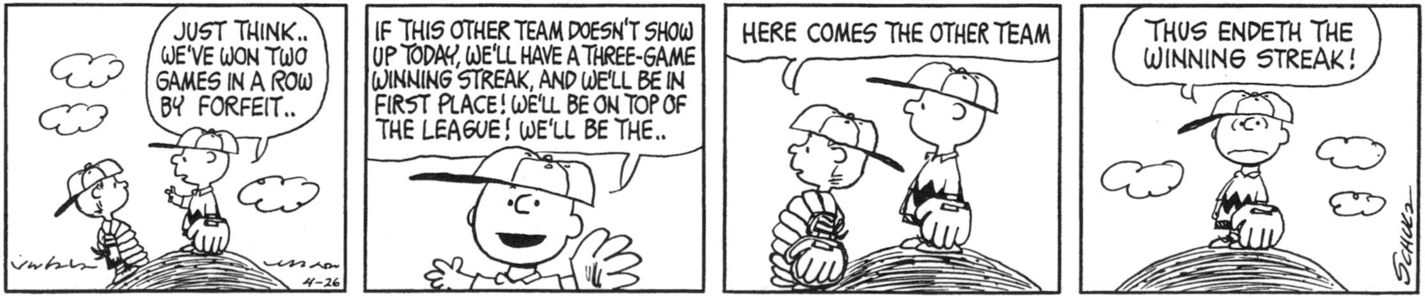
JUST THINK.. WE'VE WON TWO GAMES IN A ROW BY FORFEIT..
IF THIS OTHER TEAM DOESN'T SHOW UP TODAY, WE'LL HAVE A THREE-GAME WINNING STREAK, AND WE'LL BE IN FIRST PLACE! WE'LL BE ON TOP OF THE LEAGUE! WE'LL BE THE..
HERE COMES THE OTHER TEAM
THUS ENDETH THE WINNING STREAK!

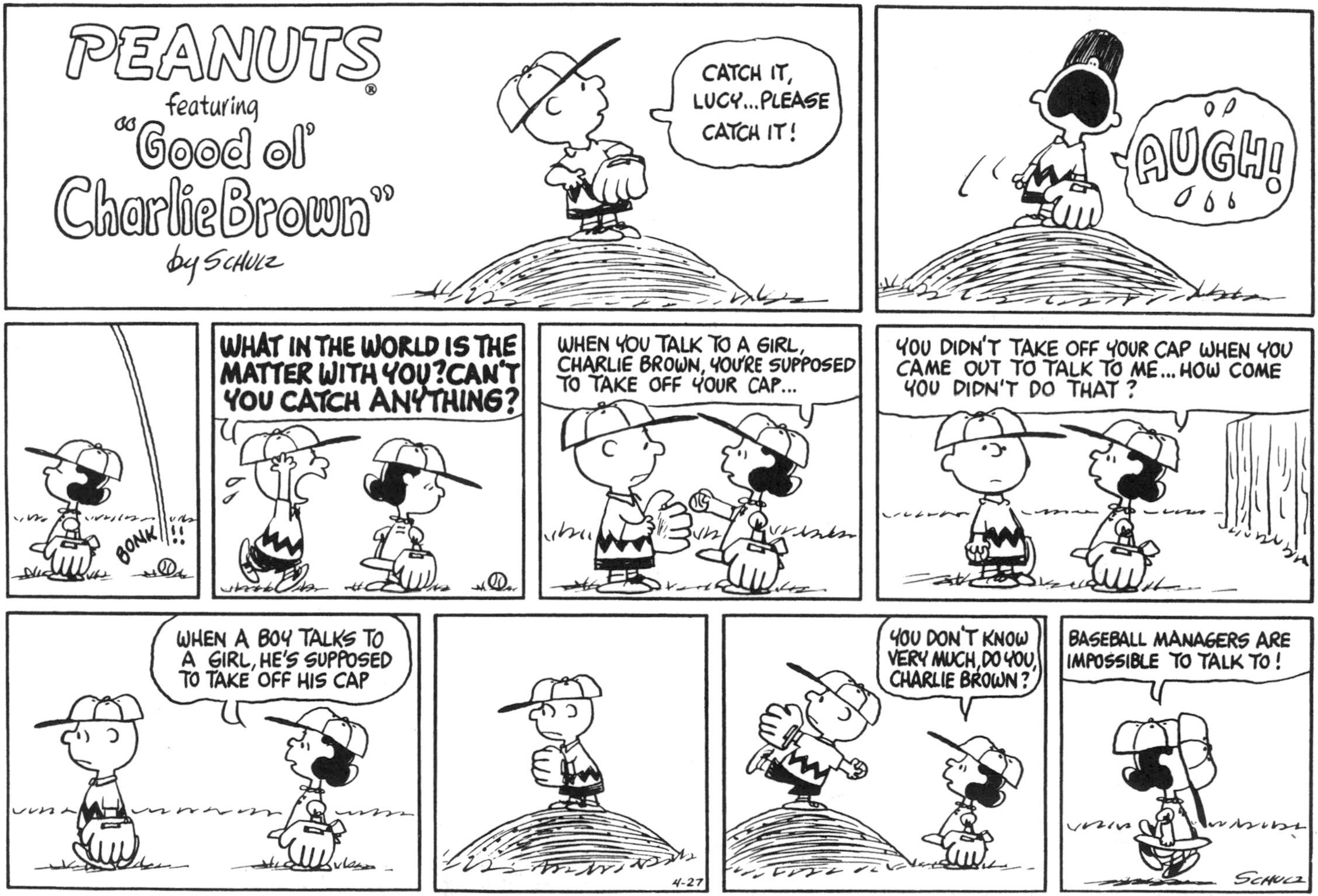
PEANUTS®
featuring "Good ol' Charlie Brown"
by SCHULZ
CATCH IT, LUCY...PLEASE CATCH IT!
AUGH!
BONK!!
WHAT IN THE WORLD IS THE MATTER WITH YOU? CAN'T YOU CATCH ANYTHING?
WHEN YOU TALK TO A GIRL, CHARLIE BROWN, YOU'RE SUPPOSED TO TAKE OFF YOUR CAP...
YOU DIDN'T TAKE OFF YOUR CAP WHEN YOU CAME OUT TO TALK TO ME... HOW COME YOU DIDN'T DO THAT?
WHEN A BOY TALKS TO A GIRL, HE'S SUPPOSED TO TAKE OFF HIS CAP
4-27
YOU DON'T KNOW VERY MUCH, DO YOU, CHARLIE BROWN?
BASEBALL MANAGERS ARE IMPOSSIBLE TO TALK TO!
SCHULZ

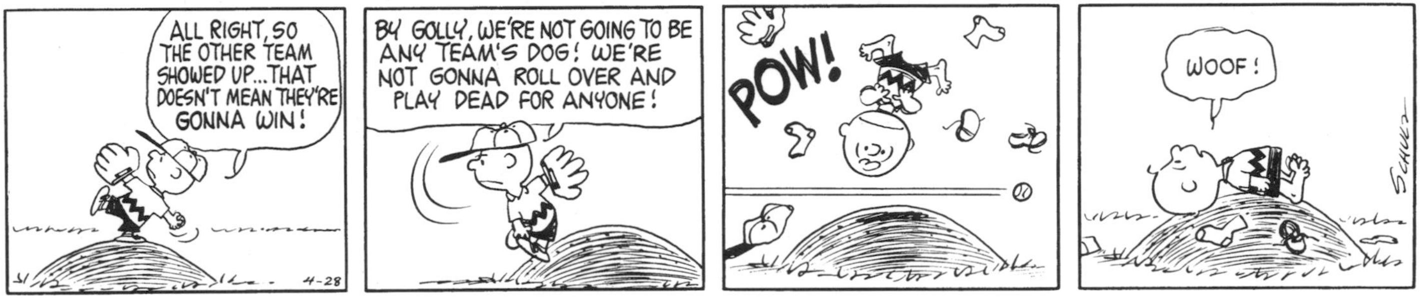
ALL RIGHT, SO THE OTHER TEAM SHOWED UP...THAT DOESN'T MEAN THEY'RE GONNA WIN!
4-28
BY GOLLY, WE'RE NOT GOING TO BE ANY TEAM'S DOG! WE'RE NOT GONNA ROLL OVER AND PLAY DEAD FOR ANYONE!
POW!
WOOF!
SCHULZ

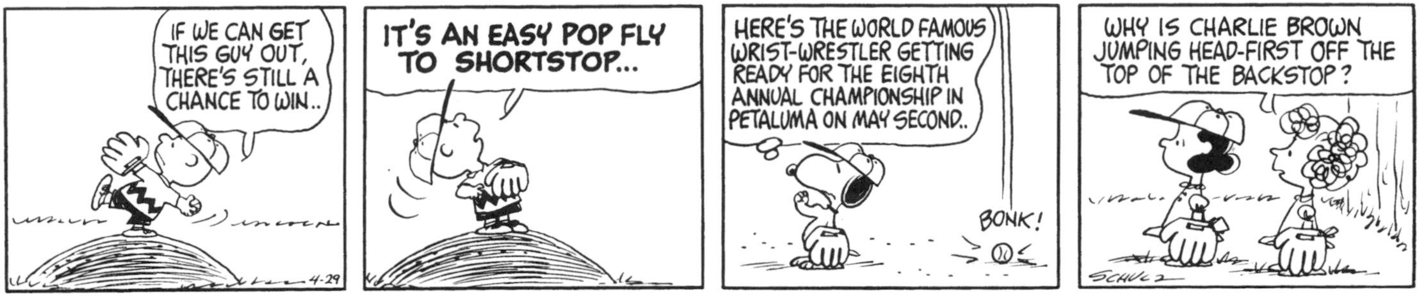
IF WE CAN GET THIS GUY OUT, THERE'S STILL A CHANCE TO WIN..
4-29
IT'S AN EASY POP FLY TO SHORTSTOP...
HERE'S THE WORLD FAMOUS WRIST-WRESTLER GETTING READY FOR THE EIGHTH ANNUAL CHAMPIONSHIP IN PETALUMA ON MAY SECOND..
BONK!
WHY IS CHARLIE BROWN JUMPING HEAD-FIRST OFF THE TOP OF THE BACKSTOP?
SCHULZ

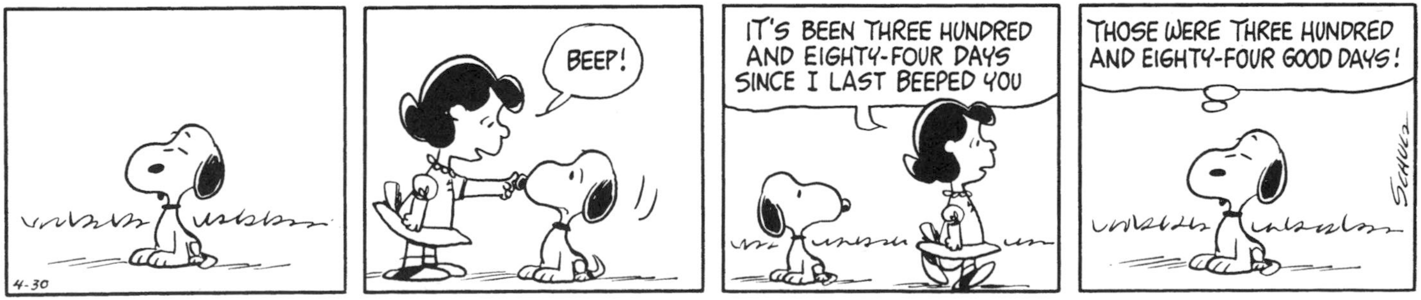
4-30
BEEP!
IT'S BEEN THREE HUNDRED AND EIGHTY-FOUR DAYS SINCE I LAST BEEPED YOU
THOSE WERE THREE HUNDRED AND EIGHTY-FOUR GOOD DAYS!
SCHULZ

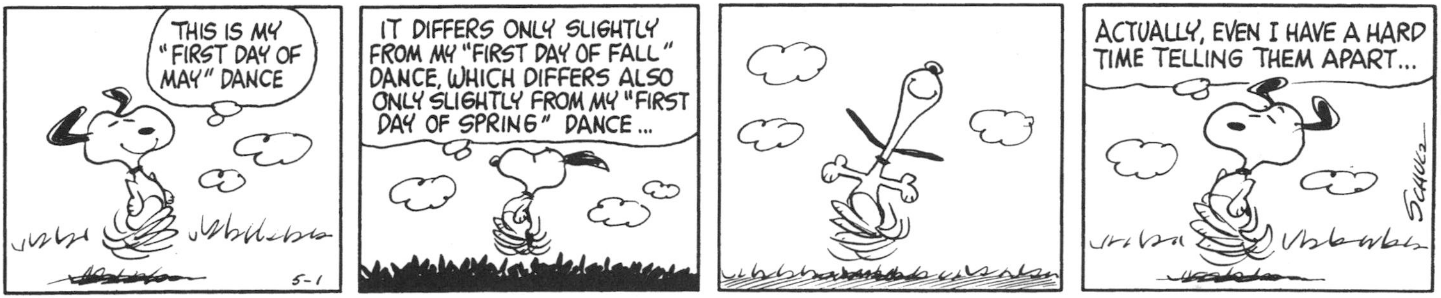
THIS IS MY "FIRST DAY OF MAY" DANCE
IT DIFFERS ONLY SLIGHTLY FROM MY "FIRST DAY OF FALL" DANCE, WHICH DIFFERS ALSO ONLY SLIGHTLY FROM MY "FIRST DAY OF SPRING" DANCE...
ACTUALLY, EVEN I HAVE A HARD TIME TELLING THEM APART...
5-1

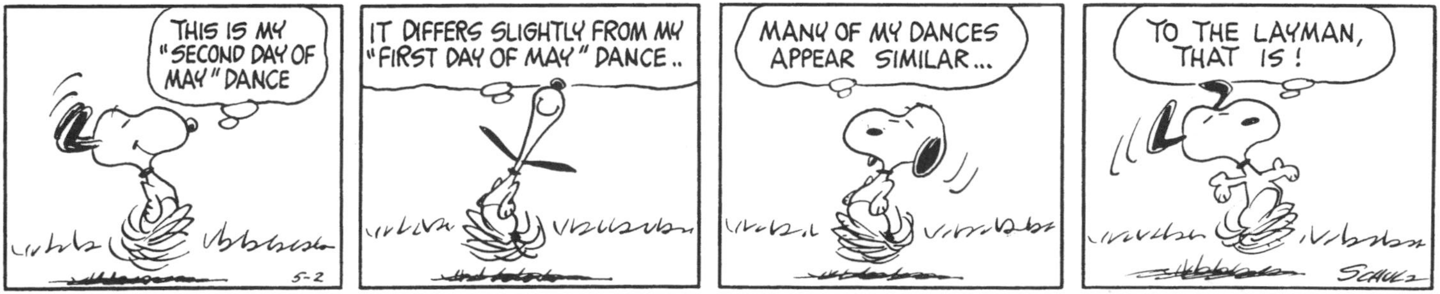
THIS IS MY "SECOND DAY OF MAY" DANCE
IT DIFFERS SLIGHTLY FROM MY "FIRST DAY OF MAY" DANCE..
MANY OF MY DANCES APPEAR SIMILAR...
TO THE LAYMAN, THAT IS!
5-2

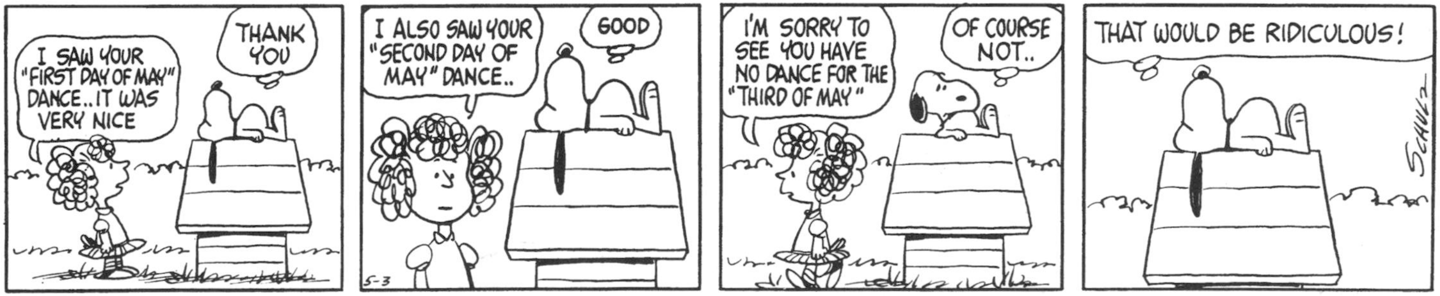
I SAW YOUR "FIRST DAY OF MAY" DANCE..IT WAS VERY NICE
THANK YOU
I ALSO SAW YOUR "SECOND DAY OF MAY" DANCE..
GOOD
I'M SORRY TO SEE YOU HAVE NO DANCE FOR THE "THIRD OF MAY"
OF COURSE NOT..
THAT WOULD BE RIDICULOUS!
5-3

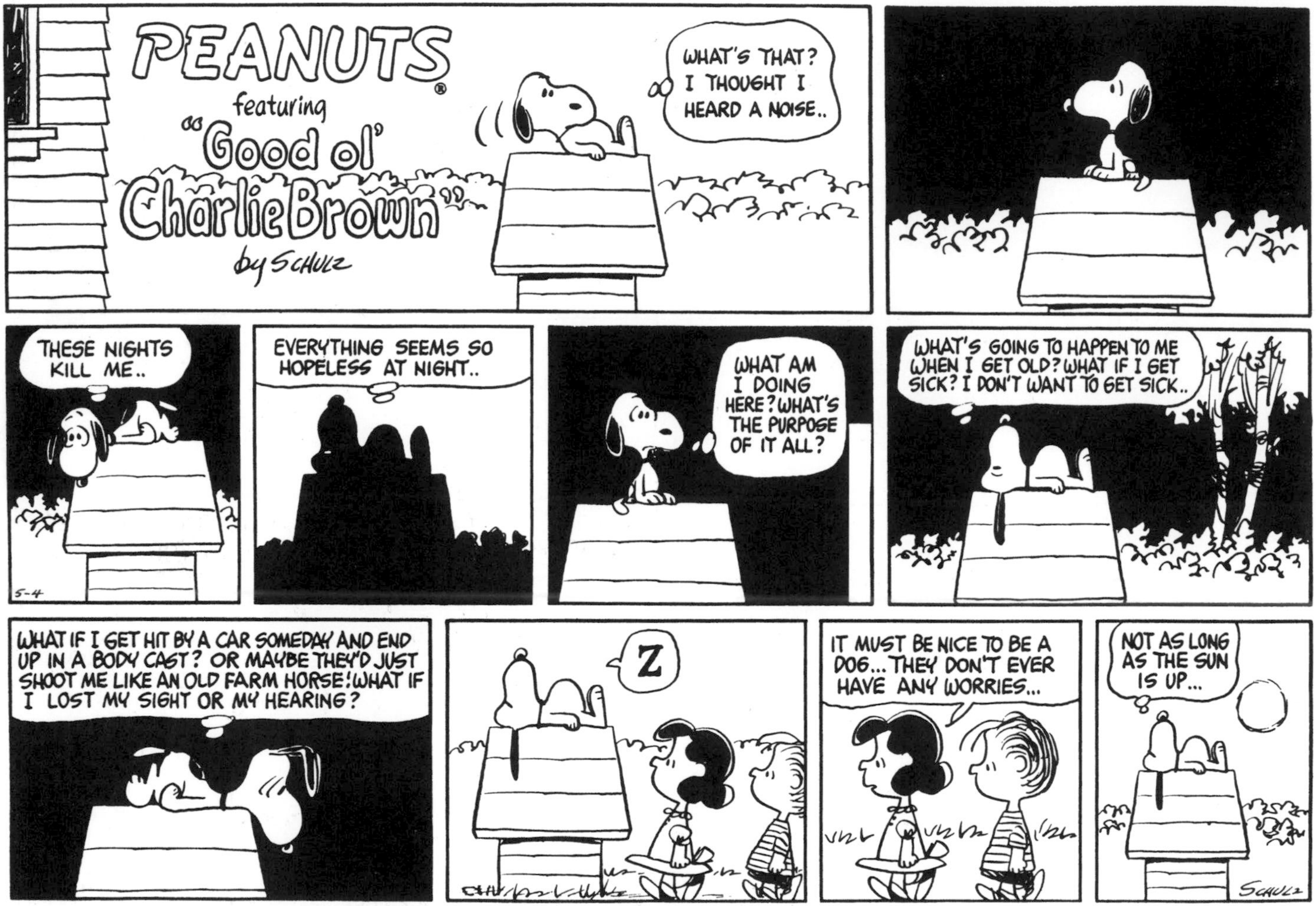
PEANUTS®
featuring "Good ol' Charlie Brown"
by SCHULZ
WHAT'S THAT? I THOUGHT I HEARD A NOISE..
THESE NIGHTS KILL ME..
5-4
EVERYTHING SEEMS SO HOPELESS AT NIGHT..
WHAT AM I DOING HERE? WHAT'S THE PURPOSE OF IT ALL?
WHAT'S GOING TO HAPPEN TO ME WHEN I GET OLD? WHAT IF I GET SICK? I DON'T WANT TO GET SICK..
WHAT IF I GET HIT BY A CAR SOMEDAY AND END UP IN A BODY CAST? OR MAYBE THEY'D JUST SHOOT ME LIKE AN OLD FARM HORSE! WHAT IF I LOST MY SIGHT OR MY HEARING?
Z
IT MUST BE NICE TO BE A DOG... THEY DON'T EVER HAVE ANY WORRIES...
NOT AS LONG AS THE SUN IS UP...
SCHULZ

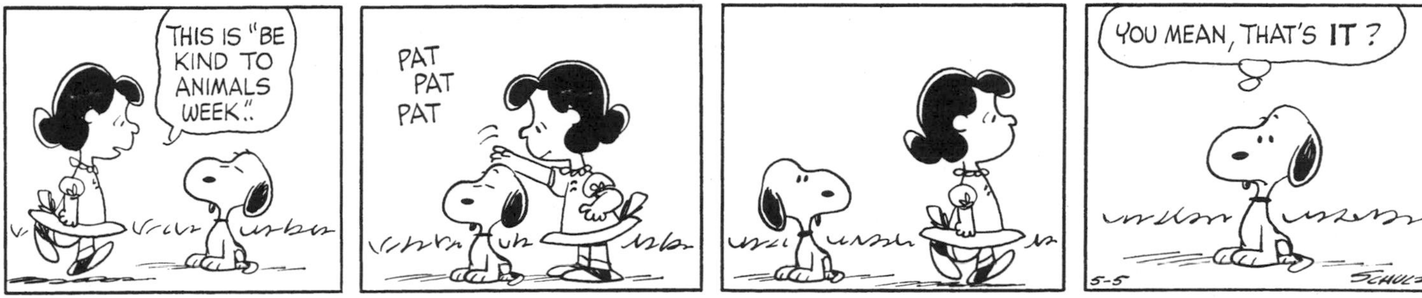
THIS IS "BE KIND TO ANIMALS WEEK"..
PAT PAT PAT
YOU MEAN, THAT'S **IT** ?
5-5
SCHULZ

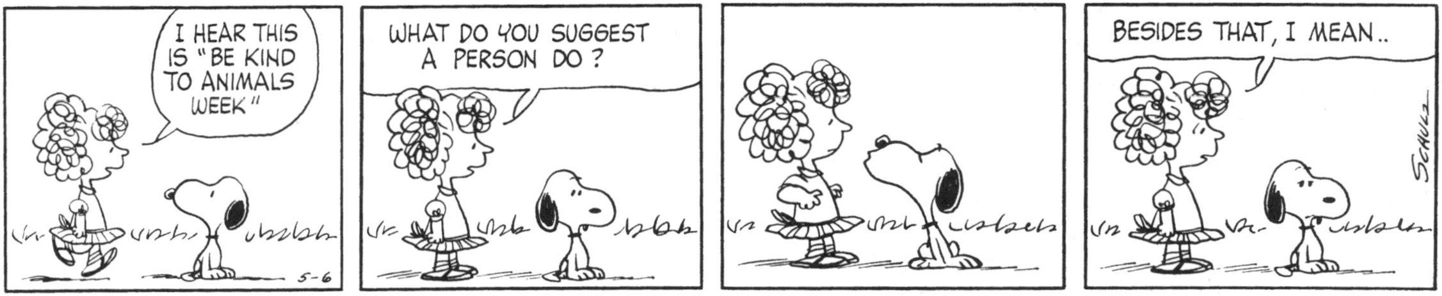
I HEAR THIS IS "BE KIND TO ANIMALS WEEK"
5-6
WHAT DO YOU SUGGEST A PERSON DO ?
BESIDES THAT, I MEAN..
SCHULZ

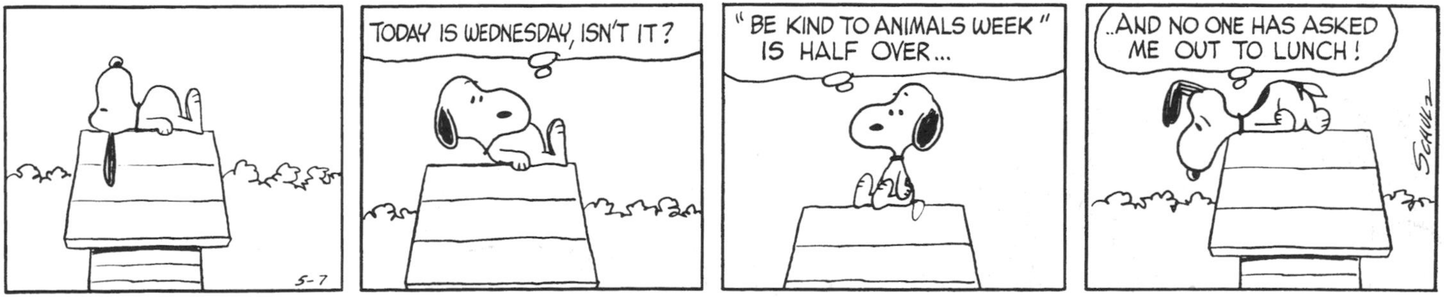
5-7
TODAY IS WEDNESDAY, ISN'T IT ?
"BE KIND TO ANIMALS WEEK" IS HALF OVER...
..AND NO ONE HAS ASKED ME OUT TO LUNCH !
SCHULZ

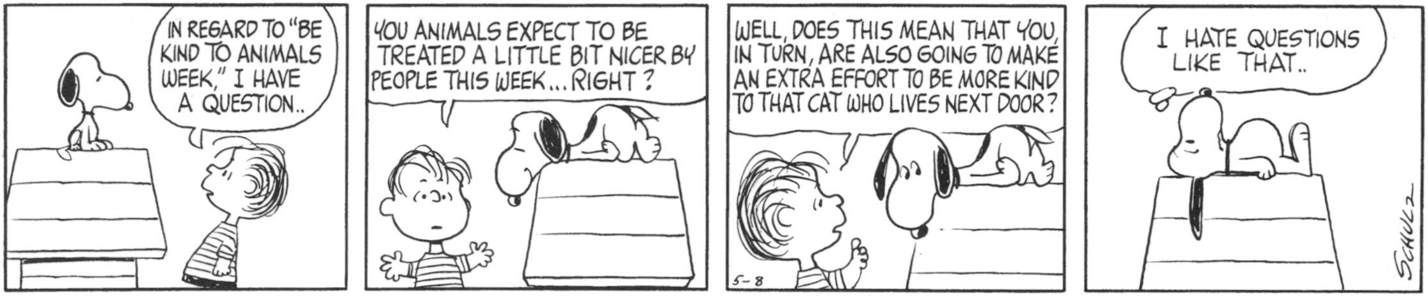
IN REGARD TO "BE KIND TO ANIMALS WEEK," I HAVE A QUESTION..
YOU ANIMALS EXPECT TO BE TREATED A LITTLE BIT NICER BY PEOPLE THIS WEEK... RIGHT?
WELL, DOES THIS MEAN THAT YOU, IN TURN, ARE ALSO GOING TO MAKE AN EXTRA EFFORT TO BE MORE KIND TO THAT CAT WHO LIVES NEXT DOOR?
I HATE QUESTIONS LIKE THAT..
5-8
SCHULZ

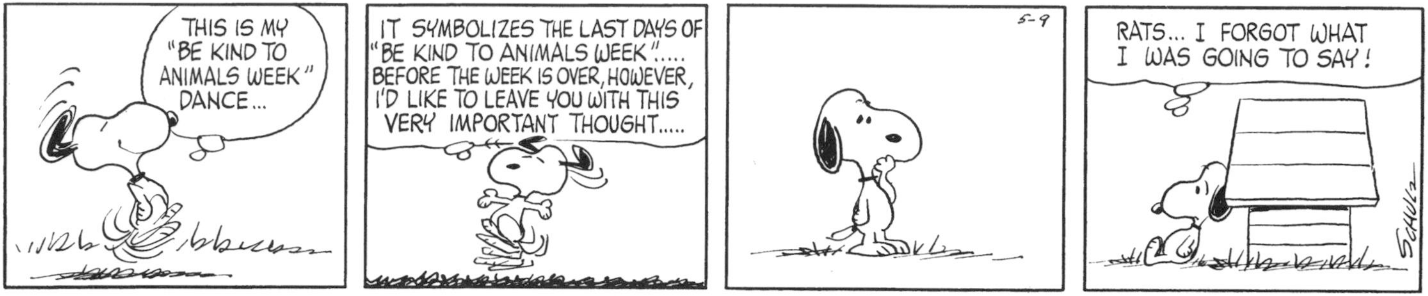
THIS IS MY "BE KIND TO ANIMALS WEEK" DANCE...
IT SYMBOLIZES THE LAST DAYS OF "BE KIND TO ANIMALS WEEK"..... BEFORE THE WEEK IS OVER, HOWEVER, I'D LIKE TO LEAVE YOU WITH THIS VERY IMPORTANT THOUGHT.....
5-9
RATS... I FORGOT WHAT I WAS GOING TO SAY!
SCHULZ

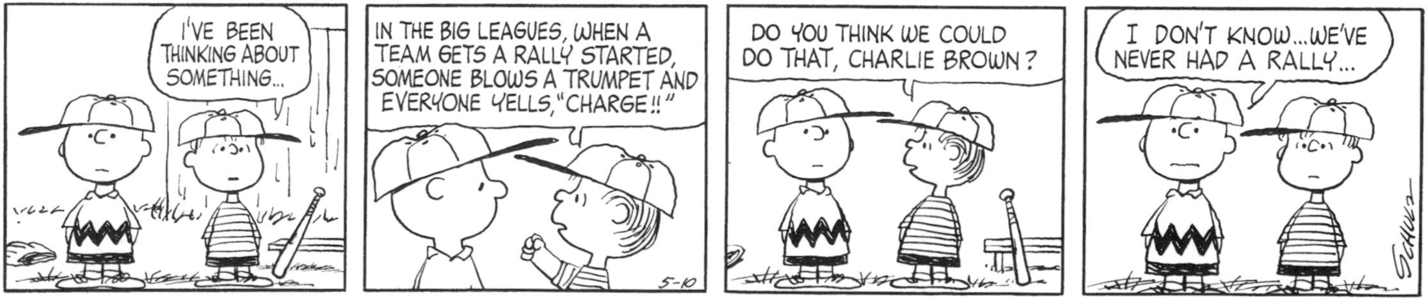
I'VE BEEN THINKING ABOUT SOMETHING...
IN THE BIG LEAGUES, WHEN A TEAM GETS A RALLY STARTED, SOMEONE BLOWS A TRUMPET AND EVERYONE YELLS, "CHARGE!!"
5-10
DO YOU THINK WE COULD DO THAT, CHARLIE BROWN?
I DON'T KNOW...WE'VE NEVER HAD A RALLY...
SCHULZ

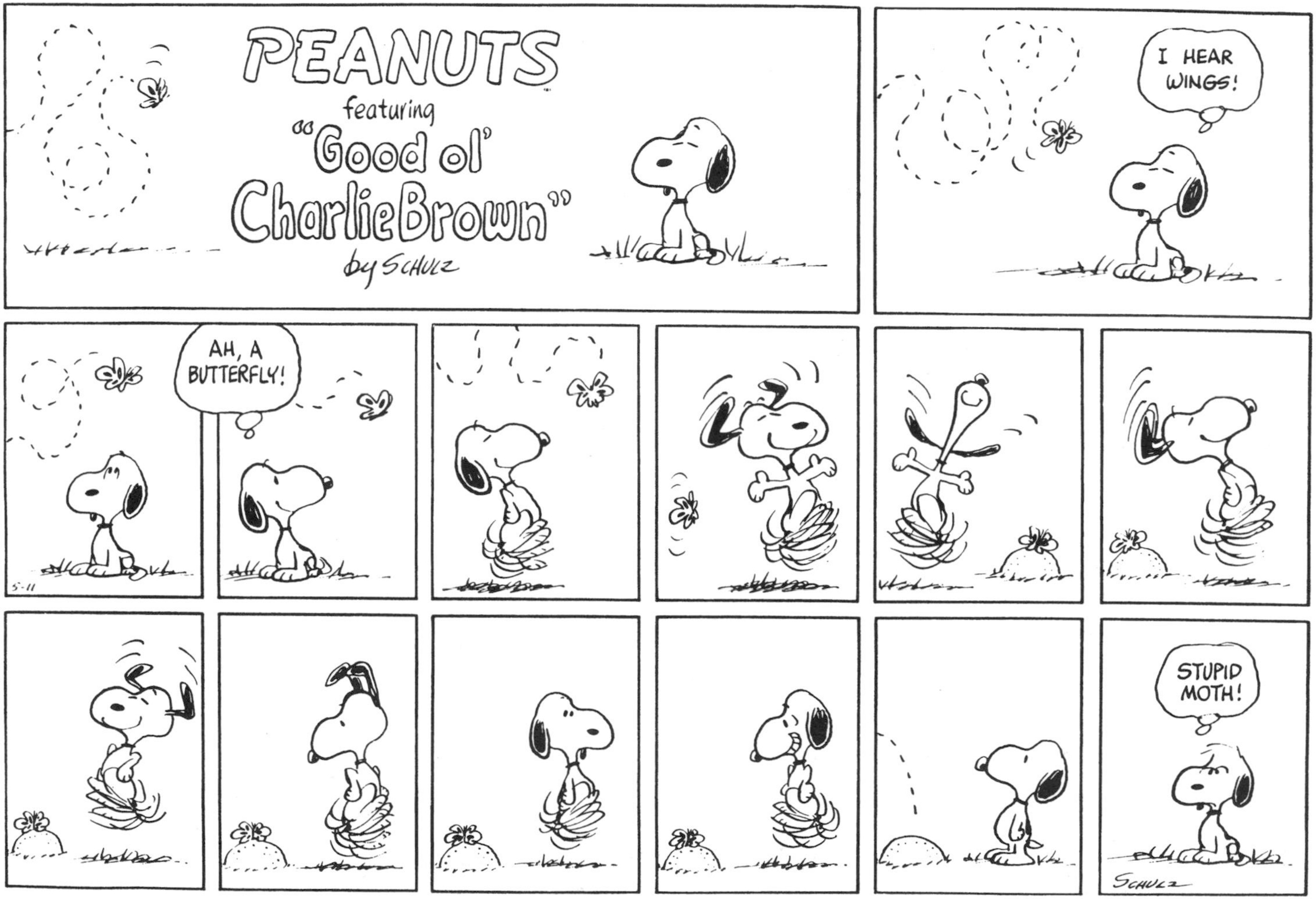
PEANUTS
featuring
"Good ol' CharlieBrown"
by SCHULZ
I HEAR WINGS!
5-11
AH, A BUTTERFLY!
STUPID MOTH!
SCHULZ

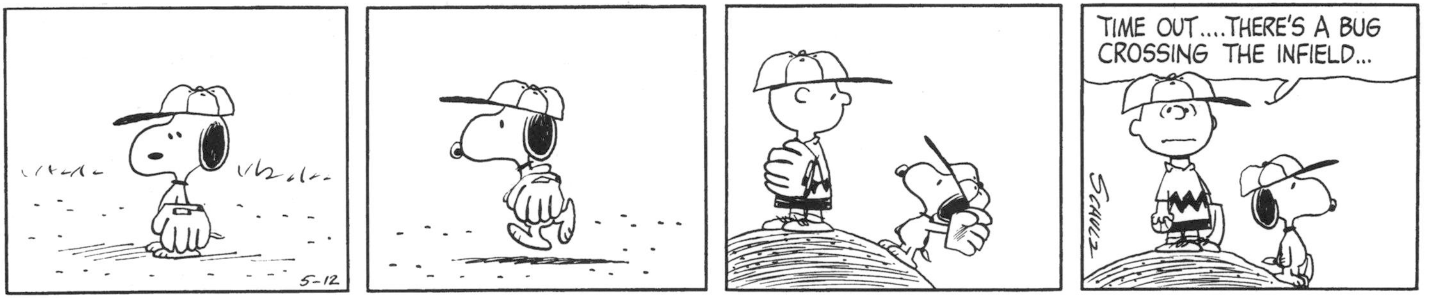
TIME OUT....THERE'S A BUG CROSSING THE INFIELD...

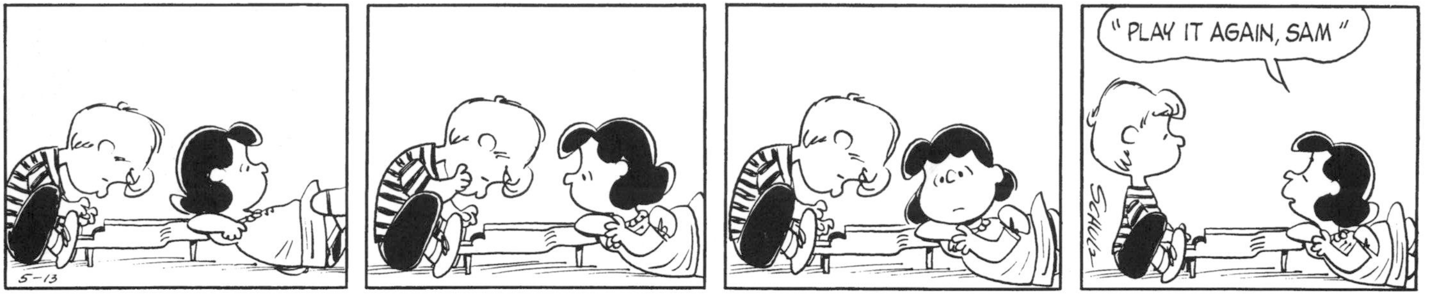
" PLAY IT AGAIN, SAM "

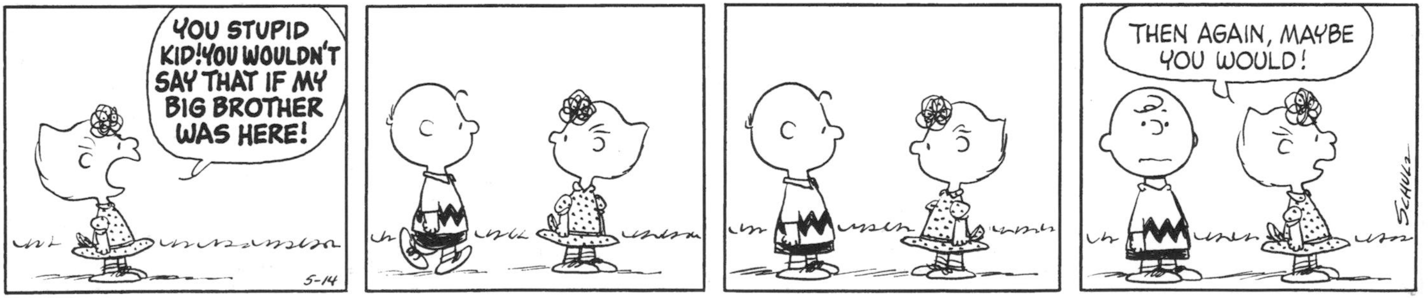
YOU STUPID KID! YOU WOULDN'T SAY THAT IF MY BIG BROTHER WAS HERE!
THEN AGAIN, MAYBE YOU WOULD!

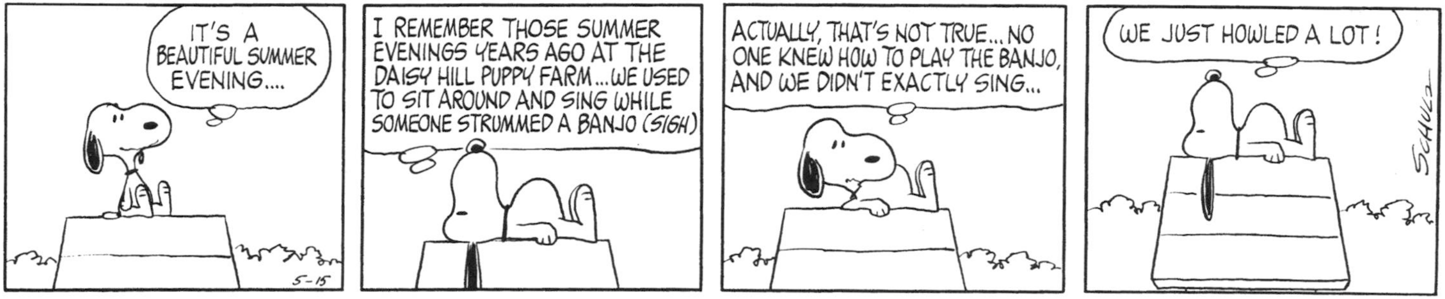
IT'S A BEAUTIFUL SUMMER EVENING....
5-15
I REMEMBER THOSE SUMMER EVENINGS YEARS AGO AT THE DAISY HILL PUPPY FARM...WE USED TO SIT AROUND AND SING WHILE SOMEONE STRUMMED A BANJO (SIGH)
ACTUALLY, THAT'S NOT TRUE... NO ONE KNEW HOW TO PLAY THE BANJO, AND WE DIDN'T EXACTLY SING...
WE JUST HOWLED A LOT!
SCHULZ

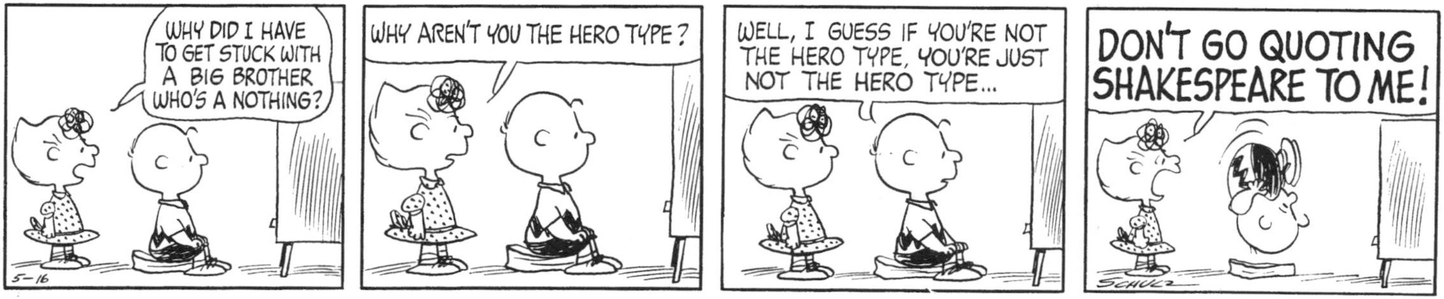
WHY DID I HAVE TO GET STUCK WITH A BIG BROTHER WHO'S A NOTHING?
5-16
WHY AREN'T YOU THE HERO TYPE?
WELL, I GUESS IF YOU'RE NOT THE HERO TYPE, YOU'RE JUST NOT THE HERO TYPE...
DON'T GO QUOTING SHAKESPEARE TO ME!
SCHULZ

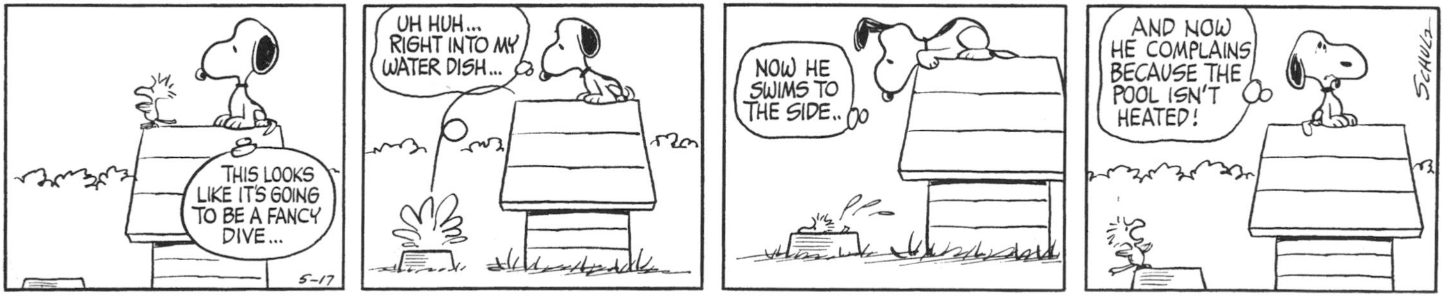
THIS LOOKS LIKE IT'S GOING TO BE A FANCY DIVE...
5-17
UH HUH... RIGHT INTO MY WATER DISH...
NOW HE SWIMS TO THE SIDE..
AND NOW HE COMPLAINS BECAUSE THE POOL ISN'T HEATED!
SCHULZ

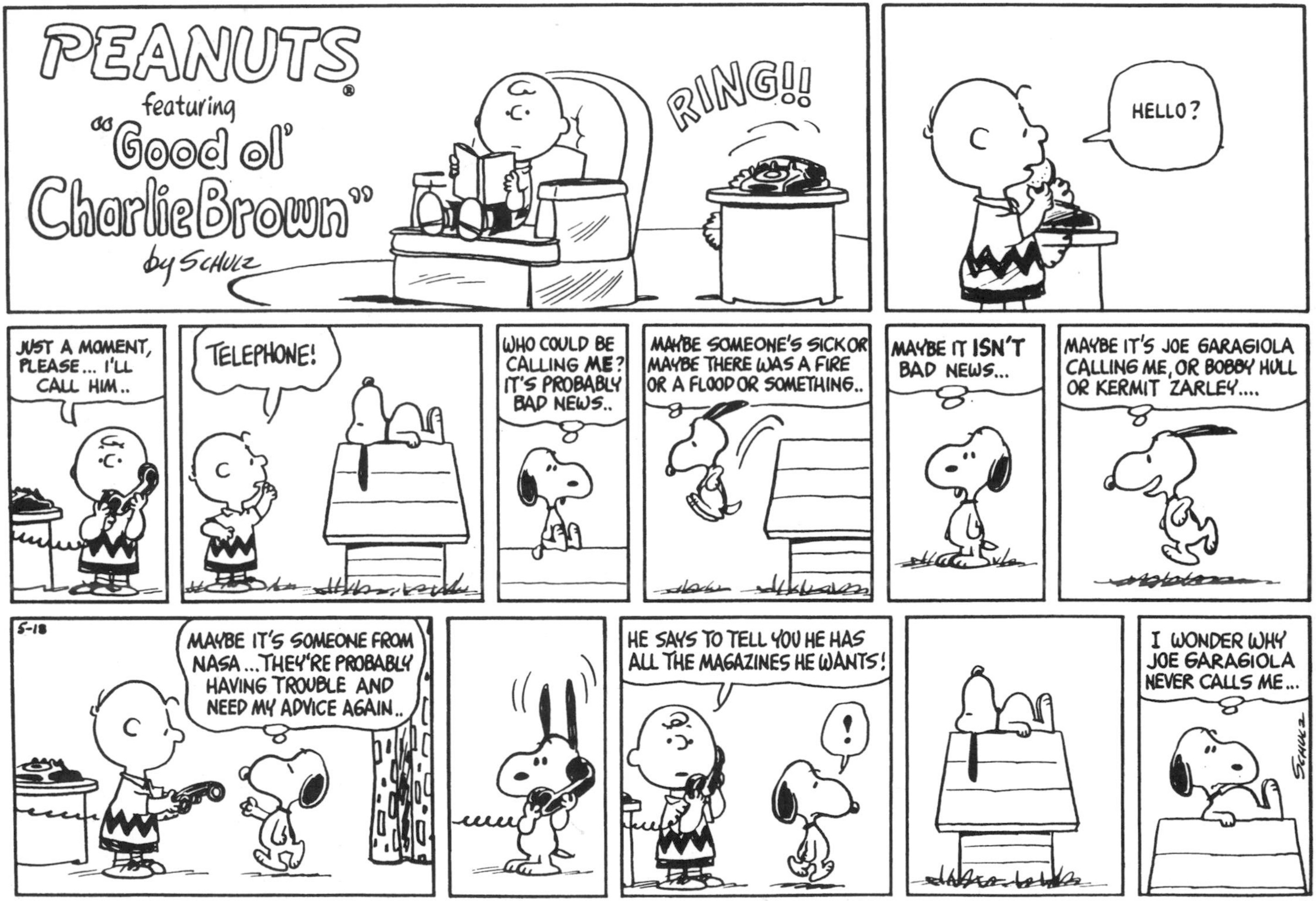

PEANUTS
featuring
"Good ol' Charlie Brown"
by SCHULZ
RING!!
HELLO?
JUST A MOMENT, PLEASE... I'LL CALL HIM..
TELEPHONE!
WHO COULD BE CALLING ME? IT'S PROBABLY BAD NEWS..
MAYBE SOMEONE'S SICK OR MAYBE THERE WAS A FIRE OR A FLOOD OR SOMETHING..
MAYBE IT ISN'T BAD NEWS...
MAYBE IT'S JOE GARAGIOLA CALLING ME, OR BOBBY HULL OR KERMIT ZARLEY....
5-18
MAYBE IT'S SOMEONE FROM NASA ...THEY'RE PROBABLY HAVING TROUBLE AND NEED MY ADVICE AGAIN..
HE SAYS TO TELL YOU HE HAS ALL THE MAGAZINES HE WANTS!
!
I WONDER WHY JOE GARAGIOLA NEVER CALLS ME...
SCHULZ

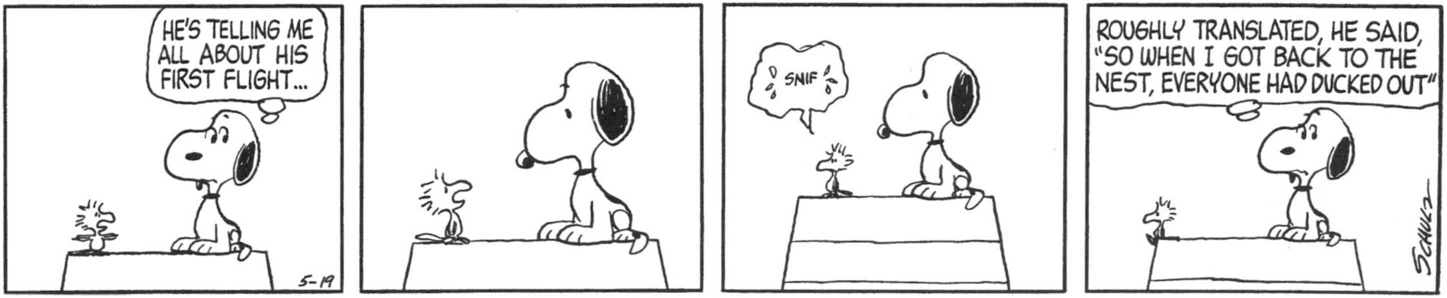
HE'S TELLING ME ALL ABOUT HIS FIRST FLIGHT...
5-19
SNIF
ROUGHLY TRANSLATED, HE SAID, "SO WHEN I GOT BACK TO THE NEST, EVERYONE HAD DUCKED OUT"
SCHULZ

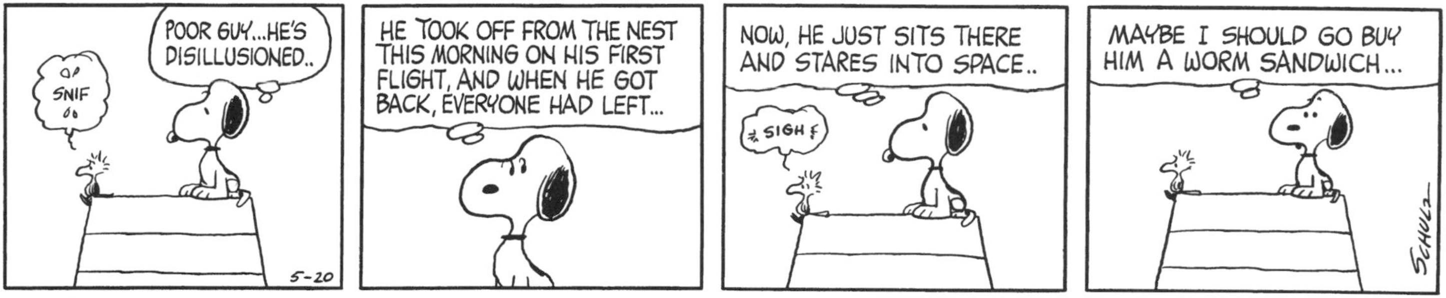
SNIF
POOR GUY...HE'S DISILLUSIONED..
5-20
HE TOOK OFF FROM THE NEST THIS MORNING ON HIS FIRST FLIGHT, AND WHEN HE GOT BACK, EVERYONE HAD LEFT...
NOW, HE JUST SITS THERE AND STARES INTO SPACE..
SIGH
MAYBE I SHOULD GO BUY HIM A WORM SANDWICH...
SCHULZ

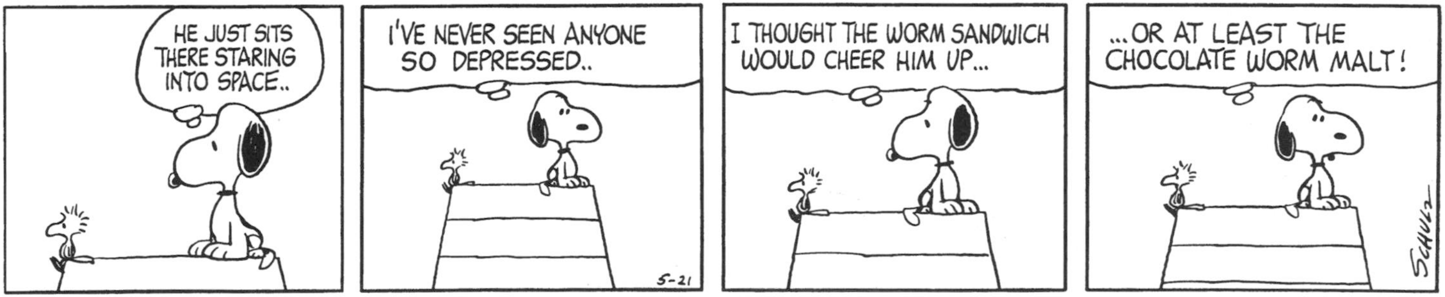
HE JUST SITS THERE STARING INTO SPACE..
I'VE NEVER SEEN ANYONE SO DEPRESSED..
5-21
I THOUGHT THE WORM SANDWICH WOULD CHEER HIM UP...
...OR AT LEAST THE CHOCOLATE WORM MALT!
SCHULZ

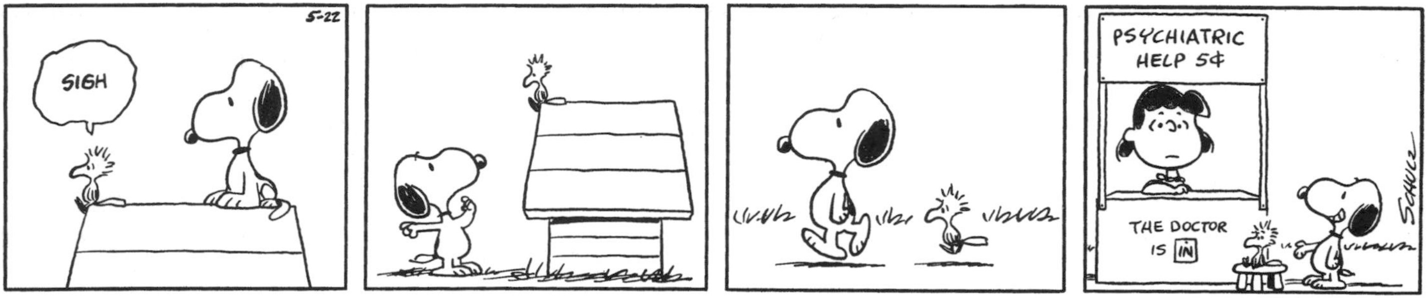
5-22
SIGH
PSYCHIATRIC HELP 5¢
THE DOCTOR IS IN

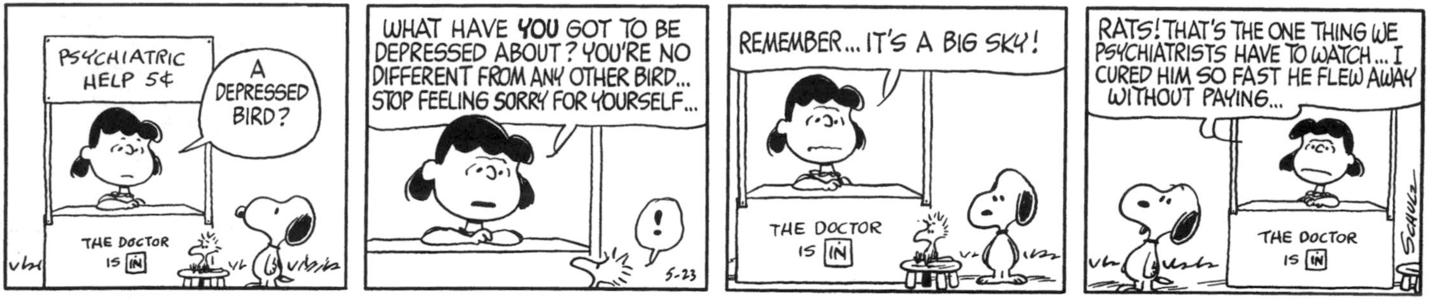
PSYCHIATRIC HELP 5¢
A DEPRESSED BIRD?
THE DOCTOR IS IN
WHAT HAVE YOU GOT TO BE DEPRESSED ABOUT? YOU'RE NO DIFFERENT FROM ANY OTHER BIRD... STOP FEELING SORRY FOR YOURSELF...
!
5-23
REMEMBER... IT'S A BIG SKY!
THE DOCTOR IS IN
RATS! THAT'S THE ONE THING WE PSYCHIATRISTS HAVE TO WATCH... I CURED HIM SO FAST HE FLEW AWAY WITHOUT PAYING...
THE DOCTOR IS IN

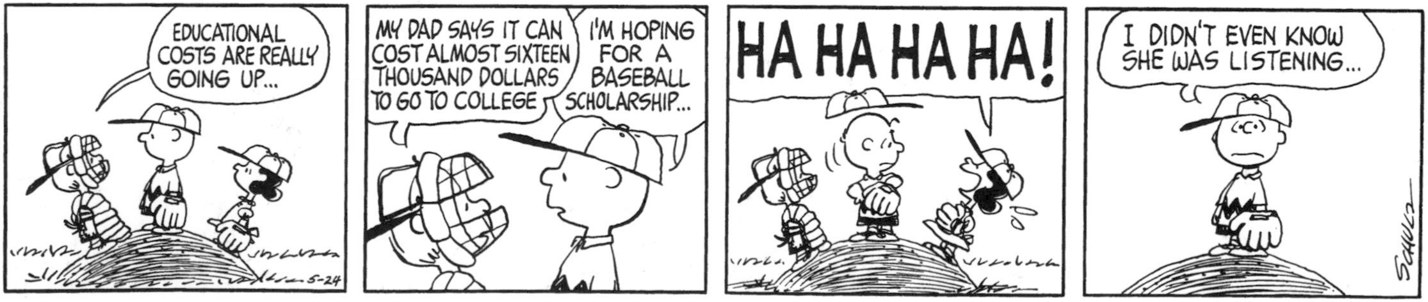
EDUCATIONAL COSTS ARE REALLY GOING UP...
5-24
MY DAD SAYS IT CAN COST ALMOST SIXTEEN THOUSAND DOLLARS TO GO TO COLLEGE
I'M HOPING FOR A BASEBALL SCHOLARSHIP...
HA HA HA HA!
I DIDN'T EVEN KNOW SHE WAS LISTENING...

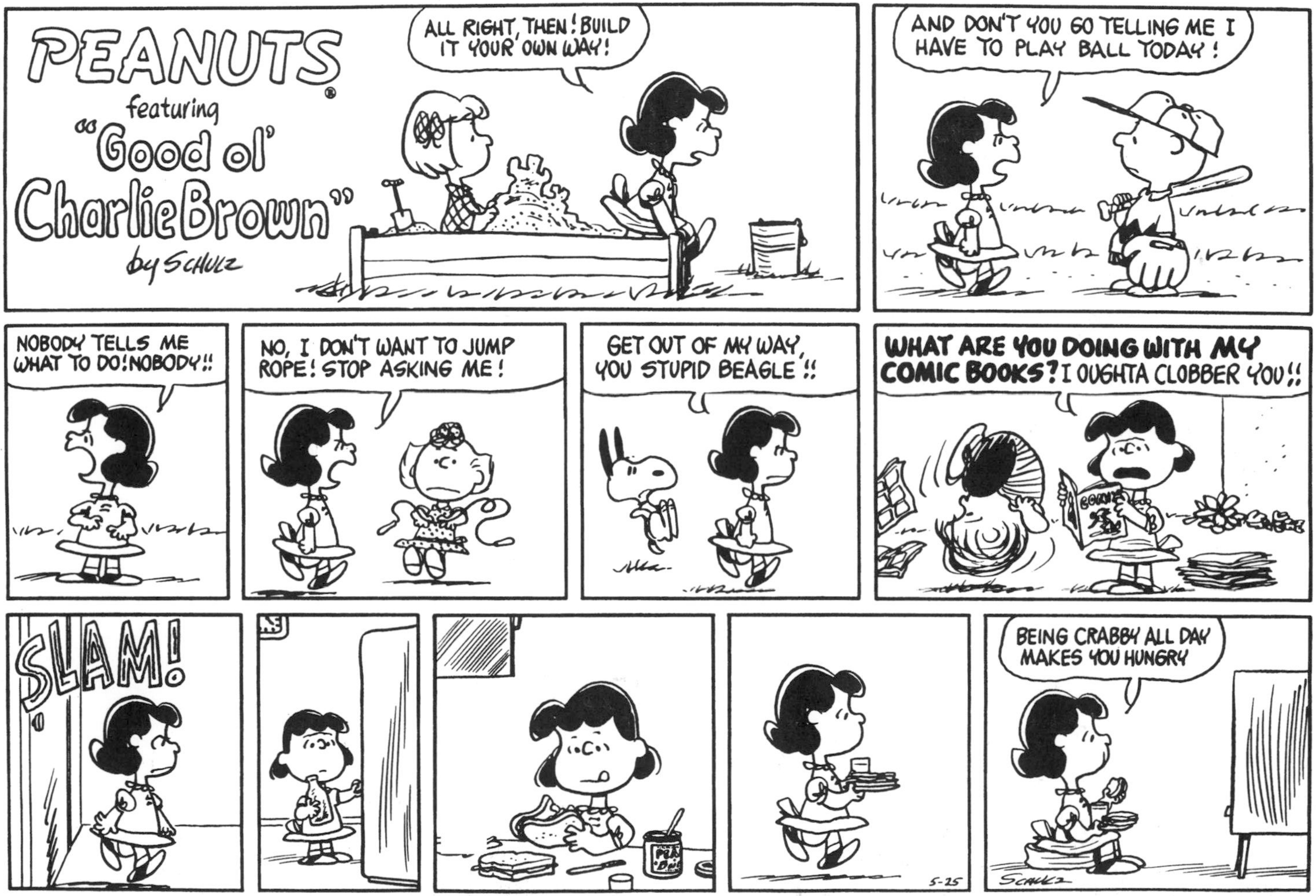
PEANUTS
featuring "Good ol' CharlieBrown"
by SCHULZ
ALL RIGHT, THEN! BUILD IT YOUR OWN WAY!
AND DON'T YOU GO TELLING ME I HAVE TO PLAY BALL TODAY!
NOBODY TELLS ME WHAT TO DO! NOBODY!!
NO, I DON'T WANT TO JUMP ROPE! STOP ASKING ME!
GET OUT OF MY WAY, YOU STUPID BEAGLE!!
WHAT ARE YOU DOING WITH MY COMIC BOOKS? I OUGHTA CLOBBER YOU!!
SLAM!
5-25
BEING CRABBY ALL DAY MAKES YOU HUNGRY
SCHULZ

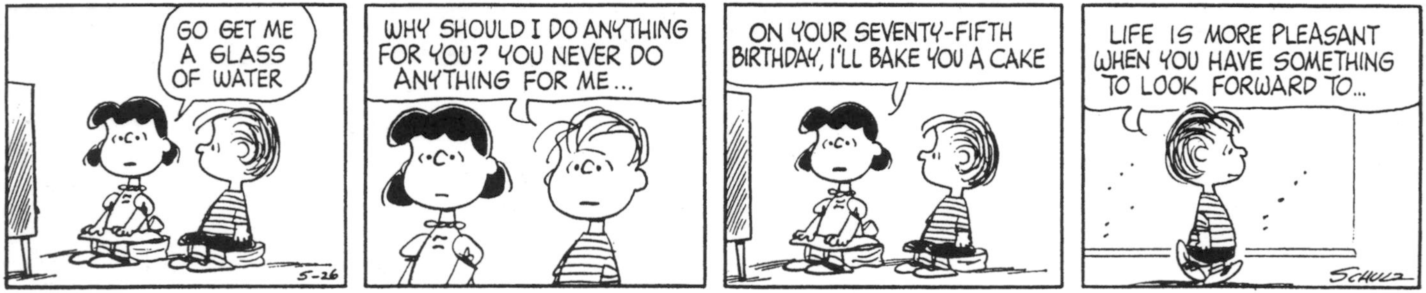
GO GET ME A GLASS OF WATER
WHY SHOULD I DO ANYTHING FOR YOU? YOU NEVER DO ANYTHING FOR ME...
ON YOUR SEVENTY-FIFTH BIRTHDAY, I'LL BAKE YOU A CAKE
LIFE IS MORE PLEASANT WHEN YOU HAVE SOMETHING TO LOOK FORWARD TO...
5-26
SCHULZ

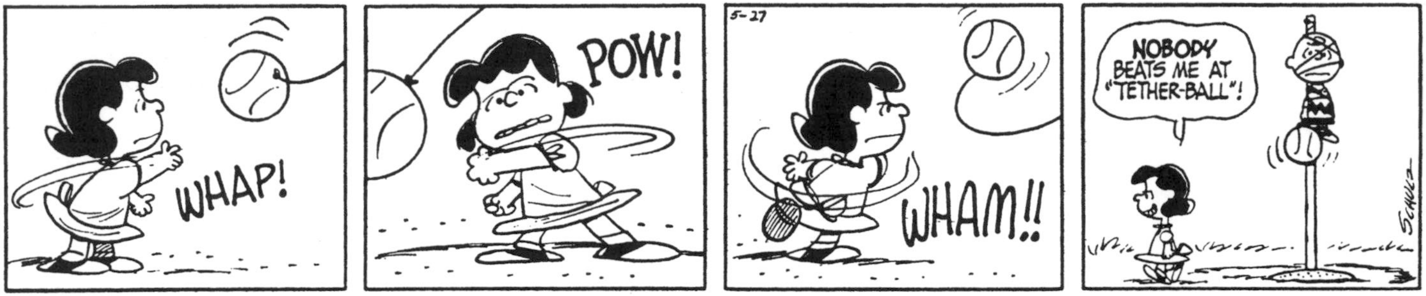
WHAP!
POW!
5-27
WHAM!!
NOBODY BEATS ME AT "TETHER-BALL"!
SCHULZ

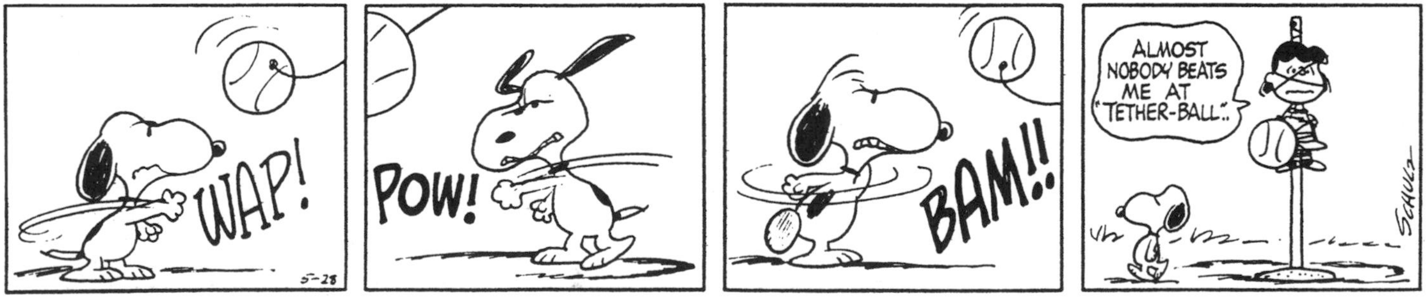
WAP!
5-28
POW!
BAM!!
ALMOST NOBODY BEATS ME AT "TETHER-BALL"..
SCHULZ

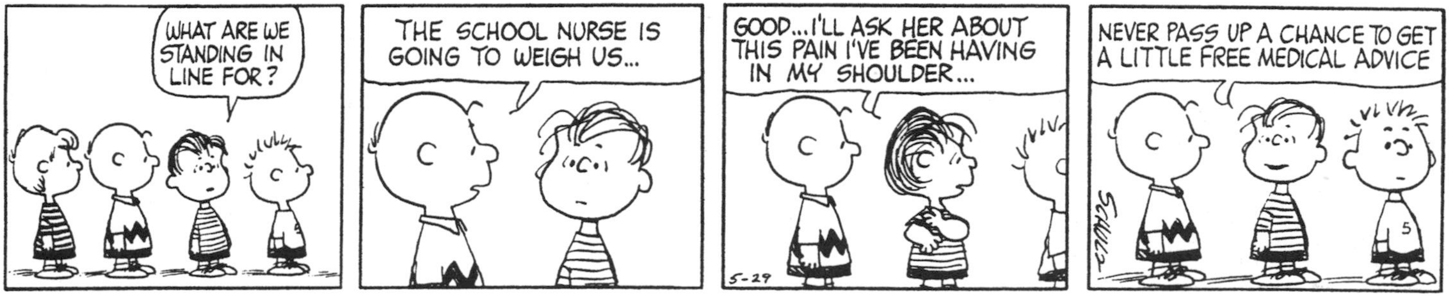
WHAT ARE WE STANDING IN LINE FOR?
THE SCHOOL NURSE IS GOING TO WEIGH US...
GOOD...I'LL ASK HER ABOUT THIS PAIN I'VE BEEN HAVING IN MY SHOULDER...
NEVER PASS UP A CHANCE TO GET A LITTLE FREE MEDICAL ADVICE

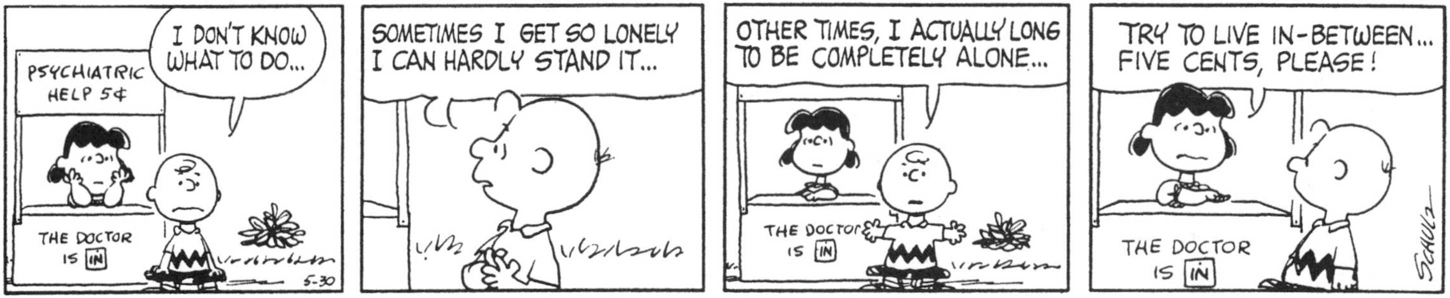
PSYCHIATRIC HELP 5¢
THE DOCTOR IS IN
I DON'T KNOW WHAT TO DO...
SOMETIMES I GET SO LONELY I CAN HARDLY STAND IT...
OTHER TIMES, I ACTUALLY LONG TO BE COMPLETELY ALONE...
THE DOCTOR IS IN
TRY TO LIVE IN-BETWEEN... FIVE CENTS, PLEASE!
THE DOCTOR IS IN

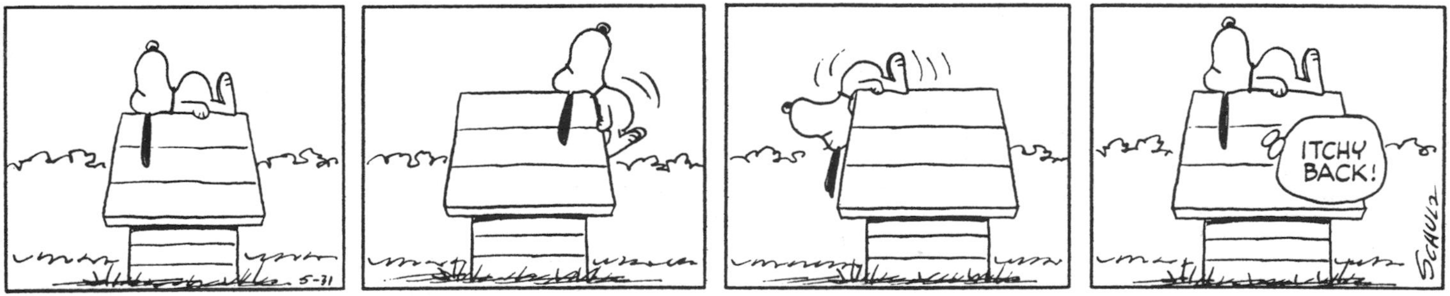
ITCHY BACK!

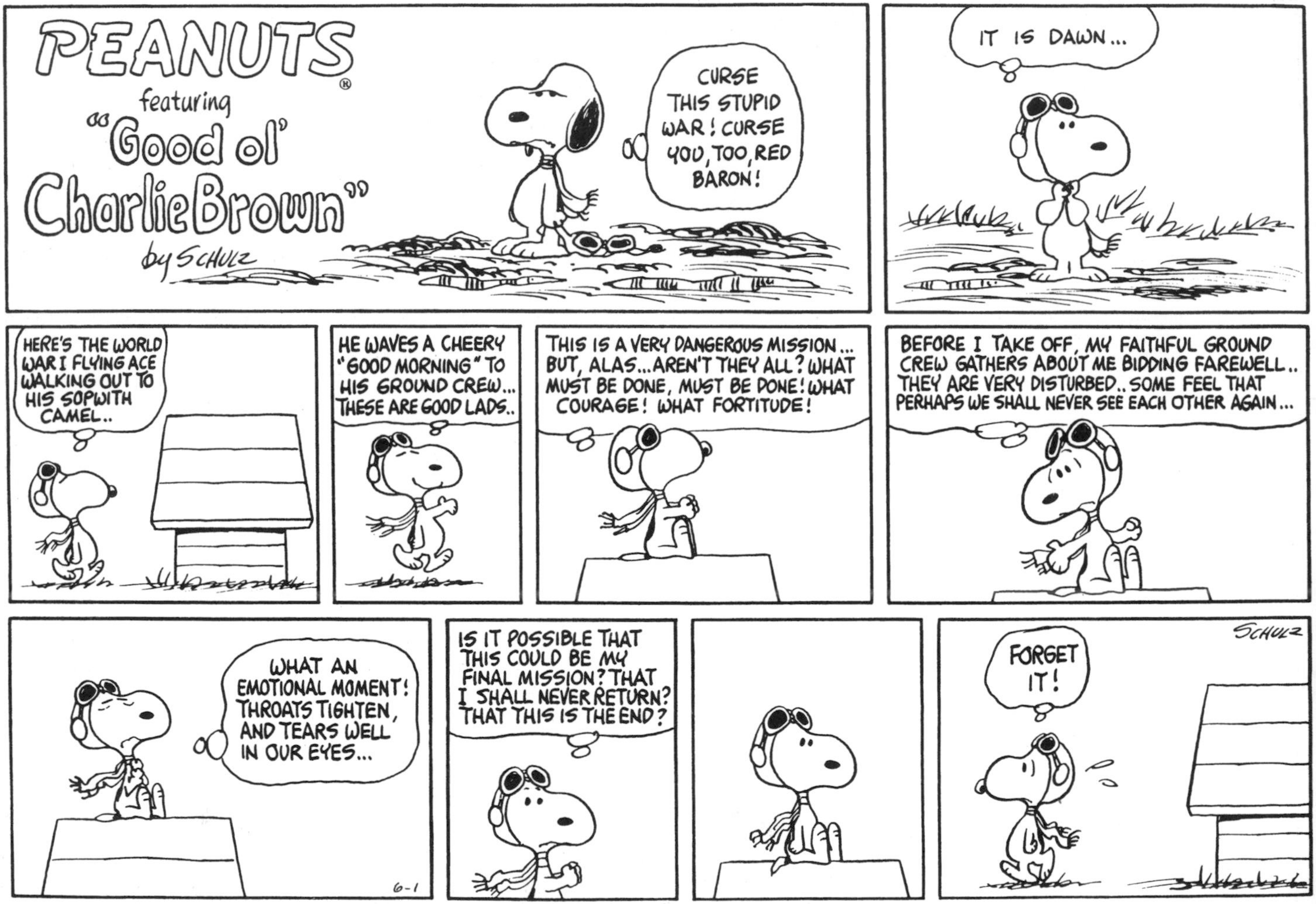
PEANUTS®
featuring "Good ol' Charlie Brown"
by SCHULZ
CURSE THIS STUPID WAR! CURSE YOU, TOO, RED BARON!
IT IS DAWN...
HERE'S THE WORLD WAR I FLYING ACE WALKING OUT TO HIS SOPWITH CAMEL..
HE WAVES A CHEERY "GOOD MORNING" TO HIS GROUND CREW... THESE ARE GOOD LADS..
THIS IS A VERY DANGEROUS MISSION... BUT, ALAS...AREN'T THEY ALL? WHAT MUST BE DONE, MUST BE DONE! WHAT COURAGE! WHAT FORTITUDE!
BEFORE I TAKE OFF, MY FAITHFUL GROUND CREW GATHERS ABOUT ME BIDDING FAREWELL.. THEY ARE VERY DISTURBED.. SOME FEEL THAT PERHAPS WE SHALL NEVER SEE EACH OTHER AGAIN...
WHAT AN EMOTIONAL MOMENT! THROATS TIGHTEN, AND TEARS WELL IN OUR EYES...
6-1
IS IT POSSIBLE THAT THIS COULD BE MY FINAL MISSION? THAT I SHALL NEVER RETURN? THAT THIS IS THE END?
SCHULZ
FORGET IT!

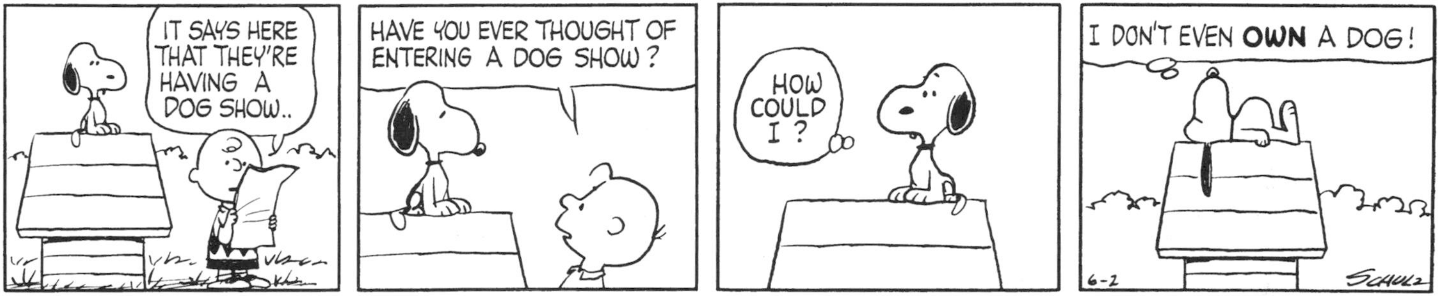
IT SAYS HERE THAT THEY'RE HAVING A DOG SHOW..
HAVE YOU EVER THOUGHT OF ENTERING A DOG SHOW?
HOW COULD I?
I DON'T EVEN **OWN** A DOG!

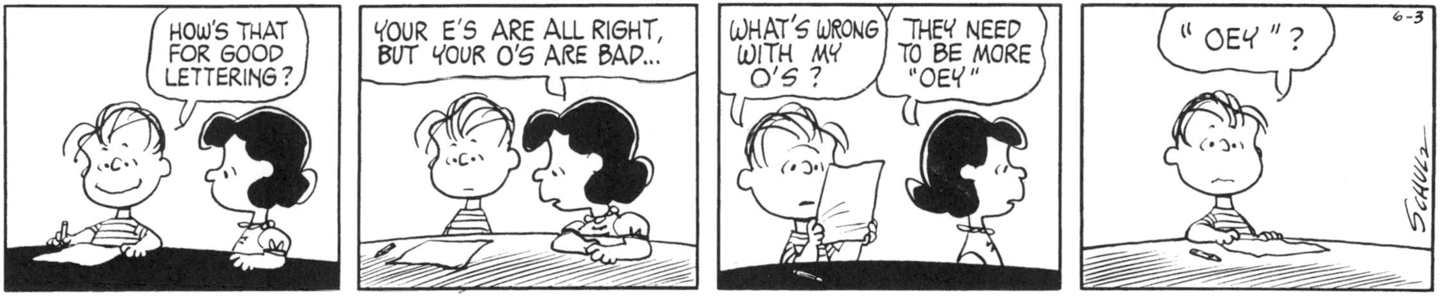
HOW'S THAT FOR GOOD LETTERING?
YOUR E'S ARE ALL RIGHT, BUT YOUR O'S ARE BAD...
WHAT'S WRONG WITH MY O'S?
THEY NEED TO BE MORE "OEY"
"OEY"?

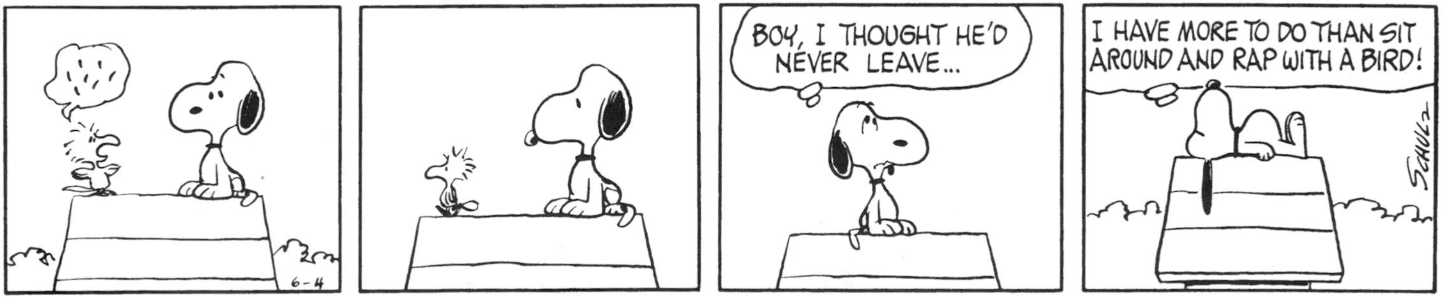
BOY, I THOUGHT HE'D NEVER LEAVE...
I HAVE MORE TO DO THAN SIT AROUND AND RAP WITH A BIRD!

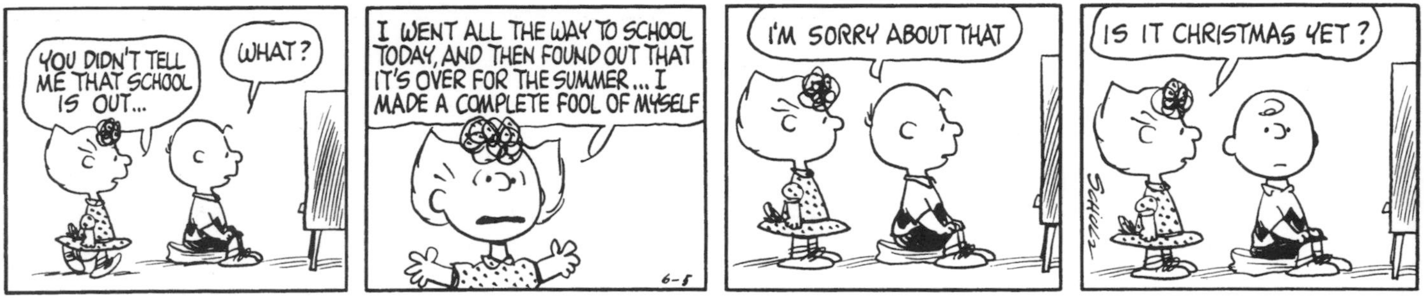
YOU DIDN'T TELL ME THAT SCHOOL IS OUT...
WHAT?
I WENT ALL THE WAY TO SCHOOL TODAY, AND THEN FOUND OUT THAT IT'S OVER FOR THE SUMMER... I MADE A COMPLETE FOOL OF MYSELF
I'M SORRY ABOUT THAT
IS IT CHRISTMAS YET?

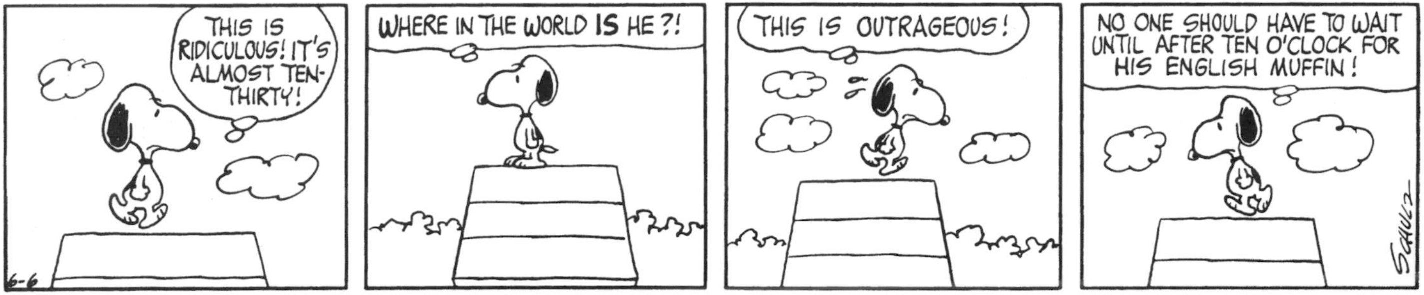
THIS IS RIDICULOUS! IT'S ALMOST TEN-THIRTY!
WHERE IN THE WORLD IS HE?!
THIS IS OUTRAGEOUS!
NO ONE SHOULD HAVE TO WAIT UNTIL AFTER TEN O'CLOCK FOR HIS ENGLISH MUFFIN!

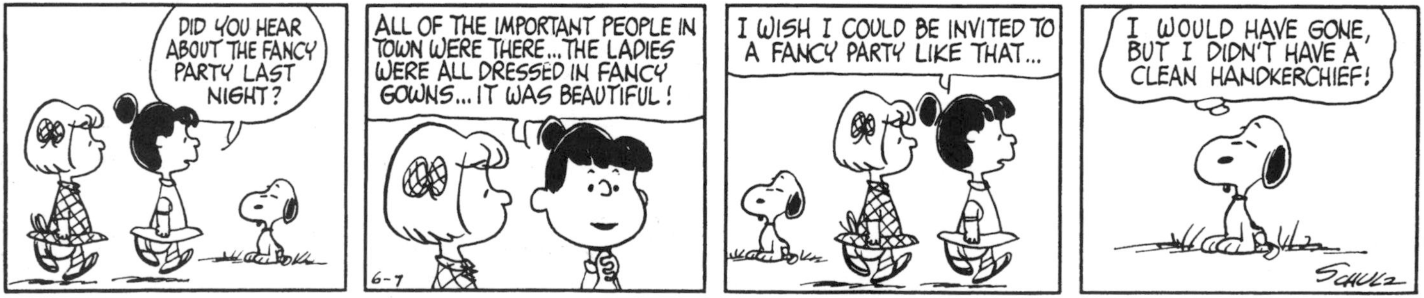
DID YOU HEAR ABOUT THE FANCY PARTY LAST NIGHT?
ALL OF THE IMPORTANT PEOPLE IN TOWN WERE THERE... THE LADIES WERE ALL DRESSED IN FANCY GOWNS... IT WAS BEAUTIFUL!
I WISH I COULD BE INVITED TO A FANCY PARTY LIKE THAT...
I WOULD HAVE GONE, BUT I DIDN'T HAVE A CLEAN HANDKERCHIEF!

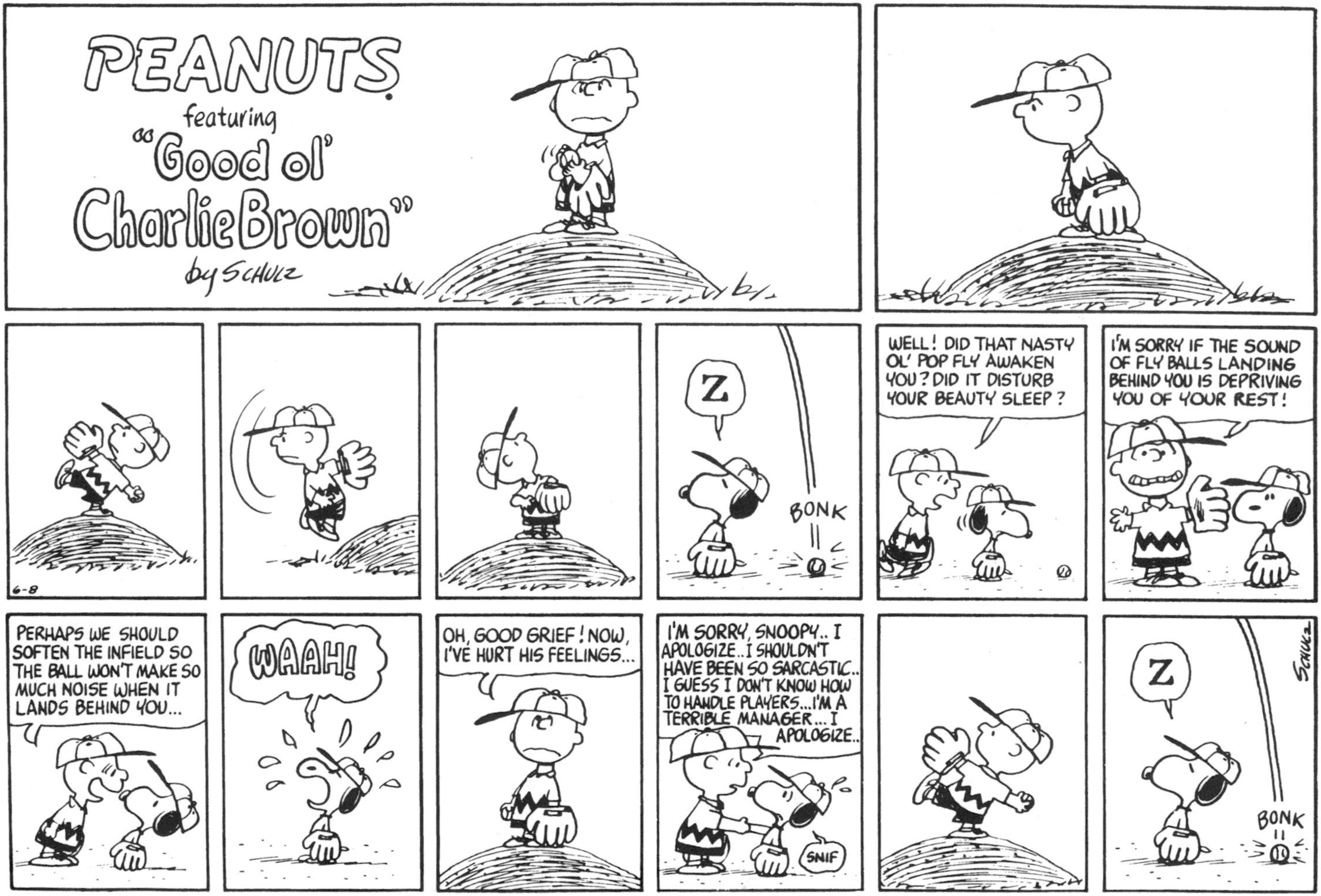
PEANUTS
featuring "Good ol' CharlieBrown"
by SCHULZ
6-8
Z
BONK
WELL! DID THAT NASTY OL' POP FLY AWAKEN YOU? DID IT DISTURB YOUR BEAUTY SLEEP?
I'M SORRY IF THE SOUND OF FLY BALLS LANDING BEHIND YOU IS DEPRIVING YOU OF YOUR REST!
PERHAPS WE SHOULD SOFTEN THE INFIELD SO THE BALL WON'T MAKE SO MUCH NOISE WHEN IT LANDS BEHIND YOU...
WAAH!
OH, GOOD GRIEF! NOW, I'VE HURT HIS FEELINGS...
I'M SORRY, SNOOPY.. I APOLOGIZE.. I SHOULDN'T HAVE BEEN SO SARCASTIC.. I GUESS I DON'T KNOW HOW TO HANDLE PLAYERS...I'M A TERRIBLE MANAGER... I APOLOGIZE..
SNIF
SCHULZ
Z
BONK

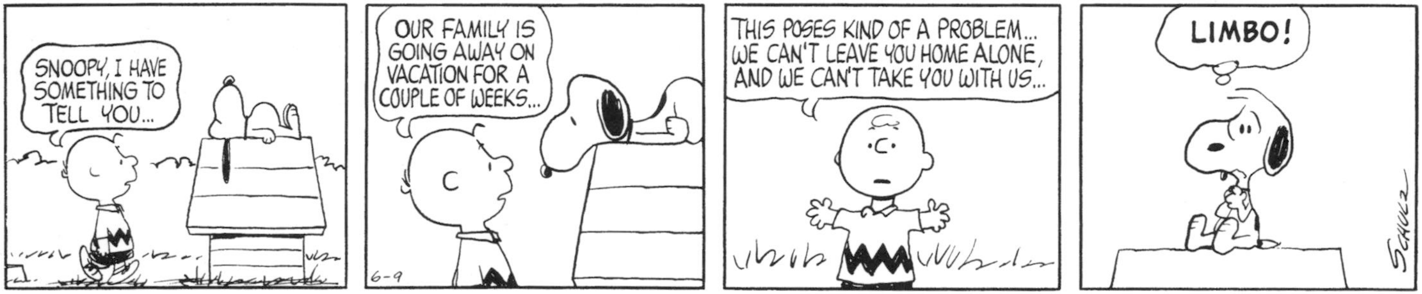
SNOOPY, I HAVE SOMETHING TO TELL YOU...
OUR FAMILY IS GOING AWAY ON VACATION FOR A COUPLE OF WEEKS...
THIS POSES KIND OF A PROBLEM... WE CAN'T LEAVE YOU HOME ALONE, AND WE CAN'T TAKE YOU WITH US...
LIMBO!

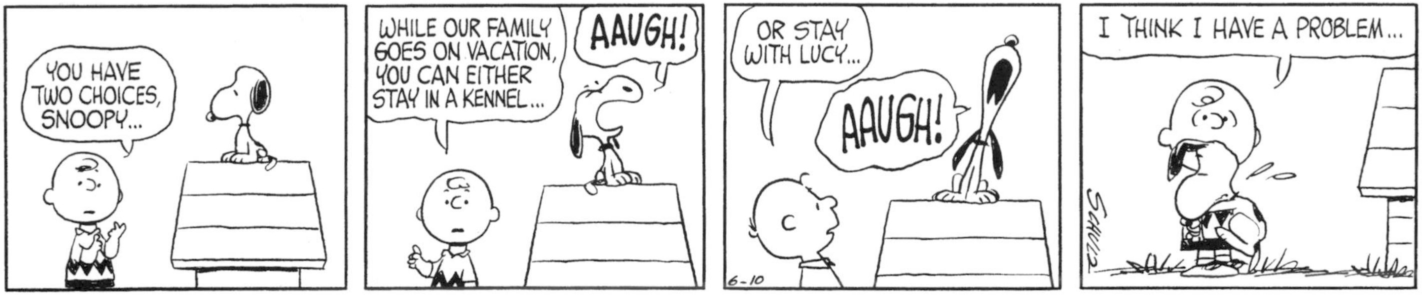
YOU HAVE TWO CHOICES, SNOOPY...
WHILE OUR FAMILY GOES ON VACATION, YOU CAN EITHER STAY IN A KENNEL...
AAUGH!
OR STAY WITH LUCY...
AAUGH!
I THINK I HAVE A PROBLEM...

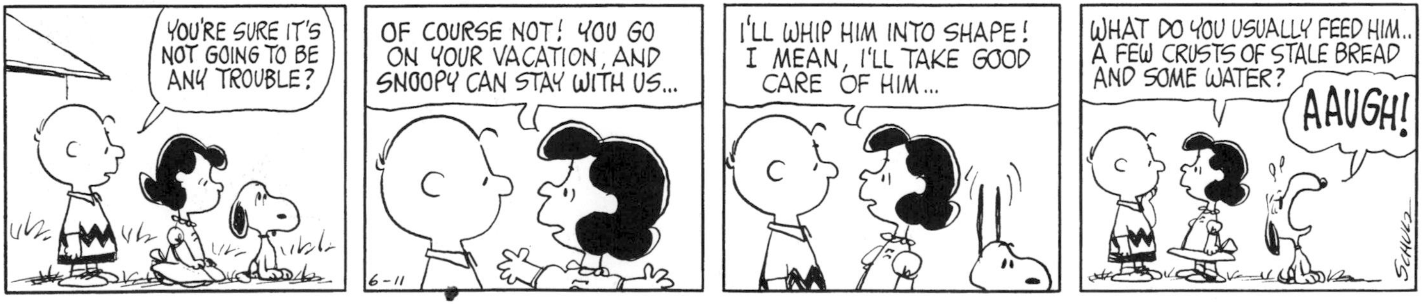
YOU'RE SURE IT'S NOT GOING TO BE ANY TROUBLE?
OF COURSE NOT! YOU GO ON YOUR VACATION, AND SNOOPY CAN STAY WITH US...
I'LL WHIP HIM INTO SHAPE! I MEAN, I'LL TAKE GOOD CARE OF HIM...
WHAT DO YOU USUALLY FEED HIM.. A FEW CRUSTS OF STALE BREAD AND SOME WATER?
AAUGH!

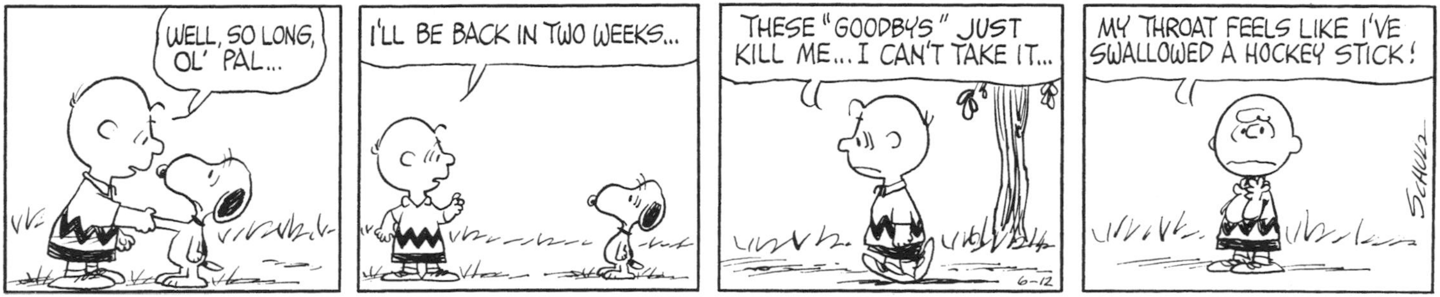
WELL, SO LONG, OL' PAL...
I'LL BE BACK IN TWO WEEKS...
THESE "GOODBYS" JUST KILL ME... I CAN'T TAKE IT...
MY THROAT FEELS LIKE I'VE SWALLOWED A HOCKEY STICK!

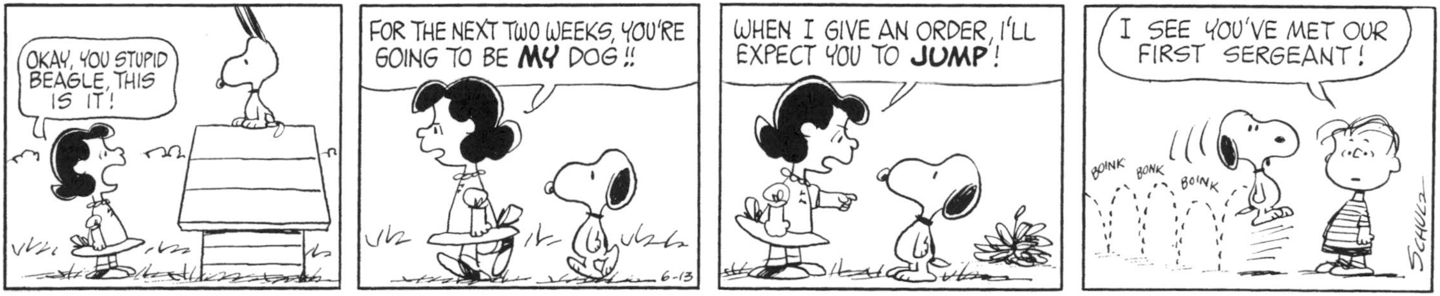
OKAY, YOU STUPID BEAGLE, THIS IS IT!
FOR THE NEXT TWO WEEKS, YOU'RE GOING TO BE **MY** DOG!!
WHEN I GIVE AN ORDER, I'LL EXPECT YOU TO **JUMP**!
BOINK
BONK
BOINK
I SEE YOU'VE MET OUR FIRST SERGEANT!

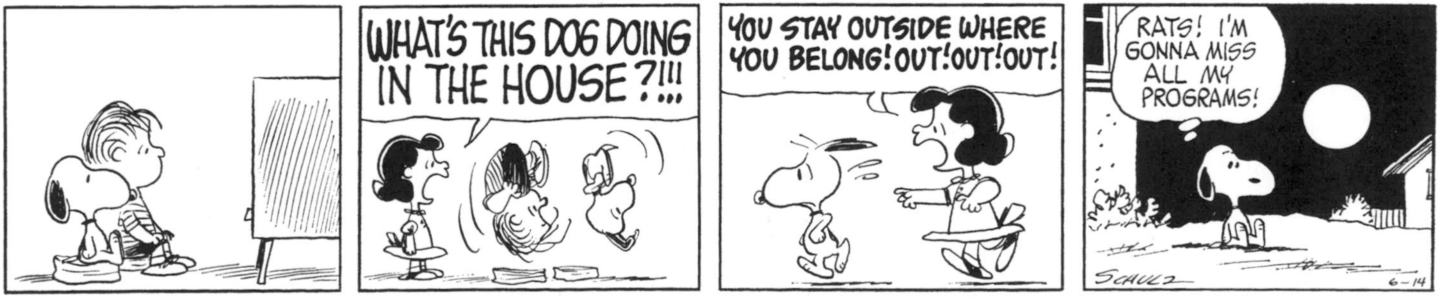
WHAT'S THIS DOG DOING IN THE HOUSE?!!!...
YOU STAY OUTSIDE WHERE YOU BELONG! OUT! OUT! OUT!
RATS! I'M GONNA MISS ALL MY PROGRAMS!

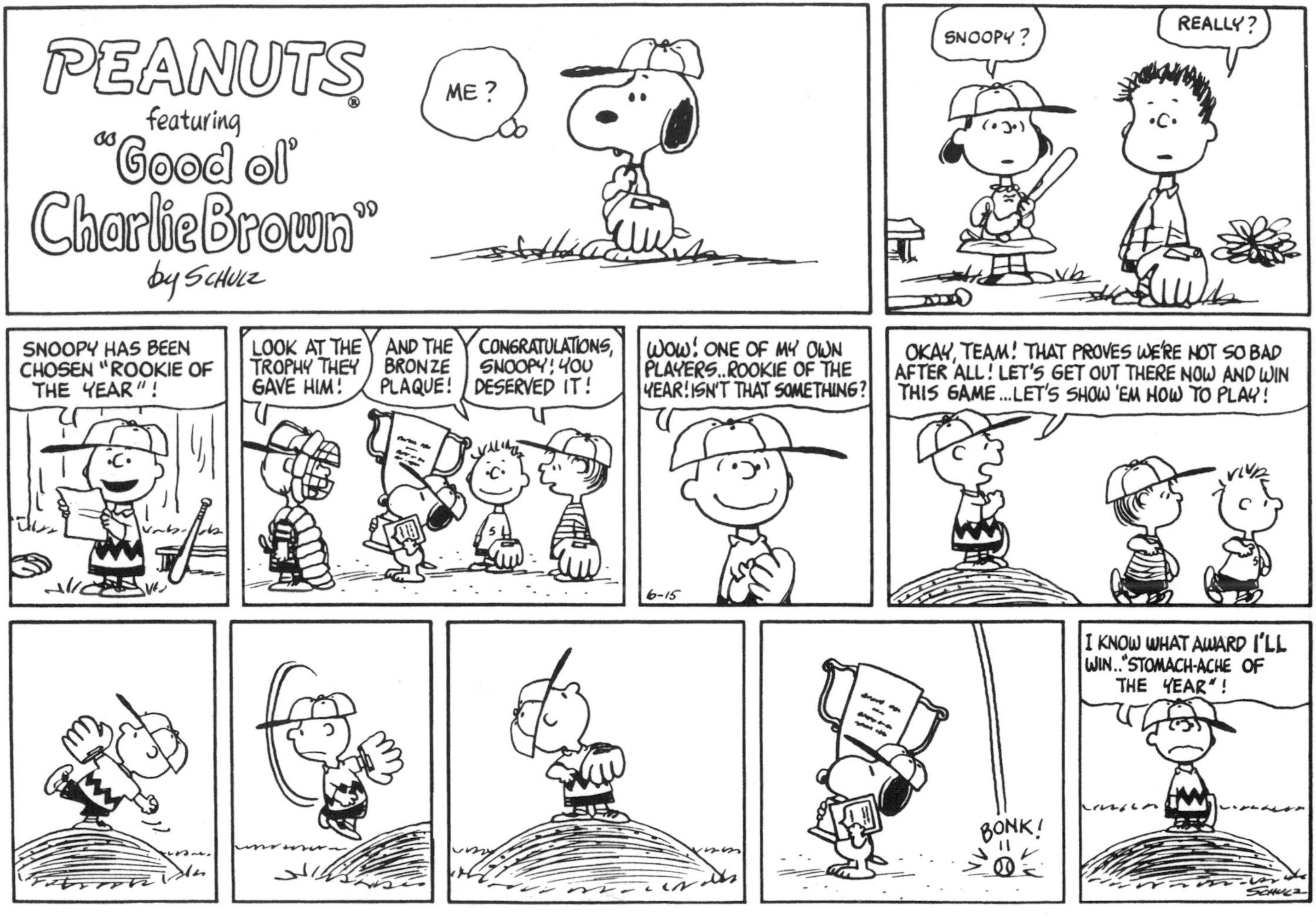
PEANUTS®
featuring "Good ol' CharlieBrown"
by SCHULZ
ME?
SNOOPY?
REALLY?
SNOOPY HAS BEEN CHOSEN "ROOKIE OF THE YEAR"!
LOOK AT THE TROPHY THEY GAVE HIM!
AND THE BRONZE PLAQUE!
CONGRATULATIONS, SNOOPY! YOU DESERVED IT!
WOW! ONE OF MY OWN PLAYERS..ROOKIE OF THE YEAR! ISN'T THAT SOMETHING?
6-15
OKAY, TEAM! THAT PROVES WE'RE NOT SO BAD AFTER ALL! LET'S GET OUT THERE NOW AND WIN THIS GAME...LET'S SHOW 'EM HOW TO PLAY!
BONK!
I KNOW WHAT AWARD I'LL WIN.."STOMACH-ACHE OF THE YEAR"!
SCHULZ

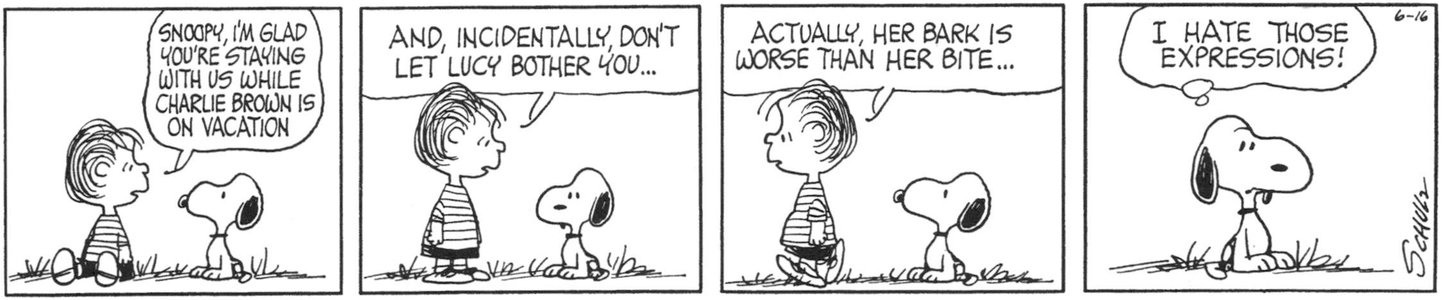
SNOOPY, I'M GLAD YOU'RE STAYING WITH US WHILE CHARLIE BROWN IS ON VACATION
AND, INCIDENTALLY, DON'T LET LUCY BOTHER YOU...
ACTUALLY, HER BARK IS WORSE THAN HER BITE...
I HATE THOSE EXPRESSIONS!
6-16
SCHULZ

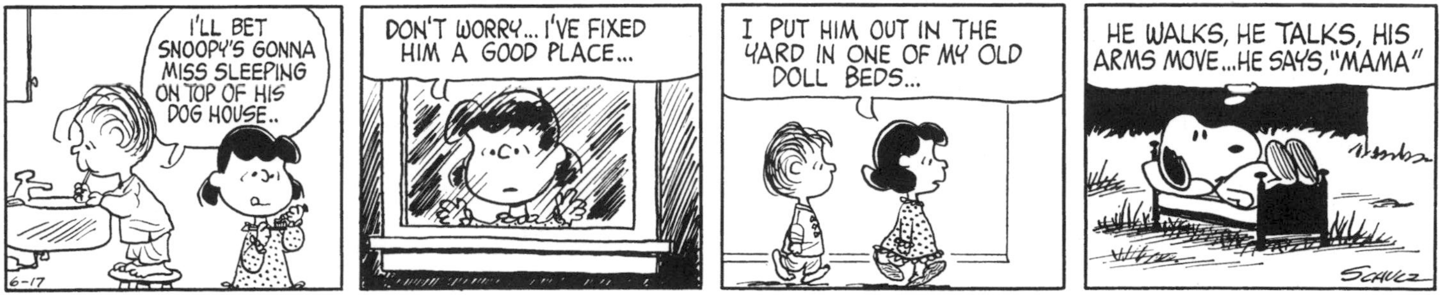
I'LL BET SNOOPY'S GONNA MISS SLEEPING ON TOP OF HIS DOG HOUSE..
6-17
DON'T WORRY... I'VE FIXED HIM A GOOD PLACE...
I PUT HIM OUT IN THE YARD IN ONE OF MY OLD DOLL BEDS...
HE WALKS, HE TALKS, HIS ARMS MOVE...HE SAYS, "MAMA"
SCHULZ

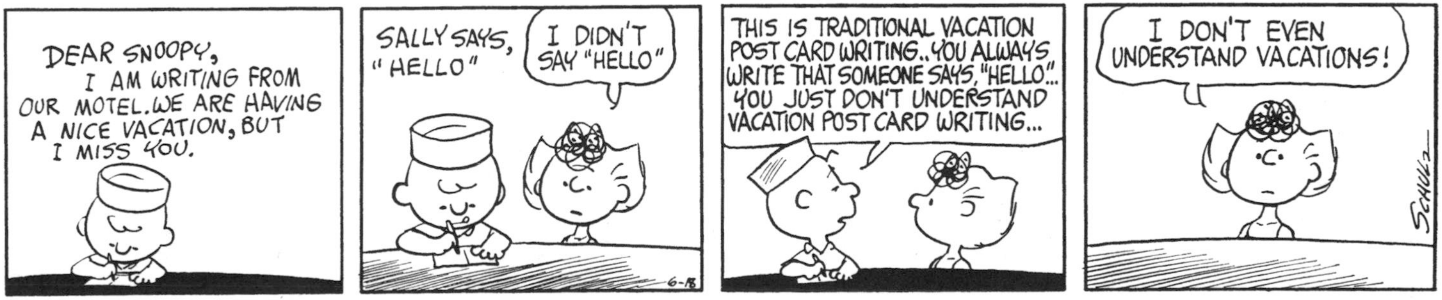
DEAR SNOOPY,
I AM WRITING FROM OUR MOTEL. WE ARE HAVING A NICE VACATION, BUT I MISS YOU.
SALLY SAYS, "HELLO"
I DIDN'T SAY "HELLO"
6-18
THIS IS TRADITIONAL VACATION POST CARD WRITING.. YOU ALWAYS WRITE THAT SOMEONE SAYS, "HELLO"... YOU JUST DON'T UNDERSTAND VACATION POST CARD WRITING...
I DON'T EVEN UNDERSTAND VACATIONS!
SCHULZ

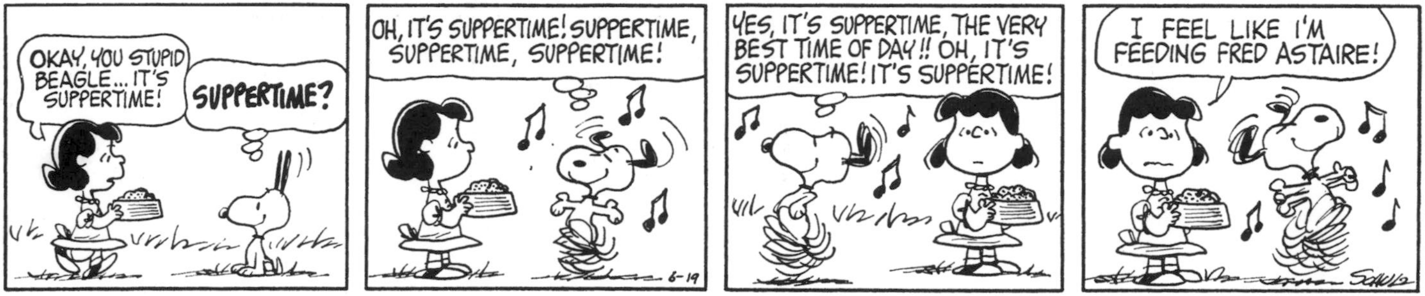
OKAY, YOU STUPID BEAGLE... IT'S SUPPERTIME!
SUPPERTIME?
OH, IT'S SUPPERTIME! SUPPERTIME, SUPPERTIME, SUPPERTIME!
6-19
YES, IT'S SUPPERTIME, THE VERY BEST TIME OF DAY!! OH, IT'S SUPPERTIME! IT'S SUPPERTIME!
I FEEL LIKE I'M FEEDING FRED ASTAIRE!
SCHULZ

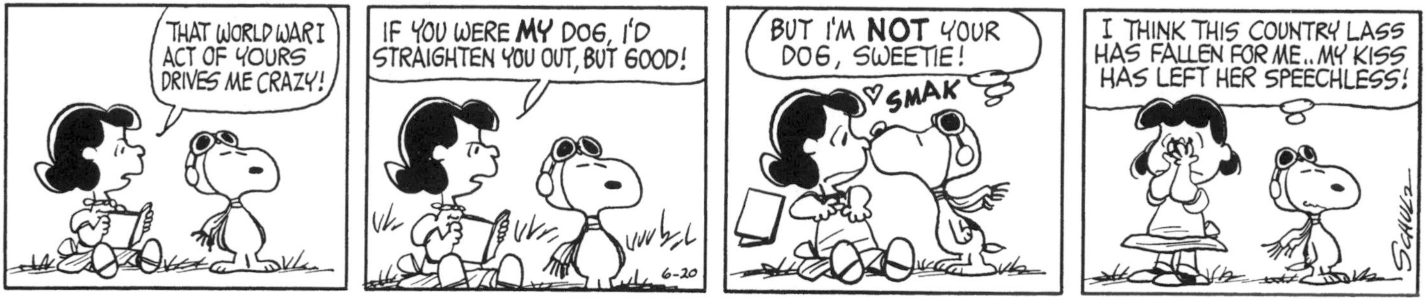
THAT WORLD WAR I ACT OF YOURS DRIVES ME CRAZY!
IF YOU WERE MY DOG, I'D STRAIGHTEN YOU OUT, BUT GOOD!
6-20
BUT I'M NOT YOUR DOG, SWEETIE!
SMAK
I THINK THIS COUNTRY LASS HAS FALLEN FOR ME.. MY KISS HAS LEFT HER SPEECHLESS!
SCHULZ

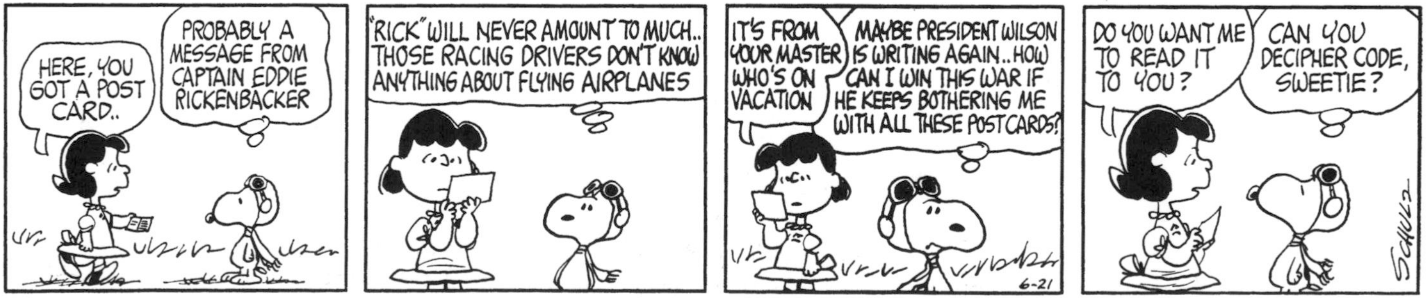
HERE, YOU GOT A POST CARD..
PROBABLY A MESSAGE FROM CAPTAIN EDDIE RICKENBACKER
"RICK" WILL NEVER AMOUNT TO MUCH.. THOSE RACING DRIVERS DON'T KNOW ANYTHING ABOUT FLYING AIRPLANES
IT'S FROM YOUR MASTER WHO'S ON VACATION
MAYBE PRESIDENT WILSON IS WRITING AGAIN...HOW CAN I WIN THIS WAR IF HE KEEPS BOTHERING ME WITH ALL THESE POSTCARDS?
6-21
DO YOU WANT ME TO READ IT TO YOU?
CAN YOU DECIPHER CODE, SWEETIE?
SCHULZ

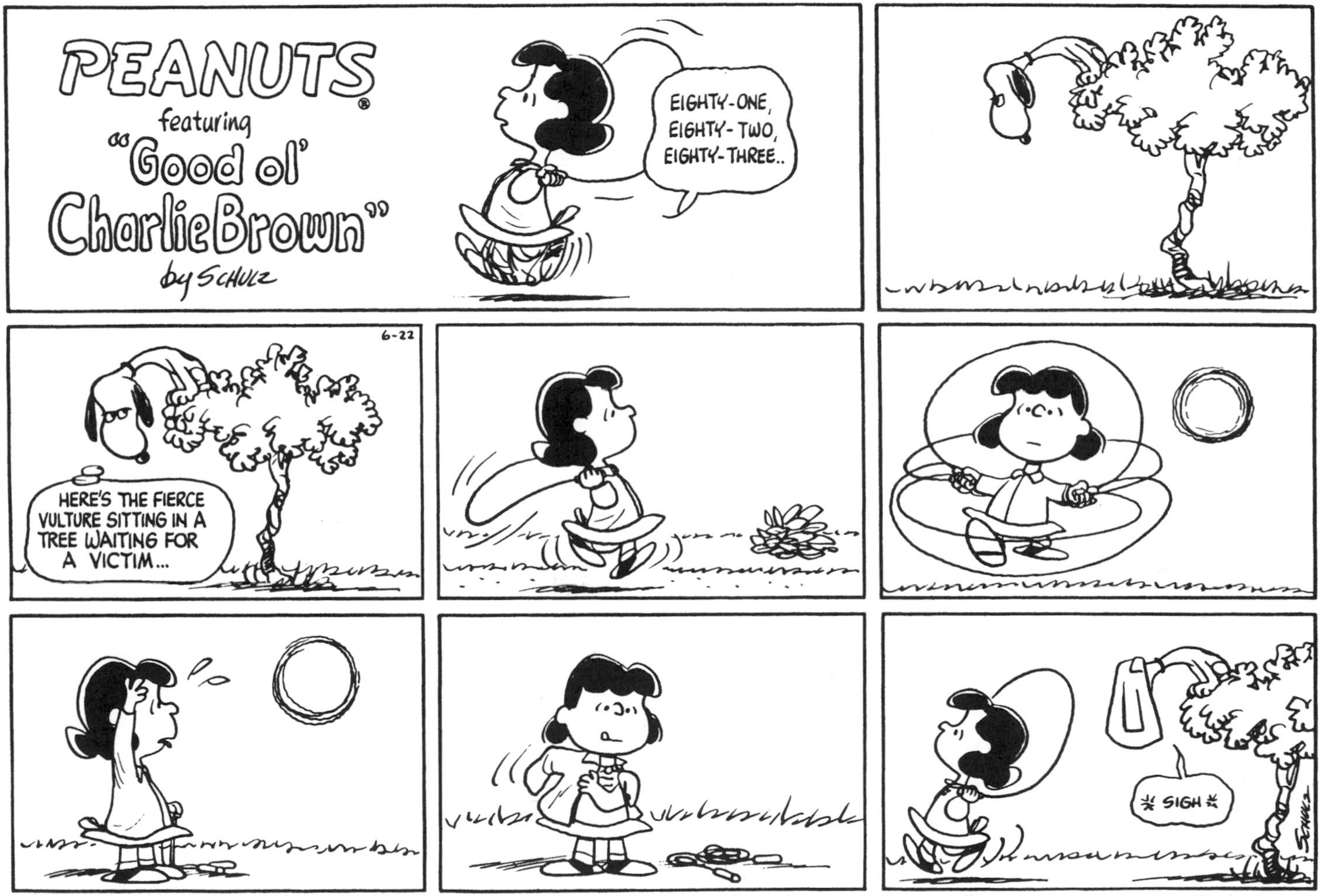
PEANUTS®
featuring
"Good ol' CharlieBrown"
by SCHULZ
EIGHTY-ONE, EIGHTY-TWO, EIGHTY-THREE..
6-22
HERE'S THE FIERCE VULTURE SITTING IN A TREE WAITING FOR A VICTIM...
* SIGH *
SCHULZ

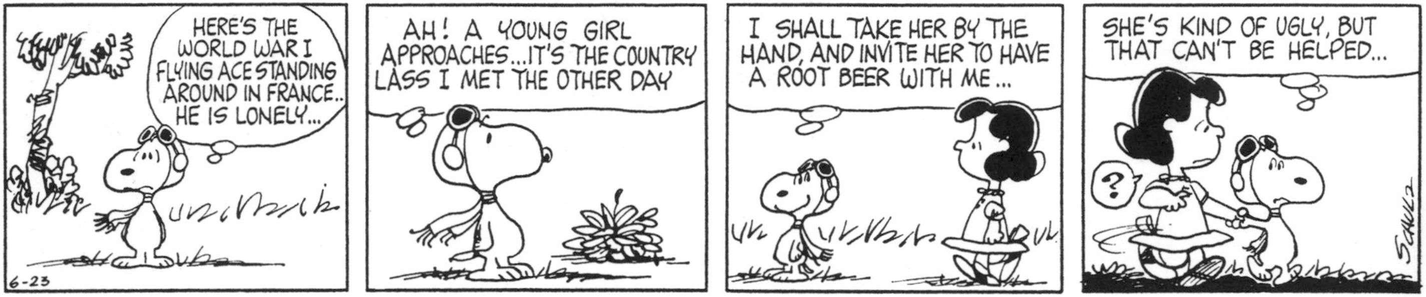
HERE'S THE WORLD WAR I FLYING ACE STANDING AROUND IN FRANCE.. HE IS LONELY...
6-23
AH! A YOUNG GIRL APPROACHES...IT'S THE COUNTRY LASS I MET THE OTHER DAY
I SHALL TAKE HER BY THE HAND, AND INVITE HER TO HAVE A ROOT BEER WITH ME...
SHE'S KIND OF UGLY, BUT THAT CAN'T BE HELPED...
?
SCHULZ

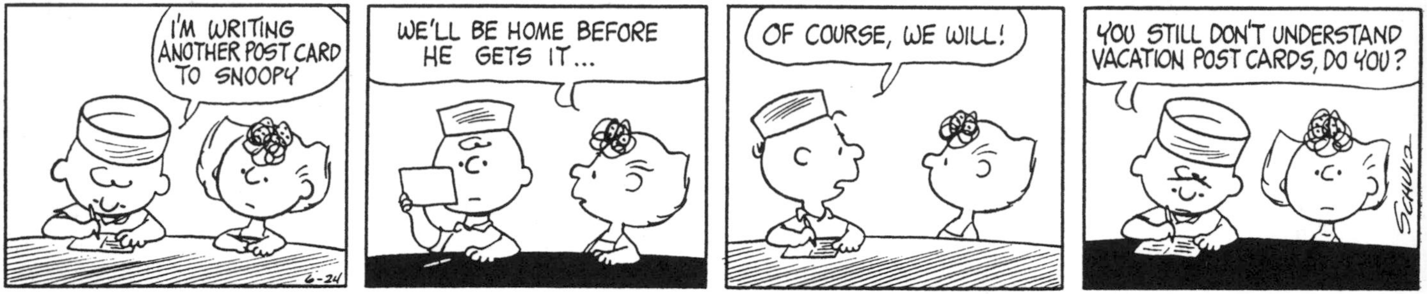
I'M WRITING ANOTHER POST CARD TO SNOOPY
6-24
WE'LL BE HOME BEFORE HE GETS IT...
OF COURSE, WE WILL!
YOU STILL DON'T UNDERSTAND VACATION POST CARDS, DO YOU?
SCHULZ

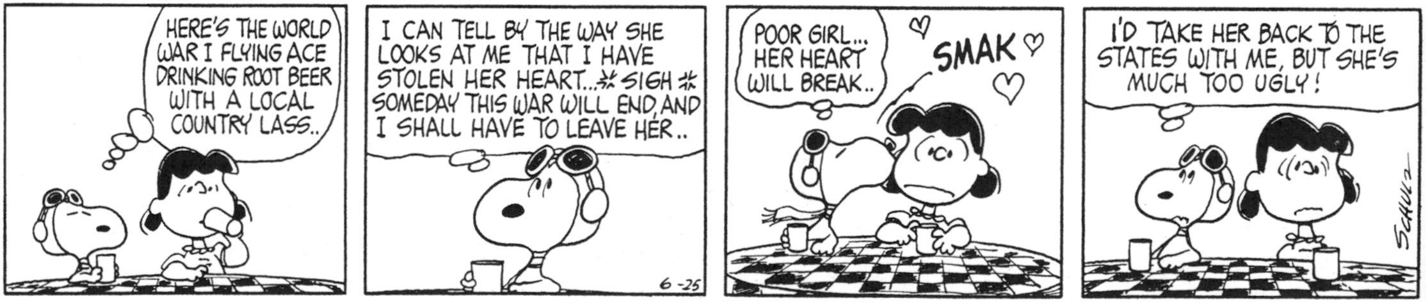
HERE'S THE WORLD WAR I FLYING ACE DRINKING ROOT BEER WITH A LOCAL COUNTRY LASS..
I CAN TELL BY THE WAY SHE LOOKS AT ME THAT I HAVE STOLEN HER HEART... SIGH SOMEDAY THIS WAR WILL END, AND I SHALL HAVE TO LEAVE HER..
6-25
POOR GIRL... HER HEART WILL BREAK..
SMAK
SCHULZ
I'D TAKE HER BACK TO THE STATES WITH ME, BUT SHE'S MUCH TOO UGLY!

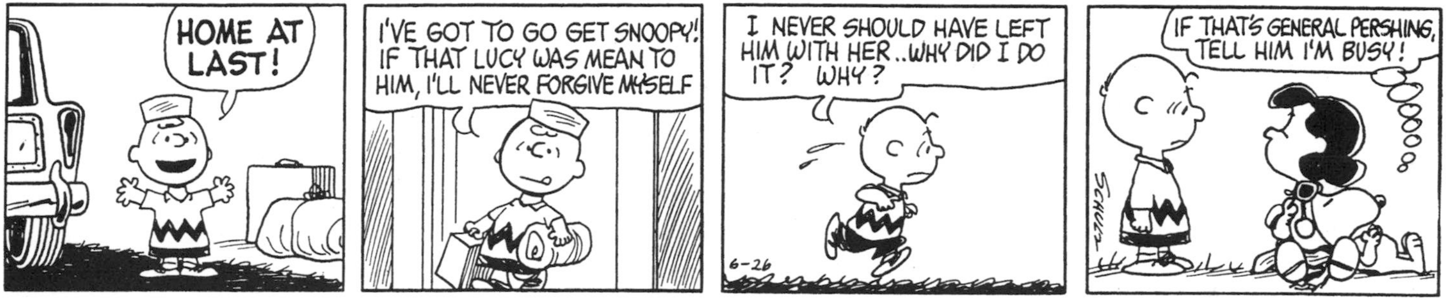
HOME AT LAST!
I'VE GOT TO GO GET SNOOPY! IF THAT LUCY WAS MEAN TO HIM, I'LL NEVER FORGIVE MYSELF
I NEVER SHOULD HAVE LEFT HIM WITH HER..WHY DID I DO IT? WHY?
IF THAT'S GENERAL PERSHING, TELL HIM I'M BUSY!

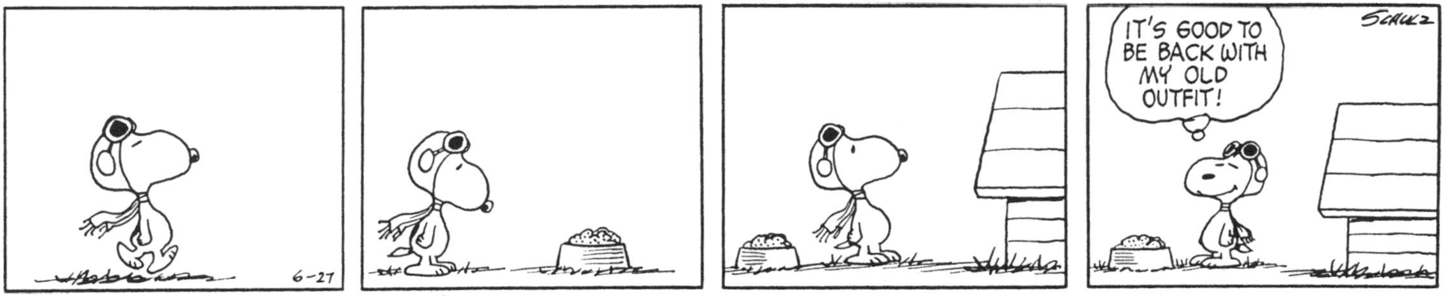
IT'S GOOD TO BE BACK WITH MY OLD OUTFIT!

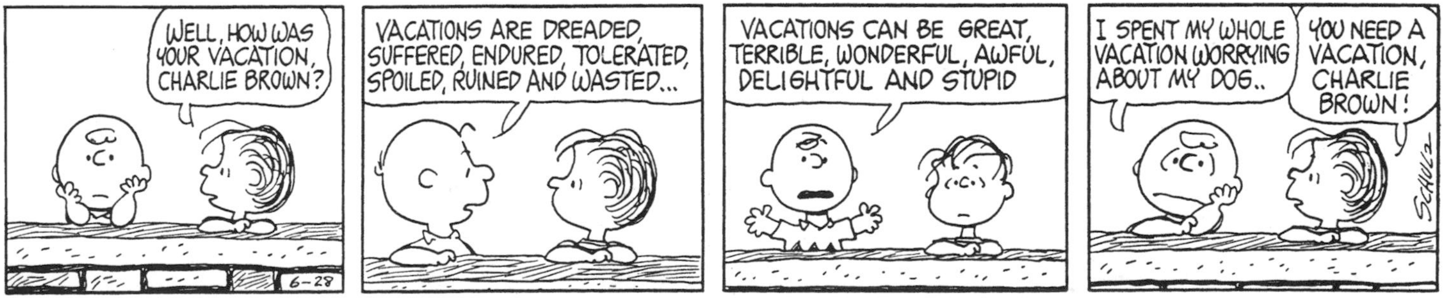
WELL, HOW WAS YOUR VACATION, CHARLIE BROWN?
VACATIONS ARE DREADED, SUFFERED, ENDURED, TOLERATED, SPOILED, RUINED AND WASTED...
VACATIONS CAN BE GREAT, TERRIBLE, WONDERFUL, AWFUL, DELIGHTFUL AND STUPID
I SPENT MY WHOLE VACATION WORRYING ABOUT MY DOG..
YOU NEED A VACATION, CHARLIE BROWN!

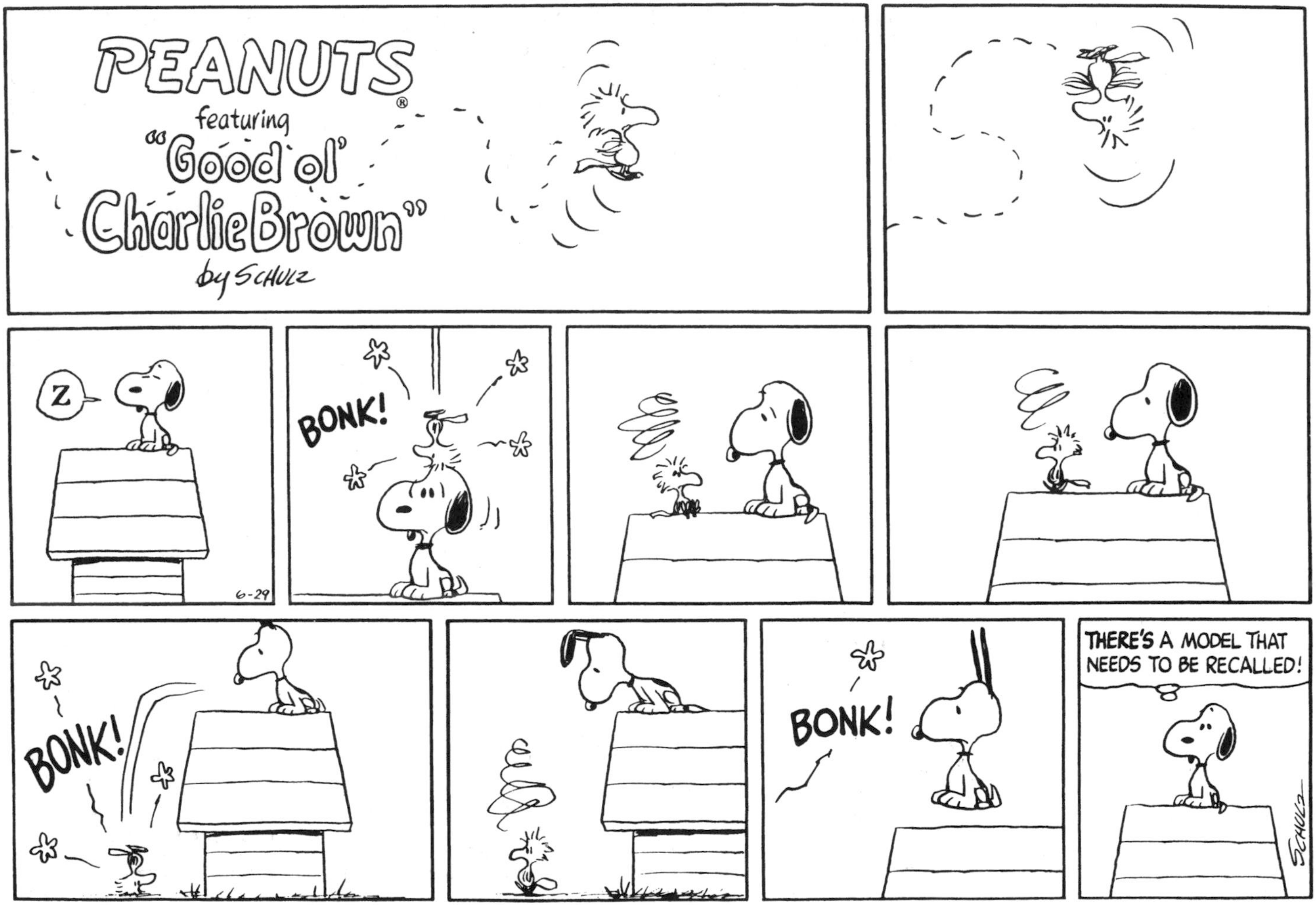
PEANUTS®
featuring
"Good ol' Charlie Brown"
by SCHULZ
Z
6-29
BONK!
BONK!
BONK!
THERE'S A MODEL THAT NEEDS TO BE RECALLED!
SCHULZ

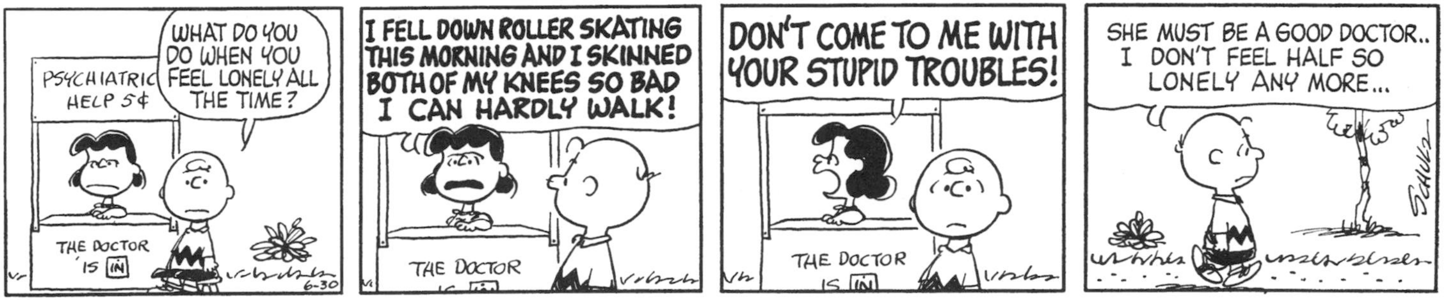
PSYCHIATRIC HELP 5¢
THE DOCTOR IS IN
WHAT DO YOU DO WHEN YOU FEEL LONELY ALL THE TIME?
6-30
I FELL DOWN ROLLER SKATING THIS MORNING AND I SKINNED BOTH OF MY KNEES SO BAD I CAN HARDLY WALK!
THE DOCTOR
DON'T COME TO ME WITH YOUR STUPID TROUBLES!
THE DOCTOR IS IN
SHE MUST BE A GOOD DOCTOR.. I DON'T FEEL HALF SO LONELY ANY MORE...
SCHULZ

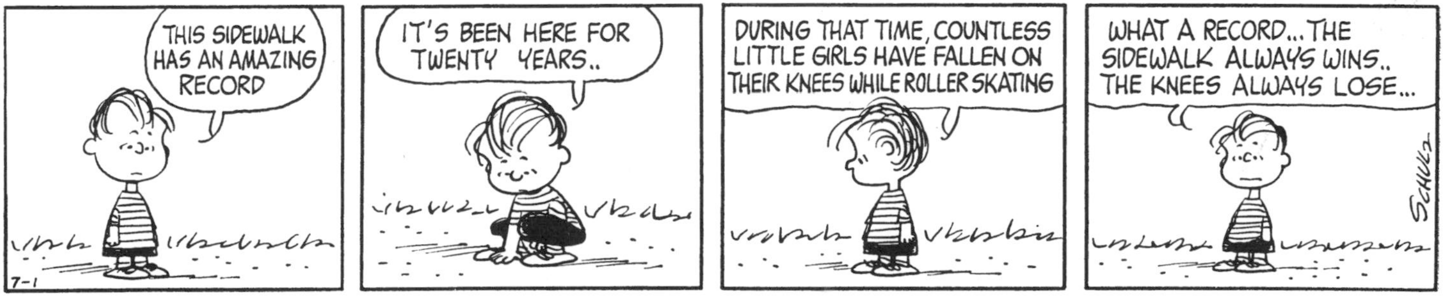
7-1
THIS SIDEWALK HAS AN AMAZING RECORD
IT'S BEEN HERE FOR TWENTY YEARS..
DURING THAT TIME, COUNTLESS LITTLE GIRLS HAVE FALLEN ON THEIR KNEES WHILE ROLLER SKATING
WHAT A RECORD... THE SIDEWALK ALWAYS WINS.. THE KNEES ALWAYS LOSE...
SCHULZ

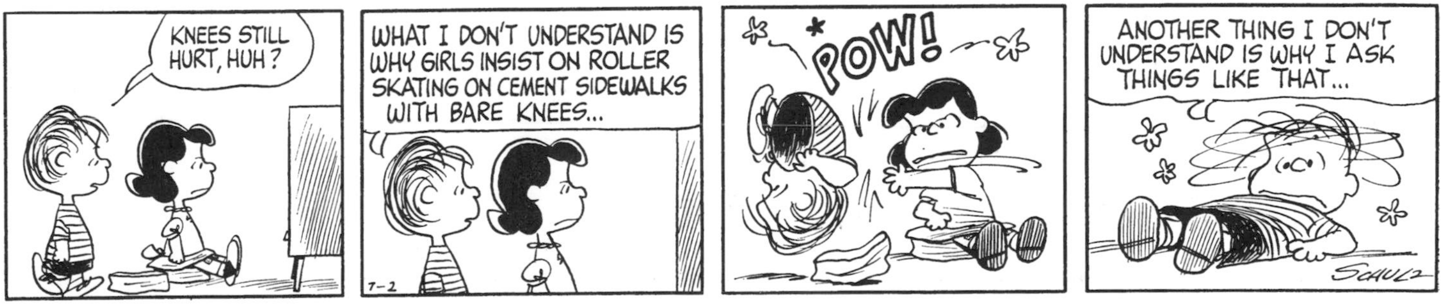
KNEES STILL HURT, HUH?
7-2
WHAT I DON'T UNDERSTAND IS WHY GIRLS INSIST ON ROLLER SKATING ON CEMENT SIDEWALKS WITH BARE KNEES...
POW!
ANOTHER THING I DON'T UNDERSTAND IS WHY I ASK THINGS LIKE THAT...
SCHULZ

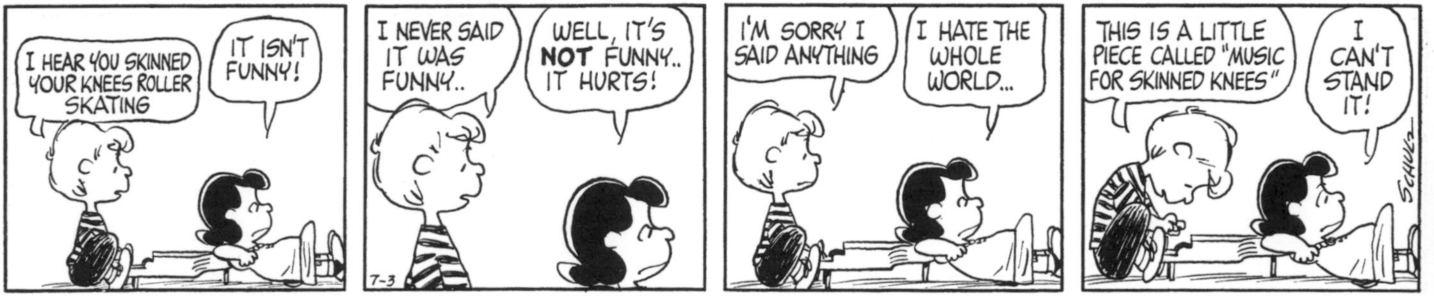
I HEAR YOU SKINNED YOUR KNEES ROLLER SKATING
IT ISN'T FUNNY!
I NEVER SAID IT WAS FUNNY..
WELL, IT'S **NOT** FUNNY.. IT HURTS!
I'M SORRY I SAID ANYTHING
I HATE THE WHOLE WORLD...
THIS IS A LITTLE PIECE CALLED "MUSIC FOR SKINNED KNEES"
I CAN'T STAND IT!

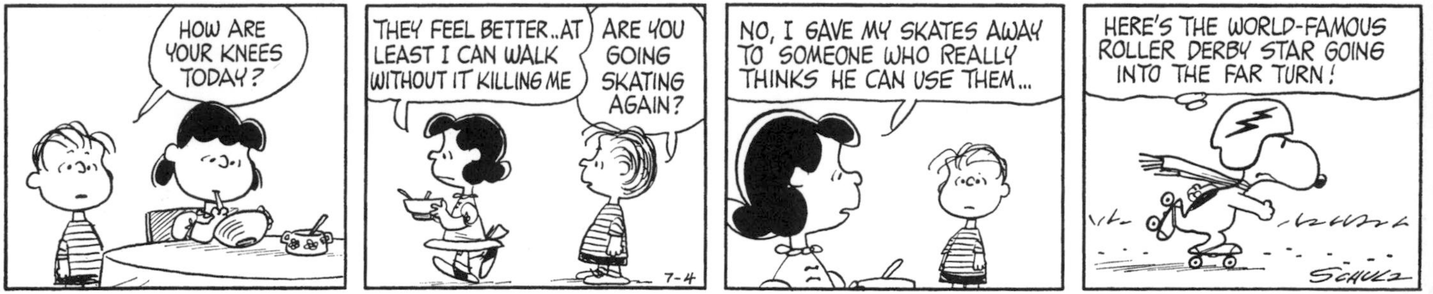
HOW ARE YOUR KNEES TODAY?
THEY FEEL BETTER..AT LEAST I CAN WALK WITHOUT IT KILLING ME
ARE YOU GOING SKATING AGAIN?
NO, I GAVE MY SKATES AWAY TO SOMEONE WHO REALLY THINKS HE CAN USE THEM...
HERE'S THE WORLD-FAMOUS ROLLER DERBY STAR GOING INTO THE FAR TURN!

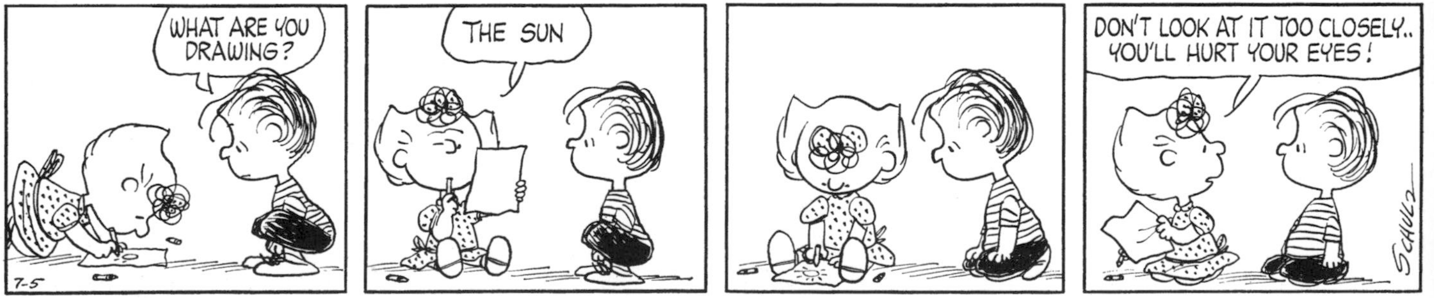
WHAT ARE YOU DRAWING?
THE SUN
DON'T LOOK AT IT TOO CLOSELY.. YOU'LL HURT YOUR EYES!

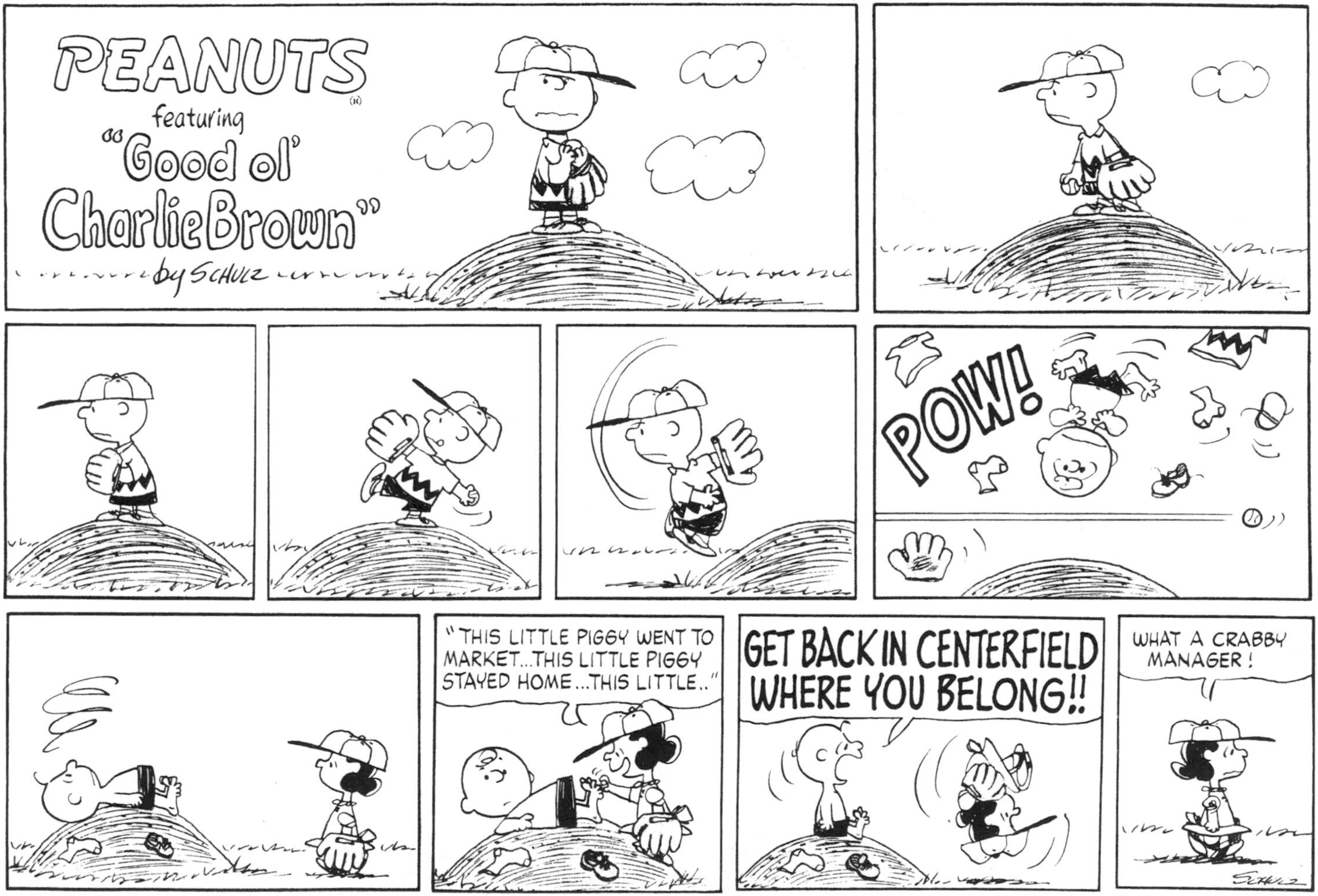
PEANUTS
featuring
"Good ol' Charlie Brown"
by SCHULZ
POW!
"THIS LITTLE PIGGY WENT TO MARKET...THIS LITTLE PIGGY STAYED HOME...THIS LITTLE.."
GET BACK IN CENTERFIELD WHERE YOU BELONG!!
WHAT A CRABBY MANAGER!
SCHULZ

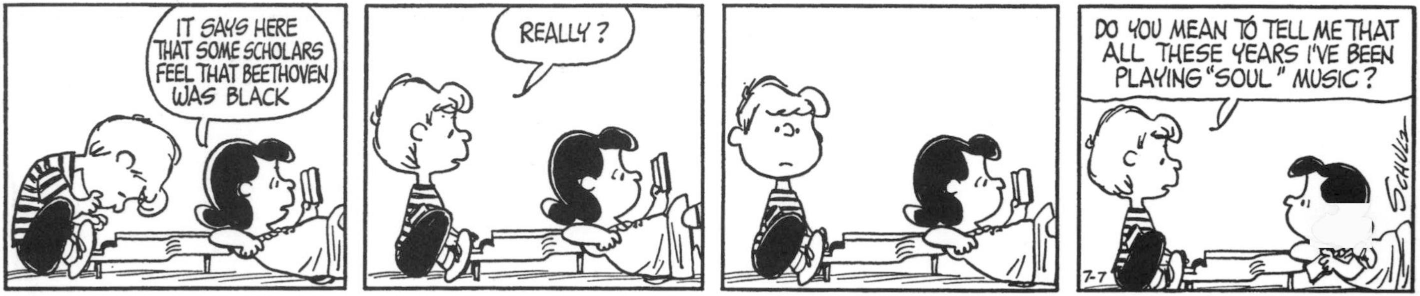
IT SAYS HERE THAT SOME SCHOLARS FEEL THAT BEETHOVEN WAS BLACK
REALLY ?
DO YOU MEAN TO TELL ME THAT ALL THESE YEARS I'VE BEEN PLAYING "SOUL" MUSIC ?

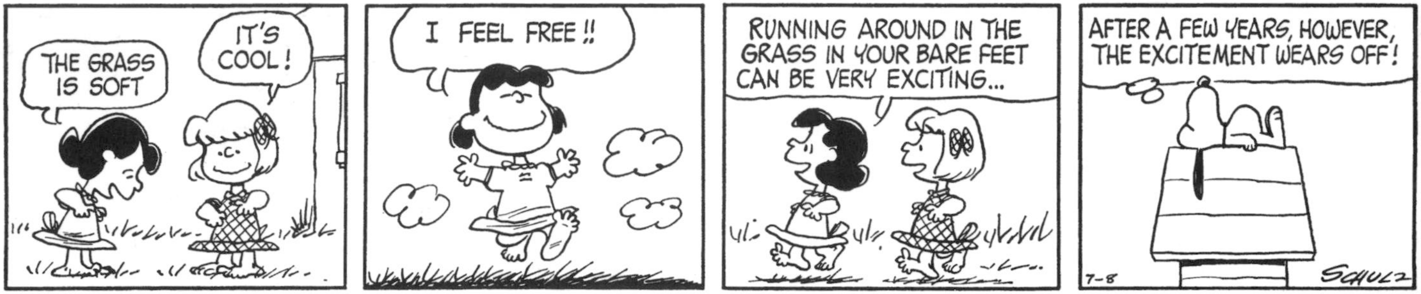
THE GRASS IS SOFT
IT'S COOL !
I FEEL FREE !!
RUNNING AROUND IN THE GRASS IN YOUR BARE FEET CAN BE VERY EXCITING...
AFTER A FEW YEARS, HOWEVER, THE EXCITEMENT WEARS OFF !

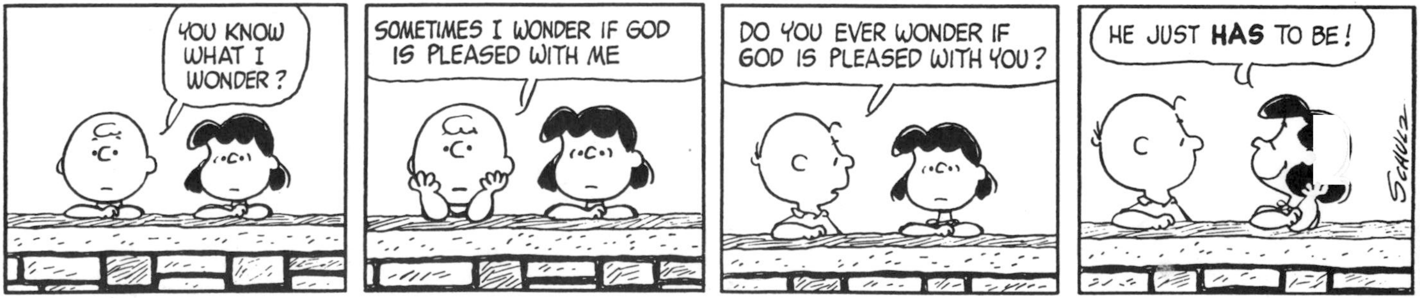
YOU KNOW WHAT I WONDER ?
SOMETIMES I WONDER IF GOD IS PLEASED WITH ME
DO YOU EVER WONDER IF GOD IS PLEASED WITH YOU ?
HE JUST HAS TO BE !

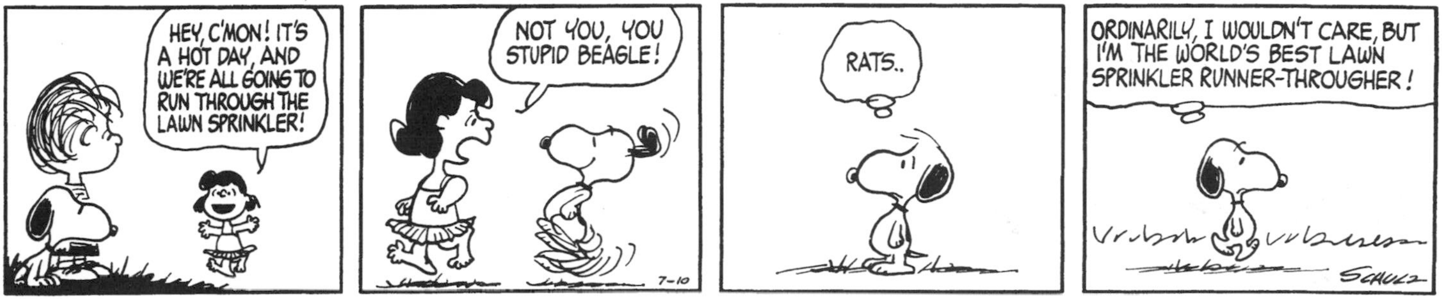
HEY, C'MON! IT'S A HOT DAY, AND WE'RE ALL GOING TO RUN THROUGH THE LAWN SPRINKLER!
NOT YOU, YOU STUPID BEAGLE!
7-10
RATS..
ORDINARILY, I WOULDN'T CARE, BUT I'M THE WORLD'S BEST LAWN SPRINKLER RUNNER-THROUGHER!
SCHULZ

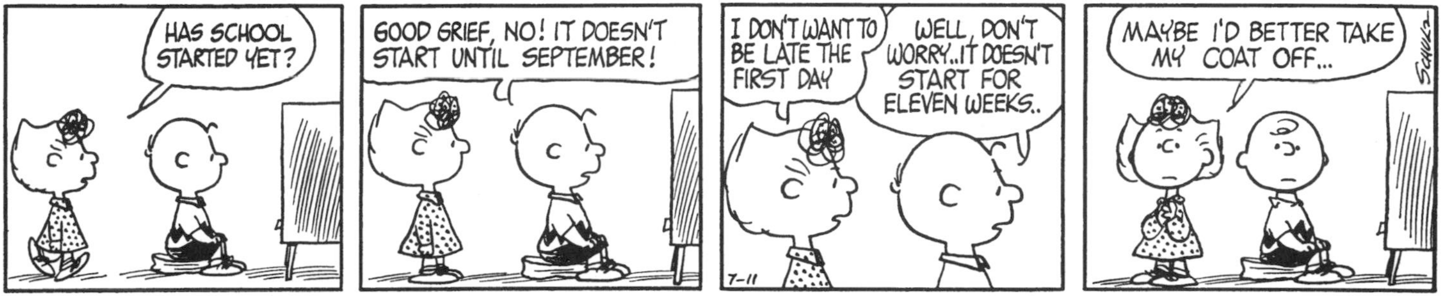
HAS SCHOOL STARTED YET?
GOOD GRIEF, NO! IT DOESN'T START UNTIL SEPTEMBER!
I DON'T WANT TO BE LATE THE FIRST DAY
WELL, DON'T WORRY..IT DOESN'T START FOR ELEVEN WEEKS..
7-11
MAYBE I'D BETTER TAKE MY COAT OFF...
SCHULZ

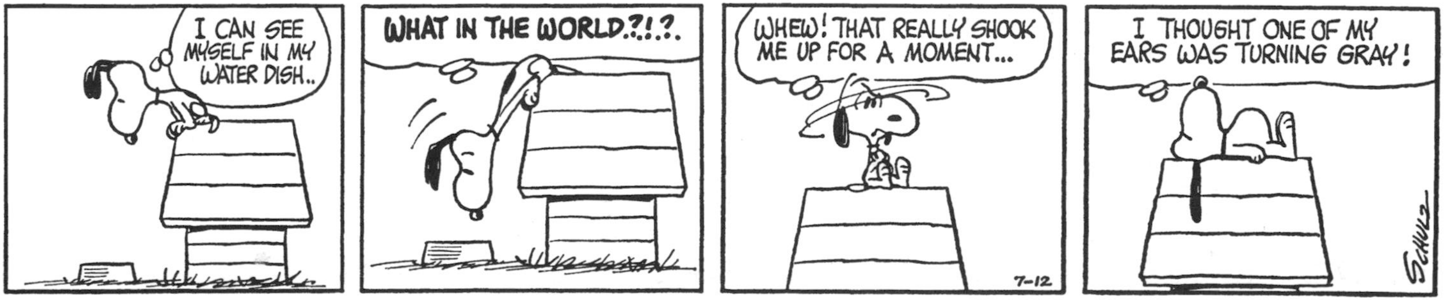
I CAN SEE MYSELF IN MY WATER DISH..
WHAT IN THE WORLD?!?!?.
WHEW! THAT REALLY SHOOK ME UP FOR A MOMENT...
7-12
I THOUGHT ONE OF MY EARS WAS TURNING GRAY!
SCHULZ

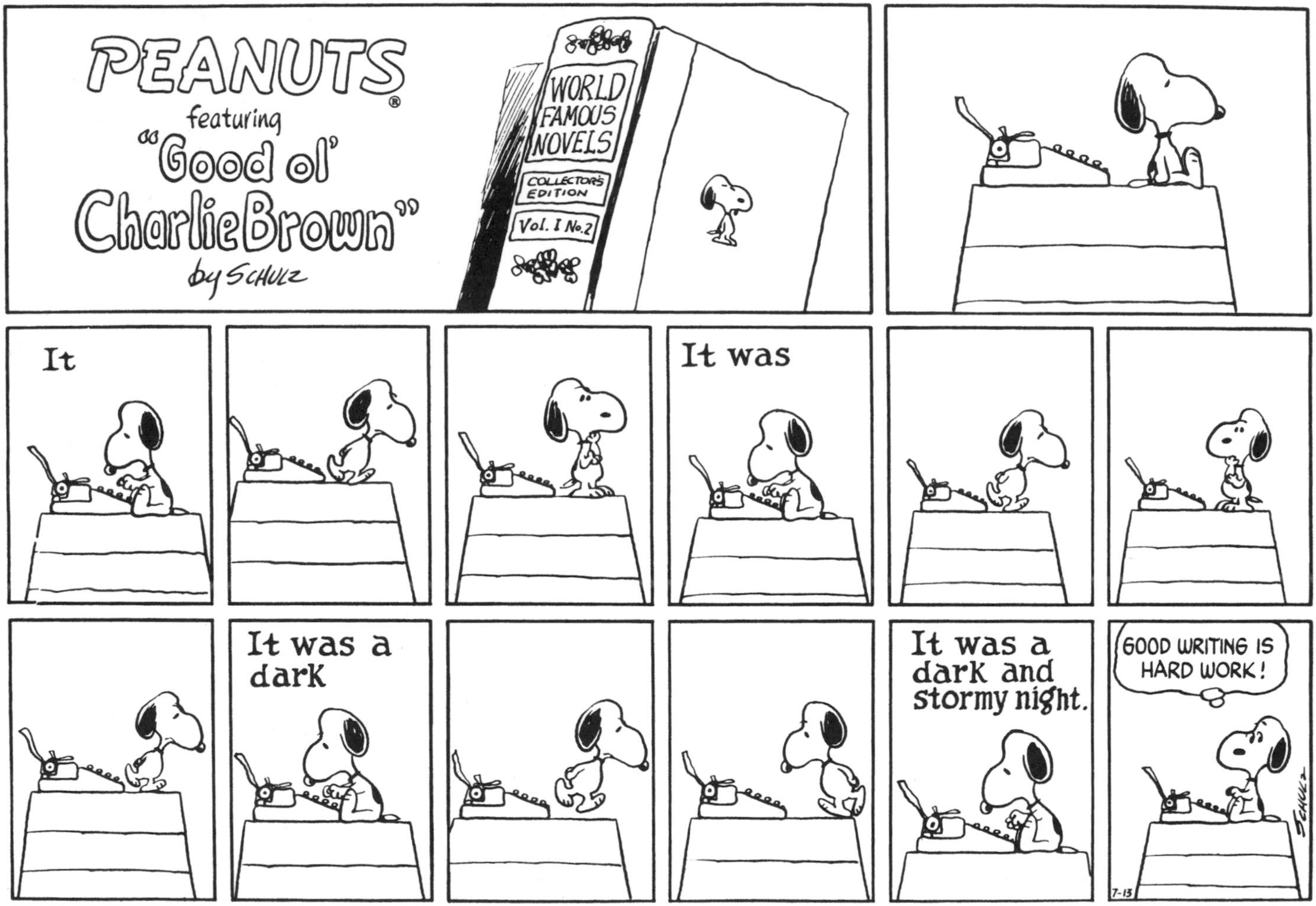
PEANUTS®
featuring
"Good ol' Charlie Brown"
by SCHULZ
WORLD FAMOUS NOVELS
COLLECTOR'S EDITION
Vol. I No. 2
It
It was
It was a dark
It was a dark and stormy night.
GOOD WRITING IS HARD WORK!
SCHULZ
7-13

Panel 1: LOOK, CHARLIE BROWN... A MOVING VAN..

Panel 2: SOMEONE NEW, I SUPPOSE..PEOPLE ARE ALWAYS COMING AND GOING..

IT'S STOPPING DOWN THERE IN THE NEXT BLOCK..

Panel 3: IT'S STOPPING IN FRONT OF THAT LITTLE RED-HAIRED GIRL'S HOUSE!

7-14

Panel 4: WHY IS MY WHOLE LIFE SUDDENLY PASSING IN FRONT OF MY EYES?!

Panel 5: THERE'S A MOVING VAN IN FRONT OF THAT LITTLE RED-HAIRED GIRL'S HOUSE!

Panel 6: SHE'S MOVING AWAY, CHARLIE BROWN... SEE? THEY'RE CARRYING OUT ALL THE FURNITURE!

Panel 7: IF SHE MOVES AWAY, YOU'LL NEVER SEE HER AGAIN.. YOU'VE GOT TO DO SOMETHING!

7-15

Panel 8: AAUGH!

I WAS HOPING FOR A MORE PRACTICAL RESPONSE

Panel 9: THAT LITTLE RED-HAIRED GIRL IS GOING TO MOVE AWAY!

7-16

Panel 10: I'VE NEVER EVEN TALKED TO HER! I THOUGHT I HAD PLENTY OF TIME... I THOUGHT I COULD WAIT UNTIL THE SIXTH-GRADE SWIM PARTY OR THE SEVENTH-GRADE CLASS PARTY...

Panel 11: OR I THOUGHT I COULD ASK HER TO THE SENIOR PROM OR LOTS OF OTHER THINGS WHEN WE GOT OLDER, BUT NOW SHE'S MOVING AWAY AND IT'S TOO LATE! IT'S TOO LATE!

Panel 12: YOU'VE GOT TO SAY GOODBY TO HER, CHARLIE BROWN!

I'VE NEVER EVEN SAID **HELLO** TO HER!!

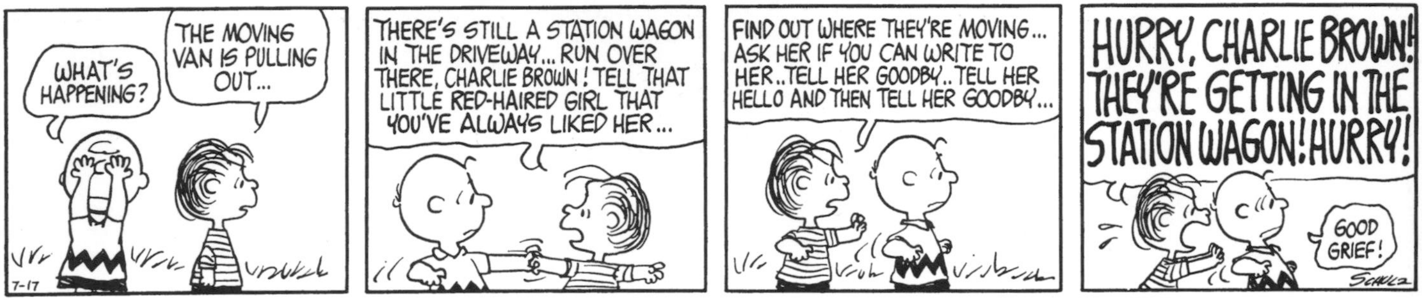
WHAT'S HAPPENING?
THE MOVING VAN IS PULLING OUT...
7-17
THERE'S STILL A STATION WAGON IN THE DRIVEWAY... RUN OVER THERE, CHARLIE BROWN! TELL THAT LITTLE RED-HAIRED GIRL THAT YOU'VE ALWAYS LIKED HER...
FIND OUT WHERE THEY'RE MOVING... ASK HER IF YOU CAN WRITE TO HER.. TELL HER GOODBY.. TELL HER HELLO AND THEN TELL HER GOODBY...
HURRY, CHARLIE BROWN! THEY'RE GETTING IN THE STATION WAGON! HURRY!
GOOD GRIEF!
SCHULZ

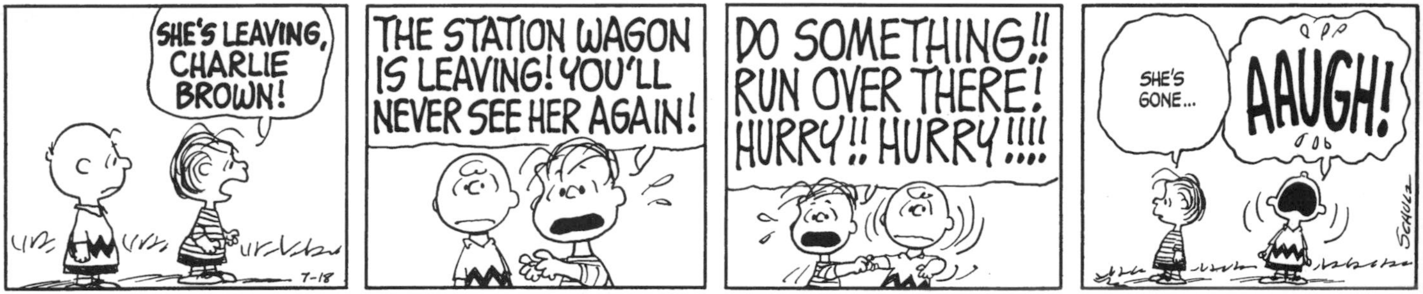
SHE'S LEAVING, CHARLIE BROWN!
7-18
THE STATION WAGON IS LEAVING! YOU'LL NEVER SEE HER AGAIN!
DO SOMETHING!! RUN OVER THERE! HURRY!! HURRY!!!!
SHE'S GONE...
AAUGH!
SCHULZ

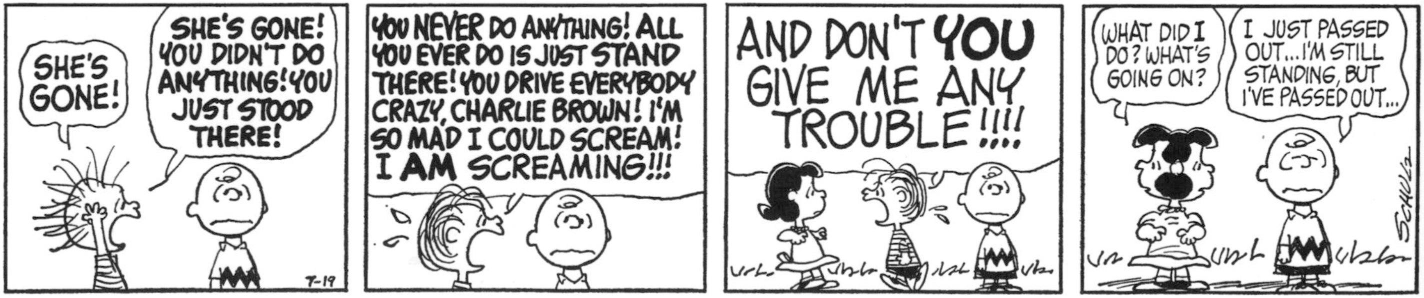
SHE'S GONE!
SHE'S GONE! YOU DIDN'T DO ANYTHING! YOU JUST STOOD THERE!
7-19
YOU NEVER DO ANYTHING! ALL YOU EVER DO IS JUST STAND THERE! YOU DRIVE EVERYBODY CRAZY, CHARLIE BROWN! I'M SO MAD I COULD SCREAM! I AM SCREAMING!!!
AND DON'T YOU GIVE ME ANY TROUBLE!!!!
WHAT DID I DO? WHAT'S GOING ON?
I JUST PASSED OUT... I'M STILL STANDING, BUT I'VE PASSED OUT...
SCHULZ

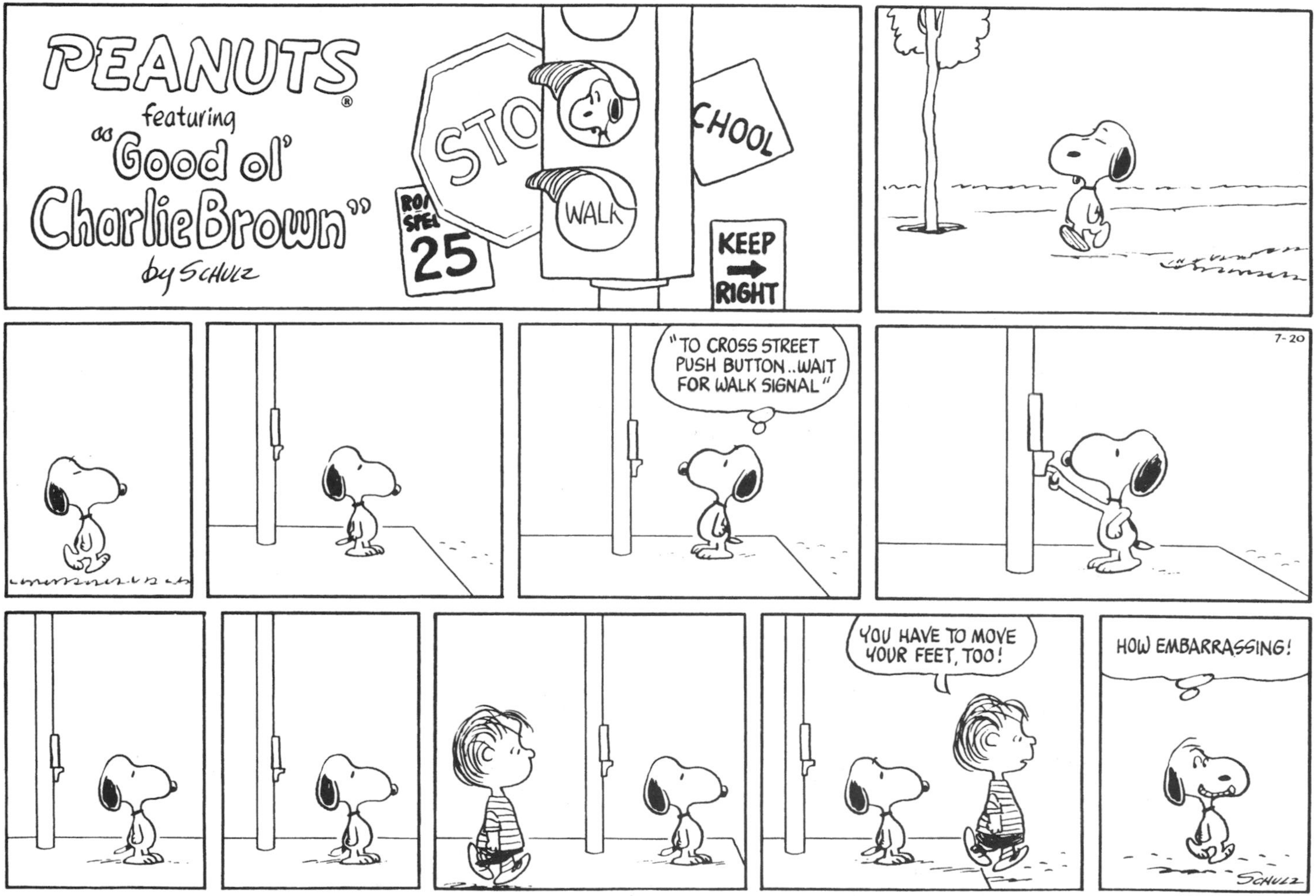
PEANUTS®
featuring
as "Good ol' Charlie Brown"
by SCHULZ
STO
WALK
CHOOL
25
KEEP
RIGHT
7-20
"TO CROSS STREET PUSH BUTTON..WAIT FOR WALK SIGNAL"
YOU HAVE TO MOVE YOUR FEET, TOO!
HOW EMBARRASSING!
SCHULZ

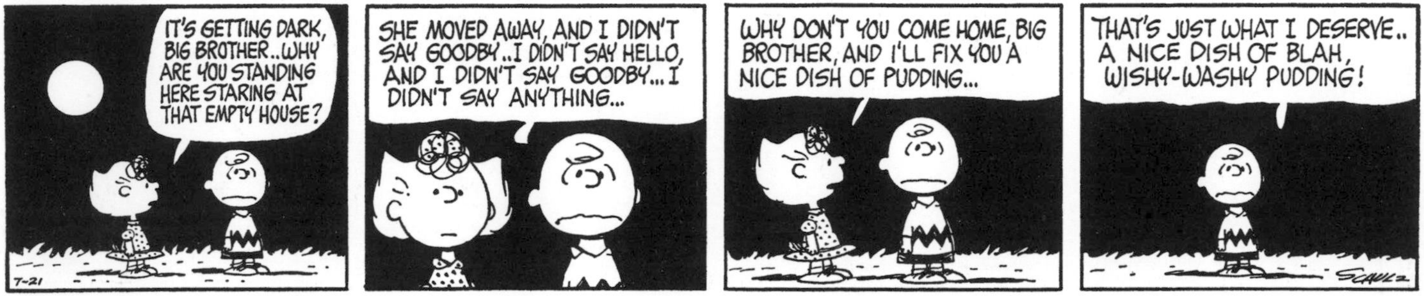
IT'S GETTING DARK, BIG BROTHER..WHY ARE YOU STANDING HERE STARING AT THAT EMPTY HOUSE?
7-21
SHE MOVED AWAY, AND I DIDN'T SAY GOODBY..I DIDN'T SAY HELLO, AND I DIDN'T SAY GOODBY...I DIDN'T SAY ANYTHING...
WHY DON'T YOU COME HOME, BIG BROTHER, AND I'LL FIX YOU A NICE DISH OF PUDDING...
THAT'S JUST WHAT I DESERVE.. A NICE DISH OF BLAH, WISHY-WASHY PUDDING!

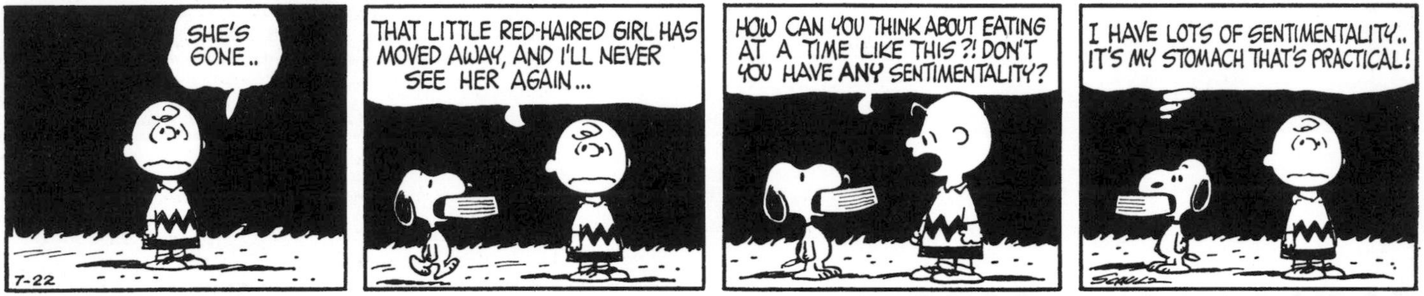
SHE'S GONE..
7-22
THAT LITTLE RED-HAIRED GIRL HAS MOVED AWAY, AND I'LL NEVER SEE HER AGAIN...
HOW CAN YOU THINK ABOUT EATING AT A TIME LIKE THIS?! DON'T YOU HAVE **ANY** SENTIMENTALITY?
I HAVE LOTS OF SENTIMENTALITY.. IT'S MY STOMACH THAT'S PRACTICAL!

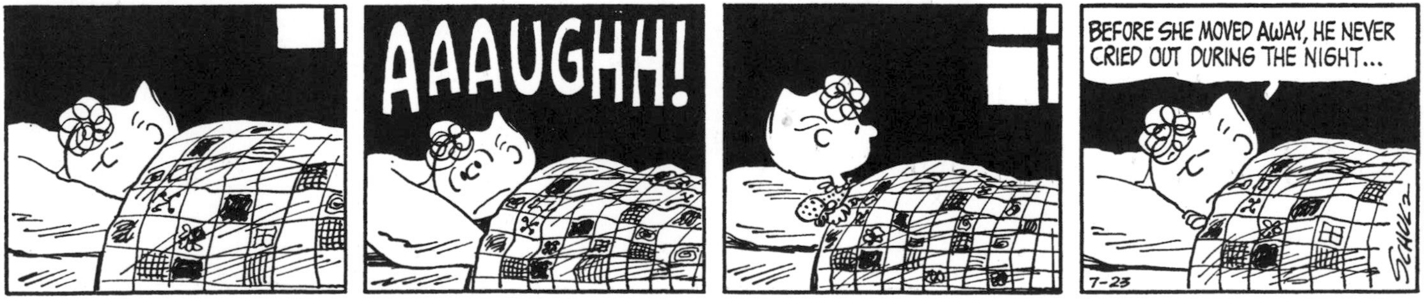
AAAUGHH!
BEFORE SHE MOVED AWAY, HE NEVER CRIED OUT DURING THE NIGHT...
7-23

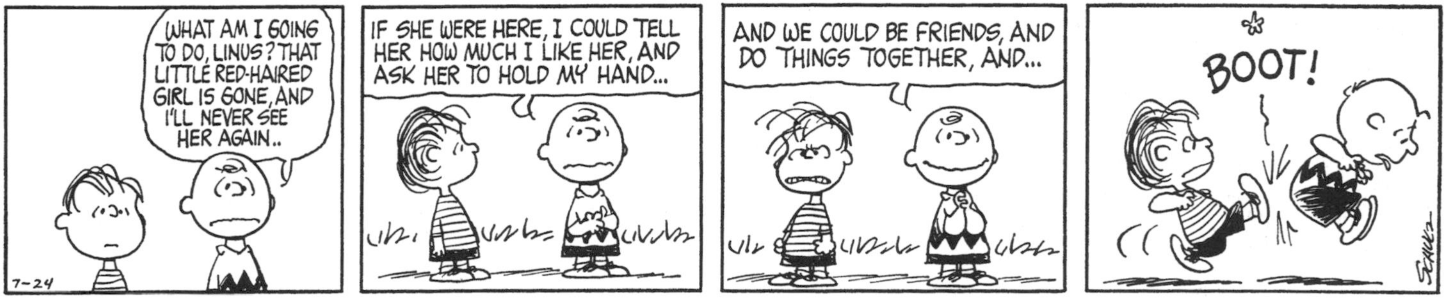
WHAT AM I GOING TO DO, LINUS? THAT LITTLE RED-HAIRED GIRL IS GONE, AND I'LL NEVER SEE HER AGAIN..
IF SHE WERE HERE, I COULD TELL HER HOW MUCH I LIKE HER, AND ASK HER TO HOLD MY HAND...
AND WE COULD BE FRIENDS, AND DO THINGS TOGETHER, AND...
BOOT!
7-24
SCHULZ

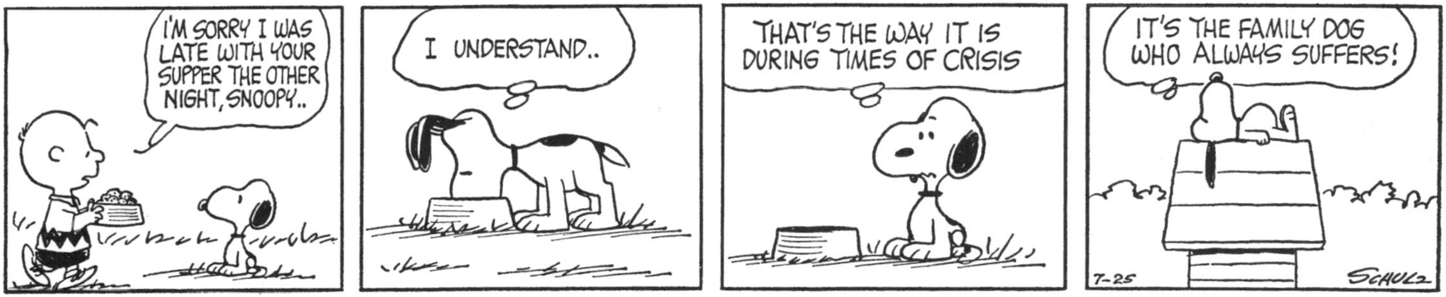
I'M SORRY I WAS LATE WITH YOUR SUPPER THE OTHER NIGHT, SNOOPY..
I UNDERSTAND..
THAT'S THE WAY IT IS DURING TIMES OF CRISIS
IT'S THE FAMILY DOG WHO ALWAYS SUFFERS!
7-25
SCHULZ

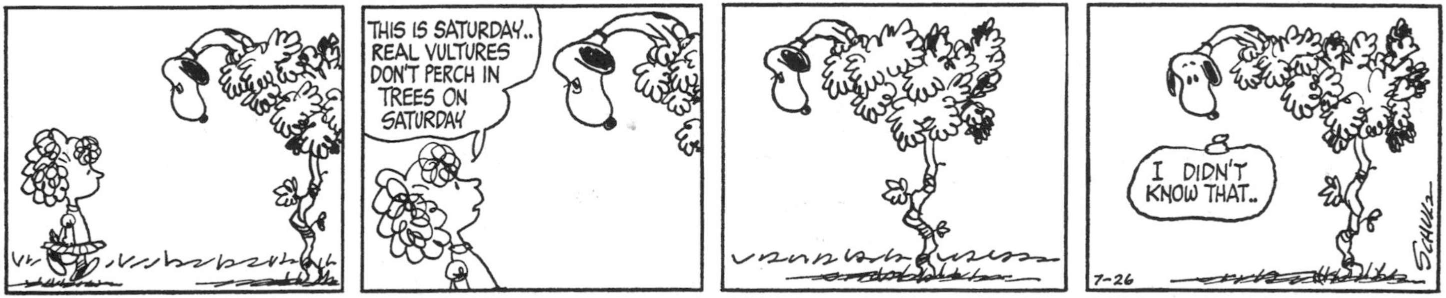
THIS IS SATURDAY.. REAL VULTURES DON'T PERCH IN TREES ON SATURDAY
I DIDN'T KNOW THAT..
7-26
SCHULZ

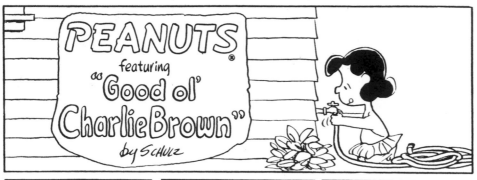

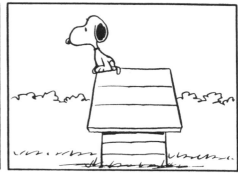

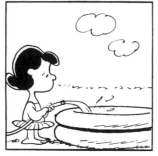

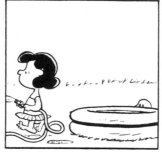

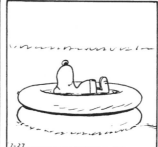

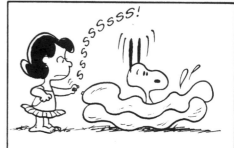

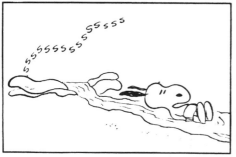

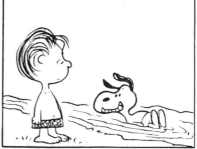

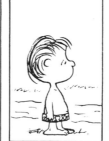

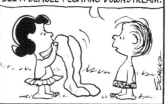

PEANUTS®
featuring
"Good ol' CharlieBrown"
by SCHULZ
SSSSSSSS!
SSSSSSSSSSSSSS
ON A WARM SUNNY DAY LIKE TODAY, IN A NEIGHBORHOOD SUCH AS OURS, IT IS NOT OFTEN THAT YOU'LL SEE A BEAGLE FLOATING DOWNSTREAM!
SCHULZ

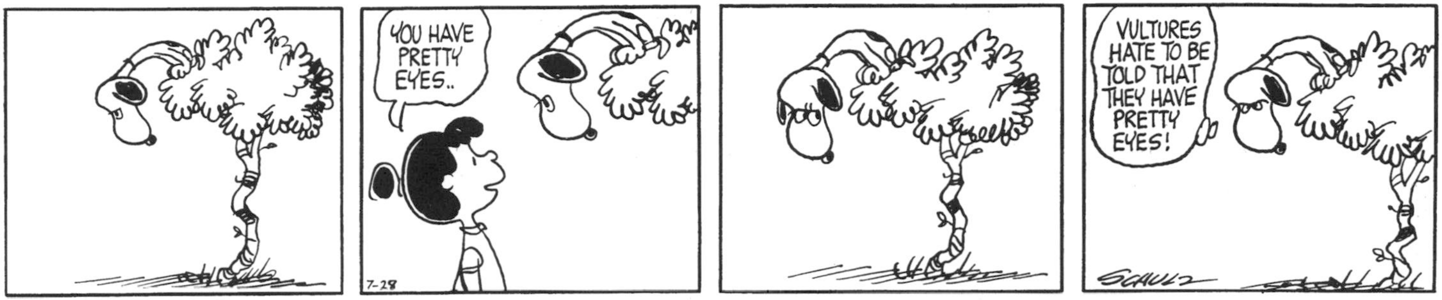
YOU HAVE PRETTY EYES..
VULTURES HATE TO BE TOLD THAT THEY HAVE PRETTY EYES!

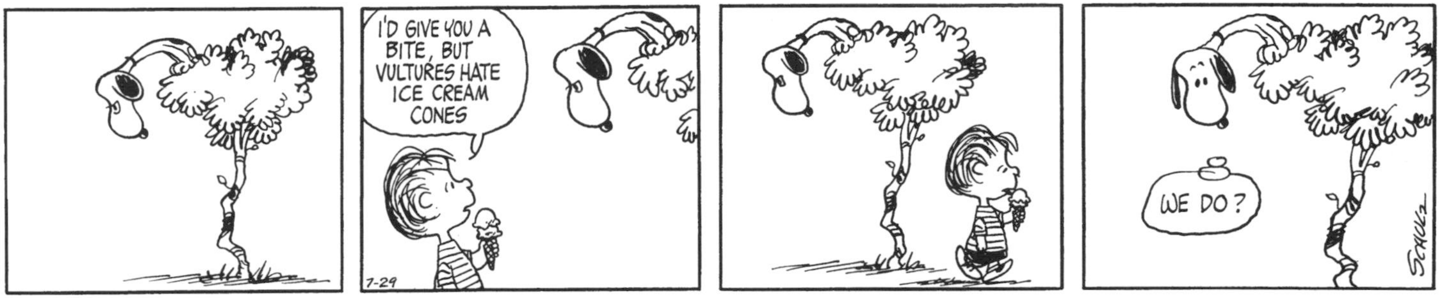
I'D GIVE YOU A BITE, BUT VULTURES HATE ICE CREAM CONES
WE DO?

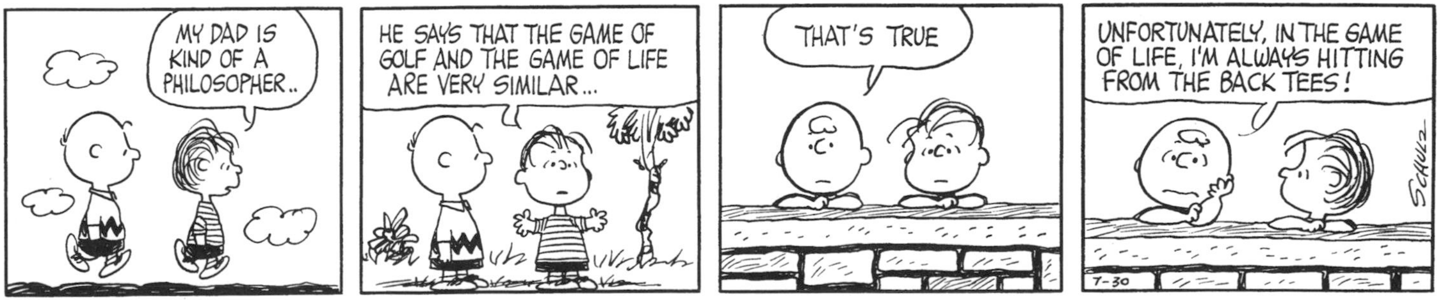
MY DAD IS KIND OF A PHILOSOPHER..
HE SAYS THAT THE GAME OF GOLF AND THE GAME OF LIFE ARE VERY SIMILAR...
THAT'S TRUE
UNFORTUNATELY, IN THE GAME OF LIFE, I'M ALWAYS HITTING FROM THE BACK TEES!

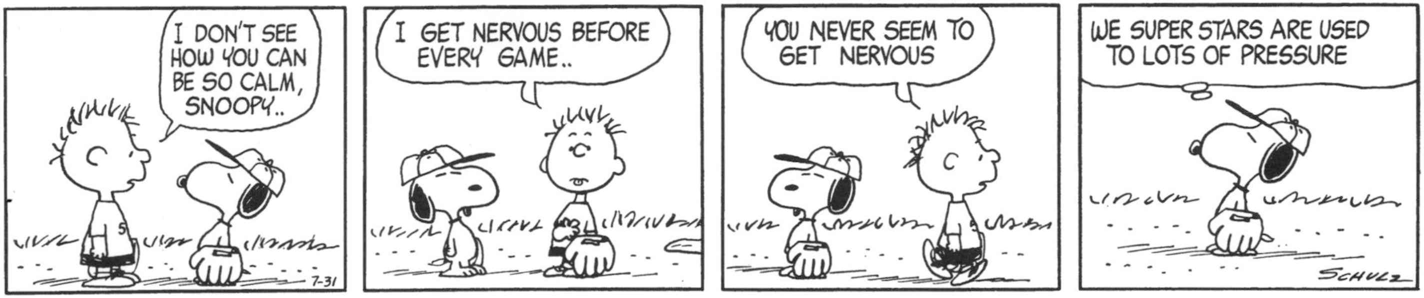
I DON'T SEE HOW YOU CAN BE SO CALM, SNOOPY..
I GET NERVOUS BEFORE EVERY GAME..
YOU NEVER SEEM TO GET NERVOUS
WE SUPER STARS ARE USED TO LOTS OF PRESSURE
7-31
SCHULZ

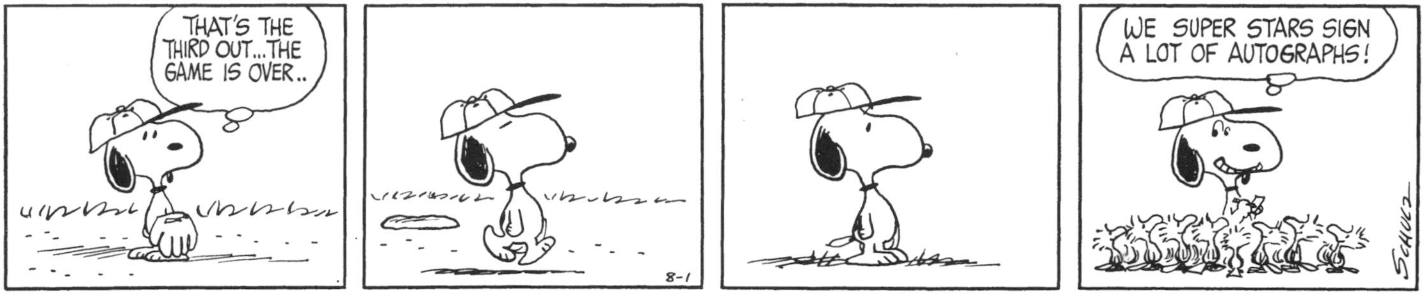
THAT'S THE THIRD OUT...THE GAME IS OVER..
8-1
WE SUPER STARS SIGN A LOT OF AUTOGRAPHS!
SCHULZ

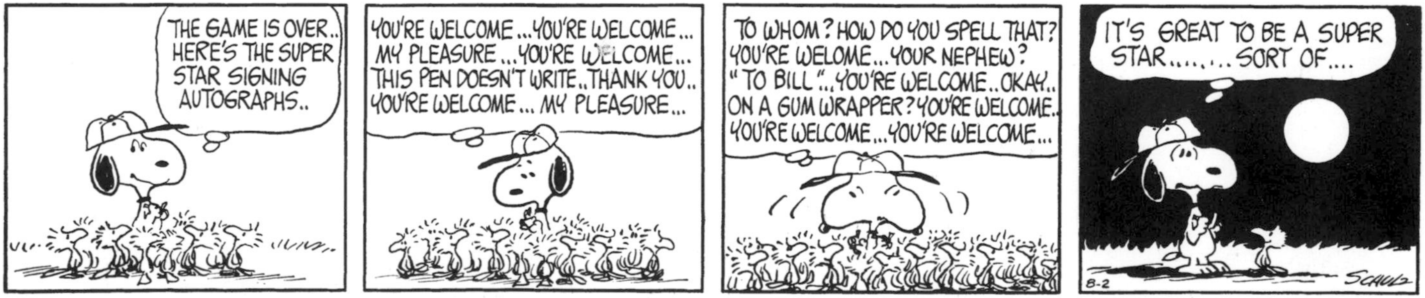
THE GAME IS OVER.. HERE'S THE SUPER STAR SIGNING AUTOGRAPHS..
YOU'RE WELCOME...YOU'RE WELCOME... MY PLEASURE...YOU'RE WELCOME... THIS PEN DOESN'T WRITE..THANK YOU.. YOU'RE WELCOME... MY PLEASURE...
TO WHOM? HOW DO YOU SPELL THAT? YOU'RE WELOME...YOUR NEPHEW? "TO BILL"..YOU'RE WELCOME..OKAY.. ON A GUM WRAPPER? YOU'RE WELCOME.. YOU'RE WELCOME...YOU'RE WELCOME...
IT'S GREAT TO BE A SUPER STAR........SORT OF....
8-2
SCHULZ

PEANUTS

featuring "Good ol' Charlie Brown"
by SCHULZ

Player's Model Trap Action

Lucille Van Pelt

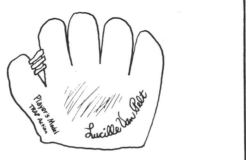

OKAY, LET'S SHOW A LITTLE LIFE OUT THERE!

?

HEY, MANAGER...SOME KID MUST HAVE LEFT HIS GLOVE HERE.. IT HAS HIS NAME ON IT..

SEE? RIGHT HERE... "WILLIE MAYS"....HE WROTE HIS NAME ON HIS GLOVE, SEE?

POOR KID..HE'S PROBABLY BEEN LOOKING ALL OVER FOR IT..WE SHOULD HAVE A "LOST AND FOUND"

8-3

I DON'T KNOW ANY KID AROUND HERE NAMED "WILLIE MAYS," DO YOU? HOW ARE WE GONNA GET IT BACK TO HIM? HE WAS PRETTY SMART PUTTING HIS NAME ON HIS GLOVE THIS WAY, THOUGH...IT'S FUNNY, I JUST DON'T REMEMBER ANY KID BY THAT NAME...

LOOK AT THE NAME ON YOUR GLOVE

WHAT?

LOOK AT YOUR OWN GLOVE... THERE'S A NAME ON IT..

"BABE RUTH"...WELL, I'LL BE! HOW IN THE WORLD DO YOU SUPPOSE I GOT HER GLOVE?!

SCHULZ

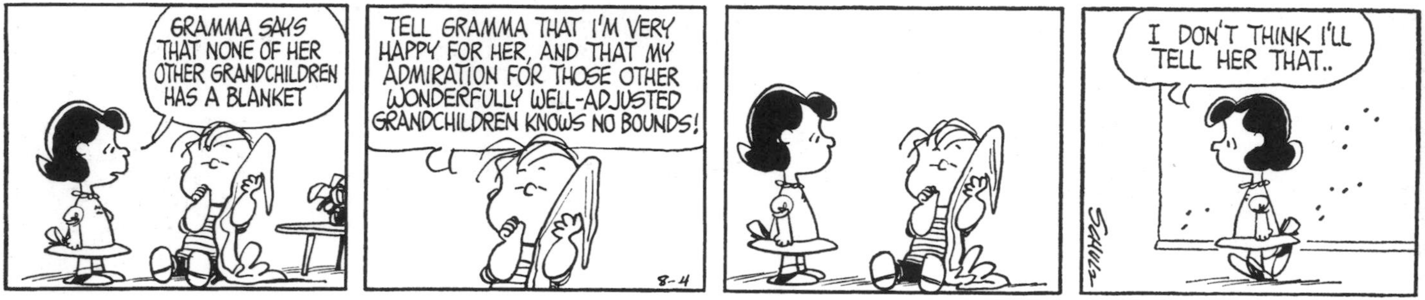
GRAMMA SAYS THAT NONE OF HER OTHER GRANDCHILDREN HAS A BLANKET
TELL GRAMMA THAT I'M VERY HAPPY FOR HER, AND THAT MY ADMIRATION FOR THOSE OTHER WONDERFULLY WELL-ADJUSTED GRANDCHILDREN KNOWS NO BOUNDS!
8-4
I DON'T THINK I'LL TELL HER THAT..
SCHULZ

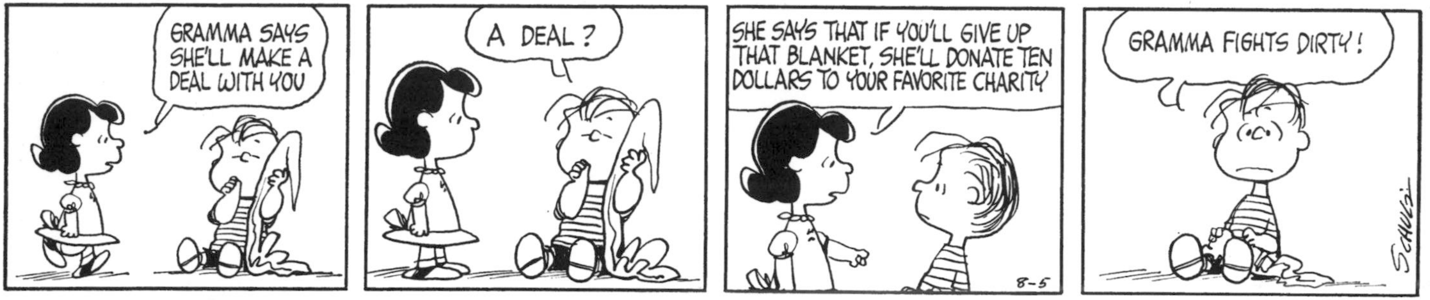
GRAMMA SAYS SHE'LL MAKE A DEAL WITH YOU
A DEAL ?
SHE SAYS THAT IF YOU'LL GIVE UP THAT BLANKET, SHE'LL DONATE TEN DOLLARS TO YOUR FAVORITE CHARITY
8-5
GRAMMA FIGHTS DIRTY!
SCHULZ

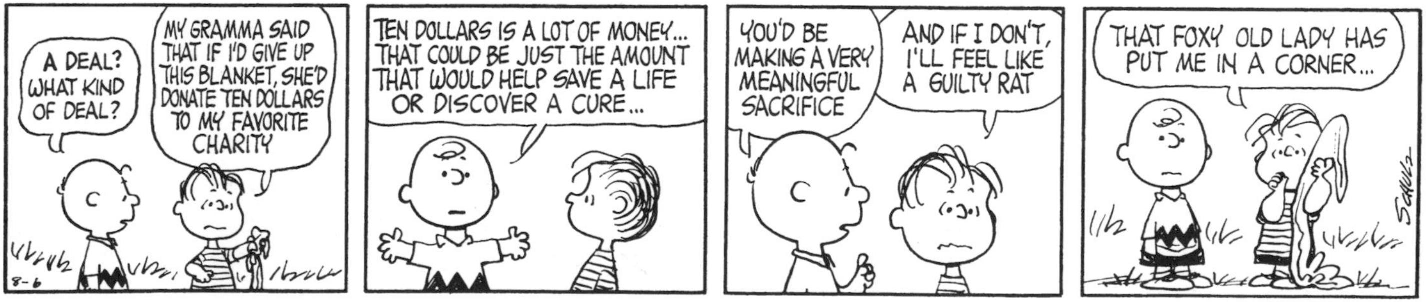
A DEAL? WHAT KIND OF DEAL?
MY GRAMMA SAID THAT IF I'D GIVE UP THIS BLANKET, SHE'D DONATE TEN DOLLARS TO MY FAVORITE CHARITY
8-6
TEN DOLLARS IS A LOT OF MONEY... THAT COULD BE JUST THE AMOUNT THAT WOULD HELP SAVE A LIFE OR DISCOVER A CURE...
YOU'D BE MAKING A VERY MEANINGFUL SACRIFICE
AND IF I DON'T, I'LL FEEL LIKE A GUILTY RAT
THAT FOXY OLD LADY HAS PUT ME IN A CORNER...
SCHULZ

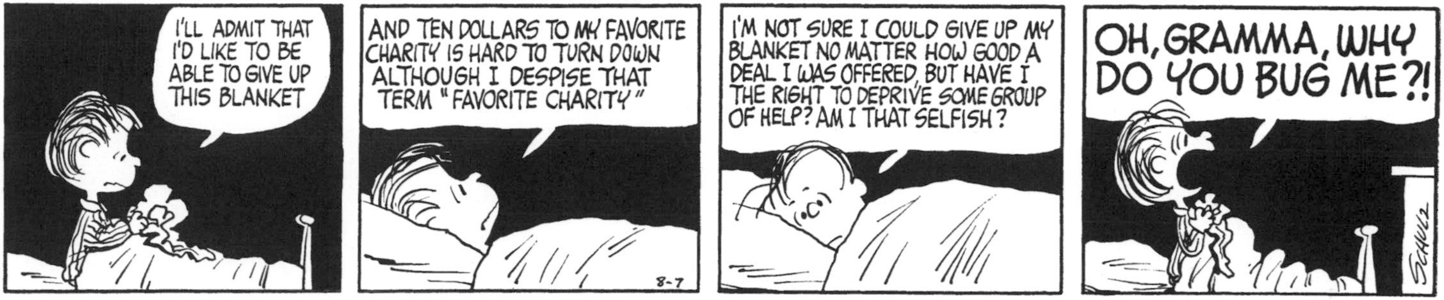
I'LL ADMIT THAT I'D LIKE TO BE ABLE TO GIVE UP THIS BLANKET
AND TEN DOLLARS TO MY FAVORITE CHARITY IS HARD TO TURN DOWN ALTHOUGH I DESPISE THAT TERM "FAVORITE CHARITY"
8-7
I'M NOT SURE I COULD GIVE UP MY BLANKET NO MATTER HOW GOOD A DEAL I WAS OFFERED, BUT HAVE I THE RIGHT TO DEPRIVE SOME GROUP OF HELP? AM I THAT SELFISH?
OH, GRAMMA, WHY DO YOU BUG ME?!
SCHULZ

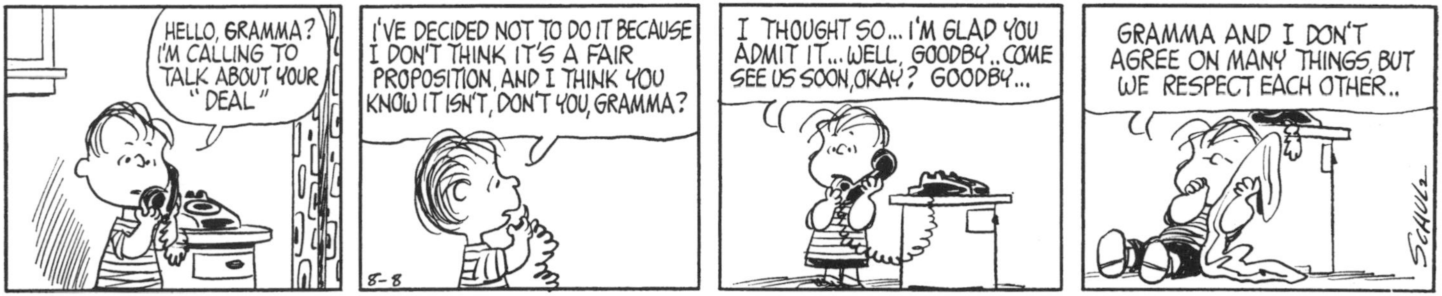
HELLO, GRAMMA? I'M CALLING TO TALK ABOUT YOUR "DEAL"
I'VE DECIDED NOT TO DO IT BECAUSE I DON'T THINK IT'S A FAIR PROPOSITION, AND I THINK YOU KNOW IT ISN'T, DON'T YOU, GRAMMA?
8-8
I THOUGHT SO... I'M GLAD YOU ADMIT IT... WELL, GOODBY.. COME SEE US SOON, OKAY? GOODBY...
GRAMMA AND I DON'T AGREE ON MANY THINGS, BUT WE RESPECT EACH OTHER..
SCHULZ

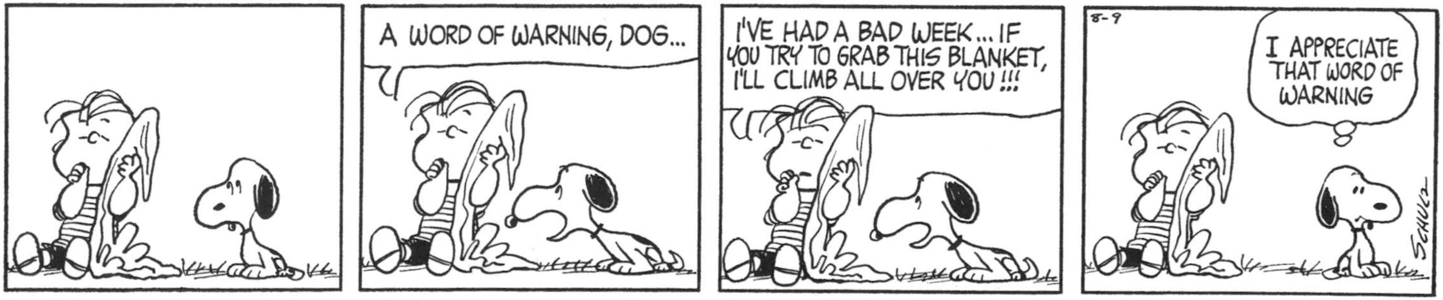
A WORD OF WARNING, DOG...
I'VE HAD A BAD WEEK... IF YOU TRY TO GRAB THIS BLANKET, I'LL CLIMB ALL OVER YOU!!!
8-9
I APPRECIATE THAT WORD OF WARNING
SCHULZ

PEANUTS
featuring
"Good ol' Charlie Brown"
by SCHULZ

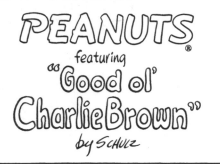

WHAT'S THIS?

"PROPOSED NEW DOG-FEEDING SCHEDULE"

"PRE-BREAKFAST SNACK..BREAKFAST..MORNING COFFEE BREAK..PRE-NOON SNACK..LUNCH..EARLY AFTERNOON SNACK..AFTERNOON TEA..PRE-DINNER SNACK..DINNER..TV SNACK..BEDTIME SNACK.. AND FINALLY, A SMALL MIDNIGHT SNACK"

HMM...WELL, I'LL TELL YOU WHAT WE'LL DO... WE'LL COMPROMISE...

YOU'LL EAT ONE MEAL A DAY LIKE EVERY OTHER DOG!!!!

I HATE THOSE COMPROMISES!

8-10   SCHULZ

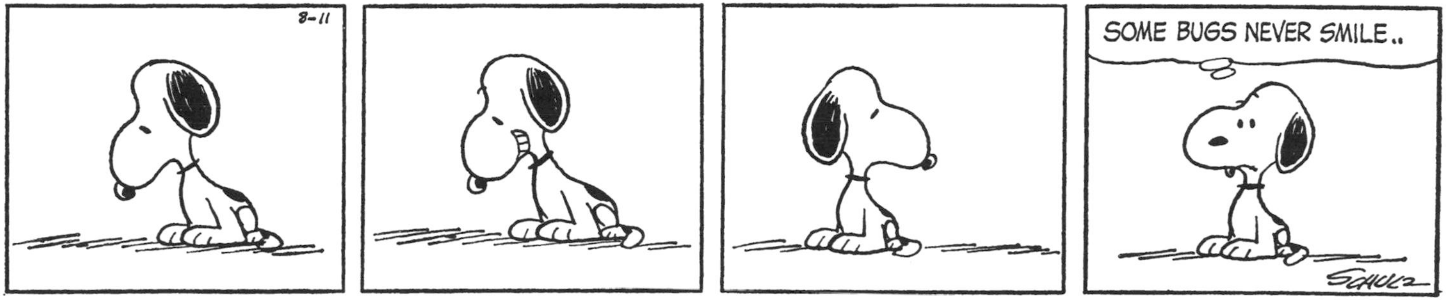
SOME BUGS NEVER SMILE..

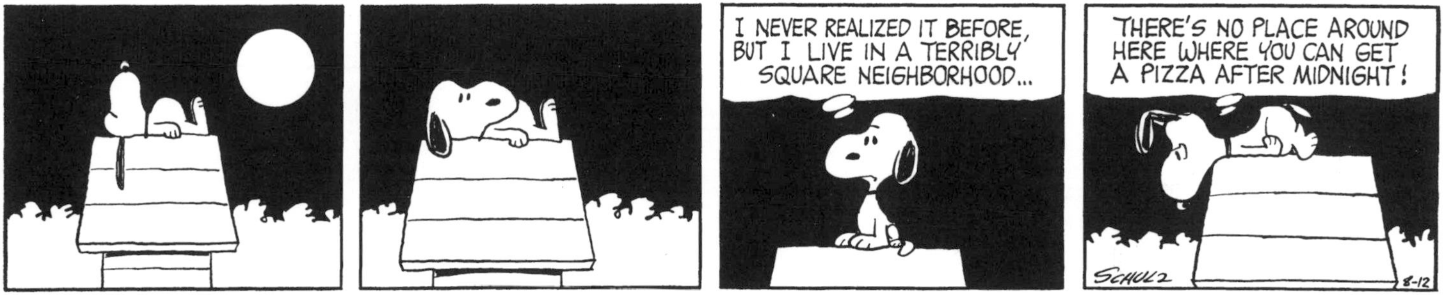
I NEVER REALIZED IT BEFORE, BUT I LIVE IN A TERRIBLY SQUARE NEIGHBORHOOD...
THERE'S NO PLACE AROUND HERE WHERE YOU CAN GET A PIZZA AFTER MIDNIGHT!

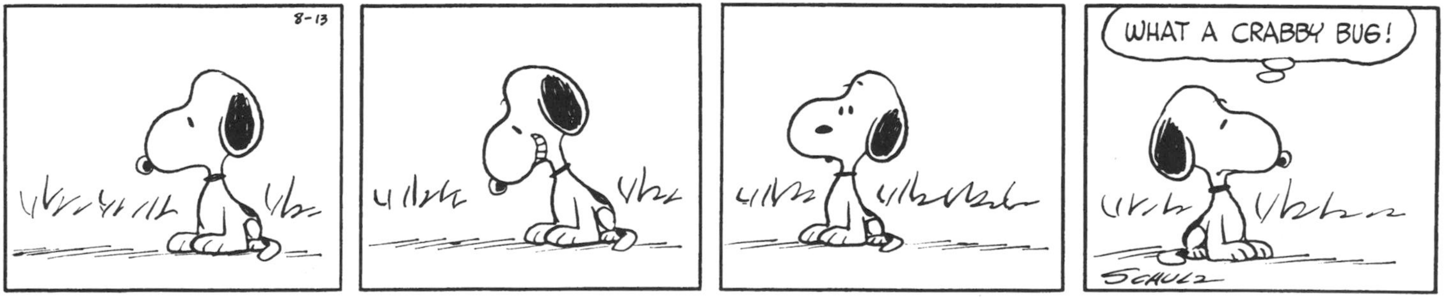
WHAT A CRABBY BUG!

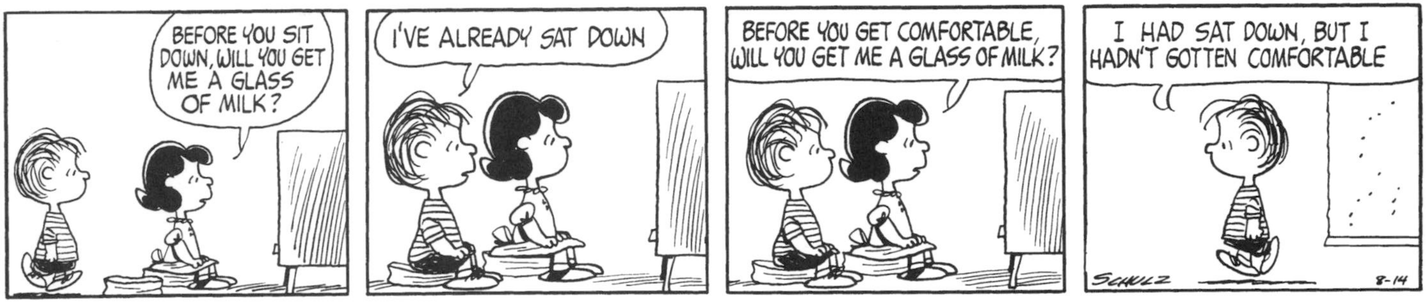
BEFORE YOU SIT DOWN, WILL YOU GET ME A GLASS OF MILK?
I'VE ALREADY SAT DOWN
BEFORE YOU GET COMFORTABLE, WILL YOU GET ME A GLASS OF MILK?
I HAD SAT DOWN, BUT I HADN'T GOTTEN COMFORTABLE
SCHULZ
8-14

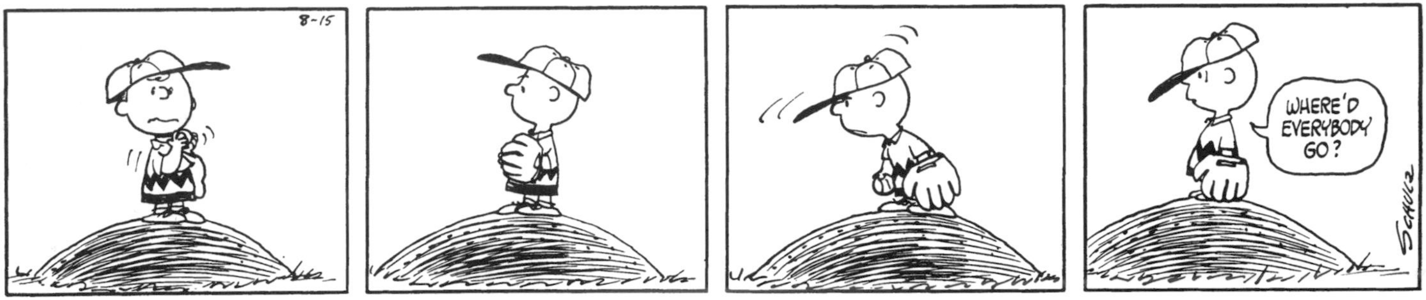
8-15
WHERE'D EVERYBODY GO?
SCHULZ

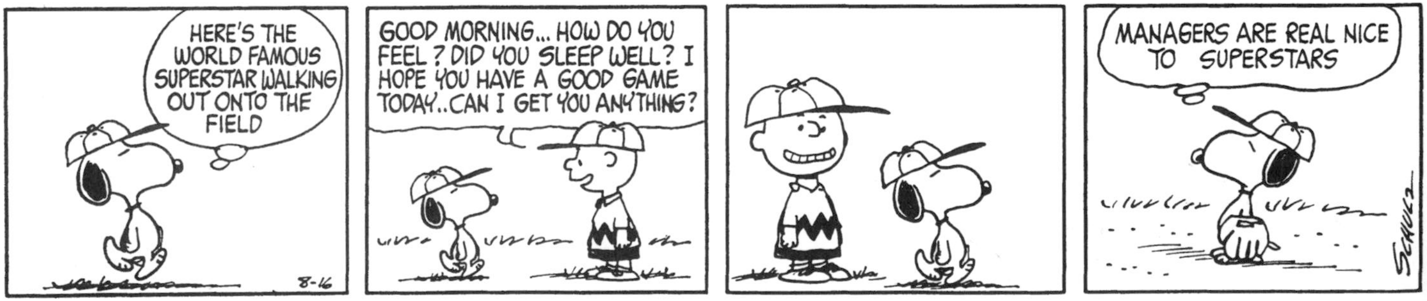
HERE'S THE WORLD FAMOUS SUPERSTAR WALKING OUT ONTO THE FIELD
8-16
GOOD MORNING... HOW DO YOU FEEL? DID YOU SLEEP WELL? I HOPE YOU HAVE A GOOD GAME TODAY..CAN I GET YOU ANYTHING?
MANAGERS ARE REAL NICE TO SUPERSTARS
SCHULZ

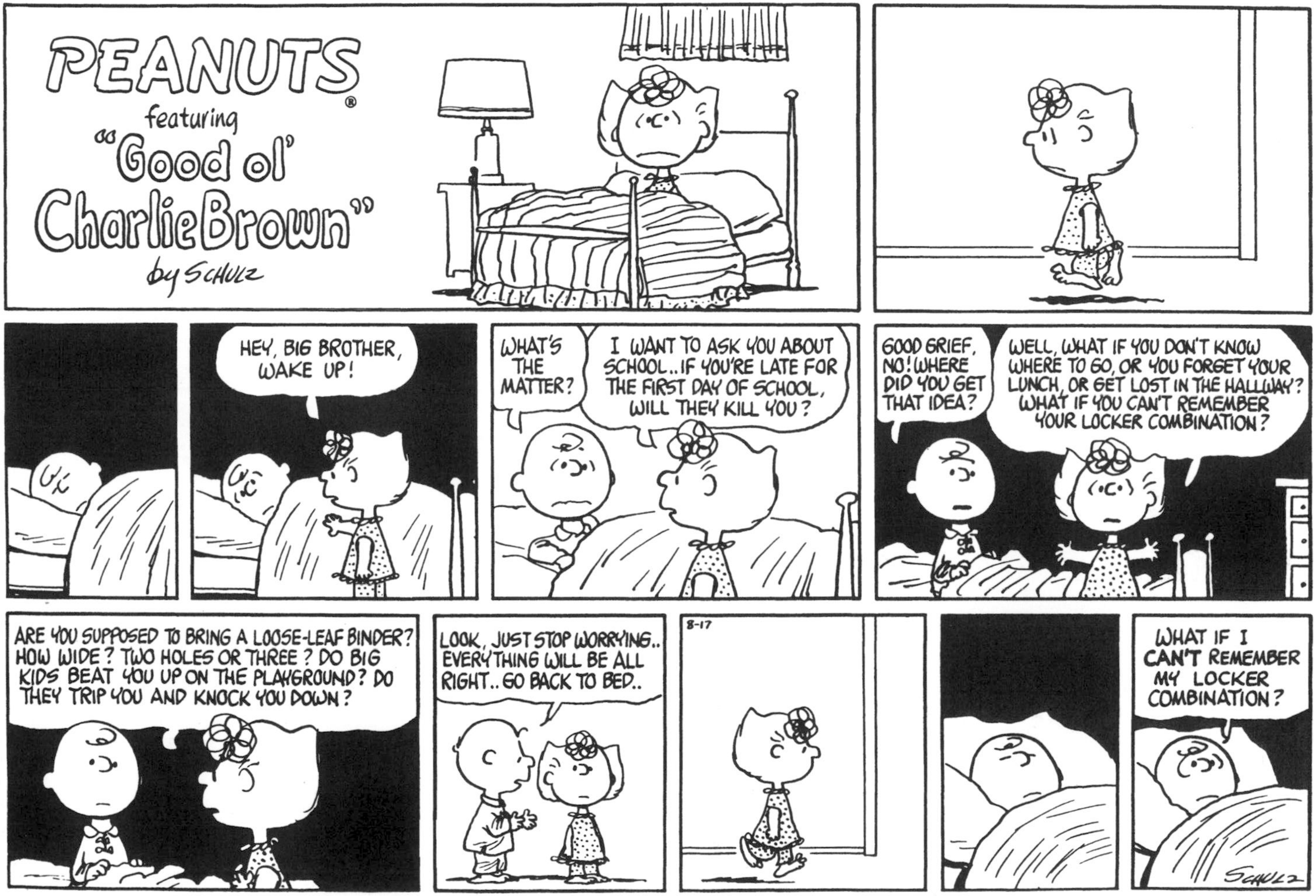
PEANUTS®
featuring
"Good ol' Charlie Brown"
by SCHULZ
HEY, BIG BROTHER, WAKE UP!
WHAT'S THE MATTER?
I WANT TO ASK YOU ABOUT SCHOOL.. IF YOU'RE LATE FOR THE FIRST DAY OF SCHOOL, WILL THEY KILL YOU?
GOOD GRIEF, NO! WHERE DID YOU GET THAT IDEA?
WELL, WHAT IF YOU DON'T KNOW WHERE TO GO, OR YOU FORGET YOUR LUNCH, OR GET LOST IN THE HALLWAY? WHAT IF YOU CAN'T REMEMBER YOUR LOCKER COMBINATION?
ARE YOU SUPPOSED TO BRING A LOOSE-LEAF BINDER? HOW WIDE? TWO HOLES OR THREE? DO BIG KIDS BEAT YOU UP ON THE PLAYGROUND? DO THEY TRIP YOU AND KNOCK YOU DOWN?
LOOK, JUST STOP WORRYING.. EVERYTHING WILL BE ALL RIGHT.. GO BACK TO BED..
8-17
WHAT IF I **CAN'T** REMEMBER MY LOCKER COMBINATION?
SCHULZ

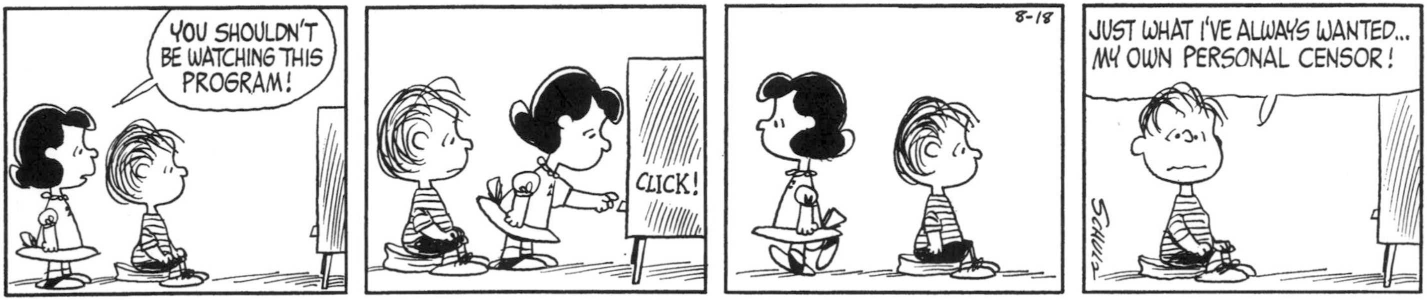
YOU SHOULDN'T BE WATCHING THIS PROGRAM!
CLICK!
8-18
JUST WHAT I'VE ALWAYS WANTED... MY OWN PERSONAL CENSOR!
SCHULZ

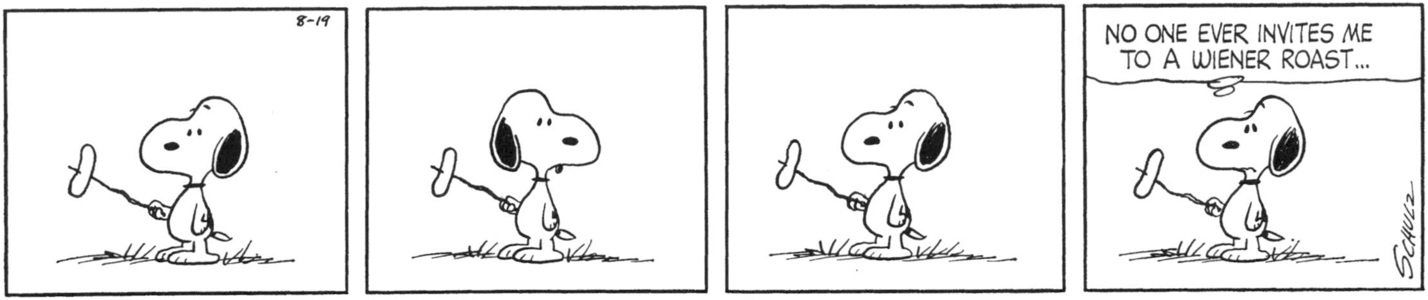
8-19
NO ONE EVER INVITES ME TO A WIENER ROAST...
SCHULZ

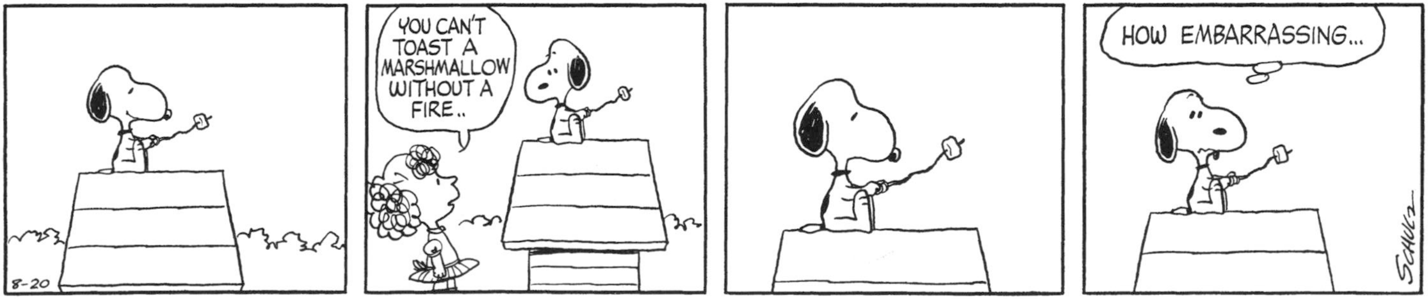
8-20
YOU CAN'T TOAST A MARSHMALLOW WITHOUT A FIRE..
HOW EMBARRASSING...
SCHULZ

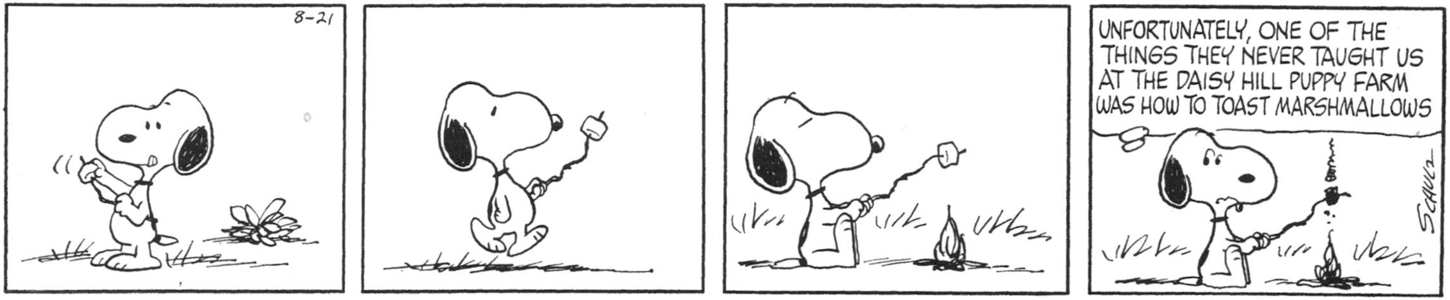
8-21
UNFORTUNATELY, ONE OF THE THINGS THEY NEVER TAUGHT US AT THE DAISY HILL PUPPY FARM WAS HOW TO TOAST MARSHMALLOWS

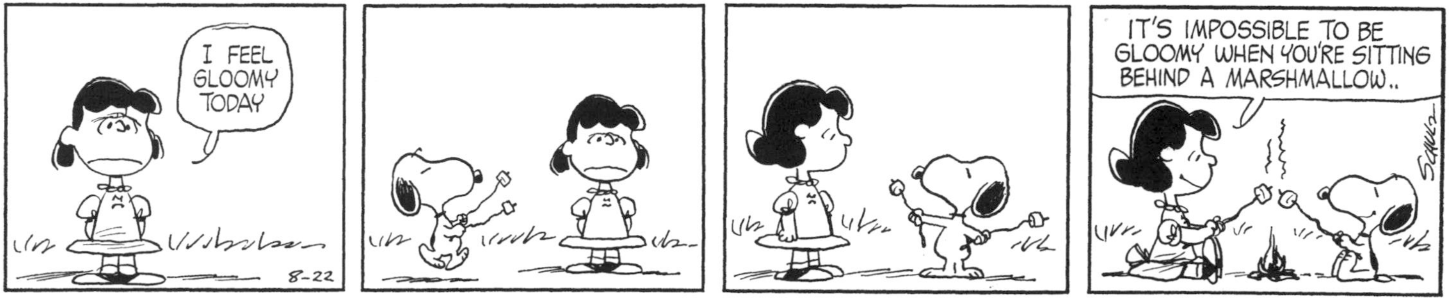
I FEEL GLOOMY TODAY
8-22
IT'S IMPOSSIBLE TO BE GLOOMY WHEN YOU'RE SITTING BEHIND A MARSHMALLOW..

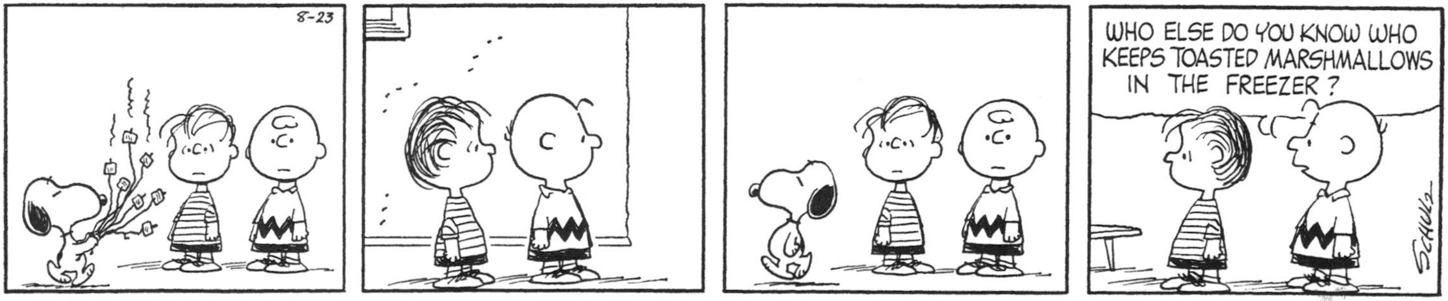
8-23
WHO ELSE DO YOU KNOW WHO KEEPS TOASTED MARSHMALLOWS IN THE FREEZER ?

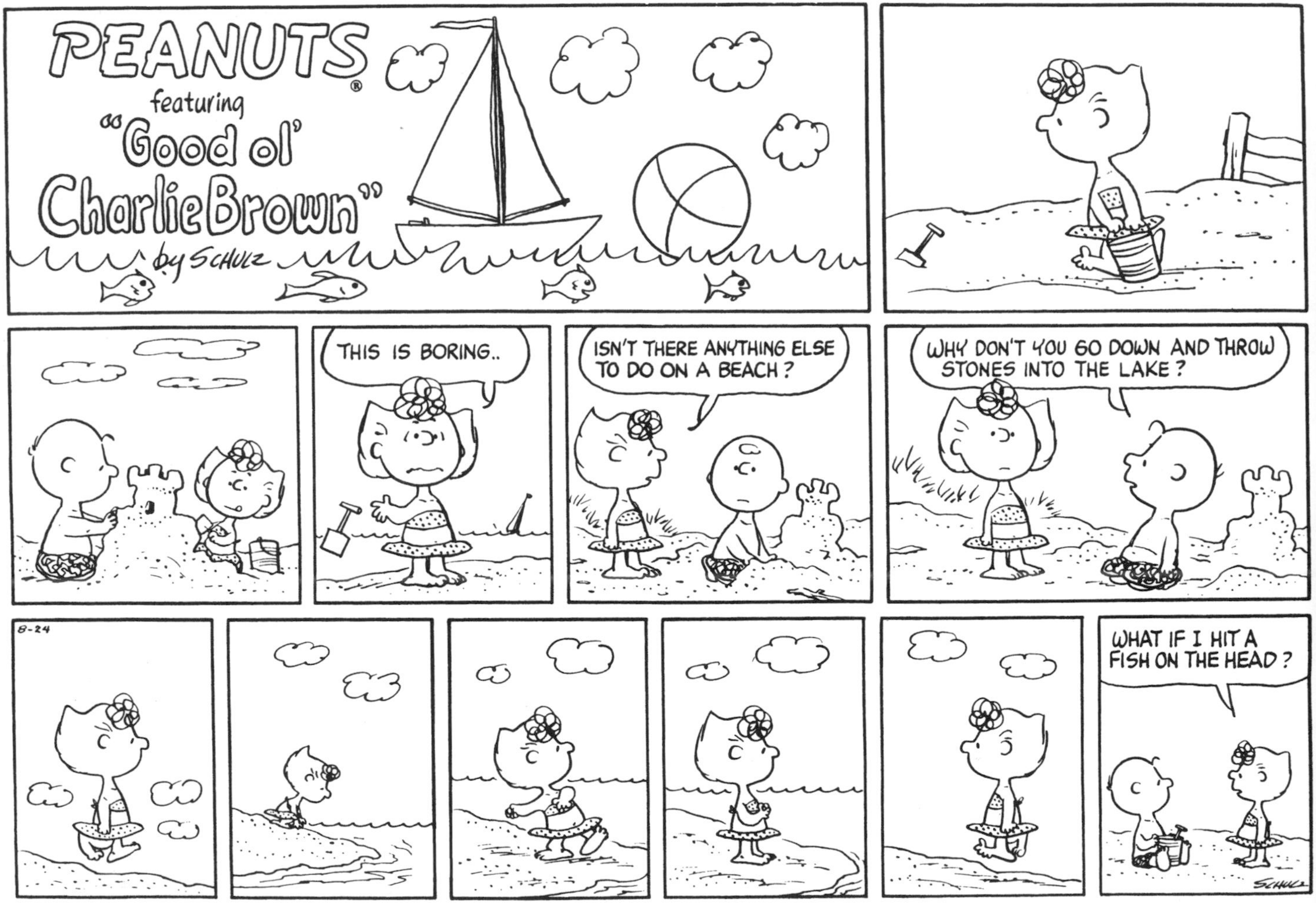
PEANUTS®
featuring "Good ol' Charlie Brown"
by SCHULZ
THIS IS BORING..
ISN'T THERE ANYTHING ELSE TO DO ON A BEACH?
WHY DON'T YOU GO DOWN AND THROW STONES INTO THE LAKE?
8-24
WHAT IF I HIT A FISH ON THE HEAD?
SCHULZ

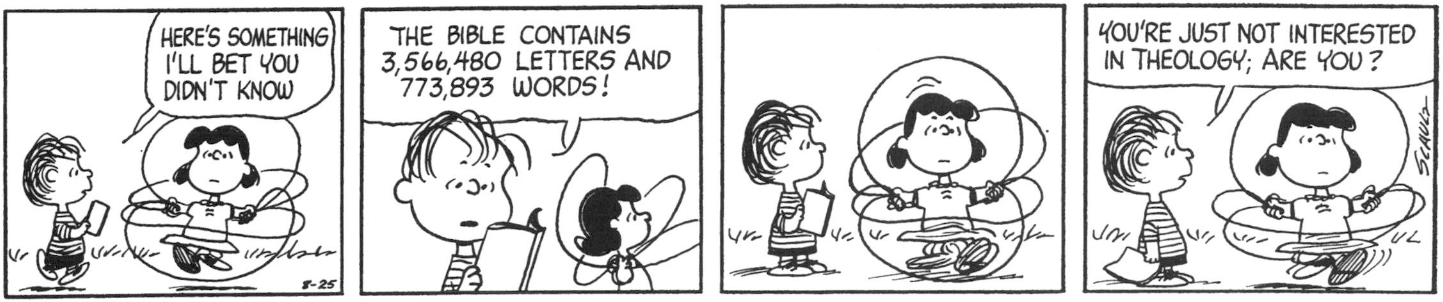
HERE'S SOMETHING I'LL BET YOU DIDN'T KNOW
THE BIBLE CONTAINS 3,566,480 LETTERS AND 773,893 WORDS!
YOU'RE JUST NOT INTERESTED IN THEOLOGY; ARE YOU?

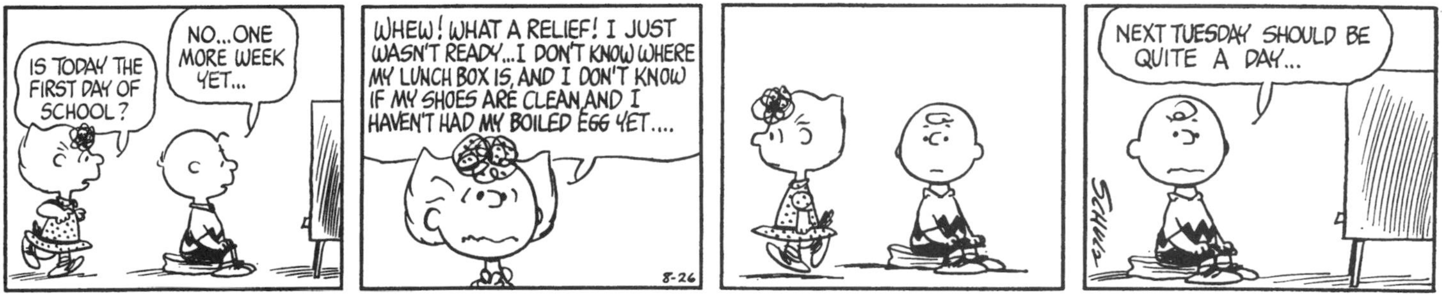
IS TODAY THE FIRST DAY OF SCHOOL?
NO...ONE MORE WEEK YET...
WHEW! WHAT A RELIEF! I JUST WASN'T READY...I DON'T KNOW WHERE MY LUNCH BOX IS, AND I DON'T KNOW IF MY SHOES ARE CLEAN AND I HAVEN'T HAD MY BOILED EGG YET....
NEXT TUESDAY SHOULD BE QUITE A DAY...

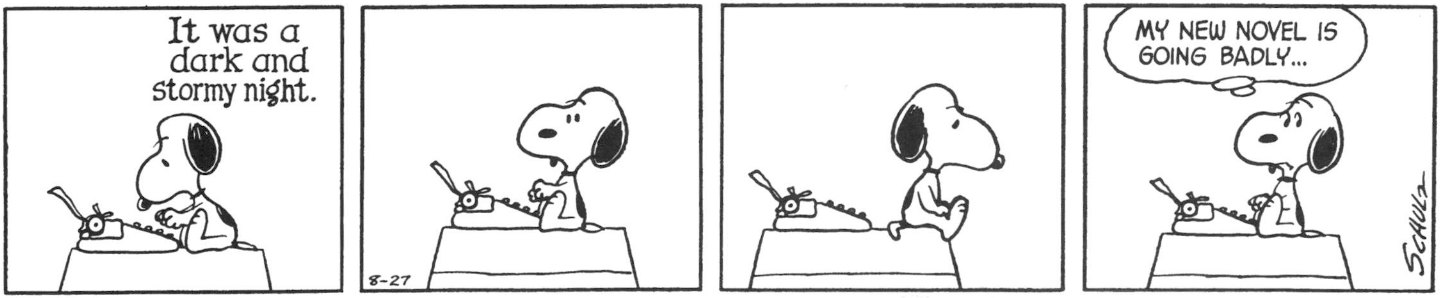
It was a dark and stormy night.
MY NEW NOVEL IS GOING BADLY...

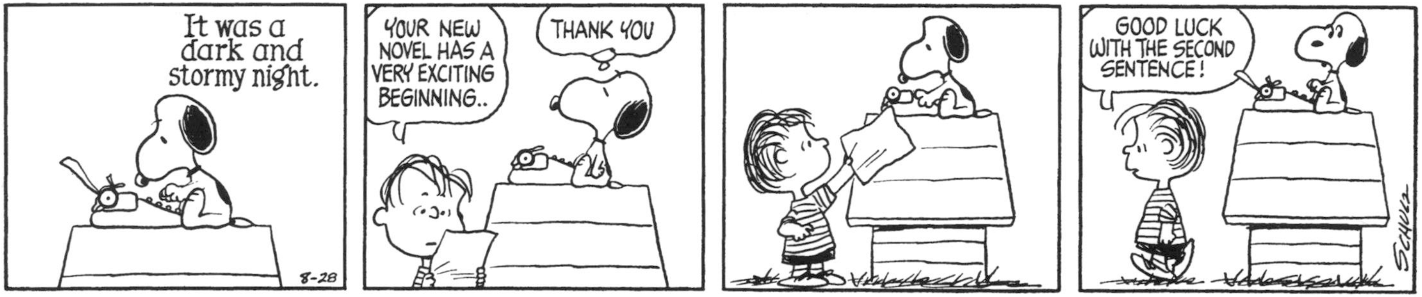
It was a dark and stormy night.
8-28
YOUR NEW NOVEL HAS A VERY EXCITING BEGINNING..
THANK YOU
GOOD LUCK WITH THE SECOND SENTENCE!
SCHULZ

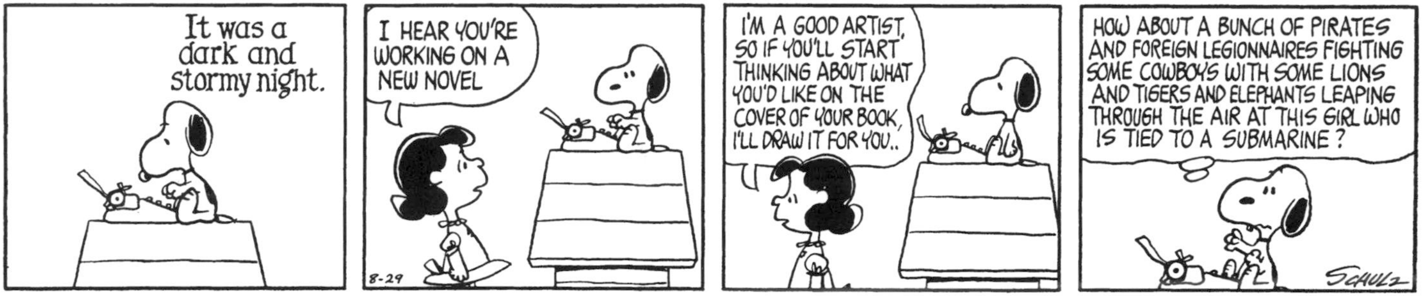
It was a dark and stormy night.
I HEAR YOU'RE WORKING ON A NEW NOVEL
8-29
I'M A GOOD ARTIST, SO IF YOU'LL START THINKING ABOUT WHAT YOU'D LIKE ON THE COVER OF YOUR BOOK, I'LL DRAW IT FOR YOU..
HOW ABOUT A BUNCH OF PIRATES AND FOREIGN LEGIONNAIRES FIGHTING SOME COWBOYS WITH SOME LIONS AND TIGERS AND ELEPHANTS LEAPING THROUGH THE AIR AT THIS GIRL WHO IS TIED TO A SUBMARINE?
SCHULZ

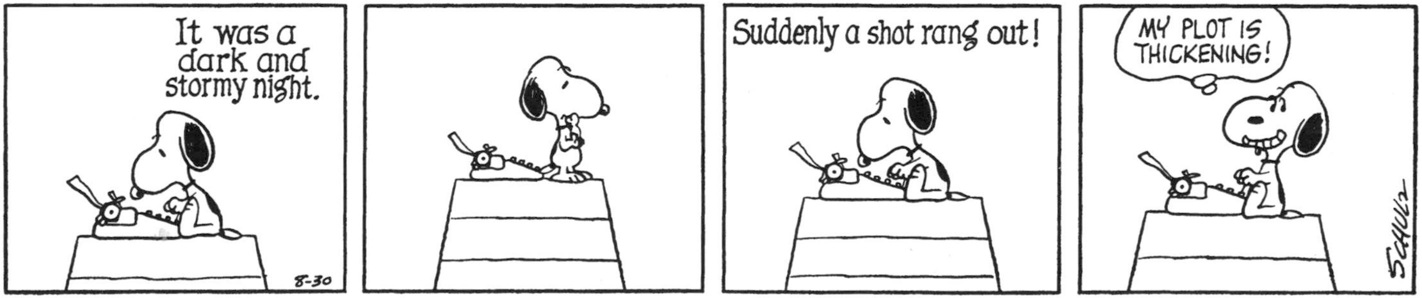
It was a dark and stormy night.
8-30
Suddenly a shot rang out!
MY PLOT IS THICKENING!
SCHULZ

PEANUTS

featuring

"Good ol' CharlieBrown"

by SCHULZ

CHARLIE
BROWN

SNOOPY

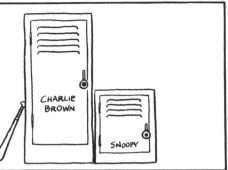

GOOD GRIEF, IT'S ALMOST NOON!

WE HAVE TO SUIT-UP FOR THE BALL GAME, SNOOPY..

HERE'S YOUR CAP...IS MINE ON RIGHT? I WANT IT STRAIGHT, BUT NOT TOO STRAIGHT...

YOURS SHOULD BE TURNED A LITTLE MORE TO THE LEFT..NOT TOO FAR BACK, EITHER, BUT NOT TOO FAR FORWARD...

WHAT DIFFERENCE DOES IT MAKE?

8-31

WHAT DIFFERENCE DOES IT MAKE? IT MAKES A LOT OF DIFFERENCE!

GIRLS JUST DON'T UNDERSTAND "SUITING-UP"!

SCHULZ

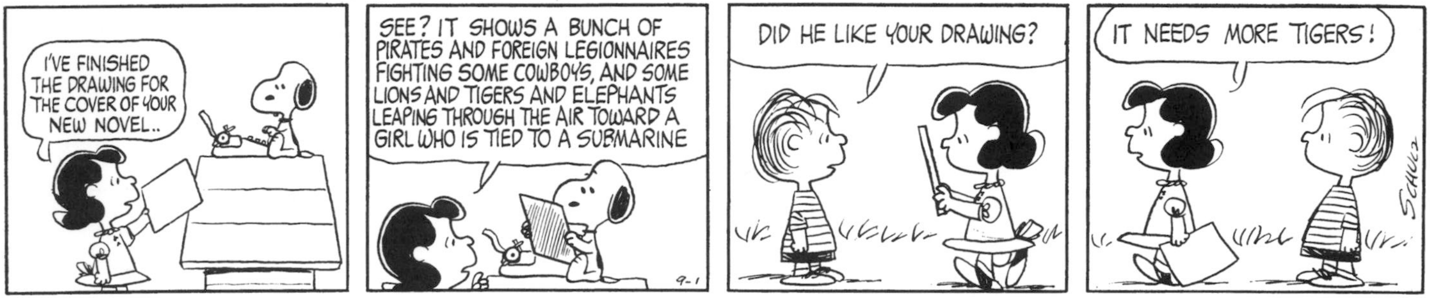
I'VE FINISHED THE DRAWING FOR THE COVER OF YOUR NEW NOVEL..
SEE? IT SHOWS A BUNCH OF PIRATES AND FOREIGN LEGIONNAIRES FIGHTING SOME COWBOYS, AND SOME LIONS AND TIGERS AND ELEPHANTS LEAPING THROUGH THE AIR TOWARD A GIRL WHO IS TIED TO A SUBMARINE
9-1
DID HE LIKE YOUR DRAWING?
IT NEEDS MORE TIGERS!
SCHULZ

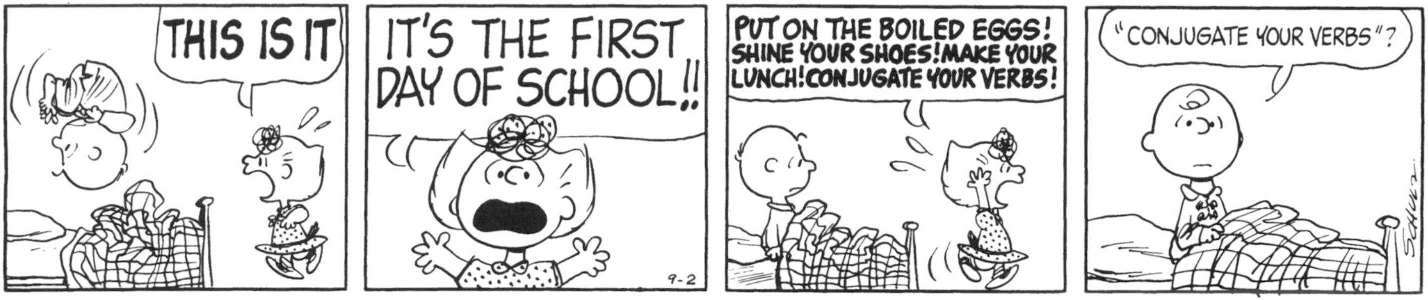
THIS IS IT
IT'S THE FIRST DAY OF SCHOOL!!
9-2
PUT ON THE BOILED EGGS! SHINE YOUR SHOES! MAKE YOUR LUNCH! CONJUGATE YOUR VERBS!
"CONJUGATE YOUR VERBS"?
SCHULZ

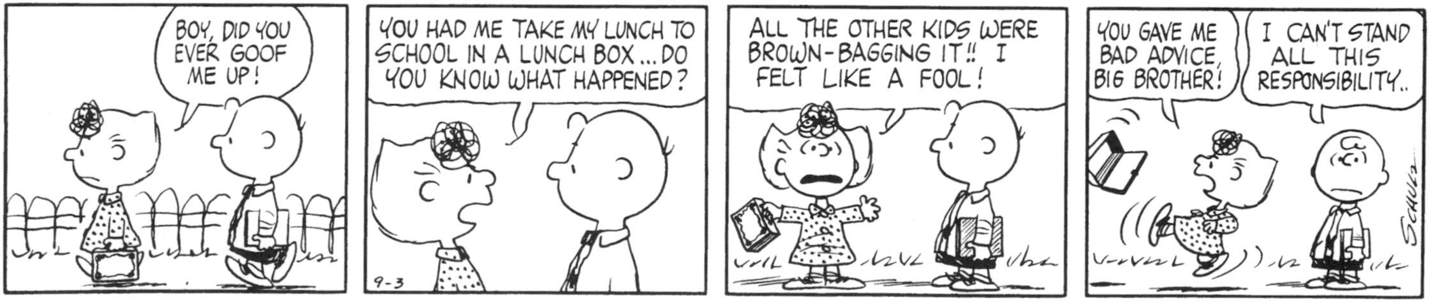
BOY, DID YOU EVER GOOF ME UP!
YOU HAD ME TAKE MY LUNCH TO SCHOOL IN A LUNCH BOX... DO YOU KNOW WHAT HAPPENED?
9-3
ALL THE OTHER KIDS WERE BROWN-BAGGING IT!! I FELT LIKE A FOOL!
YOU GAVE ME BAD ADVICE, BIG BROTHER!
I CAN'T STAND ALL THIS RESPONSIBILITY..
SCHULZ

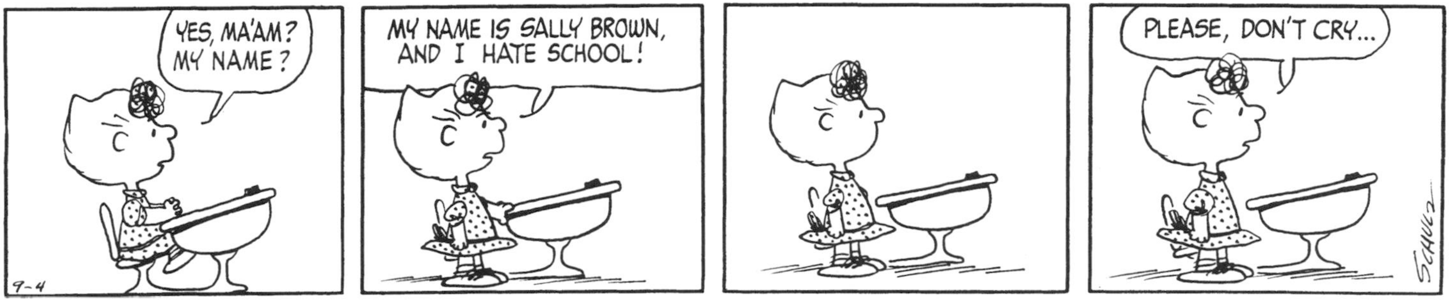
YES, MA'AM? MY NAME?
MY NAME IS SALLY BROWN, AND I HATE SCHOOL!
PLEASE, DON'T CRY...
9-4
SCHULZ

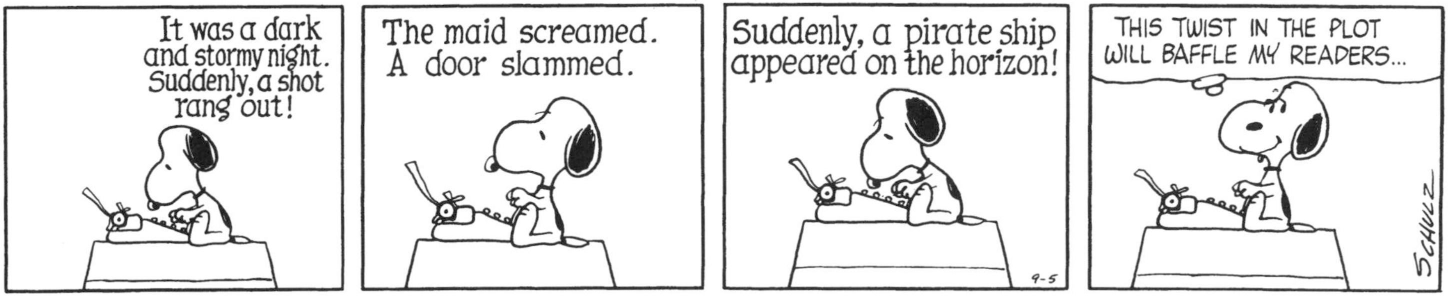
It was a dark and stormy night. Suddenly, a shot rang out!
The maid screamed. A door slammed.
Suddenly, a pirate ship appeared on the horizon!
THIS TWIST IN THE PLOT WILL BAFFLE MY READERS...
9-5
SCHULZ

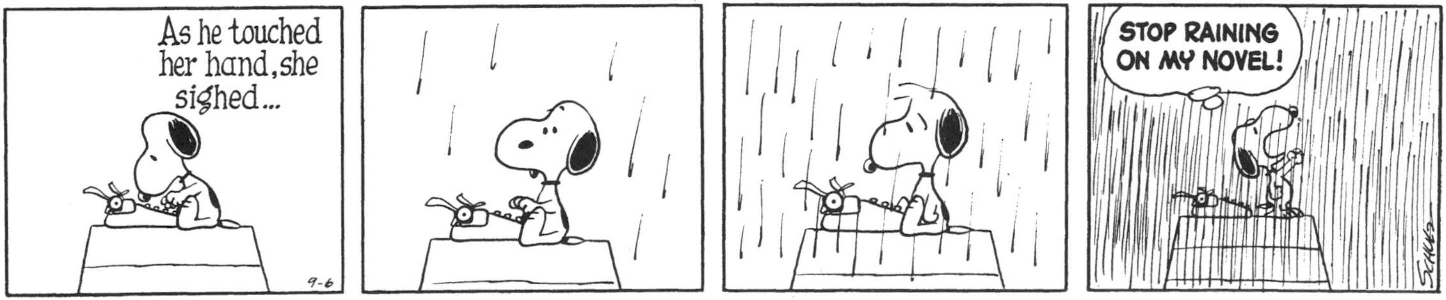
As he touched her hand, she sighed...
STOP RAINING ON MY NOVEL!
9-6
SCHULZ

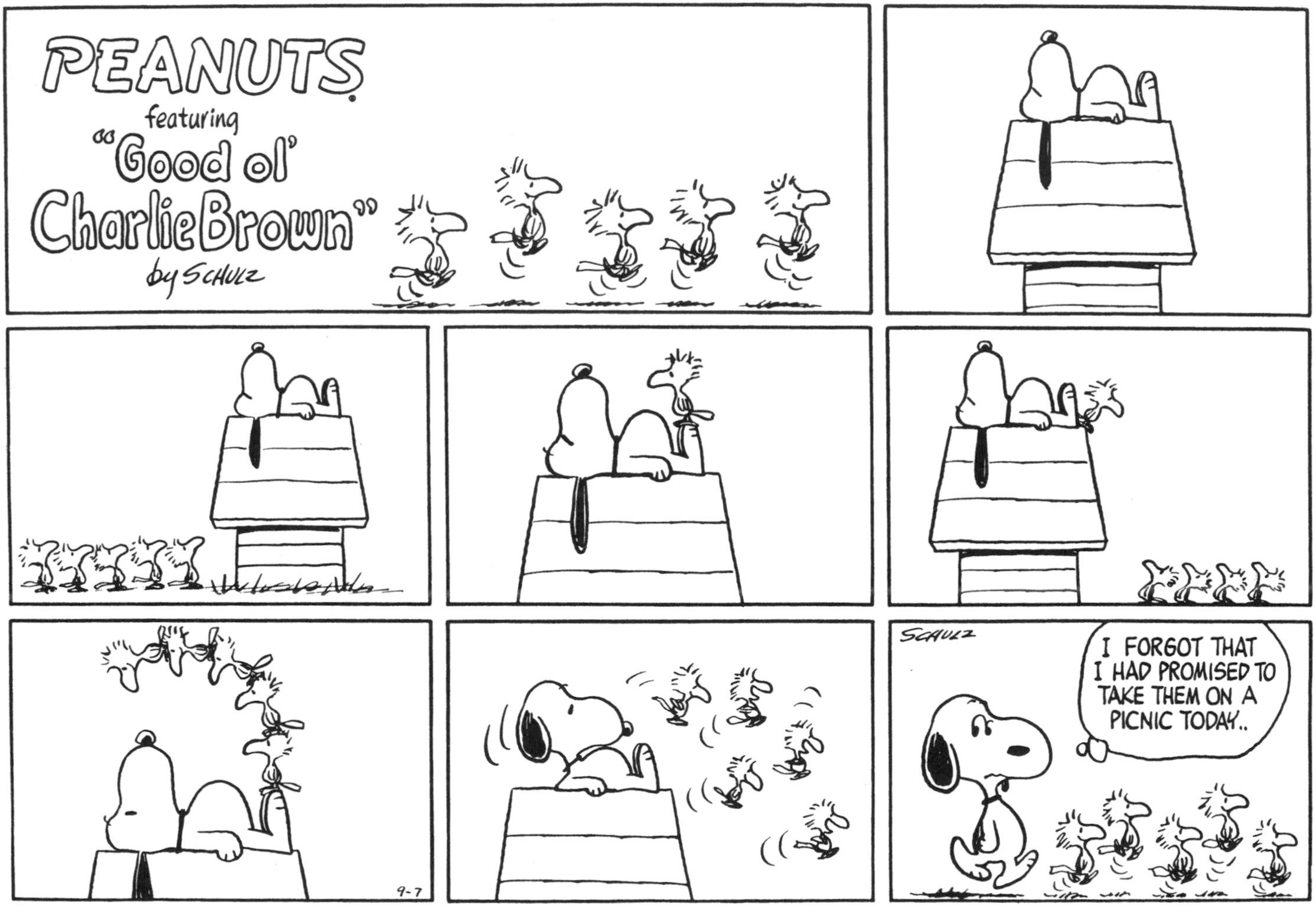
PEANUTS
featuring
"Good ol' Charlie Brown"
by SCHULZ
9-7
SCHULZ
I FORGOT THAT I HAD PROMISED TO TAKE THEM ON A PICNIC TODAY..

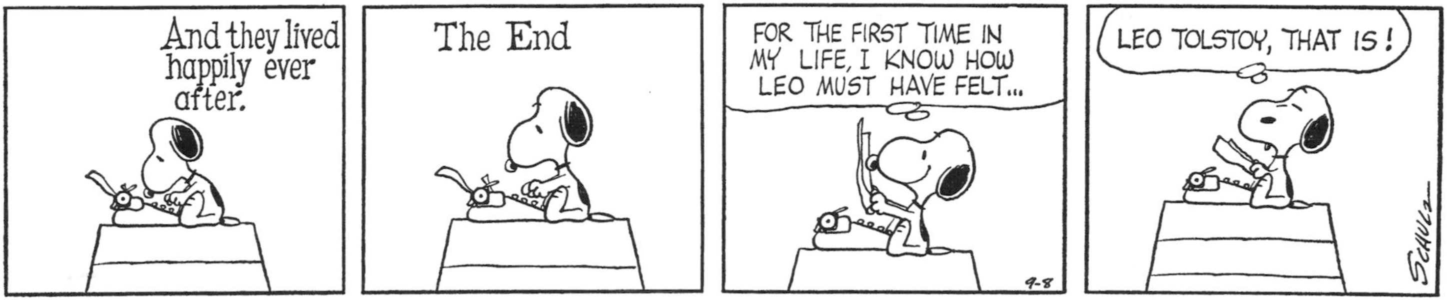
And they lived happily ever after.
The End
FOR THE FIRST TIME IN MY LIFE, I KNOW HOW LEO MUST HAVE FELT...
9-8
LEO TOLSTOY, THAT IS!
SCHULZ

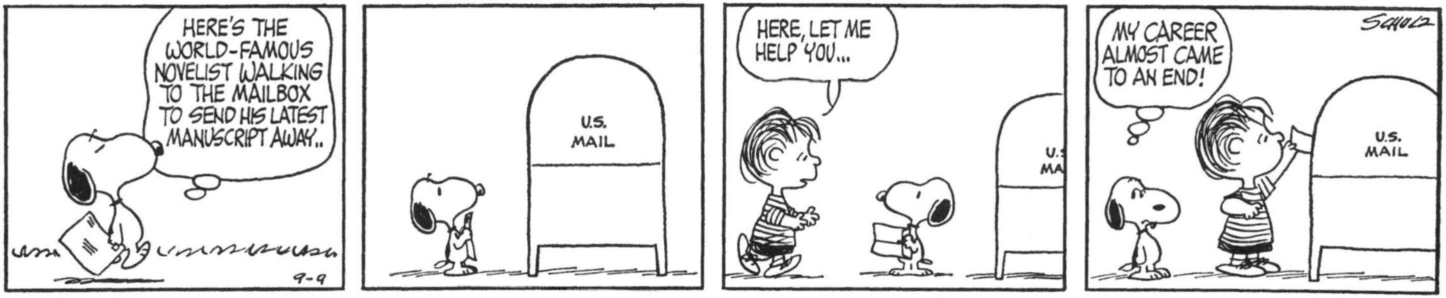
HERE'S THE WORLD-FAMOUS NOVELIST WALKING TO THE MAILBOX TO SEND HIS LATEST MANUSCRIPT AWAY..
9-9
U.S. MAIL
HERE, LET ME HELP YOU...
SCHULZ
MY CAREER ALMOST CAME TO AN END!
U.S. MAIL

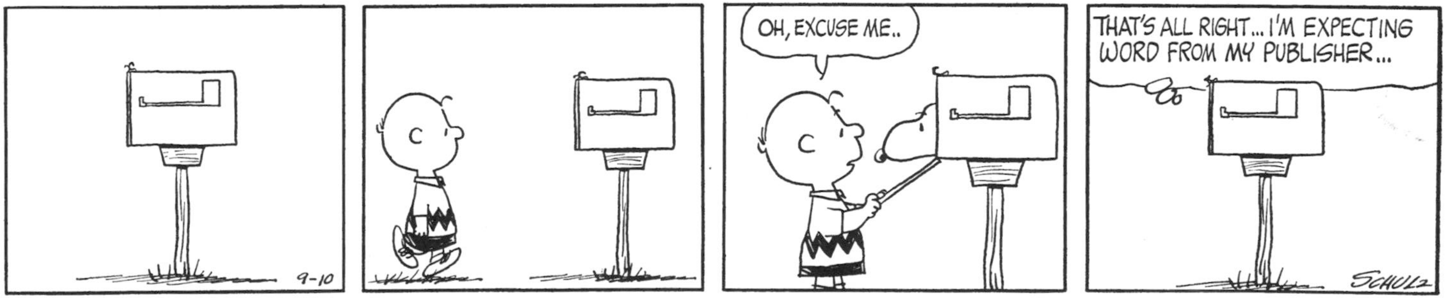
9-10
OH, EXCUSE ME..
THAT'S ALL RIGHT... I'M EXPECTING WORD FROM MY PUBLISHER...
SCHULZ

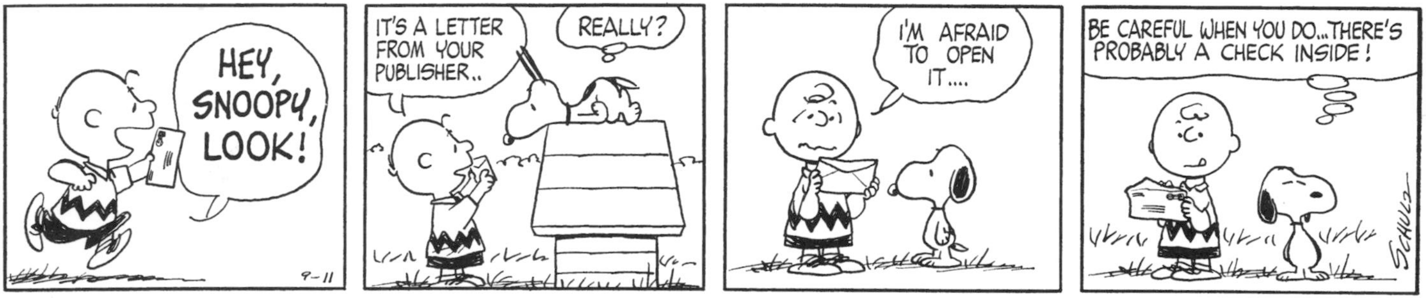
HEY, SNOOPY, LOOK!
9-11
IT'S A LETTER FROM YOUR PUBLISHER..
REALLY?
I'M AFRAID TO OPEN IT....
BE CAREFUL WHEN YOU DO...THERE'S PROBABLY A CHECK INSIDE!
SCHULZ

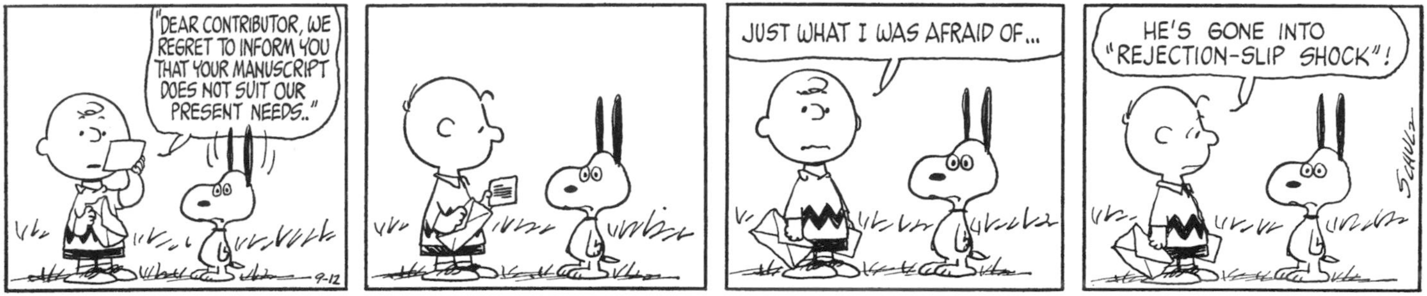
"DEAR CONTRIBUTOR, WE REGRET TO INFORM YOU THAT YOUR MANUSCRIPT DOES NOT SUIT OUR PRESENT NEEDS.."
9-12
JUST WHAT I WAS AFRAID OF...
HE'S GONE INTO "REJECTION-SLIP SHOCK"!
SCHULZ

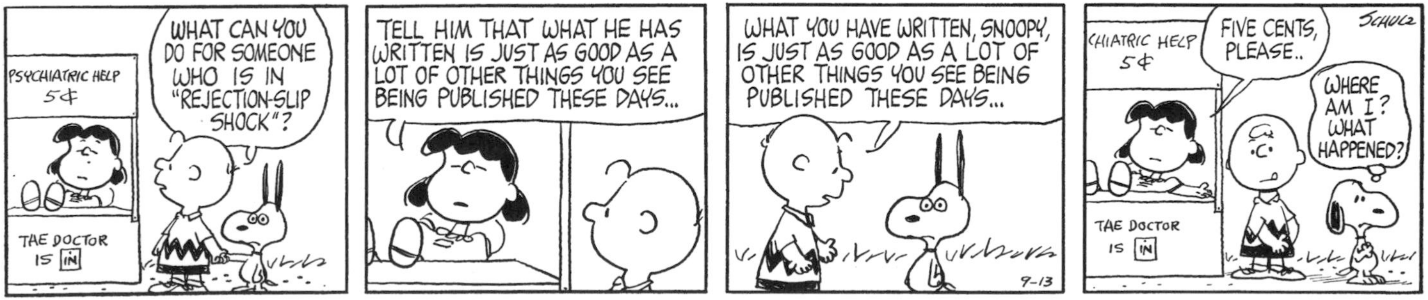
PSYCHIATRIC HELP 5¢
WHAT CAN YOU DO FOR SOMEONE WHO IS IN "REJECTION-SLIP SHOCK"?
THE DOCTOR IS IN
TELL HIM THAT WHAT HE HAS WRITTEN IS JUST AS GOOD AS A LOT OF OTHER THINGS YOU SEE BEING PUBLISHED THESE DAYS...
WHAT YOU HAVE WRITTEN, SNOOPY, IS JUST AS GOOD AS A LOT OF OTHER THINGS YOU SEE BEING PUBLISHED THESE DAYS...
9-13
SCHULZ
CHIATRIC HELP 5¢
FIVE CENTS, PLEASE..
WHERE AM I? WHAT HAPPENED?
THE DOCTOR IS IN

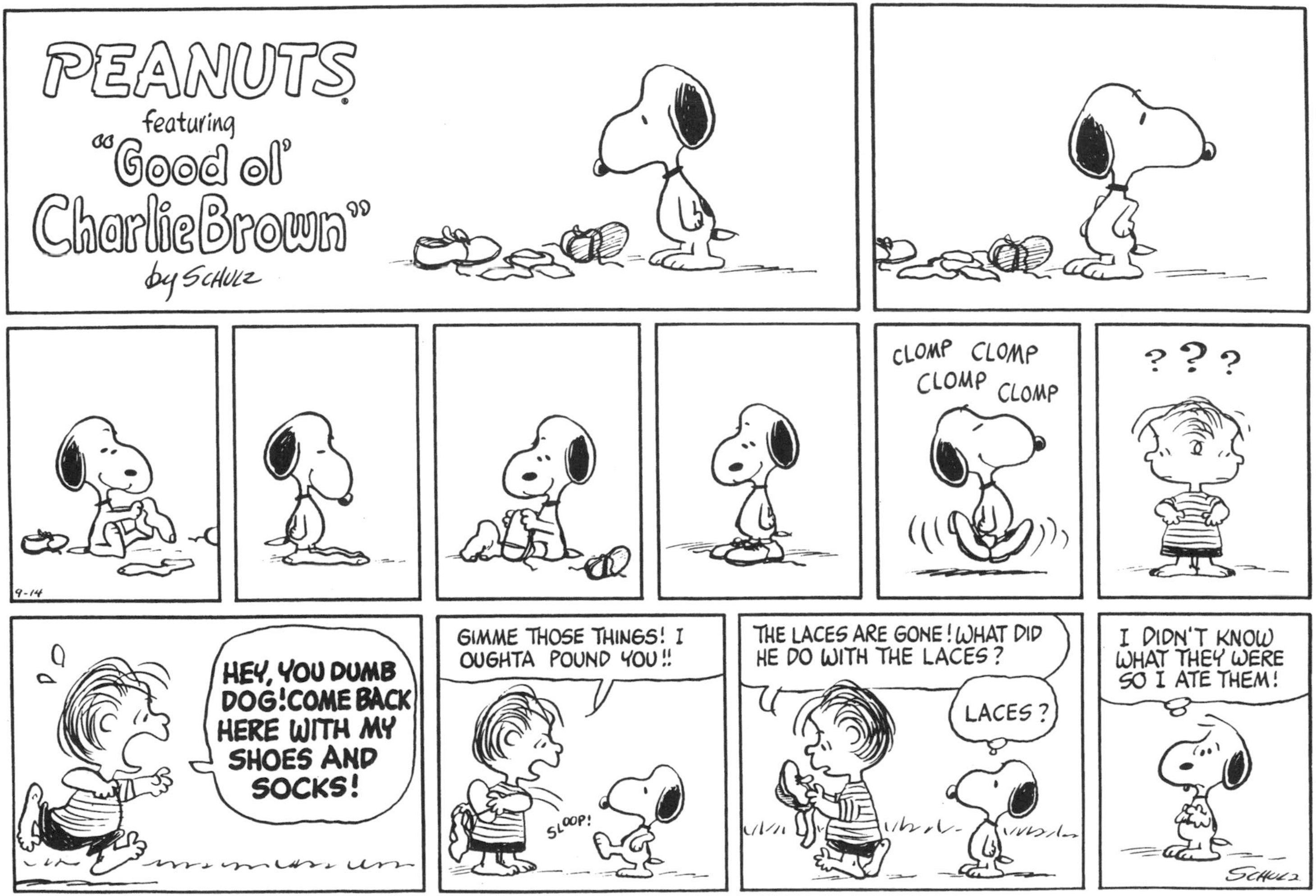
PEANUTS
featuring
"Good ol' Charlie Brown"
by SCHULZ
CLOMP CLOMP
CLOMP CLOMP
? ? ?
HEY, YOU DUMB DOG! COME BACK HERE WITH MY SHOES AND SOCKS!
GIMME THOSE THINGS! I OUGHTA POUND YOU!!
SLOOP!
THE LACES ARE GONE! WHAT DID HE DO WITH THE LACES?
LACES?
I DIDN'T KNOW WHAT THEY WERE SO I ATE THEM!
SCHULZ

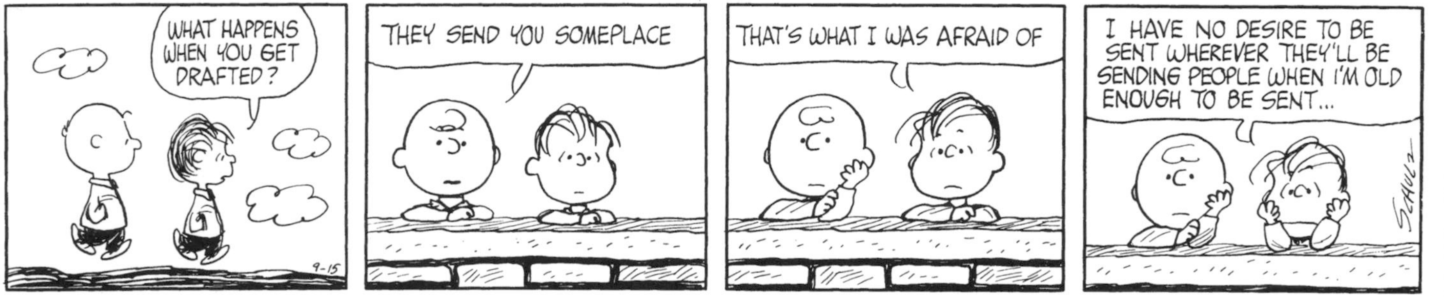
WHAT HAPPENS WHEN YOU GET DRAFTED?
9-15
THEY SEND YOU SOMEPLACE
THAT'S WHAT I WAS AFRAID OF
I HAVE NO DESIRE TO BE SENT WHEREVER THEY'LL BE SENDING PEOPLE WHEN I'M OLD ENOUGH TO BE SENT...
SCHULZ

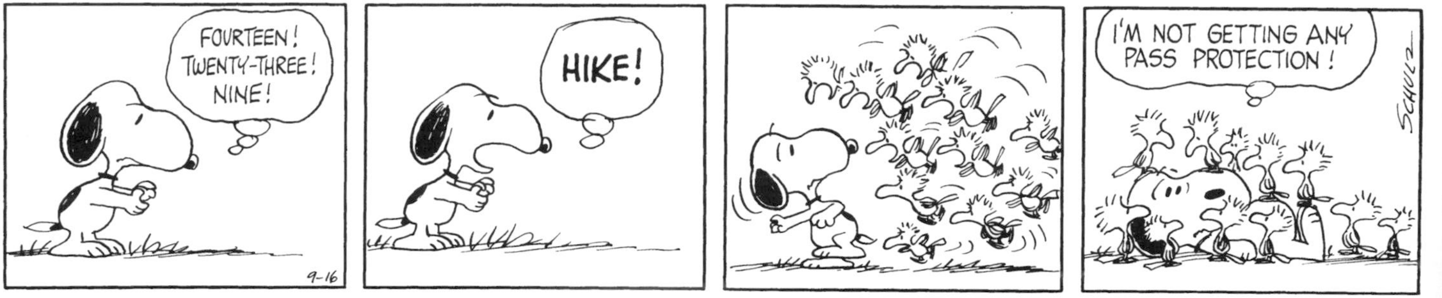
FOURTEEN! TWENTY-THREE! NINE!
9-16
HIKE!
I'M NOT GETTING ANY PASS PROTECTION!
SCHULZ

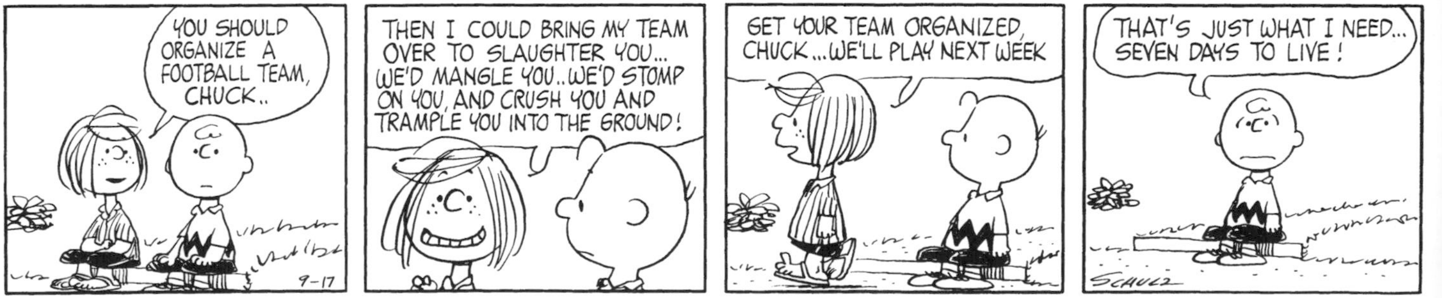
YOU SHOULD ORGANIZE A FOOTBALL TEAM, CHUCK..
9-17
THEN I COULD BRING MY TEAM OVER TO SLAUGHTER YOU... WE'D MANGLE YOU..WE'D STOMP ON YOU, AND CRUSH YOU AND TRAMPLE YOU INTO THE GROUND!
GET YOUR TEAM ORGANIZED, CHUCK...WE'LL PLAY NEXT WEEK
THAT'S JUST WHAT I NEED... SEVEN DAYS TO LIVE!
SCHULZ

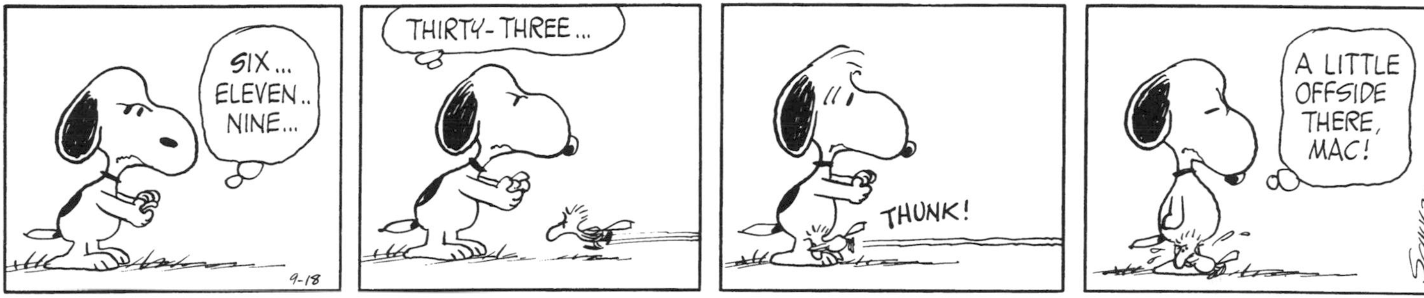
SIX... ELEVEN.. NINE...
9-18
THIRTY-THREE...
THUNK!
A LITTLE OFFSIDE THERE, MAC!
SCHULZ

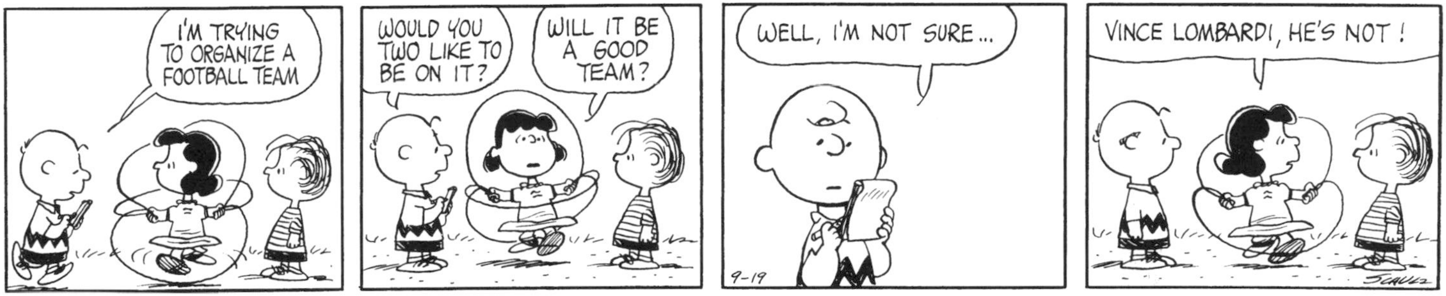
I'M TRYING TO ORGANIZE A FOOTBALL TEAM
WOULD YOU TWO LIKE TO BE ON IT?
WILL IT BE A GOOD TEAM?
WELL, I'M NOT SURE...
9-19
VINCE LOMBARDI, HE'S NOT!
SCHULZ

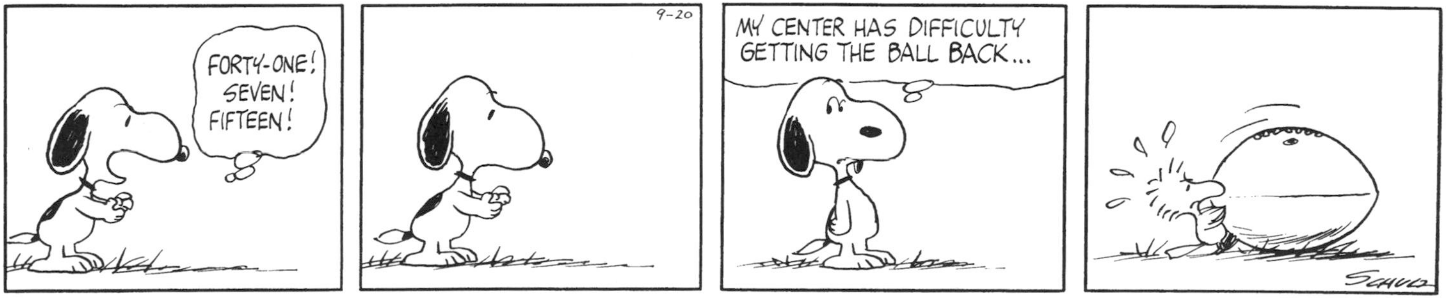
FORTY-ONE! SEVEN! FIFTEEN!
9-20
MY CENTER HAS DIFFICULTY GETTING THE BALL BACK...
SCHULZ

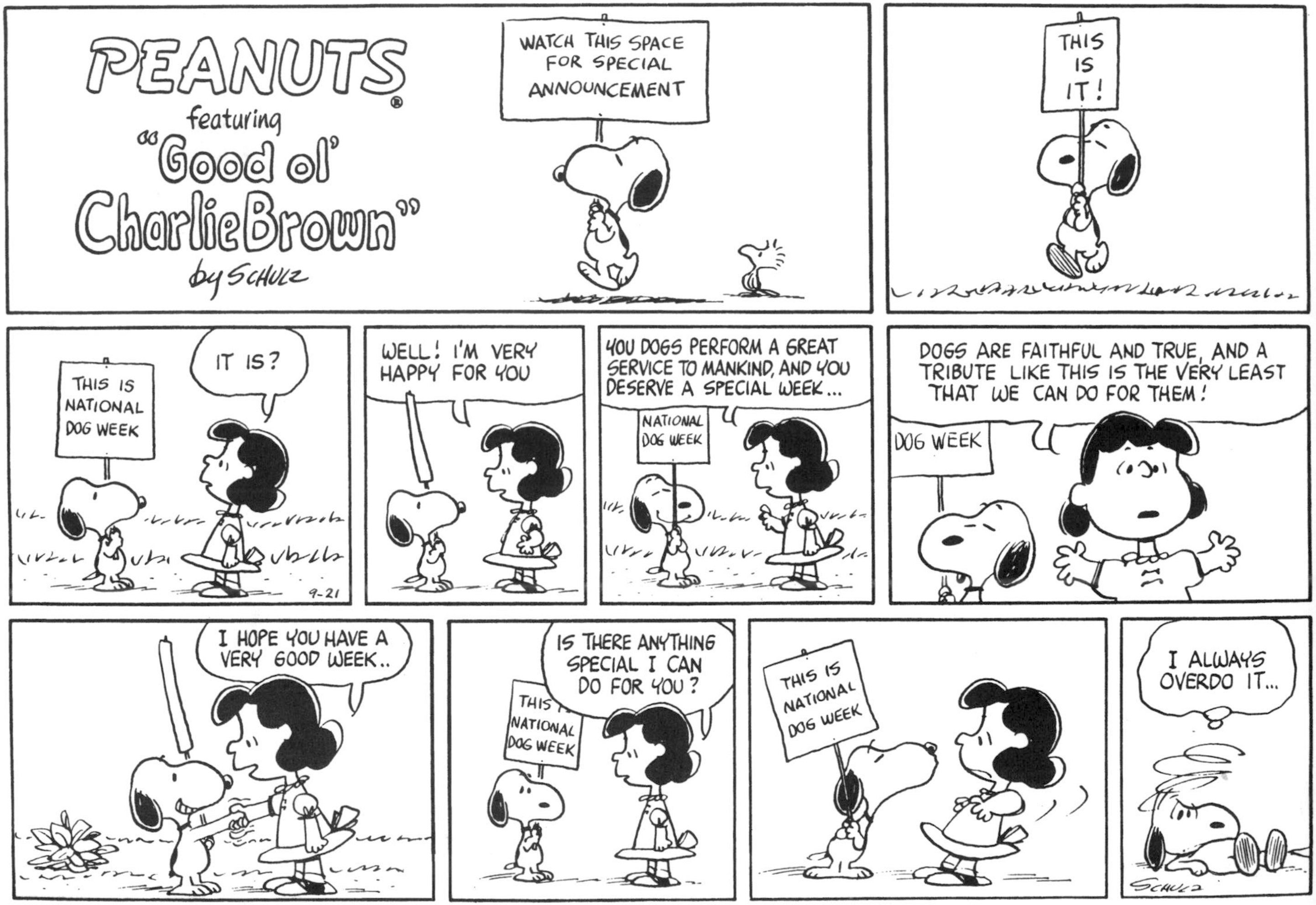
PEANUTS®
featuring "Good ol' Charlie Brown"
by SCHULZ
WATCH THIS SPACE FOR SPECIAL ANNOUNCEMENT
THIS IS IT!
THIS IS NATIONAL DOG WEEK
IT IS?
9-21
WELL! I'M VERY HAPPY FOR YOU
YOU DOGS PERFORM A GREAT SERVICE TO MANKIND, AND YOU DESERVE A SPECIAL WEEK...
NATIONAL DOG WEEK
DOGS ARE FAITHFUL AND TRUE, AND A TRIBUTE LIKE THIS IS THE VERY LEAST THAT WE CAN DO FOR THEM!
DOG WEEK
I HOPE YOU HAVE A VERY GOOD WEEK..
IS THERE ANYTHING SPECIAL I CAN DO FOR YOU?
NATIONAL DOG WEEK
THIS IS NATIONAL DOG WEEK
I ALWAYS OVERDO IT...
SCHULZ

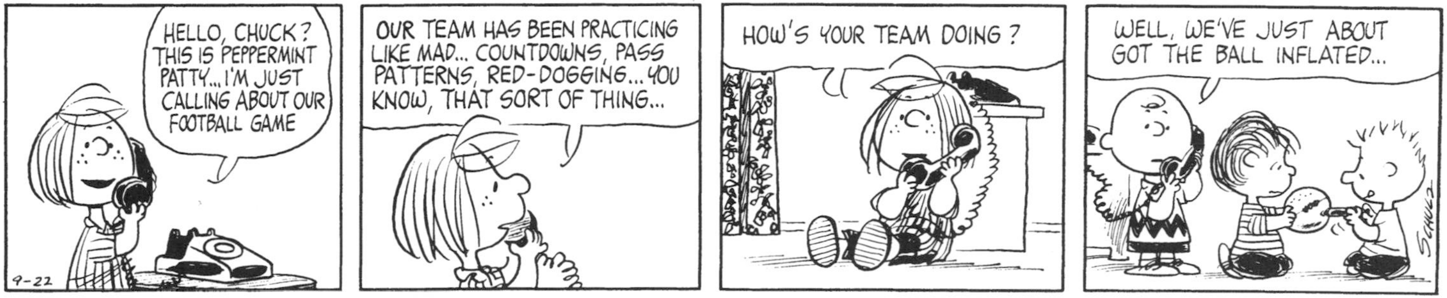
HELLO, CHUCK? THIS IS PEPPERMINT PATTY... I'M JUST CALLING ABOUT OUR FOOTBALL GAME
9-22
OUR TEAM HAS BEEN PRACTICING LIKE MAD... COUNTDOWNS, PASS PATTERNS, RED-DOGGING... YOU KNOW, THAT SORT OF THING...
HOW'S YOUR TEAM DOING?
WELL, WE'VE JUST ABOUT GOT THE BALL INFLATED...
SCHULZ

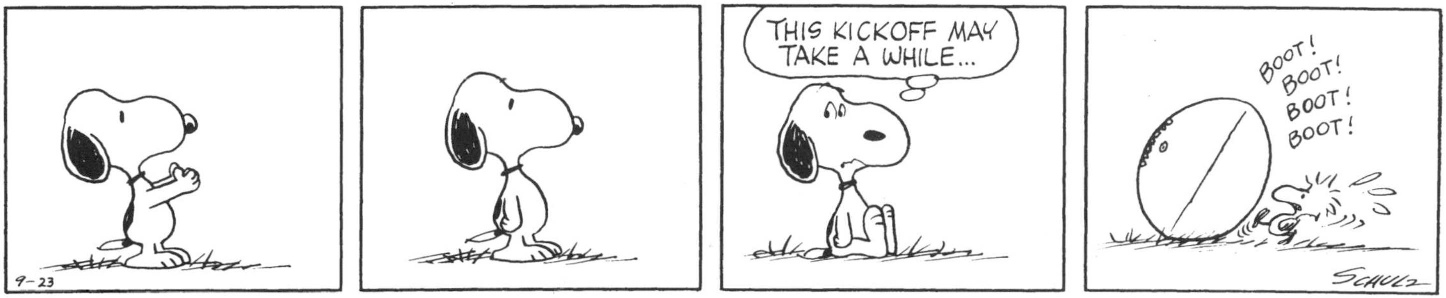
9-23
THIS KICKOFF MAY TAKE A WHILE...
BOOT!
BOOT!
BOOT!
BOOT!
SCHULZ

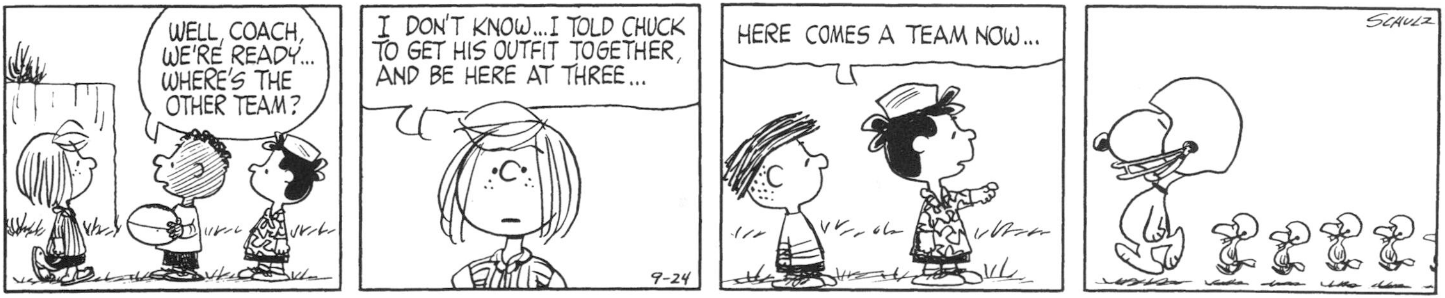
WELL, COACH, WE'RE READY... WHERE'S THE OTHER TEAM?
I DON'T KNOW... I TOLD CHUCK TO GET HIS OUTFIT TOGETHER, AND BE HERE AT THREE...
9-24
HERE COMES A TEAM NOW...
SCHULZ

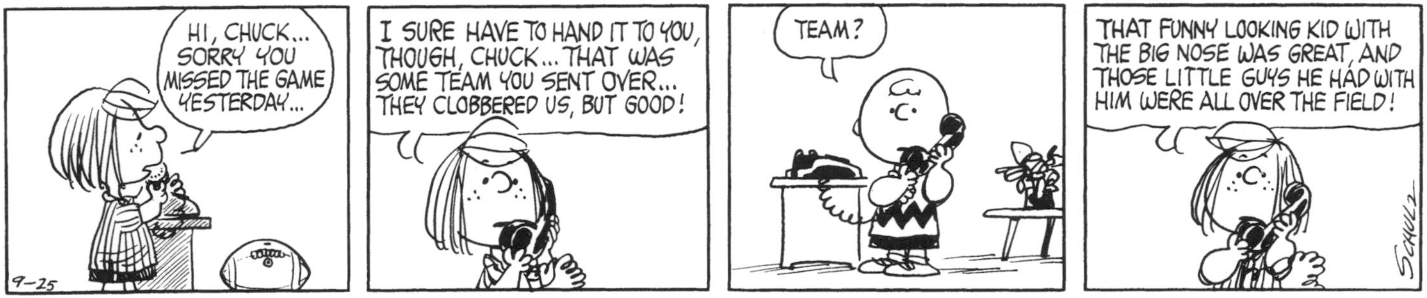
HI, CHUCK... SORRY YOU MISSED THE GAME YESTERDAY...
9-25
I SURE HAVE TO HAND IT TO YOU, THOUGH, CHUCK... THAT WAS SOME TEAM YOU SENT OVER... THEY CLOBBERED US, BUT GOOD!
TEAM?
THAT FUNNY LOOKING KID WITH THE BIG NOSE WAS GREAT, AND THOSE LITTLE GUYS HE HAD WITH HIM WERE ALL OVER THE FIELD!
SCHULZ

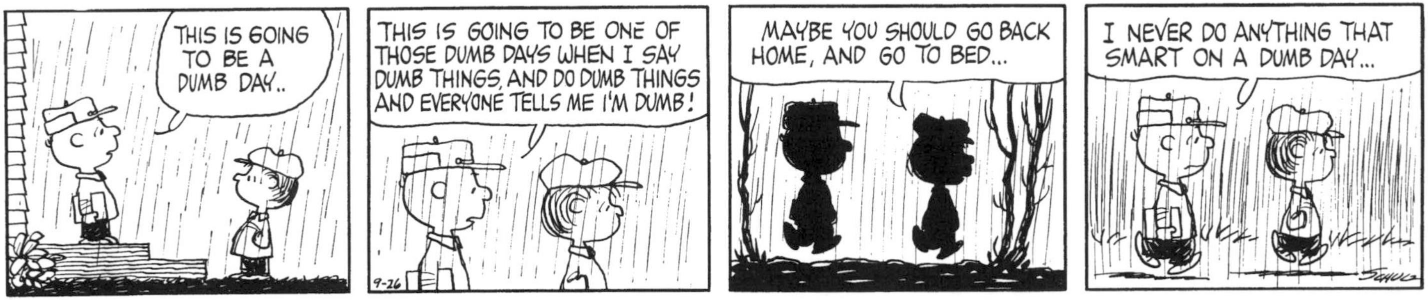
THIS IS GOING TO BE A DUMB DAY..
THIS IS GOING TO BE ONE OF THOSE DUMB DAYS WHEN I SAY DUMB THINGS, AND DO DUMB THINGS AND EVERYONE TELLS ME I'M DUMB!
9-26
MAYBE YOU SHOULD GO BACK HOME, AND GO TO BED...
I NEVER DO ANYTHING THAT SMART ON A DUMB DAY...
SCHULZ

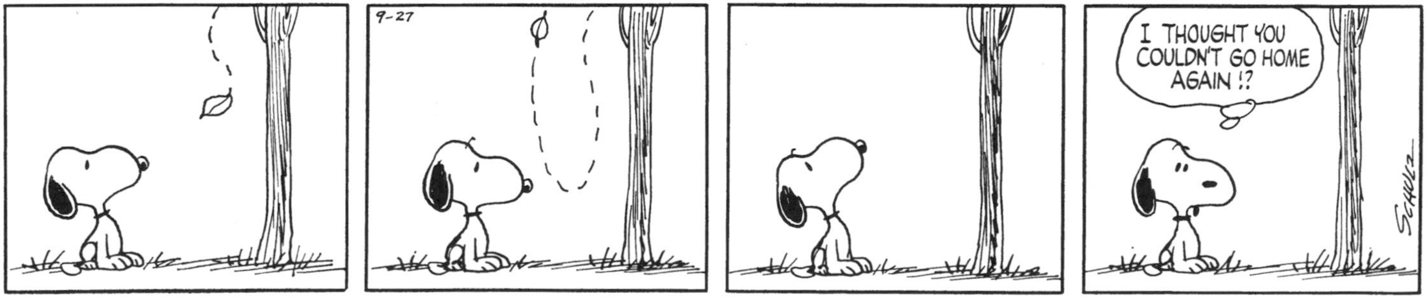
9-27
I THOUGHT YOU COULDN'T GO HOME AGAIN!?
SCHULZ

PEANUTS
featuring
"Good ol' Charlie Brown"
by SCHULZ

CHARLIE BROWN?

CHARLIE BROWN, I HAVE A GREAT IDEA..I'LL HOLD THE FOOTBALL LIKE THIS, AND YOU COME RUNNING UP AND KICK IT...

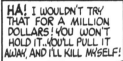

HA! I WOULDN'T TRY THAT FOR A MILLION DOLLARS! YOU WON'T HOLD IT..YOU'LL PULL IT AWAY, AND I'LL KILL MYSELF!

WAAH! YOU DON'T TRUST ME!

YOU THINK I'M NO GOOD! YOU HAVE NO FAITH IN ME!

DON'T CRY, LUCY... I APOLOGIZE..I'M SORRY.. PLEASE, DON'T CRY...

YOU HOLD THE BALL, AND I'LL COME RUNNING UP AND KICK IT...

SNIF

AAUGH!

WUMP!

NEVER LISTEN TO A WOMAN'S TEARS, CHARLIE BROWN!

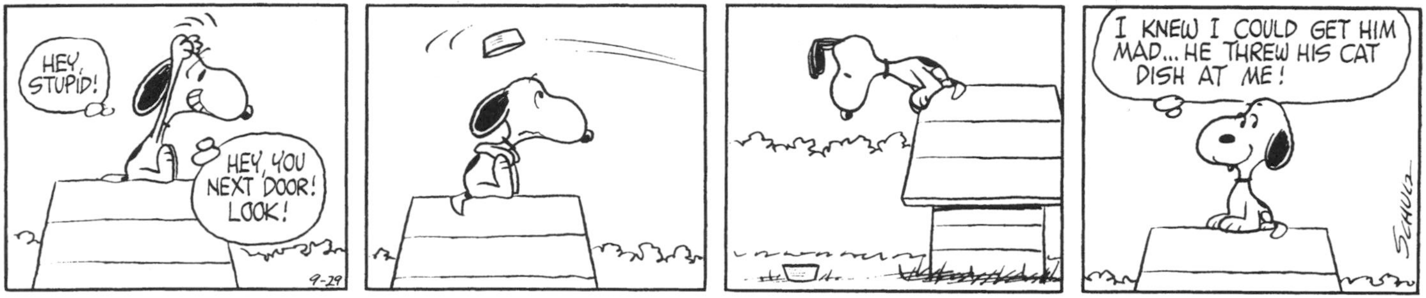
HEY, STUPID!
HEY, YOU NEXT DOOR! LOOK!
I KNEW I COULD GET HIM MAD... HE THREW HIS CAT DISH AT ME!
9-29
SCHULZ

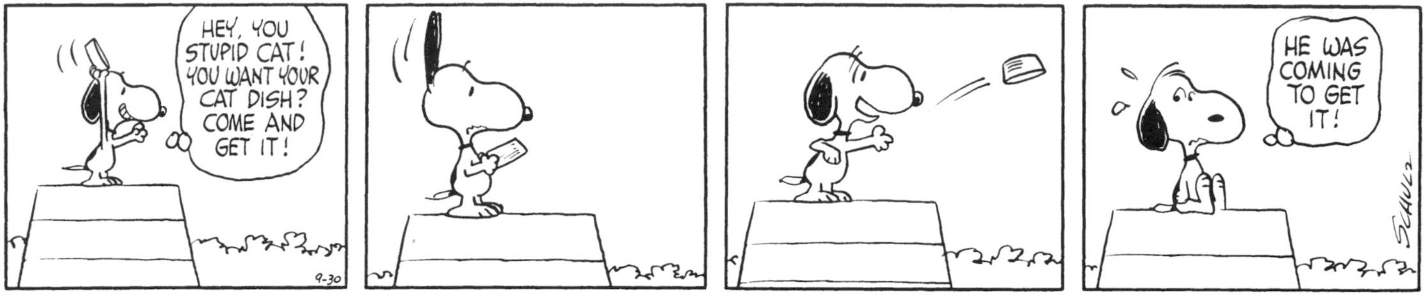
HEY, YOU STUPID CAT! YOU WANT YOUR CAT DISH? COME AND GET IT!
HE WAS COMING TO GET IT!
9-30
SCHULZ

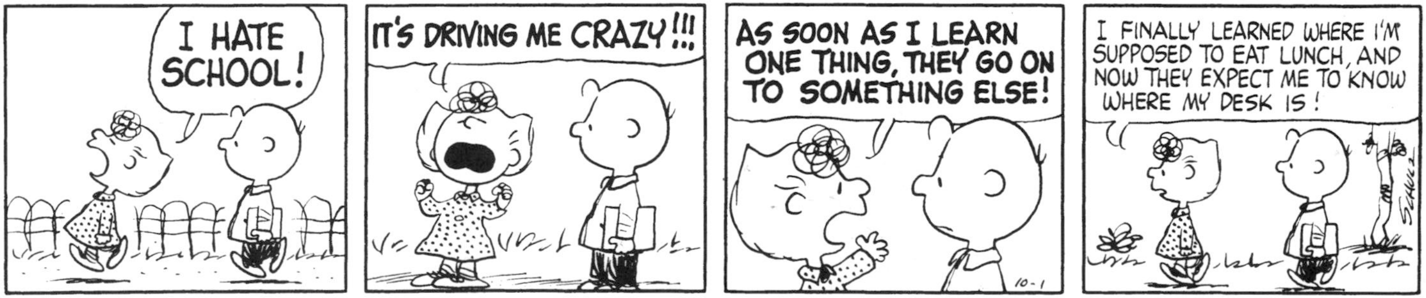
I HATE SCHOOL!
IT'S DRIVING ME CRAZY!!!
AS SOON AS I LEARN ONE THING, THEY GO ON TO SOMETHING ELSE!
I FINALLY LEARNED WHERE I'M SUPPOSED TO EAT LUNCH, AND NOW THEY EXPECT ME TO KNOW WHERE MY DESK IS!
10-1
SCHULZ

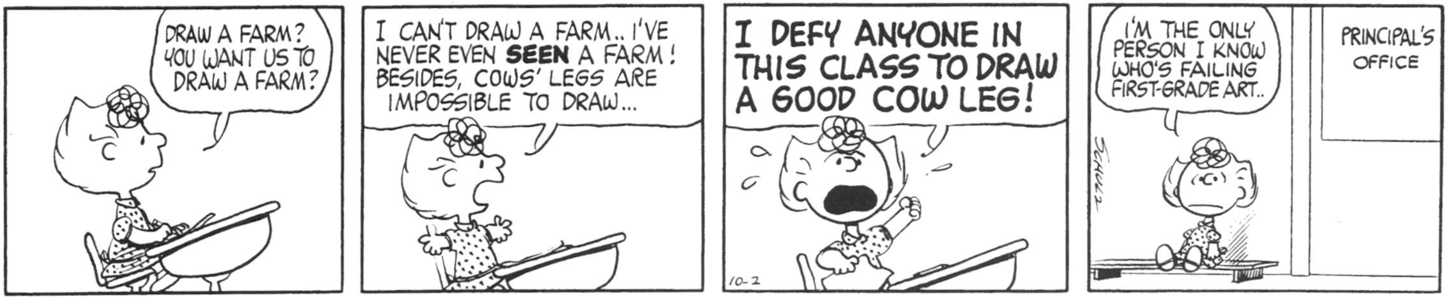
DRAW A FARM? YOU WANT US TO DRAW A FARM?
I CAN'T DRAW A FARM.. I'VE NEVER EVEN **SEEN** A FARM! BESIDES, COWS' LEGS ARE IMPOSSIBLE TO DRAW...
I DEFY ANYONE IN THIS CLASS TO DRAW A GOOD COW LEG!
10-2
I'M THE ONLY PERSON I KNOW WHO'S FAILING FIRST-GRADE ART..
PRINCIPAL'S OFFICE
SCHULZ

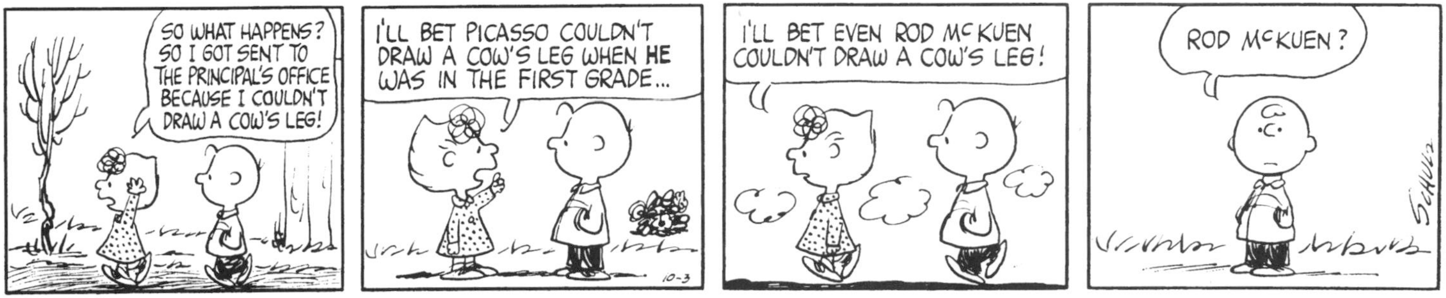
SO WHAT HAPPENS? SO I GOT SENT TO THE PRINCIPAL'S OFFICE BECAUSE I COULDN'T DRAW A COW'S LEG!
I'LL BET PICASSO COULDN'T DRAW A COW'S LEG WHEN **HE** WAS IN THE FIRST GRADE...
10-3
I'LL BET EVEN ROD McKUEN COULDN'T DRAW A COW'S LEG!
ROD McKUEN?
SCHULZ

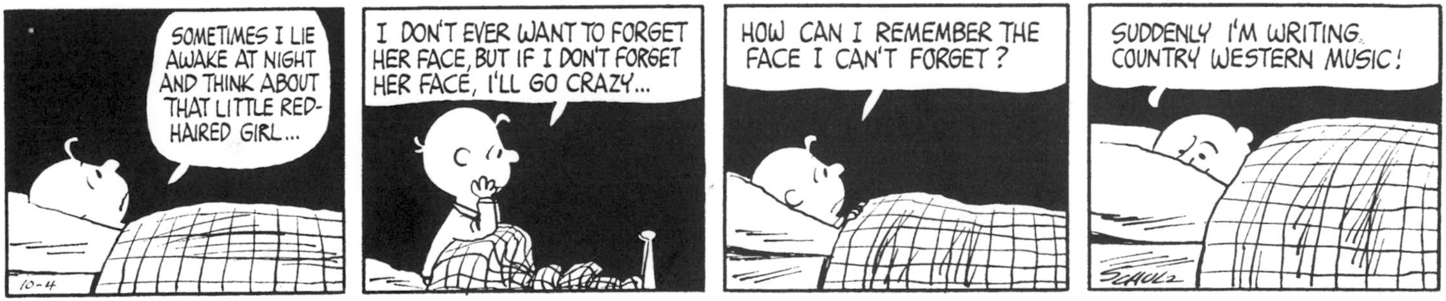
SOMETIMES I LIE AWAKE AT NIGHT AND THINK ABOUT THAT LITTLE RED-HAIRED GIRL...
10-4
I DON'T EVER WANT TO FORGET HER FACE, BUT IF I DON'T FORGET HER FACE, I'LL GO CRAZY...
HOW CAN I REMEMBER THE FACE I CAN'T FORGET?
SUDDENLY I'M WRITING COUNTRY WESTERN MUSIC!
SCHULZ

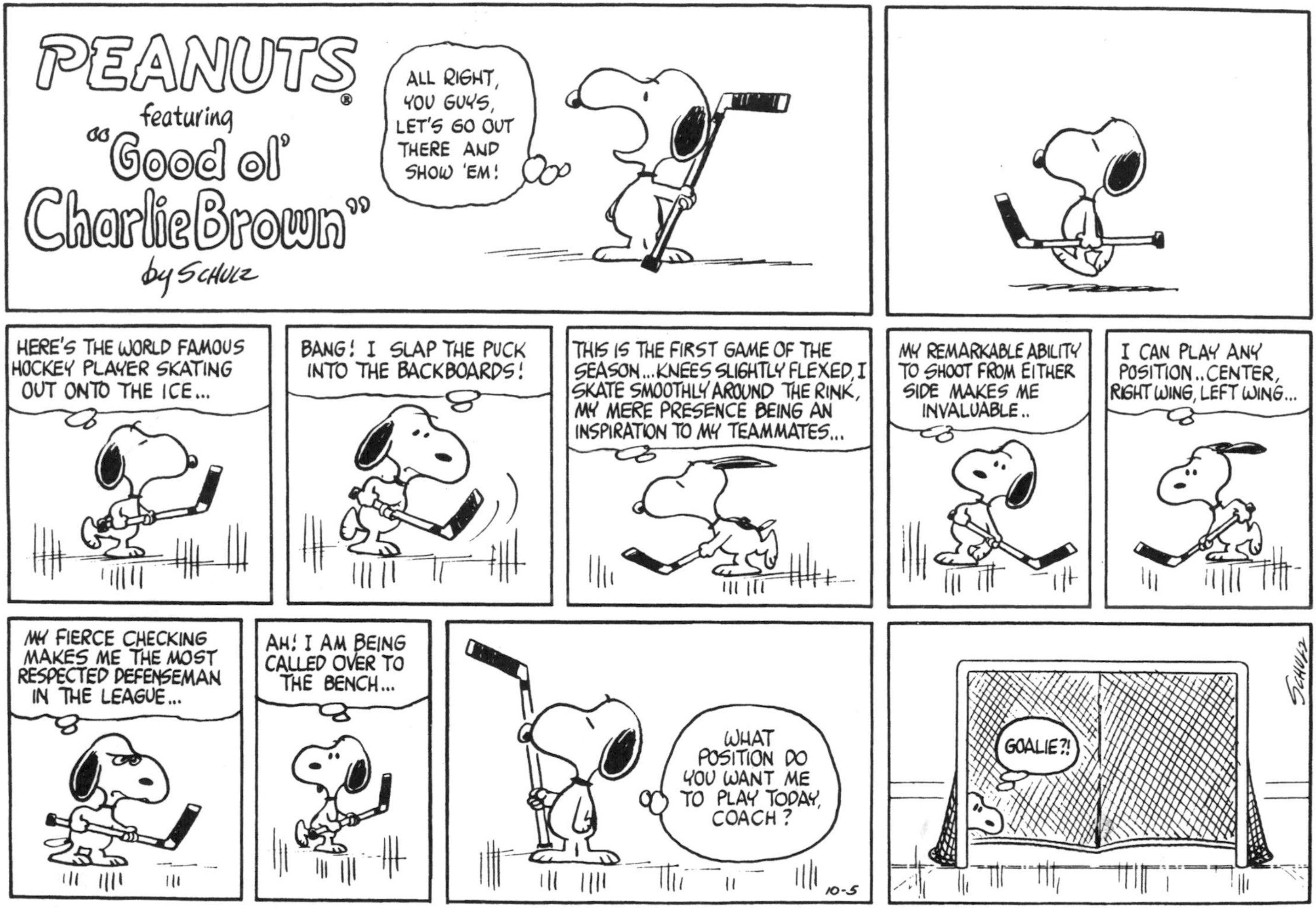
PEANUTS®
featuring "Good ol' Charlie Brown"
by SCHULZ
ALL RIGHT, YOU GUYS, LET'S GO OUT THERE AND SHOW 'EM!
HERE'S THE WORLD FAMOUS HOCKEY PLAYER SKATING OUT ONTO THE ICE...
BANG! I SLAP THE PUCK INTO THE BACKBOARDS!
THIS IS THE FIRST GAME OF THE SEASON...KNEES SLIGHTLY FLEXED, I SKATE SMOOTHLY AROUND THE RINK, MY MERE PRESENCE BEING AN INSPIRATION TO MY TEAMMATES...
MY REMARKABLE ABILITY TO SHOOT FROM EITHER SIDE MAKES ME INVALUABLE..
I CAN PLAY ANY POSITION..CENTER, RIGHT WING, LEFT WING...
MY FIERCE CHECKING MAKES ME THE MOST RESPECTED DEFENSEMAN IN THE LEAGUE...
AH! I AM BEING CALLED OVER TO THE BENCH...
WHAT POSITION DO YOU WANT ME TO PLAY TODAY, COACH?
10-5
GOALIE?!
SCHULZ

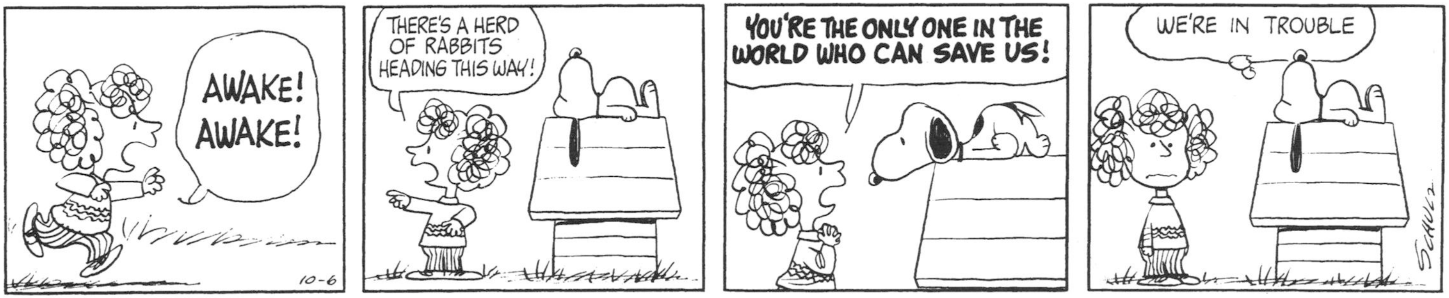
AWAKE! AWAKE!
10-6
THERE'S A HERD OF RABBITS HEADING THIS WAY!
YOU'RE THE ONLY ONE IN THE WORLD WHO CAN SAVE US!
WE'RE IN TROUBLE
SCHULZ

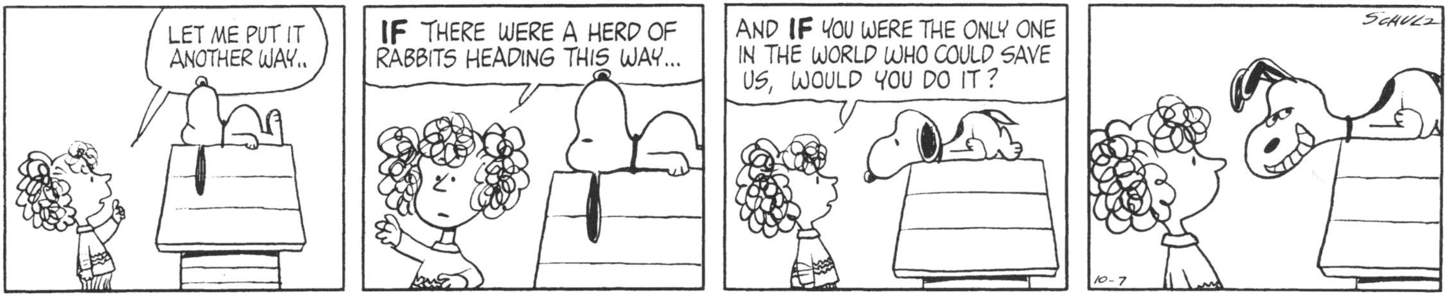
LET ME PUT IT ANOTHER WAY..
IF THERE WERE A HERD OF RABBITS HEADING THIS WAY...
AND IF YOU WERE THE ONLY ONE IN THE WORLD WHO COULD SAVE US, WOULD YOU DO IT?
SCHULZ
10-7

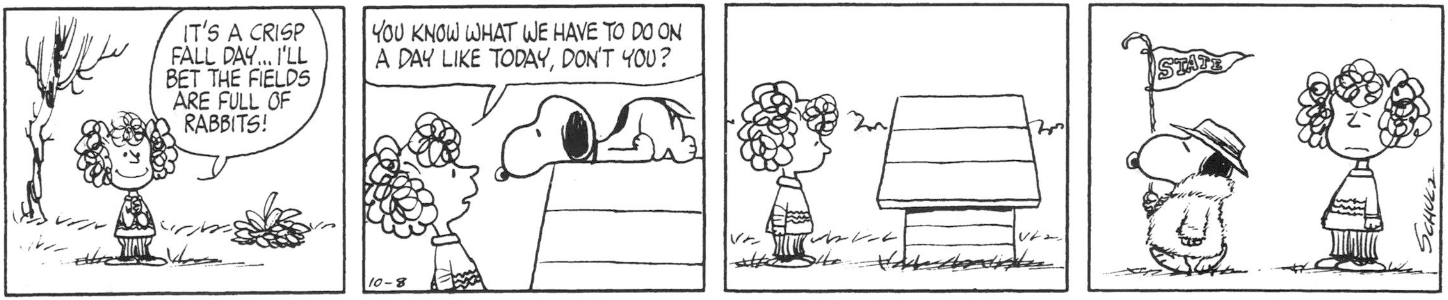
IT'S A CRISP FALL DAY... I'LL BET THE FIELDS ARE FULL OF RABBITS!
YOU KNOW WHAT WE HAVE TO DO ON A DAY LIKE TODAY, DON'T YOU?
10-8
STATE
SCHULZ

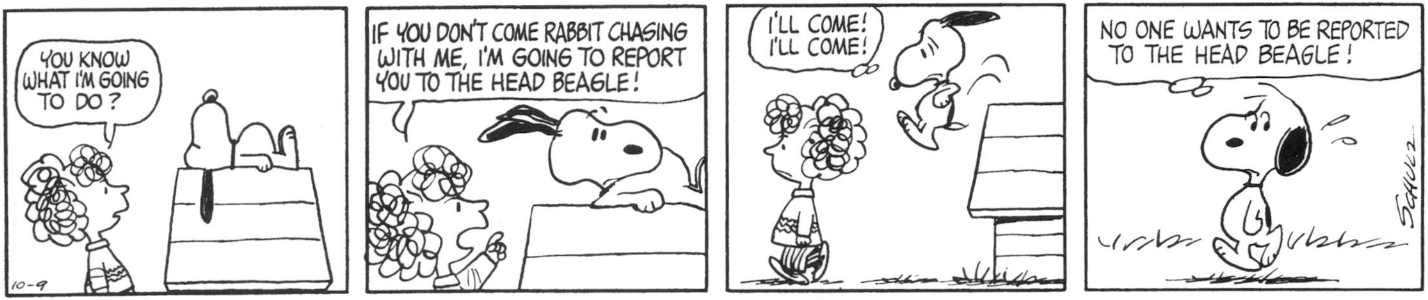
YOU KNOW WHAT I'M GOING TO DO?
10-9
IF YOU DON'T COME RABBIT CHASING WITH ME, I'M GOING TO REPORT YOU TO THE HEAD BEAGLE!
I'LL COME! I'LL COME!
NO ONE WANTS TO BE REPORTED TO THE HEAD BEAGLE!
SCHULZ

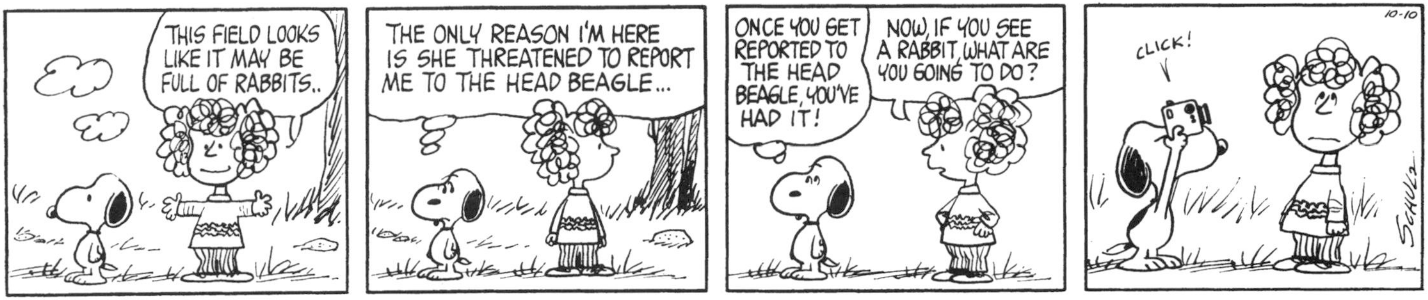
THIS FIELD LOOKS LIKE IT MAY BE FULL OF RABBITS..
THE ONLY REASON I'M HERE IS SHE THREATENED TO REPORT ME TO THE HEAD BEAGLE...
ONCE YOU GET REPORTED TO THE HEAD BEAGLE, YOU'VE HAD IT!
NOW, IF YOU SEE A RABBIT, WHAT ARE YOU GOING TO DO?
10-10
CLICK!
SCHULZ

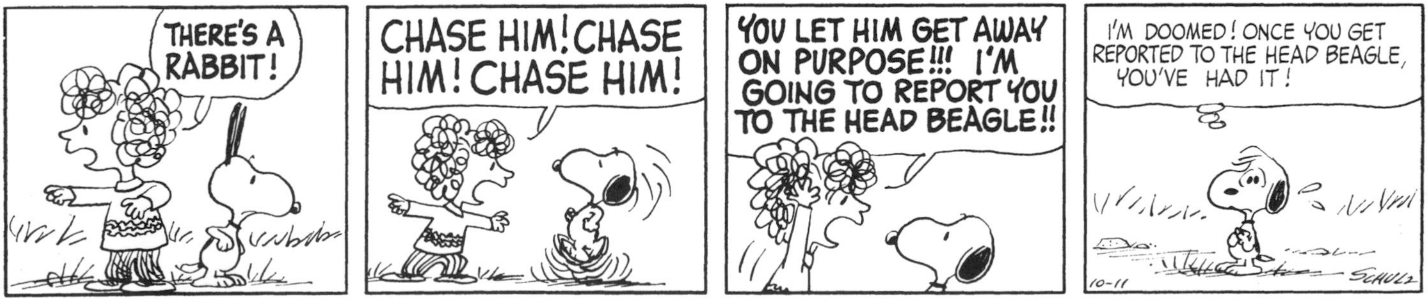
THERE'S A RABBIT!
CHASE HIM! CHASE HIM! CHASE HIM!
YOU LET HIM GET AWAY ON PURPOSE!!! I'M GOING TO REPORT YOU TO THE HEAD BEAGLE!!
I'M DOOMED! ONCE YOU GET REPORTED TO THE HEAD BEAGLE, YOU'VE HAD IT!
10-11
SCHULZ

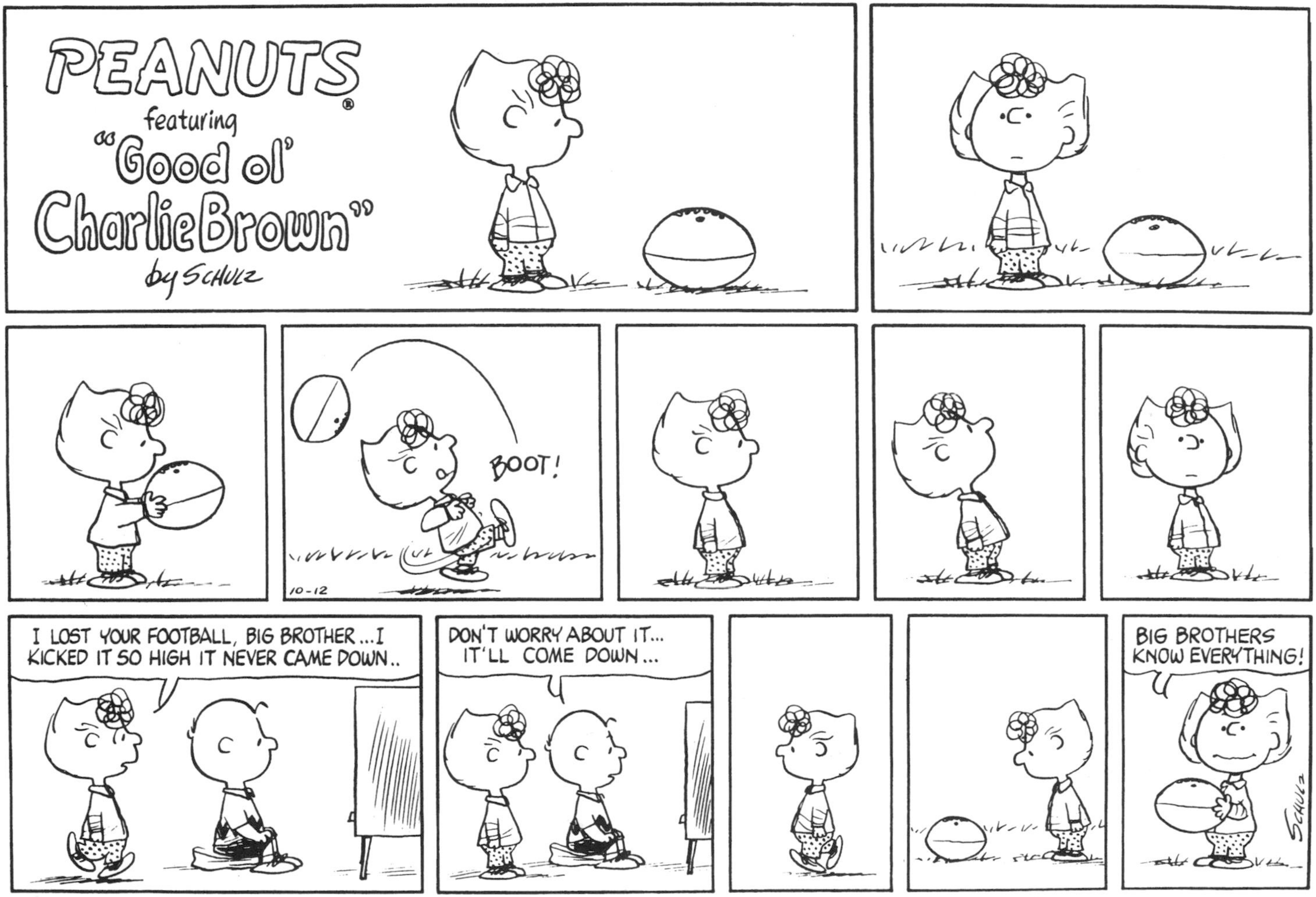
PEANUTS®
featuring
"Good ol' Charlie Brown"
by SCHULZ
BOOT!
10-12
I LOST YOUR FOOTBALL, BIG BROTHER...I KICKED IT SO HIGH IT NEVER CAME DOWN..
DON'T WORRY ABOUT IT... IT'LL COME DOWN...
BIG BROTHERS KNOW EVERYTHING!
SCHULZ

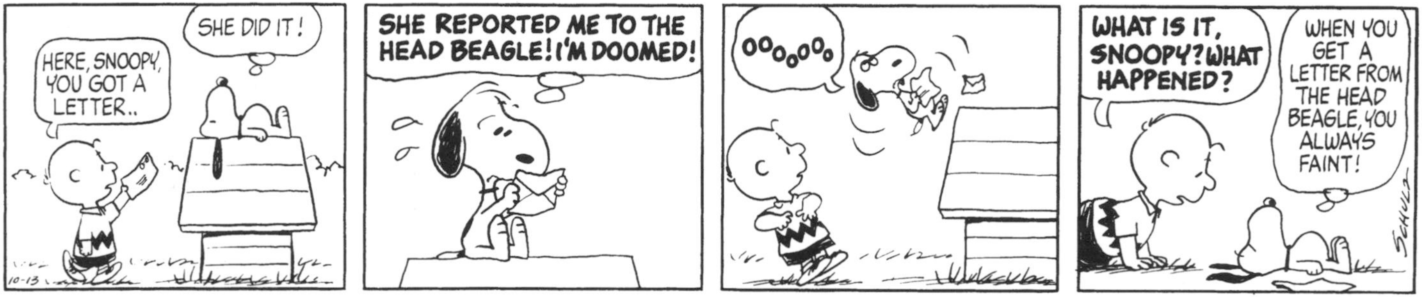
HERE, SNOOPY, YOU GOT A LETTER..
SHE DID IT!
10-13
SHE REPORTED ME TO THE HEAD BEAGLE! I'M DOOMED!
OOOOOOO
WHAT IS IT, SNOOPY? WHAT HAPPENED?
WHEN YOU GET A LETTER FROM THE HEAD BEAGLE, YOU ALWAYS FAINT!
SCHULZ

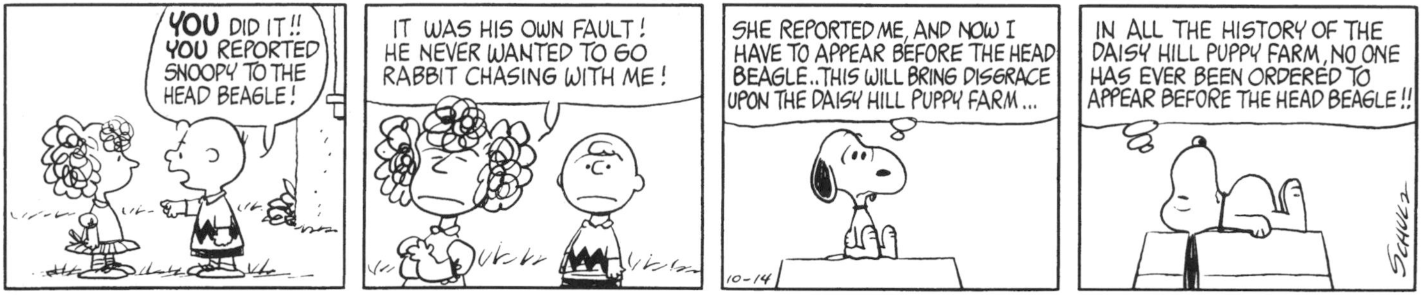
YOU DID IT!! YOU REPORTED SNOOPY TO THE HEAD BEAGLE!
IT WAS HIS OWN FAULT! HE NEVER WANTED TO GO RABBIT CHASING WITH ME!
SHE REPORTED ME, AND NOW I HAVE TO APPEAR BEFORE THE HEAD BEAGLE..THIS WILL BRING DISGRACE UPON THE DAISY HILL PUPPY FARM...
10-14
IN ALL THE HISTORY OF THE DAISY HILL PUPPY FARM, NO ONE HAS EVER BEEN ORDERED TO APPEAR BEFORE THE HEAD BEAGLE!!
SCHULZ

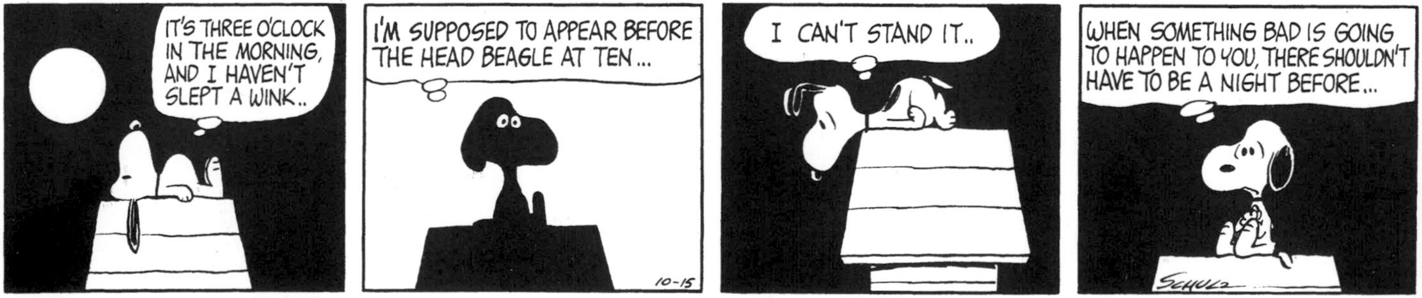
IT'S THREE O'CLOCK IN THE MORNING, AND I HAVEN'T SLEPT A WINK..
I'M SUPPOSED TO APPEAR BEFORE THE HEAD BEAGLE AT TEN...
10-15
I CAN'T STAND IT..
WHEN SOMETHING BAD IS GOING TO HAPPEN TO YOU, THERE SHOULDN'T HAVE TO BE A NIGHT BEFORE...
SCHULZ

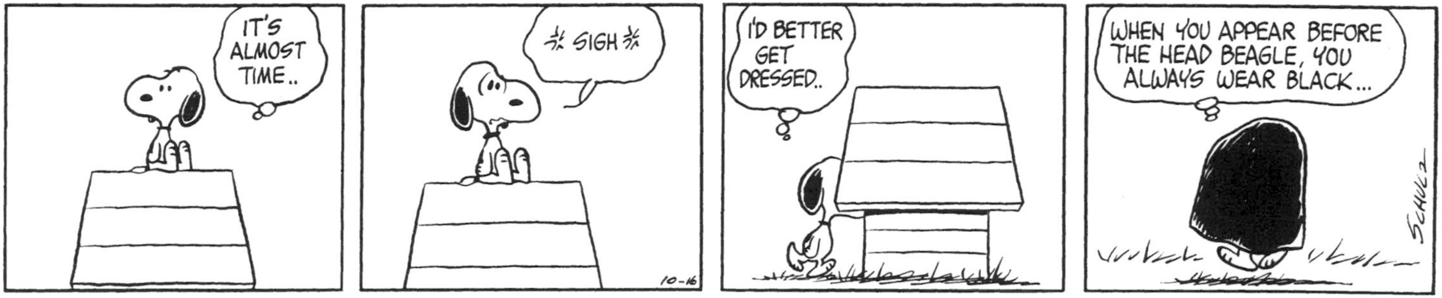
IT'S ALMOST TIME..
SIGH
I'D BETTER GET DRESSED..
WHEN YOU APPEAR BEFORE THE HEAD BEAGLE, YOU ALWAYS WEAR BLACK...
10-16
SCHULZ

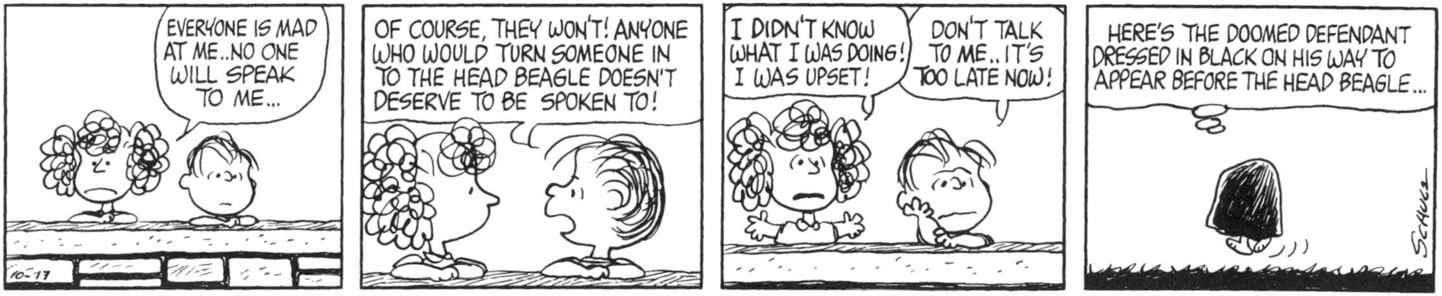
EVERYONE IS MAD AT ME..NO ONE WILL SPEAK TO ME...
OF COURSE, THEY WON'T! ANYONE WHO WOULD TURN SOMEONE IN TO THE HEAD BEAGLE DOESN'T DESERVE TO BE SPOKEN TO!
I DIDN'T KNOW WHAT I WAS DOING! I WAS UPSET!
DON'T TALK TO ME.. IT'S TOO LATE NOW!
HERE'S THE DOOMED DEFENDANT DRESSED IN BLACK ON HIS WAY TO APPEAR BEFORE THE HEAD BEAGLE...
10-17
SCHULZ

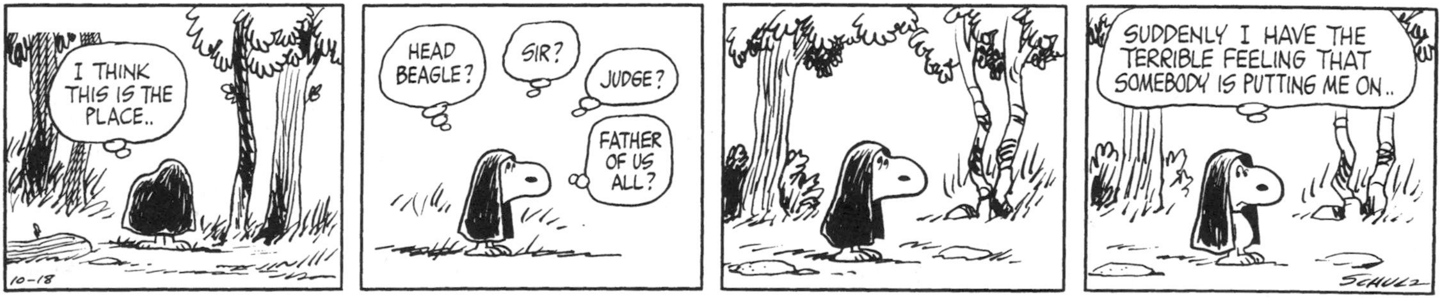
I THINK THIS IS THE PLACE..
HEAD BEAGLE?
SIR?
JUDGE?
FATHER OF US ALL?
SUDDENLY I HAVE THE TERRIBLE FEELING THAT SOMEBODY IS PUTTING ME ON..
10-18
SCHULZ

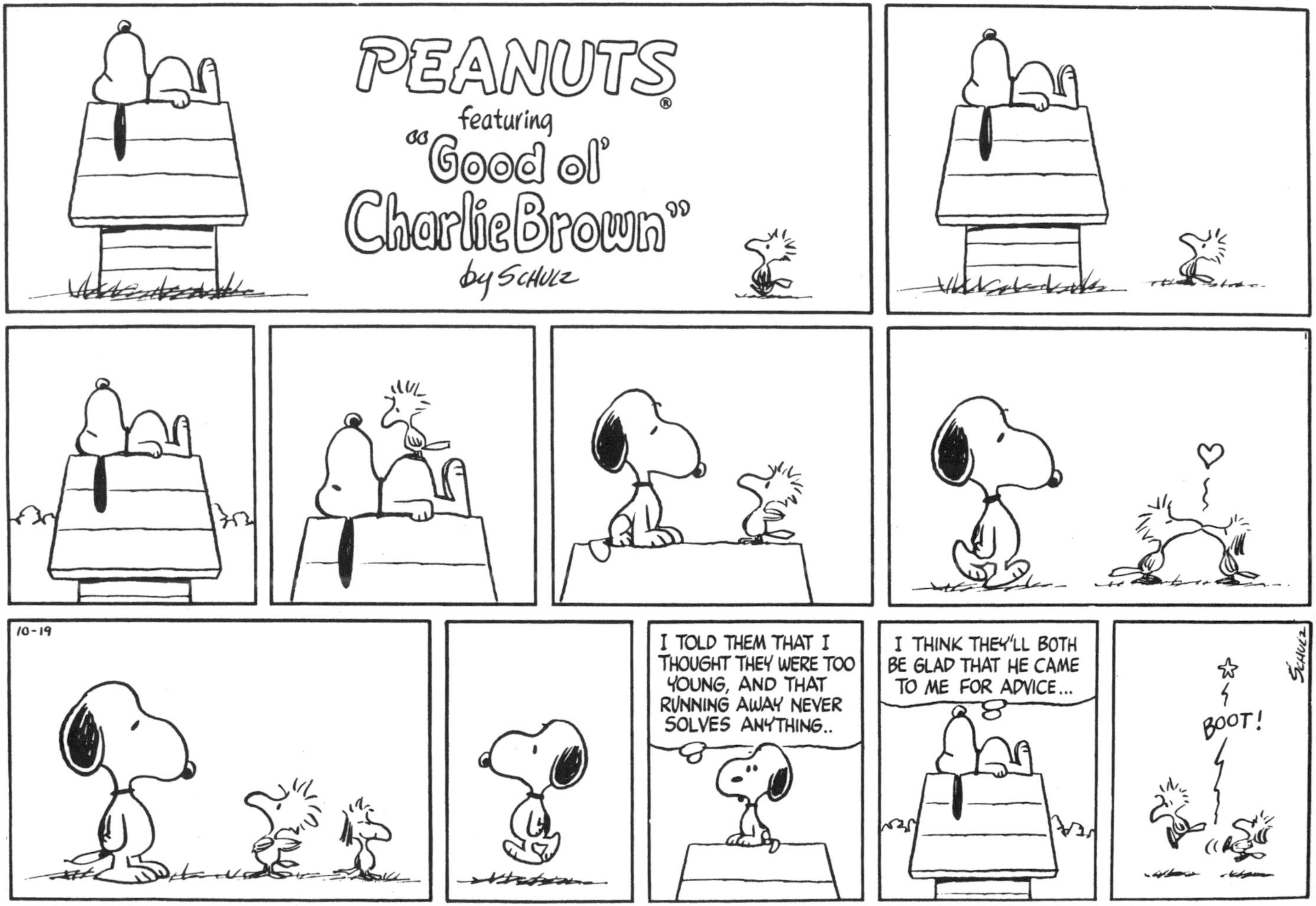
PEANUTS®
featuring
"Good ol' CharlieBrown"
by SCHULZ
10-19
I TOLD THEM THAT I THOUGHT THEY WERE TOO YOUNG, AND THAT RUNNING AWAY NEVER SOLVES ANYTHING..
I THINK THEY'LL BOTH BE GLAD THAT HE CAME TO ME FOR ADVICE...
BOOT!
SCHULZ

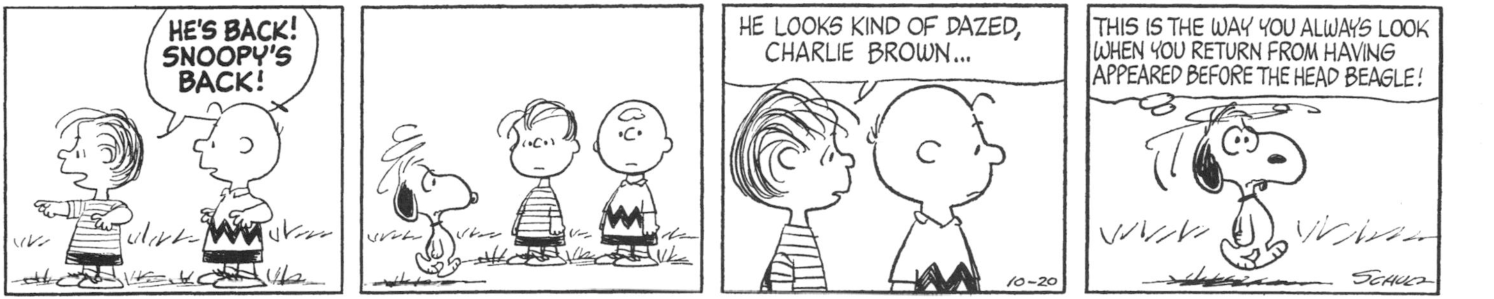
HE'S BACK! SNOOPY'S BACK!
HE LOOKS KIND OF DAZED, CHARLIE BROWN...
THIS IS THE WAY YOU ALWAYS LOOK WHEN YOU RETURN FROM HAVING APPEARED BEFORE THE HEAD BEAGLE!
10-20
SCHULZ

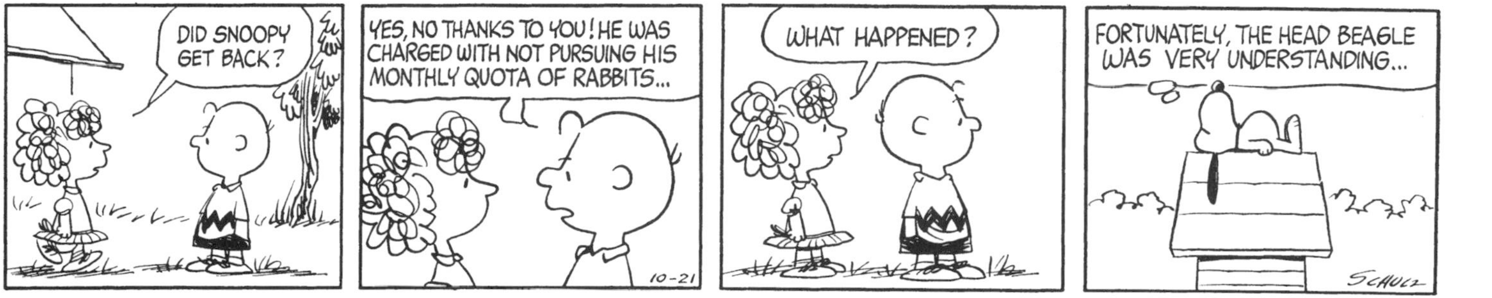
DID SNOOPY GET BACK?
YES, NO THANKS TO YOU! HE WAS CHARGED WITH NOT PURSUING HIS MONTHLY QUOTA OF RABBITS...
10-21
WHAT HAPPENED?
FORTUNATELY, THE HEAD BEAGLE WAS VERY UNDERSTANDING...
SCHULZ

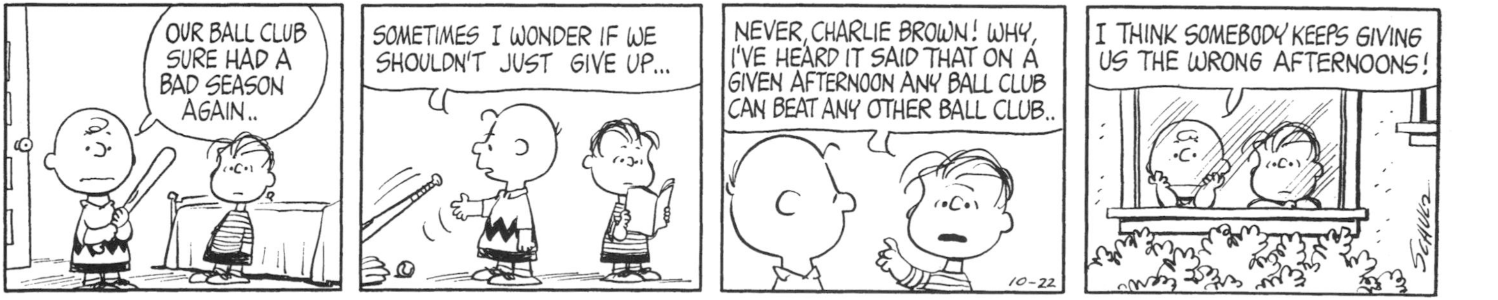
OUR BALL CLUB SURE HAD A BAD SEASON AGAIN..
SOMETIMES I WONDER IF WE SHOULDN'T JUST GIVE UP...
NEVER, CHARLIE BROWN! WHY, I'VE HEARD IT SAID THAT ON A GIVEN AFTERNOON ANY BALL CLUB CAN BEAT ANY OTHER BALL CLUB..
10-22
I THINK SOMEBODY KEEPS GIVING US THE WRONG AFTERNOONS!
SCHULZ

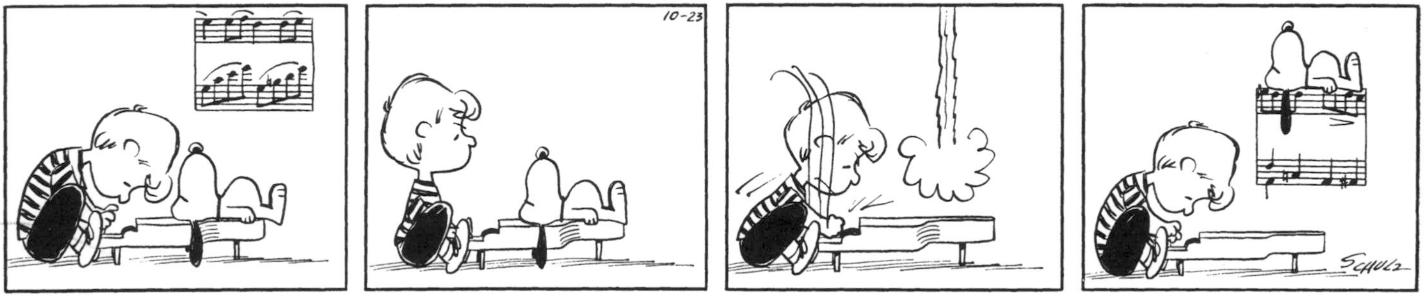
10-23
SCHULZ

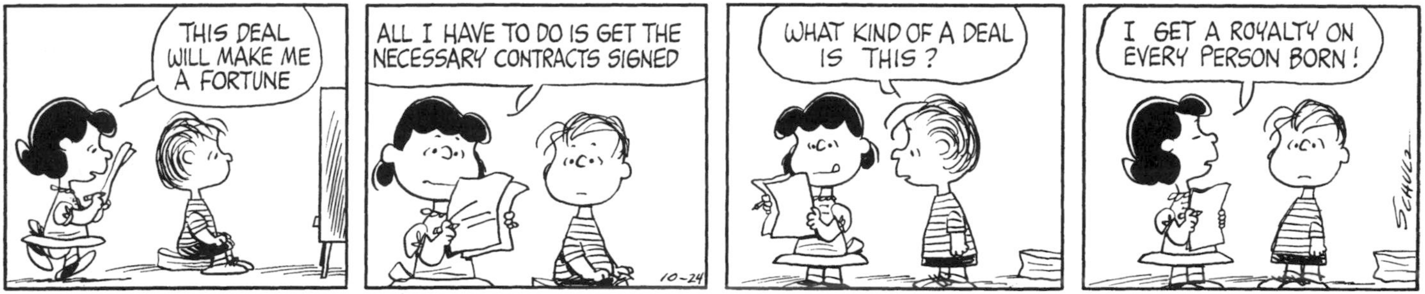
THIS DEAL WILL MAKE ME A FORTUNE
ALL I HAVE TO DO IS GET THE NECESSARY CONTRACTS SIGNED
10-24
WHAT KIND OF A DEAL IS THIS ?
I GET A ROYALTY ON EVERY PERSON BORN !
SCHULZ

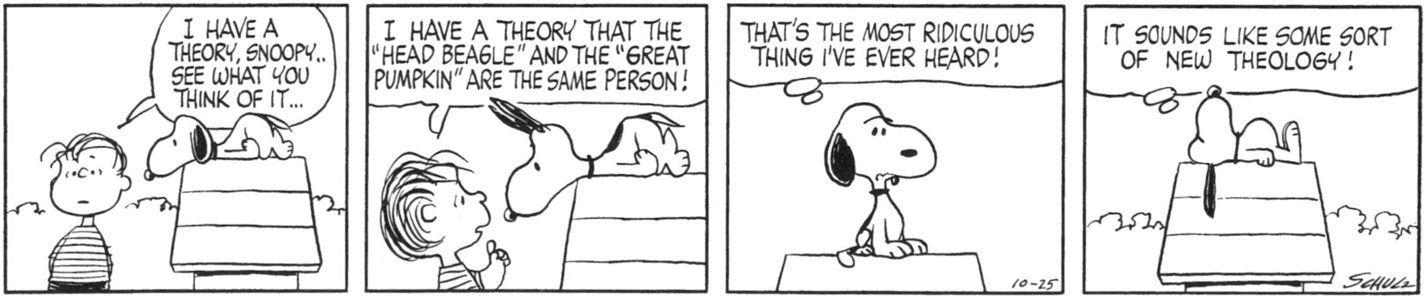
I HAVE A THEORY, SNOOPY.. SEE WHAT YOU THINK OF IT...
I HAVE A THEORY THAT THE "HEAD BEAGLE" AND THE "GREAT PUMPKIN" ARE THE SAME PERSON !
THAT'S THE MOST RIDICULOUS THING I'VE EVER HEARD !
10-25
IT SOUNDS LIKE SOME SORT OF NEW THEOLOGY !
SCHULZ

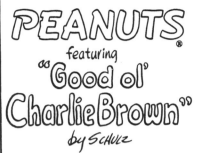

PEANUTS featuring "Good ol' Charlie Brown" by Schulz

GO! GO! GO!

FANTASTIC!

CHARLIE BROWN, I JUST SAW THE MOST UNBELIEVABLE FOOTBALL GAME EVER PLAYED...

WHAT A COMEBACK!

THE HOME TEAM WAS BEHIND SIX-TO-NOTHING WITH ONLY THREE SECONDS TO PLAY...THEY HAD THE BALL ON THEIR OWN ONE-YARD LINE...

10-26

THE QUARTERBACK TOOK THE BALL, FADED BACK BEHIND HIS OWN GOAL POSTS AND THREW A PERFECT PASS TO THE LEFT END, WHO WHIRLED AWAY FROM FOUR GUYS AND RAN ALL THE WAY FOR A TOUCHDOWN! THE FANS WENT WILD! YOU SHOULD HAVE SEEN THEM!

PEOPLE WERE JUMPING UP AND DOWN, AND WHEN THEY KICKED THE EXTRA POINT, THOUSANDS OF PEOPLE RAN OUT ONTO THE FIELD LAUGHING AND SCREAMING! THE FANS AND THE PLAYERS WERE SO HAPPY THEY WERE ROLLING ON THE GROUND AND HUGGING EACH OTHER AND DANCING AND EVERYTHING!

IT WAS FANTASTIC!

HOW DID THE OTHER TEAM FEEL?

SCHULZ

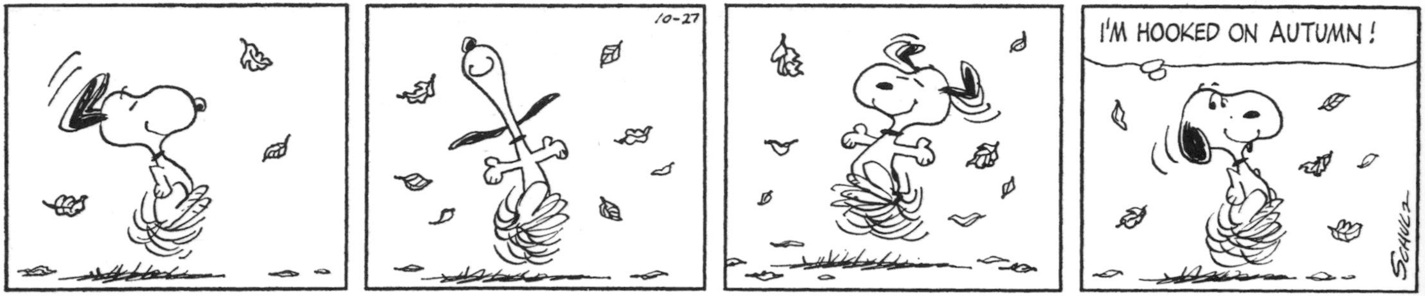
10-27
I'M HOOKED ON AUTUMN!
SCHULZ

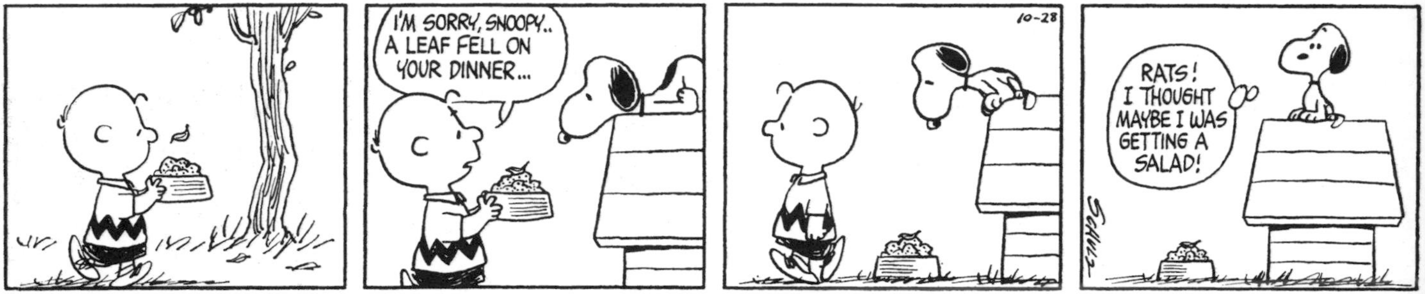
I'M SORRY, SNOOPY.. A LEAF FELL ON YOUR DINNER...
10-28
RATS! I THOUGHT MAYBE I WAS GETTING A SALAD!
SCHULZ

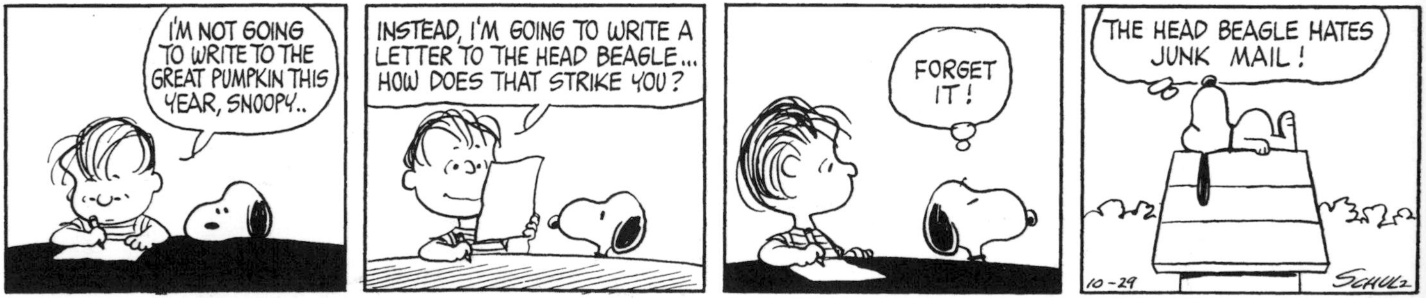
I'M NOT GOING TO WRITE TO THE GREAT PUMPKIN THIS YEAR, SNOOPY..
INSTEAD, I'M GOING TO WRITE A LETTER TO THE HEAD BEAGLE... HOW DOES THAT STRIKE YOU?
FORGET IT!
THE HEAD BEAGLE HATES JUNK MAIL!
10-29
SCHULZ

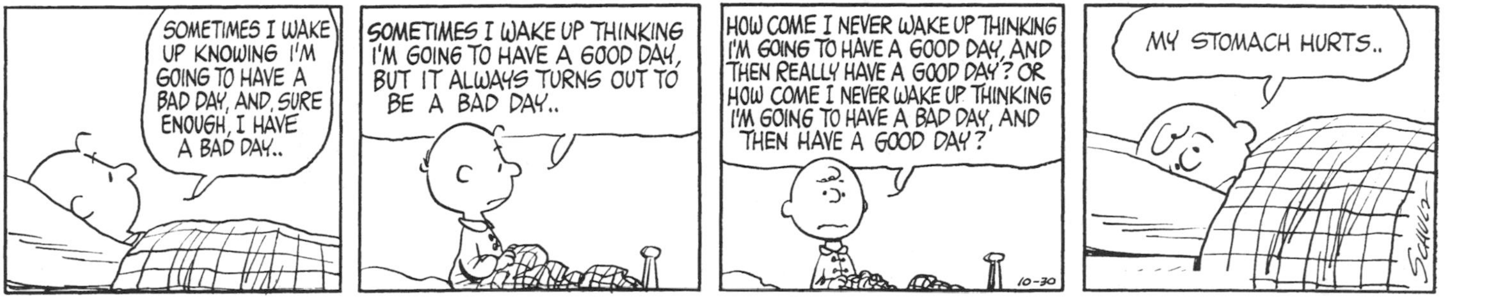
SOMETIMES I WAKE UP KNOWING I'M GOING TO HAVE A BAD DAY, AND, SURE ENOUGH, I HAVE A BAD DAY..
SOMETIMES I WAKE UP THINKING I'M GOING TO HAVE A GOOD DAY, BUT IT ALWAYS TURNS OUT TO BE A BAD DAY..
HOW COME I NEVER WAKE UP THINKING I'M GOING TO HAVE A GOOD DAY, AND THEN REALLY HAVE A GOOD DAY? OR HOW COME I NEVER WAKE UP THINKING I'M GOING TO HAVE A BAD DAY, AND THEN HAVE A GOOD DAY?
10-30
MY STOMACH HURTS..
SCHULZ

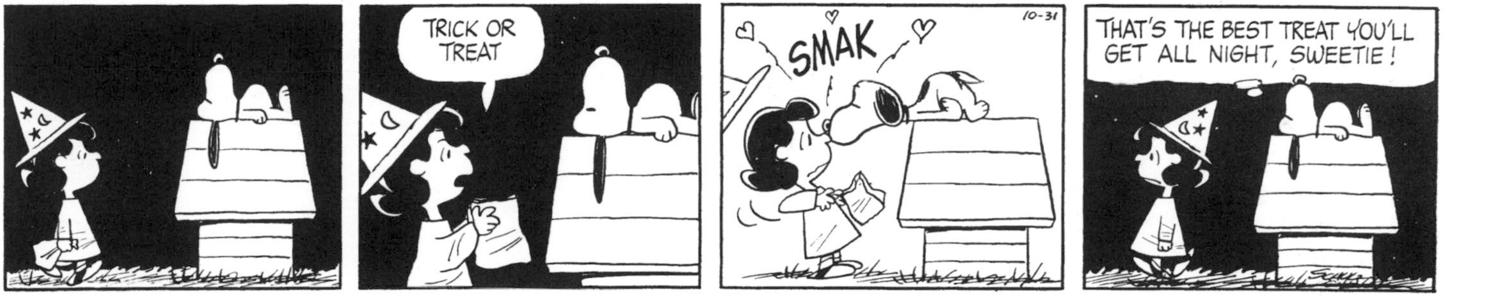
TRICK OR TREAT
10-31
SMAK
THAT'S THE BEST TREAT YOU'LL GET ALL NIGHT, SWEETIE!

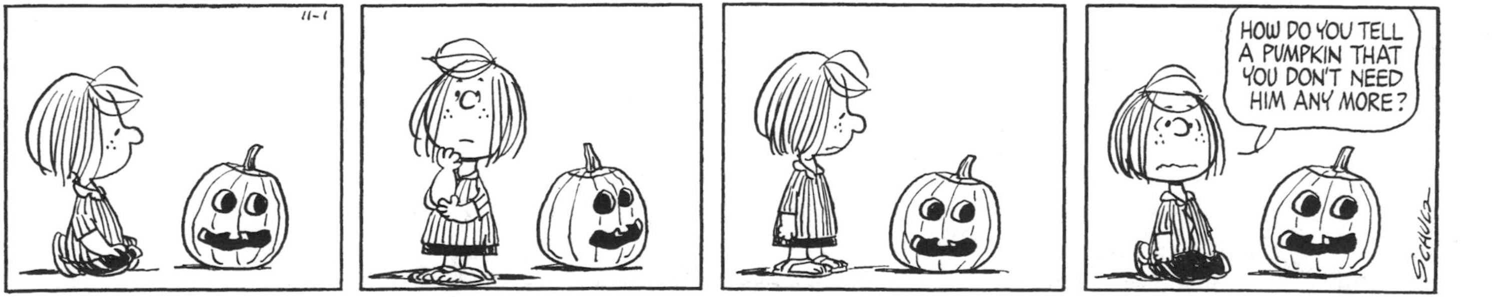
11-1
HOW DO YOU TELL A PUMPKIN THAT YOU DON'T NEED HIM ANY MORE?
SCHULZ

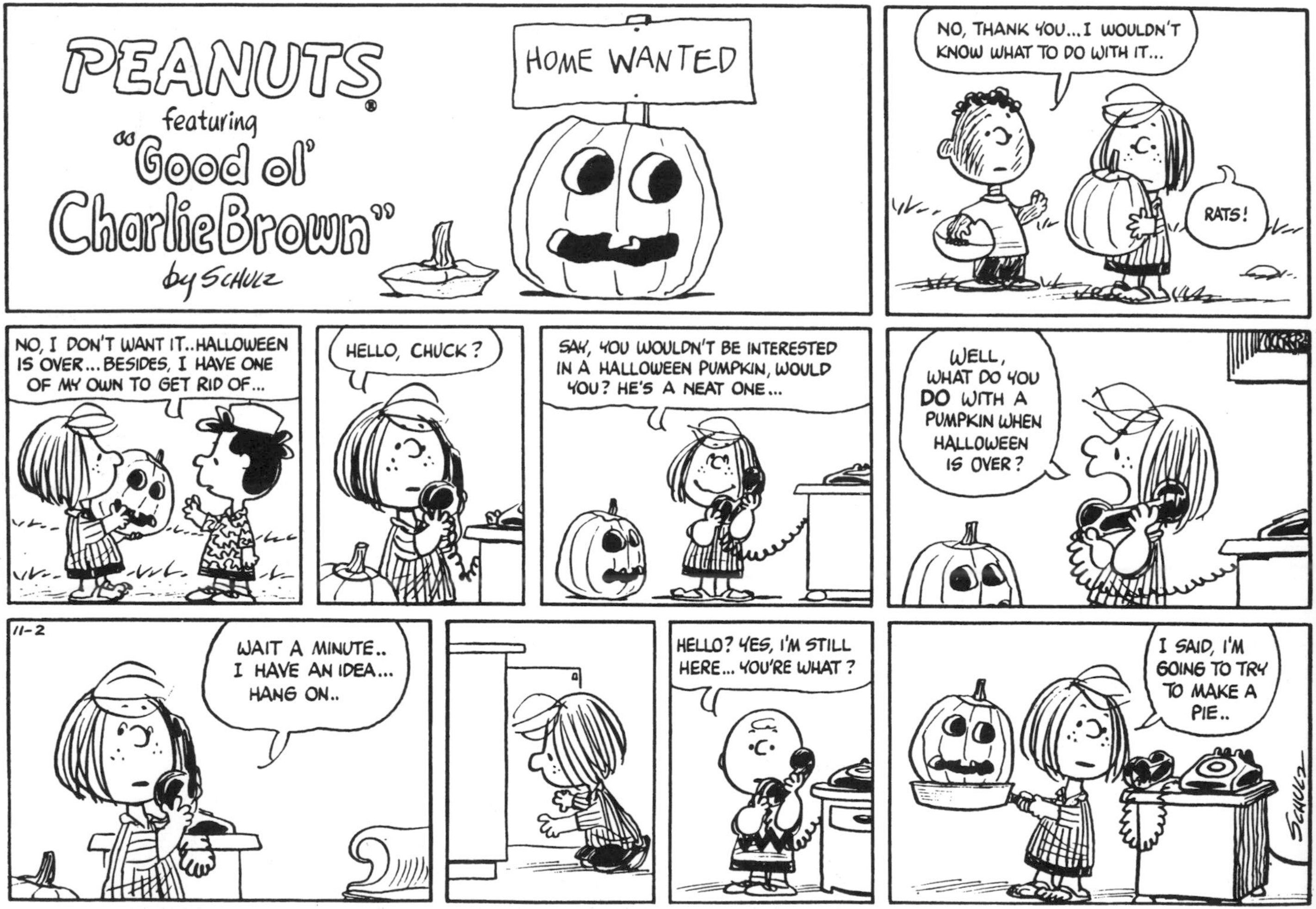
PEANUTS®
featuring "Good ol' Charlie Brown"
by SCHULZ
HOME WANTED
NO, THANK YOU... I WOULDN'T KNOW WHAT TO DO WITH IT...
RATS!
NO, I DON'T WANT IT.. HALLOWEEN IS OVER... BESIDES, I HAVE ONE OF MY OWN TO GET RID OF...
HELLO, CHUCK?
SAY, YOU WOULDN'T BE INTERESTED IN A HALLOWEEN PUMPKIN, WOULD YOU? HE'S A NEAT ONE...
WELL, WHAT DO YOU DO WITH A PUMPKIN WHEN HALLOWEEN IS OVER?
11-2
WAIT A MINUTE.. I HAVE AN IDEA... HANG ON..
HELLO? YES, I'M STILL HERE... YOU'RE WHAT?
I SAID, I'M GOING TO TRY TO MAKE A PIE..
SCHULZ

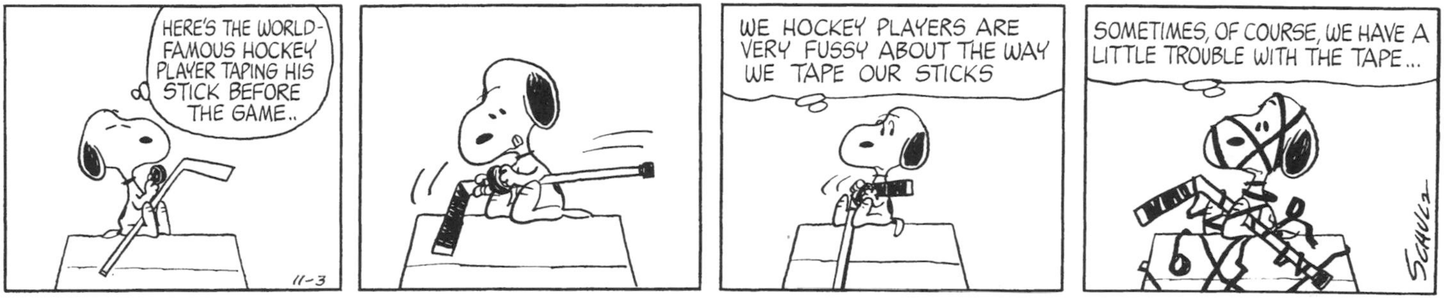
HERE'S THE WORLD-FAMOUS HOCKEY PLAYER TAPING HIS STICK BEFORE THE GAME..
WE HOCKEY PLAYERS ARE VERY FUSSY ABOUT THE WAY WE TAPE OUR STICKS
SOMETIMES, OF COURSE, WE HAVE A LITTLE TROUBLE WITH THE TAPE...

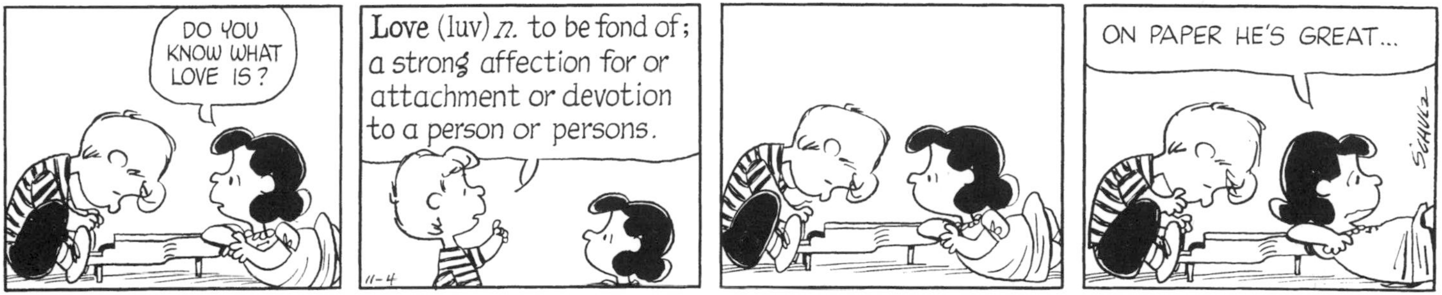
DO YOU KNOW WHAT LOVE IS ?
Love (luv) n. to be fond of; a strong affection for or attachment or devotion to a person or persons.
ON PAPER HE'S GREAT...

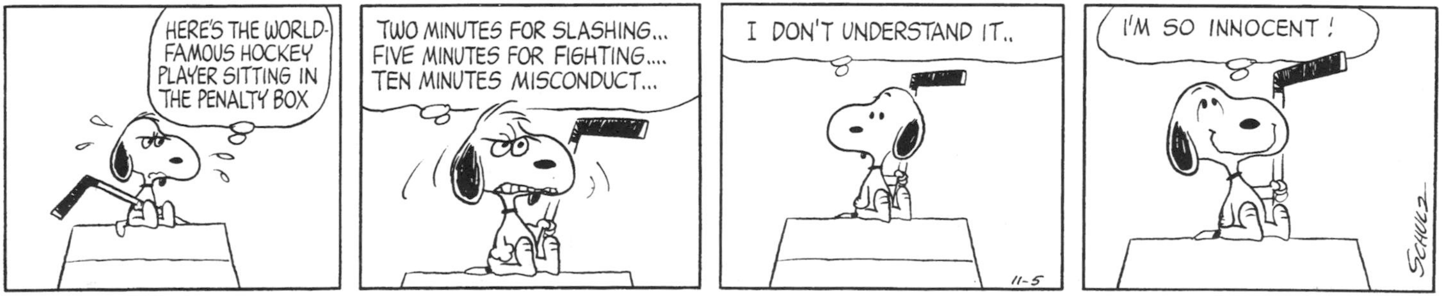
HERE'S THE WORLD-FAMOUS HOCKEY PLAYER SITTING IN THE PENALTY BOX
TWO MINUTES FOR SLASHING... FIVE MINUTES FOR FIGHTING.... TEN MINUTES MISCONDUCT...
I DON'T UNDERSTAND IT..
I'M SO INNOCENT !

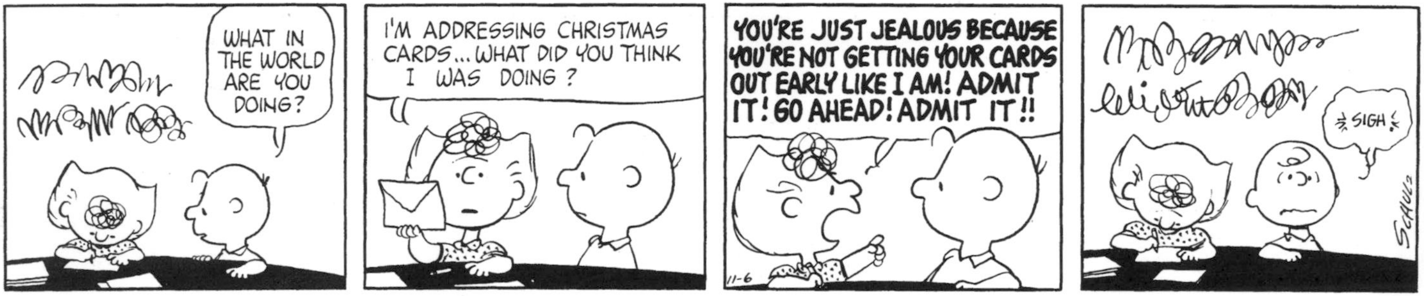
WHAT IN THE WORLD ARE YOU DOING?
I'M ADDRESSING CHRISTMAS CARDS... WHAT DID YOU THINK I WAS DOING?
YOU'RE JUST JEALOUS BECAUSE YOU'RE NOT GETTING YOUR CARDS OUT EARLY LIKE I AM! ADMIT IT! GO AHEAD! ADMIT IT!!
11-6
SIGH
SCHULZ

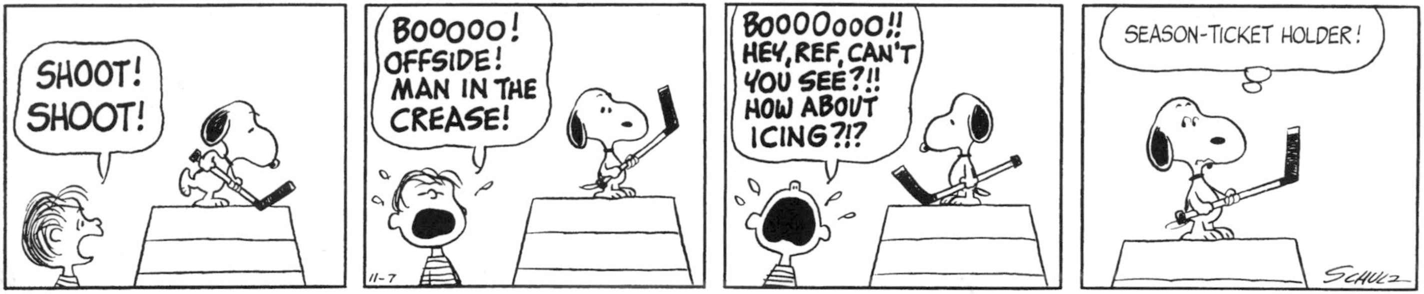
SHOOT! SHOOT!
BOOOOO! OFFSIDE! MAN IN THE CREASE!
11-7
BOOOOooo!! HEY, REF, CAN'T YOU SEE?!! HOW ABOUT ICING?!?
SEASON-TICKET HOLDER!
SCHULZ

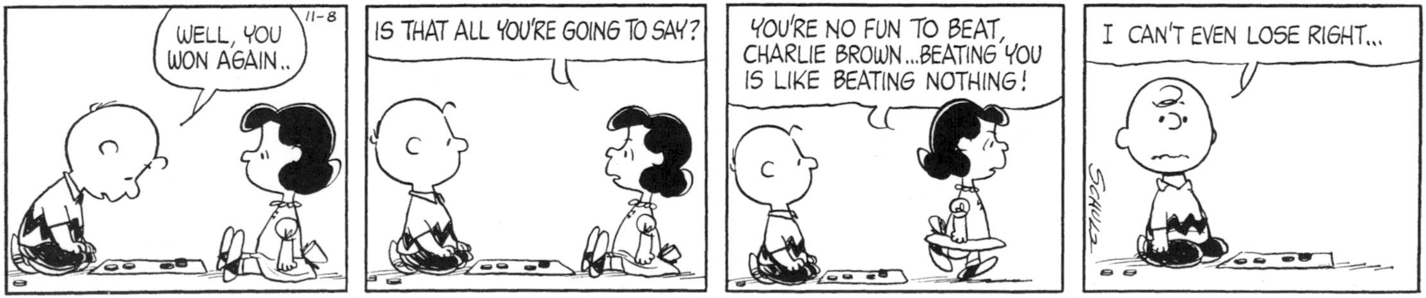
11-8
WELL, YOU WON AGAIN..
IS THAT ALL YOU'RE GOING TO SAY?
YOU'RE NO FUN TO BEAT, CHARLIE BROWN...BEATING YOU IS LIKE BEATING NOTHING!
I CAN'T EVEN LOSE RIGHT...
SCHULZ

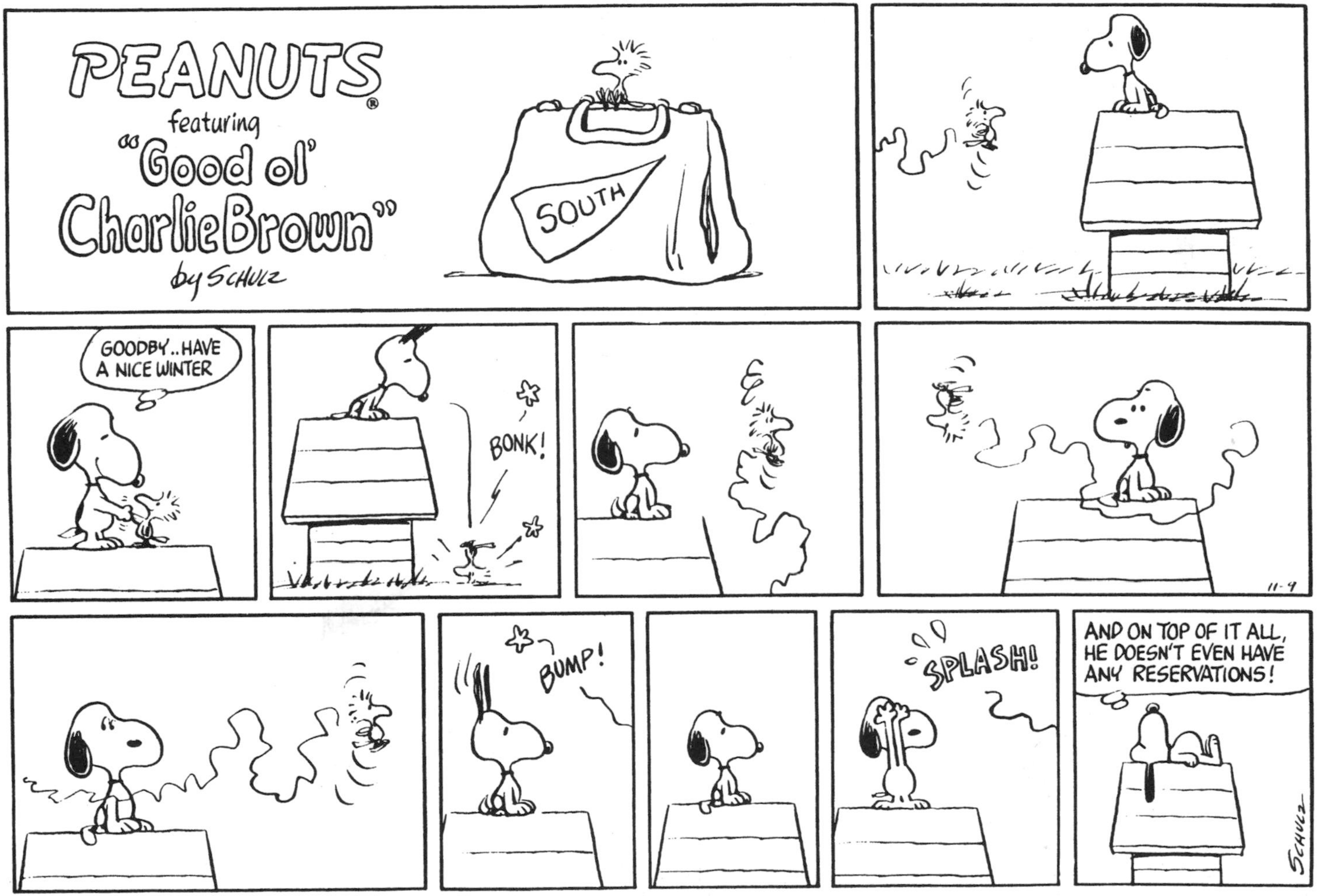
PEANUTS®
featuring
"Good ol' Charlie Brown"
by SCHULZ
SOUTH
GOODBY.. HAVE A NICE WINTER
BONK!
11-9
BUMP!
SPLASH!
AND ON TOP OF IT ALL, HE DOESN'T EVEN HAVE ANY RESERVATIONS!
SCHULZ

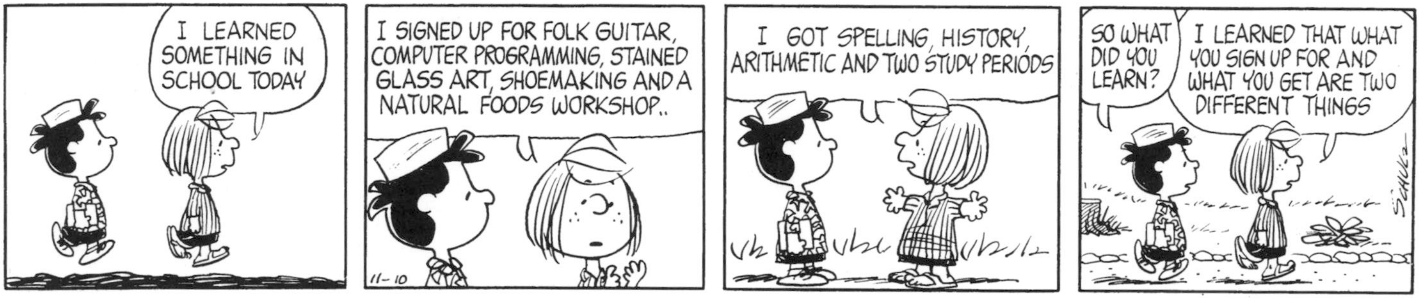
I LEARNED SOMETHING IN SCHOOL TODAY
I SIGNED UP FOR FOLK GUITAR, COMPUTER PROGRAMMING, STAINED GLASS ART, SHOEMAKING AND A NATURAL FOODS WORKSHOP..
11-10
I GOT SPELLING, HISTORY, ARITHMETIC AND TWO STUDY PERIODS
SO WHAT DID YOU LEARN?
I LEARNED THAT WHAT YOU SIGN UP FOR AND WHAT YOU GET ARE TWO DIFFERENT THINGS
SCHULZ

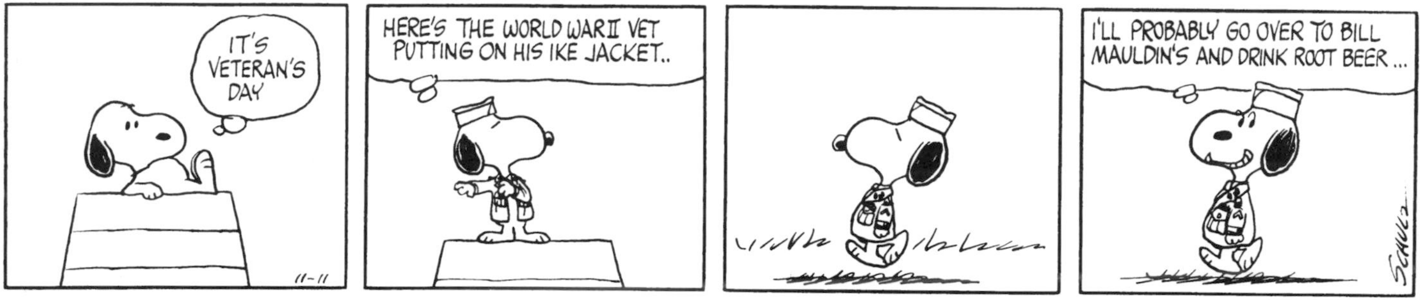
IT'S VETERAN'S DAY
11-11
HERE'S THE WORLD WAR II VET PUTTING ON HIS IKE JACKET..
I'LL PROBABLY GO OVER TO BILL MAULDIN'S AND DRINK ROOT BEER ...
SCHULZ

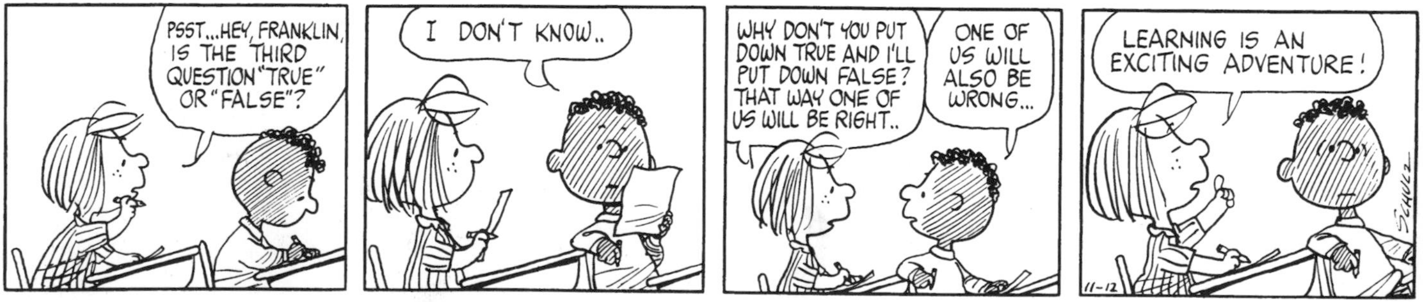
PSST...HEY, FRANKLIN, IS THE THIRD QUESTION "TRUE" OR "FALSE"?
I DON'T KNOW..
WHY DON'T YOU PUT DOWN TRUE AND I'LL PUT DOWN FALSE? THAT WAY ONE OF US WILL BE RIGHT..
ONE OF US WILL ALSO BE WRONG...
LEARNING IS AN EXCITING ADVENTURE!
11-12
SCHULZ

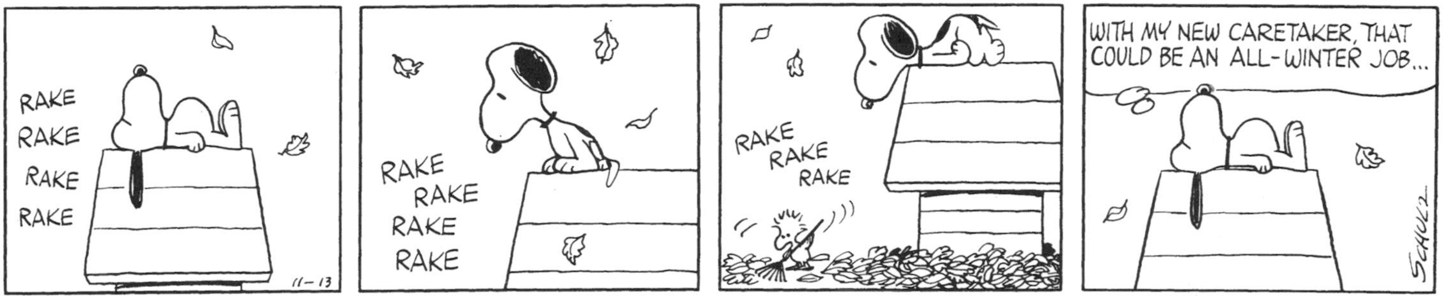
RAKE RAKE RAKE RAKE
11-13
RAKE RAKE RAKE RAKE
RAKE RAKE RAKE
WITH MY NEW CARETAKER, THAT COULD BE AN ALL-WINTER JOB...
SCHULZ

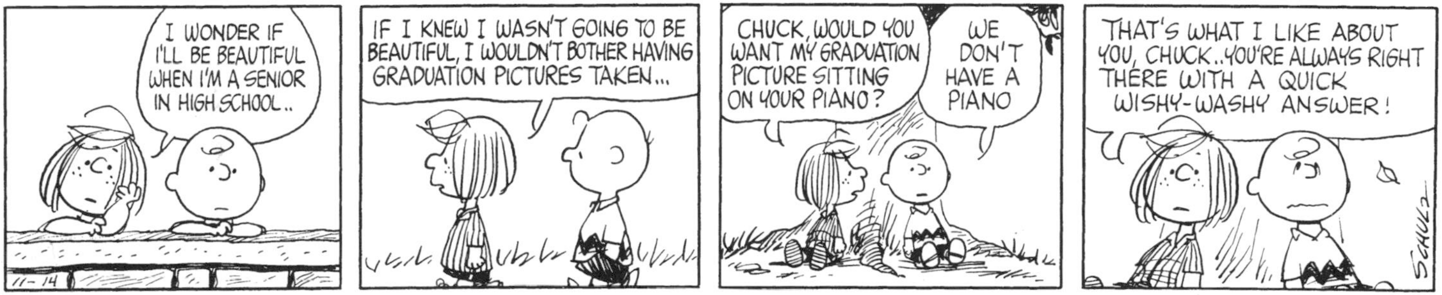
I WONDER IF I'LL BE BEAUTIFUL WHEN I'M A SENIOR IN HIGH SCHOOL..
11-14
IF I KNEW I WASN'T GOING TO BE BEAUTIFUL, I WOULDN'T BOTHER HAVING GRADUATION PICTURES TAKEN...
CHUCK, WOULD YOU WANT MY GRADUATION PICTURE SITTING ON YOUR PIANO?
WE DON'T HAVE A PIANO
THAT'S WHAT I LIKE ABOUT YOU, CHUCK..YOU'RE ALWAYS RIGHT THERE WITH A QUICK WISHY-WASHY ANSWER!
SCHULZ

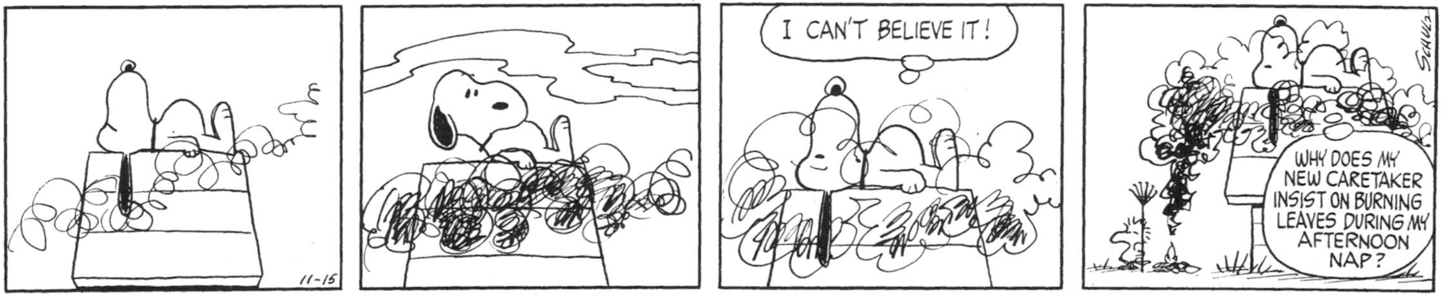
11-15
I CAN'T BELIEVE IT!
SCHULZ
WHY DOES MY NEW CARETAKER INSIST ON BURNING LEAVES DURING MY AFTERNOON NAP?

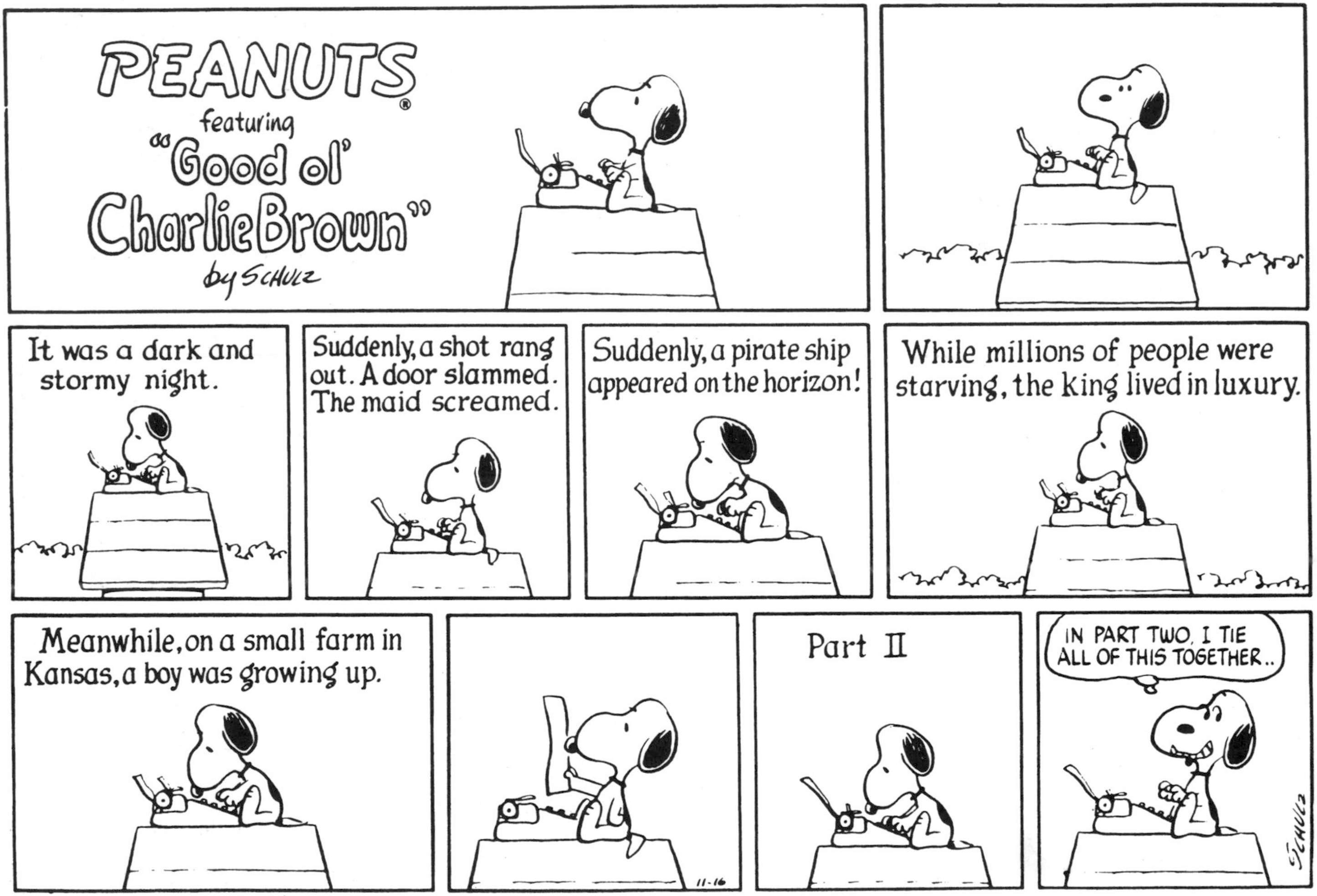
PEANUTS®
featuring
"Good ol' Charlie Brown"
by SCHULZ
It was a dark and stormy night.
Suddenly, a shot rang out. A door slammed. The maid screamed.
Suddenly, a pirate ship appeared on the horizon!
While millions of people were starving, the king lived in luxury.
Meanwhile, on a small farm in Kansas, a boy was growing up.
11-16
Part II
IN PART TWO, I TIE ALL OF THIS TOGETHER..
SCHULZ

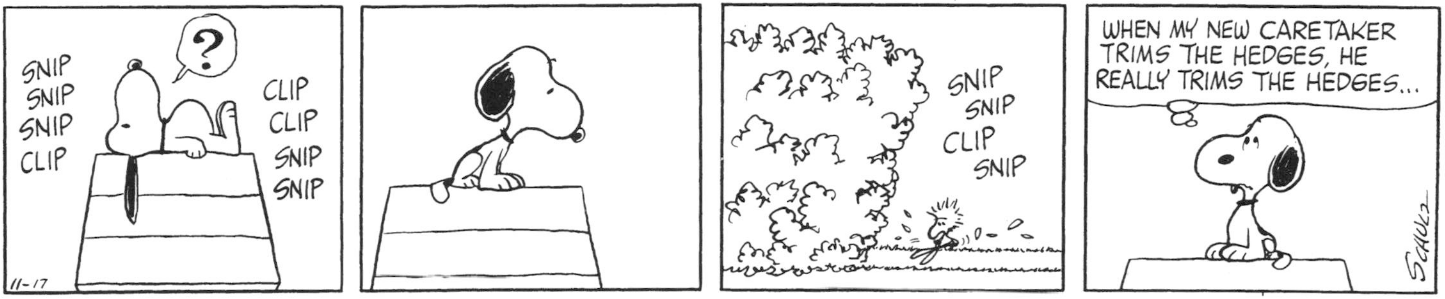
SNIP
SNIP
SNIP
CLIP
?
CLIP
CLIP
SNIP
SNIP
11-17
SNIP
SNIP
CLIP
SNIP
WHEN MY NEW CARETAKER TRIMS THE HEDGES, HE REALLY TRIMS THE HEDGES...
SCHULZ

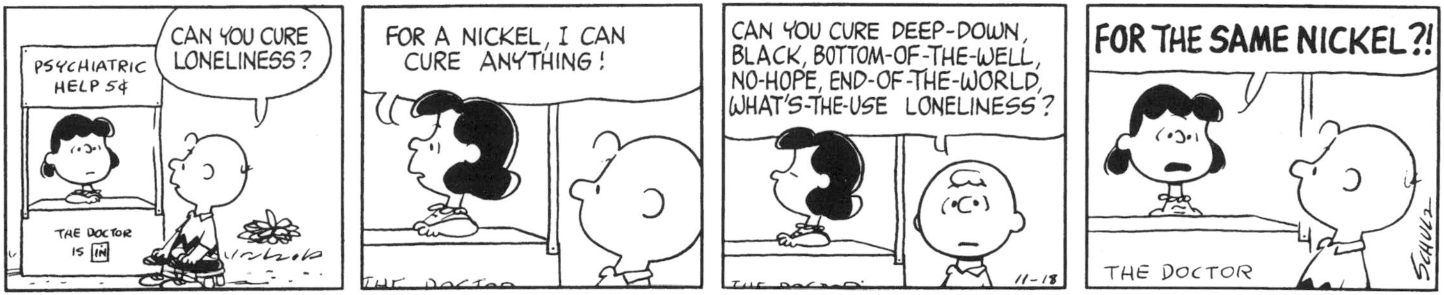
PSYCHIATRIC HELP 5¢
THE DOCTOR IS IN
CAN YOU CURE LONELINESS?
FOR A NICKEL, I CAN CURE ANYTHING!
CAN YOU CURE DEEP-DOWN, BLACK, BOTTOM-OF-THE-WELL, NO-HOPE, END-OF-THE-WORLD, WHAT'S-THE-USE LONELINESS?
11-18
FOR THE SAME NICKEL?!
THE DOCTOR
SCHULZ

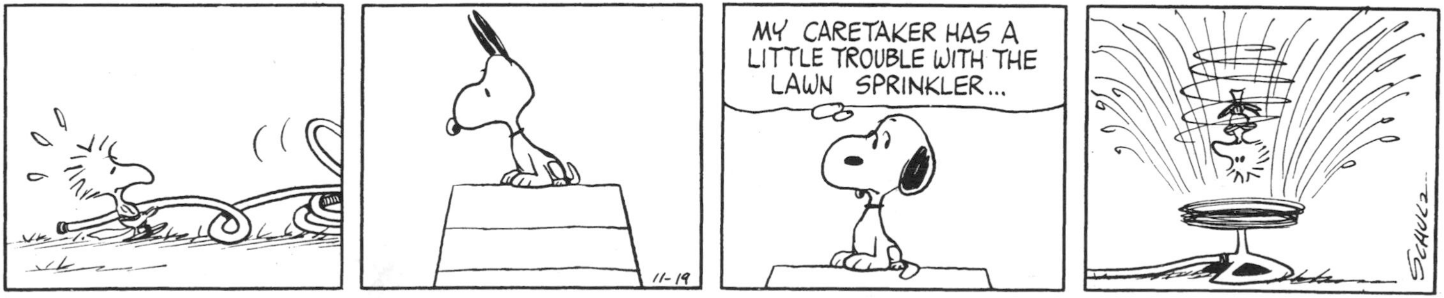
11-19
MY CARETAKER HAS A LITTLE TROUBLE WITH THE LAWN SPRINKLER...
SCHULZ

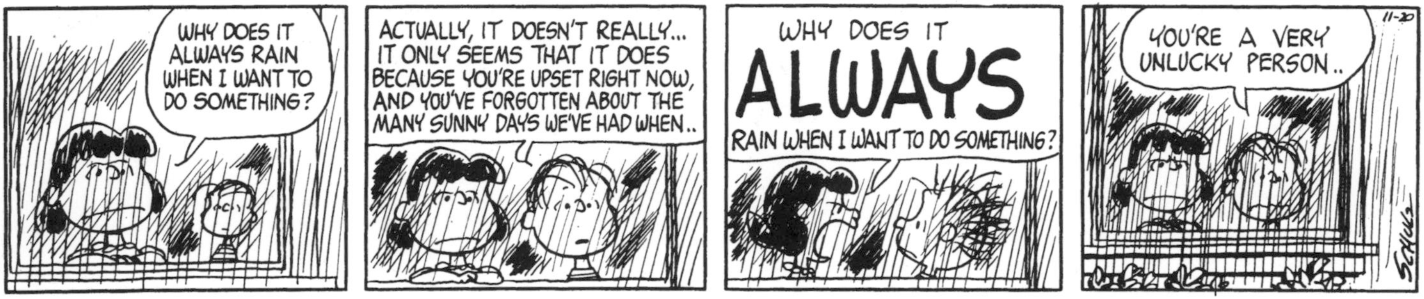
WHY DOES IT ALWAYS RAIN WHEN I WANT TO DO SOMETHING?
ACTUALLY, IT DOESN'T REALLY... IT ONLY SEEMS THAT IT DOES BECAUSE YOU'RE UPSET RIGHT NOW, AND YOU'VE FORGOTTEN ABOUT THE MANY SUNNY DAYS WE'VE HAD WHEN..
WHY DOES IT ALWAYS RAIN WHEN I WANT TO DO SOMETHING?
11-20
YOU'RE A VERY UNLUCKY PERSON..
SCHULZ

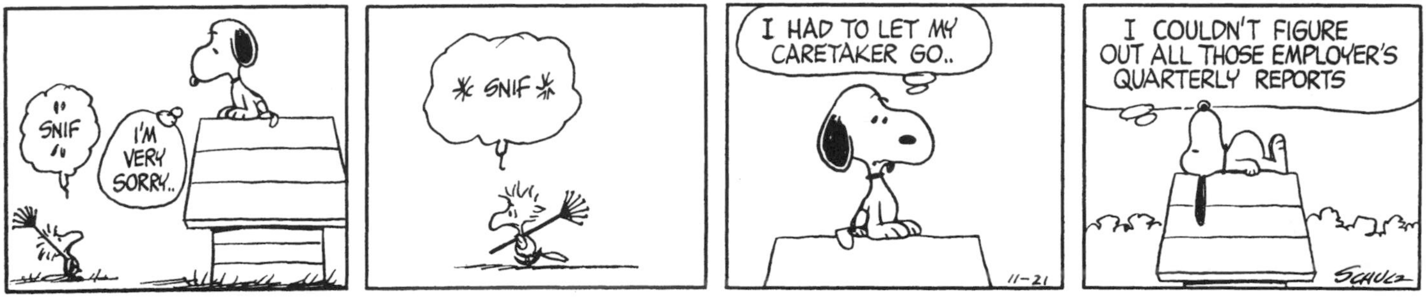
SNIF
I'M VERY SORRY..
SNIF
I HAD TO LET MY CARETAKER GO..
11-21
I COULDN'T FIGURE OUT ALL THOSE EMPLOYER'S QUARTERLY REPORTS
SCHULZ

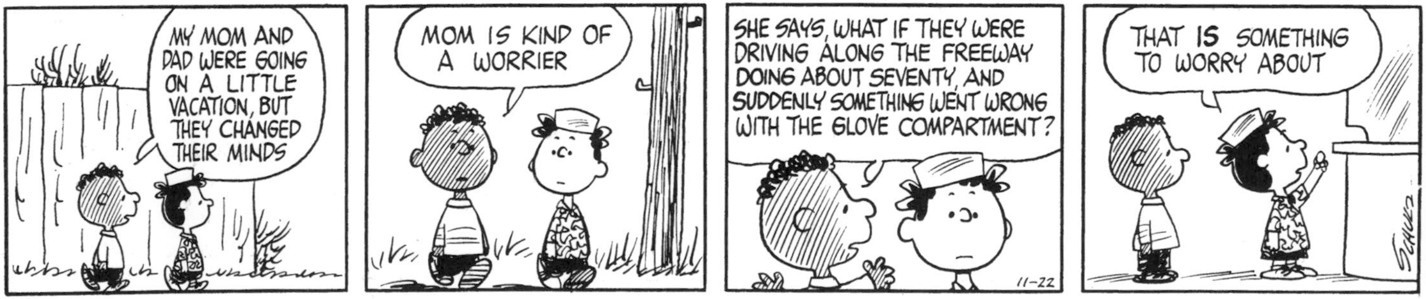
MY MOM AND DAD WERE GOING ON A LITTLE VACATION, BUT THEY CHANGED THEIR MINDS
MOM IS KIND OF A WORRIER
SHE SAYS, WHAT IF THEY WERE DRIVING ALONG THE FREEWAY DOING ABOUT SEVENTY, AND SUDDENLY SOMETHING WENT WRONG WITH THE GLOVE COMPARTMENT?
11-22
THAT IS SOMETHING TO WORRY ABOUT
SCHULZ

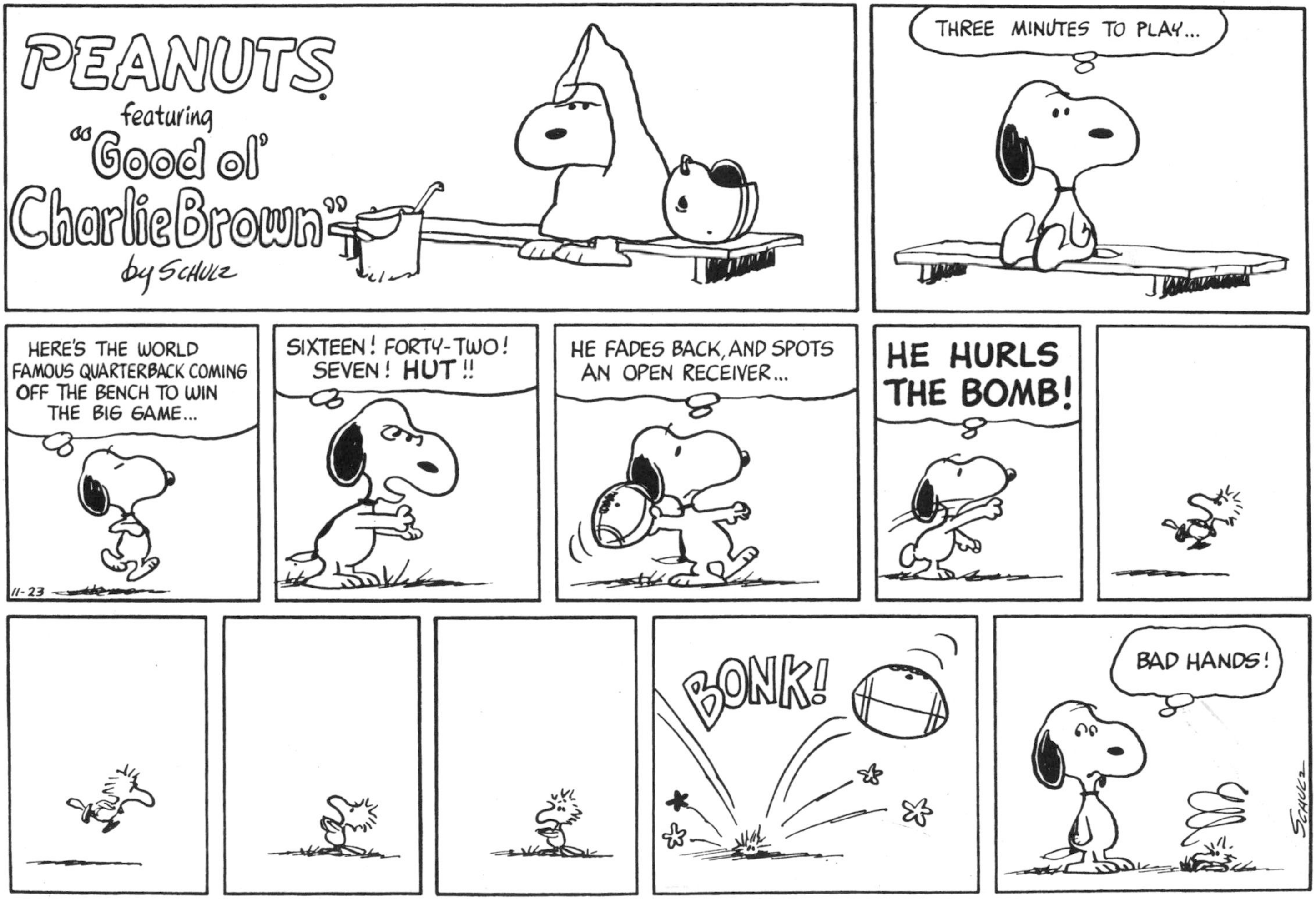
PEANUTS
featuring
"Good ol' CharlieBrown"
by SCHULZ
THREE MINUTES TO PLAY...
HERE'S THE WORLD FAMOUS QUARTERBACK COMING OFF THE BENCH TO WIN THE BIG GAME...
11-23
SIXTEEN! FORTY-TWO! SEVEN! HUT!!
HE FADES BACK, AND SPOTS AN OPEN RECEIVER...
HE HURLS THE BOMB!
BONK!
BAD HANDS!
SCHULZ

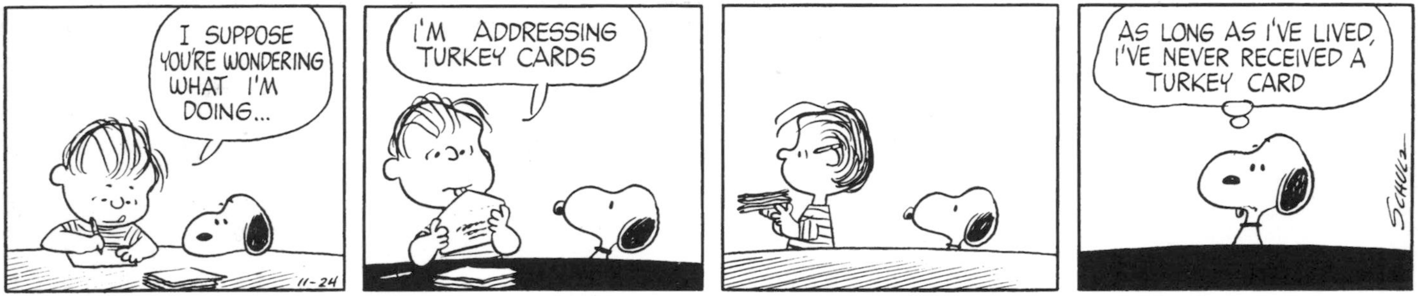
I SUPPOSE YOU'RE WONDERING WHAT I'M DOING...
11-24
I'M ADDRESSING TURKEY CARDS
AS LONG AS I'VE LIVED, I'VE NEVER RECEIVED A TURKEY CARD
SCHULZ

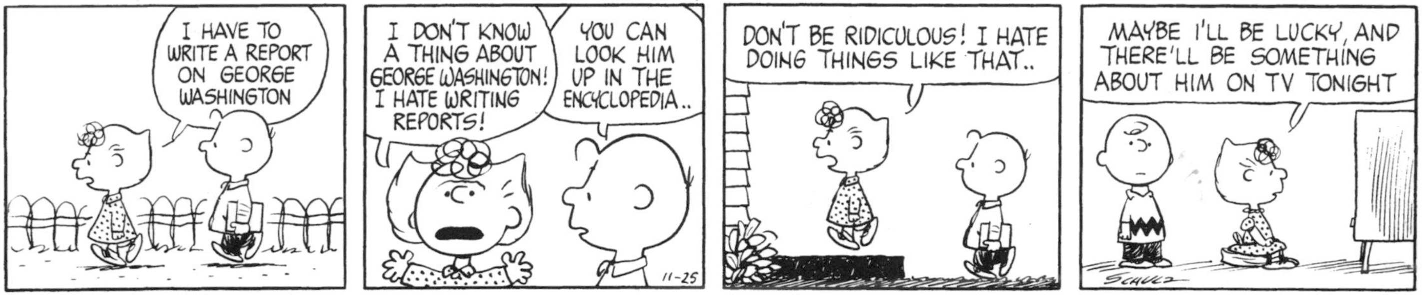
I HAVE TO WRITE A REPORT ON GEORGE WASHINGTON
I DON'T KNOW A THING ABOUT GEORGE WASHINGTON! I HATE WRITING REPORTS!
YOU CAN LOOK HIM UP IN THE ENCYCLOPEDIA..
11-25
DON'T BE RIDICULOUS! I HATE DOING THINGS LIKE THAT..
MAYBE I'LL BE LUCKY, AND THERE'LL BE SOMETHING ABOUT HIM ON TV TONIGHT
SCHULZ

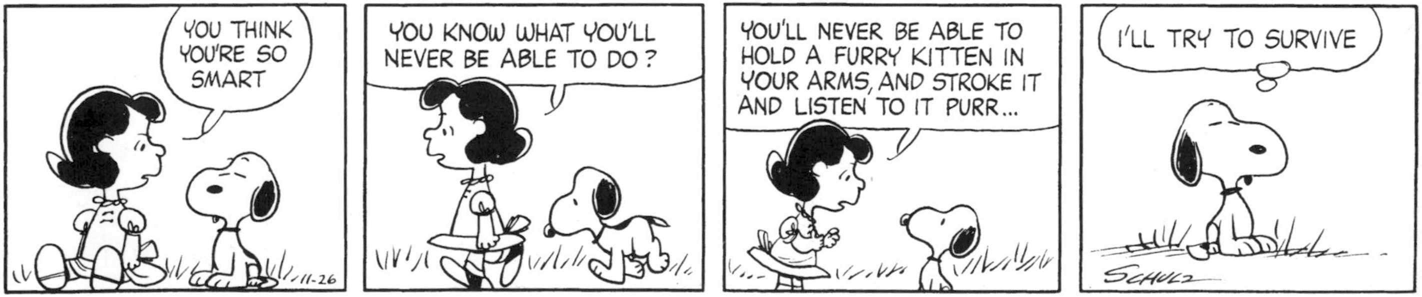
YOU THINK YOU'RE SO SMART
11-26
YOU KNOW WHAT YOU'LL NEVER BE ABLE TO DO?
YOU'LL NEVER BE ABLE TO HOLD A FURRY KITTEN IN YOUR ARMS, AND STROKE IT AND LISTEN TO IT PURR...
I'LL TRY TO SURVIVE
SCHULZ

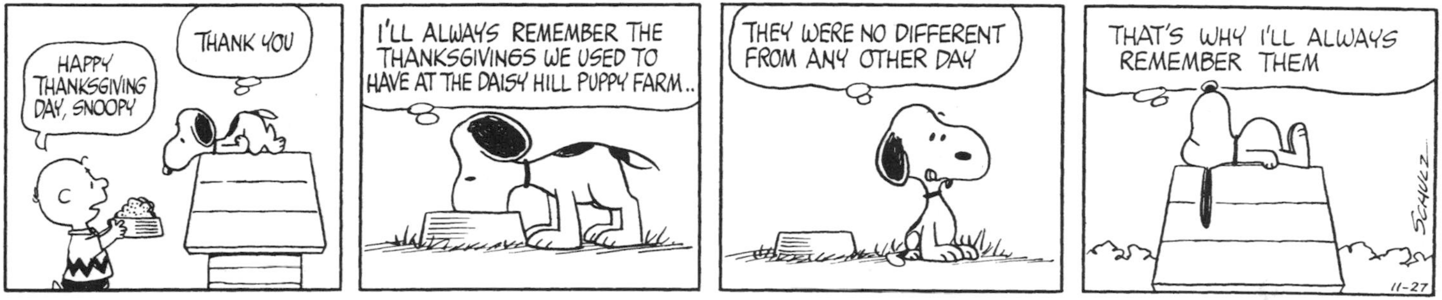
HAPPY THANKSGIVING DAY, SNOOPY
THANK YOU
I'LL ALWAYS REMEMBER THE THANKSGIVINGS WE USED TO HAVE AT THE DAISY HILL PUPPY FARM..
THEY WERE NO DIFFERENT FROM ANY OTHER DAY
THAT'S WHY I'LL ALWAYS REMEMBER THEM
SCHULZ
11-27

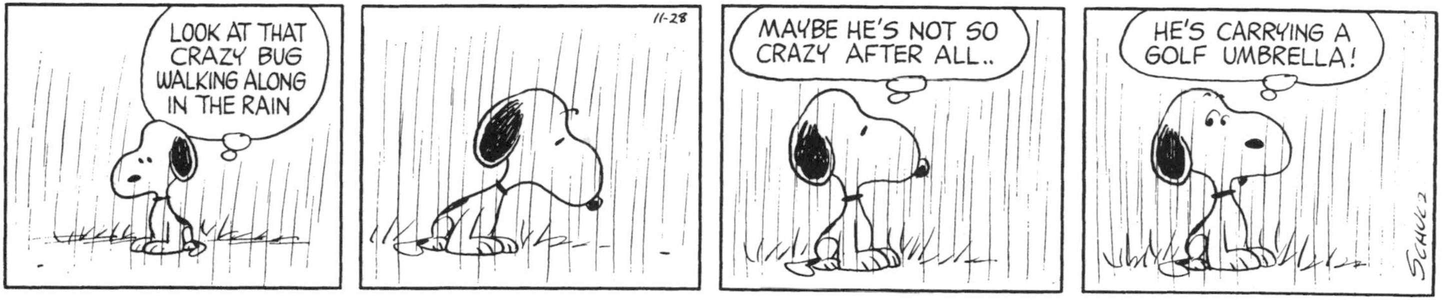
LOOK AT THAT CRAZY BUG WALKING ALONG IN THE RAIN
11-28
MAYBE HE'S NOT SO CRAZY AFTER ALL..
HE'S CARRYING A GOLF UMBRELLA!
SCHULZ

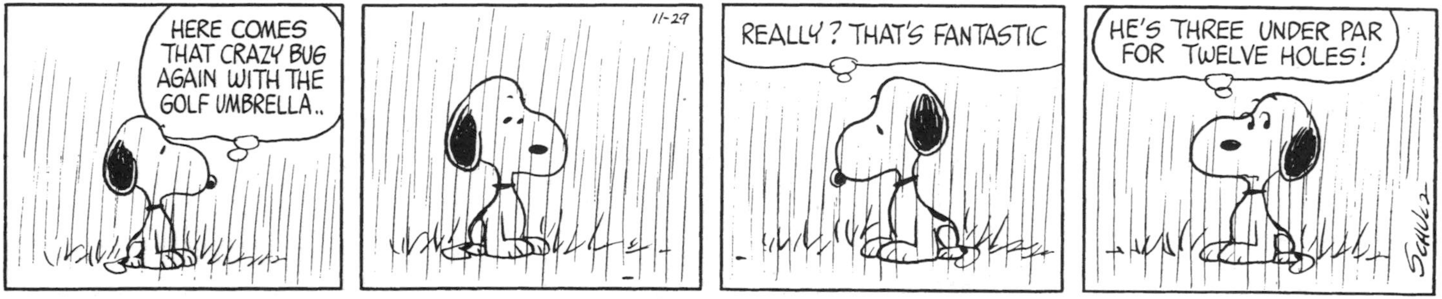
HERE COMES THAT CRAZY BUG AGAIN WITH THE GOLF UMBRELLA..
11-29
REALLY? THAT'S FANTASTIC
HE'S THREE UNDER PAR FOR TWELVE HOLES!
SCHULZ

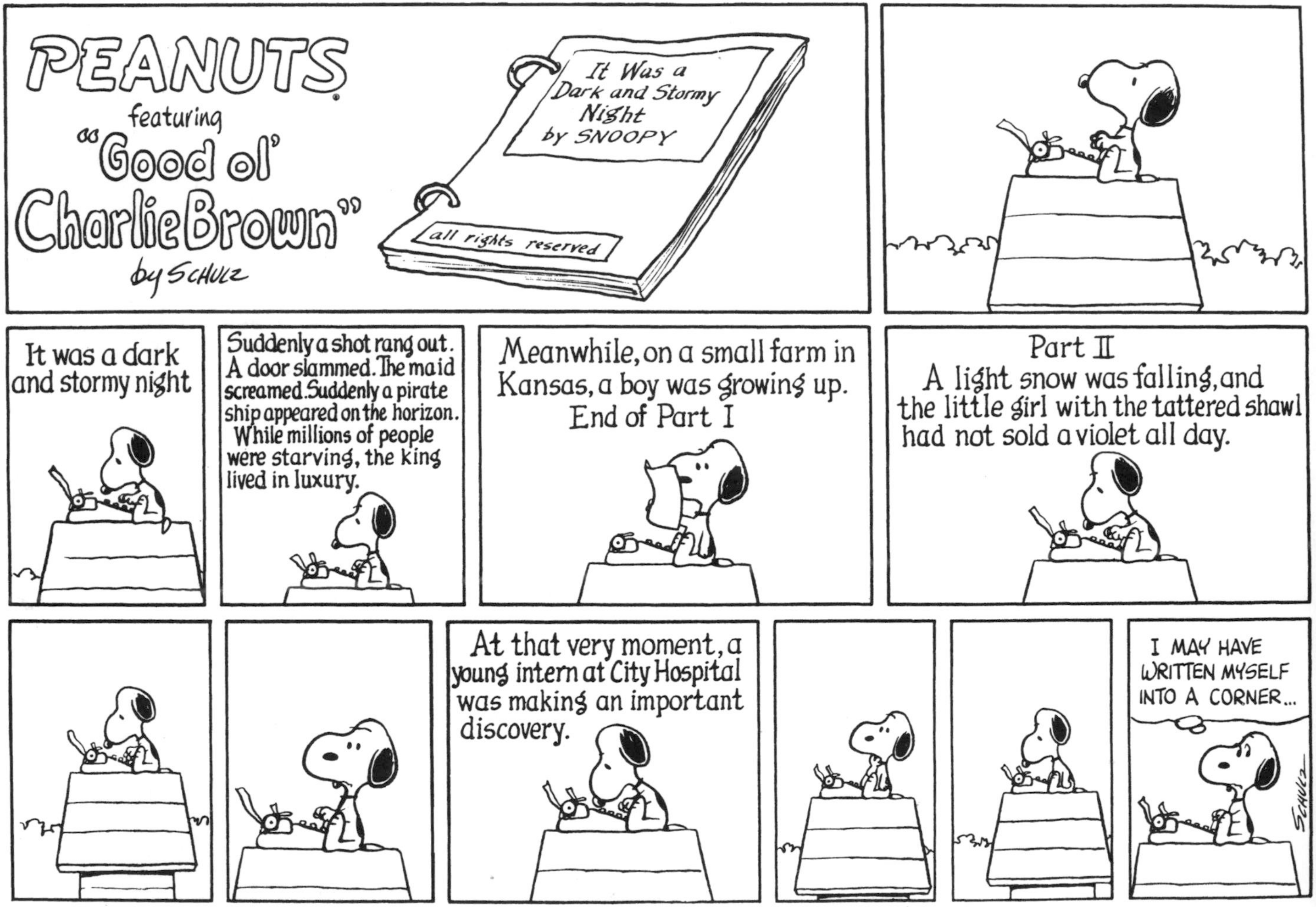
PEANUTS
featuring
"Good ol' Charlie Brown"
by SCHULZ
It Was a Dark and Stormy Night by SNOOPY
all rights reserved
It was a dark and stormy night
Suddenly a shot rang out. A door slammed. The maid screamed. Suddenly a pirate ship appeared on the horizon. While millions of people were starving, the king lived in luxury.
Meanwhile, on a small farm in Kansas, a boy was growing up. End of Part I
Part II A light snow was falling, and the little girl with the tattered shawl had not sold a violet all day.
At that very moment, a young intern at City Hospital was making an important discovery.
I MAY HAVE WRITTEN MYSELF INTO A CORNER...
SCHULZ

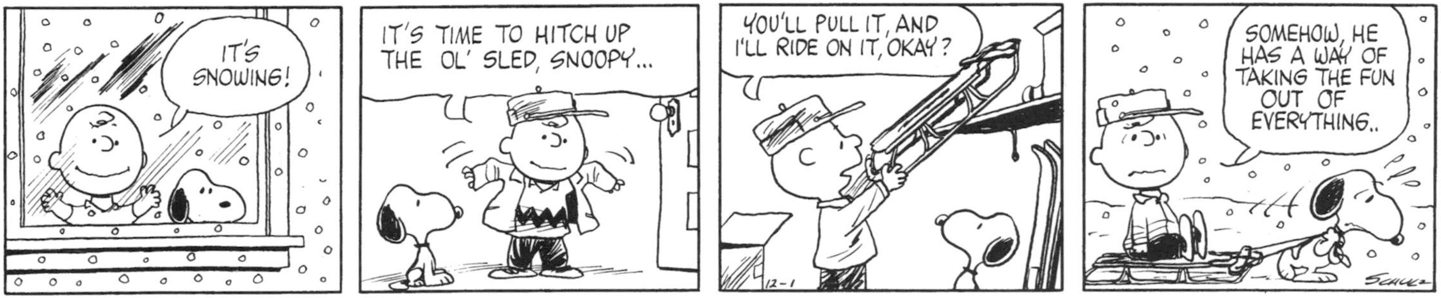
IT'S SNOWING!
IT'S TIME TO HITCH UP THE OL' SLED, SNOOPY...
YOU'LL PULL IT, AND I'LL RIDE ON IT, OKAY?
12-1
SOMEHOW, HE HAS A WAY OF TAKING THE FUN OUT OF EVERYTHING..
SCHULZ

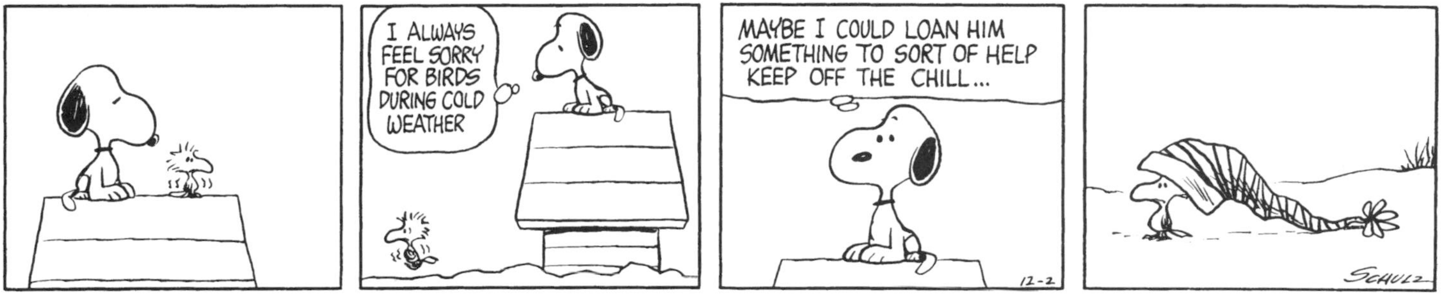
I ALWAYS FEEL SORRY FOR BIRDS DURING COLD WEATHER
MAYBE I COULD LOAN HIM SOMETHING TO SORT OF HELP KEEP OFF THE CHILL...
12-2
SCHULZ

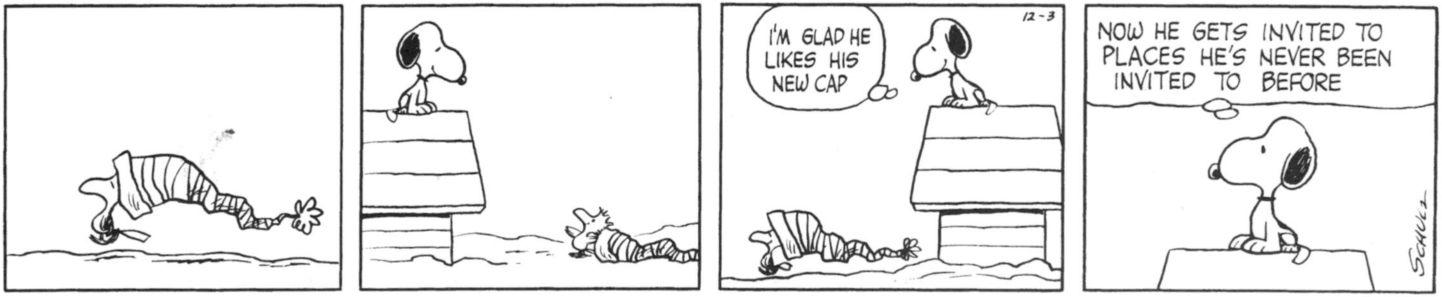
I'M GLAD HE LIKES HIS NEW CAP
12-3
NOW HE GETS INVITED TO PLACES HE'S NEVER BEEN INVITED TO BEFORE
SCHULZ

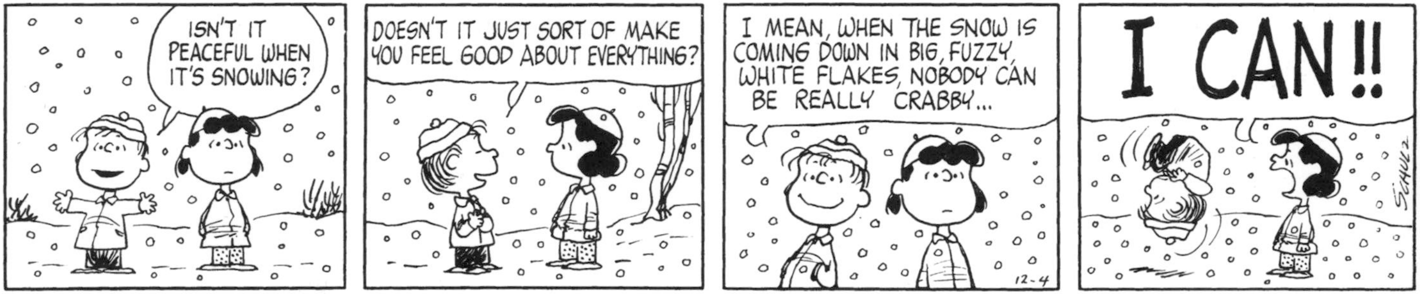
ISN'T IT PEACEFUL WHEN IT'S SNOWING?
DOESN'T IT JUST SORT OF MAKE YOU FEEL GOOD ABOUT EVERYTHING?
I MEAN, WHEN THE SNOW IS COMING DOWN IN BIG, FUZZY, WHITE FLAKES, NOBODY CAN BE REALLY CRABBY...
12-4
I CAN!!
SCHULZ

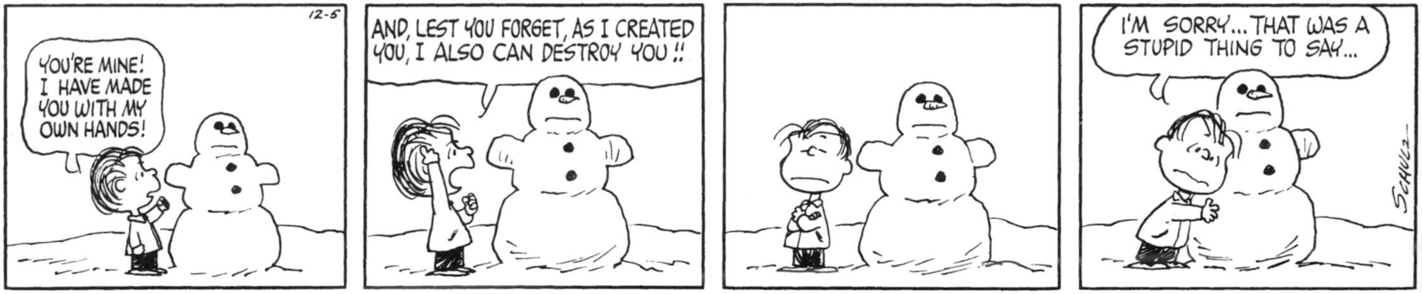
12-5
YOU'RE MINE! I HAVE MADE YOU WITH MY OWN HANDS!
AND, LEST YOU FORGET, AS I CREATED YOU, I ALSO CAN DESTROY YOU!!
I'M SORRY... THAT WAS A STUPID THING TO SAY...
SCHULZ

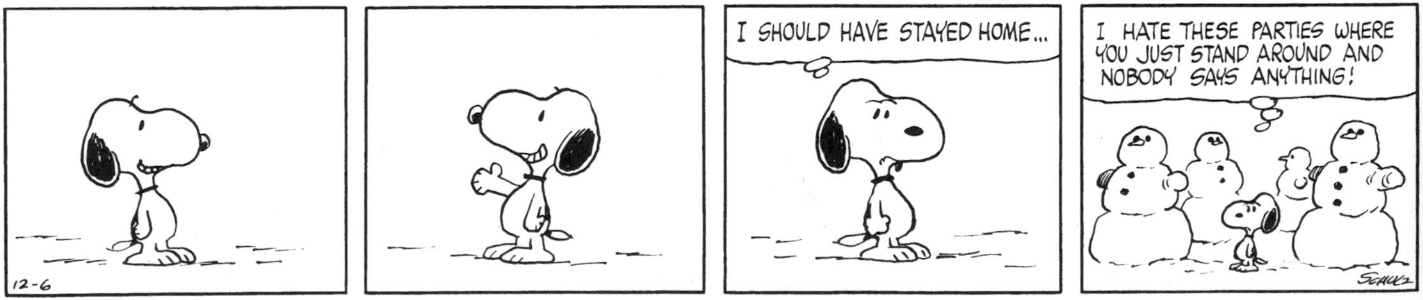
12-6
I SHOULD HAVE STAYED HOME...
I HATE THESE PARTIES WHERE YOU JUST STAND AROUND AND NOBODY SAYS ANYTHING!
SCHULZ

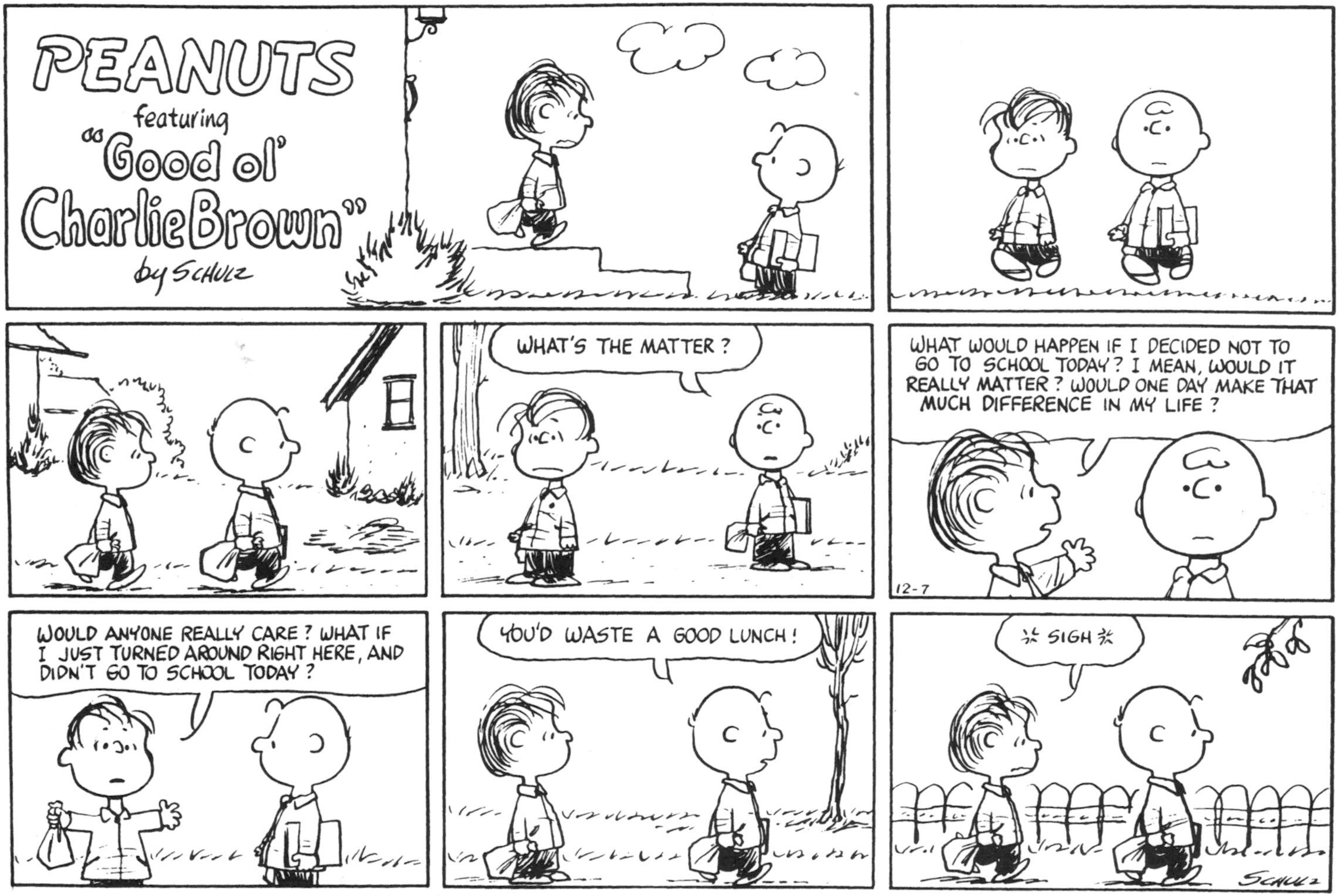
PEANUTS
featuring
"Good ol' CharlieBrown"
by SCHULZ
WHAT'S THE MATTER?
WHAT WOULD HAPPEN IF I DECIDED NOT TO GO TO SCHOOL TODAY? I MEAN, WOULD IT REALLY MATTER? WOULD ONE DAY MAKE THAT MUCH DIFFERENCE IN MY LIFE?
12-7
WOULD ANYONE REALLY CARE? WHAT IF I JUST TURNED AROUND RIGHT HERE, AND DIDN'T GO TO SCHOOL TODAY?
YOU'D WASTE A GOOD LUNCH!
SIGH
SCHULZ

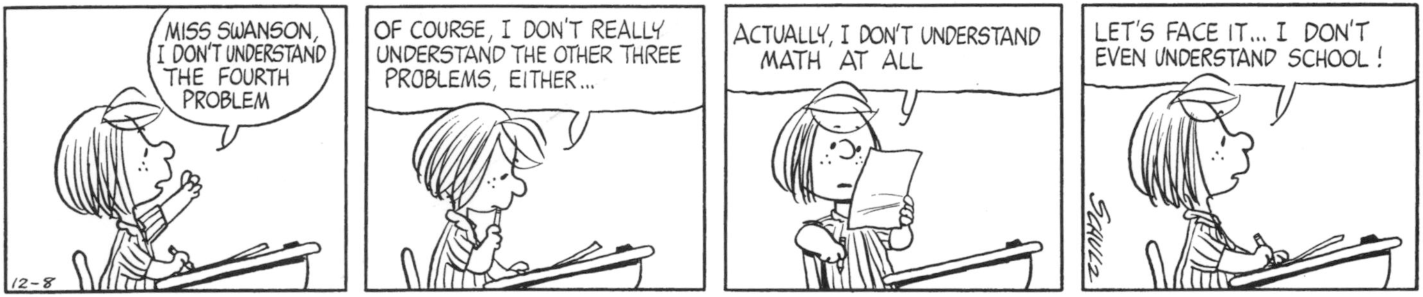
12-8
MISS SWANSON, I DON'T UNDERSTAND THE FOURTH PROBLEM
OF COURSE, I DON'T REALLY UNDERSTAND THE OTHER THREE PROBLEMS, EITHER...
ACTUALLY, I DON'T UNDERSTAND MATH AT ALL
LET'S FACE IT... I DON'T EVEN UNDERSTAND SCHOOL!
SCHULZ

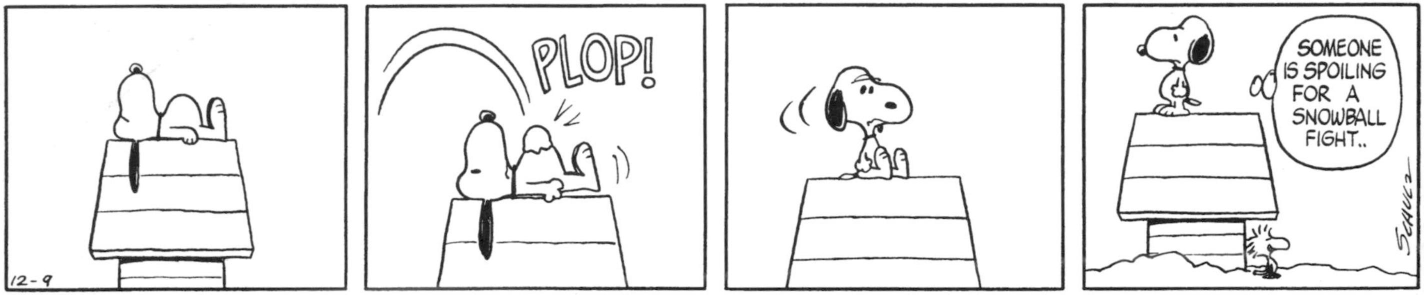
12-9
PLOP!
SOMEONE IS SPOILING FOR A SNOWBALL FIGHT..
SCHULZ

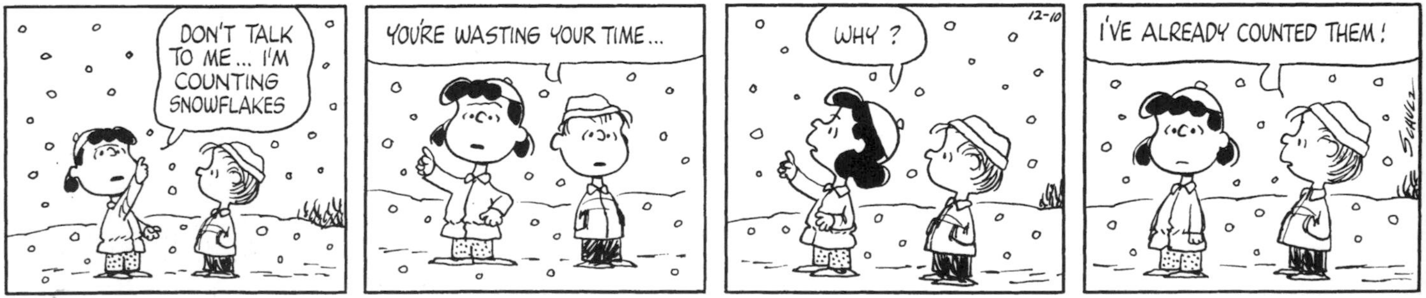
DON'T TALK TO ME... I'M COUNTING SNOWFLAKES
YOU'RE WASTING YOUR TIME...
12-10
WHY?
I'VE ALREADY COUNTED THEM!
SCHULZ

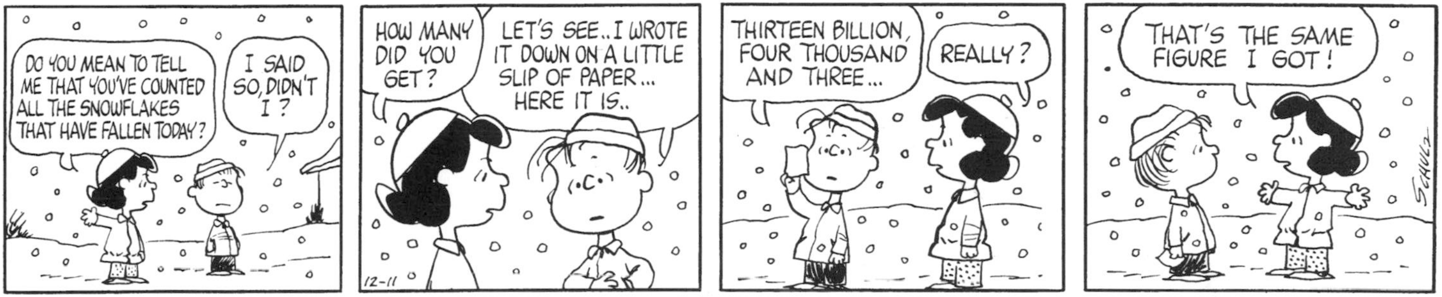
DO YOU MEAN TO TELL ME THAT YOU'VE COUNTED ALL THE SNOWFLAKES THAT HAVE FALLEN TODAY?
I SAID SO, DIDN'T I ?
HOW MANY DID YOU GET?
LET'S SEE..I WROTE IT DOWN ON A LITTLE SLIP OF PAPER... HERE IT IS..
12-11
THIRTEEN BILLION, FOUR THOUSAND AND THREE...
REALLY?
THAT'S THE SAME FIGURE I GOT!
SCHULZ

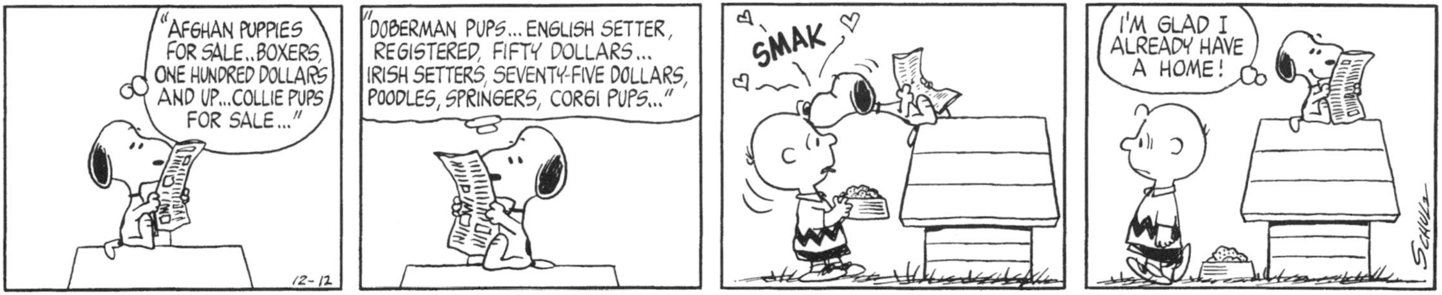
"AFGHAN PUPPIES FOR SALE..BOXERS, ONE HUNDRED DOLLARS AND UP...COLLIE PUPS FOR SALE..."
12-12
"DOBERMAN PUPS...ENGLISH SETTER, REGISTERED, FIFTY DOLLARS... IRISH SETTERS, SEVENTY-FIVE DOLLARS, POODLES, SPRINGERS, CORGI PUPS..."
SMAK
I'M GLAD I ALREADY HAVE A HOME!
SCHULZ

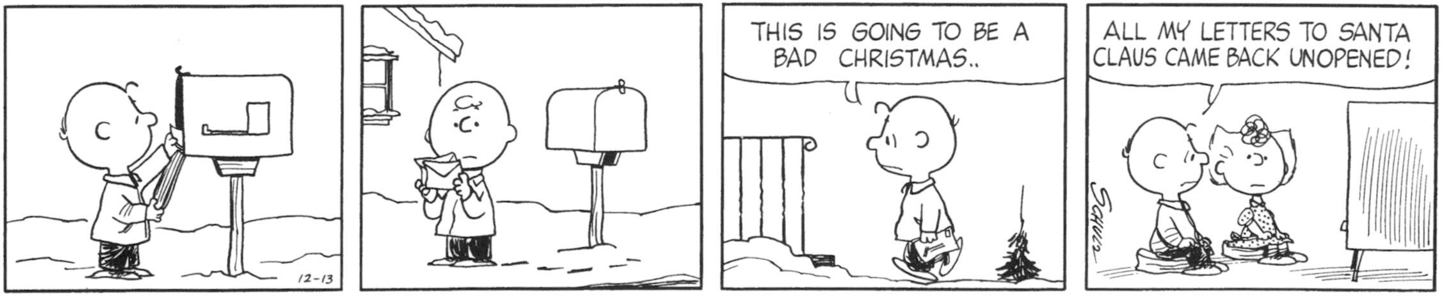
12-13
THIS IS GOING TO BE A BAD CHRISTMAS..
ALL MY LETTERS TO SANTA CLAUS CAME BACK UNOPENED!
SCHULZ

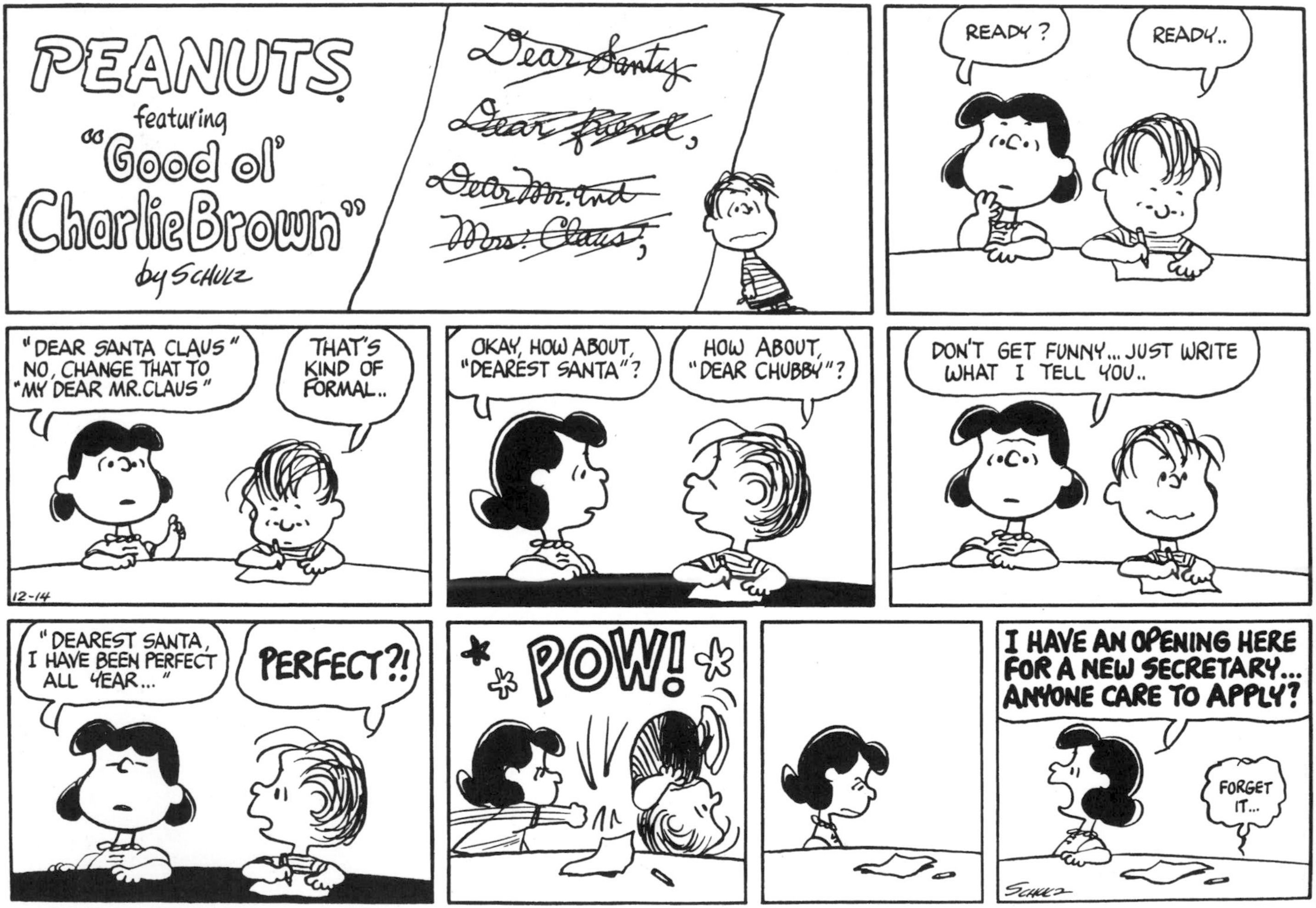
PEANUTS
featuring
"Good ol' Charlie Brown"
by SCHULZ
Dear Santy
Dear friend,
Dear Mr. and
Mrs. Claus,
READY?
READY..
"DEAR SANTA CLAUS" NO, CHANGE THAT TO "MY DEAR MR. CLAUS"
THAT'S KIND OF FORMAL..
12-14
OKAY, HOW ABOUT, "DEAREST SANTA"?
HOW ABOUT, "DEAR CHUBBY"?
DON'T GET FUNNY... JUST WRITE WHAT I TELL YOU..
"DEAREST SANTA, I HAVE BEEN PERFECT ALL YEAR..."
PERFECT?!
POW!
I HAVE AN OPENING HERE FOR A NEW SECRETARY... ANYONE CARE TO APPLY?
FORGET IT...
SCHULZ

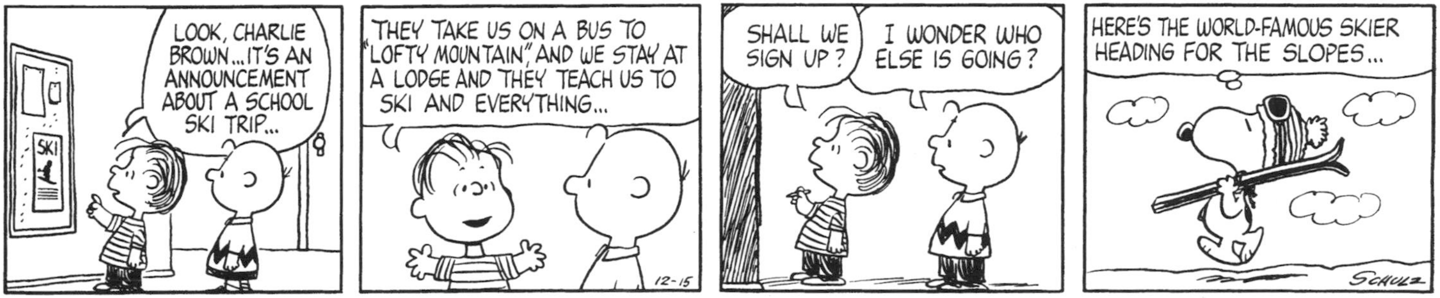
LOOK, CHARLIE BROWN...IT'S AN ANNOUNCEMENT ABOUT A SCHOOL SKI TRIP...
SKI
"THEY TAKE US ON A BUS TO "LOFTY MOUNTAIN," AND WE STAY AT A LODGE AND THEY TEACH US TO SKI AND EVERYTHING...
12-15
SHALL WE SIGN UP?
I WONDER WHO ELSE IS GOING?
HERE'S THE WORLD-FAMOUS SKIER HEADING FOR THE SLOPES...
SCHULZ

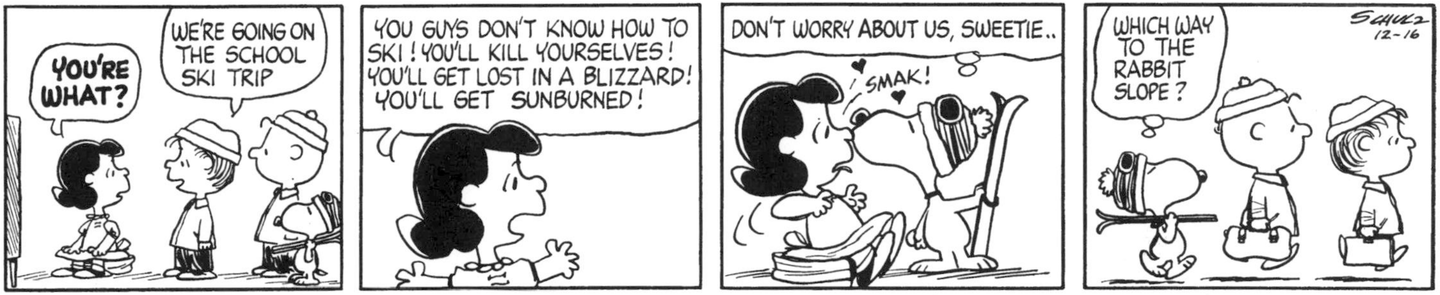
WE'RE GOING ON THE SCHOOL SKI TRIP
YOU'RE WHAT?
YOU GUYS DON'T KNOW HOW TO SKI! YOU'LL KILL YOURSELVES! YOU'LL GET LOST IN A BLIZZARD! YOU'LL GET SUNBURNED!
DON'T WORRY ABOUT US, SWEETIE..
SMAK!
SCHULZ 12-16
WHICH WAY TO THE RABBIT SLOPE?

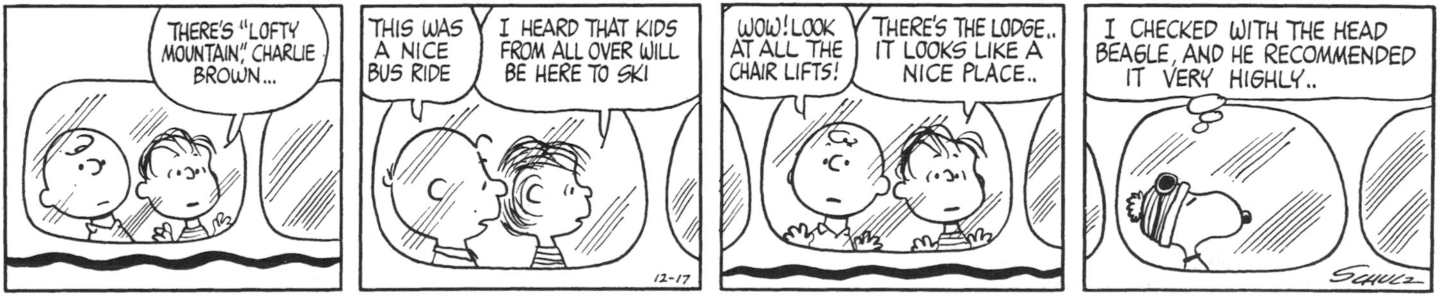
THERE'S "LOFTY MOUNTAIN," CHARLIE BROWN...
THIS WAS A NICE BUS RIDE
I HEARD THAT KIDS FROM ALL OVER WILL BE HERE TO SKI
12-17
WOW! LOOK AT ALL THE CHAIR LIFTS!
THERE'S THE LODGE.. IT LOOKS LIKE A NICE PLACE..
I CHECKED WITH THE HEAD BEAGLE, AND HE RECOMMENDED IT VERY HIGHLY..
SCHULZ

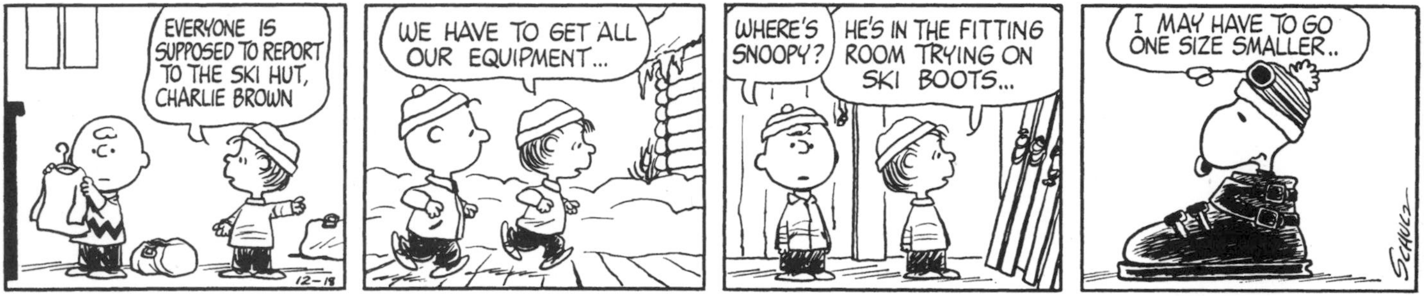
EVERYONE IS SUPPOSED TO REPORT TO THE SKI HUT, CHARLIE BROWN
12-18
WE HAVE TO GET ALL OUR EQUIPMENT...
WHERE'S SNOOPY?
HE'S IN THE FITTING ROOM TRYING ON SKI BOOTS...
I MAY HAVE TO GO ONE SIZE SMALLER..
SCHULZ

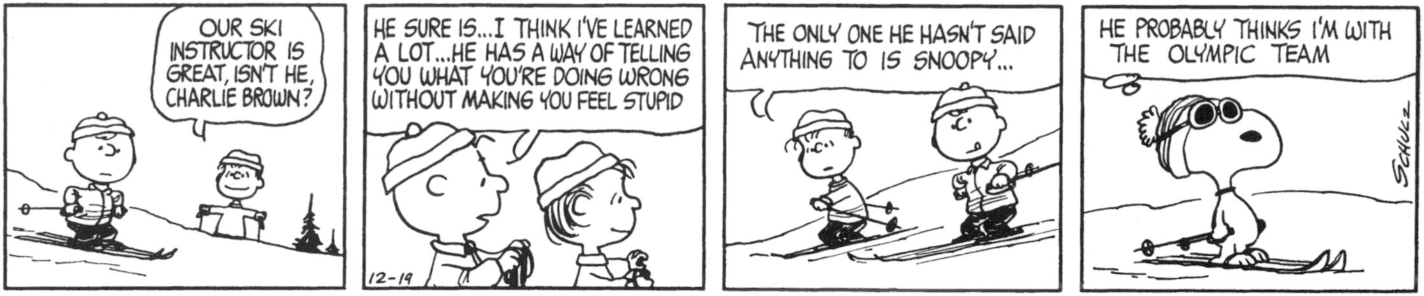
OUR SKI INSTRUCTOR IS GREAT, ISN'T HE, CHARLIE BROWN?
HE SURE IS...I THINK I'VE LEARNED A LOT...HE HAS A WAY OF TELLING YOU WHAT YOU'RE DOING WRONG WITHOUT MAKING YOU FEEL STUPID
12-19
THE ONLY ONE HE HASN'T SAID ANYTHING TO IS SNOOPY...
HE PROBABLY THINKS I'M WITH THE OLYMPIC TEAM
SCHULZ

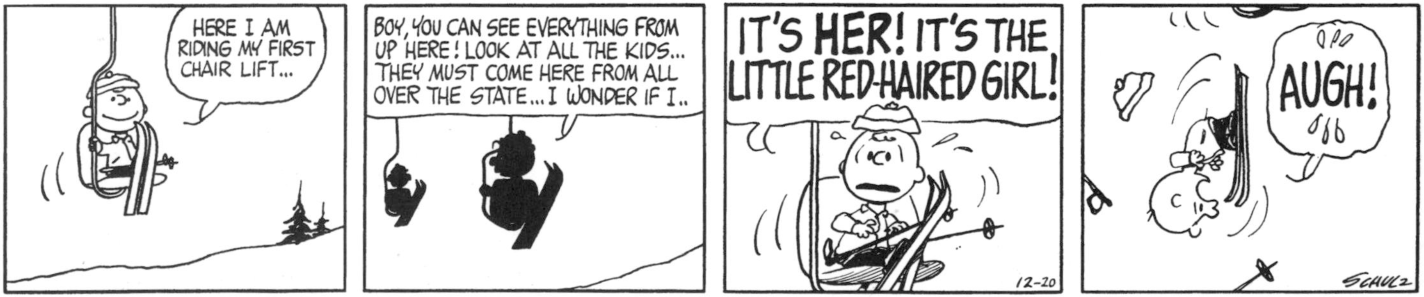
HERE I AM RIDING MY FIRST CHAIR LIFT...
BOY, YOU CAN SEE EVERYTHING FROM UP HERE! LOOK AT ALL THE KIDS... THEY MUST COME HERE FROM ALL OVER THE STATE...I WONDER IF I..
IT'S HER! IT'S THE LITTLE RED-HAIRED GIRL!
12-20
AUGH!
SCHULZ

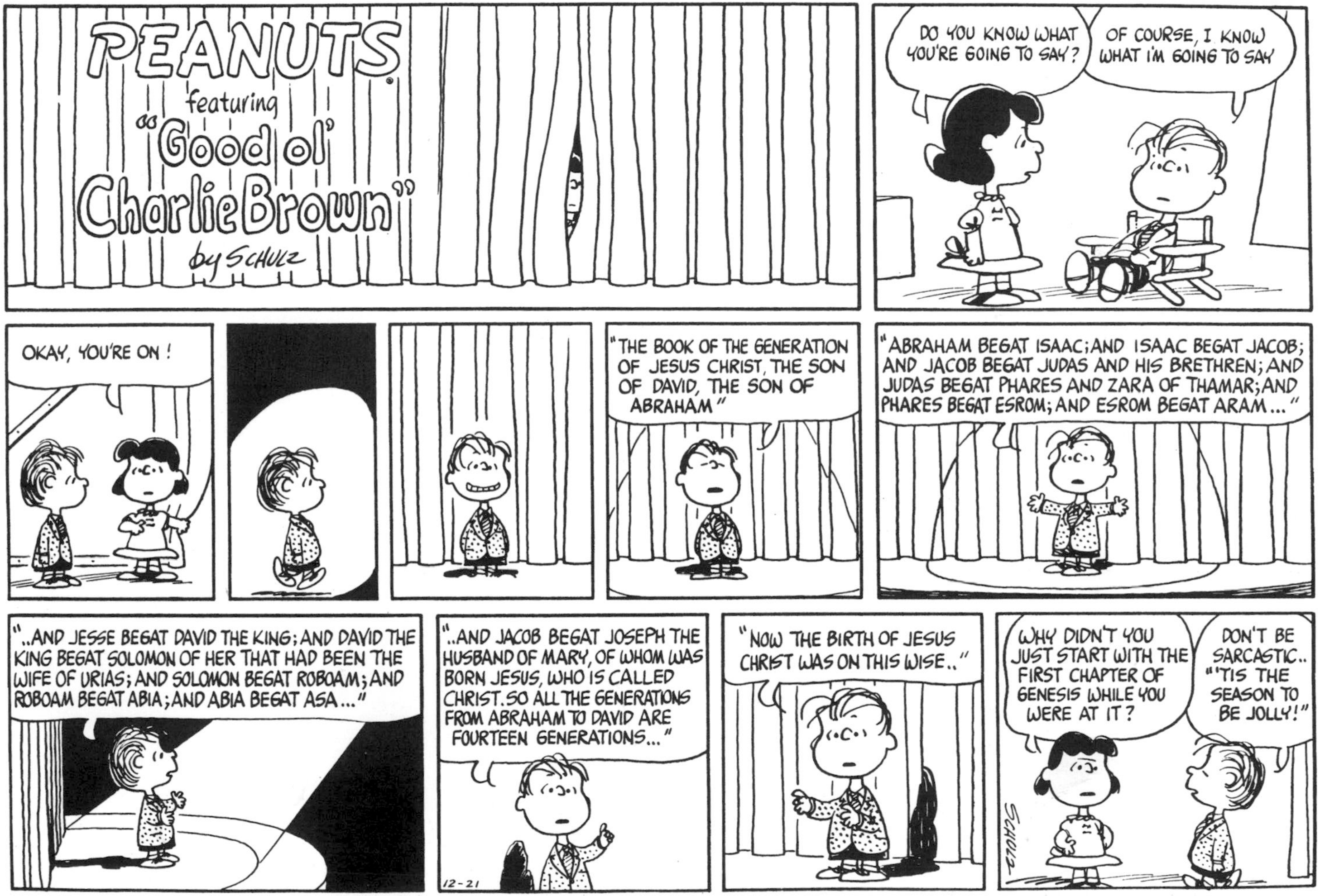
PEANUTS
featuring "Good ol' Charlie Brown"
by SCHULZ
DO YOU KNOW WHAT YOU'RE GOING TO SAY?
OF COURSE, I KNOW WHAT I'M GOING TO SAY
OKAY, YOU'RE ON!
"THE BOOK OF THE GENERATION OF JESUS CHRIST, THE SON OF DAVID, THE SON OF ABRAHAM"
"ABRAHAM BEGAT ISAAC; AND ISAAC BEGAT JACOB; AND JACOB BEGAT JUDAS AND HIS BRETHREN; AND JUDAS BEGAT PHARES AND ZARA OF THAMAR; AND PHARES BEGAT ESROM; AND ESROM BEGAT ARAM..."
"..AND JESSE BEGAT DAVID THE KING; AND DAVID THE KING BEGAT SOLOMON OF HER THAT HAD BEEN THE WIFE OF URIAS; AND SOLOMON BEGAT ROBOAM; AND ROBOAM BEGAT ABIA; AND ABIA BEGAT ASA..."
"..AND JACOB BEGAT JOSEPH THE HUSBAND OF MARY, OF WHOM WAS BORN JESUS, WHO IS CALLED CHRIST. SO ALL THE GENERATIONS FROM ABRAHAM TO DAVID ARE FOURTEEN GENERATIONS..."
12-21
"NOW THE BIRTH OF JESUS CHRIST WAS ON THIS WISE.."
WHY DIDN'T YOU JUST START WITH THE FIRST CHAPTER OF GENESIS WHILE YOU WERE AT IT?
DON'T BE SARCASTIC.. "'TIS THE SEASON TO BE JOLLY!"
SCHULZ

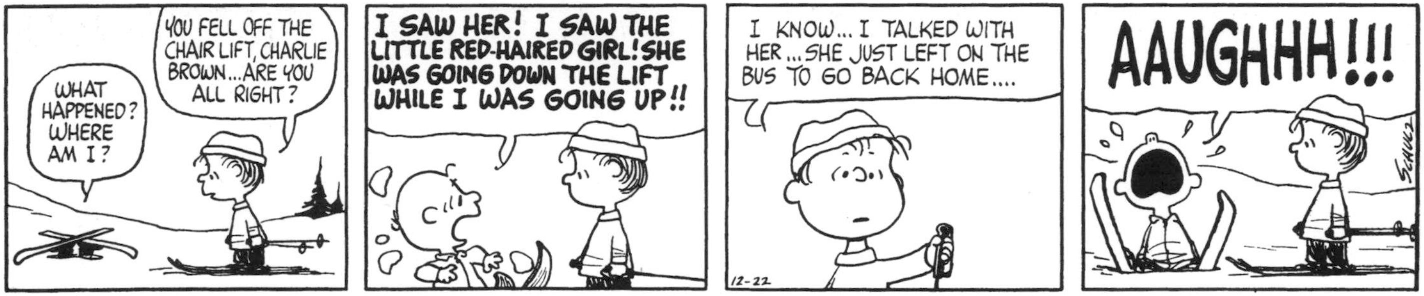
WHAT HAPPENED? WHERE AM I?
YOU FELL OFF THE CHAIR LIFT, CHARLIE BROWN...ARE YOU ALL RIGHT?
I SAW HER! I SAW THE LITTLE RED-HAIRED GIRL! SHE WAS GOING DOWN THE LIFT WHILE I WAS GOING UP!!
I KNOW... I TALKED WITH HER ... SHE JUST LEFT ON THE BUS TO GO BACK HOME....
12-22
AAUGHHH!!!
SCHULZ

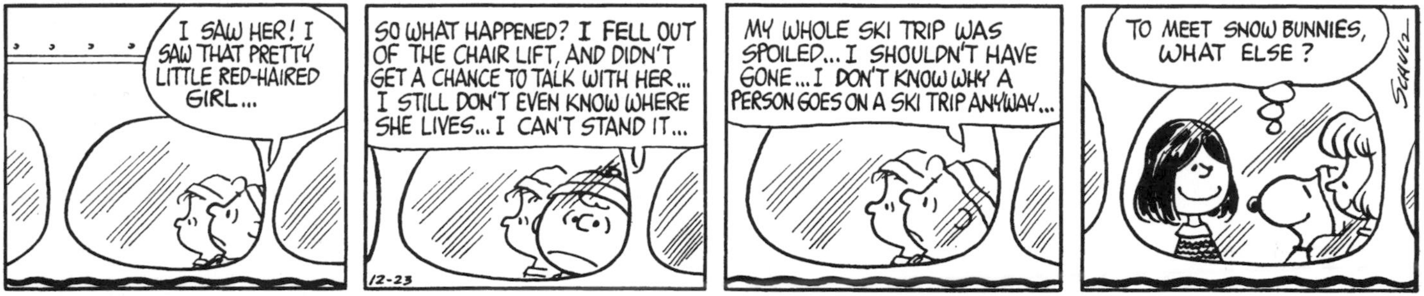
I SAW HER! I SAW THAT PRETTY LITTLE RED-HAIRED GIRL...
SO WHAT HAPPENED? I FELL OUT OF THE CHAIR LIFT, AND DIDN'T GET A CHANCE TO TALK WITH HER... I STILL DON'T EVEN KNOW WHERE SHE LIVES... I CAN'T STAND IT...
12-23
MY WHOLE SKI TRIP WAS SPOILED... I SHOULDN'T HAVE GONE... I DON'T KNOW WHY A PERSON GOES ON A SKI TRIP ANYWAY...
TO MEET SNOW BUNNIES, WHAT ELSE?
SCHULZ

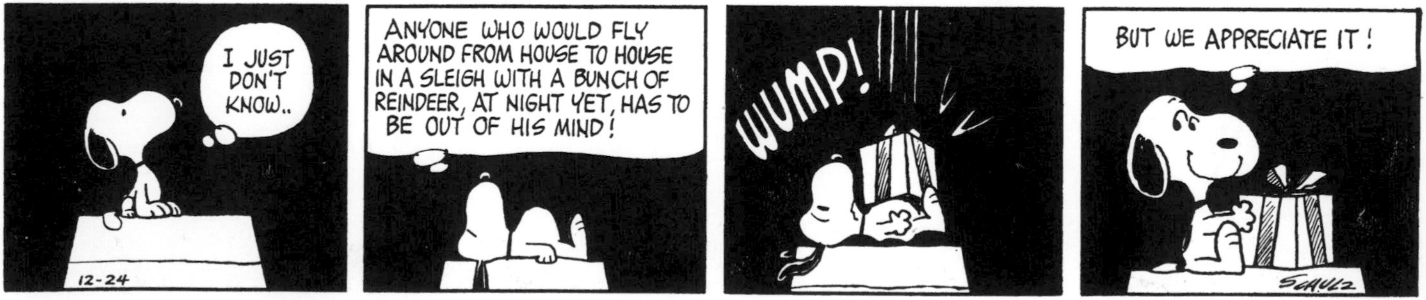
I JUST DON'T KNOW..
12-24
ANYONE WHO WOULD FLY AROUND FROM HOUSE TO HOUSE IN A SLEIGH WITH A BUNCH OF REINDEER, AT NIGHT YET, HAS TO BE OUT OF HIS MIND!
WUMP!
BUT WE APPRECIATE IT!
SCHULZ

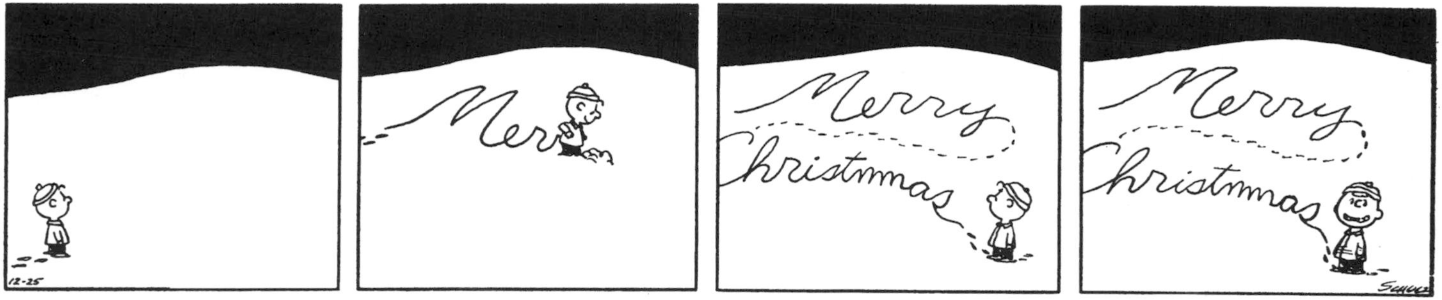
12-25
Mer
Merry
Christmas
Merry
Christmas
SCHULZ

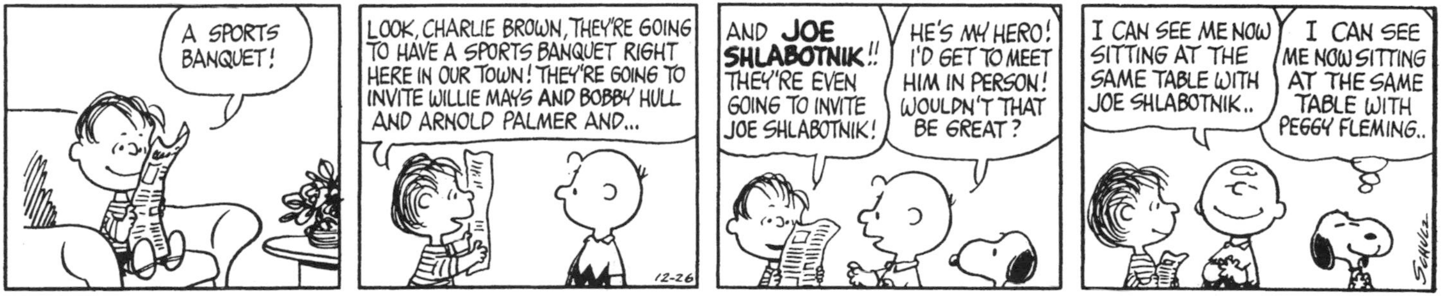
A SPORTS BANQUET!
LOOK, CHARLIE BROWN, THEY'RE GOING TO HAVE A SPORTS BANQUET RIGHT HERE IN OUR TOWN! THEY'RE GOING TO INVITE WILLIE MAYS AND BOBBY HULL AND ARNOLD PALMER AND...
12-26
AND JOE SHLABOTNIK!! THEY'RE EVEN GOING TO INVITE JOE SHLABOTNIK!
HE'S MY HERO! I'D GET TO MEET HIM IN PERSON! WOULDN'T THAT BE GREAT?
I CAN SEE ME NOW SITTING AT THE SAME TABLE WITH JOE SHLABOTNIK..
I CAN SEE ME NOW SITTING AT THE SAME TABLE WITH PEGGY FLEMING..
SCHULZ

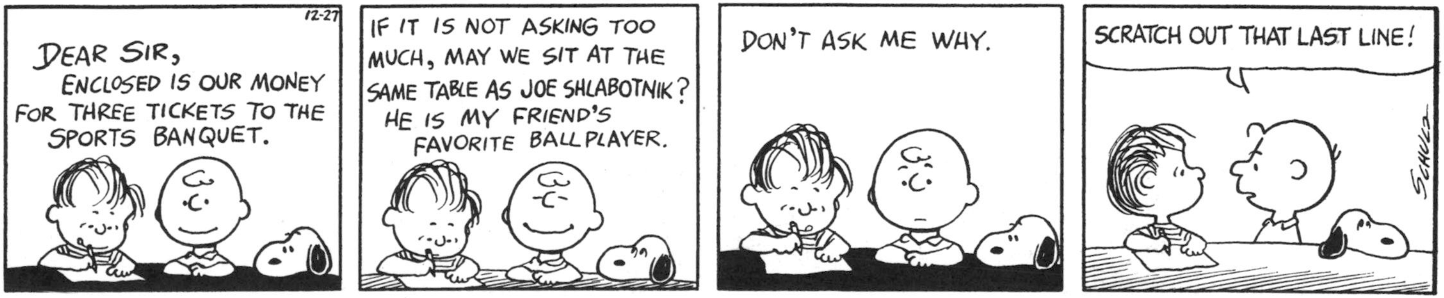
12-27
DEAR SIR,
ENCLOSED IS OUR MONEY FOR THREE TICKETS TO THE SPORTS BANQUET.
IF IT IS NOT ASKING TOO MUCH, MAY WE SIT AT THE SAME TABLE AS JOE SHLABOTNIK? HE IS MY FRIEND'S FAVORITE BALLPLAYER.
DON'T ASK ME WHY.
SCRATCH OUT THAT LAST LINE!
SCHULZ

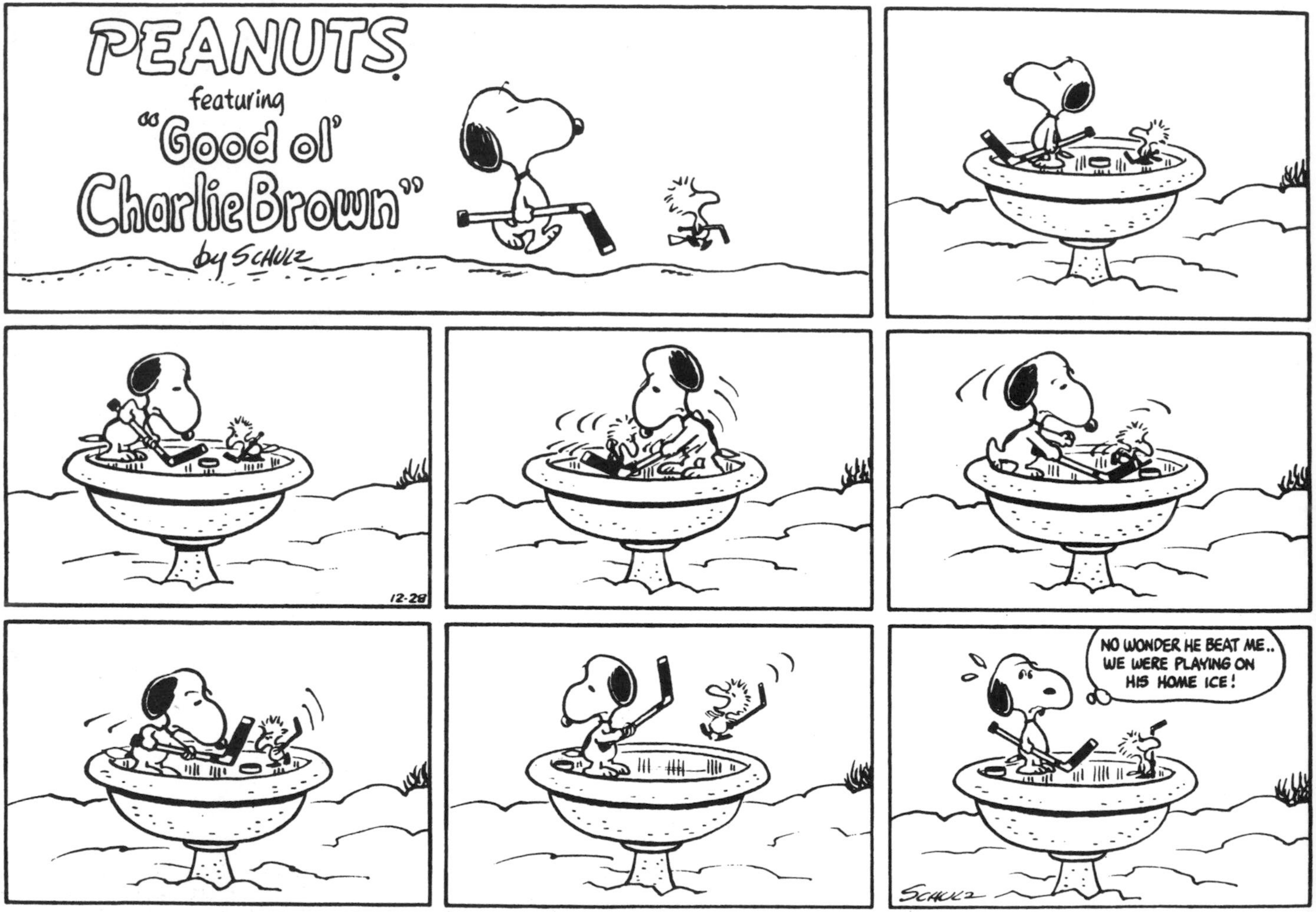
PEANUTS
featuring
"Good ol' Charlie Brown"
by SCHULZ
12-28
NO WONDER HE BEAT ME..
WE WERE PLAYING ON
HIS HOME ICE!
SCHULZ

Panel 1: WHAT ARE YOU ALL DRESSED UP FOR?

Panel 2: CHARLIE BROWN, SNOOPY AND I ARE GOING TO A SPORTS BANQUET... WE'RE GOING TO BE DINING WITH FAMOUS ATHLETES!

Panel 3: YOU'LL PROBABLY MAKE A FOOL OUT OF YOURSELF BY USING THE WRONG FORK...

Panel 4: FORK?

Panel 5: LOOK AT ALL THE FAMOUS ATHLETES, CHARLIE BROWN

WHERE'S PEGGY FLEMING?

Panel 6: THERE'S JOE GARAGIOLA, AND JACK NICKLAUS, AND BOBBY ORR, AND FRED GLOVER, AND HANK AARON, AND PANCHO GONZALES AND..

Panel 7: WHERE'S JOE SHLABOTNIK? HE'S SUPPOSED TO BE SITTING AT OUR TABLE...

Panel 8: HE'LL BE HERE..HE'S PROBABLY SIGNING AUTOGRAPHS OR SOMETHING..

THERE'S PEGGY! HI, SWEETIE, REMEMBER ME?

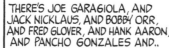

Panel 9: WHERE'S JOE SHLABOTNIK?

HE'LL BE HERE! WHEN JOE SHLABOTNIK SAYS HE'S GOING TO DO SOMETHING, HE DOES IT!

THERE'S PATTY BERG.. HI, SWEETIE!

Panel 10: I REMEMBER ONE GAME LAST YEAR... HE CAME UP TO BAT IN THE NINTH INNING, AND SAID HE WAS GOING TO HIT A HOME RUN...

Panel 11: DID HE?

NO, HE POPPED UP...BUT HE RAN IT OUT!

OOO! THERE'S CAROL MANN...

Panel 12: I'M GLAD YOU HAVE FAITH IN YOUR HERO, CHARLIE BROWN

HE'LL BE HERE... HE PROBABLY STOPPED TO FIX A FLAT TIRE ON SOME ELDERLY PERSON'S CAR....

HI, SWEETIE!

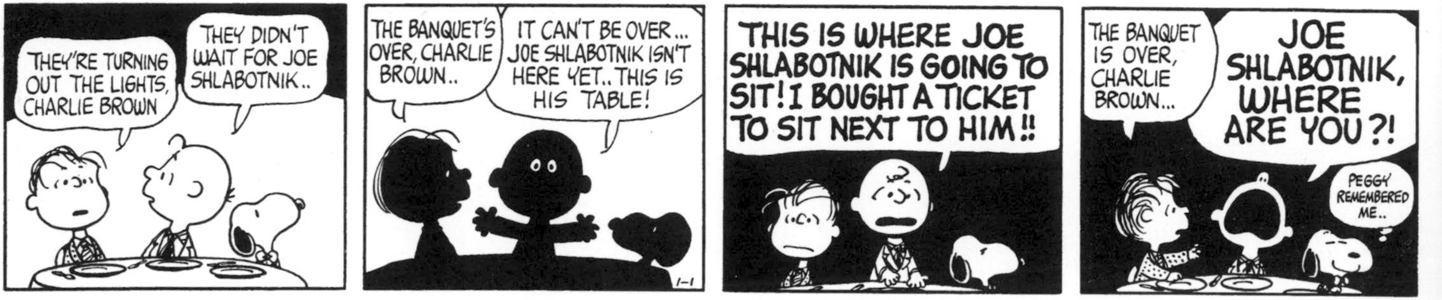
THEY'RE TURNING OUT THE LIGHTS, CHARLIE BROWN
THEY DIDN'T WAIT FOR JOE SHLABOTNIK..
THE BANQUET'S OVER, CHARLIE BROWN..
IT CAN'T BE OVER... JOE SHLABOTNIK ISN'T HERE YET.. THIS IS HIS TABLE!
THIS IS WHERE JOE SHLABOTNIK IS GOING TO SIT! I BOUGHT A TICKET TO SIT NEXT TO HIM!!
THE BANQUET IS OVER, CHARLIE BROWN...
JOE SHLABOTNIK, WHERE ARE YOU?!
PEGGY REMEMBERED ME..
1-1

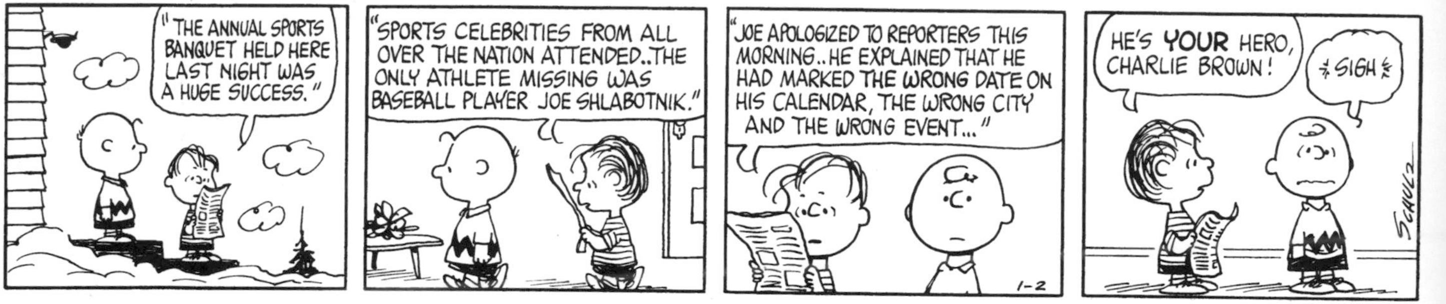
"THE ANNUAL SPORTS BANQUET HELD HERE LAST NIGHT WAS A HUGE SUCCESS."
"SPORTS CELEBRITIES FROM ALL OVER THE NATION ATTENDED..THE ONLY ATHLETE MISSING WAS BASEBALL PLAYER JOE SHLABOTNIK."
"JOE APOLOGIZED TO REPORTERS THIS MORNING..HE EXPLAINED THAT HE HAD MARKED THE WRONG DATE ON HIS CALENDAR, THE WRONG CITY AND THE WRONG EVENT..."
HE'S YOUR HERO, CHARLIE BROWN!
SIGH
1-2
SCHULZ

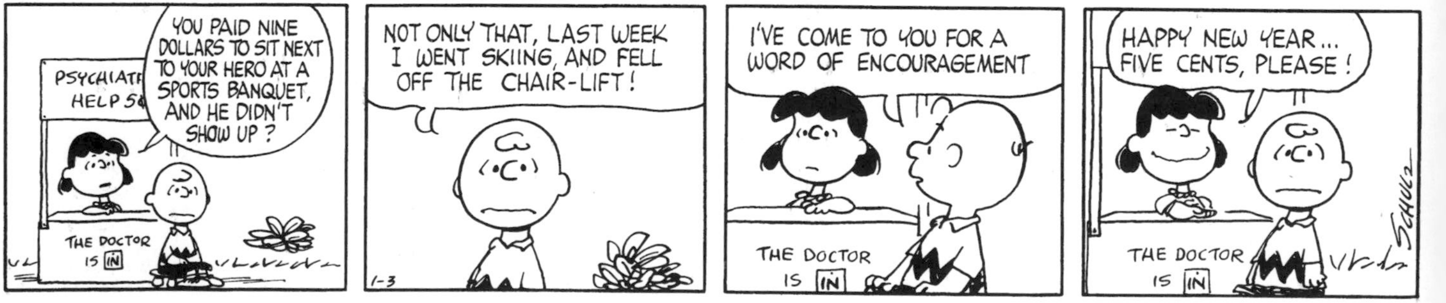
PSYCHIATR
HELP 5¢
YOU PAID NINE DOLLARS TO SIT NEXT TO YOUR HERO AT A SPORTS BANQUET, AND HE DIDN'T SHOW UP?
THE DOCTOR IS IN
NOT ONLY THAT, LAST WEEK I WENT SKIING, AND FELL OFF THE CHAIR-LIFT!
1-3
I'VE COME TO YOU FOR A WORD OF ENCOURAGEMENT
THE DOCTOR IS IN
HAPPY NEW YEAR... FIVE CENTS, PLEASE!
THE DOCTOR IS IN
SCHULZ

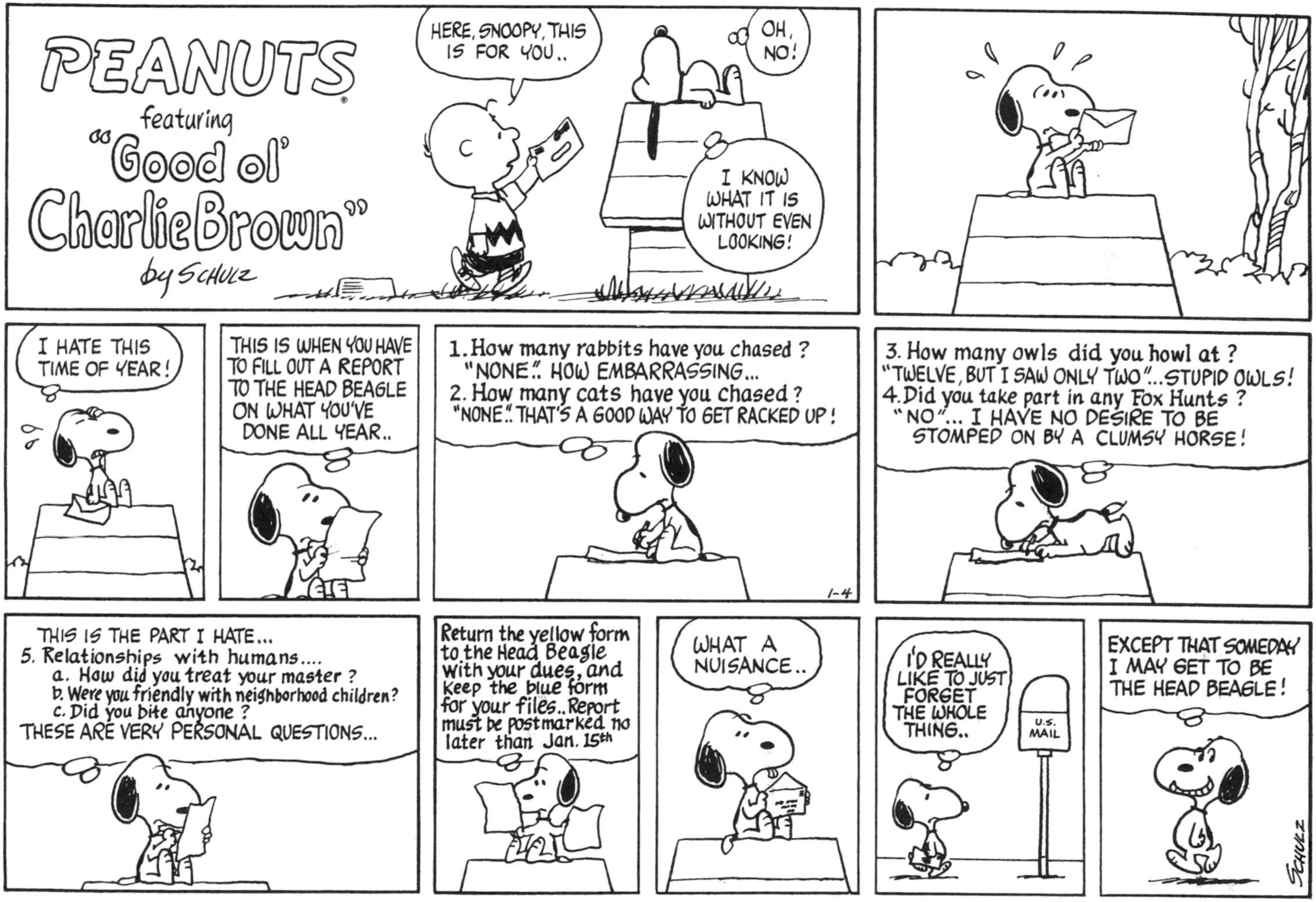
PEANUTS
featuring "Good ol' Charlie Brown"
by SCHULZ
HERE, SNOOPY, THIS IS FOR YOU..
OH, NO!
I KNOW WHAT IT IS WITHOUT EVEN LOOKING!
I HATE THIS TIME OF YEAR!
THIS IS WHEN YOU HAVE TO FILL OUT A REPORT TO THE HEAD BEAGLE ON WHAT YOU'VE DONE ALL YEAR..
1. How many rabbits have you chased ?
"NONE". HOW EMBARRASSING...
2. How many cats have you chased ?
"NONE". THAT'S A GOOD WAY TO GET RACKED UP!
1-4
3. How many owls did you howl at ?
"TWELVE, BUT I SAW ONLY TWO"... STUPID OWLS!
4. Did you take part in any Fox Hunts ?
"NO"... I HAVE NO DESIRE TO BE STOMPED ON BY A CLUMSY HORSE!
THIS IS THE PART I HATE...
5. Relationships with humans....
a. How did you treat your master ?
b. Were you friendly with neighborhood children?
c. Did you bite anyone ?
THESE ARE VERY PERSONAL QUESTIONS...
Return the yellow form to the Head Beagle with your dues, and keep the blue form for your files.. Report must be postmarked no later than Jan. 15th
WHAT A NUISANCE..
I'D REALLY LIKE TO JUST FORGET THE WHOLE THING..
U.S. MAIL
EXCEPT THAT SOMEDAY I MAY GET TO BE THE HEAD BEAGLE!
SCHULZ

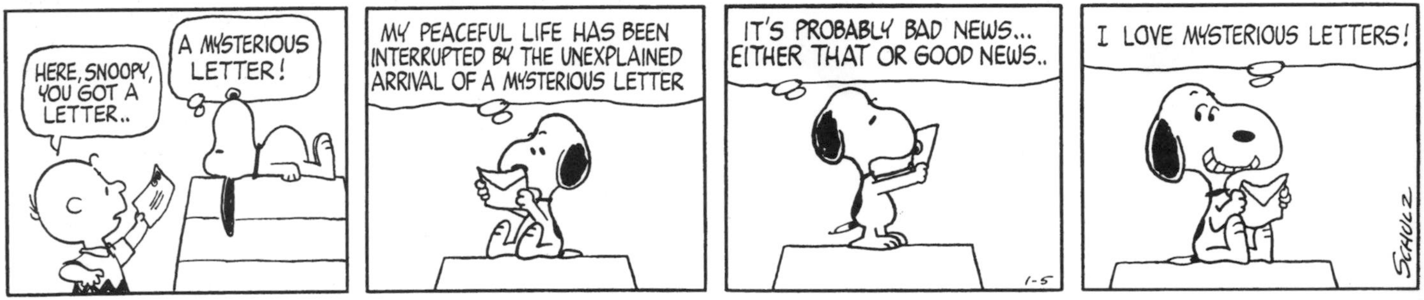

HERE, SNOOPY, YOU GOT A LETTER..
A MYSTERIOUS LETTER!
MY PEACEFUL LIFE HAS BEEN INTERRUPTED BY THE UNEXPLAINED ARRIVAL OF A MYSTERIOUS LETTER
IT'S PROBABLY BAD NEWS... EITHER THAT OR GOOD NEWS..
I LOVE MYSTERIOUS LETTERS!

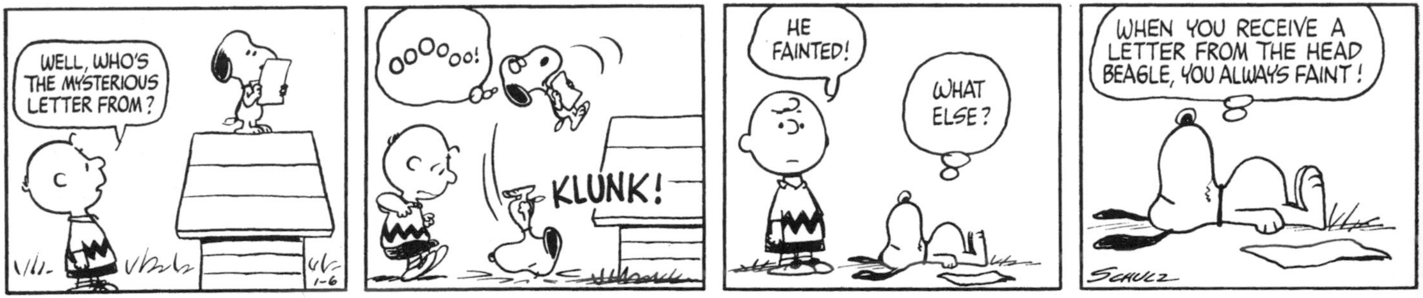

WELL, WHO'S THE MYSTERIOUS LETTER FROM?
OOOOoo!
KLUNK!
HE FAINTED!
WHAT ELSE?
WHEN YOU RECEIVE A LETTER FROM THE HEAD BEAGLE, YOU ALWAYS FAINT!

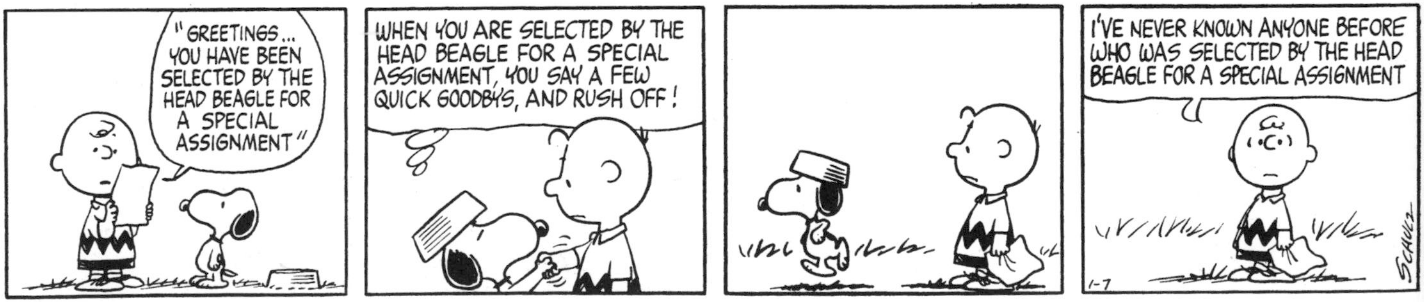

"GREETINGS... YOU HAVE BEEN SELECTED BY THE HEAD BEAGLE FOR A SPECIAL ASSIGNMENT"
WHEN YOU ARE SELECTED BY THE HEAD BEAGLE FOR A SPECIAL ASSIGNMENT, YOU SAY A FEW QUICK GOODBYS, AND RUSH OFF!
I'VE NEVER KNOWN ANYONE BEFORE WHO WAS SELECTED BY THE HEAD BEAGLE FOR A SPECIAL ASSIGNMENT

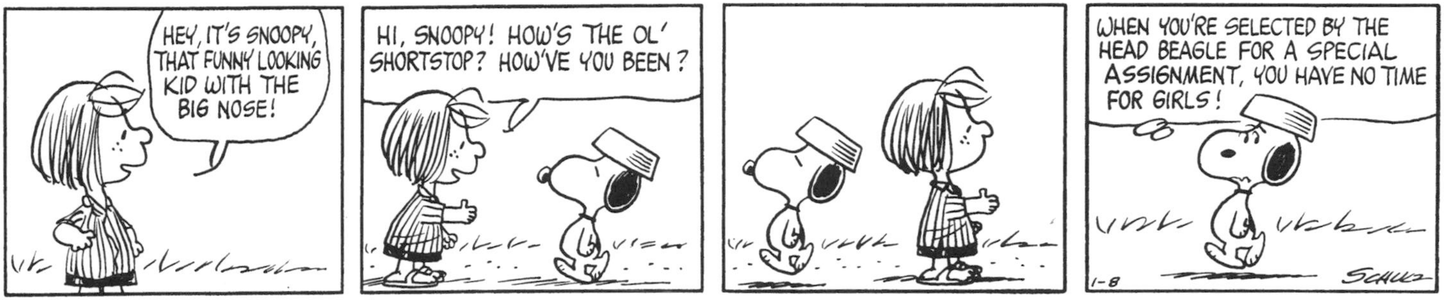
HEY, IT'S SNOOPY, THAT FUNNY LOOKING KID WITH THE BIG NOSE!
HI, SNOOPY! HOW'S THE OL' SHORTSTOP? HOW'VE YOU BEEN?
WHEN YOU'RE SELECTED BY THE HEAD BEAGLE FOR A SPECIAL ASSIGNMENT, YOU HAVE NO TIME FOR GIRLS!
1-8
SCHULZ

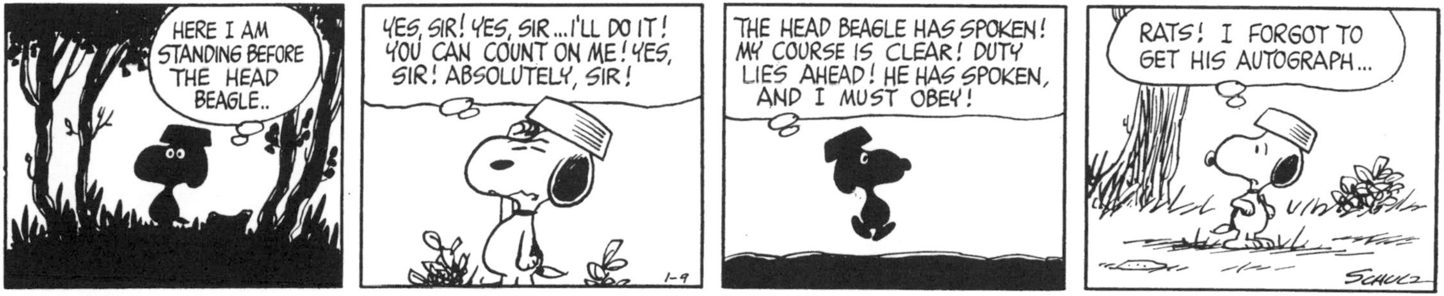
HERE I AM STANDING BEFORE THE HEAD BEAGLE..
YES, SIR! YES, SIR...I'LL DO IT! YOU CAN COUNT ON ME! YES, SIR! ABSOLUTELY, SIR!
1-9
THE HEAD BEAGLE HAS SPOKEN! MY COURSE IS CLEAR! DUTY LIES AHEAD! HE HAS SPOKEN, AND I MUST OBEY!
RATS! I FORGOT TO GET HIS AUTOGRAPH...
SCHULZ

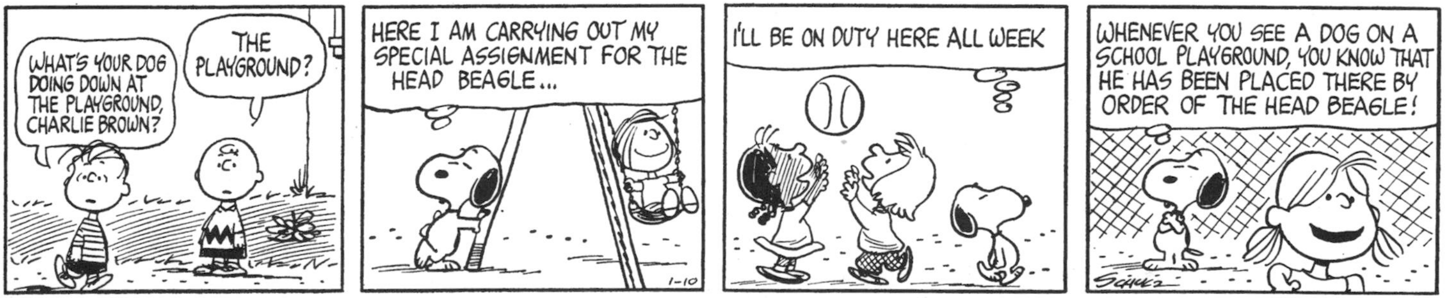
WHAT'S YOUR DOG DOING DOWN AT THE PLAYGROUND, CHARLIE BROWN?
THE PLAYGROUND?
HERE I AM CARRYING OUT MY SPECIAL ASSIGNMENT FOR THE HEAD BEAGLE...
1-10
I'LL BE ON DUTY HERE ALL WEEK
WHENEVER YOU SEE A DOG ON A SCHOOL PLAYGROUND, YOU KNOW THAT HE HAS BEEN PLACED THERE BY ORDER OF THE HEAD BEAGLE!
SCHULZ

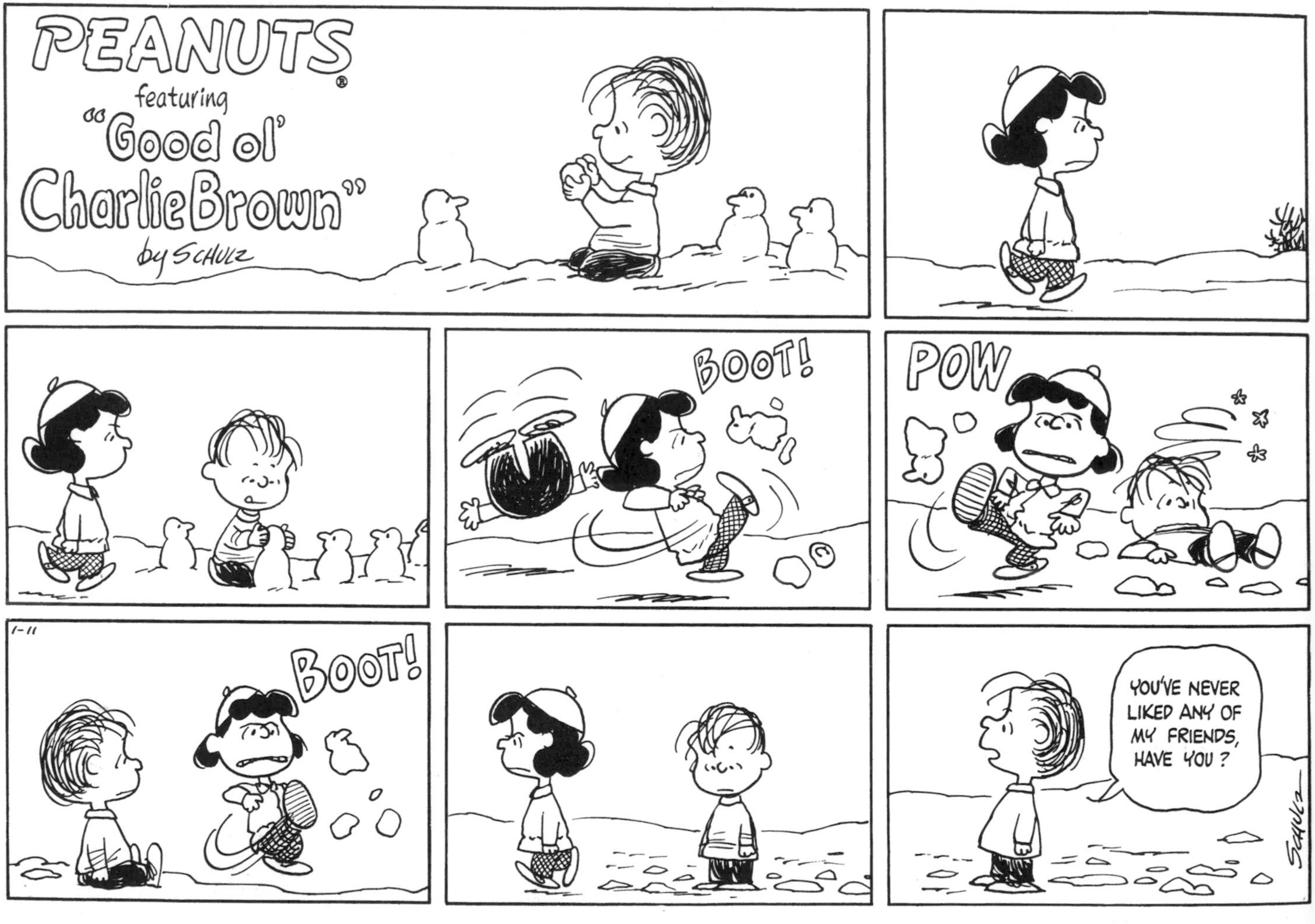
PEANUTS®
featuring
"Good ol' Charlie Brown"
by SCHULZ
BOOT!
POW
1-11
BOOT!
YOU'VE NEVER LIKED ANY OF MY FRIENDS, HAVE YOU ?
SCHULZ

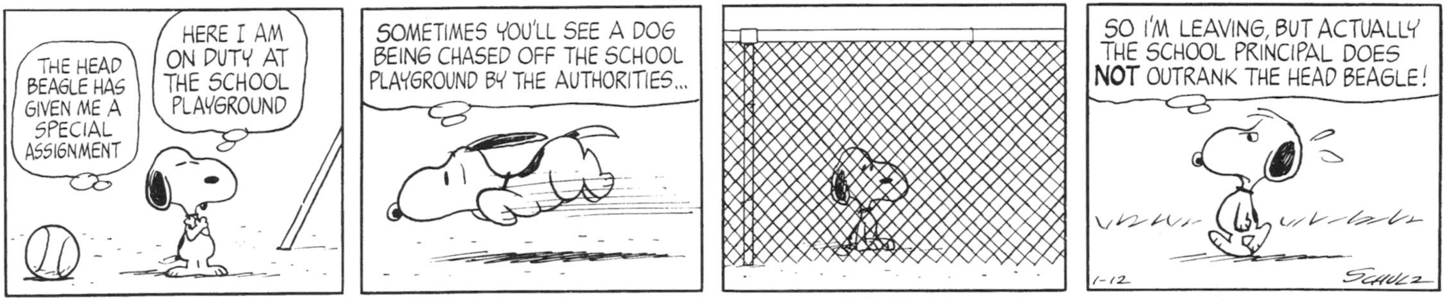
HERE I AM ON DUTY AT THE SCHOOL PLAYGROUND
THE HEAD BEAGLE HAS GIVEN ME A SPECIAL ASSIGNMENT
SOMETIMES YOU'LL SEE A DOG BEING CHASED OFF THE SCHOOL PLAYGROUND BY THE AUTHORITIES...
SO I'M LEAVING, BUT ACTUALLY THE SCHOOL PRINCIPAL DOES NOT OUTRANK THE HEAD BEAGLE!
1-12
SCHULZ

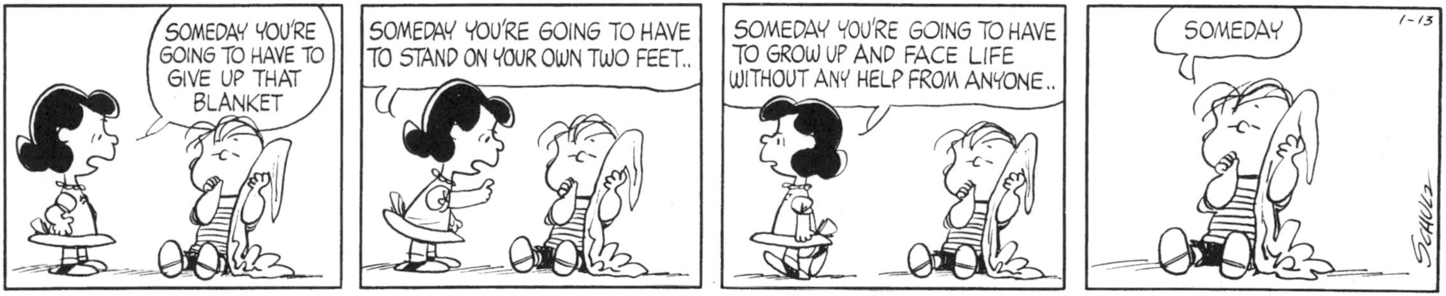
SOMEDAY YOU'RE GOING TO HAVE TO GIVE UP THAT BLANKET
SOMEDAY YOU'RE GOING TO HAVE TO STAND ON YOUR OWN TWO FEET..
SOMEDAY YOU'RE GOING TO HAVE TO GROW UP AND FACE LIFE WITHOUT ANY HELP FROM ANYONE..
SOMEDAY
1-13
SCHULZ

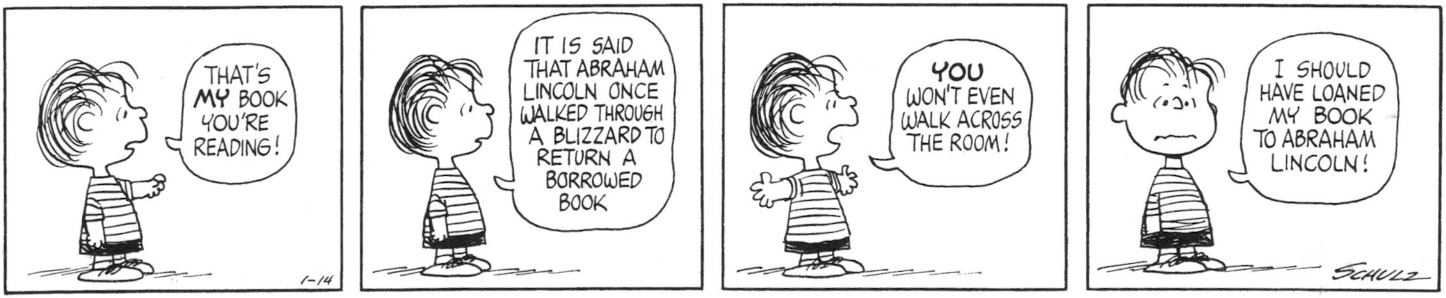
THAT'S MY BOOK YOU'RE READING!
1-14
IT IS SAID THAT ABRAHAM LINCOLN ONCE WALKED THROUGH A BLIZZARD TO RETURN A BORROWED BOOK
YOU WON'T EVEN WALK ACROSS THE ROOM!
I SHOULD HAVE LOANED MY BOOK TO ABRAHAM LINCOLN!
SCHULZ

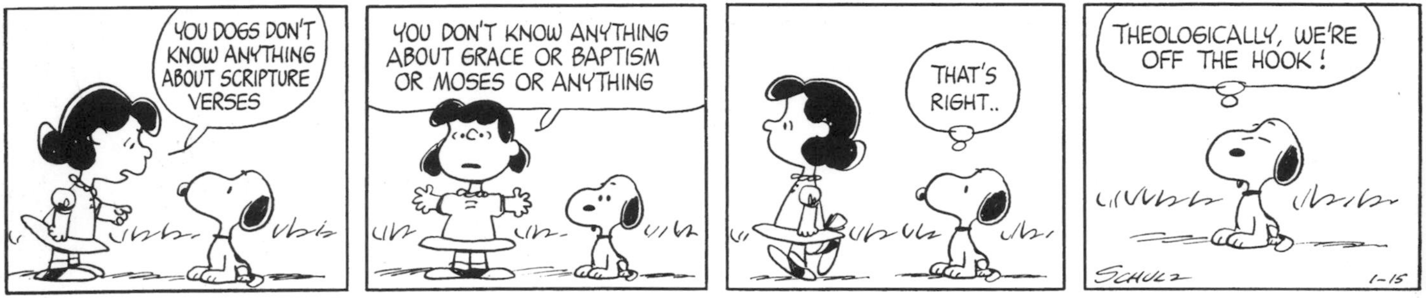
YOU DOGS DON'T KNOW ANYTHING ABOUT SCRIPTURE VERSES
YOU DON'T KNOW ANYTHING ABOUT GRACE OR BAPTISM OR MOSES OR ANYTHING
THAT'S RIGHT..
THEOLOGICALLY, WE'RE OFF THE HOOK!
SCHULZ
1-15

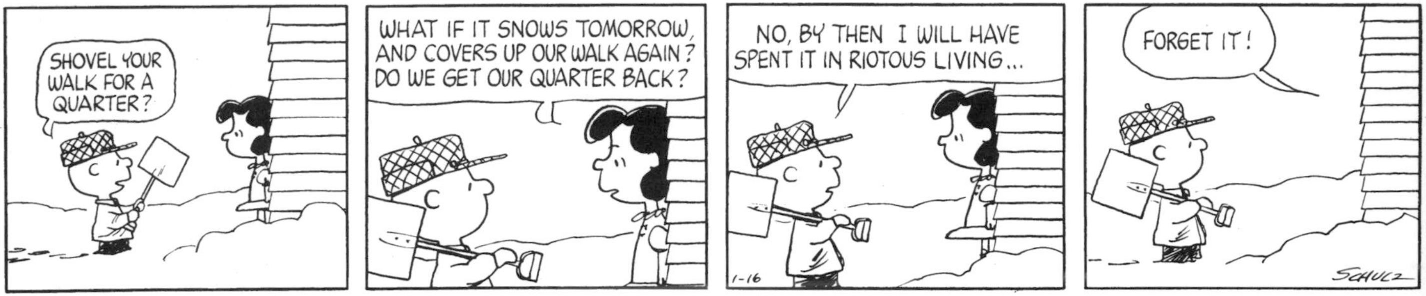
SHOVEL YOUR WALK FOR A QUARTER?
WHAT IF IT SNOWS TOMORROW, AND COVERS UP OUR WALK AGAIN? DO WE GET OUR QUARTER BACK?
NO, BY THEN I WILL HAVE SPENT IT IN RIOTOUS LIVING...
1-16
FORGET IT!
SCHULZ

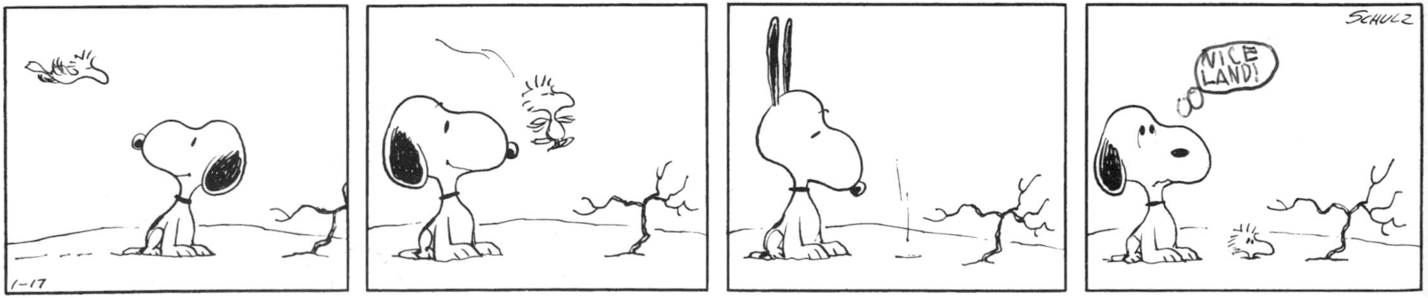
1-17
SCHULZ
NICE LAND!

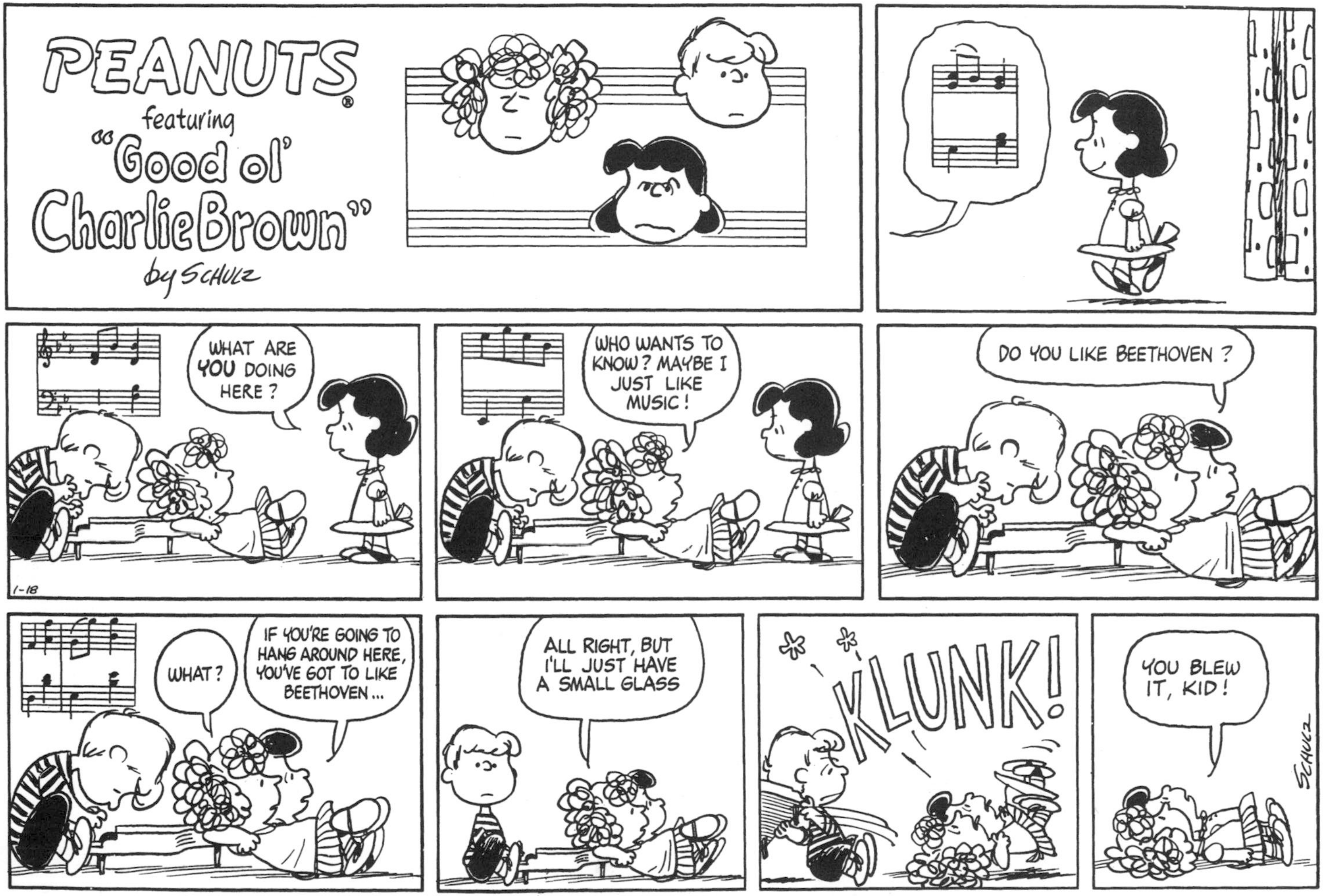
PEANUTS®
featuring
"Good ol' CharlieBrown"
by SCHULZ
WHAT ARE YOU DOING HERE ?
WHO WANTS TO KNOW ? MAYBE I JUST LIKE MUSIC !
DO YOU LIKE BEETHOVEN ?
WHAT ?
IF YOU'RE GOING TO HANG AROUND HERE, YOU'VE GOT TO LIKE BEETHOVEN ...
ALL RIGHT, BUT I'LL JUST HAVE A SMALL GLASS
KLUNK!
YOU BLEW IT, KID !
SCHULZ
1-18

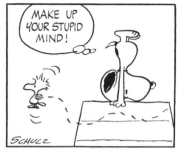

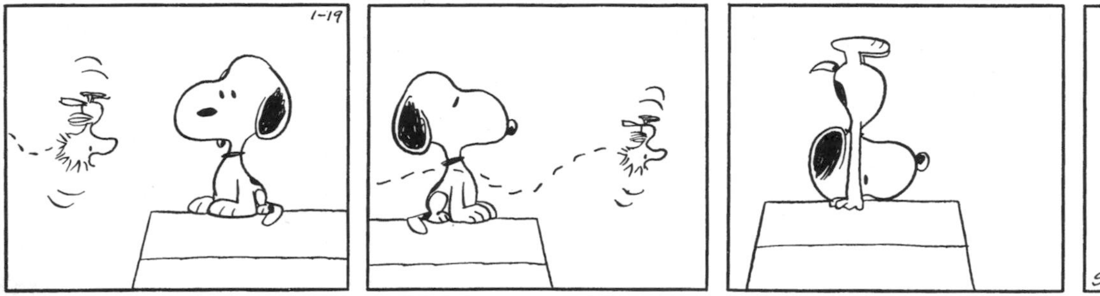
MAKE UP YOUR STUPID MIND!

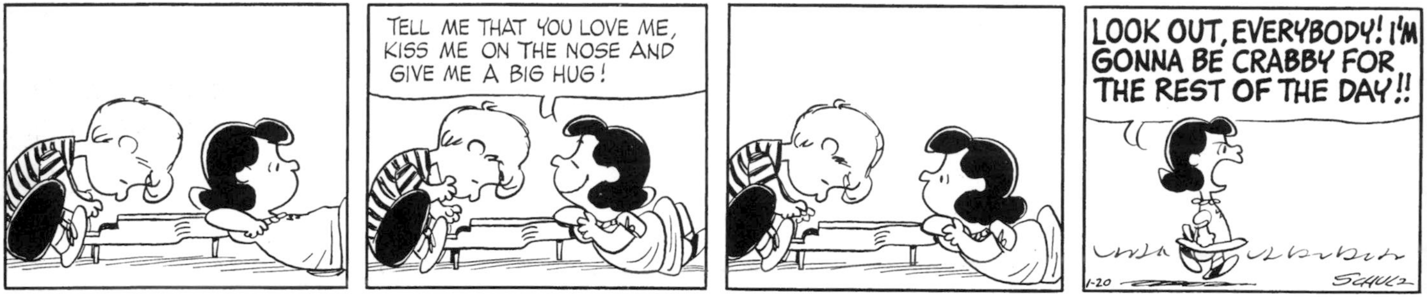
TELL ME THAT YOU LOVE ME, KISS ME ON THE NOSE AND GIVE ME A BIG HUG!
LOOK OUT, EVERYBODY! I'M GONNA BE CRABBY FOR THE REST OF THE DAY!!

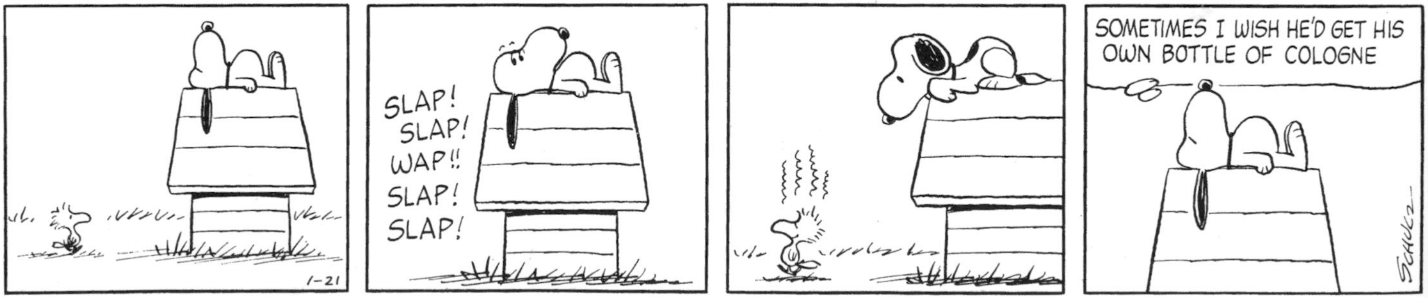
SLAP! SLAP! WAP!! SLAP! SLAP!
SOMETIMES I WISH HE'D GET HIS OWN BOTTLE OF COLOGNE

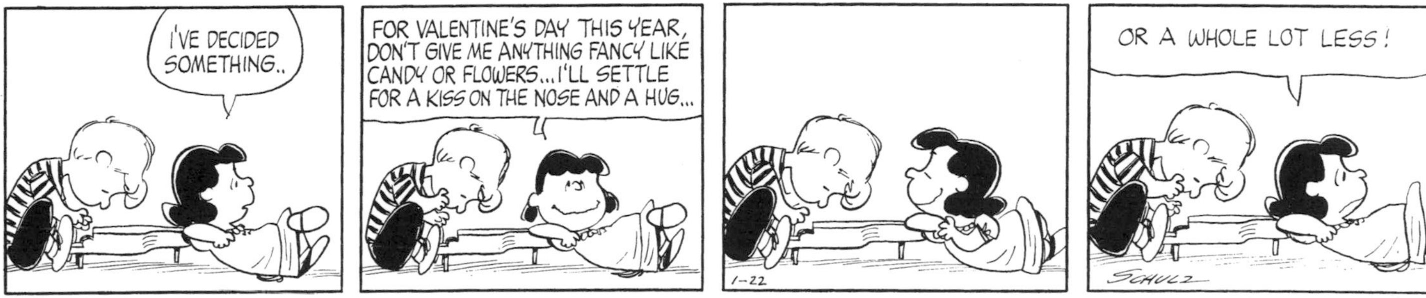
I'VE DECIDED SOMETHING..
FOR VALENTINE'S DAY THIS YEAR, DON'T GIVE ME ANYTHING FANCY LIKE CANDY OR FLOWERS...I'LL SETTLE FOR A KISS ON THE NOSE AND A HUG...
OR A WHOLE LOT LESS!

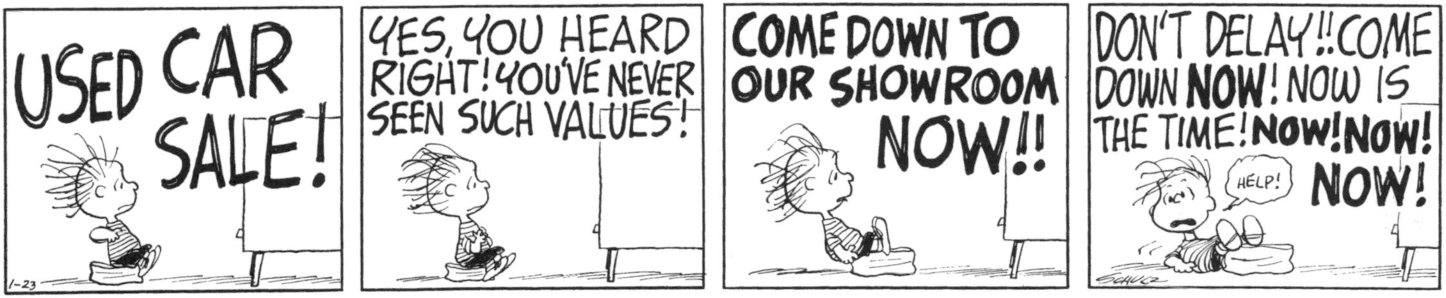
USED CAR SALE!
YES, YOU HEARD RIGHT! YOU'VE NEVER SEEN SUCH VALUES!
COME DOWN TO OUR SHOWROOM NOW!!
DON'T DELAY!! COME DOWN NOW! NOW IS THE TIME! NOW! NOW! NOW!
HELP!

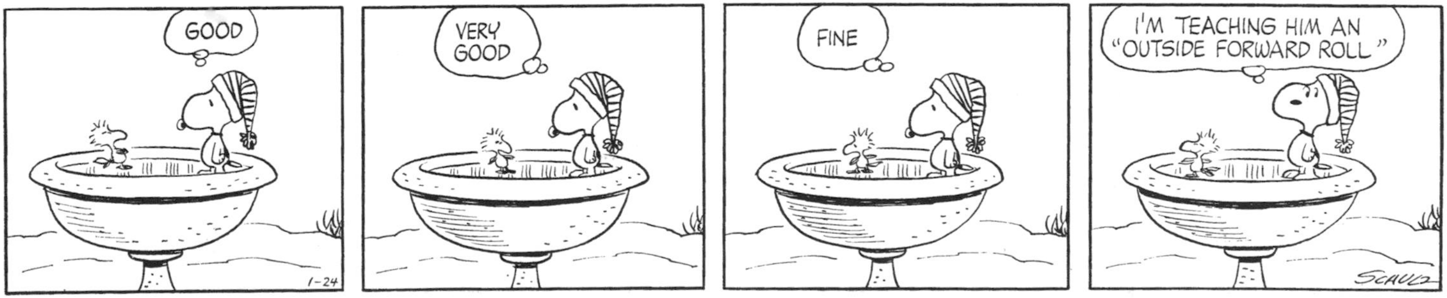
GOOD
VERY GOOD
FINE
I'M TEACHING HIM AN "OUTSIDE FORWARD ROLL"

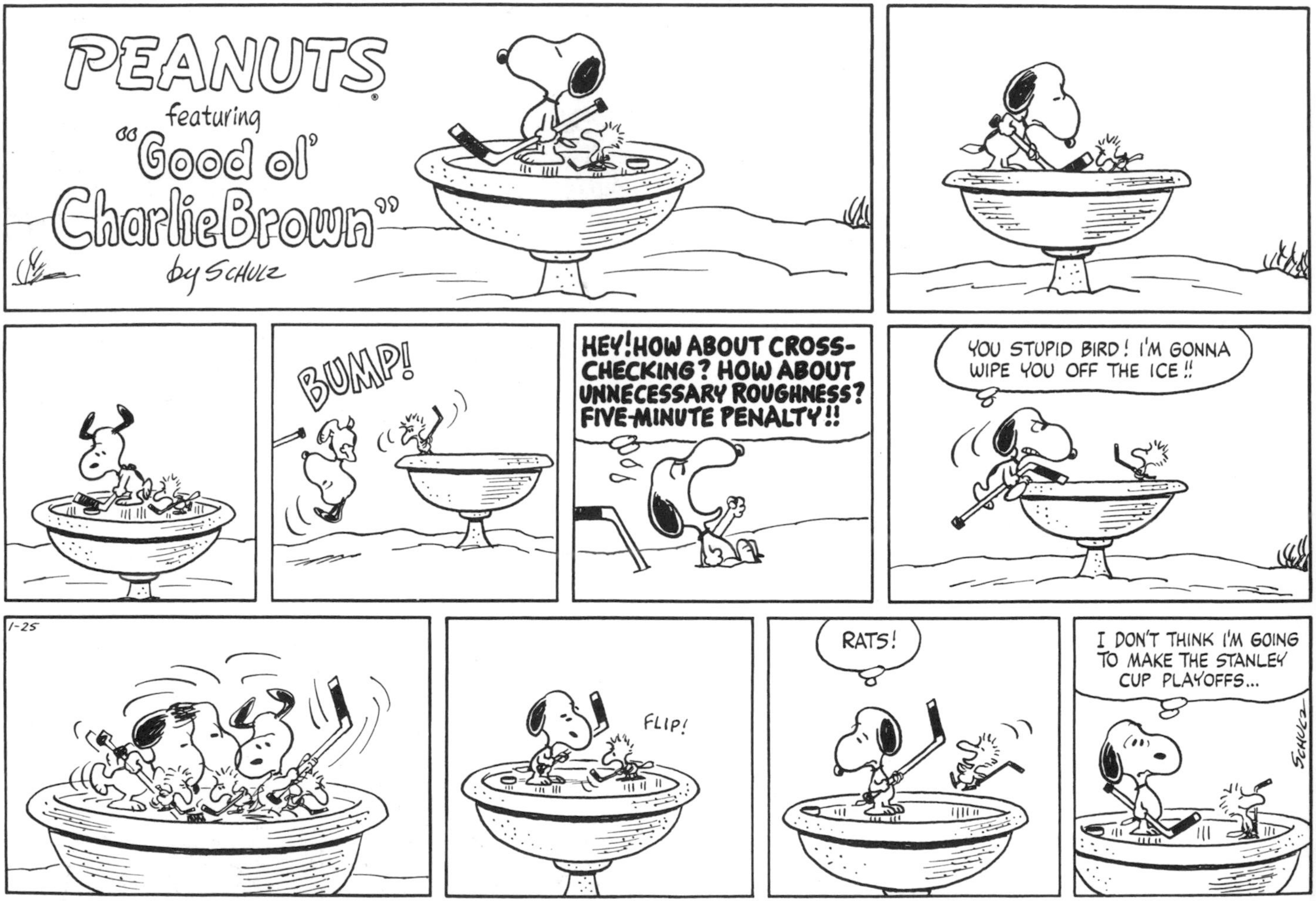
PEANUTS
featuring
"Good ol' CharlieBrown"
by SCHULZ
BUMP!
HEY! HOW ABOUT CROSS-CHECKING? HOW ABOUT UNNECESSARY ROUGHNESS? FIVE-MINUTE PENALTY!!
YOU STUPID BIRD! I'M GONNA WIPE YOU OFF THE ICE!!
1-25
FLIP!
RATS!
I DON'T THINK I'M GOING TO MAKE THE STANLEY CUP PLAYOFFS...
SCHULZ

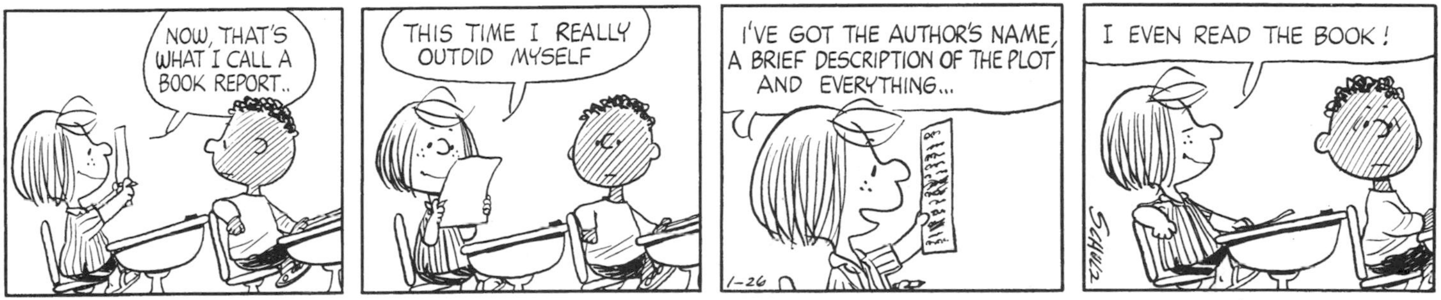
NOW, THAT'S WHAT I CALL A BOOK REPORT..
THIS TIME I REALLY OUTDID MYSELF
I'VE GOT THE AUTHOR'S NAME, A BRIEF DESCRIPTION OF THE PLOT AND EVERYTHING...
I EVEN READ THE BOOK!

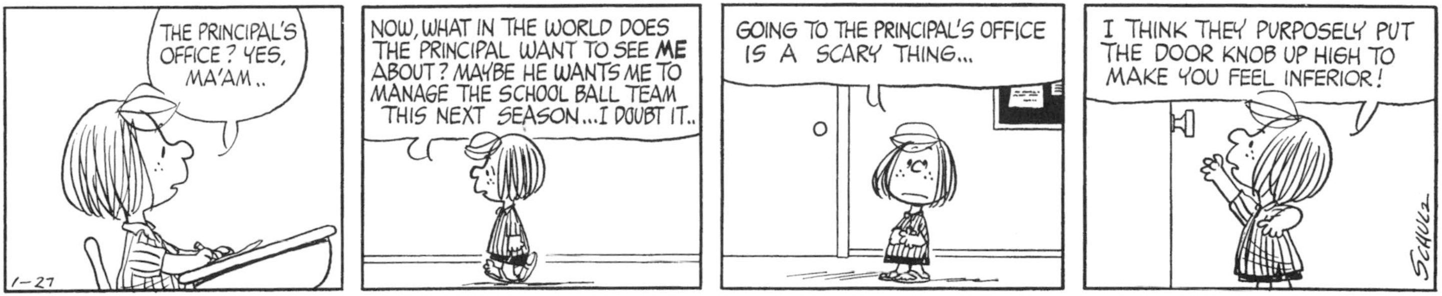
THE PRINCIPAL'S OFFICE? YES, MA'AM..
NOW, WHAT IN THE WORLD DOES THE PRINCIPAL WANT TO SEE ME ABOUT? MAYBE HE WANTS ME TO MANAGE THE SCHOOL BALL TEAM THIS NEXT SEASON...I DOUBT IT..
GOING TO THE PRINCIPAL'S OFFICE IS A SCARY THING...
I THINK THEY PURPOSELY PUT THE DOOR KNOB UP HIGH TO MAKE YOU FEEL INFERIOR!

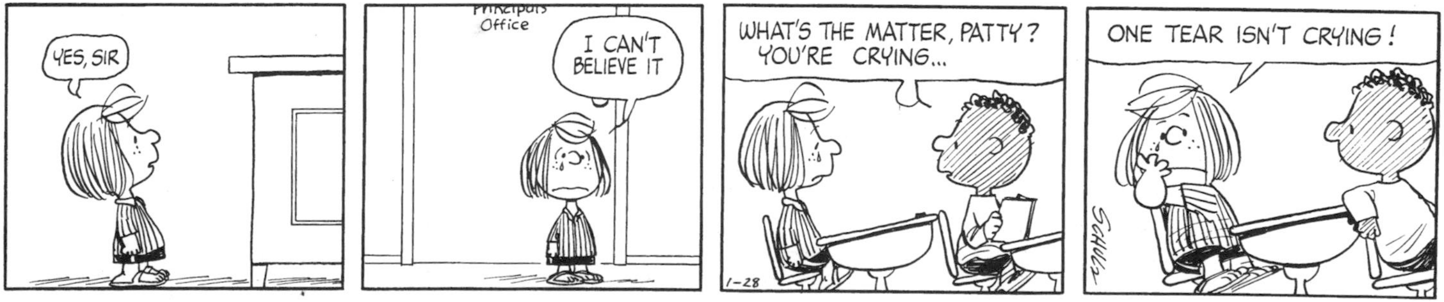
YES, SIR
Office
I CAN'T BELIEVE IT
WHAT'S THE MATTER, PATTY? YOU'RE CRYING...
ONE TEAR ISN'T CRYING!

Peppermint Patty: HELLO, CHUCK? I NEED YOUR HELP.. I NEED SOMEONE TO TALK TO

Peppermint Patty: GUESS WHAT HAPPENED...THEY WON'T LET ME WEAR MY SANDALS TO SCHOOL ANY MORE..IT'S AGAINST THE DRESS CODE...WHAT AM I GOING TO DO? I NEED YOUR ADVICE...

1-29

Charlie Brown: WELL, I...I...I DON'T KNOW...I... YOU...I...I...IT...YOU....I..I..I....

THANKS, CHUCK.. click!

SIGH

Peppermint Patty: I SAW A PAIR OF SANDALS IN A STORE ONE DAY, AND I ASKED MY DAD IF I COULD HAVE THEM..

Peppermint Patty: HE SAID, "YOU MOST CERTAINLY MAY HAVE THEM BECAUSE YOU ARE A RARE GEM!" NOW, THEY SAY I CAN'T WEAR THEM TO SCHOOL ANY MORE BECAUSE OF THE DRESS CODE..WHAT AM I GOING TO DO? I LOVE MY SANDALS...SNIF!

1-30

SMAK!

I KISSED AWAY A TEAR!

THEY SAY IT'S THE SCHOOL DRESS CODE, LINUS..

I CAN'T WEAR MY SANDALS TO SCHOOL ANY MORE... I'M REALLY UPSET... SNIF!

SMAK!

1-31

AND THEN THIS WEIRD KID WITH THE BIG NOSE KEEPS KISSING ME!

WE ALL NEED SOMEONE TO KISS AWAY OUR TEARS

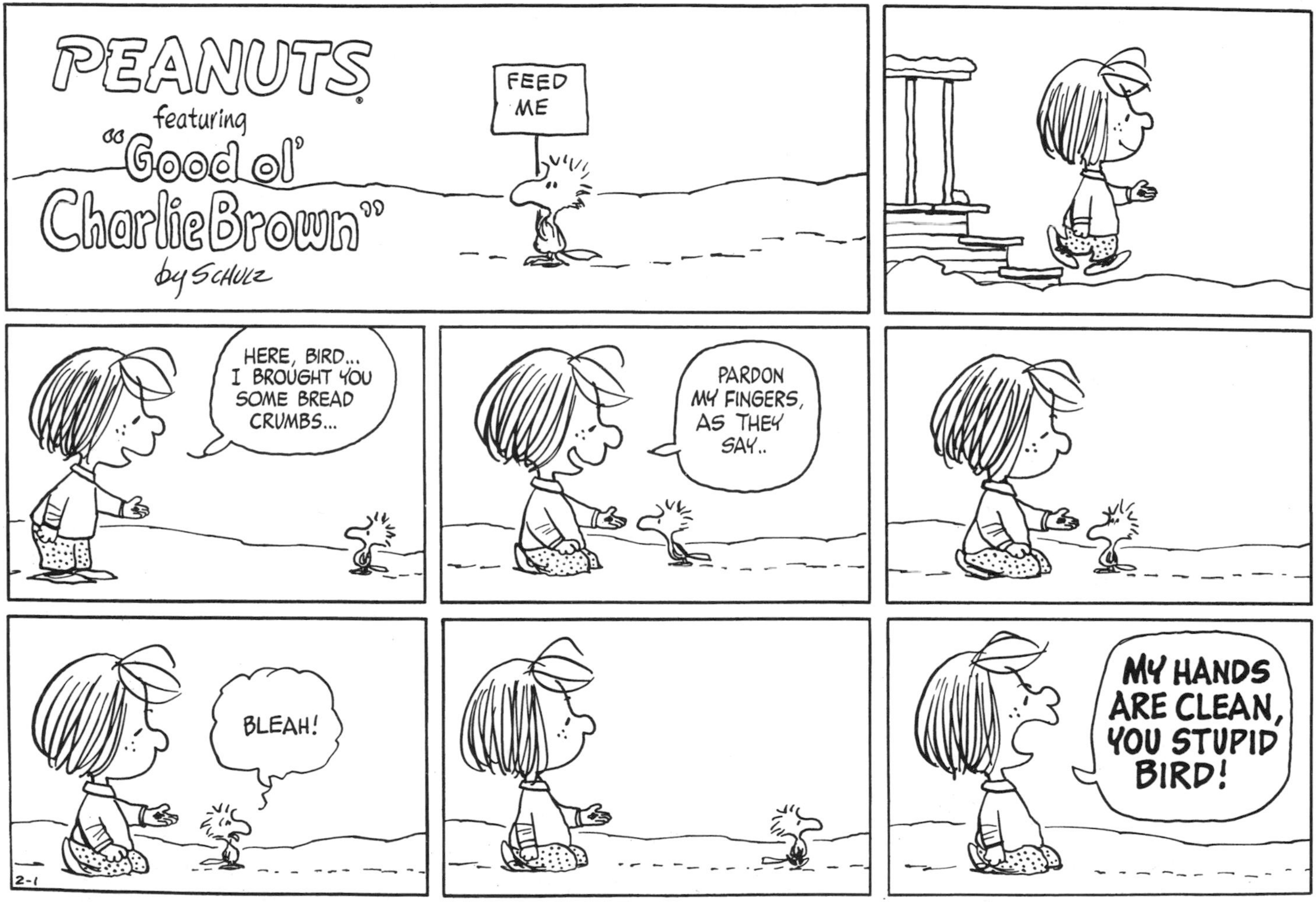
PEANUTS
featuring
"Good ol' Charlie Brown"
by SCHULZ
FEED ME
HERE, BIRD... I BROUGHT YOU SOME BREAD CRUMBS...
PARDON MY FINGERS, AS THEY SAY..
BLEAH!
2-1
MY HANDS ARE CLEAN, YOU STUPID BIRD!

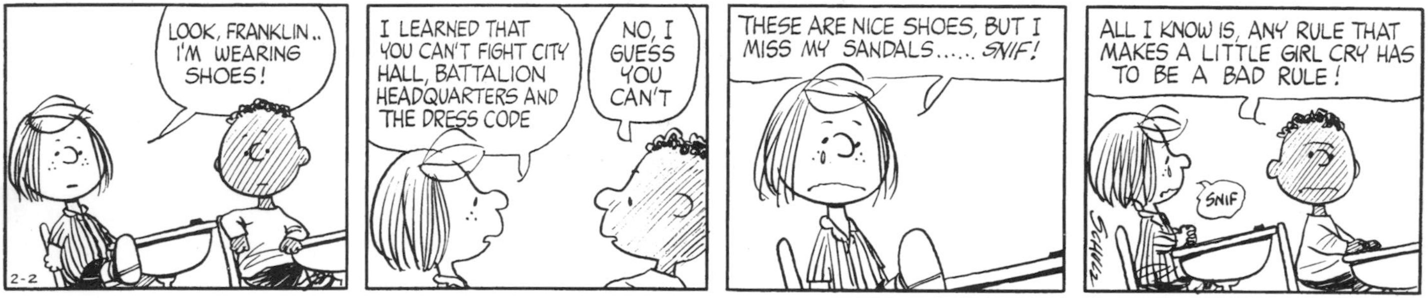
2-2
LOOK, FRANKLIN.. I'M WEARING SHOES!
I LEARNED THAT YOU CAN'T FIGHT CITY HALL, BATTALION HEADQUARTERS AND THE DRESS CODE
NO, I GUESS YOU CAN'T
THESE ARE NICE SHOES, BUT I MISS MY SANDALS..... SNIF!
ALL I KNOW IS, ANY RULE THAT MAKES A LITTLE GIRL CRY HAS TO BE A BAD RULE!
SNIF
SCHULZ

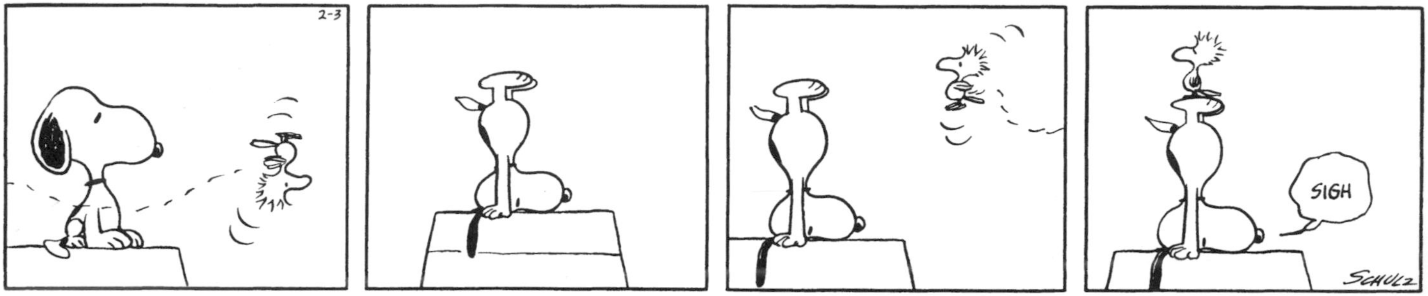
2-3
SIGH
SCHULZ

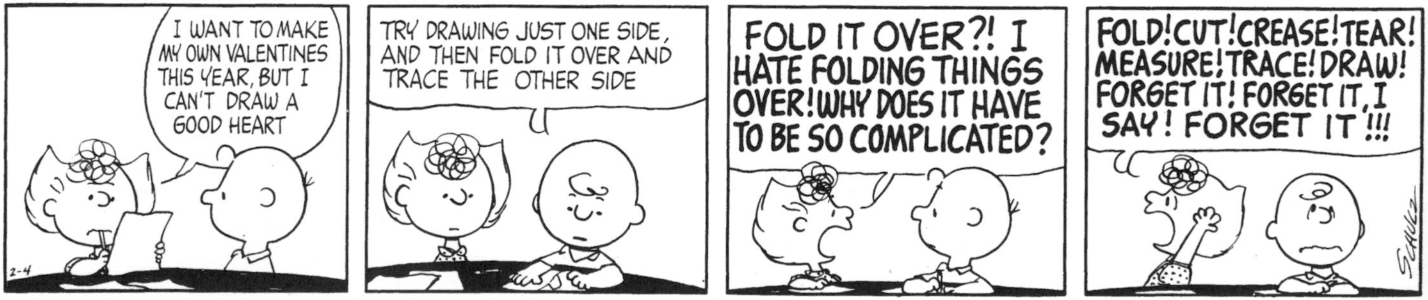
2-4
I WANT TO MAKE MY OWN VALENTINES THIS YEAR, BUT I CAN'T DRAW A GOOD HEART
TRY DRAWING JUST ONE SIDE, AND THEN FOLD IT OVER AND TRACE THE OTHER SIDE
FOLD IT OVER?! I HATE FOLDING THINGS OVER! WHY DOES IT HAVE TO BE SO COMPLICATED?
FOLD! CUT! CREASE! TEAR! MEASURE! TRACE! DRAW! FORGET IT! FORGET IT, I SAY! FORGET IT!!!
SCHULZ

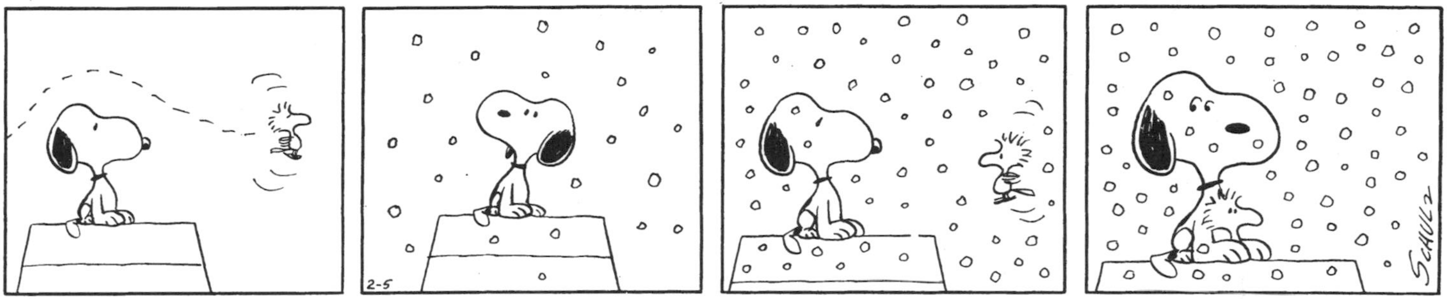
2-5
SCHULZ

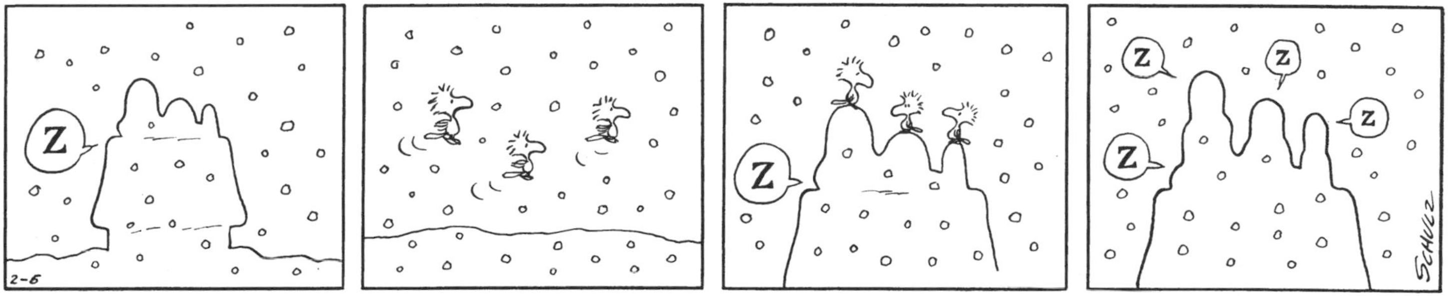
Z
2-6
Z
Z
Z
Z
Z
SCHULZ

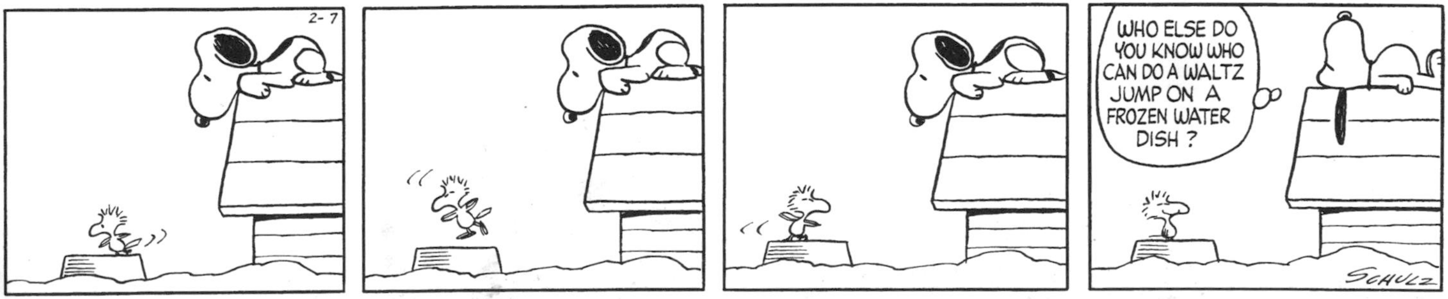
2-7
WHO ELSE DO YOU KNOW WHO CAN DO A WALTZ JUMP ON A FROZEN WATER DISH ?
SCHULZ

PEANUTS

featuring

"Good ol' Charlie Brown"

by SCHULZ

TRZIC
Kamnik
VRHNIKA

HERE I AM PRACTICING FOR THE WORLD FIGURE-SKATING CHAMPIONSHIP IN YUGOSLAVIA..

2-8

I'LL PROBABLY CATCH A FLIGHT OUT OF NEW YORK ON FEBRUARY TWENTY-SEVENTH ...

I'LL ARRIVE IN ZURICH IN THE MORNING, AND CONNECT WITH ANOTHER FLIGHT TO ZAGREB...

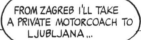

FROM ZAGREB I'LL TAKE A PRIVATE MOTORCOACH TO LJUBLJANA ...

AS I RECALL, WE GO UP HIGHWAY NINETY-FOUR ABOUT A HUNDRED MILES...

I'LL GET UP SUNDAY MORNING IN LJUBLJANA, HAVE A GREAT BREAKFAST, AND THEN ...

GET OFF THE ICE, YOU STUPID BEAGLE!

THEN AGAIN, I MAY JUST STAY HOME AND WATCH THE WHOLE THING ON TV ...

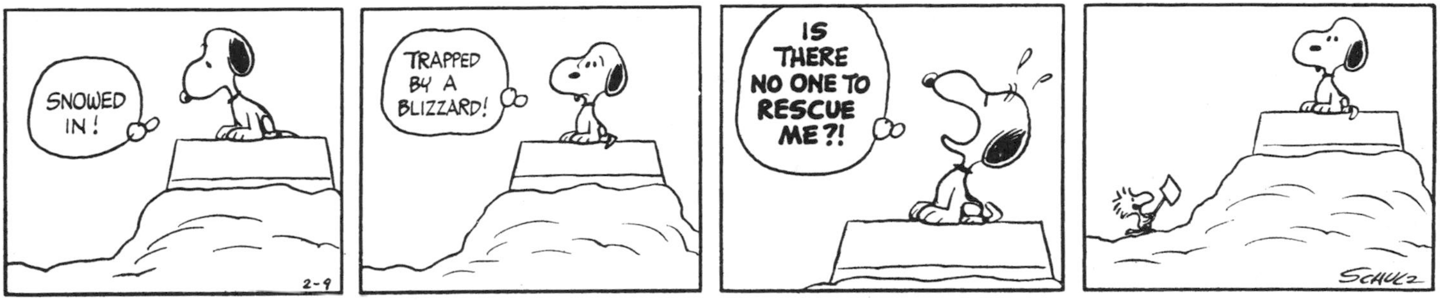
SNOWED IN!
2-9
TRAPPED BY A BLIZZARD!
IS THERE NO ONE TO RESCUE ME?!
SCHULZ

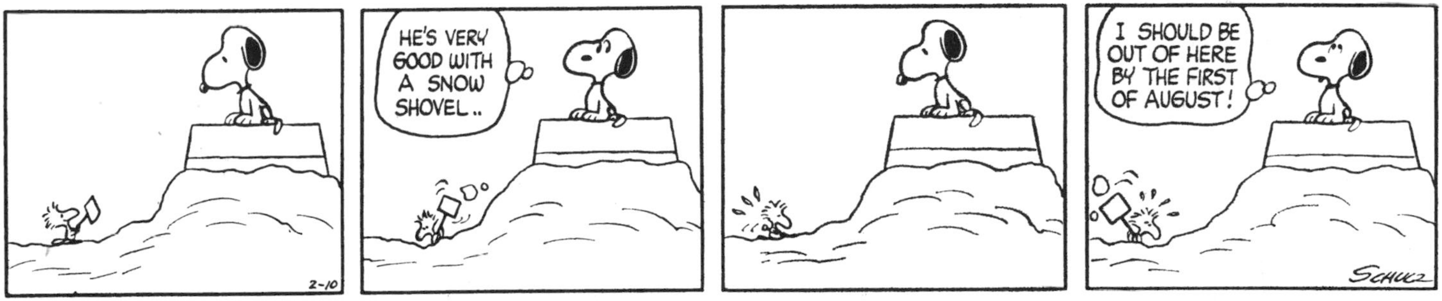
2-10
HE'S VERY GOOD WITH A SNOW SHOVEL..
I SHOULD BE OUT OF HERE BY THE FIRST OF AUGUST!
SCHULZ

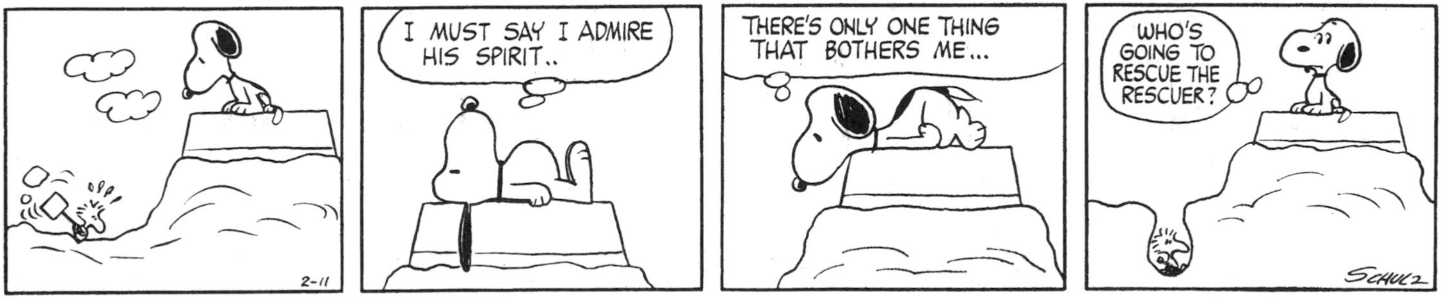
2-11
I MUST SAY I ADMIRE HIS SPIRIT..
THERE'S ONLY ONE THING THAT BOTHERS ME...
WHO'S GOING TO RESCUE THE RESCUER?
SCHULZ

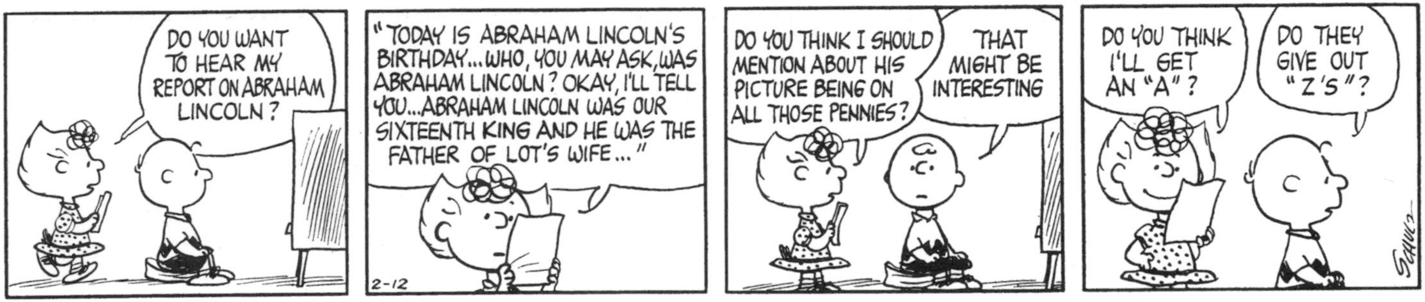
DO YOU WANT TO HEAR MY REPORT ON ABRAHAM LINCOLN?
"TODAY IS ABRAHAM LINCOLN'S BIRTHDAY...WHO, YOU MAY ASK, WAS ABRAHAM LINCOLN? OKAY, I'LL TELL YOU...ABRAHAM LINCOLN WAS OUR SIXTEENTH KING AND HE WAS THE FATHER OF LOT'S WIFE..."
2-12
DO YOU THINK I SHOULD MENTION ABOUT HIS PICTURE BEING ON ALL THOSE PENNIES?
THAT MIGHT BE INTERESTING
DO YOU THINK I'LL GET AN "A"?
DO THEY GIVE OUT "Z'S"?
SCHULZ

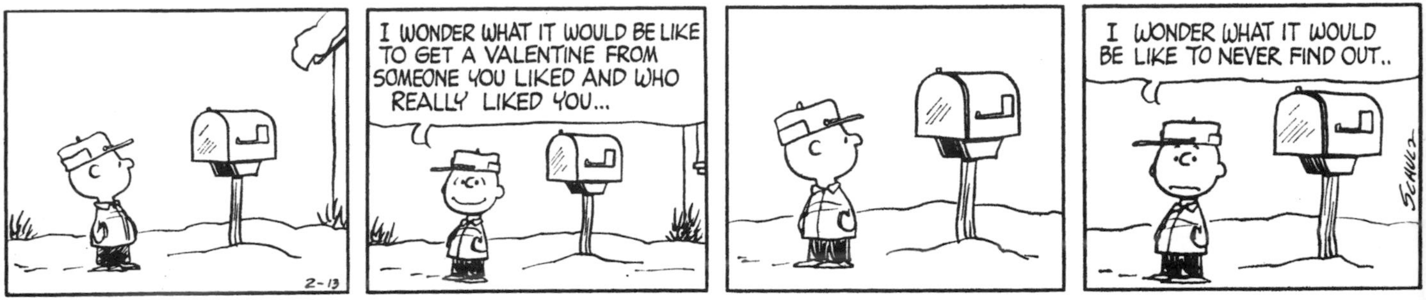
2-13
I WONDER WHAT IT WOULD BE LIKE TO GET A VALENTINE FROM SOMEONE YOU LIKED AND WHO REALLY LIKED YOU...
I WONDER WHAT IT WOULD BE LIKE TO NEVER FIND OUT..
SCHULZ

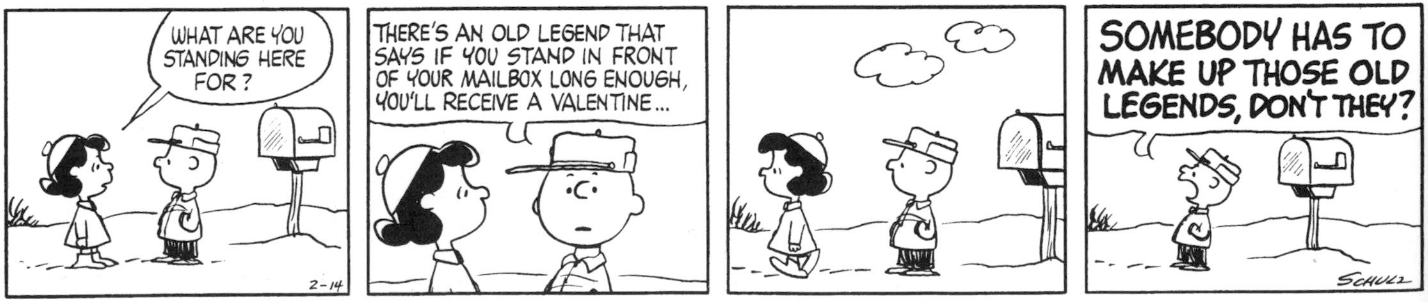
WHAT ARE YOU STANDING HERE FOR?
2-14
THERE'S AN OLD LEGEND THAT SAYS IF YOU STAND IN FRONT OF YOUR MAILBOX LONG ENOUGH, YOU'LL RECEIVE A VALENTINE...
SOMEBODY HAS TO MAKE UP THOSE OLD LEGENDS, DON'T THEY?
SCHULZ

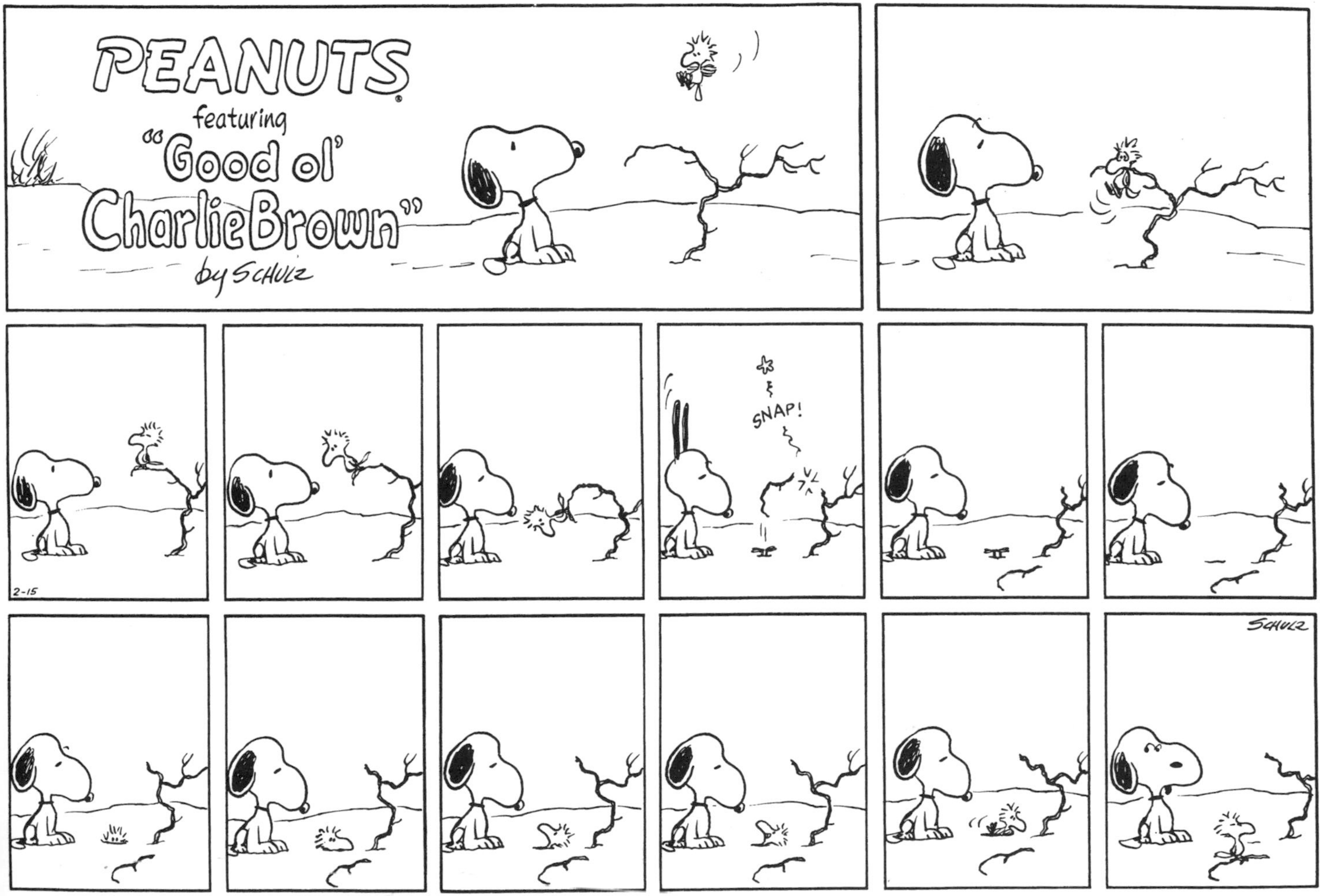
PEANUTS®
featuring
"Good ol' Charlie Brown"
by SCHULZ
2-15
SNAP!
SCHULZ

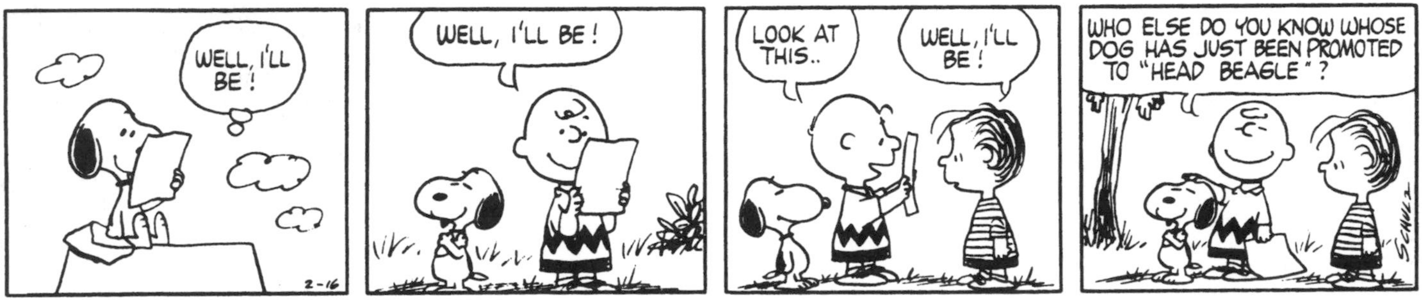
WELL, I'LL BE!
WELL, I'LL BE!
LOOK AT THIS..
WELL, I'LL BE!
WHO ELSE DO YOU KNOW WHOSE DOG HAS JUST BEEN PROMOTED TO "HEAD BEAGLE"?
2-16
SCHULZ

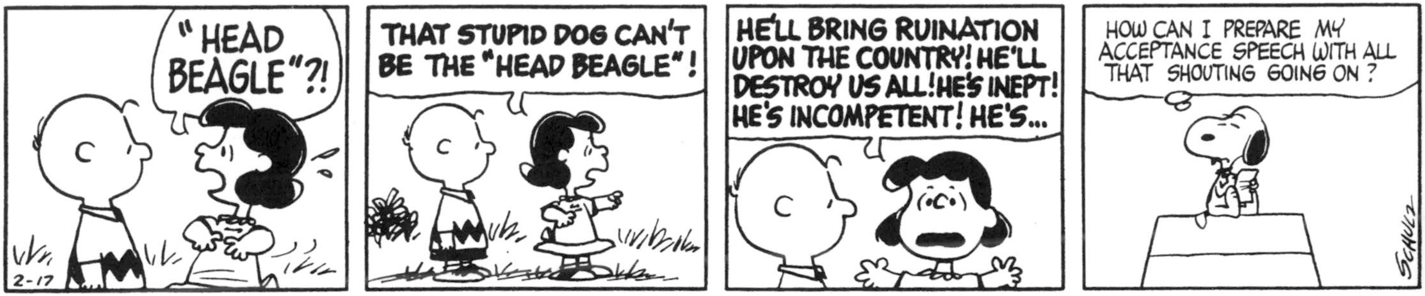
"HEAD BEAGLE"?!
2-17
THAT STUPID DOG CAN'T BE THE "HEAD BEAGLE"!
HE'LL BRING RUINATION UPON THE COUNTRY! HE'LL DESTROY US ALL! HE'S INEPT! HE'S INCOMPETENT! HE'S...
HOW CAN I PREPARE MY ACCEPTANCE SPEECH WITH ALL THAT SHOUTING GOING ON?
SCHULZ

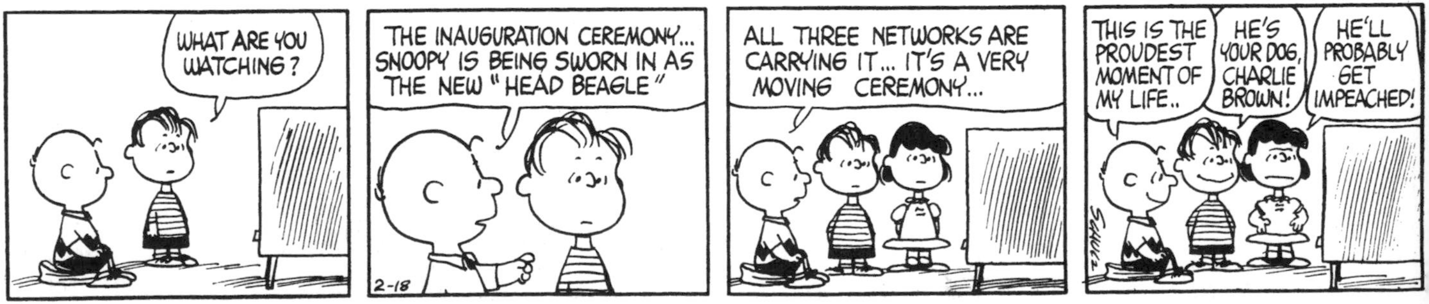
WHAT ARE YOU WATCHING?
THE INAUGURATION CEREMONY... SNOOPY IS BEING SWORN IN AS THE NEW "HEAD BEAGLE"
2-18
ALL THREE NETWORKS ARE CARRYING IT... IT'S A VERY MOVING CEREMONY...
THIS IS THE PROUDEST MOMENT OF MY LIFE..
HE'S YOUR DOG, CHARLIE BROWN!
HE'LL PROBABLY GET IMPEACHED!
SCHULZ

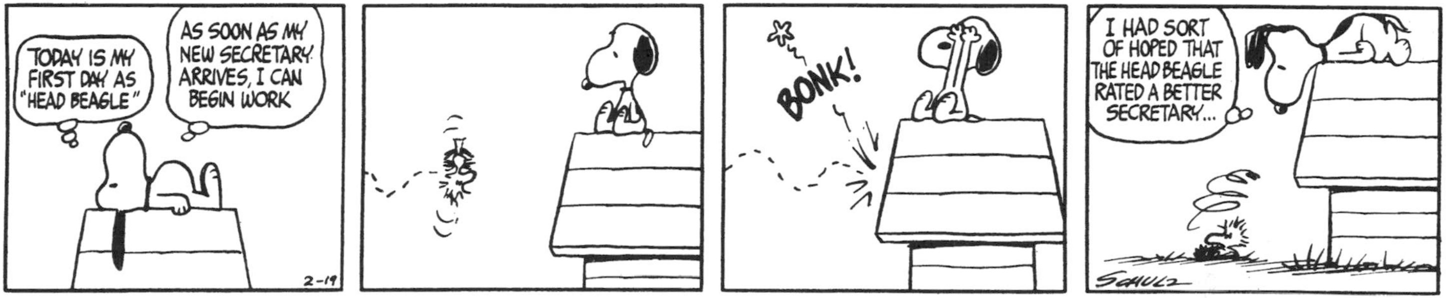
TODAY IS MY FIRST DAY AS "HEAD BEAGLE"
AS SOON AS MY NEW SECRETARY ARRIVES, I CAN BEGIN WORK
BONK!
I HAD SORT OF HOPED THAT THE HEAD BEAGLE RATED A BETTER SECRETARY...
2-19
SCHULZ

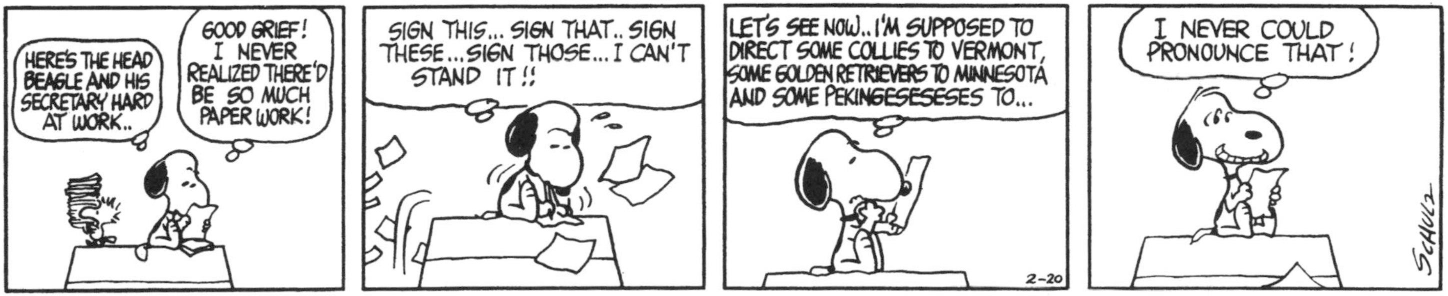
HERE'S THE HEAD BEAGLE AND HIS SECRETARY HARD AT WORK..
GOOD GRIEF! I NEVER REALIZED THERE'D BE SO MUCH PAPER WORK!
SIGN THIS... SIGN THAT.. SIGN THESE...SIGN THOSE...I CAN'T STAND IT!!
LET'S SEE NOW..I'M SUPPOSED TO DIRECT SOME COLLIES TO VERMONT, SOME GOLDEN RETRIEVERS TO MINNESOTA AND SOME PEKINGESESESES TO...
2-20
I NEVER COULD PRONOUNCE THAT!
SCHULZ

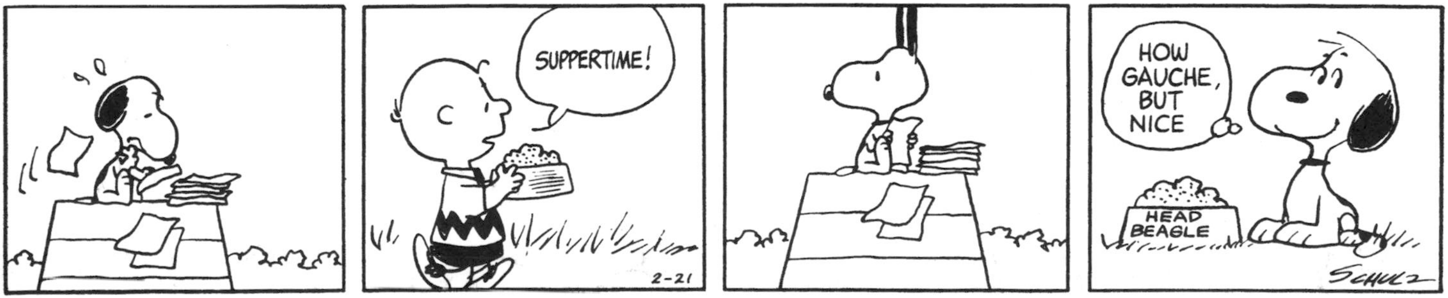
SUPPERTIME!
2-21
HOW GAUCHE, BUT NICE
HEAD BEAGLE
SCHULZ

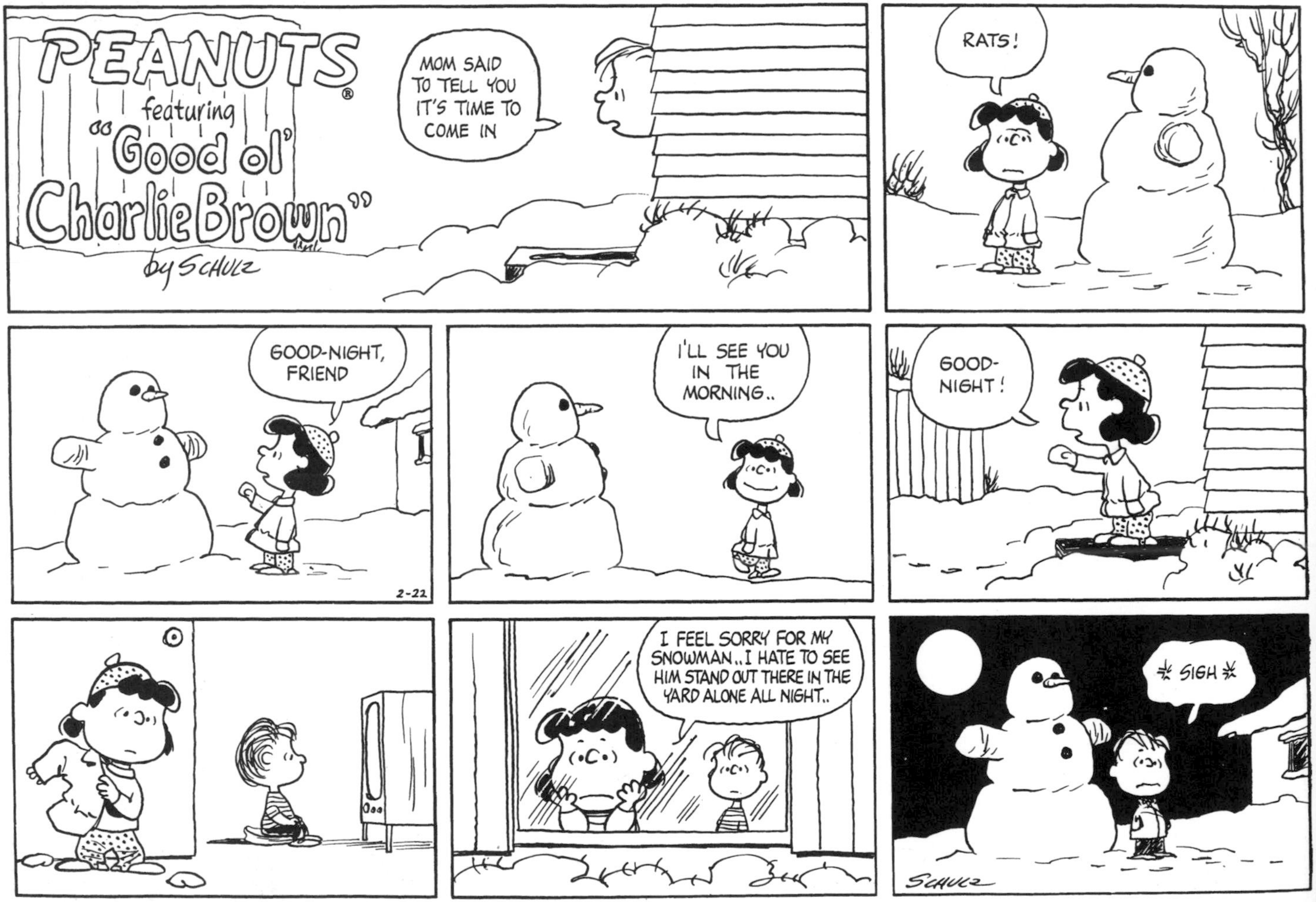
PEANUTS®
featuring "Good ol' Charlie Brown"
by SCHULZ
MOM SAID TO TELL YOU IT'S TIME TO COME IN
RATS!
GOOD-NIGHT, FRIEND
I'LL SEE YOU IN THE MORNING..
GOOD-NIGHT!
I FEEL SORRY FOR MY SNOWMAN..I HATE TO SEE HIM STAND OUT THERE IN THE YARD ALONE ALL NIGHT..
SIGH
SCHULZ

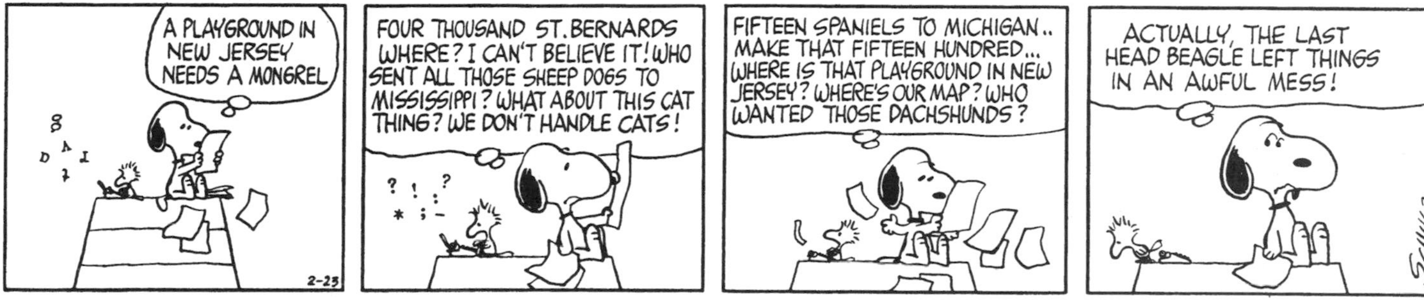
A PLAYGROUND IN NEW JERSEY NEEDS A MONGREL
FOUR THOUSAND ST. BERNARDS WHERE? I CAN'T BELIEVE IT! WHO SENT ALL THOSE SHEEP DOGS TO MISSISSIPPI? WHAT ABOUT THIS CAT THING? WE DON'T HANDLE CATS!
FIFTEEN SPANIELS TO MICHIGAN.. MAKE THAT FIFTEEN HUNDRED... WHERE IS THAT PLAYGROUND IN NEW JERSEY? WHERE'S OUR MAP? WHO WANTED THOSE DACHSHUNDS?
ACTUALLY, THE LAST HEAD BEAGLE LEFT THINGS IN AN AWFUL MESS!

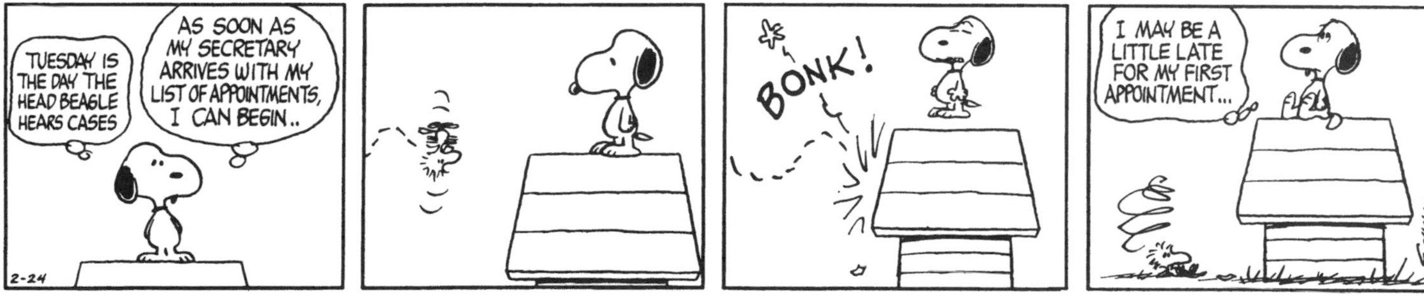
TUESDAY IS THE DAY THE HEAD BEAGLE HEARS CASES
AS SOON AS MY SECRETARY ARRIVES WITH MY LIST OF APPOINTMENTS, I CAN BEGIN..
BONK!
I MAY BE A LITTLE LATE FOR MY FIRST APPOINTMENT...

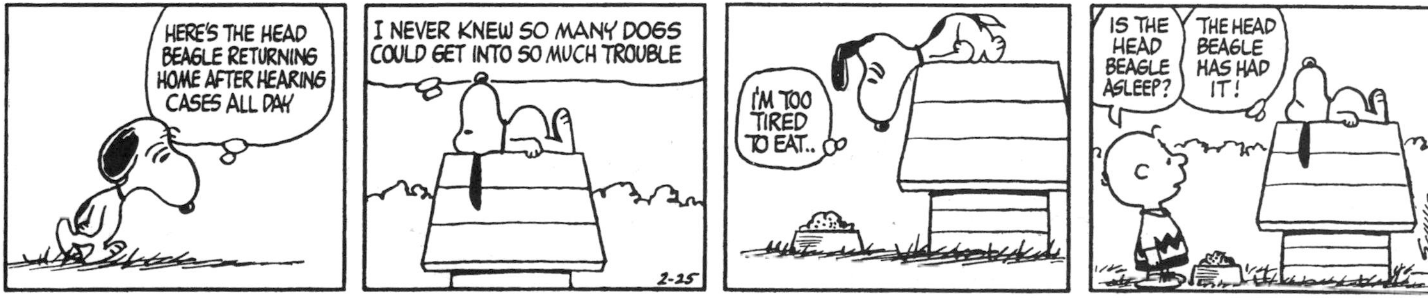
HERE'S THE HEAD BEAGLE RETURNING HOME AFTER HEARING CASES ALL DAY
I NEVER KNEW SO MANY DOGS COULD GET INTO SO MUCH TROUBLE
I'M TOO TIRED TO EAT..
IS THE HEAD BEAGLE ASLEEP?
THE HEAD BEAGLE HAS HAD IT!

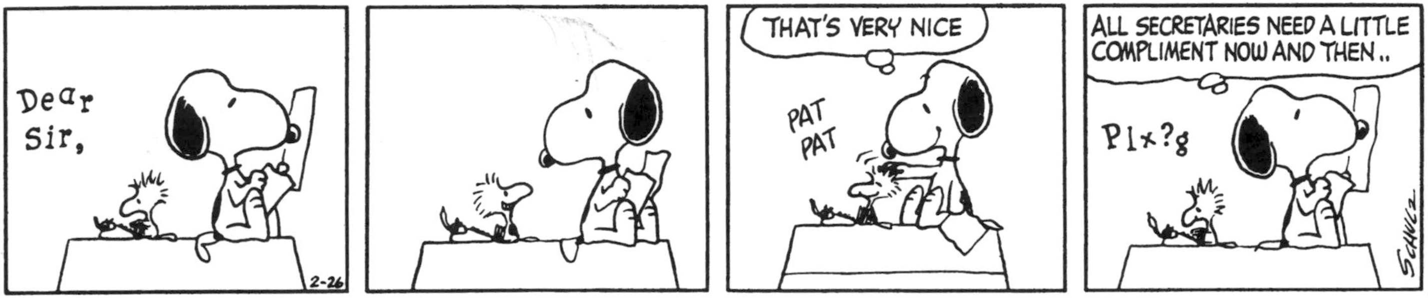
Dear Sir,
2-26
THAT'S VERY NICE
PAT PAT
ALL SECRETARIES NEED A LITTLE COMPLIMENT NOW AND THEN..
Plx?g
SCHULZ

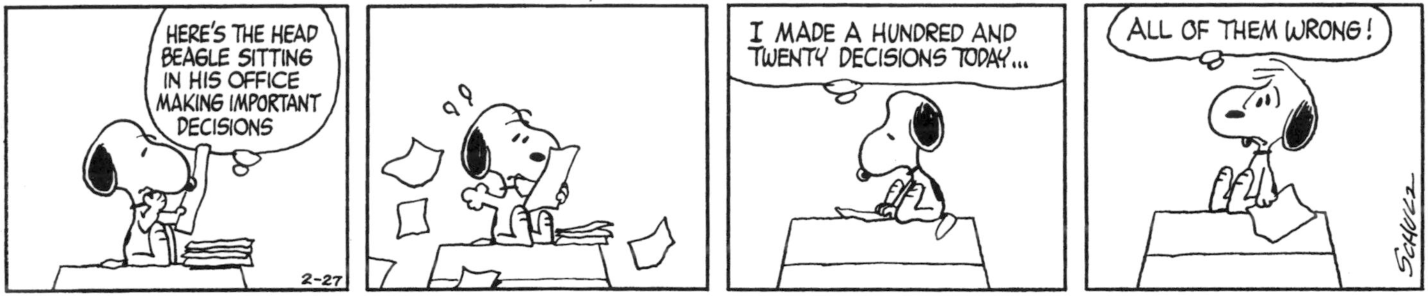
HERE'S THE HEAD BEAGLE SITTING IN HIS OFFICE MAKING IMPORTANT DECISIONS
2-27
I MADE A HUNDRED AND TWENTY DECISIONS TODAY...
ALL OF THEM WRONG!
SCHULZ

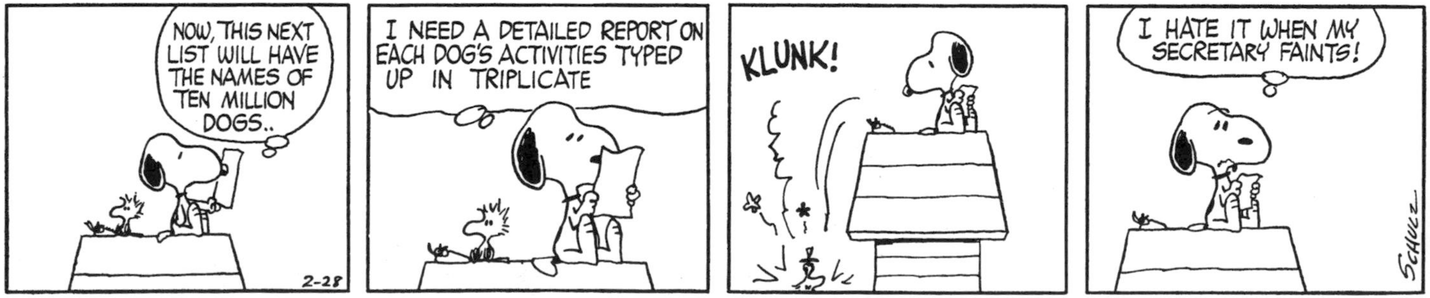
NOW, THIS NEXT LIST WILL HAVE THE NAMES OF TEN MILLION DOGS..
2-28
I NEED A DETAILED REPORT ON EACH DOG'S ACTIVITIES TYPED UP IN TRIPLICATE
KLUNK!
I HATE IT WHEN MY SECRETARY FAINTS!
SCHULZ

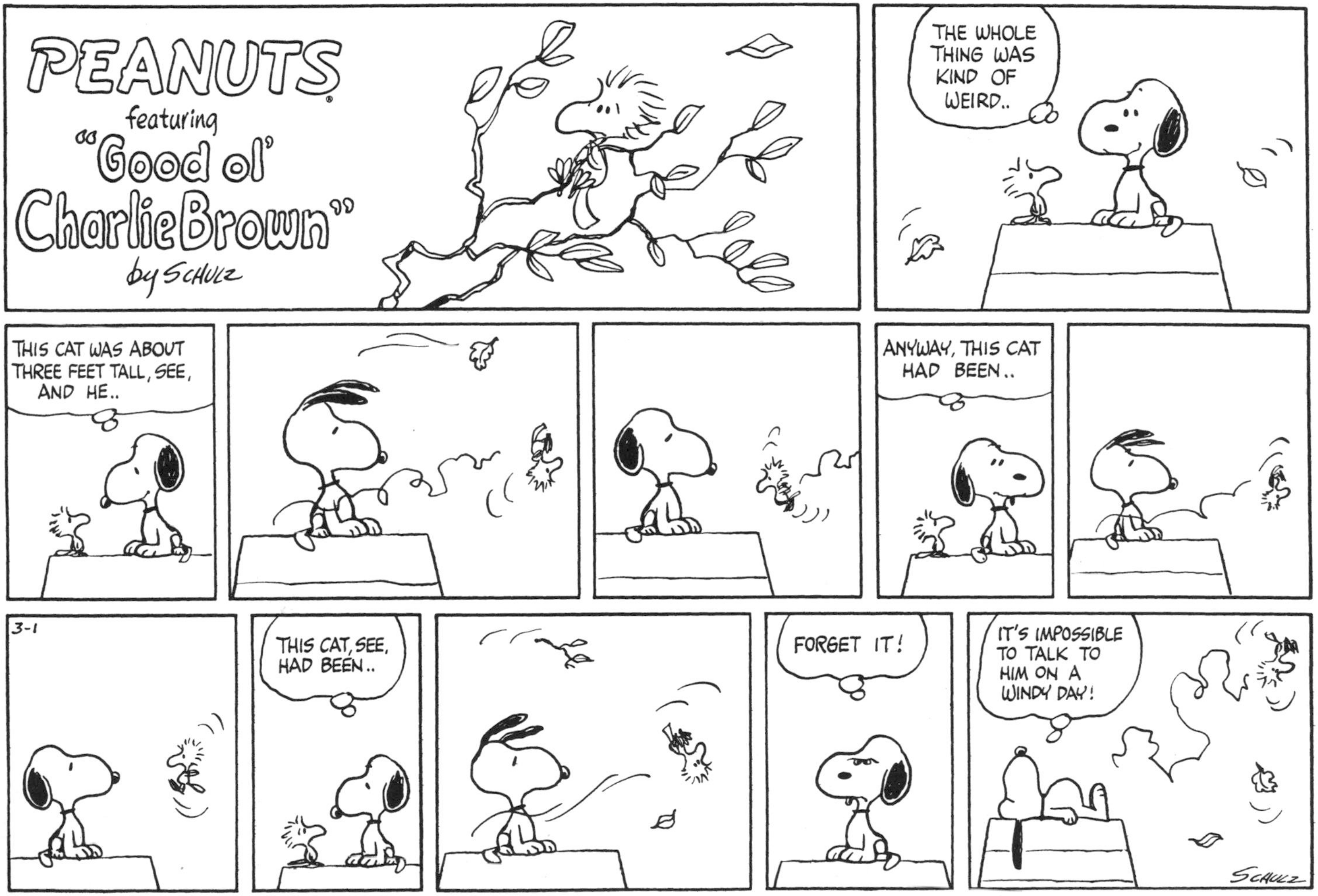
PEANUTS
featuring "Good ol' Charlie Brown"
by SCHULZ
THE WHOLE THING WAS KIND OF WEIRD..
THIS CAT WAS ABOUT THREE FEET TALL, SEE, AND HE..
ANYWAY, THIS CAT HAD BEEN..
3-1
THIS CAT, SEE, HAD BEEN..
FORGET IT!
IT'S IMPOSSIBLE TO TALK TO HIM ON A WINDY DAY!
SCHULZ

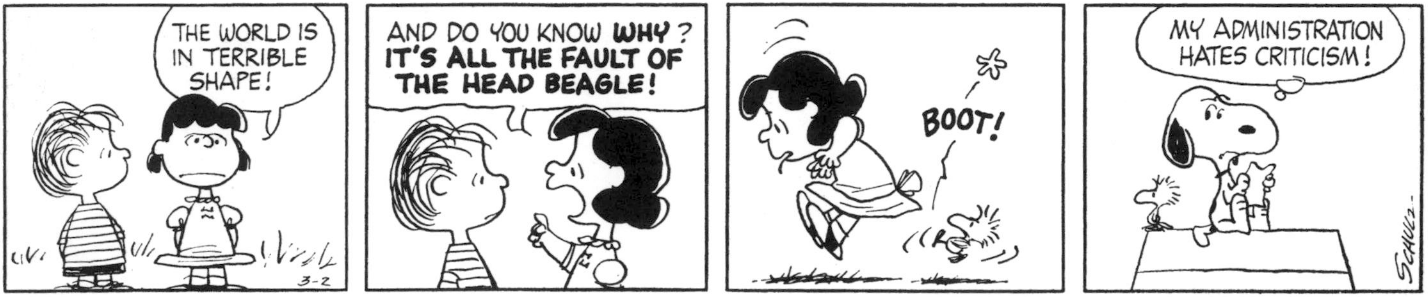
THE WORLD IS IN TERRIBLE SHAPE!
3-2
AND DO YOU KNOW WHY? IT'S ALL THE FAULT OF THE HEAD BEAGLE!
BOOT!
MY ADMINISTRATION HATES CRITICISM!
SCHULZ

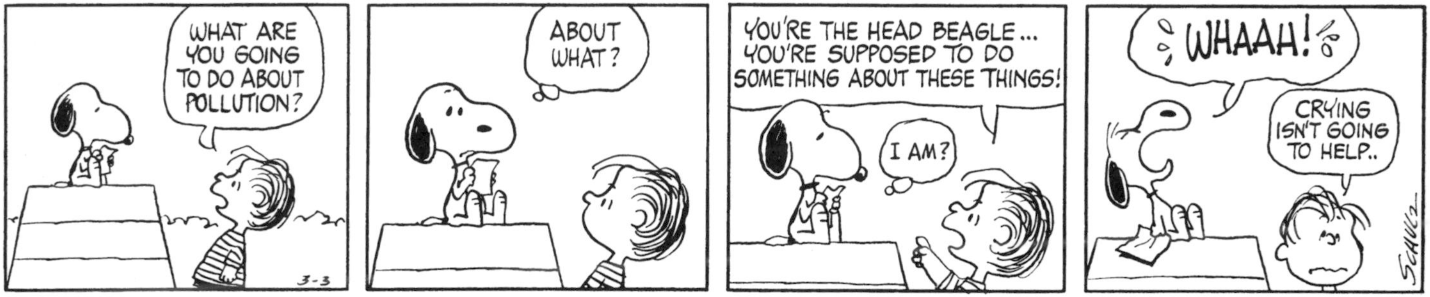
WHAT ARE YOU GOING TO DO ABOUT POLLUTION?
3-3
ABOUT WHAT?
YOU'RE THE HEAD BEAGLE... YOU'RE SUPPOSED TO DO SOMETHING ABOUT THESE THINGS!
I AM?
WHAAAH!
CRYING ISN'T GOING TO HELP..
SCHULZ

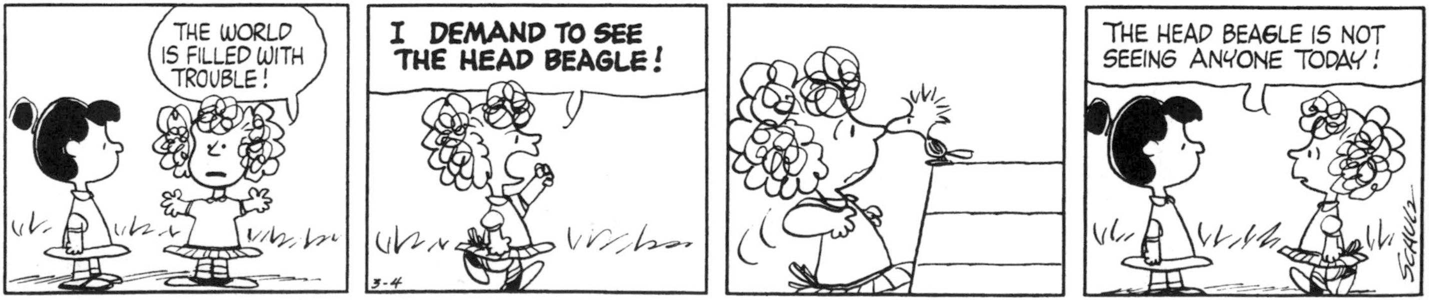
THE WORLD IS FILLED WITH TROUBLE!
I DEMAND TO SEE THE HEAD BEAGLE!
3-4
THE HEAD BEAGLE IS NOT SEEING ANYONE TODAY!
SCHULZ

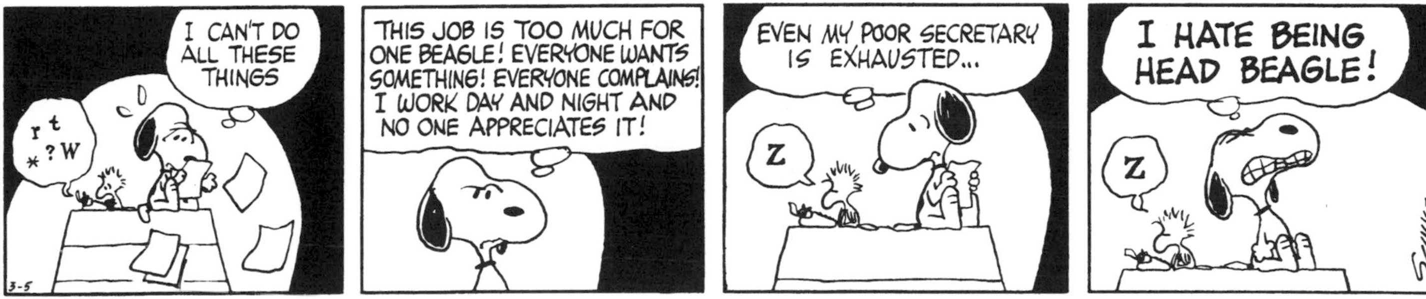
I CAN'T DO ALL THESE THINGS
r t * ? W
3-5
THIS JOB IS TOO MUCH FOR ONE BEAGLE! EVERYONE WANTS SOMETHING! EVERYONE COMPLAINS! I WORK DAY AND NIGHT AND NO ONE APPRECIATES IT!
EVEN MY POOR SECRETARY IS EXHAUSTED...
Z
I HATE BEING HEAD BEAGLE!
Z
SCHULZ

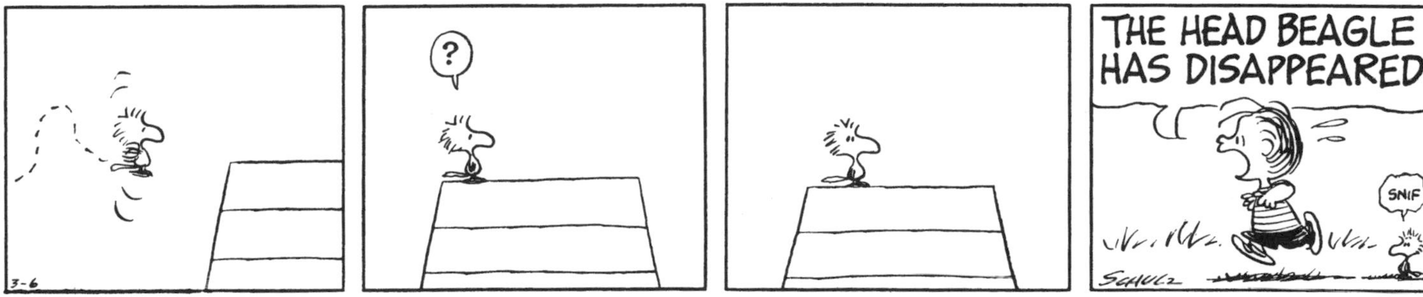
3-6
?
THE HEAD BEAGLE HAS DISAPPEARED!
SNIF
SCHULZ

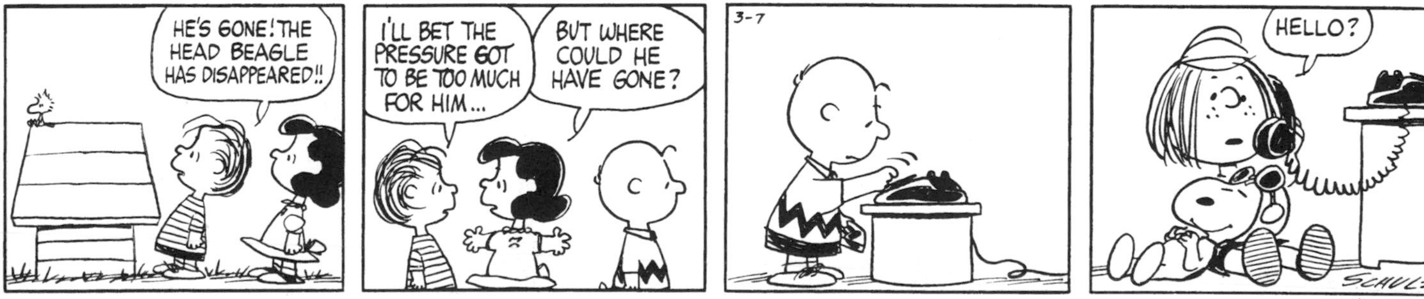
HE'S GONE! THE HEAD BEAGLE HAS DISAPPEARED!!
I'LL BET THE PRESSURE GOT TO BE TOO MUCH FOR HIM...
BUT WHERE COULD HE HAVE GONE?
3-7
HELLO?
SCHULZ

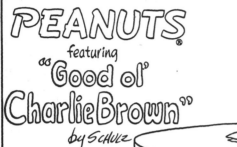

PEANUTS featuring "Good ol' Charlie Brown" by SCHULZ

JOE SHLABOT

JOE SHLABOTNIK FAN CLUB NEWS

VOLUME I NO. 1

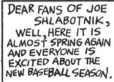

DEAR FANS OF JOE SHLABOTNIK, WELL, HERE IT IS ALMOST SPRING AGAIN AND EVERYONE IS EXCITED ABOUT THE NEW BASEBALL SEASON.

OUR HERO WILL BE PLAYING FOR HILLCREST IN THE GREEN GRASS LEAGUE AGAIN.

I REALLY SHOULD HAVE SOME PHOTOGRAPHS IN MY FAN MAGAZINE TO GIVE IT SOME CLASS, BUT I DON'T KNOW HOW TO PRINT THEM...

LAST YEAR JOE BATTED .143 AND MADE SOME SPECTACULAR CATCHES OF ROUTINE FLY BALLS. HE ALSO THREW OUT A RUNNER WHO HAD FALLEN DOWN BETWEEN FIRST AND SECOND.

WELL, FANS, THERE IT IS. REMEMBER, THIS LITTLE OL' FAN MAGAZINE IS YOURS. WE WELCOME *YOUR* COMMENTS.

WHO NEEDS IT?

I SHOULDN'T HAVE WELCOMED HER COMMENTS...

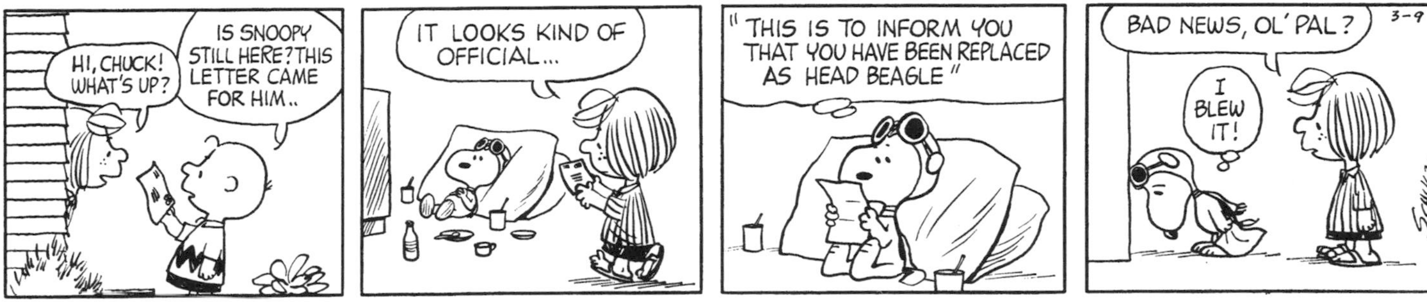
HI, CHUCK! WHAT'S UP?
IS SNOOPY STILL HERE? THIS LETTER CAME FOR HIM..
IT LOOKS KIND OF OFFICIAL...
"THIS IS TO INFORM YOU THAT YOU HAVE BEEN REPLACED AS HEAD BEAGLE"
BAD NEWS, OL' PAL?
3-9
I BLEW IT!
SCHULZ

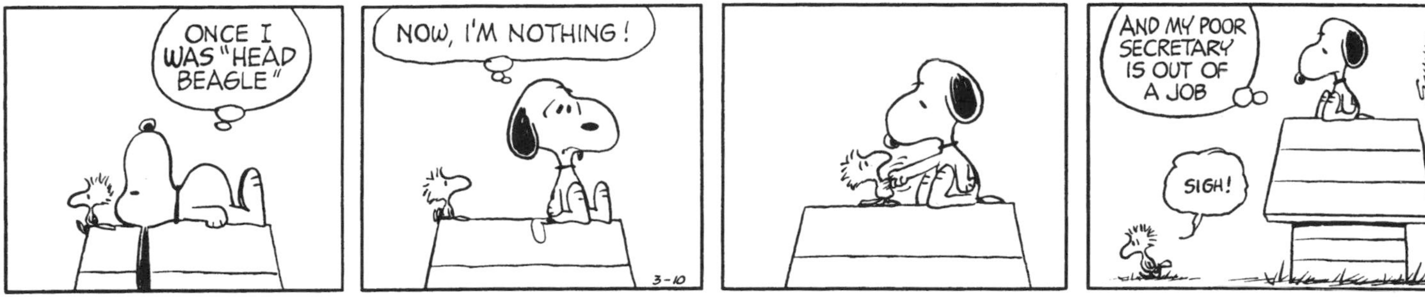
ONCE I WAS "HEAD BEAGLE"
NOW, I'M NOTHING!
3-10
AND MY POOR SECRETARY IS OUT OF A JOB
SIGH!
SCHULZ

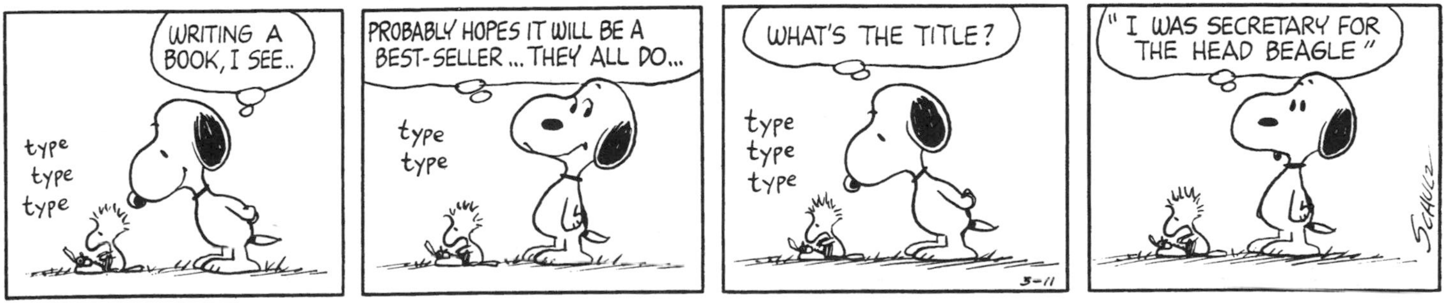
WRITING A BOOK, I SEE..
type type type
PROBABLY HOPES IT WILL BE A BEST-SELLER... THEY ALL DO...
type type
WHAT'S THE TITLE?
type type type
3-11
"I WAS SECRETARY FOR THE HEAD BEAGLE"
SCHULZ

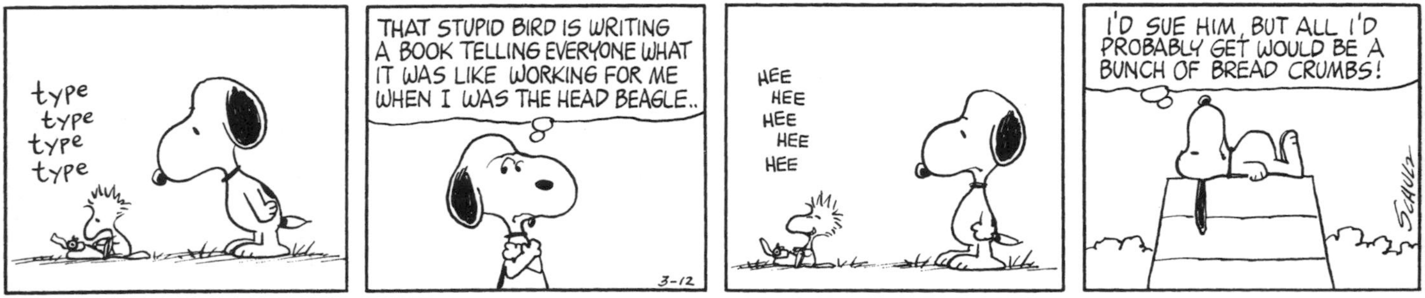
type
type
type
type
THAT STUPID BIRD IS WRITING A BOOK TELLING EVERYONE WHAT IT WAS LIKE WORKING FOR ME WHEN I WAS THE HEAD BEAGLE..
3-12
HEE
HEE
HEE
HEE
HEE
I'D SUE HIM, BUT ALL I'D PROBABLY GET WOULD BE A BUNCH OF BREAD CRUMBS!
SCHULZ

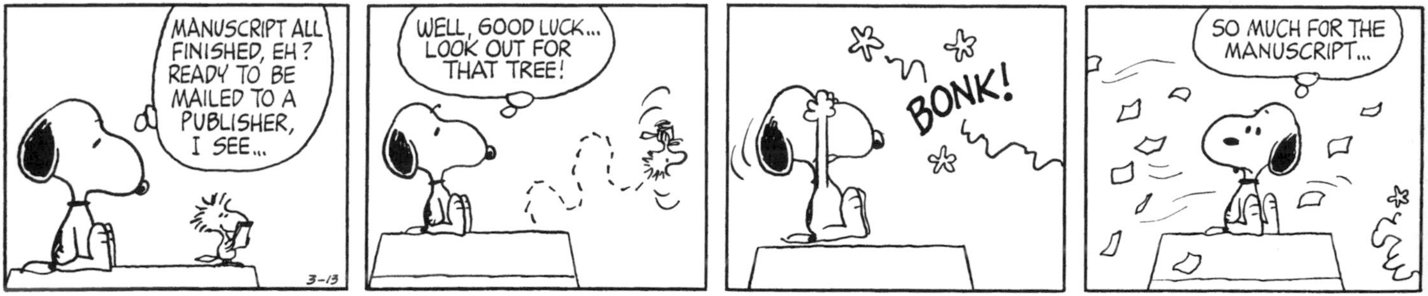
MANUSCRIPT ALL FINISHED, EH? READY TO BE MAILED TO A PUBLISHER, I SEE...
3-13
WELL, GOOD LUCK... LOOK OUT FOR THAT TREE!
BONK!
SO MUCH FOR THE MANUSCRIPT...

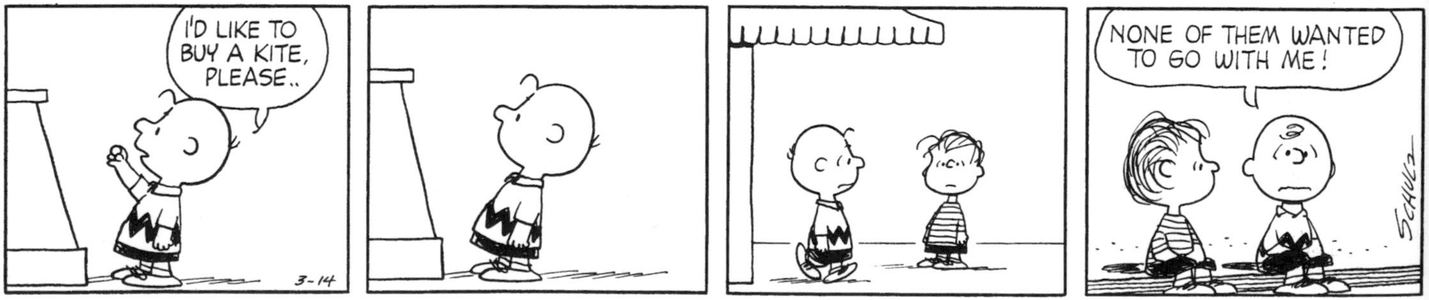
I'D LIKE TO BUY A KITE, PLEASE..
3-14
NONE OF THEM WANTED TO GO WITH ME!
SCHULZ

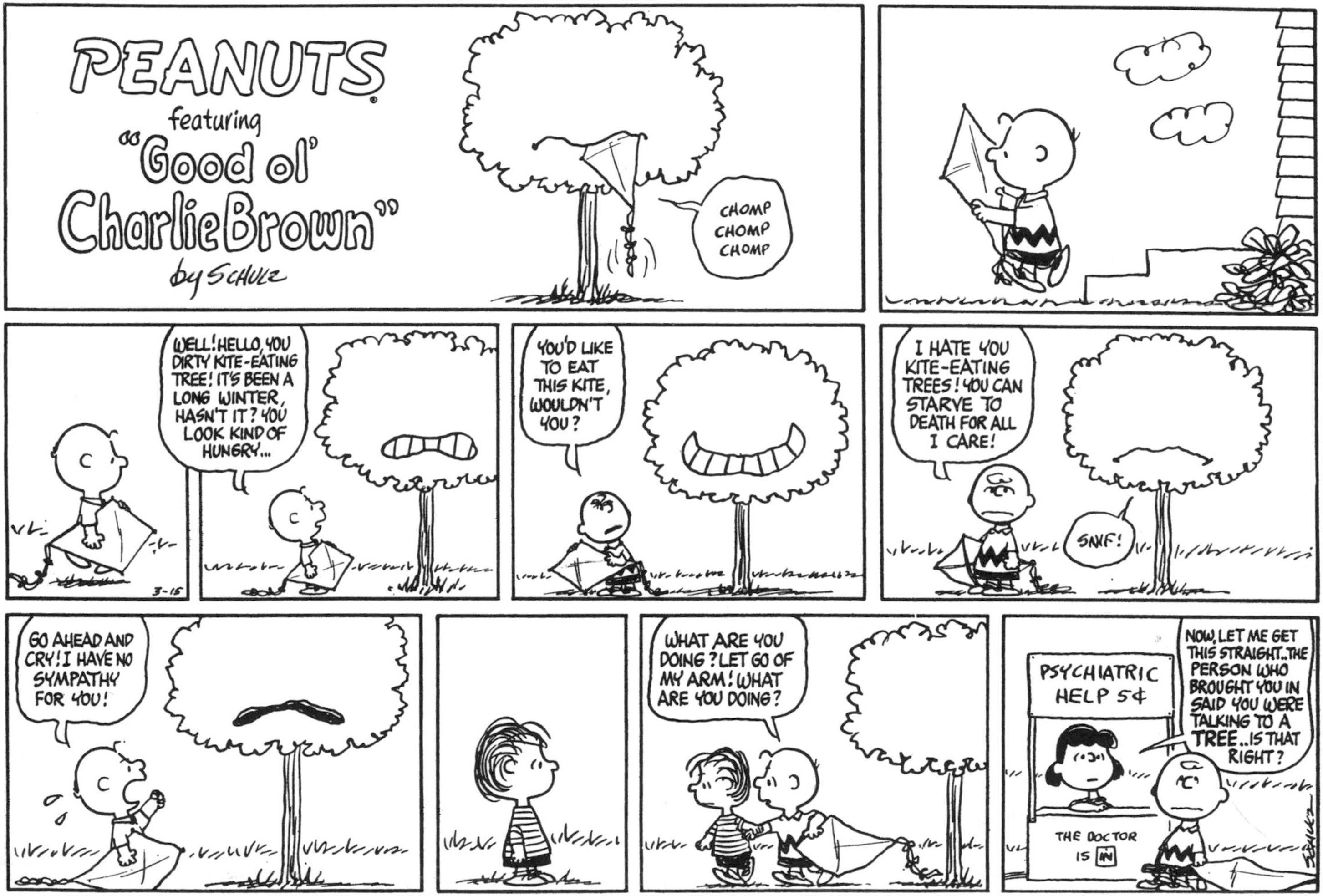
PEANUTS
featuring
"Good ol' Charlie Brown"
by SCHULZ
CHOMP CHOMP CHOMP
3-15
WELL! HELLO, YOU DIRTY KITE-EATING TREE! IT'S BEEN A LONG WINTER, HASN'T IT? YOU LOOK KIND OF HUNGRY...
YOU'D LIKE TO EAT THIS KITE, WOULDN'T YOU?
I HATE YOU KITE-EATING TREES! YOU CAN STARVE TO DEATH FOR ALL I CARE!
SNIF!
GO AHEAD AND CRY! I HAVE NO SYMPATHY FOR YOU!
WHAT ARE YOU DOING? LET GO OF MY ARM! WHAT ARE YOU DOING?
PSYCHIATRIC HELP 5¢
THE DOCTOR IS IN
NOW, LET ME GET THIS STRAIGHT.. THE PERSON WHO BROUGHT YOU IN SAID YOU WERE TALKING TO A TREE.. IS THAT RIGHT?
SCHULZ

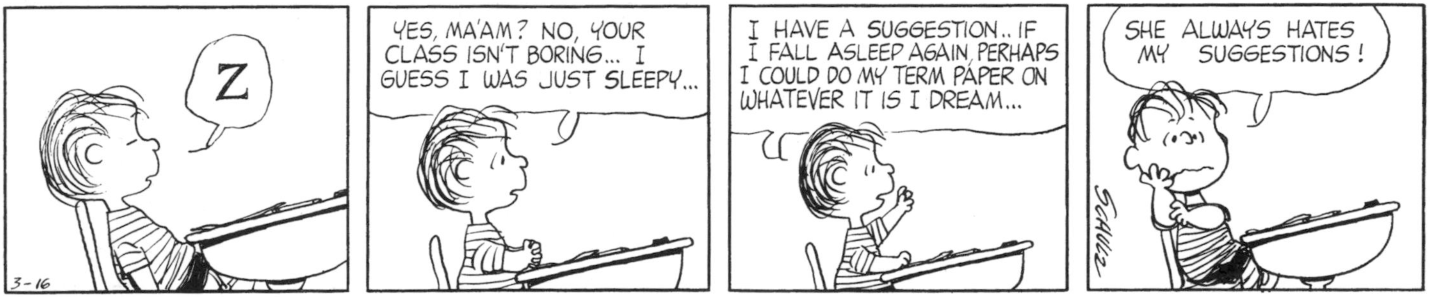
Z
YES, MA'AM? NO, YOUR CLASS ISN'T BORING... I GUESS I WAS JUST SLEEPY...
I HAVE A SUGGESTION.. IF I FALL ASLEEP AGAIN, PERHAPS I COULD DO MY TERM PAPER ON WHATEVER IT IS I DREAM...
SHE ALWAYS HATES MY SUGGESTIONS!
3-16
SCHULZ

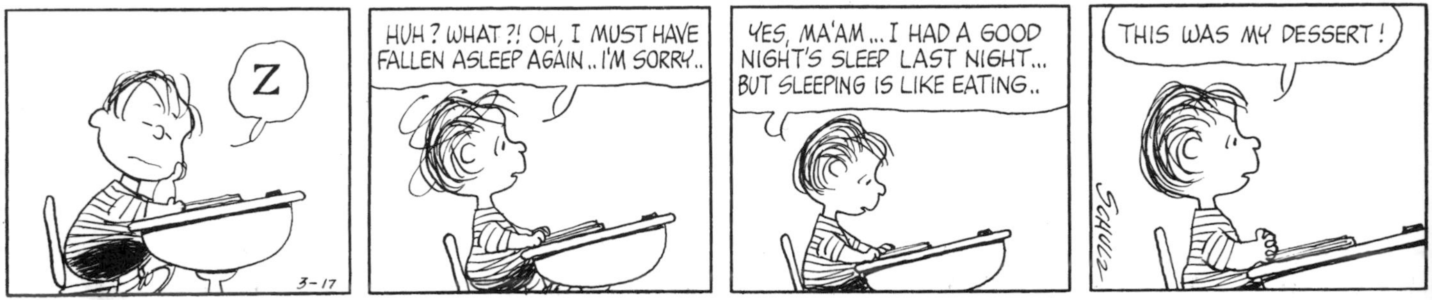
Z
HUH? WHAT?! OH, I MUST HAVE FALLEN ASLEEP AGAIN.. I'M SORRY..
YES, MA'AM... I HAD A GOOD NIGHT'S SLEEP LAST NIGHT... BUT SLEEPING IS LIKE EATING..
THIS WAS MY DESSERT!
3-17
SCHULZ

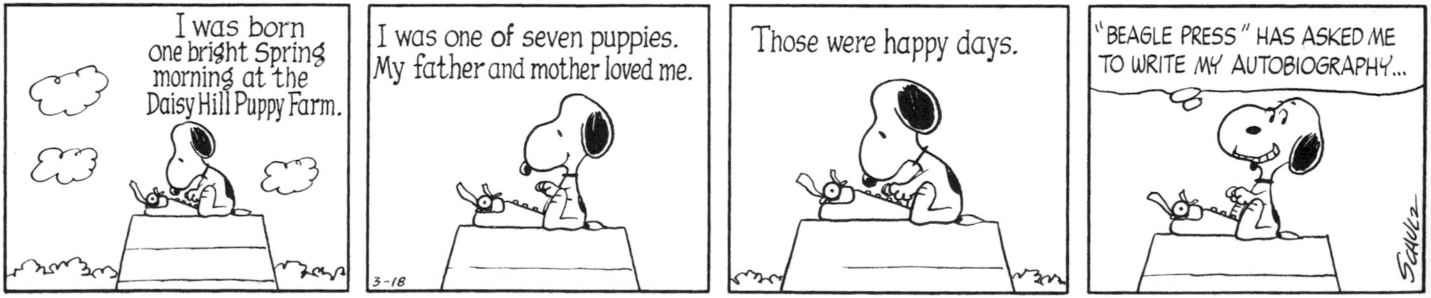
I was born one bright Spring morning at the Daisy Hill Puppy Farm.
I was one of seven puppies. My father and mother loved me.
Those were happy days.
"BEAGLE PRESS" HAS ASKED ME TO WRITE MY AUTOBIOGRAPHY...
3-18
SCHULZ

Although my early years were good, gray clouds soon appeared in my sky.

My life has been one of many hardships.

HARDSHIPS?!

WADDYAMEAN, HARDSHIPS?! I'VE TAKEN GOOD CARE OF YOU! YOU'VE NEVER HAD A HARDSHIP IN YOUR LIFE!

I HAVEN'T?

3-19

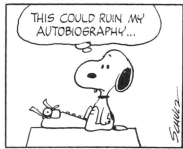

THIS COULD RUIN MY AUTOBIOGRAPHY...

In my life I have known a lot of

3-20

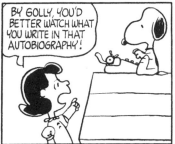

BY GOLLY, YOU'D BETTER WATCH WHAT YOU WRITE IN THAT AUTOBIOGRAPHY!

IF YOU SAY ANYTHING BAD ABOUT ME, I'LL KICK YOUR DOG DISH!

weird characters.

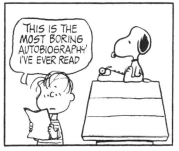

THIS IS THE MOST BORING AUTOBIOGRAPHY I'VE EVER READ

YOU'VE LIVED A VERY DULL LIFE... NO ONE WILL WANT TO READ ABOUT IT..

3-21

EVERYTHING THAT HAPPENED TO YOU ONLY HAPPENED IN YOUR IMAGINATION

I'LL IMAGINE THAT I'VE SOLD A MILLION COPIES!

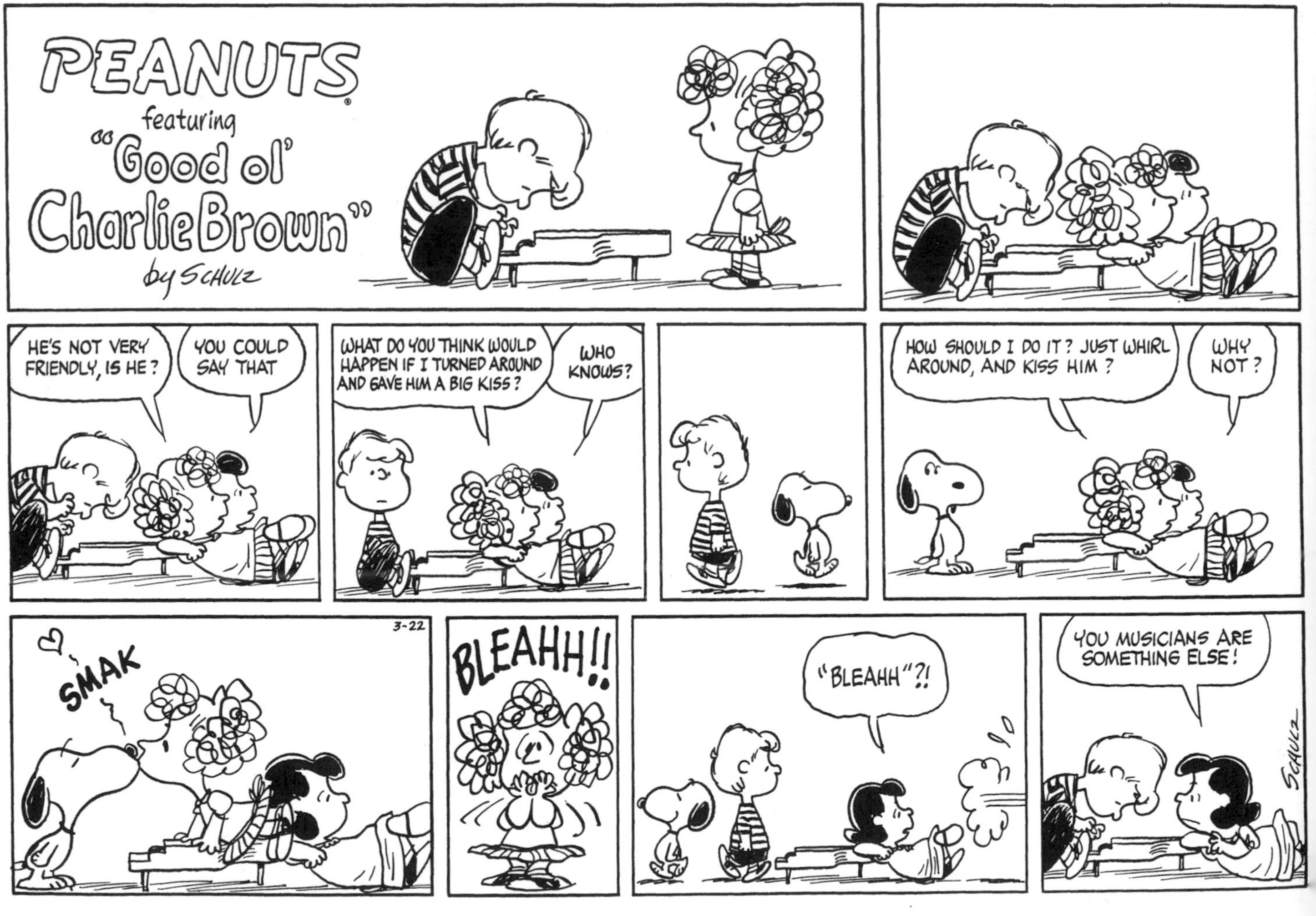
PEANUTS
featuring
"Good ol' Charlie Brown"
by SCHULZ
HE'S NOT VERY FRIENDLY, IS HE?
YOU COULD SAY THAT
WHAT DO YOU THINK WOULD HAPPEN IF I TURNED AROUND AND GAVE HIM A BIG KISS?
WHO KNOWS?
HOW SHOULD I DO IT? JUST WHIRL AROUND, AND KISS HIM?
WHY NOT?
3-22
SMAK
BLEAHH!!
"BLEAHH"?!
YOU MUSICIANS ARE SOMETHING ELSE!
SCHULZ

PSYCHIATRIC HELP 5¢

THE DOCTOR IS [IN]

PSYCHIATRIC HELP 5¢

KLUNK!!

THE DOCTOR IS [IN]

PSYCHIATRIC HELP 5¢

THE DOCTOR IS [IN]

THAT'S THE SORT OF THING THEY DON'T WARN YOU ABOUT IN MEDICAL SCHOOL...

THE DOCTOR

IS IT CHRISTMAS YET?

NO, NOT FOR ANOTHER NINE MONTHS

THEN I DON'T SUPPOSE I SHOULD HANG UP THIS STOCKING...

NOW I REMEMBER WHAT I WAS GOING TO GET HER **LAST** CHRISTMAS...A CALENDAR!

WHAT'S THIS?

A CALENDAR.. I BOUGHT IT FOR YOU SO YOU'D BE ABLE TO TELL WHEN CHRISTMAS COMES AND THINGS LIKE THAT..

IT'S GOT **NUMBERS** ON IT! I CAN'T UNDERSTAND SOMETHING WITH **NUMBERS** ALL OVER IT!!

WHY DO YOU WANT TO GIVE ME SOMETHING SO COMPLICATED?

WHY CAN'T PEOPLE GIVE SIMPLE THINGS? WHY DOES EVERYTHING HAVE TO BE SO COMPLICATED?!

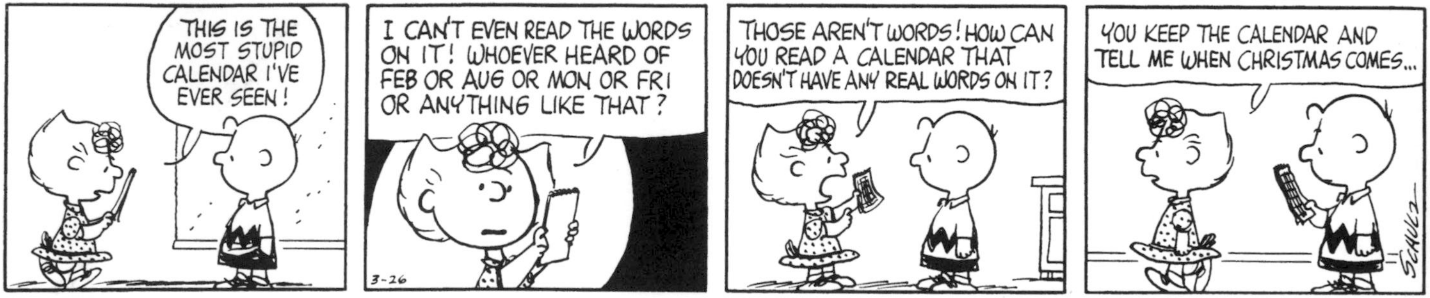
THIS IS THE MOST STUPID CALENDAR I'VE EVER SEEN!
I CAN'T EVEN READ THE WORDS ON IT! WHOEVER HEARD OF FEB OR AUG OR MON OR FRI OR ANYTHING LIKE THAT?
3-26
THOSE AREN'T WORDS! HOW CAN YOU READ A CALENDAR THAT DOESN'T HAVE ANY REAL WORDS ON IT?
YOU KEEP THE CALENDAR AND TELL ME WHEN CHRISTMAS COMES...

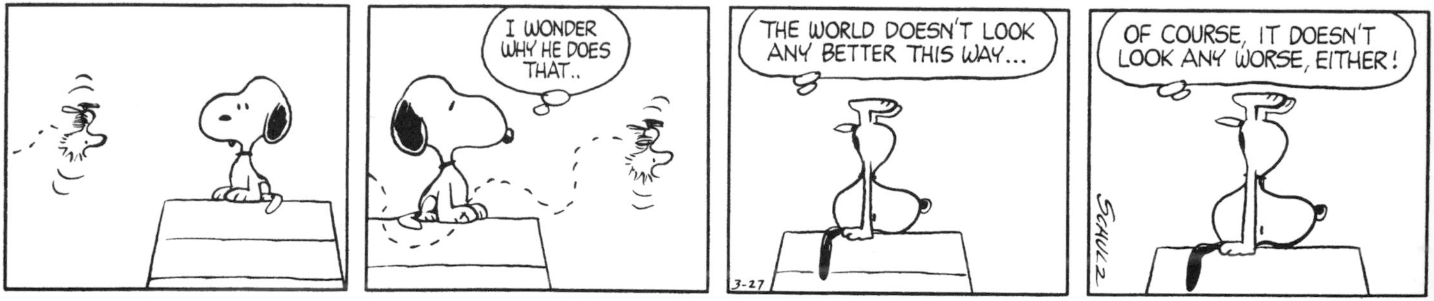
I WONDER WHY HE DOES THAT..
THE WORLD DOESN'T LOOK ANY BETTER THIS WAY...
3-27
OF COURSE, IT DOESN'T LOOK ANY WORSE, EITHER!

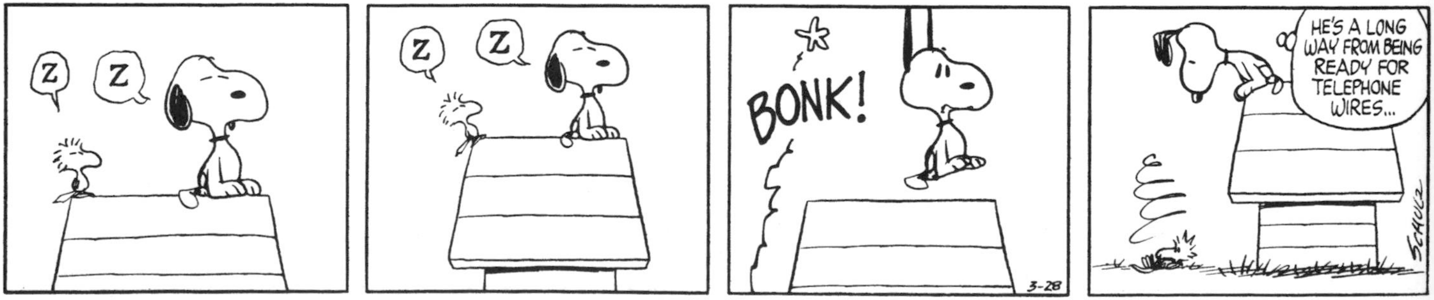
Z
Z
Z
Z
BONK!
3-28
HE'S A LONG WAY FROM BEING READY FOR TELEPHONE WIRES...

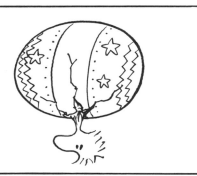

PEANUTS featuring "Good ol' CharlieBrown" by SCHULZ

Z

3-29

BONK!

Z

SCHULZ

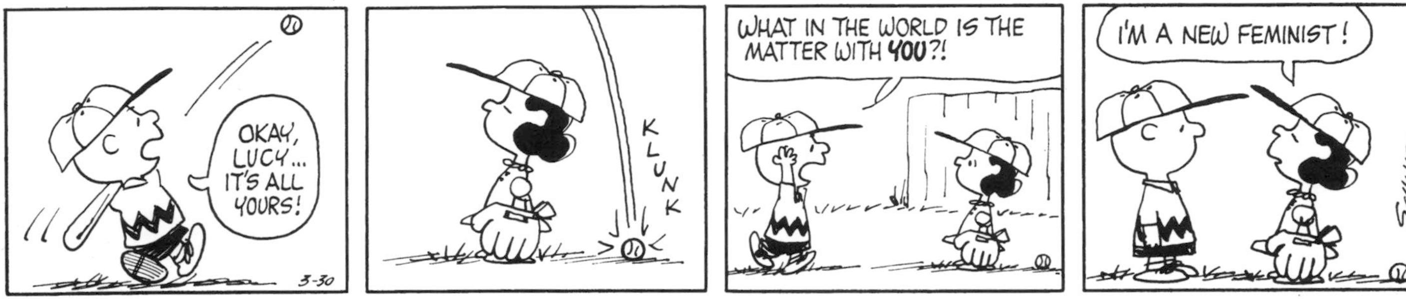
OKAY, LUCY... IT'S ALL YOURS!
3-30
KLUNK
WHAT IN THE WORLD IS THE MATTER WITH **YOU**?!
I'M A NEW FEMINIST!
SCHULZ

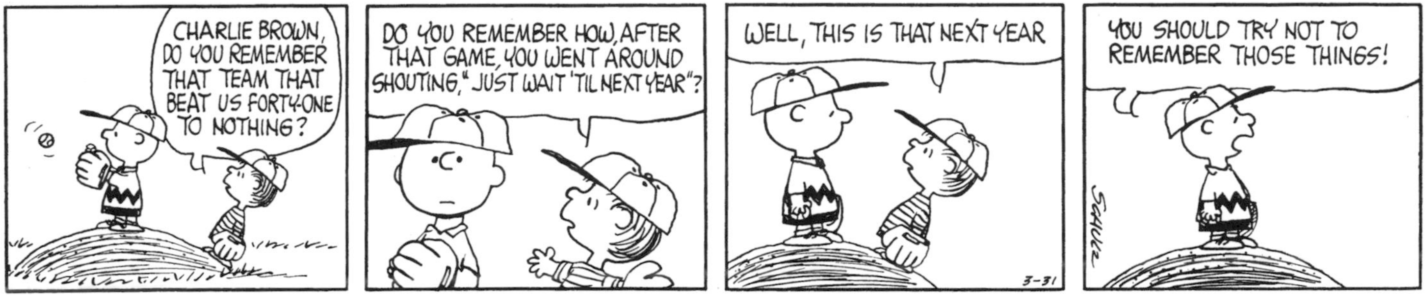
CHARLIE BROWN, DO YOU REMEMBER THAT TEAM THAT BEAT US FORTY-ONE TO NOTHING?
DO YOU REMEMBER HOW, AFTER THAT GAME, YOU WENT AROUND SHOUTING, "JUST WAIT 'TIL NEXT YEAR"?
WELL, THIS IS THAT NEXT YEAR
3-31
YOU SHOULD TRY NOT TO REMEMBER THOSE THINGS!
SCHULZ

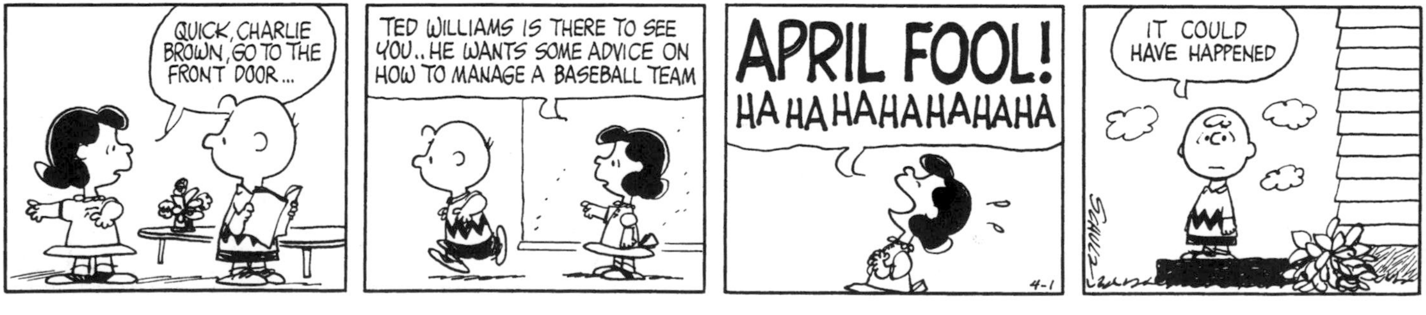
QUICK, CHARLIE BROWN, GO TO THE FRONT DOOR...
TED WILLIAMS IS THERE TO SEE YOU.. HE WANTS SOME ADVICE ON HOW TO MANAGE A BASEBALL TEAM
APRIL FOOL!
HA HA HAHAHAHAHAHA
4-1
IT COULD HAVE HAPPENED
SCHULZ

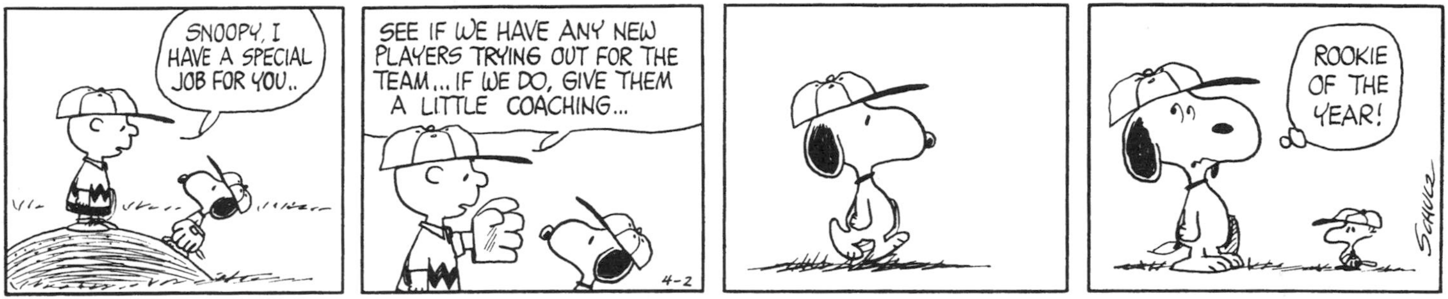
SNOOPY, I HAVE A SPECIAL JOB FOR YOU..
SEE IF WE HAVE ANY NEW PLAYERS TRYING OUT FOR THE TEAM... IF WE DO, GIVE THEM A LITTLE COACHING...
4-2
ROOKIE OF THE YEAR!
SCHULZ

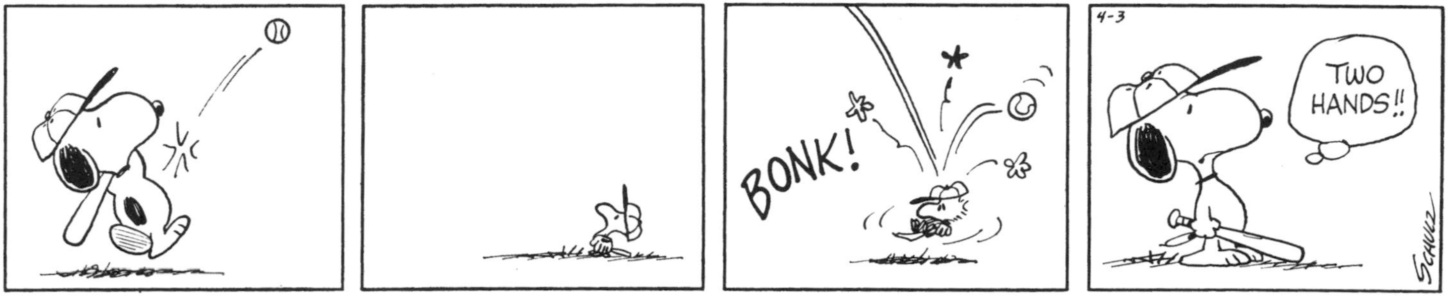
BONK!
4-3
TWO HANDS!!
SCHULZ

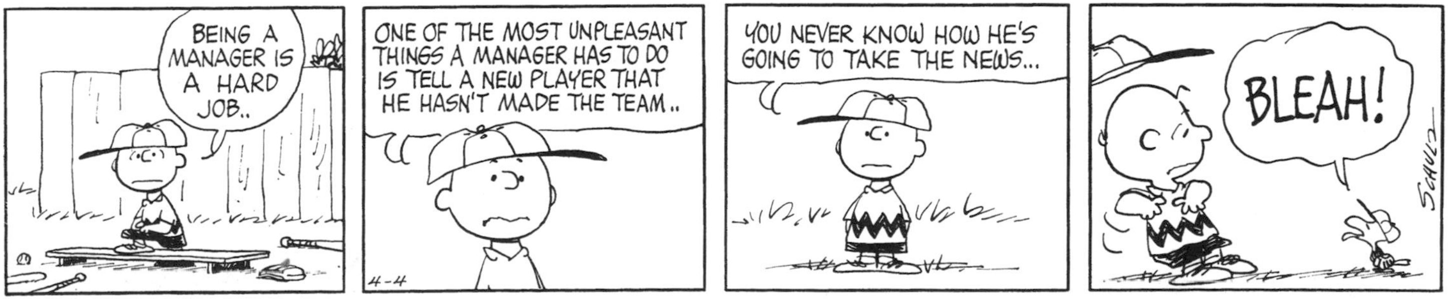
BEING A MANAGER IS A HARD JOB..
ONE OF THE MOST UNPLEASANT THINGS A MANAGER HAS TO DO IS TELL A NEW PLAYER THAT HE HASN'T MADE THE TEAM..
4-4
YOU NEVER KNOW HOW HE'S GOING TO TAKE THE NEWS...
BLEAH!
SCHULZ

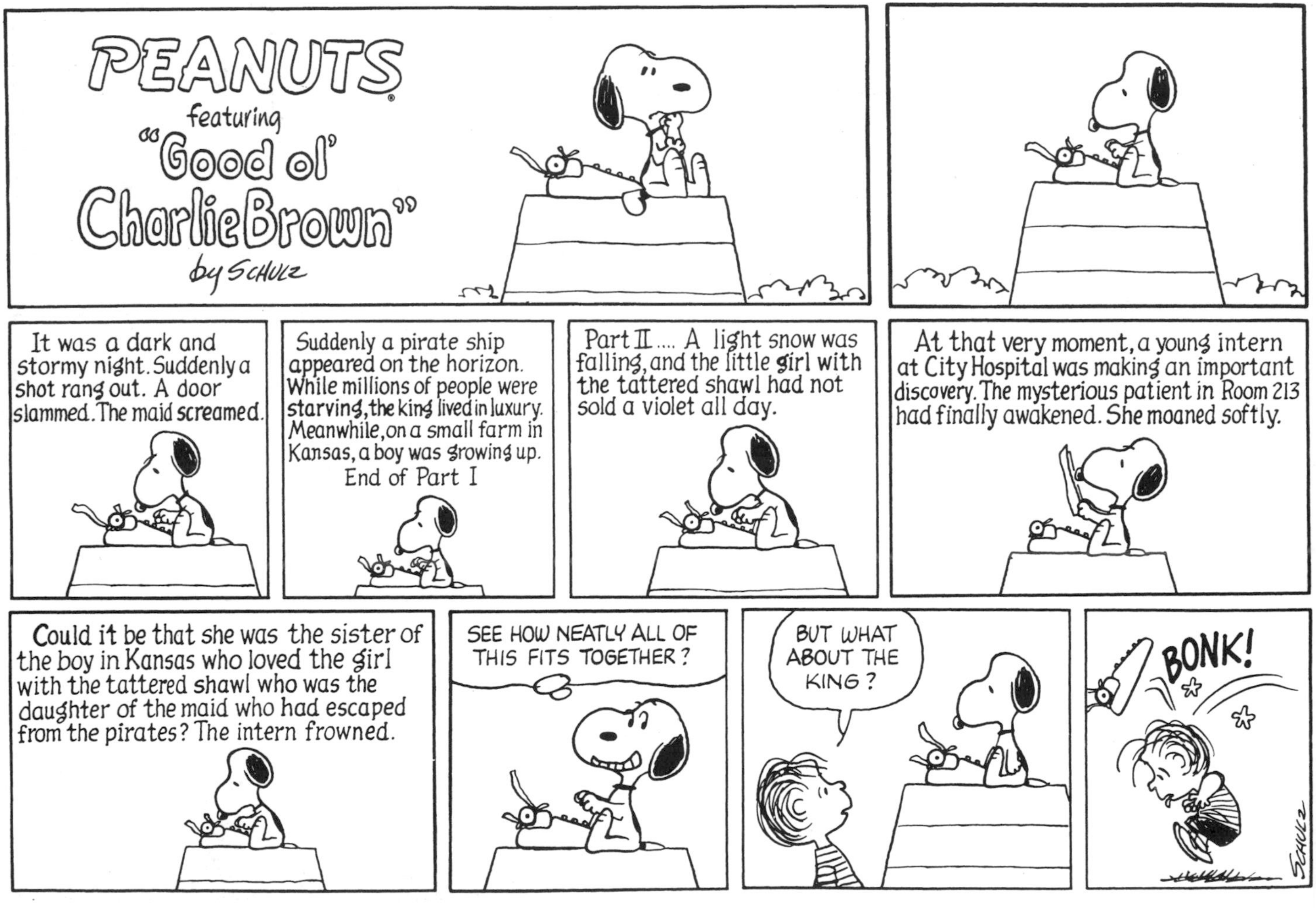
PEANUTS
featuring
"Good ol' Charlie Brown"
by SCHULZ
It was a dark and stormy night. Suddenly a shot rang out. A door slammed. The maid screamed.
Suddenly a pirate ship appeared on the horizon. While millions of people were starving, the king lived in luxury. Meanwhile, on a small farm in Kansas, a boy was growing up.
End of Part I
Part II .... A light snow was falling, and the little girl with the tattered shawl had not sold a violet all day.
At that very moment, a young intern at City Hospital was making an important discovery. The mysterious patient in Room 213 had finally awakened. She moaned softly.
Could it be that she was the sister of the boy in Kansas who loved the girl with the tattered shawl who was the daughter of the maid who had escaped from the pirates? The intern frowned.
SEE HOW NEATLY ALL OF THIS FITS TOGETHER?
BUT WHAT ABOUT THE KING?
BONK!
SCHULZ

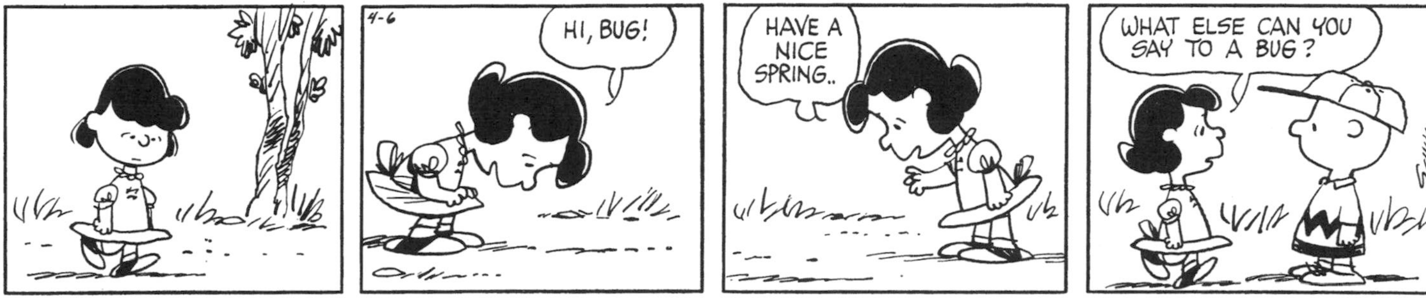
4-6
HI, BUG!
HAVE A NICE SPRING..
WHAT ELSE CAN YOU SAY TO A BUG?
SCHULZ

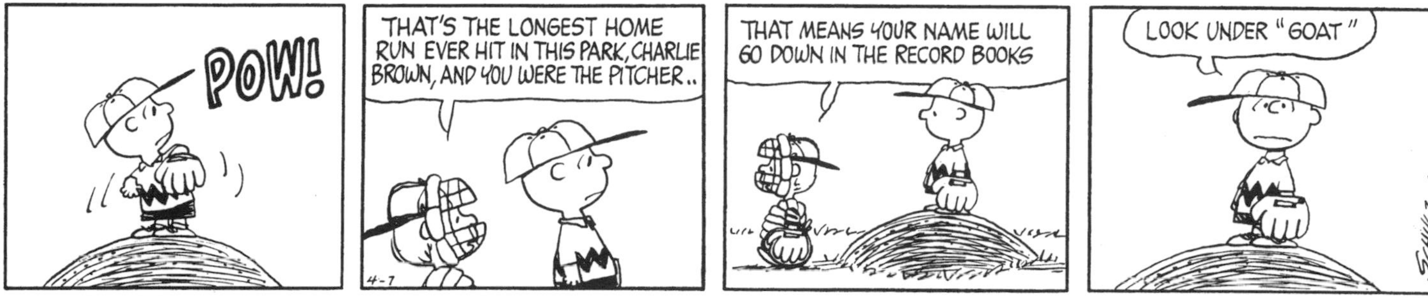
POW!
THAT'S THE LONGEST HOME RUN EVER HIT IN THIS PARK, CHARLIE BROWN, AND YOU WERE THE PITCHER..
4-7
THAT MEANS YOUR NAME WILL GO DOWN IN THE RECORD BOOKS
LOOK UNDER "GOAT"
SCHULZ

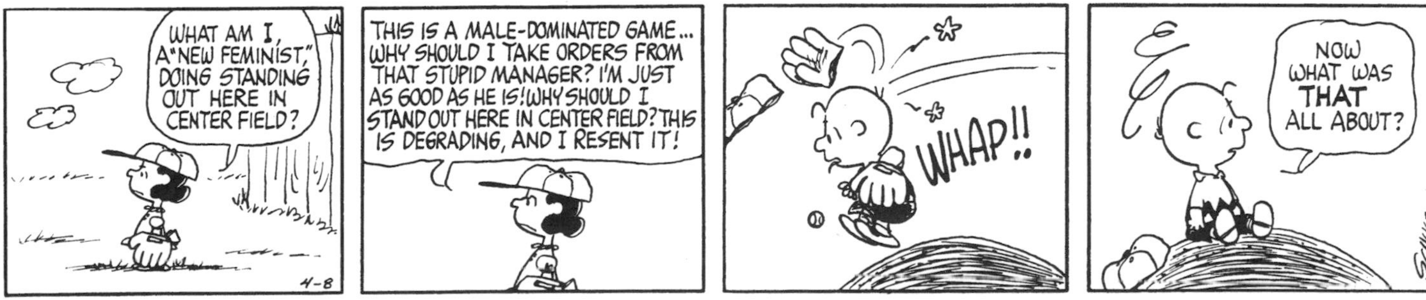
WHAT AM I, A "NEW FEMINIST," DOING STANDING OUT HERE IN CENTER FIELD?
4-8
THIS IS A MALE-DOMINATED GAME... WHY SHOULD I TAKE ORDERS FROM THAT STUPID MANAGER? I'M JUST AS GOOD AS HE IS! WHY SHOULD I STAND OUT HERE IN CENTER FIELD? THIS IS DEGRADING, AND I RESENT IT!
WHAP!!
NOW WHAT WAS THAT ALL ABOUT?
SCHULZ

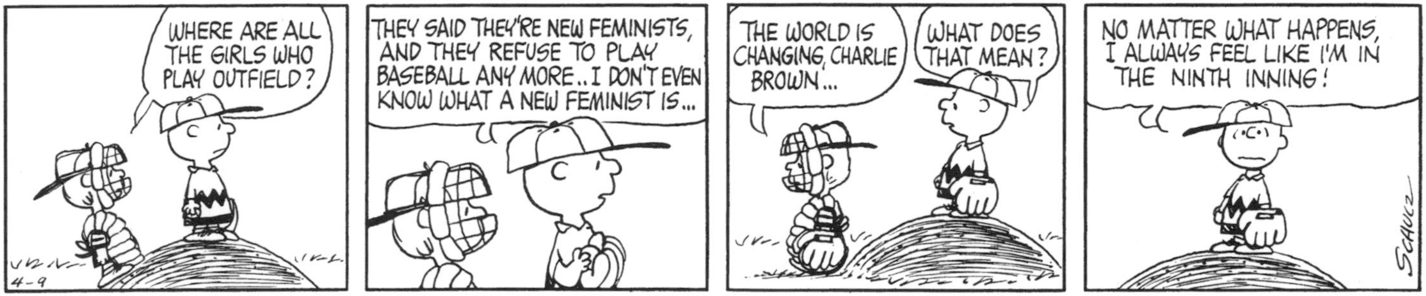
WHERE ARE ALL THE GIRLS WHO PLAY OUTFIELD?
THEY SAID THEY'RE NEW FEMINISTS, AND THEY REFUSE TO PLAY BASEBALL ANY MORE..I DON'T EVEN KNOW WHAT A NEW FEMINIST IS...
THE WORLD IS CHANGING, CHARLIE BROWN...
WHAT DOES THAT MEAN?
NO MATTER WHAT HAPPENS, I ALWAYS FEEL LIKE I'M IN THE NINTH INNING!

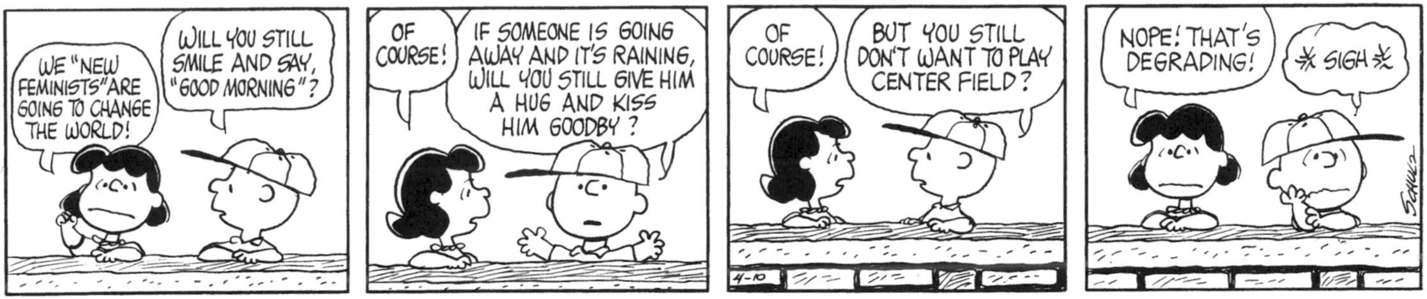
WE "NEW FEMINISTS" ARE GOING TO CHANGE THE WORLD!
WILL YOU STILL SMILE AND SAY, "GOOD MORNING"?
OF COURSE!
IF SOMEONE IS GOING AWAY AND IT'S RAINING, WILL YOU STILL GIVE HIM A HUG AND KISS HIM GOODBY?
OF COURSE!
BUT YOU STILL DON'T WANT TO PLAY CENTER FIELD?
NOPE! THAT'S DEGRADING!
SIGH

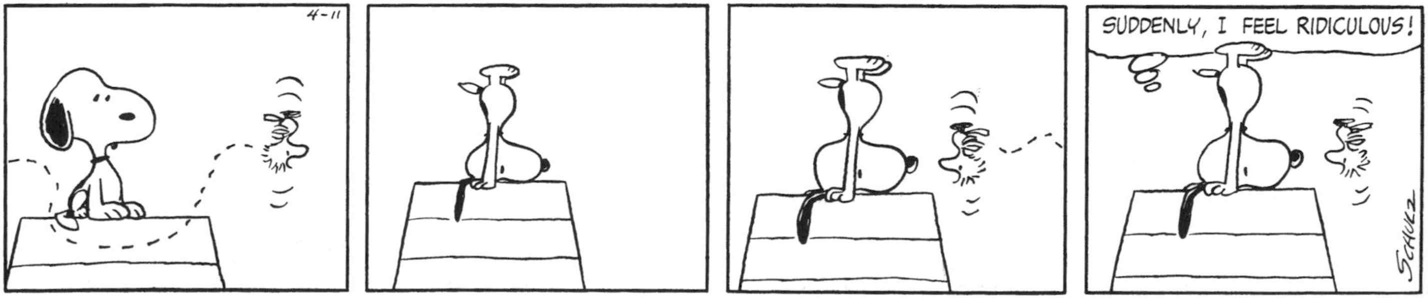
SUDDENLY, I FEEL RIDICULOUS!

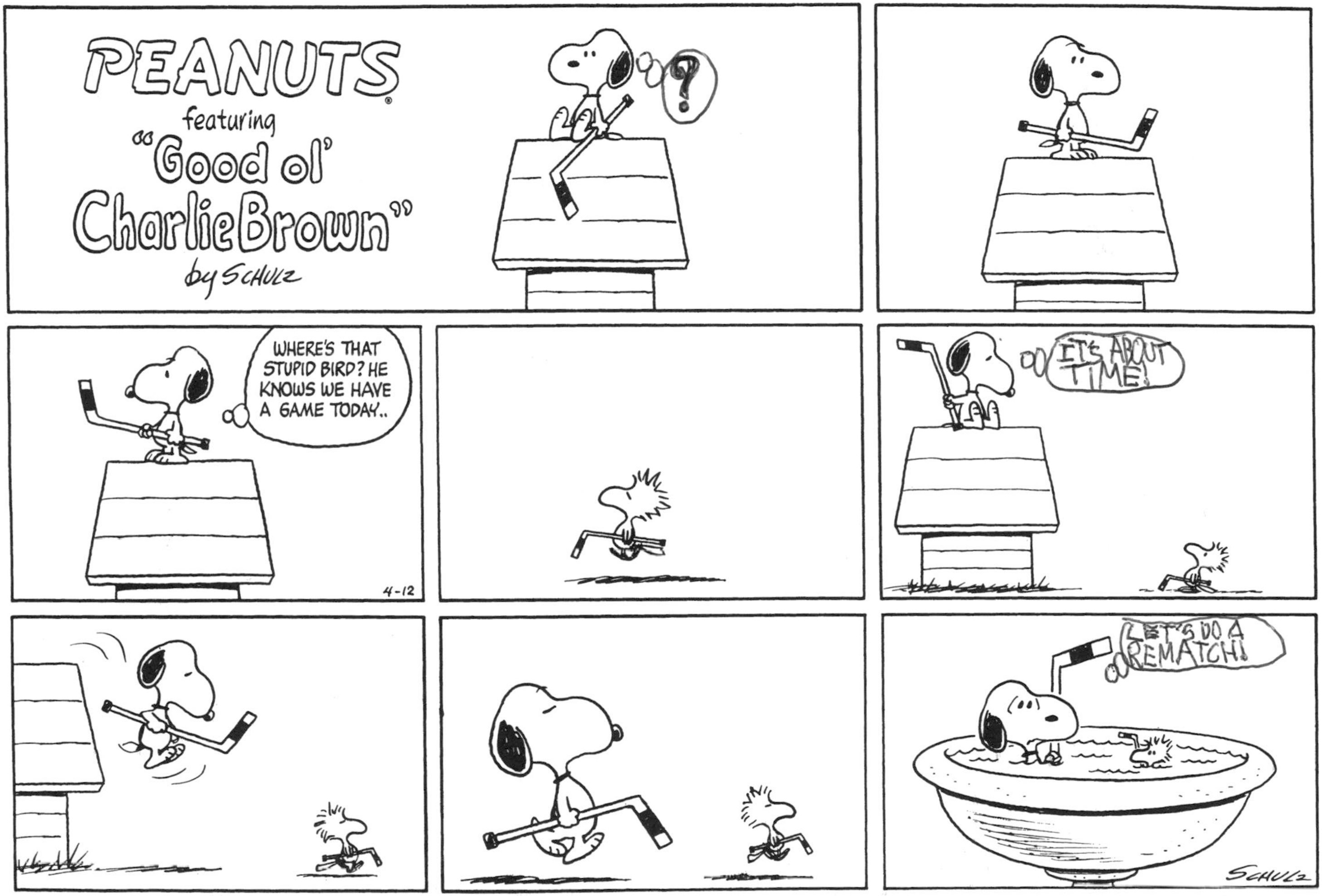
PEANUTS
featuring
"Good ol' Charlie Brown"
by SCHULZ
?
WHERE'S THAT STUPID BIRD? HE KNOWS WE HAVE A GAME TODAY..
4-12
IT'S ABOUT TIME!
LET'S DO A REMATCH!
SCHULZ

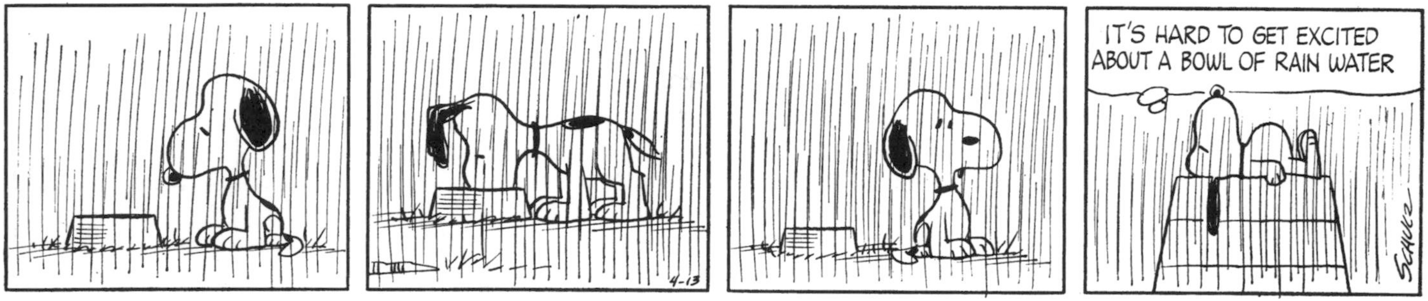
4-13
IT'S HARD TO GET EXCITED ABOUT A BOWL OF RAIN WATER
SCHULZ

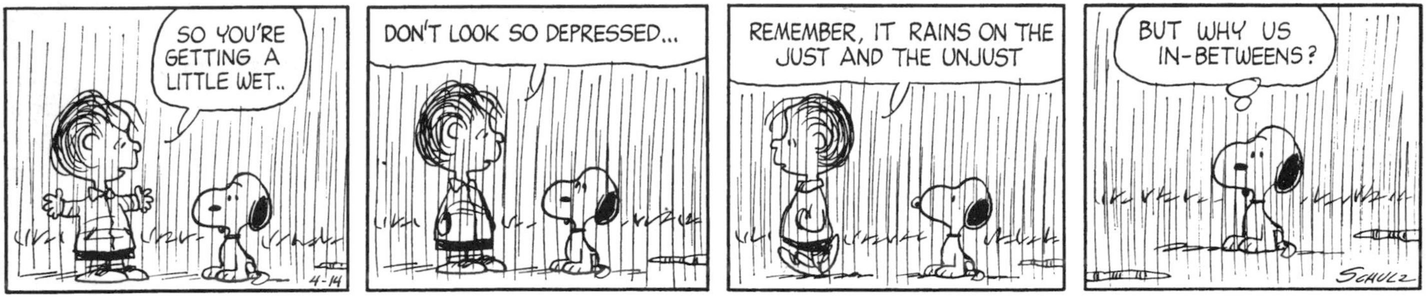
SO YOU'RE GETTING A LITTLE WET..
4-14
DON'T LOOK SO DEPRESSED...
REMEMBER, IT RAINS ON THE JUST AND THE UNJUST
BUT WHY US IN-BETWEENS?
SCHULZ

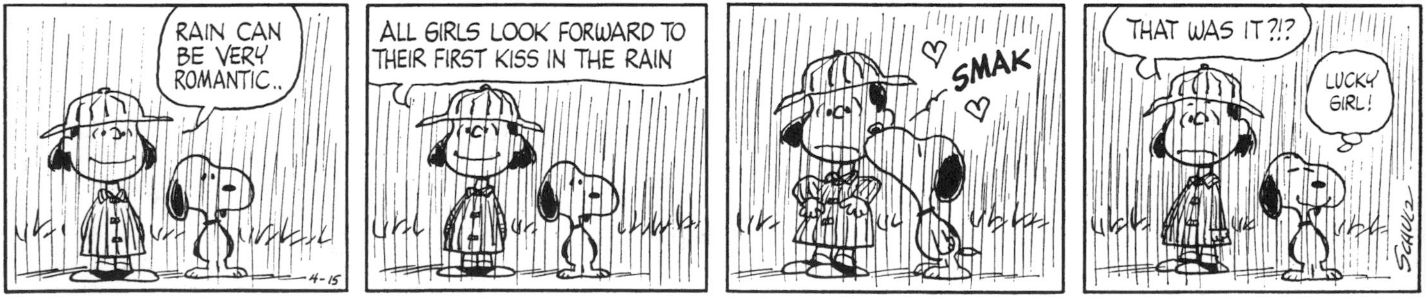
RAIN CAN BE VERY ROMANTIC..
4-15
ALL GIRLS LOOK FORWARD TO THEIR FIRST KISS IN THE RAIN
SMAK
THAT WAS IT?!?
LUCKY GIRL!
SCHULZ

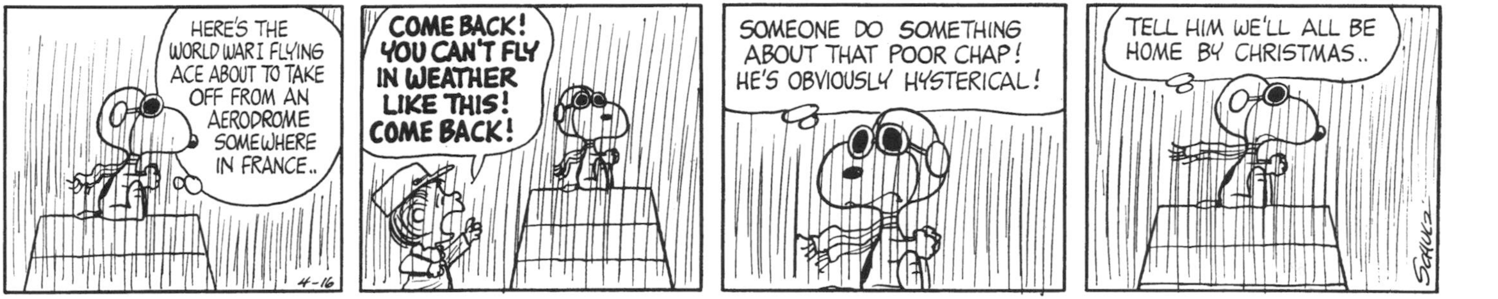
HERE'S THE WORLD WAR I FLYING ACE ABOUT TO TAKE OFF FROM AN AERODROME SOMEWHERE IN FRANCE..
4-16
COME BACK! YOU CAN'T FLY IN WEATHER LIKE THIS! COME BACK!
SOMEONE DO SOMETHING ABOUT THAT POOR CHAP! HE'S OBVIOUSLY HYSTERICAL!
TELL HIM WE'LL ALL BE HOME BY CHRISTMAS..
SCHULZ

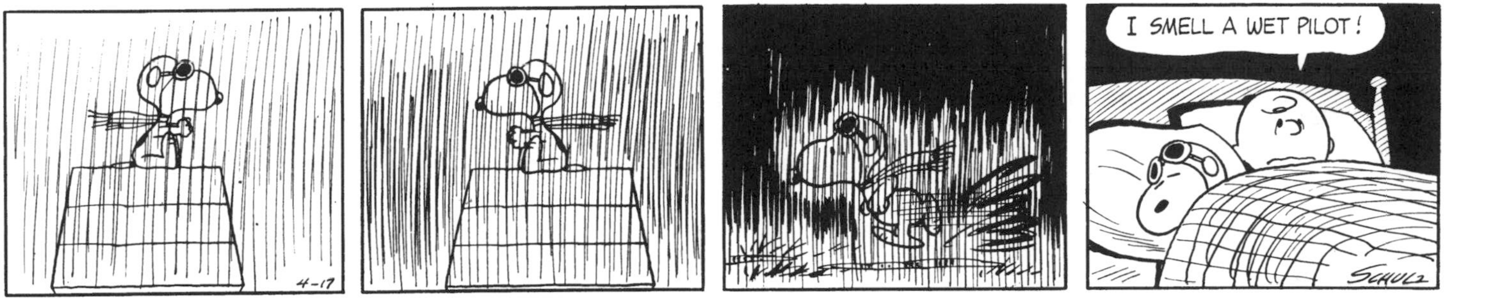
4-17
I SMELL A WET PILOT!
SCHULZ

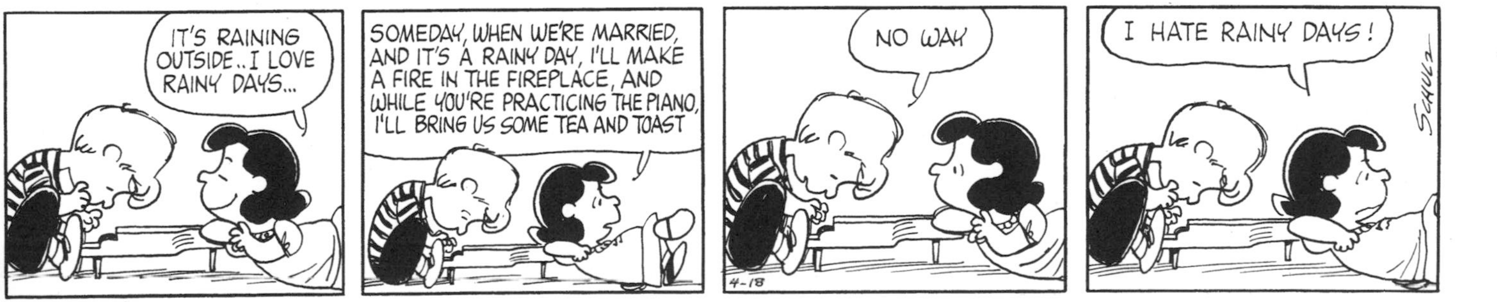
IT'S RAINING OUTSIDE..I LOVE RAINY DAYS...
SOMEDAY, WHEN WE'RE MARRIED, AND IT'S A RAINY DAY, I'LL MAKE A FIRE IN THE FIREPLACE, AND WHILE YOU'RE PRACTICING THE PIANO, I'LL BRING US SOME TEA AND TOAST
NO WAY
4-18
I HATE RAINY DAYS!
SCHULZ

PEANUTS
featuring
"Good ol' Charlie Brown"
by Schulz

| THAT'S A NICE BALLOON | THANK YOU.. |

| WHAT DOES IT DO? | IT DOESN'T DO ANYTHING EXCEPT MAYBE FLY IF I LET GO OF IT.. |

4-19

WHY DON'T YOU PAINT THE WORD "LOVE" ON IT, AND LET IT FLY OFF SOMEPLACE?

| THIS MAY CHANGE THE LIFE OF THE PERSON WHO FINDS IT... | MAYBE SOME PERSON WHO IS DEPRESSED WILL FIND IT, AND BE ENCOURAGED TO CARRY ON |

| MAYBE SOME GREAT LEADER WILL FIND IT, AND BE INSPIRED TO SEEK WORLD PEACE | GO, BALLOON! CARRY YOUR MESSAGE OF LOVE! |

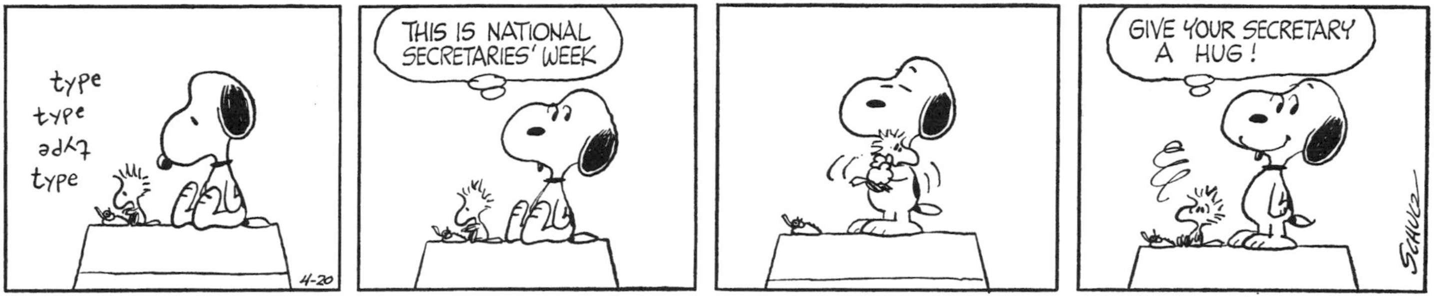
type
type
type
type
4-20
THIS IS NATIONAL SECRETARIES' WEEK
GIVE YOUR SECRETARY A HUG!
SCHULZ

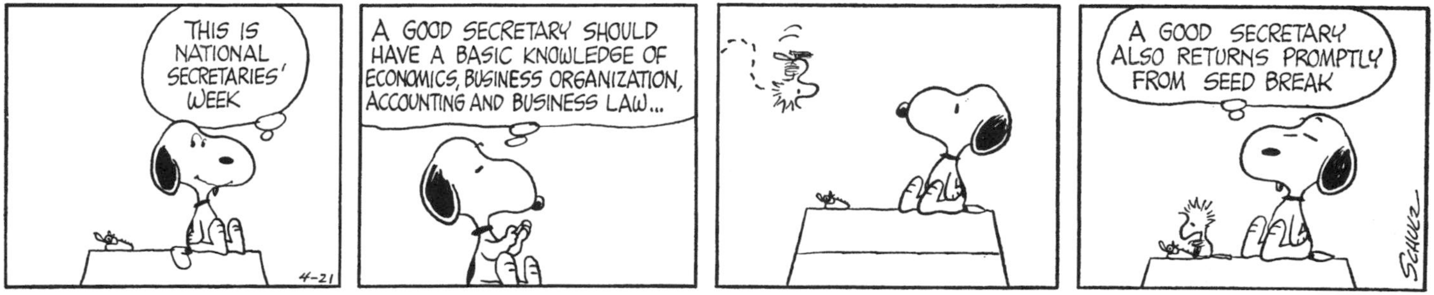
THIS IS NATIONAL SECRETARIES' WEEK
4-21
A GOOD SECRETARY SHOULD HAVE A BASIC KNOWLEDGE OF ECONOMICS, BUSINESS ORGANIZATION, ACCOUNTING AND BUSINESS LAW...
A GOOD SECRETARY ALSO RETURNS PROMPTLY FROM SEED BREAK
SCHULZ

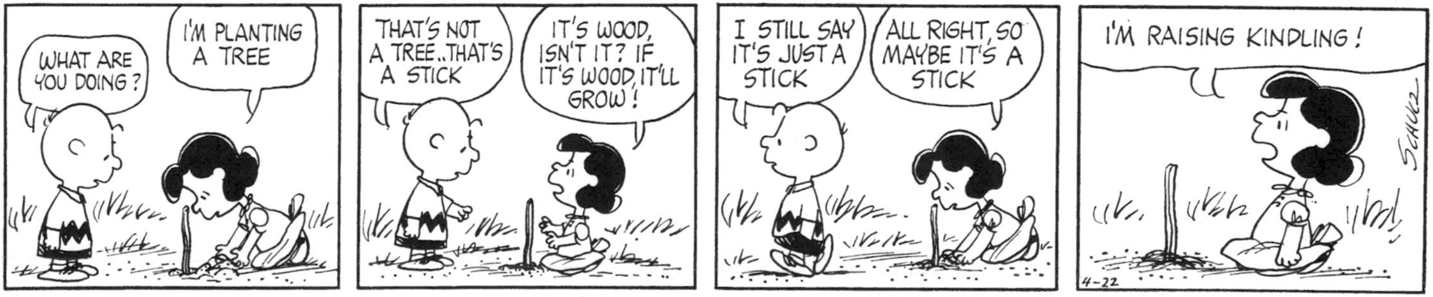
WHAT ARE YOU DOING?
I'M PLANTING A TREE
THAT'S NOT A TREE..THAT'S A STICK
IT'S WOOD, ISN'T IT? IF IT'S WOOD, IT'LL GROW!
I STILL SAY IT'S JUST A STICK
ALL RIGHT, SO MAYBE IT'S A STICK
I'M RAISING KINDLING!
SCHULZ
4-22

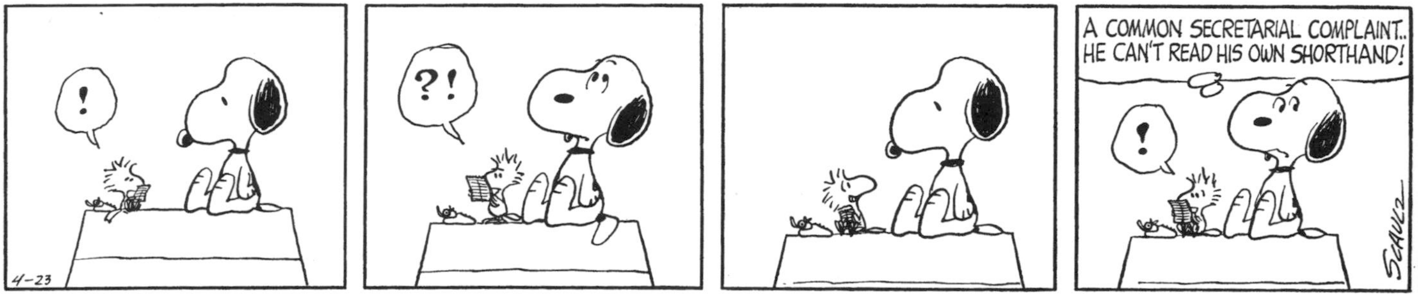
4-23
!
?!
A COMMON SECRETARIAL COMPLAINT.. HE CAN'T READ HIS OWN SHORTHAND!
!
SCHULZ

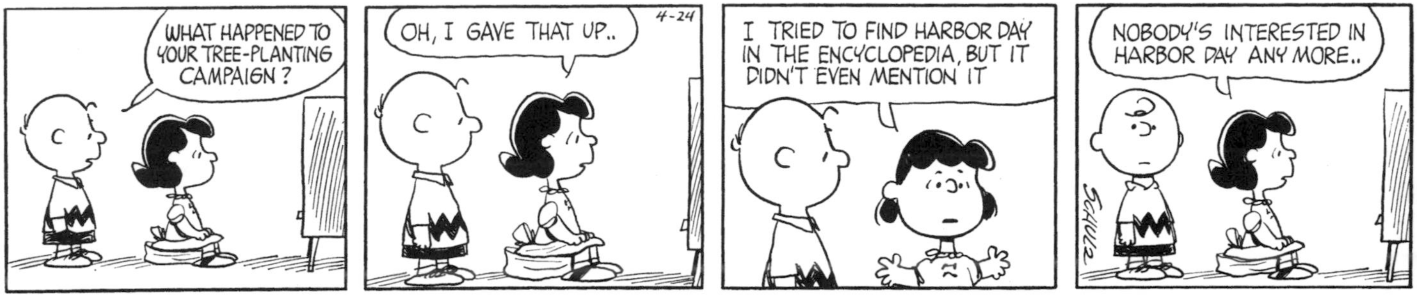
WHAT HAPPENED TO YOUR TREE-PLANTING CAMPAIGN?
4-24
OH, I GAVE THAT UP..
I TRIED TO FIND HARBOR DAY IN THE ENCYCLOPEDIA, BUT IT DIDN'T EVEN MENTION IT
NOBODY'S INTERESTED IN HARBOR DAY ANY MORE..
SCHULZ

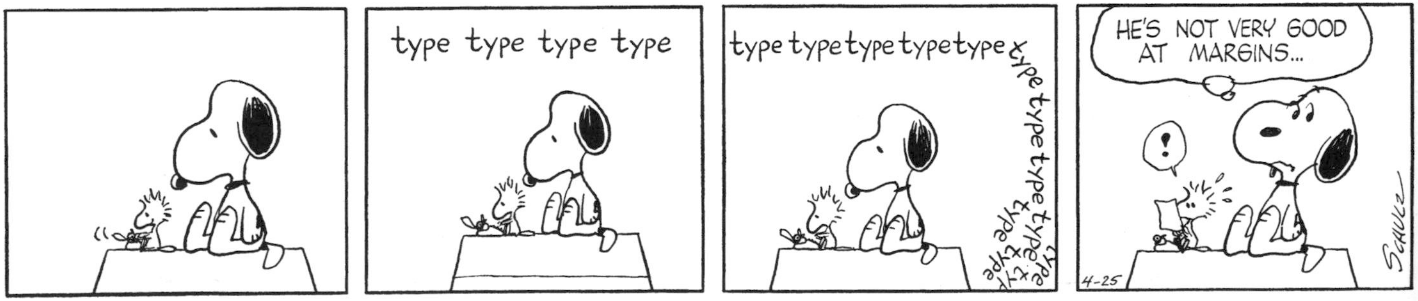
type type type type
typetypetypetypetype
HE'S NOT VERY GOOD AT MARGINS...
!
SCHULZ
4-25

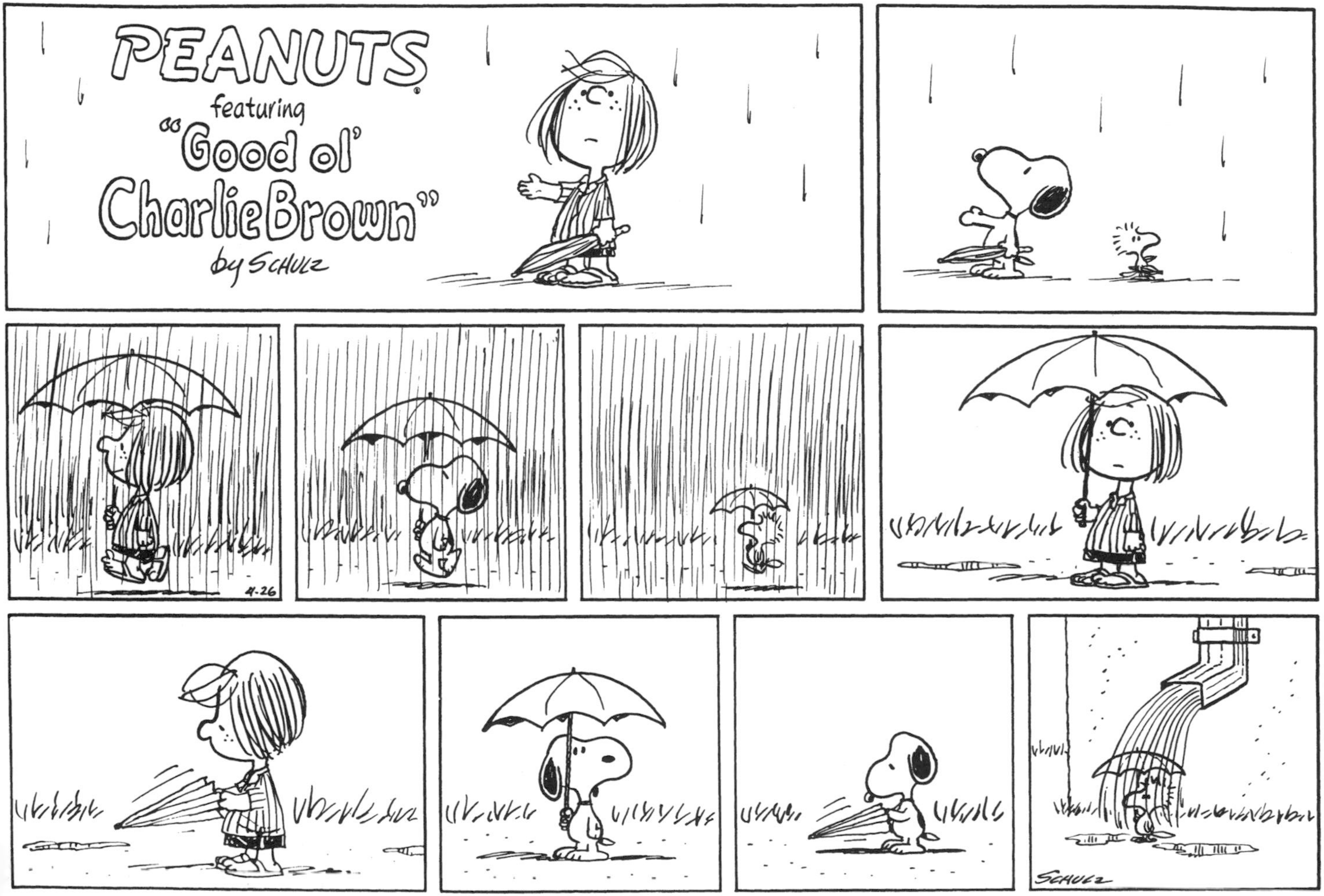
PEANUTS
featuring
"Good ol' Charlie Brown"
by SCHULZ
4-26
SCHULZ

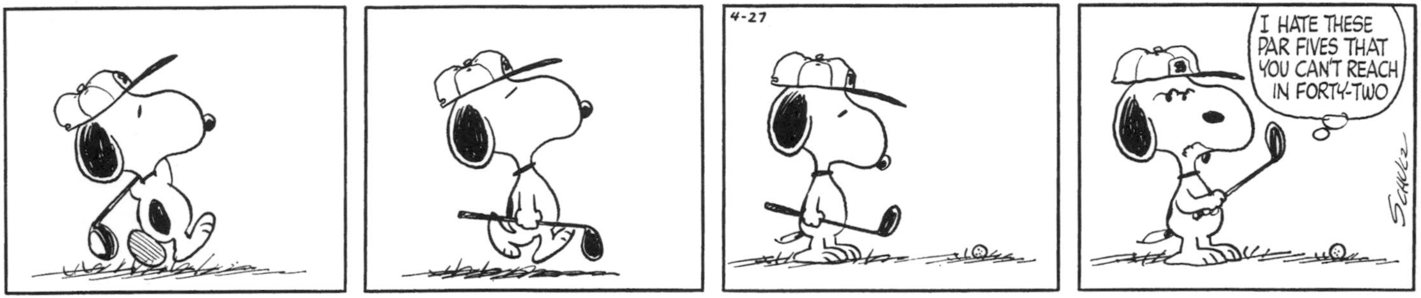
4-27
I HATE THESE PAR FIVES THAT YOU CAN'T REACH IN FORTY-TWO

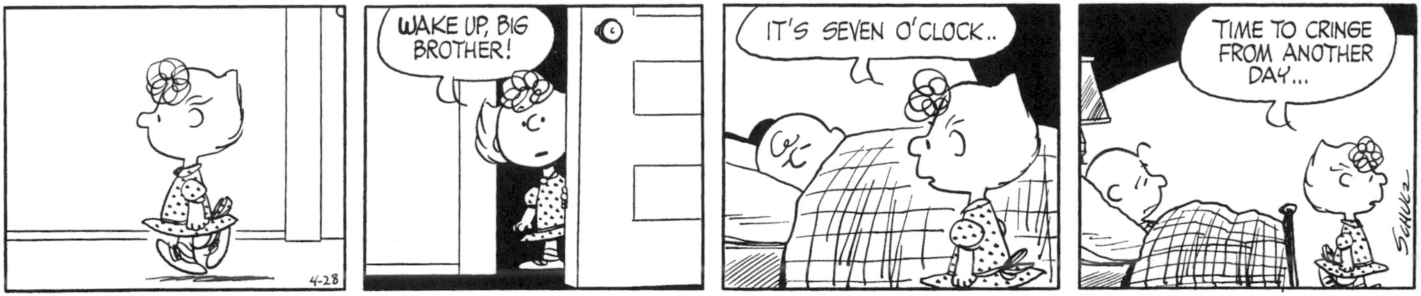
4-28
WAKE UP, BIG BROTHER!
IT'S SEVEN O'CLOCK..
TIME TO CRINGE FROM ANOTHER DAY...

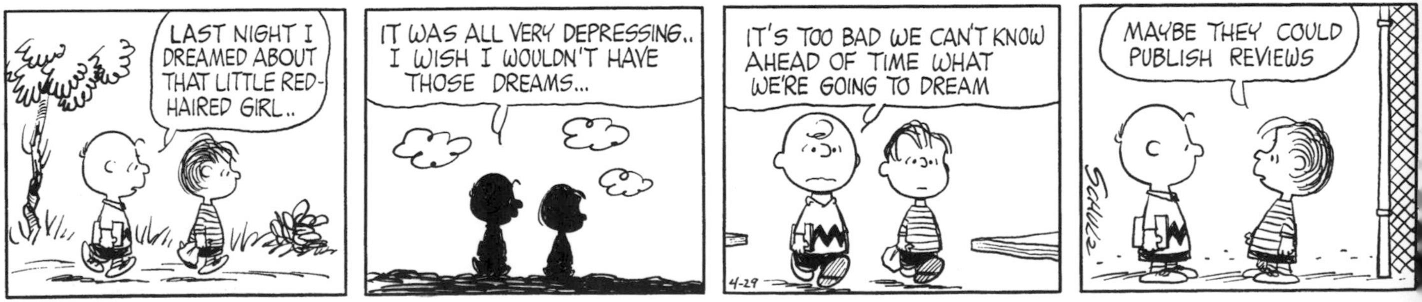
LAST NIGHT I DREAMED ABOUT THAT LITTLE RED-HAIRED GIRL..
IT WAS ALL VERY DEPRESSING.. I WISH I WOULDN'T HAVE THOSE DREAMS...
IT'S TOO BAD WE CAN'T KNOW AHEAD OF TIME WHAT WE'RE GOING TO DREAM
4-29
MAYBE THEY COULD PUBLISH REVIEWS

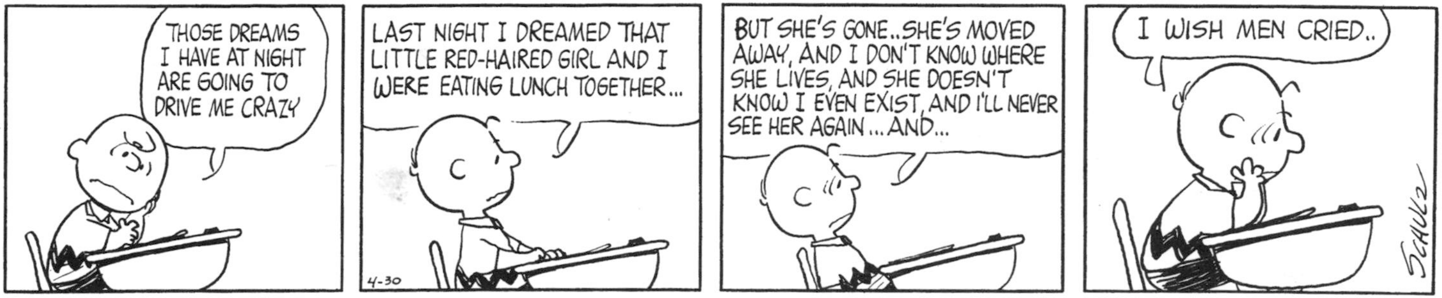
THOSE DREAMS I HAVE AT NIGHT ARE GOING TO DRIVE ME CRAZY
LAST NIGHT I DREAMED THAT LITTLE RED-HAIRED GIRL AND I WERE EATING LUNCH TOGETHER...
BUT SHE'S GONE..SHE'S MOVED AWAY, AND I DON'T KNOW WHERE SHE LIVES, AND SHE DOESN'T KNOW I EVEN EXIST, AND I'LL NEVER SEE HER AGAIN...AND...
I WISH MEN CRIED..

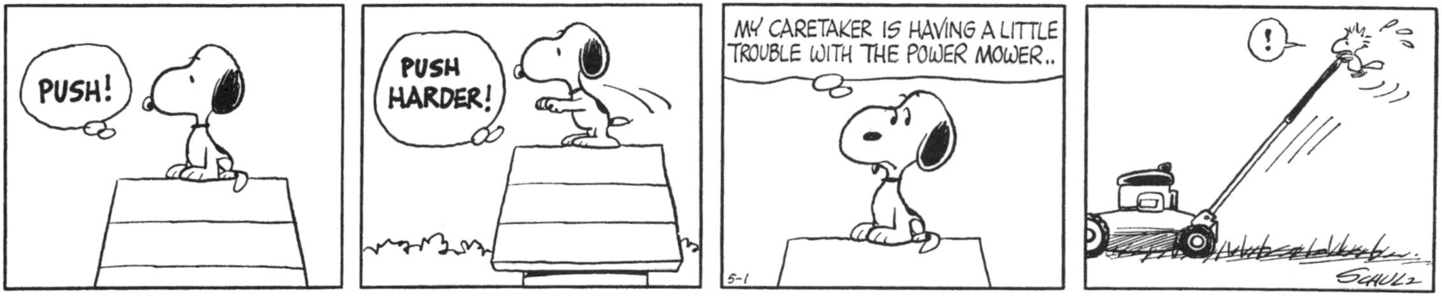
PUSH!
PUSH HARDER!
MY CARETAKER IS HAVING A LITTLE TROUBLE WITH THE POWER MOWER..
!

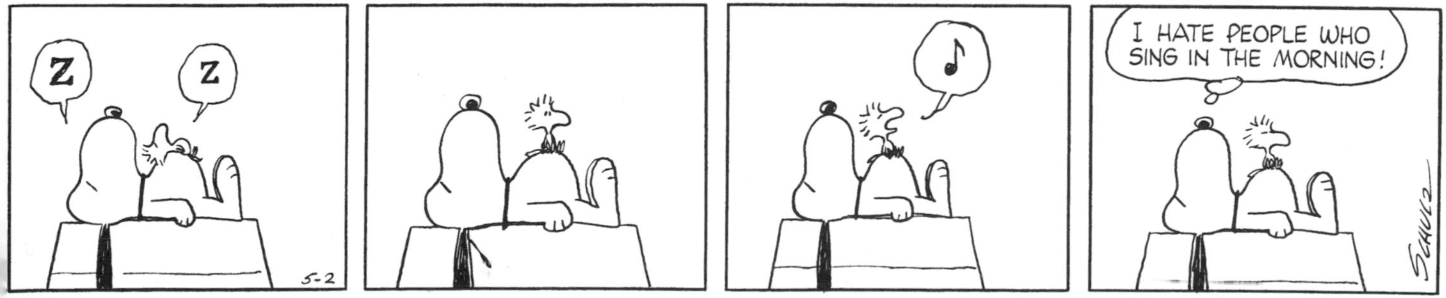
Z
Z
I HATE PEOPLE WHO SING IN THE MORNING!

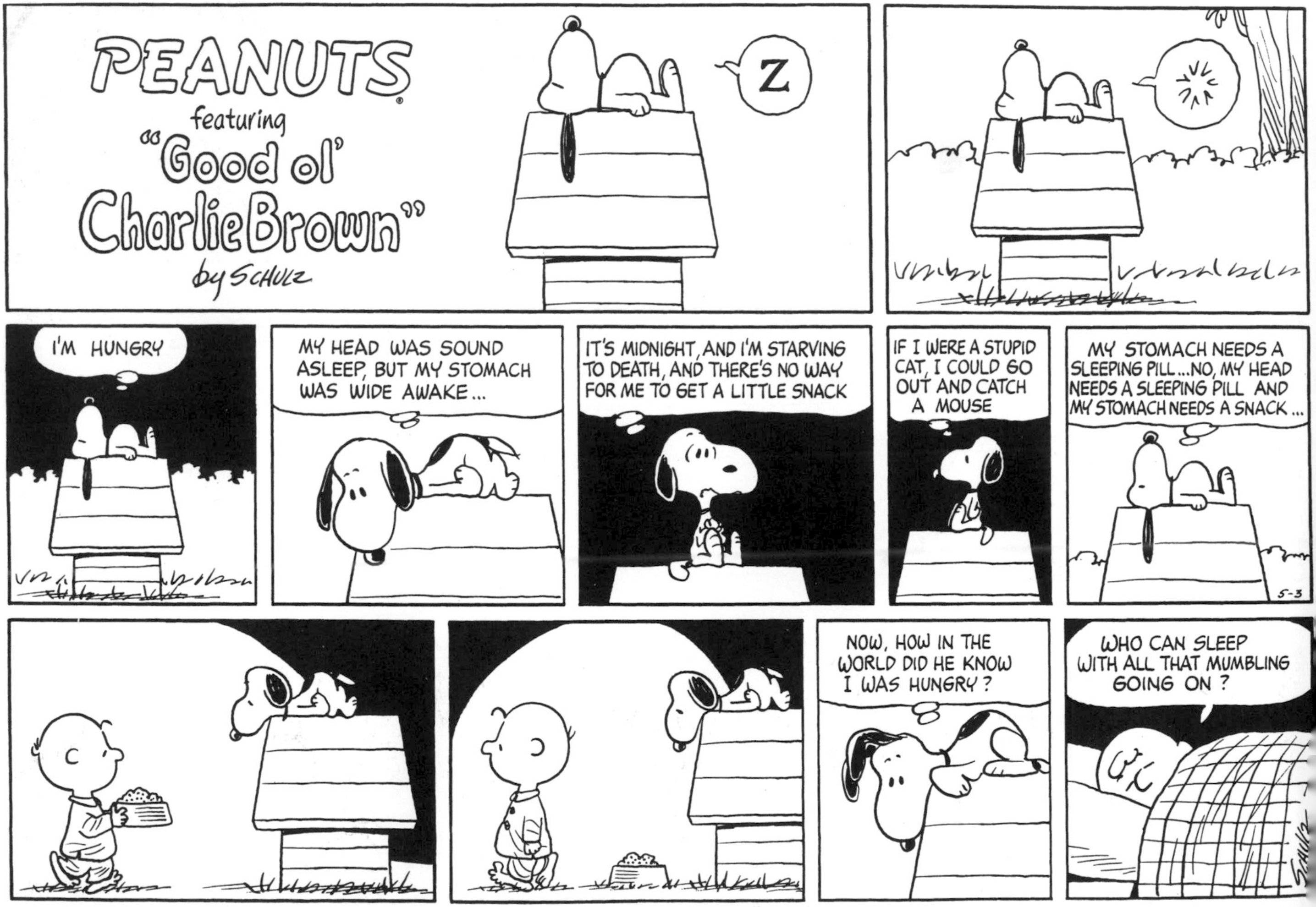
PEANUTS
featuring
"Good ol' Charlie Brown"
by SCHULZ
Z
I'M HUNGRY
MY HEAD WAS SOUND ASLEEP, BUT MY STOMACH WAS WIDE AWAKE...
IT'S MIDNIGHT, AND I'M STARVING TO DEATH, AND THERE'S NO WAY FOR ME TO GET A LITTLE SNACK
IF I WERE A STUPID CAT, I COULD GO OUT AND CATCH A MOUSE
MY STOMACH NEEDS A SLEEPING PILL...NO, MY HEAD NEEDS A SLEEPING PILL AND MY STOMACH NEEDS A SNACK...
5-3
NOW, HOW IN THE WORLD DID HE KNOW I WAS HUNGRY?
WHO CAN SLEEP WITH ALL THAT MUMBLING GOING ON?
SCHULZ

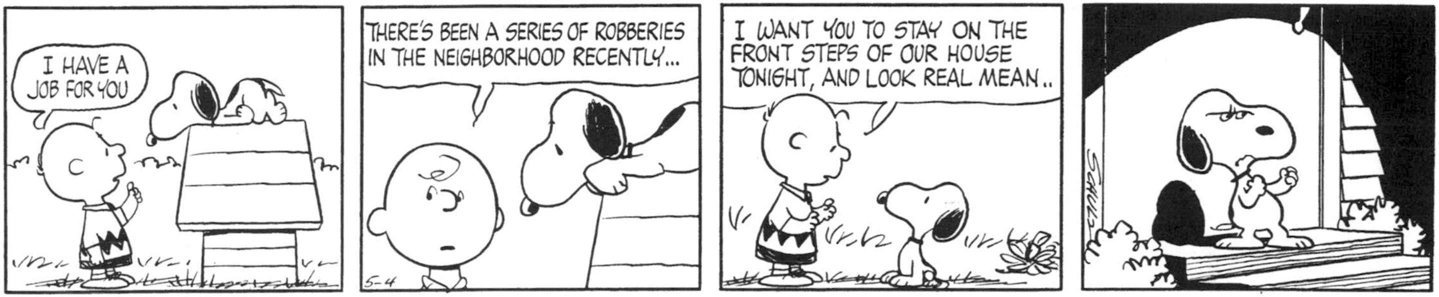
I HAVE A JOB FOR YOU
THERE'S BEEN A SERIES OF ROBBERIES IN THE NEIGHBORHOOD RECENTLY...
I WANT YOU TO STAY ON THE FRONT STEPS OF OUR HOUSE TONIGHT, AND LOOK REAL MEAN..

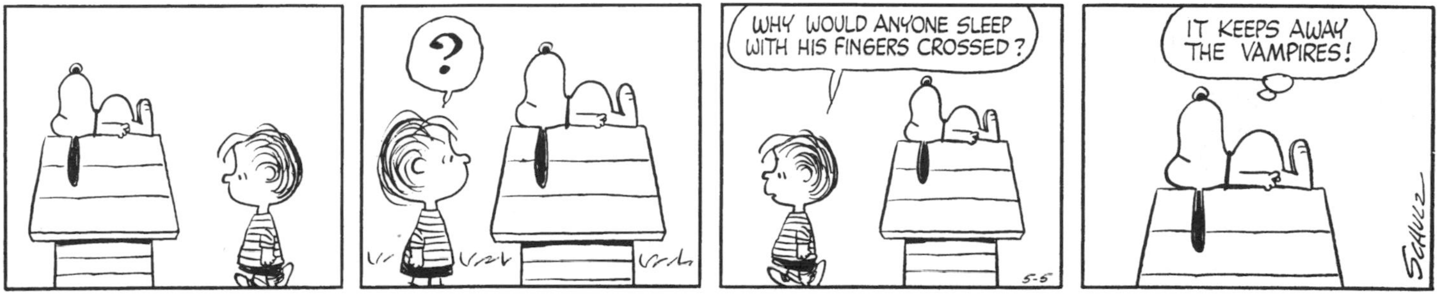
?
WHY WOULD ANYONE SLEEP WITH HIS FINGERS CROSSED?
IT KEEPS AWAY THE VAMPIRES!

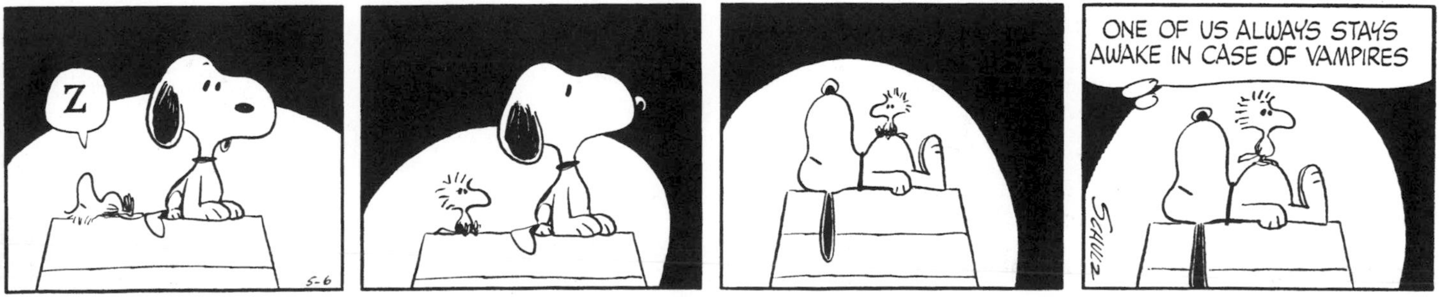
Z
ONE OF US ALWAYS STAYS AWAKE IN CASE OF VAMPIRES

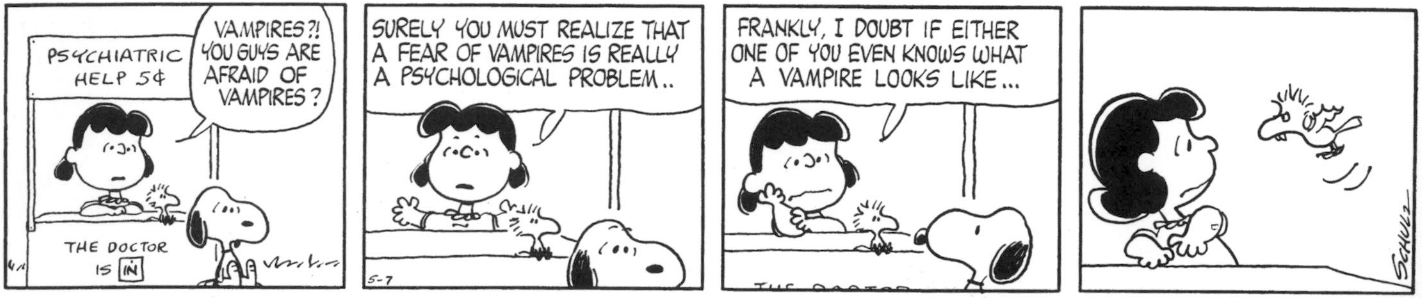
PSYCHIATRIC HELP 5¢
THE DOCTOR IS IN
VAMPIRES?! YOU GUYS ARE AFRAID OF VAMPIRES?
SURELY YOU MUST REALIZE THAT A FEAR OF VAMPIRES IS REALLY A PSYCHOLOGICAL PROBLEM..
FRANKLY, I DOUBT IF EITHER ONE OF YOU EVEN KNOWS WHAT A VAMPIRE LOOKS LIKE...
SCHULZ

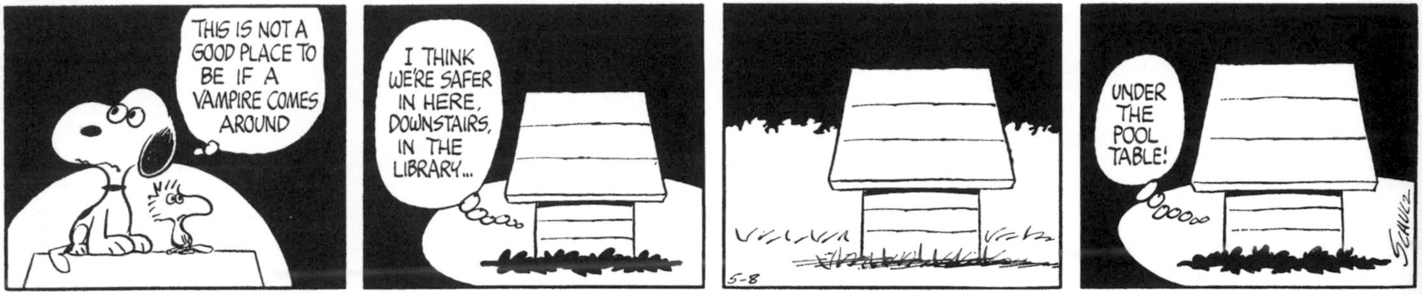
THIS IS NOT A GOOD PLACE TO BE IF A VAMPIRE COMES AROUND
I THINK WE'RE SAFER IN HERE, DOWNSTAIRS, IN THE LIBRARY...
UNDER THE POOL TABLE!
SCHULZ

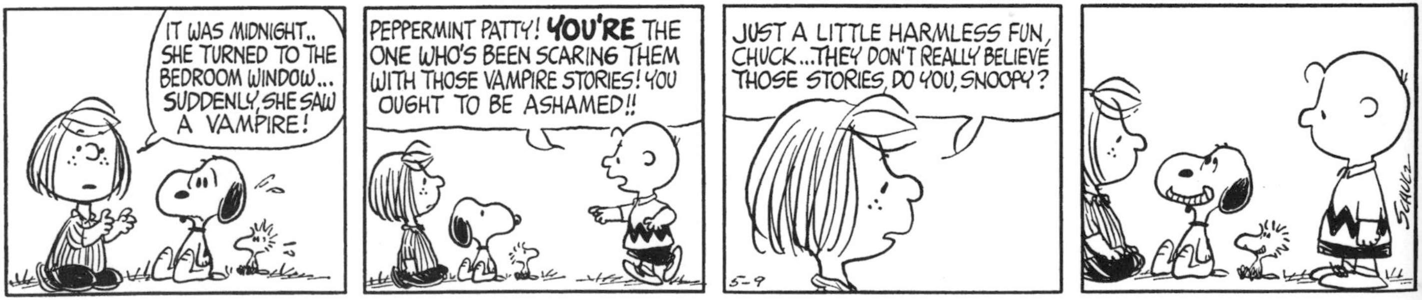
IT WAS MIDNIGHT.. SHE TURNED TO THE BEDROOM WINDOW... SUDDENLY, SHE SAW A VAMPIRE!
PEPPERMINT PATTY! YOU'RE THE ONE WHO'S BEEN SCARING THEM WITH THOSE VAMPIRE STORIES! YOU OUGHT TO BE ASHAMED!!
JUST A LITTLE HARMLESS FUN, CHUCK...THEY DON'T REALLY BELIEVE THOSE STORIES, DO YOU, SNOOPY?
SCHULZ

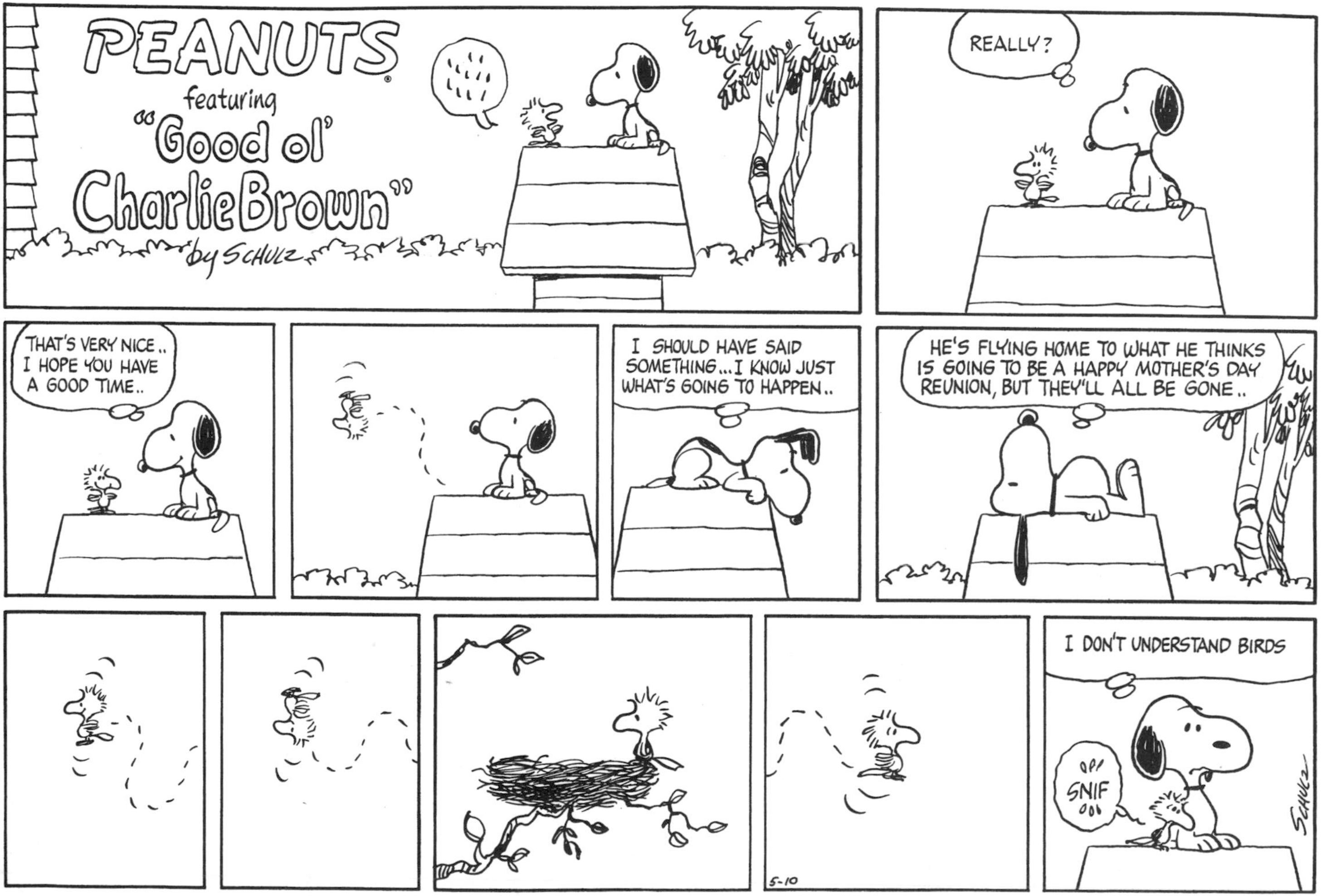
PEANUTS
featuring
"Good ol' CharlieBrown"
by SCHULZ
REALLY?
THAT'S VERY NICE.. I HOPE YOU HAVE A GOOD TIME..
I SHOULD HAVE SAID SOMETHING... I KNOW JUST WHAT'S GOING TO HAPPEN..
HE'S FLYING HOME TO WHAT HE THINKS IS GOING TO BE A HAPPY MOTHER'S DAY REUNION, BUT THEY'LL ALL BE GONE..
5-10
I DON'T UNDERSTAND BIRDS
SNIF
SCHULZ

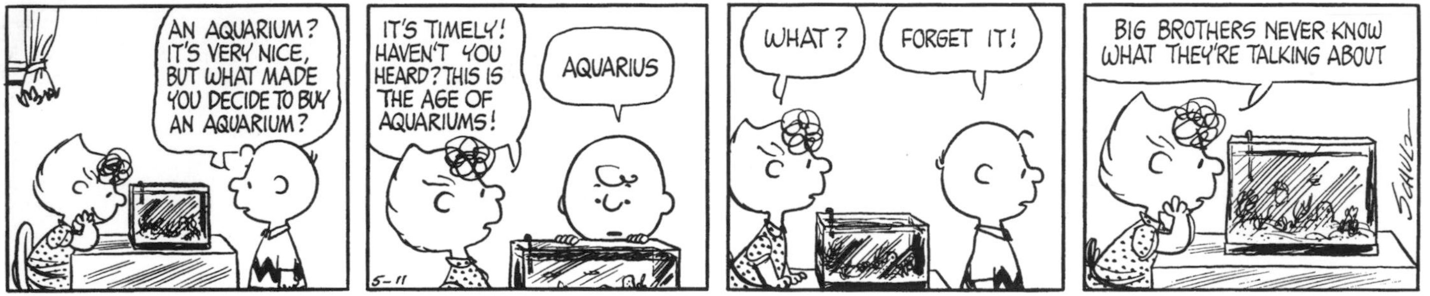
AN AQUARIUM? IT'S VERY NICE, BUT WHAT MADE YOU DECIDE TO BUY AN AQUARIUM?
IT'S TIMELY! HAVEN'T YOU HEARD? THIS IS THE AGE OF AQUARIUMS!
AQUARIUS
5-11
WHAT?
FORGET IT!
BIG BROTHERS NEVER KNOW WHAT THEY'RE TALKING ABOUT
SCHULZ

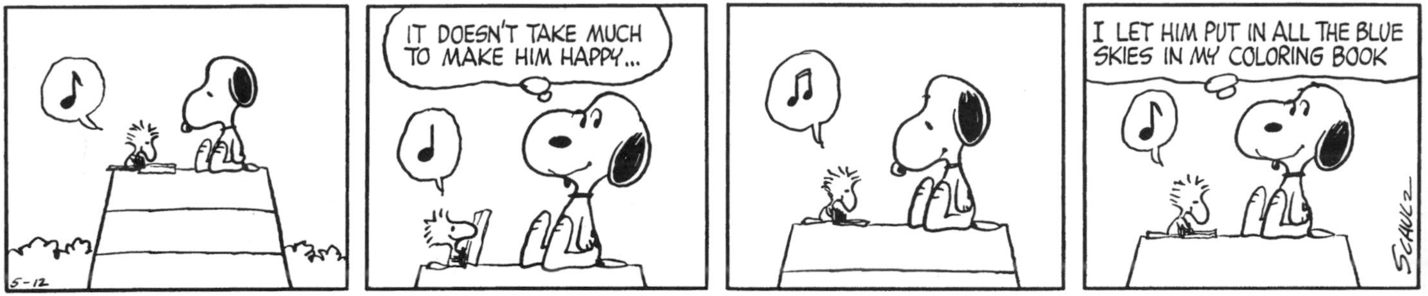
♪
5-12
IT DOESN'T TAKE MUCH TO MAKE HIM HAPPY...
♩
♫
I LET HIM PUT IN ALL THE BLUE SKIES IN MY COLORING BOOK
♪
SCHULZ

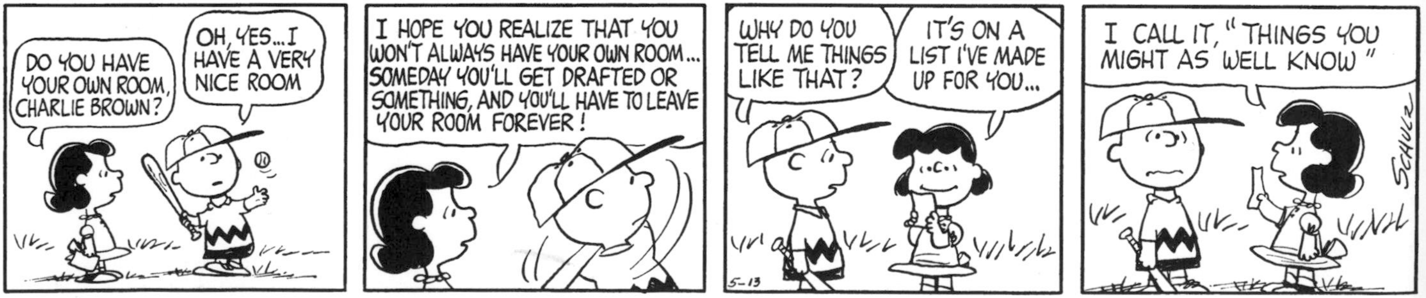
DO YOU HAVE YOUR OWN ROOM, CHARLIE BROWN?
OH, YES...I HAVE A VERY NICE ROOM
I HOPE YOU REALIZE THAT YOU WON'T ALWAYS HAVE YOUR OWN ROOM... SOMEDAY YOU'LL GET DRAFTED OR SOMETHING, AND YOU'LL HAVE TO LEAVE YOUR ROOM FOREVER!
WHY DO YOU TELL ME THINGS LIKE THAT?
IT'S ON A LIST I'VE MADE UP FOR YOU...
5-13
I CALL IT, "THINGS YOU MIGHT AS WELL KNOW"
SCHULZ

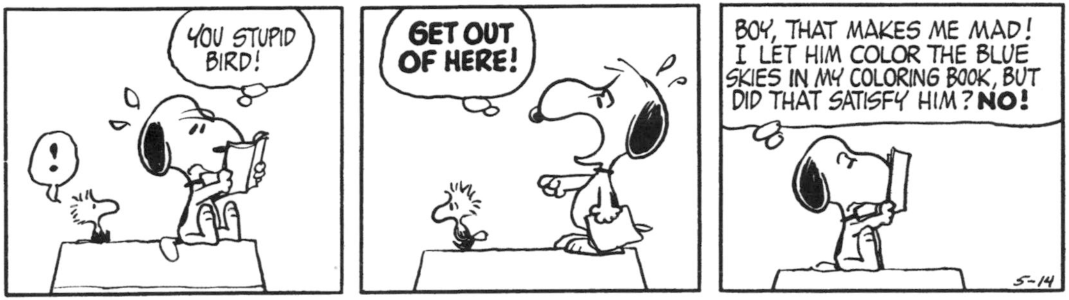
YOU STUPID BIRD!
!
GET OUT OF HERE!
BOY, THAT MAKES ME MAD! I LET HIM COLOR THE BLUE SKIES IN MY COLORING BOOK, BUT DID THAT SATISFY HIM? NO!
5-14
HE COLORED IN THE GRASS, THE TREES AND ALL THE BUNNIES!!
SCHULZ

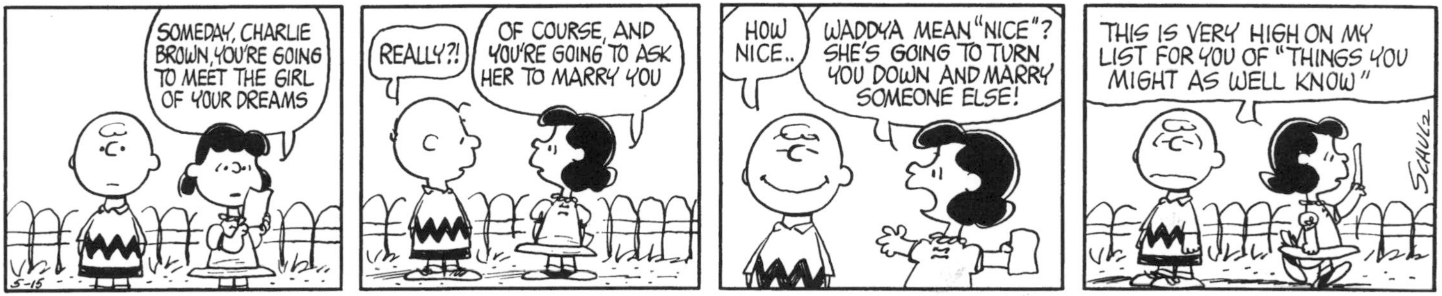
SOMEDAY, CHARLIE BROWN, YOU'RE GOING TO MEET THE GIRL OF YOUR DREAMS
5-15
REALLY?!
OF COURSE, AND YOU'RE GOING TO ASK HER TO MARRY YOU
HOW NICE..
WADDYA MEAN "NICE"? SHE'S GOING TO TURN YOU DOWN AND MARRY SOMEONE ELSE!
THIS IS VERY HIGH ON MY LIST FOR YOU OF "THINGS YOU MIGHT AS WELL KNOW"
SCHULZ

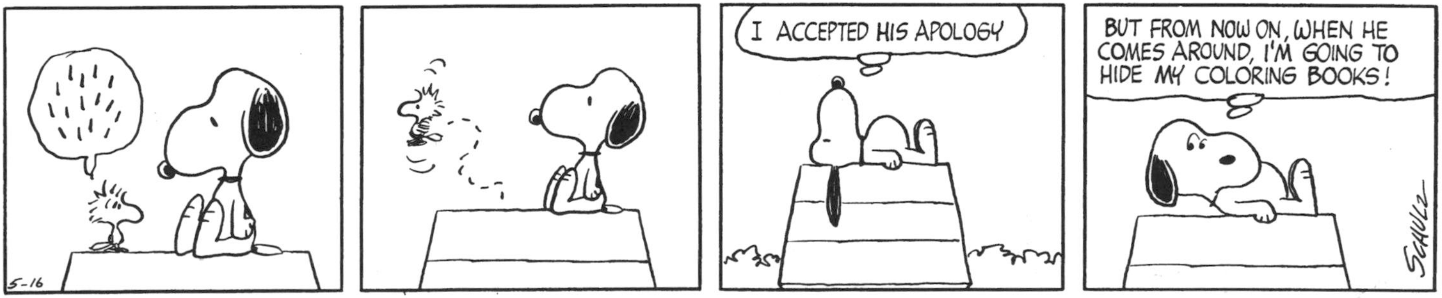
5-16
I ACCEPTED HIS APOLOGY
BUT FROM NOW ON, WHEN HE COMES AROUND, I'M GOING TO HIDE MY COLORING BOOKS!
SCHULZ

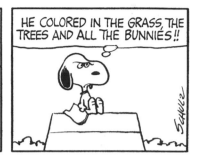

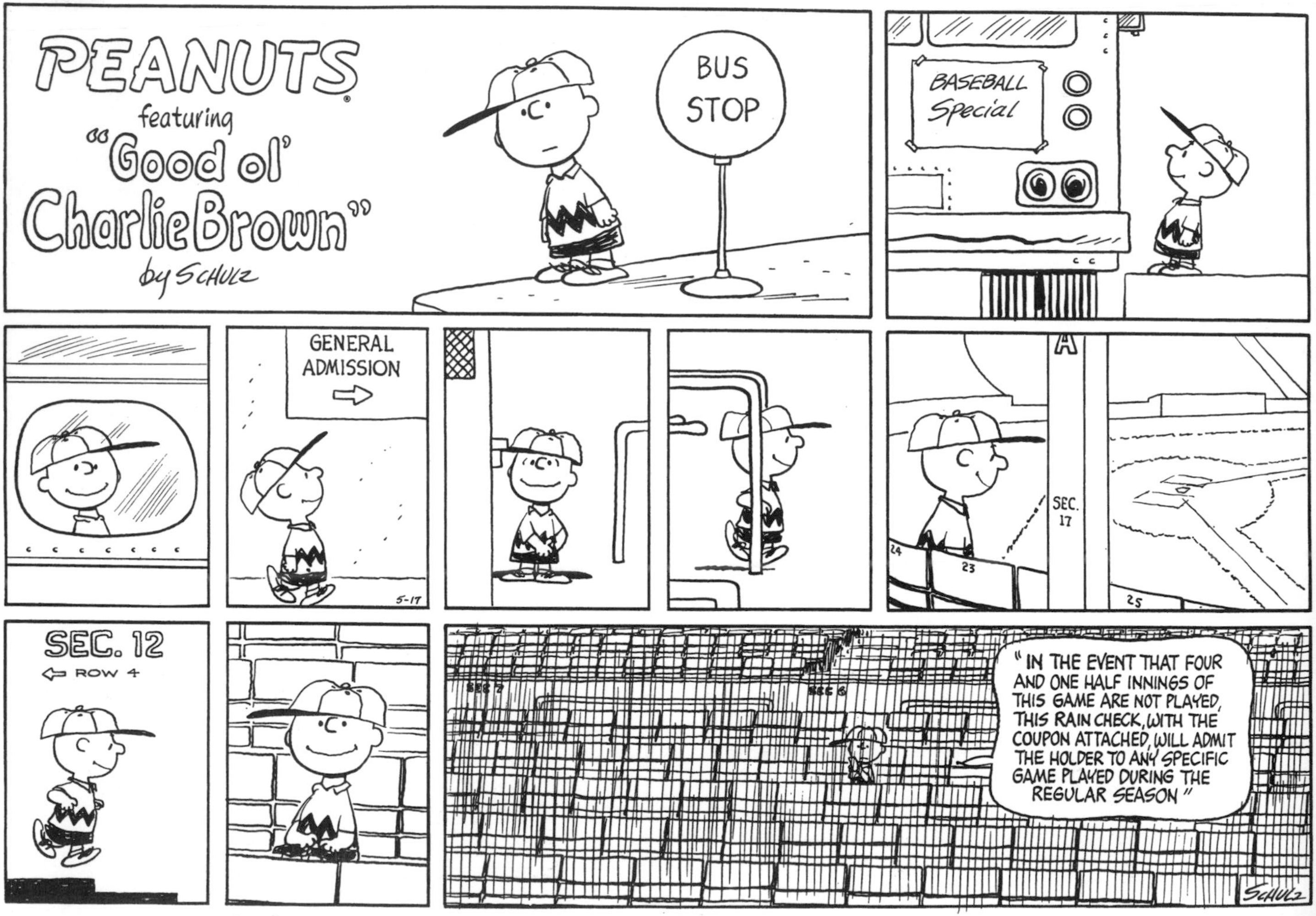
PEANUTS
featuring
"Good ol' CharlieBrown"
by SCHULZ
BUS STOP
BASEBALL Special
GENERAL ADMISSION
5-17
A
SEC. 17
24
23
25
SEC. 12
ROW 4
" IN THE EVENT THAT FOUR AND ONE HALF INNINGS OF THIS GAME ARE NOT PLAYED, THIS RAIN CHECK, WITH THE COUPON ATTACHED, WILL ADMIT THE HOLDER TO ANY SPECIFIC GAME PLAYED DURING THE REGULAR SEASON "
SCHULZ

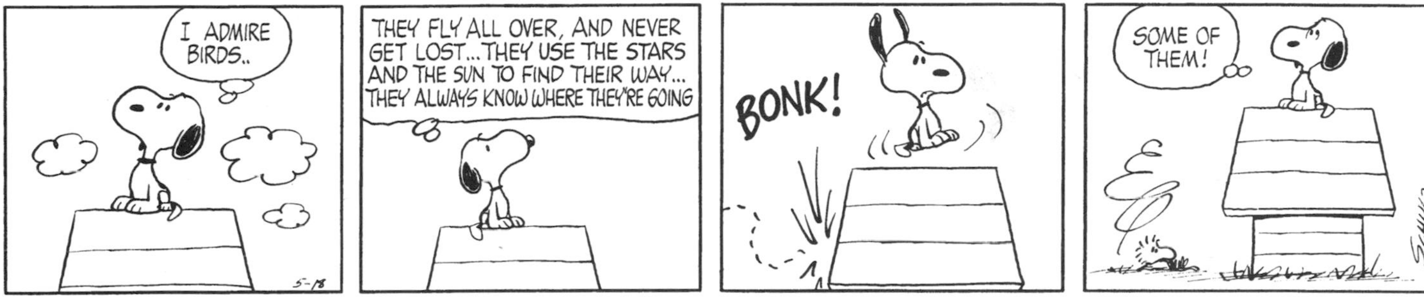
I ADMIRE BIRDS..
5-18
THEY FLY ALL OVER, AND NEVER GET LOST...THEY USE THE STARS AND THE SUN TO FIND THEIR WAY... THEY ALWAYS KNOW WHERE THEY'RE GOING
BONK!
SOME OF THEM!
SCHULZ

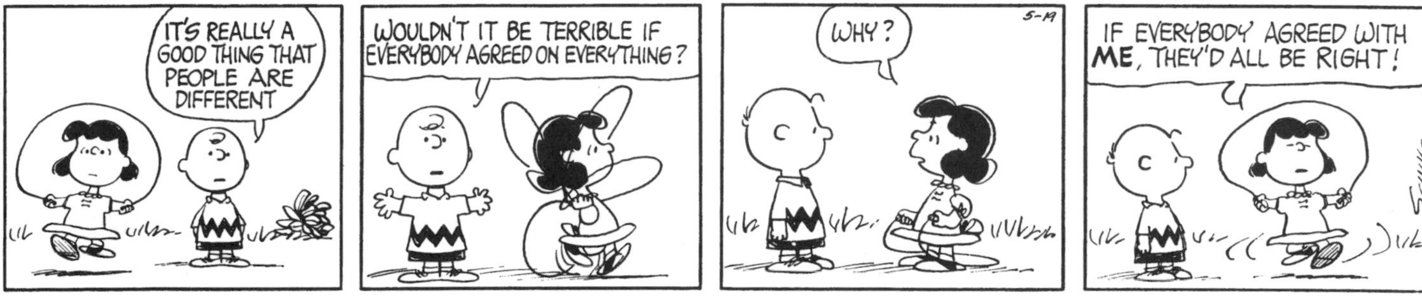
IT'S REALLY A GOOD THING THAT PEOPLE ARE DIFFERENT
WOULDN'T IT BE TERRIBLE IF EVERYBODY AGREED ON EVERYTHING?
5-19
WHY?
IF EVERYBODY AGREED WITH ME, THEY'D ALL BE RIGHT!
SCHULZ

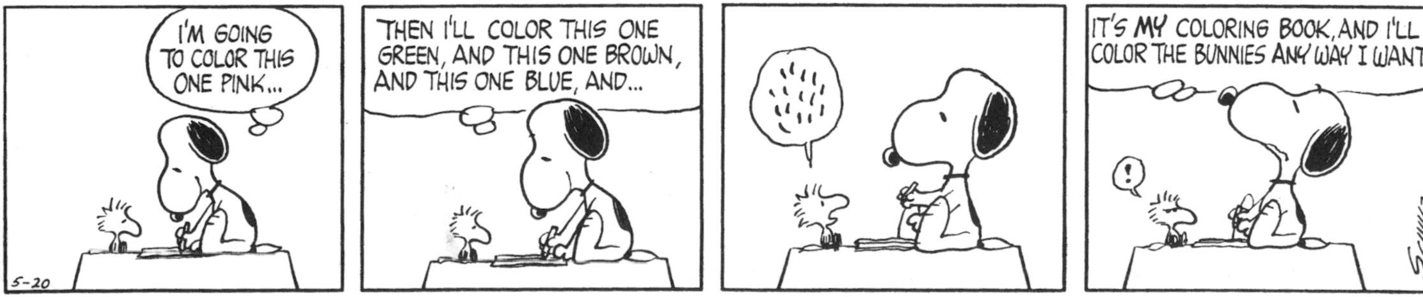
I'M GOING TO COLOR THIS ONE PINK...
5-20
THEN I'LL COLOR THIS ONE GREEN, AND THIS ONE BROWN, AND THIS ONE BLUE, AND...
IT'S MY COLORING BOOK, AND I'LL COLOR THE BUNNIES ANY WAY I WANT!
!
SCHULZ

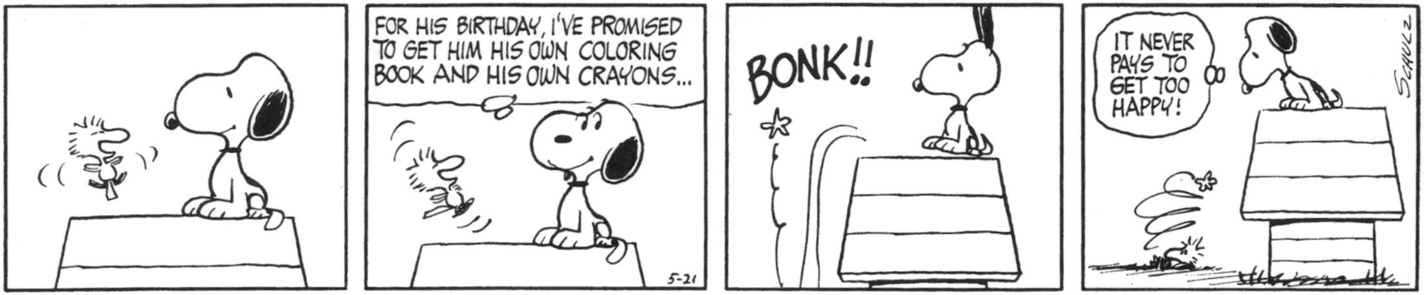
FOR HIS BIRTHDAY, I'VE PROMISED TO GET HIM HIS OWN COLORING BOOK AND HIS OWN CRAYONS...
5-21
BONK!!
IT NEVER PAYS TO GET TOO HAPPY!
SCHULZ

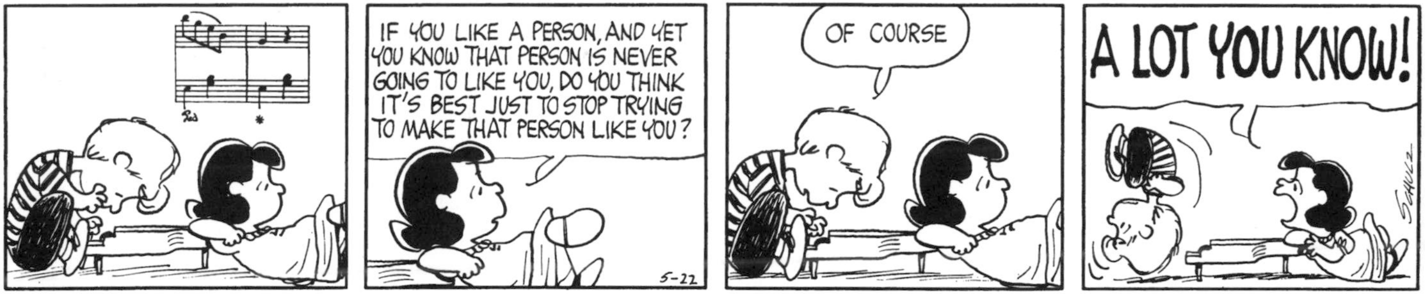
IF YOU LIKE A PERSON, AND YET YOU KNOW THAT PERSON IS NEVER GOING TO LIKE YOU, DO YOU THINK IT'S BEST JUST TO STOP TRYING TO MAKE THAT PERSON LIKE YOU?
5-22
OF COURSE
A LOT YOU KNOW!
SCHULZ

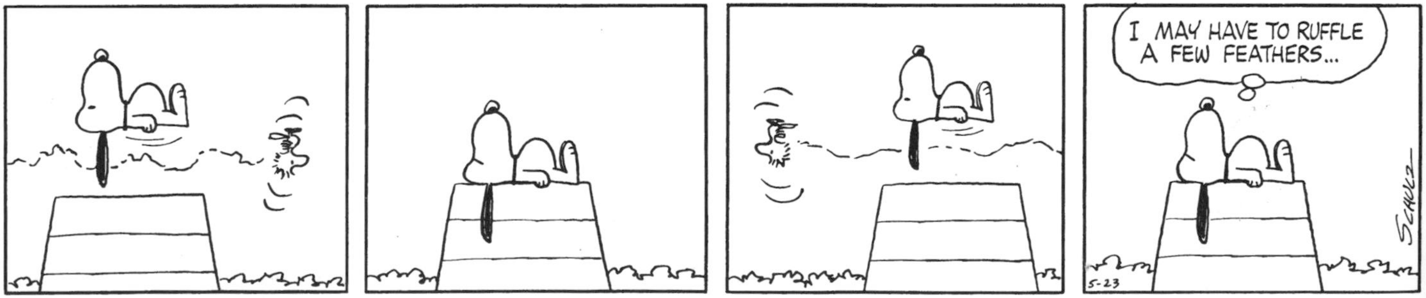
I MAY HAVE TO RUFFLE A FEW FEATHERS...
SCHULZ
5-23

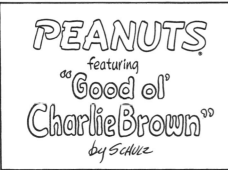

PEANUTS featuring "Good ol' Charlie Brown" by Schulz

PSYCHIATRIC HELP 5¢

TALK IS "CHEEP"

PSYCHIATRIC HELP 5¢

THE DOCTOR IS IN

WHAT'S THIS?

DO YOU THINK I'M GOING TO SIT HERE AND TELL ALL MY PROBLEMS TO A CHICKEN?

HE'S NOT A CHICKEN!

I DON'T CARE IF HE'S AN EAGLE! I'M NOT GOING TO TALK TO HIM!

THE DOCTOR IS IN

HELP 5¢

I'M SORRY, BUT I GUESS YOU'LL HAVE TO LEAVE US ALONE..

THE DOCTOR

BLEAH!

SOMETIMES I WONDER WHY I COME TO THIS PLACE...

E DOCTOR IS IN

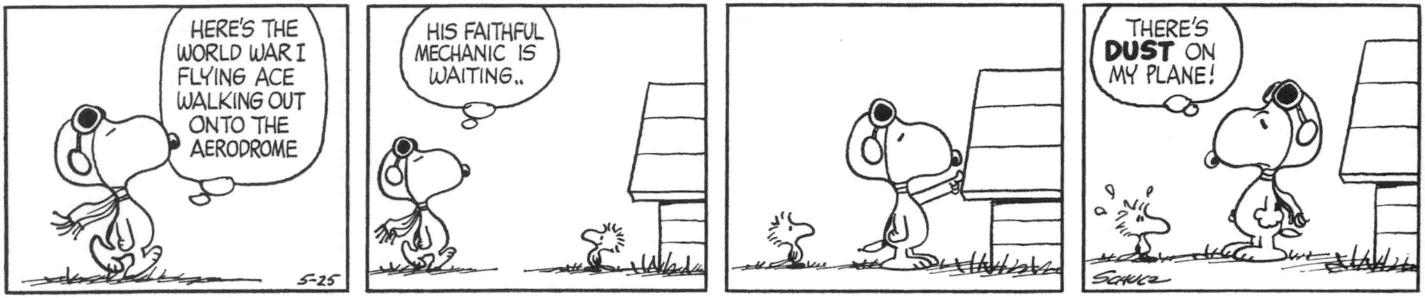
HERE'S THE WORLD WAR I FLYING ACE WALKING OUT ONTO THE AERODROME
5-25
HIS FAITHFUL MECHANIC IS WAITING..
THERE'S **DUST** ON MY PLANE!
SCHULZ

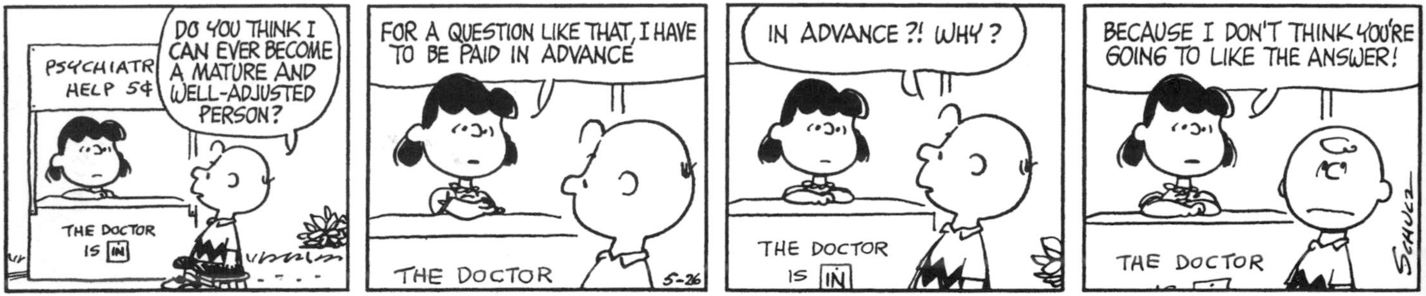
PSYCHIATR HELP 5¢
THE DOCTOR IS IN
DO YOU THINK I CAN EVER BECOME A MATURE AND WELL-ADJUSTED PERSON?
FOR A QUESTION LIKE THAT, I HAVE TO BE PAID IN ADVANCE
THE DOCTOR
5-26
IN ADVANCE?! WHY?
THE DOCTOR IS IN
BECAUSE I DON'T THINK YOU'RE GOING TO LIKE THE ANSWER!
THE DOCTOR
SCHULZ

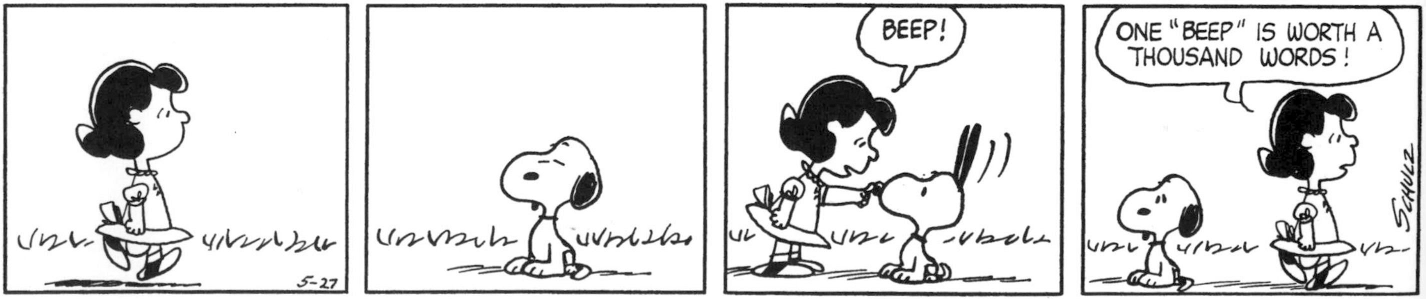
5-27
BEEP!
ONE "BEEP" IS WORTH A THOUSAND WORDS!
SCHULZ

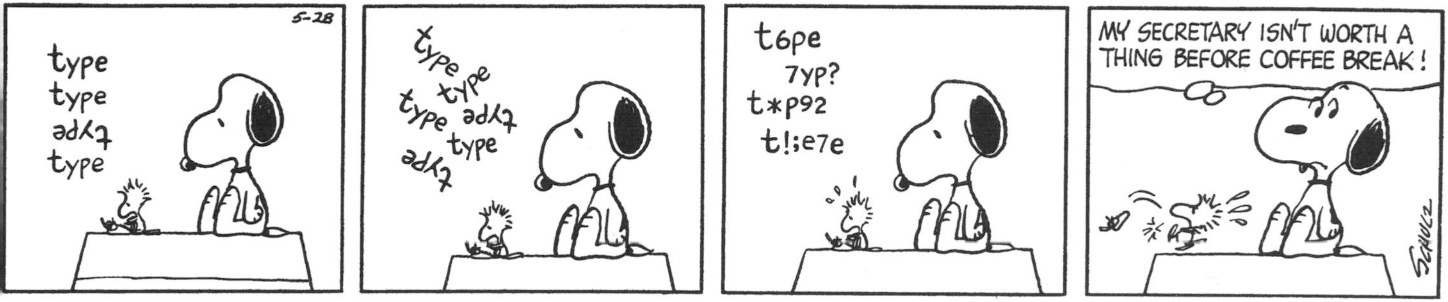
5-28
type
type
type
type
type
type
type
type
type
type
t6pe
7yp?
t*p92
t!;e7e
MY SECRETARY ISN'T WORTH A THING BEFORE COFFEE BREAK!
SCHULZ

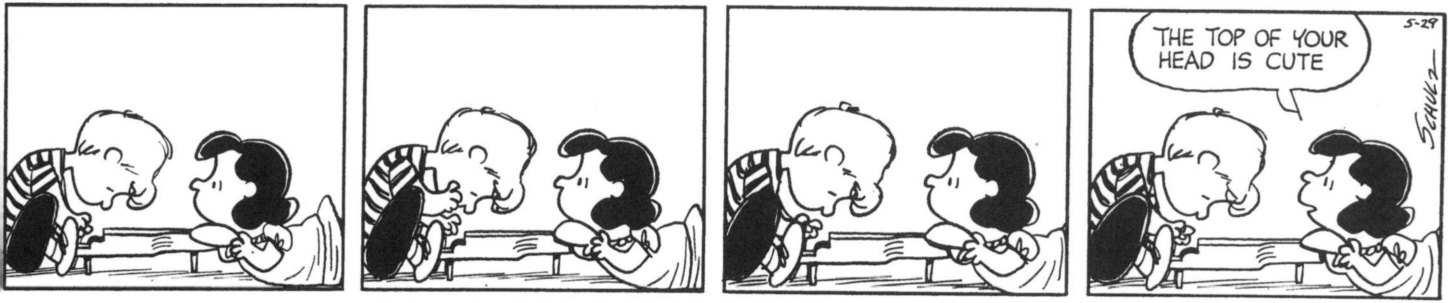
5-29
THE TOP OF YOUR HEAD IS CUTE
SCHULZ

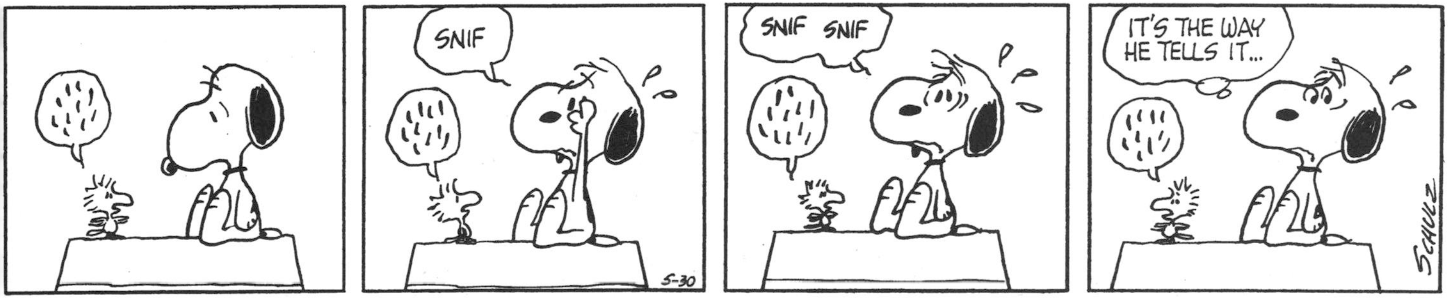
SNIF
5-30
SNIF SNIF
IT'S THE WAY HE TELLS IT...
SCHULZ

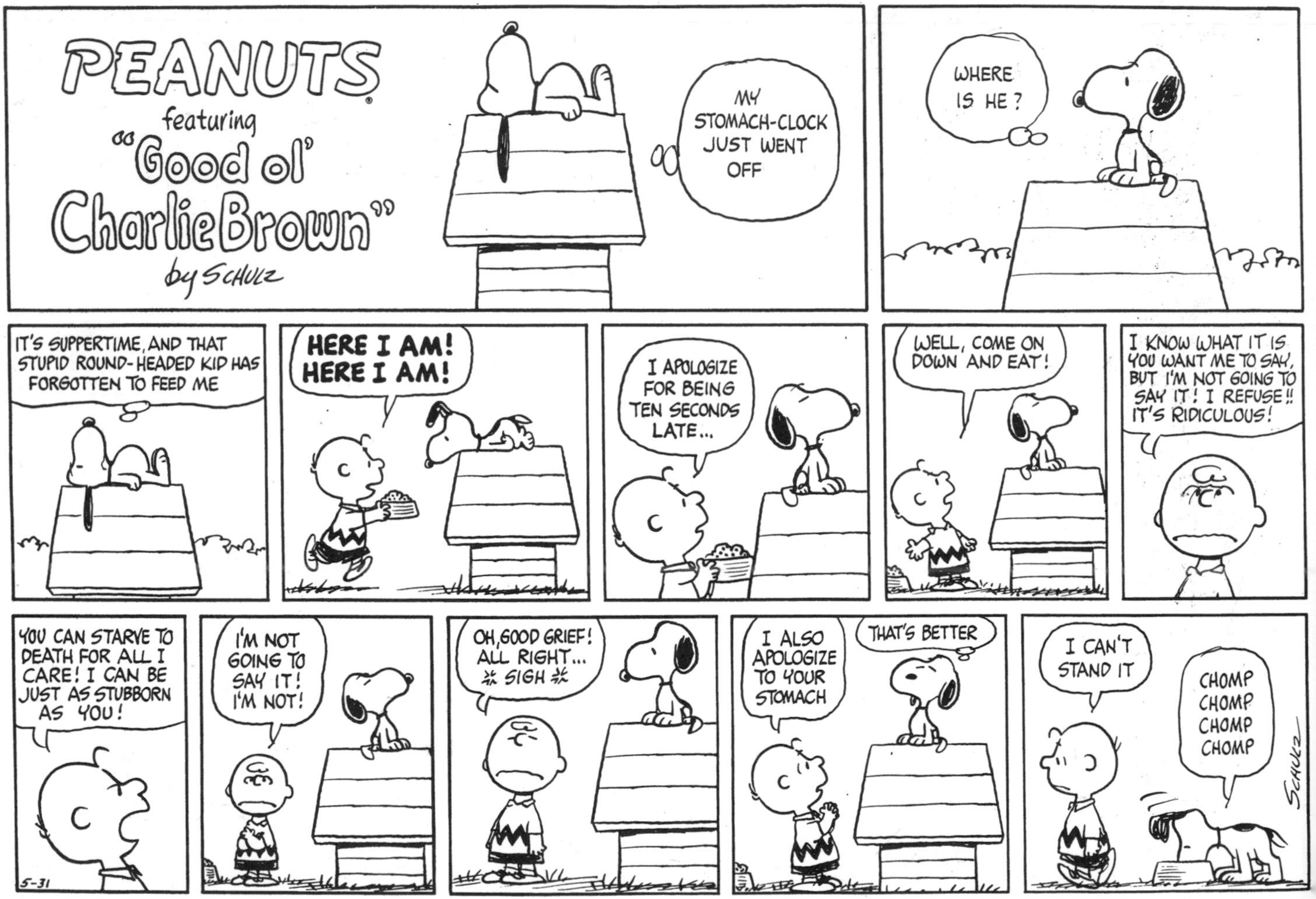
PEANUTS
featuring
"Good ol' CharlieBrown"
by SCHULZ
MY STOMACH-CLOCK JUST WENT OFF
WHERE IS HE ?
IT'S SUPPERTIME, AND THAT STUPID ROUND-HEADED KID HAS FORGOTTEN TO FEED ME
HERE I AM! HERE I AM!
I APOLOGIZE FOR BEING TEN SECONDS LATE...
WELL, COME ON DOWN AND EAT!
I KNOW WHAT IT IS YOU WANT ME TO SAY, BUT I'M NOT GOING TO SAY IT! I REFUSE!! IT'S RIDICULOUS!
YOU CAN STARVE TO DEATH FOR ALL I CARE! I CAN BE JUST AS STUBBORN AS YOU!
5-31
I'M NOT GOING TO SAY IT! I'M NOT!
OH, GOOD GRIEF! ALL RIGHT... SIGH
I ALSO APOLOGIZE TO YOUR STOMACH
THAT'S BETTER
I CAN'T STAND IT
CHOMP CHOMP CHOMP CHOMP
SCHULZ

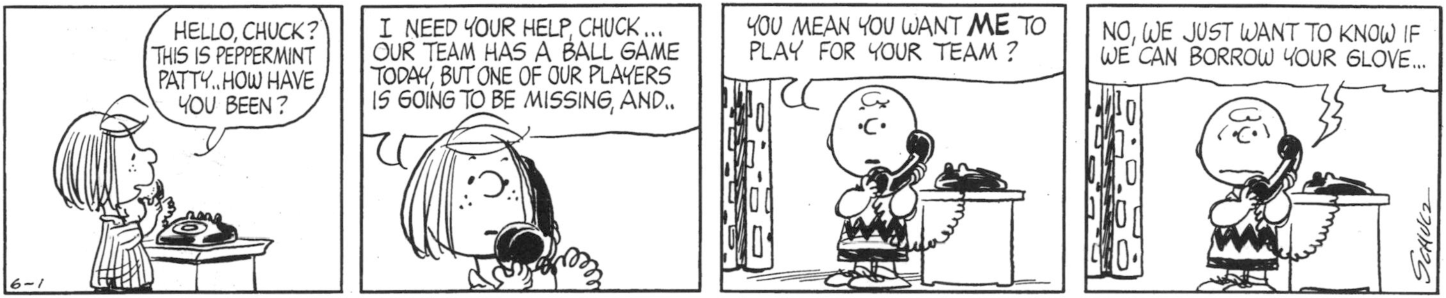
HELLO, CHUCK? THIS IS PEPPERMINT PATTY.. HOW HAVE YOU BEEN?
I NEED YOUR HELP, CHUCK... OUR TEAM HAS A BALL GAME TODAY, BUT ONE OF OUR PLAYERS IS GOING TO BE MISSING, AND..
YOU MEAN YOU WANT **ME** TO PLAY FOR YOUR TEAM?
NO, WE JUST WANT TO KNOW IF WE CAN BORROW YOUR GLOVE...
6-1
SCHULZ

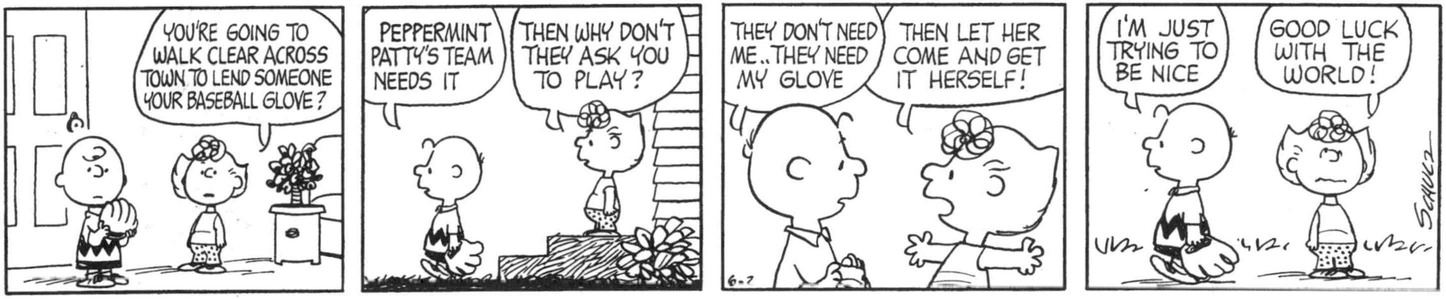
YOU'RE GOING TO WALK CLEAR ACROSS TOWN TO LEND SOMEONE YOUR BASEBALL GLOVE?
PEPPERMINT PATTY'S TEAM NEEDS IT
THEN WHY DON'T THEY ASK YOU TO PLAY?
THEY DON'T NEED ME.. THEY NEED MY GLOVE
THEN LET HER COME AND GET IT HERSELF!
I'M JUST TRYING TO BE NICE
GOOD LUCK WITH THE WORLD!
6-2
SCHULZ

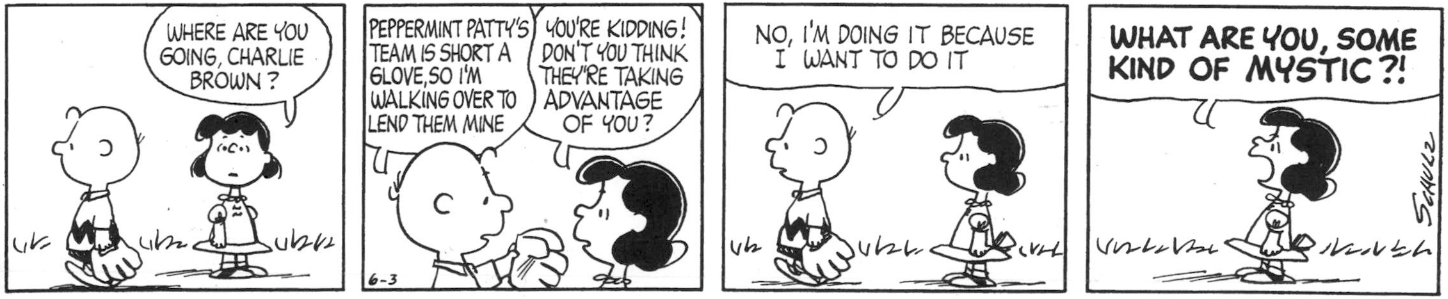
WHERE ARE YOU GOING, CHARLIE BROWN?
PEPPERMINT PATTY'S TEAM IS SHORT A GLOVE, SO I'M WALKING OVER TO LEND THEM MINE
YOU'RE KIDDING! DON'T YOU THINK THEY'RE TAKING ADVANTAGE OF YOU?
NO, I'M DOING IT BECAUSE I WANT TO DO IT
WHAT ARE YOU, SOME KIND OF MYSTIC?!
6-3
SCHULZ

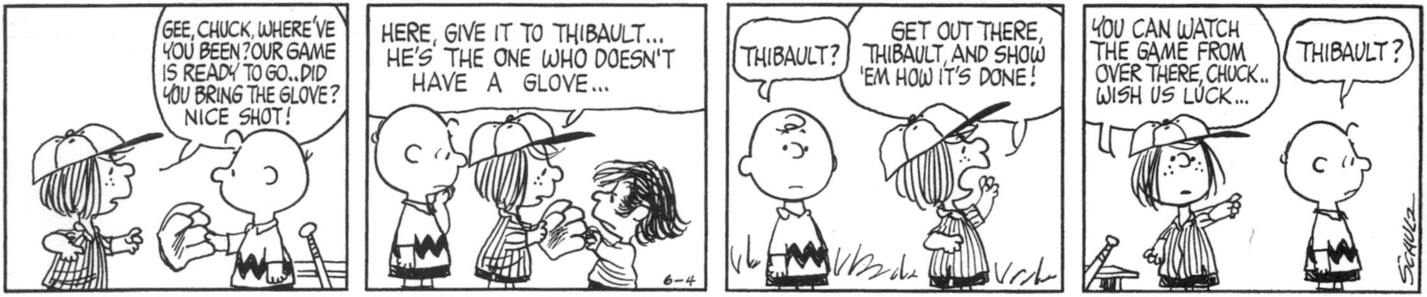
GEE, CHUCK, WHERE'VE YOU BEEN? OUR GAME IS READY TO GO..DID YOU BRING THE GLOVE? NICE SHOT!
HERE, GIVE IT TO THIBAULT... HE'S THE ONE WHO DOESN'T HAVE A GLOVE...
6-4
THIBAULT?
GET OUT THERE, THIBAULT, AND SHOW 'EM HOW IT'S DONE!
YOU CAN WATCH THE GAME FROM OVER THERE, CHUCK.. WISH US LUCK...
THIBAULT?
SCHULZ

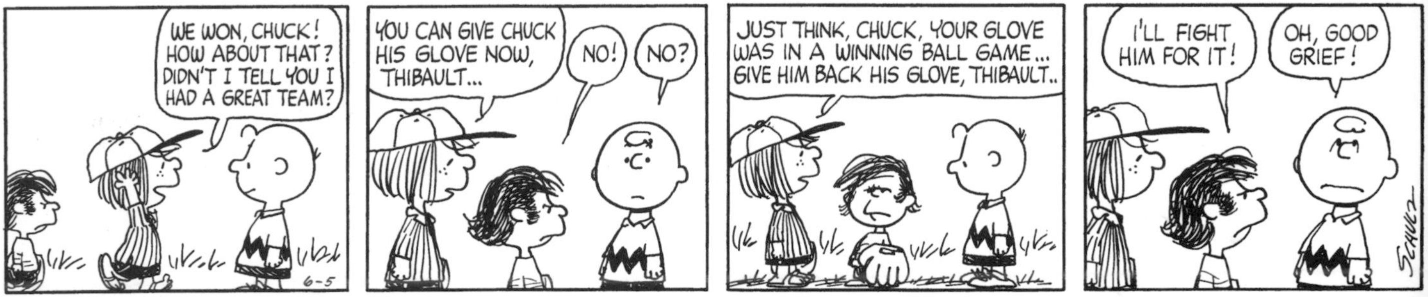
WE WON, CHUCK! HOW ABOUT THAT? DIDN'T I TELL YOU I HAD A GREAT TEAM?
6-5
YOU CAN GIVE CHUCK HIS GLOVE NOW, THIBAULT...
NO!
NO?
JUST THINK, CHUCK, YOUR GLOVE WAS IN A WINNING BALL GAME... GIVE HIM BACK HIS GLOVE, THIBAULT..
I'LL FIGHT HIM FOR IT!
OH, GOOD GRIEF!
SCHULZ

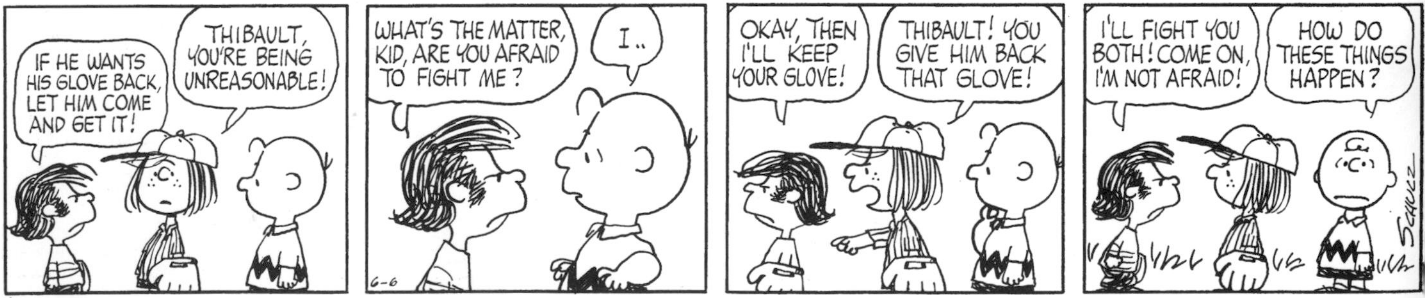
IF HE WANTS HIS GLOVE BACK, LET HIM COME AND GET IT!
THIBAULT, YOU'RE BEING UNREASONABLE!
WHAT'S THE MATTER, KID, ARE YOU AFRAID TO FIGHT ME?
I..
6-6
OKAY, THEN I'LL KEEP YOUR GLOVE!
THIBAULT! YOU GIVE HIM BACK THAT GLOVE!
I'LL FIGHT YOU BOTH! COME ON, I'M NOT AFRAID!
HOW DO THESE THINGS HAPPEN?
SCHULZ

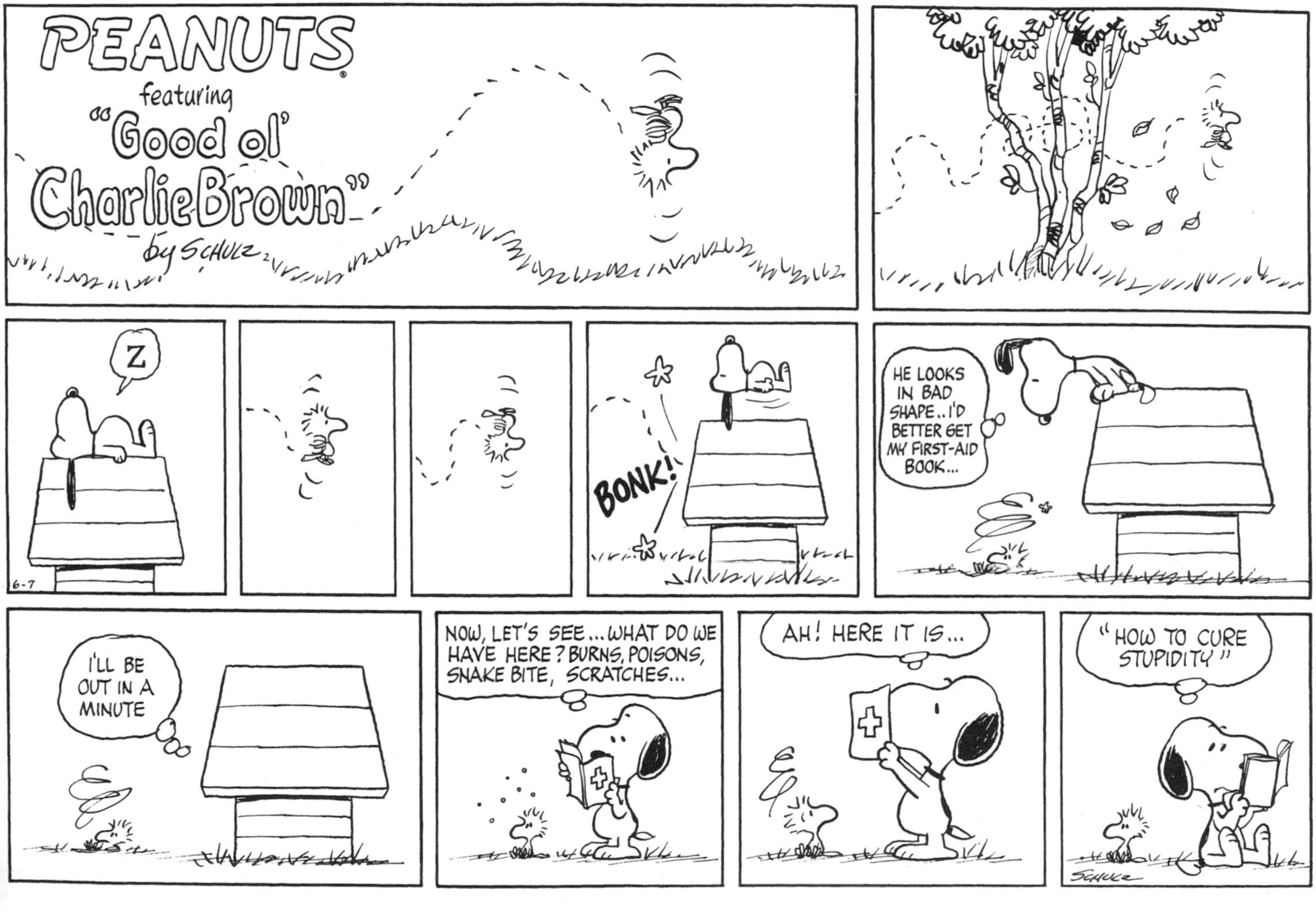

PEANUTS
featuring
"Good ol' Charlie Brown"
by SCHULZ
Z
6-7
BONK!
HE LOOKS IN BAD SHAPE..I'D BETTER GET MY FIRST-AID BOOK...
I'LL BE OUT IN A MINUTE
NOW, LET'S SEE...WHAT DO WE HAVE HERE? BURNS, POISONS, SNAKE BITE, SCRATCHES...
AH! HERE IT IS...
"HOW TO CURE STUPIDITY"
SCHULZ

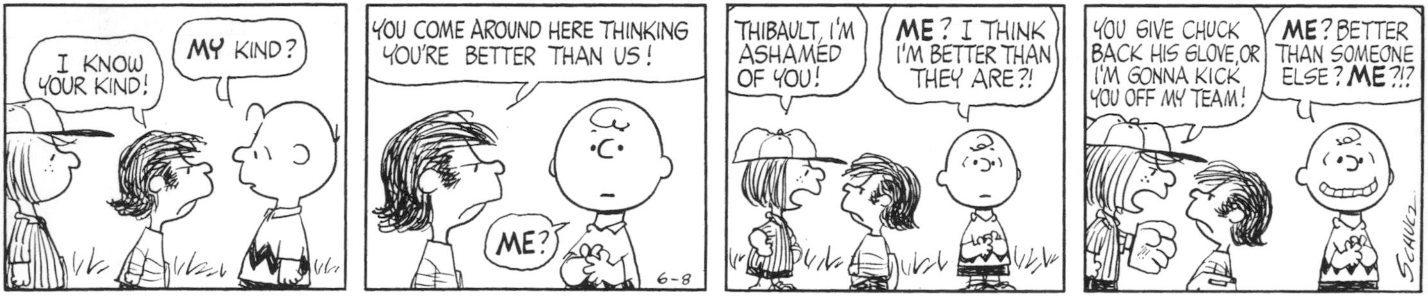
I KNOW YOUR KIND!
MY KIND?
YOU COME AROUND HERE THINKING YOU'RE BETTER THAN US!
ME?
6-8
THIBAULT, I'M ASHAMED OF YOU!
ME? I THINK I'M BETTER THAN THEY ARE?!
YOU GIVE CHUCK BACK HIS GLOVE, OR I'M GONNA KICK YOU OFF MY TEAM!
ME? BETTER THAN SOMEONE ELSE? ME?!?
SCHULZ

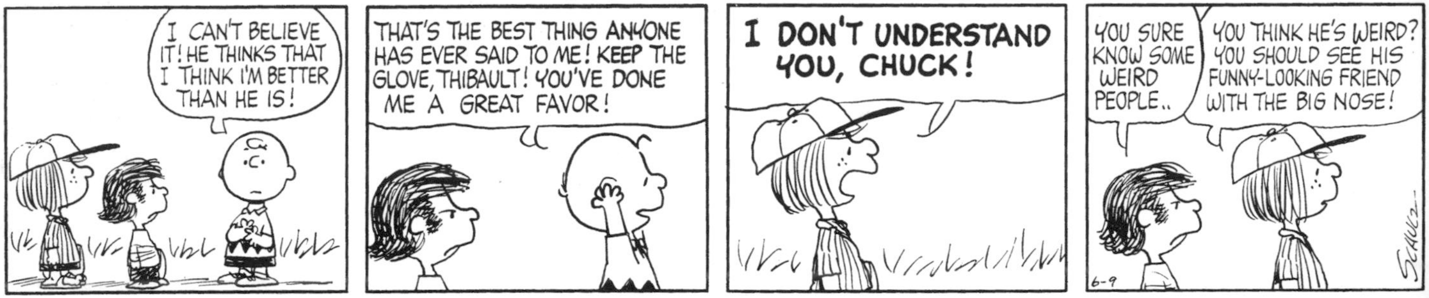
I CAN'T BELIEVE IT! HE THINKS THAT I THINK I'M BETTER THAN HE IS!
THAT'S THE BEST THING ANYONE HAS EVER SAID TO ME! KEEP THE GLOVE, THIBAULT! YOU'VE DONE ME A GREAT FAVOR!
I DON'T UNDERSTAND YOU, CHUCK!
YOU SURE KNOW SOME WEIRD PEOPLE..
YOU THINK HE'S WEIRD? YOU SHOULD SEE HIS FUNNY-LOOKING FRIEND WITH THE BIG NOSE!
SCHULZ
6-9

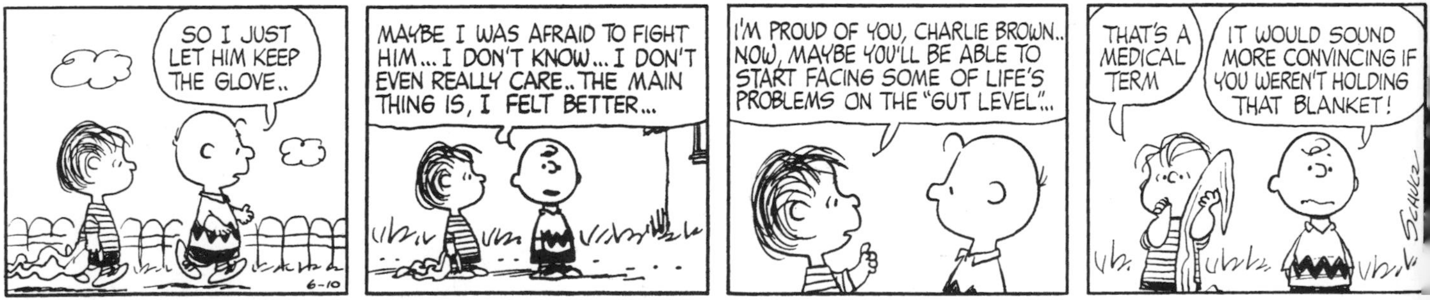
SO I JUST LET HIM KEEP THE GLOVE..
6-10
MAYBE I WAS AFRAID TO FIGHT HIM... I DON'T KNOW... I DON'T EVEN REALLY CARE.. THE MAIN THING IS, I FELT BETTER...
I'M PROUD OF YOU, CHARLIE BROWN.. NOW, MAYBE YOU'LL BE ABLE TO START FACING SOME OF LIFE'S PROBLEMS ON THE "GUT LEVEL"...
THAT'S A MEDICAL TERM
IT WOULD SOUND MORE CONVINCING IF YOU WEREN'T HOLDING THAT BLANKET!
SCHULZ

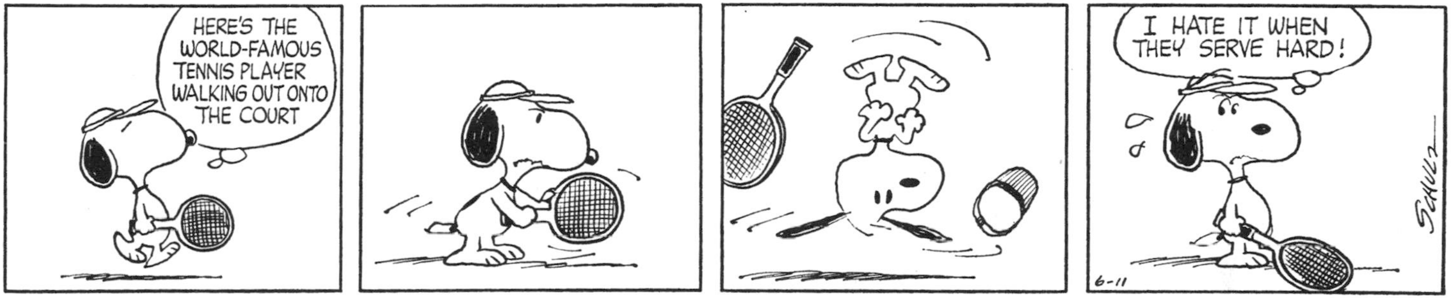
HERE'S THE WORLD-FAMOUS TENNIS PLAYER WALKING OUT ONTO THE COURT
I HATE IT WHEN THEY SERVE HARD!
6-11
SCHULZ

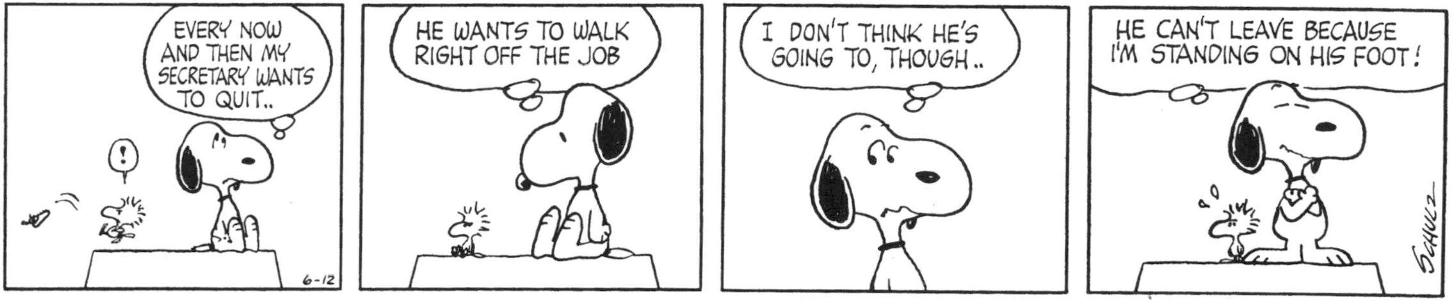
EVERY NOW AND THEN MY SECRETARY WANTS TO QUIT..
!
6-12
HE WANTS TO WALK RIGHT OFF THE JOB
I DON'T THINK HE'S GOING TO, THOUGH..
HE CAN'T LEAVE BECAUSE I'M STANDING ON HIS FOOT!
SCHULZ

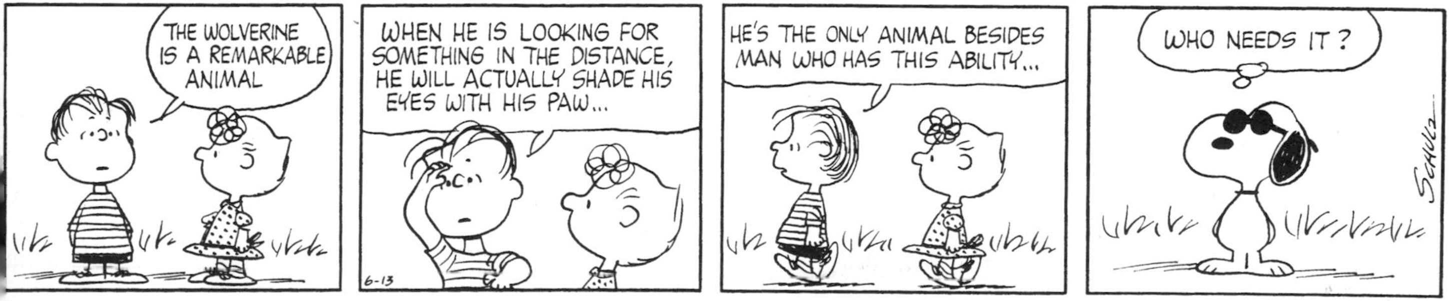
THE WOLVERINE IS A REMARKABLE ANIMAL
WHEN HE IS LOOKING FOR SOMETHING IN THE DISTANCE, HE WILL ACTUALLY SHADE HIS EYES WITH HIS PAW...
6-13
HE'S THE ONLY ANIMAL BESIDES MAN WHO HAS THIS ABILITY...
WHO NEEDS IT?
SCHULZ

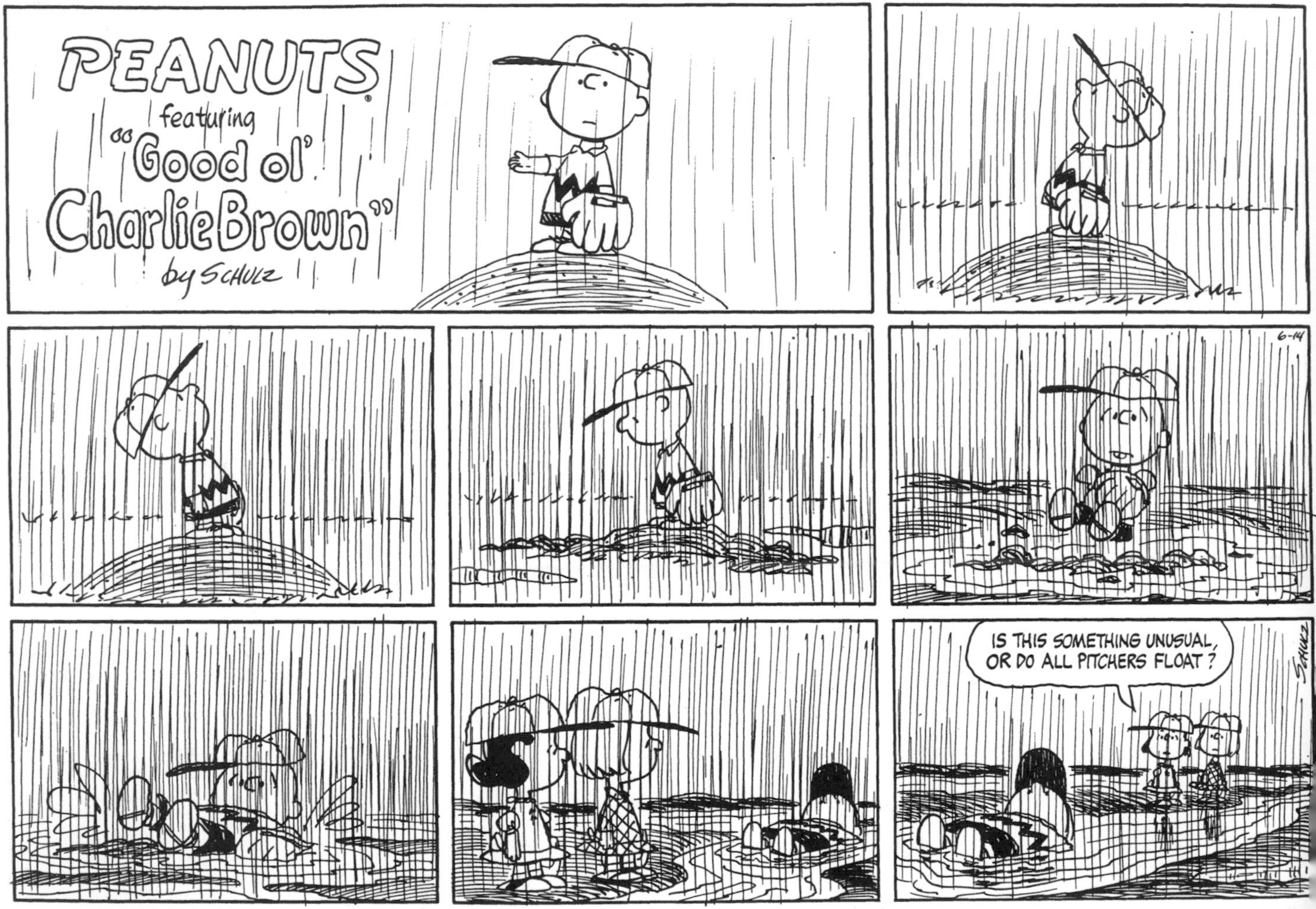
PEANUTS
featuring
"Good ol' Charlie Brown"
by SCHULZ
6-14
IS THIS SOMETHING UNUSUAL, OR DO ALL PITCHERS FLOAT?
SCHULZ

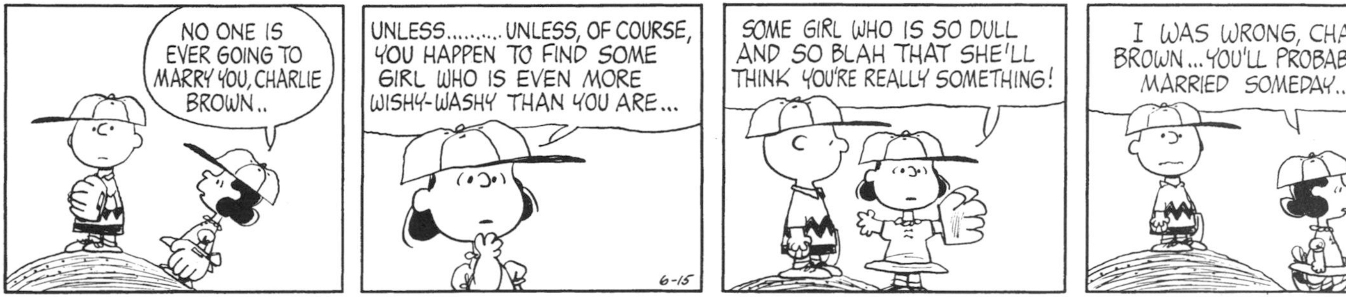
NO ONE IS EVER GOING TO MARRY YOU, CHARLIE BROWN..
UNLESS.......... UNLESS, OF COURSE, YOU HAPPEN TO FIND SOME GIRL WHO IS EVEN MORE WISHY-WASHY THAN YOU ARE...
6-15
SOME GIRL WHO IS SO DULL AND SO BLAH THAT SHE'LL THINK YOU'RE REALLY SOMETHING!
I WAS WRONG, CHARLIE BROWN... YOU'LL PROBABLY GET MARRIED SOMEDAY...
SCHULZ

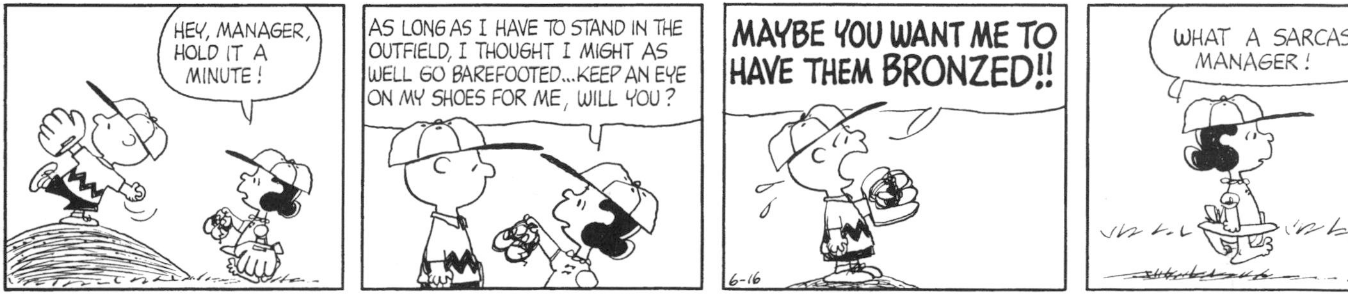
HEY, MANAGER, HOLD IT A MINUTE!
AS LONG AS I HAVE TO STAND IN THE OUTFIELD, I THOUGHT I MIGHT AS WELL GO BAREFOOTED... KEEP AN EYE ON MY SHOES FOR ME, WILL YOU?
MAYBE YOU WANT ME TO HAVE THEM BRONZED!!
6-16
WHAT A SARCASTIC MANAGER!
SCHULZ

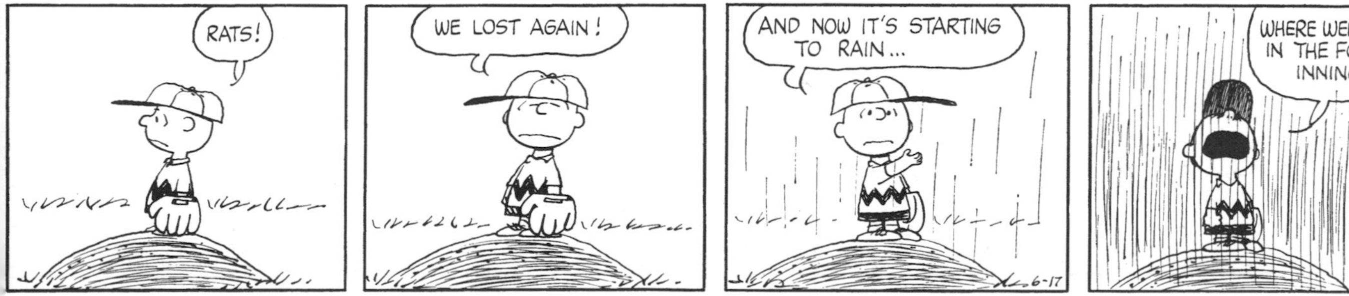
RATS!
WE LOST AGAIN!
AND NOW IT'S STARTING TO RAIN...
6-17
WHERE WERE YOU IN THE FOURTH INNING?!
SCHULZ

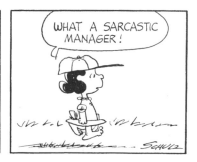

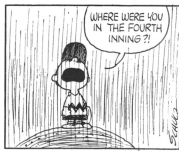

RATS! I CAN'T STAND LOSING ALL THE TIME!

THERE MUST BE SOMETHING WRONG WITH ME...

I USED TO COME HOME AND HURL MY GLOVE INTO THE CLOSET..

6-18

NOW, I CAN'T EVEN HIT THE CLOSET!

I THINK I'LL DO MY SUMMER SCHOOL THEME ON JOHNNY SEBASTIAN BACH..

NOT "JOHNNY"... "JOHANN"!

THAT'S WHAT I SAID..."JOHANNY"

NOT "JOHANNY"! JOHANN!! JOHANN SEBASTIAN BACH!

WHAT ABOUT HIM?

MAYBE I'LL WRITE ABOUT BOBBY ORR...

6-19

6-20

I ALWAYS HAVE TO REMIND HIM ABOUT SITTING AT LEAST SIX FEET FROM MY COLOR TV...

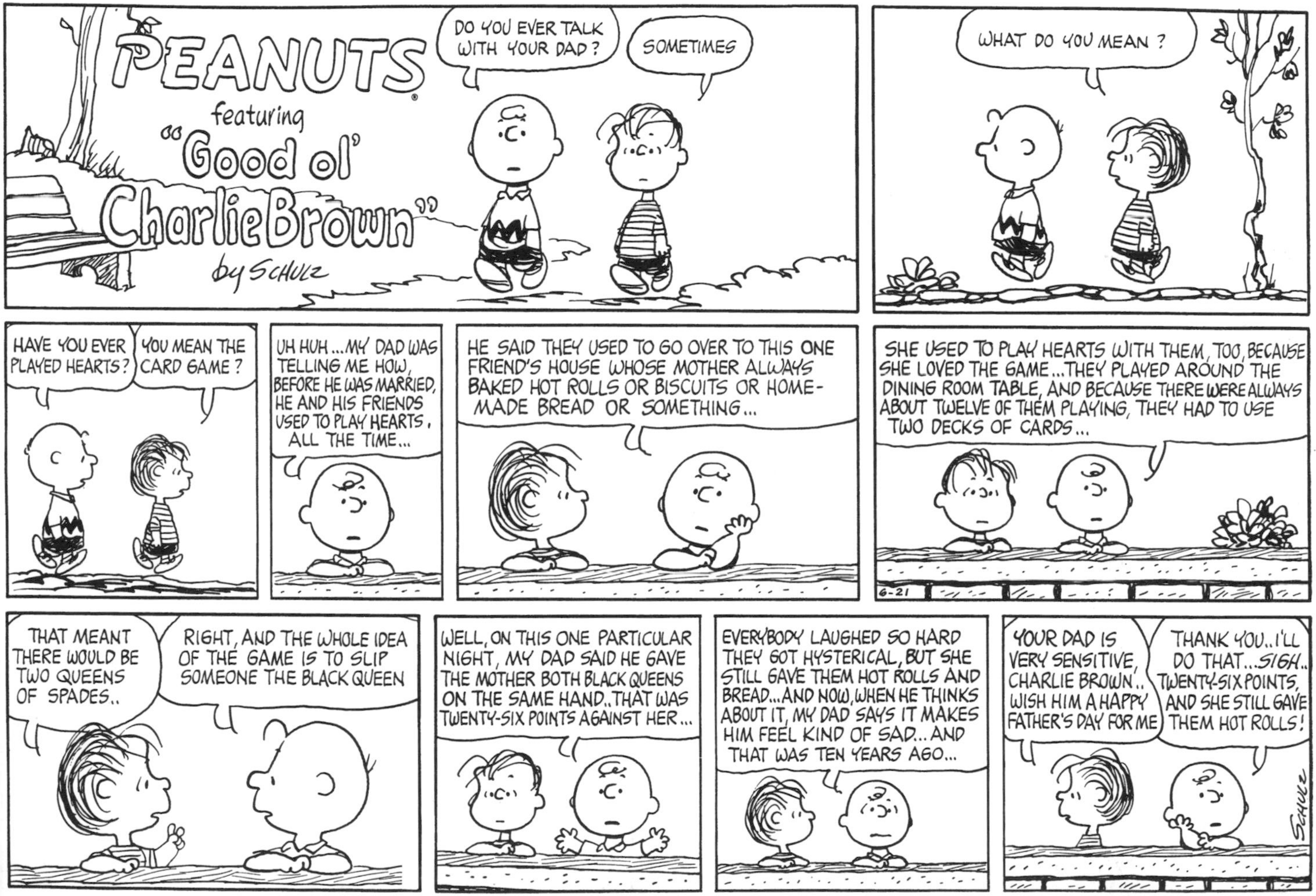
PEANUTS
featuring "Good ol' Charlie Brown"
by SCHULZ
DO YOU EVER TALK WITH YOUR DAD?
SOMETIMES
WHAT DO YOU MEAN?
HAVE YOU EVER PLAYED HEARTS?
YOU MEAN THE CARD GAME?
UH HUH ...MY DAD WAS TELLING ME HOW, BEFORE HE WAS MARRIED, HE AND HIS FRIENDS USED TO PLAY HEARTS, ALL THE TIME...
HE SAID THEY USED TO GO OVER TO THIS ONE FRIEND'S HOUSE WHOSE MOTHER ALWAYS BAKED HOT ROLLS OR BISCUITS OR HOME-MADE BREAD OR SOMETHING...
SHE USED TO PLAY HEARTS WITH THEM, TOO, BECAUSE SHE LOVED THE GAME...THEY PLAYED AROUND THE DINING ROOM TABLE, AND BECAUSE THERE WERE ALWAYS ABOUT TWELVE OF THEM PLAYING, THEY HAD TO USE TWO DECKS OF CARDS...
6-21
THAT MEANT THERE WOULD BE TWO QUEENS OF SPADES..
RIGHT, AND THE WHOLE IDEA OF THE GAME IS TO SLIP SOMEONE THE BLACK QUEEN
WELL, ON THIS ONE PARTICULAR NIGHT, MY DAD SAID HE GAVE THE MOTHER BOTH BLACK QUEENS ON THE SAME HAND..THAT WAS TWENTY-SIX POINTS AGAINST HER...
EVERYBODY LAUGHED SO HARD THEY GOT HYSTERICAL, BUT SHE STILL GAVE THEM HOT ROLLS AND BREAD...AND NOW, WHEN HE THINKS ABOUT IT, MY DAD SAYS IT MAKES HIM FEEL KIND OF SAD...AND THAT WAS TEN YEARS AGO...
YOUR DAD IS VERY SENSITIVE, CHARLIE BROWN.. WISH HIM A HAPPY FATHER'S DAY FOR ME
THANK YOU..I'LL DO THAT...SIGH.. TWENTY-SIX POINTS, AND SHE STILL GAVE THEM HOT ROLLS!
SCHULZ

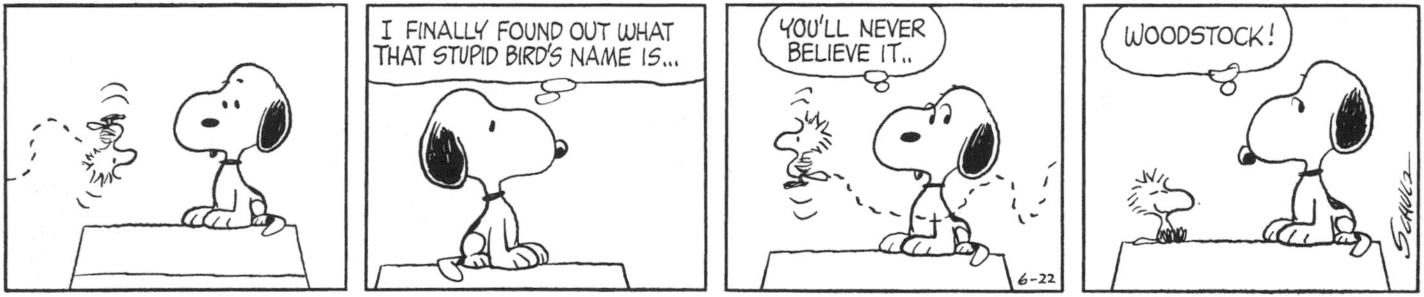
I FINALLY FOUND OUT WHAT THAT STUPID BIRD'S NAME IS...
YOU'LL NEVER BELIEVE IT..
6-22
WOODSTOCK!
SCHULZ

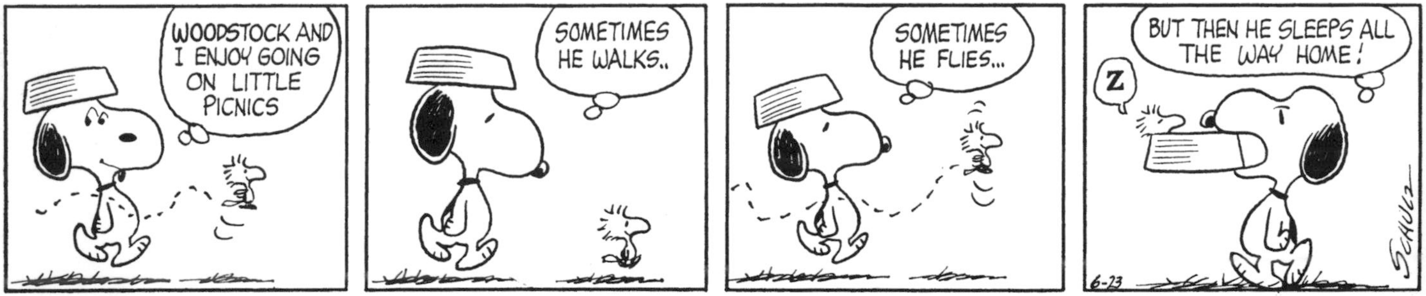
WOODSTOCK AND I ENJOY GOING ON LITTLE PICNICS
SOMETIMES HE WALKS..
SOMETIMES HE FLIES...
BUT THEN HE SLEEPS ALL THE WAY HOME!
Z
6-23
SCHULZ

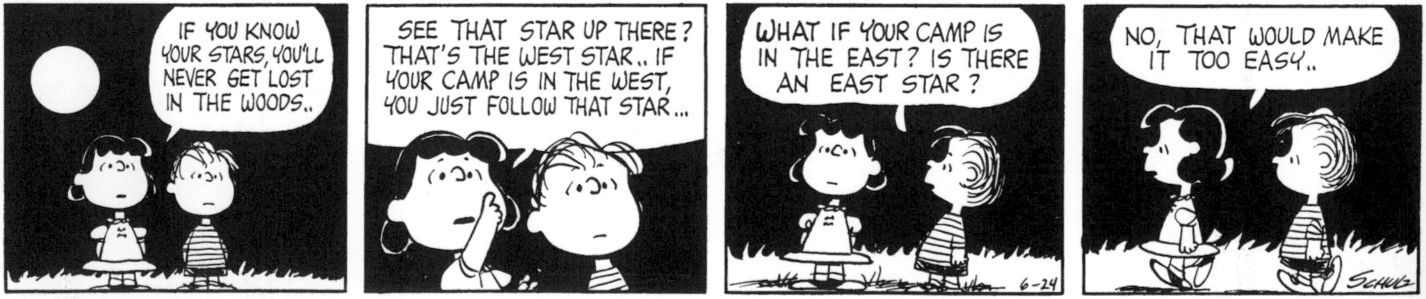
IF YOU KNOW YOUR STARS, YOU'LL NEVER GET LOST IN THE WOODS..
SEE THAT STAR UP THERE? THAT'S THE WEST STAR.. IF YOUR CAMP IS IN THE WEST, YOU JUST FOLLOW THAT STAR...
WHAT IF YOUR CAMP IS IN THE EAST? IS THERE AN EAST STAR?
6-24
NO, THAT WOULD MAKE IT TOO EASY..
SCHULZ

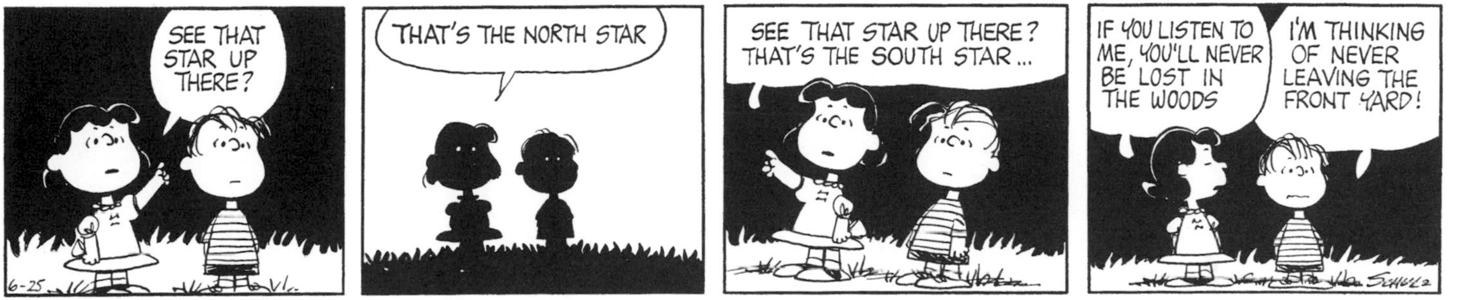
SEE THAT STAR UP THERE?
THAT'S THE NORTH STAR
SEE THAT STAR UP THERE? THAT'S THE SOUTH STAR...
IF YOU LISTEN TO ME, YOU'LL NEVER BE LOST IN THE WOODS
I'M THINKING OF NEVER LEAVING THE FRONT YARD!
6-25
SCHULZ

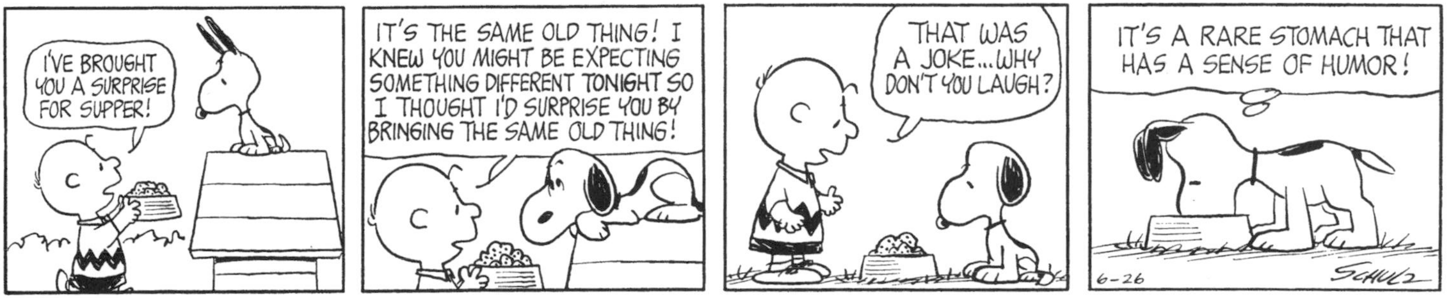
I'VE BROUGHT YOU A SURPRISE FOR SUPPER!
IT'S THE SAME OLD THING! I KNEW YOU MIGHT BE EXPECTING SOMETHING DIFFERENT TONIGHT SO I THOUGHT I'D SURPRISE YOU BY BRINGING THE SAME OLD THING!
THAT WAS A JOKE...WHY DON'T YOU LAUGH?
IT'S A RARE STOMACH THAT HAS A SENSE OF HUMOR!
6-26
SCHULZ

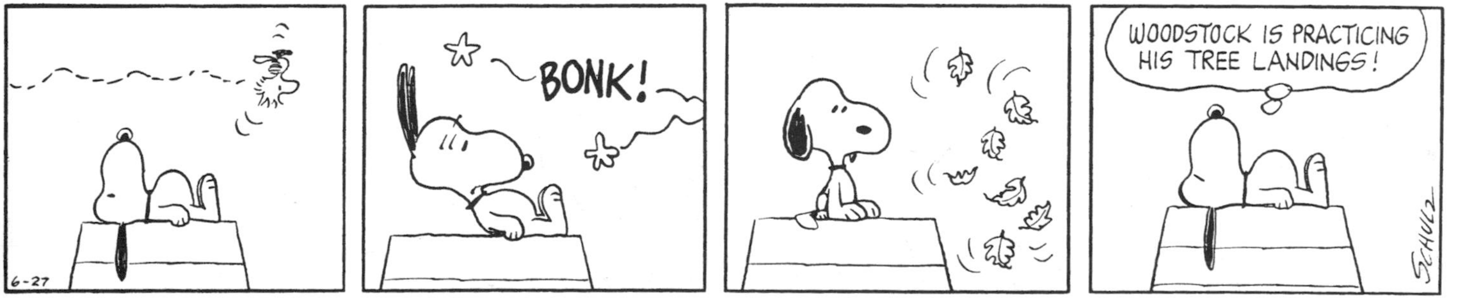
6-27
BONK!
WOODSTOCK IS PRACTICING HIS TREE LANDINGS!
SCHULZ

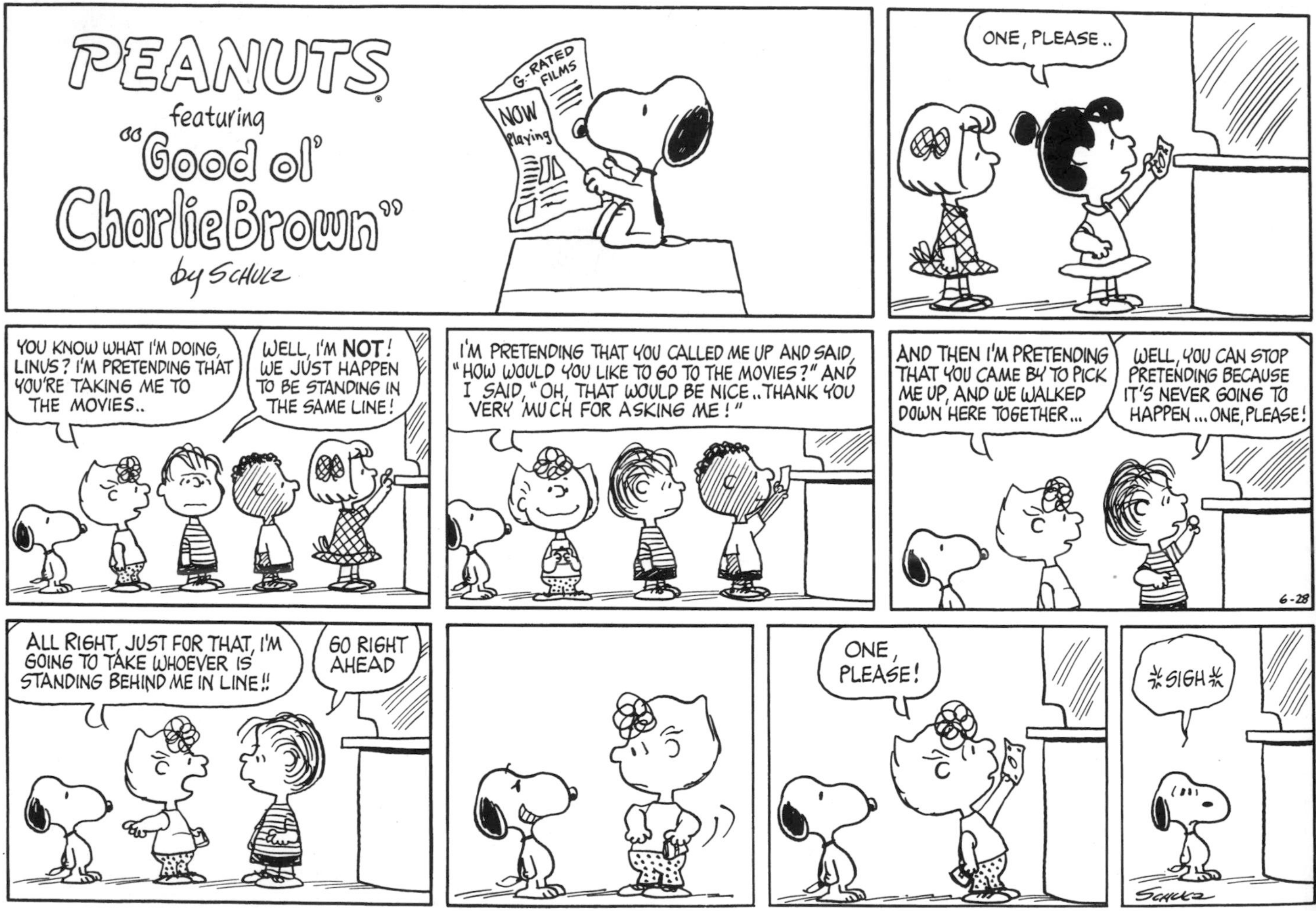
PEANUTS
featuring
"Good ol' Charlie Brown"
by SCHULZ
G-RATED FILMS
NOW Playing
ONE, PLEASE..
YOU KNOW WHAT I'M DOING, LINUS? I'M PRETENDING THAT YOU'RE TAKING ME TO THE MOVIES..
WELL, I'M NOT! WE JUST HAPPEN TO BE STANDING IN THE SAME LINE!
I'M PRETENDING THAT YOU CALLED ME UP AND SAID, "HOW WOULD YOU LIKE TO GO TO THE MOVIES?" AND I SAID, "OH, THAT WOULD BE NICE..THANK YOU VERY MUCH FOR ASKING ME!"
AND THEN I'M PRETENDING THAT YOU CAME BY TO PICK ME UP, AND WE WALKED DOWN HERE TOGETHER...
WELL, YOU CAN STOP PRETENDING BECAUSE IT'S NEVER GOING TO HAPPEN...ONE, PLEASE!
6-28
ALL RIGHT, JUST FOR THAT, I'M GOING TO TAKE WHOEVER IS STANDING BEHIND ME IN LINE!!
GO RIGHT AHEAD
ONE, PLEASE!
SIGH
SCHULZ

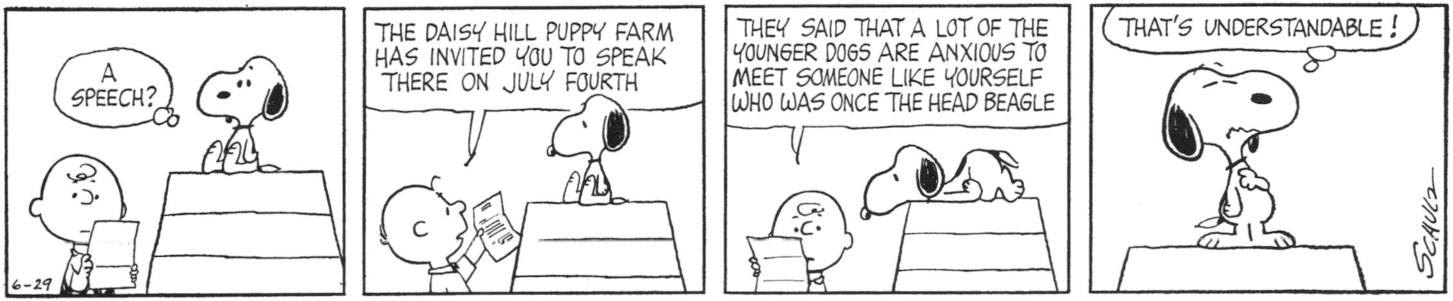
A SPEECH?
THE DAISY HILL PUPPY FARM HAS INVITED YOU TO SPEAK THERE ON JULY FOURTH
THEY SAID THAT A LOT OF THE YOUNGER DOGS ARE ANXIOUS TO MEET SOMEONE LIKE YOURSELF WHO WAS ONCE THE HEAD BEAGLE
THAT'S UNDERSTANDABLE!
6-29
SCHULZ

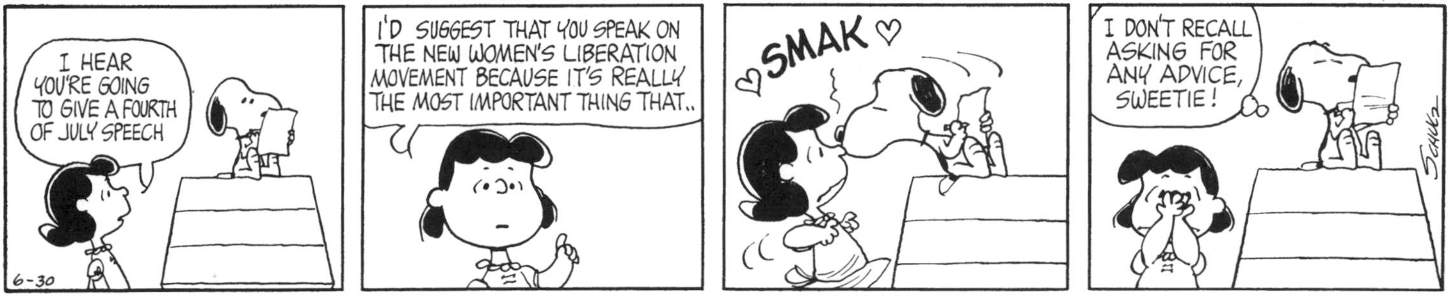
I HEAR YOU'RE GOING TO GIVE A FOURTH OF JULY SPEECH
I'D SUGGEST THAT YOU SPEAK ON THE NEW WOMEN'S LIBERATION MOVEMENT BECAUSE IT'S REALLY THE MOST IMPORTANT THING THAT..
SMAK
I DON'T RECALL ASKING FOR ANY ADVICE, SWEETIE!
6-30
SCHULZ

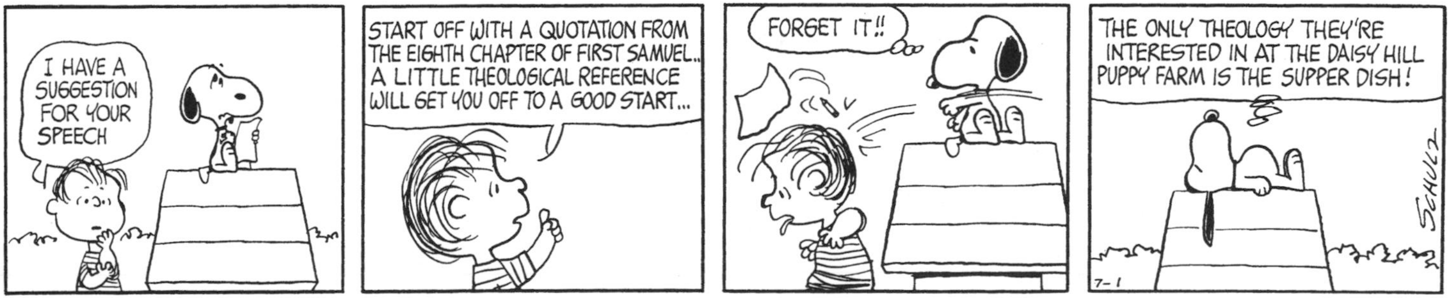
I HAVE A SUGGESTION FOR YOUR SPEECH
START OFF WITH A QUOTATION FROM THE EIGHTH CHAPTER OF FIRST SAMUEL.. A LITTLE THEOLOGICAL REFERENCE WILL GET YOU OFF TO A GOOD START...
FORGET IT!!
THE ONLY THEOLOGY THEY'RE INTERESTED IN AT THE DAISY HILL PUPPY FARM IS THE SUPPER DISH!
7-1
SCHULZ

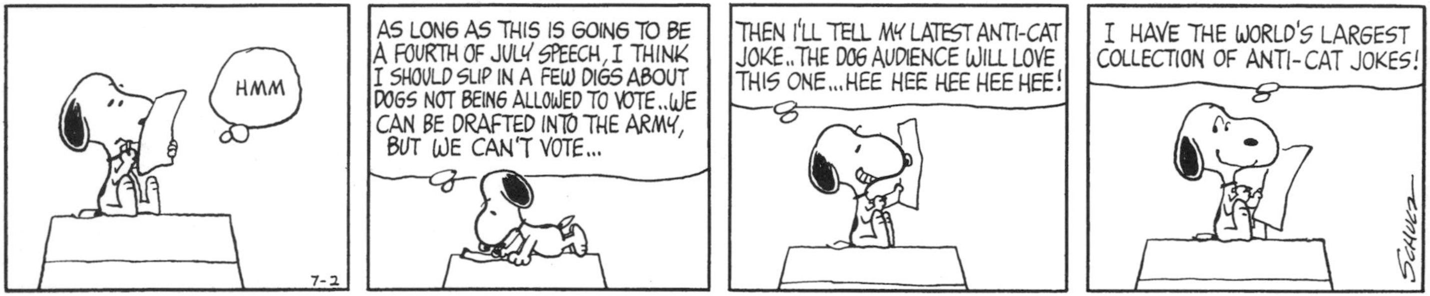
HMM
7-2
AS LONG AS THIS IS GOING TO BE A FOURTH OF JULY SPEECH, I THINK I SHOULD SLIP IN A FEW DIGS ABOUT DOGS NOT BEING ALLOWED TO VOTE..WE CAN BE DRAFTED INTO THE ARMY, BUT WE CAN'T VOTE...
THEN I'LL TELL MY LATEST ANTI-CAT JOKE..THE DOG AUDIENCE WILL LOVE THIS ONE...HEE HEE HEE HEE HEE!
I HAVE THE WORLD'S LARGEST COLLECTION OF ANTI-CAT JOKES!
SCHULZ

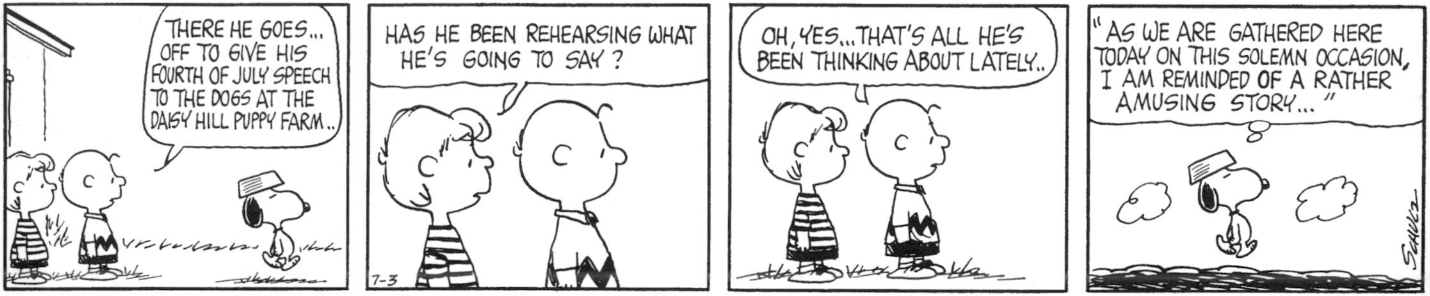
THERE HE GOES... OFF TO GIVE HIS FOURTH OF JULY SPEECH TO THE DOGS AT THE DAISY HILL PUPPY FARM..
HAS HE BEEN REHEARSING WHAT HE'S GOING TO SAY ?
7-3
OH, YES...THAT'S ALL HE'S BEEN THINKING ABOUT LATELY..
"AS WE ARE GATHERED HERE TODAY ON THIS SOLEMN OCCASION, I AM REMINDED OF A RATHER AMUSING STORY..."
SCHULZ

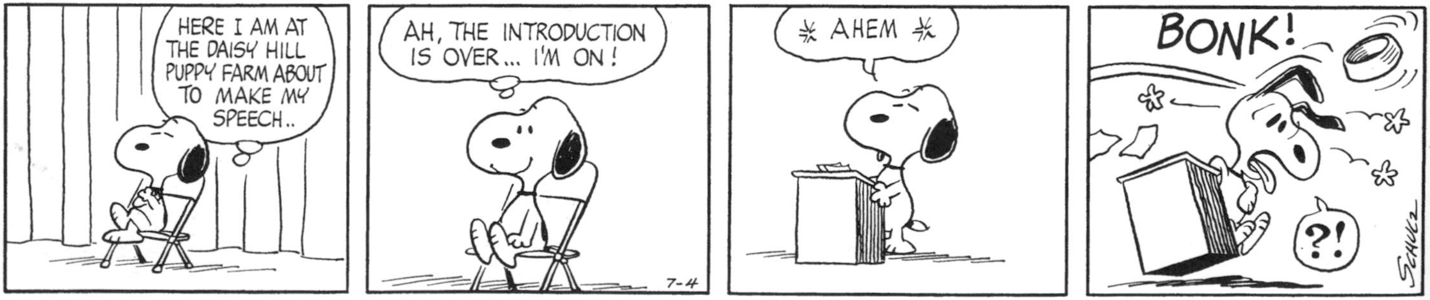
HERE I AM AT THE DAISY HILL PUPPY FARM ABOUT TO MAKE MY SPEECH..
AH, THE INTRODUCTION IS OVER... I'M ON!
7-4
AHEM
BONK!
?!
SCHULZ

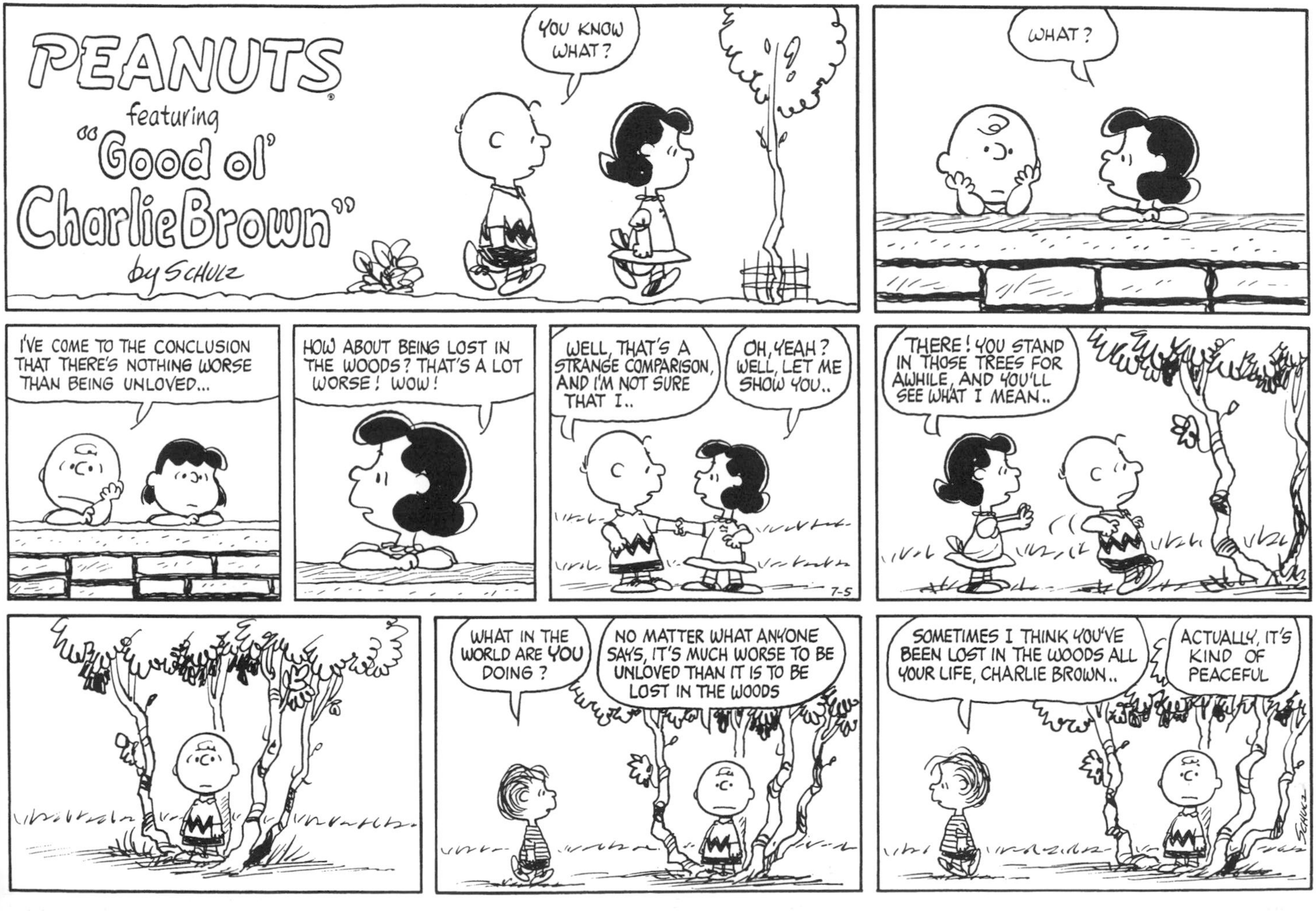
PEANUTS
featuring
"Good ol' Charlie Brown"
by SCHULZ
YOU KNOW WHAT?
WHAT?
I'VE COME TO THE CONCLUSION THAT THERE'S NOTHING WORSE THAN BEING UNLOVED...
HOW ABOUT BEING LOST IN THE WOODS? THAT'S A LOT WORSE! WOW!
WELL, THAT'S A STRANGE COMPARISON, AND I'M NOT SURE THAT I..
OH, YEAH? WELL, LET ME SHOW YOU..
7-5
THERE! YOU STAND IN THOSE TREES FOR AWHILE, AND YOU'LL SEE WHAT I MEAN..
WHAT IN THE WORLD ARE YOU DOING?
NO MATTER WHAT ANYONE SAYS, IT'S MUCH WORSE TO BE UNLOVED THAN IT IS TO BE LOST IN THE WOODS
SOMETIMES I THINK YOU'VE BEEN LOST IN THE WOODS ALL YOUR LIFE, CHARLIE BROWN..
ACTUALLY, IT'S KIND OF PEACEFUL
SCHULZ

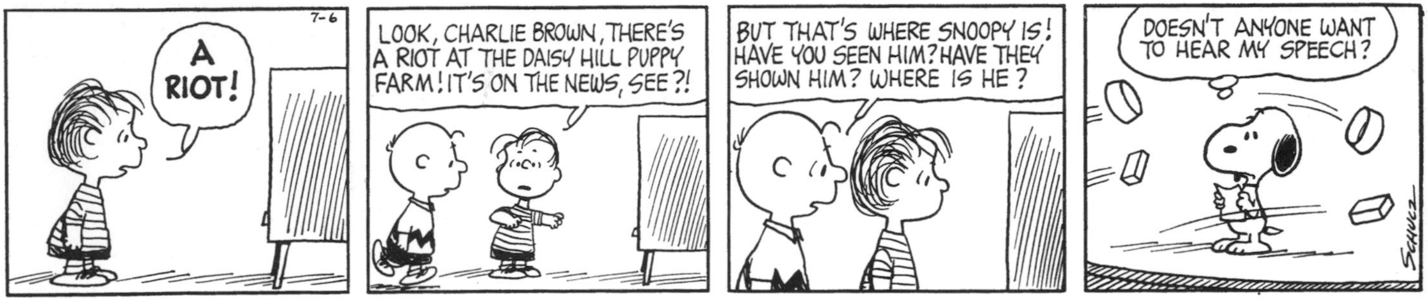
7-6
A RIOT!
LOOK, CHARLIE BROWN, THERE'S A RIOT AT THE DAISY HILL PUPPY FARM! IT'S ON THE NEWS, SEE?!
BUT THAT'S WHERE SNOOPY IS! HAVE YOU SEEN HIM? HAVE THEY SHOWN HIM? WHERE IS HE?
DOESN'T ANYONE WANT TO HEAR MY SPEECH?
SCHULZ

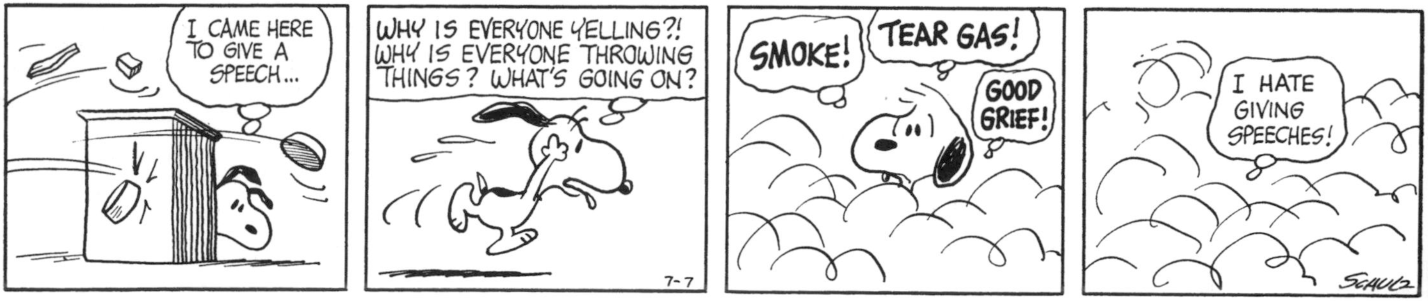
I CAME HERE TO GIVE A SPEECH...
WHY IS EVERYONE YELLING?! WHY IS EVERYONE THROWING THINGS? WHAT'S GOING ON?
7-7
SMOKE!
TEAR GAS!
GOOD GRIEF!
I HATE GIVING SPEECHES!
SCHULZ

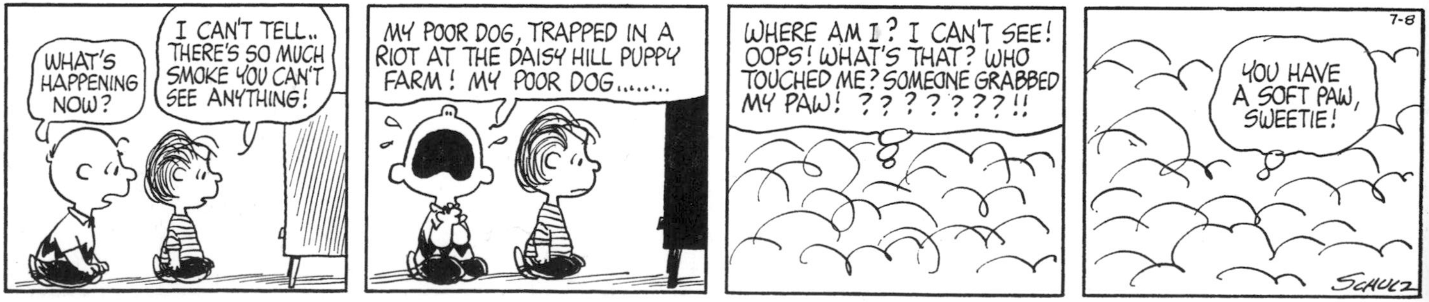
WHAT'S HAPPENING NOW?
I CAN'T TELL.. THERE'S SO MUCH SMOKE YOU CAN'T SEE ANYTHING!
MY POOR DOG, TRAPPED IN A RIOT AT THE DAISY HILL PUPPY FARM! MY POOR DOG.......
WHERE AM I? I CAN'T SEE! OOPS! WHAT'S THAT? WHO TOUCHED ME? SOMEONE GRABBED MY PAW! ???????!!
7-8
YOU HAVE A SOFT PAW, SWEETIE!
SCHULZ

YOU'RE BACK!

WHAT HAPPENED? WE SAW THE RIOT ON TV! DID YOU GET HURT? ARE YOU ALL RIGHT?

WHAT HAPPENED?

7-9

SHE HAD THE SOFTEST PAWS.... ❊ SIGH ❊

ACCORDING TO THE PAPER, THE RIOT WAS ABOUT WAR DOGS...

APPARENTLY THERE'S BEEN SOME TROUBLE ABOUT DOGS BEING SENT TO VIET NAM, AND THEN NOT GETTING BACK...

ALL I KNOW IS, I WENT TO THE DAISY HILL PUPPY FARM TO MAKE A SPEECH... I GOT WHOMPED WITH A DOG DISH, TRAPPED IN A RIOT, LOST IN THE SMOKE.....

7-10

AND THEN I MET "HER"!

GOOD GRIEF!

Dear Sweetie, Have you missed me?

I think about you all the time. I can hardly wait until Sunday morning. Don't forget.

7-11

O O O O O O O O O O O
X X X X X X X X X X X
♡ ♡ ♡ ♡ ♡ ♡ S.W.A.K.

CHEW ALONG DOTTED LINE

I THINK I'M IN LOVE!

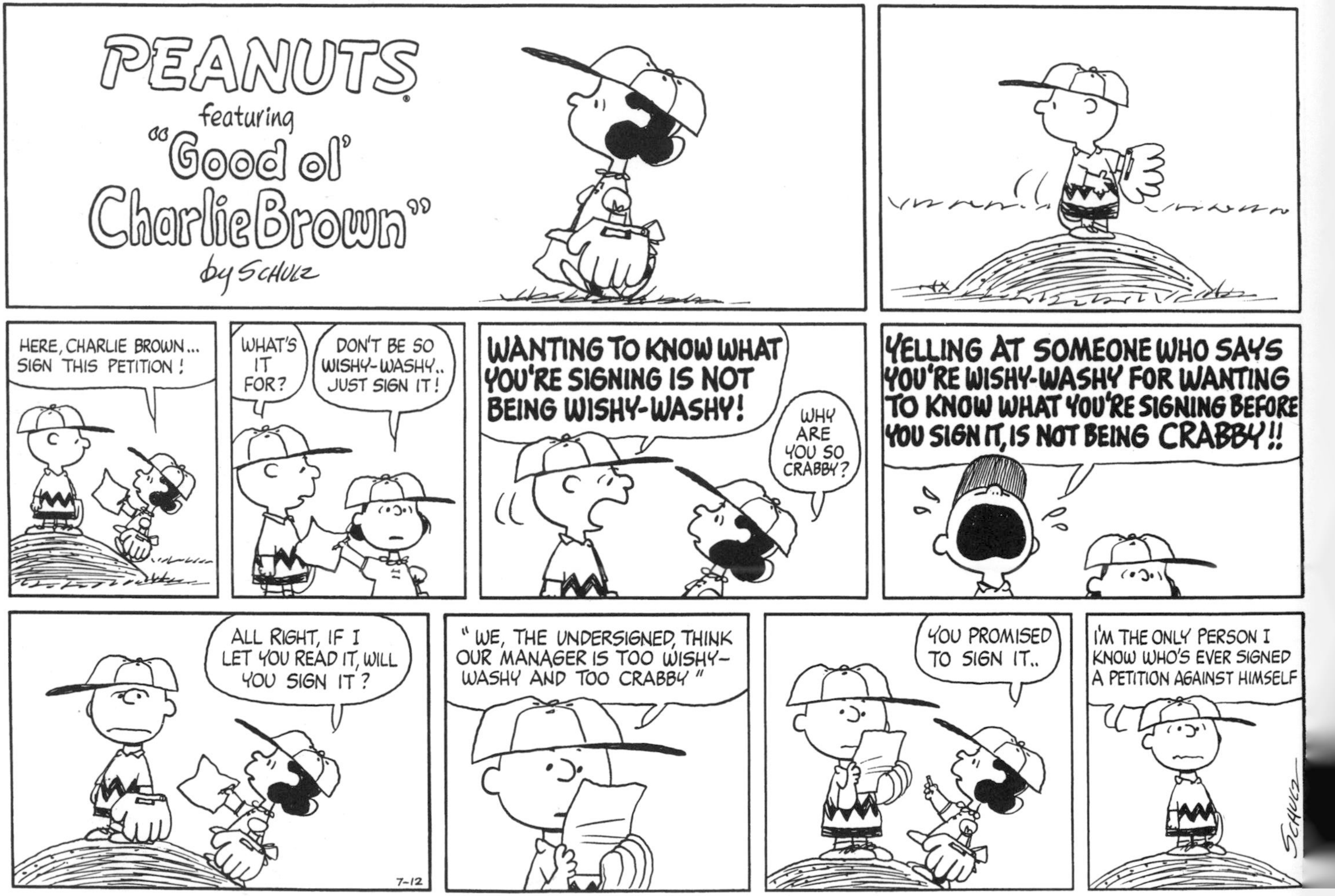
PEANUTS
featuring "Good ol' Charlie Brown"
by SCHULZ
HERE, CHARLIE BROWN... SIGN THIS PETITION!
WHAT'S IT FOR?
DON'T BE SO WISHY-WASHY.. JUST SIGN IT!
WANTING TO KNOW WHAT YOU'RE SIGNING IS NOT BEING WISHY-WASHY!
WHY ARE YOU SO CRABBY?
YELLING AT SOMEONE WHO SAYS YOU'RE WISHY-WASHY FOR WANTING TO KNOW WHAT YOU'RE SIGNING BEFORE YOU SIGN IT, IS NOT BEING CRABBY!!
ALL RIGHT, IF I LET YOU READ IT, WILL YOU SIGN IT?
7-12
"WE, THE UNDERSIGNED, THINK OUR MANAGER IS TOO WISHY-WASHY AND TOO CRABBY"
YOU PROMISED TO SIGN IT..
I'M THE ONLY PERSON I KNOW WHO'S EVER SIGNED A PETITION AGAINST HIMSELF
SCHULZ

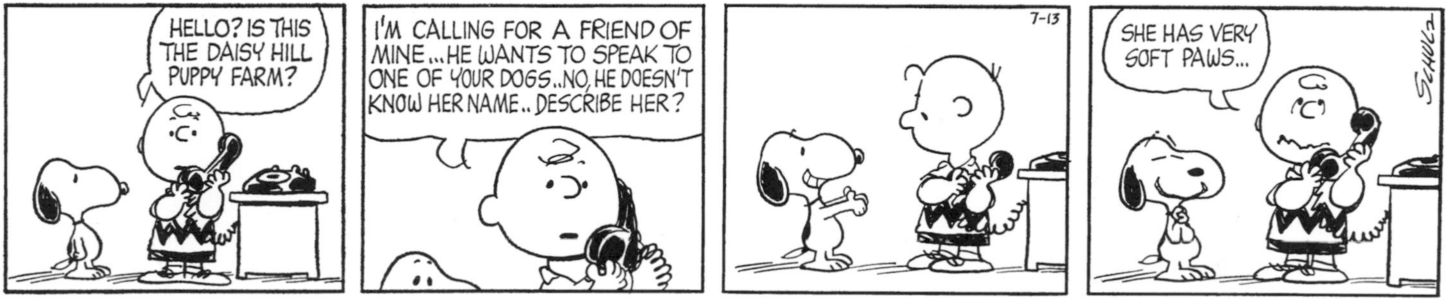
HELLO? IS THIS THE DAISY HILL PUPPY FARM?
I'M CALLING FOR A FRIEND OF MINE...HE WANTS TO SPEAK TO ONE OF YOUR DOGS..NO, HE DOESN'T KNOW HER NAME.. DESCRIBE HER?
SHE HAS VERY SOFT PAWS...

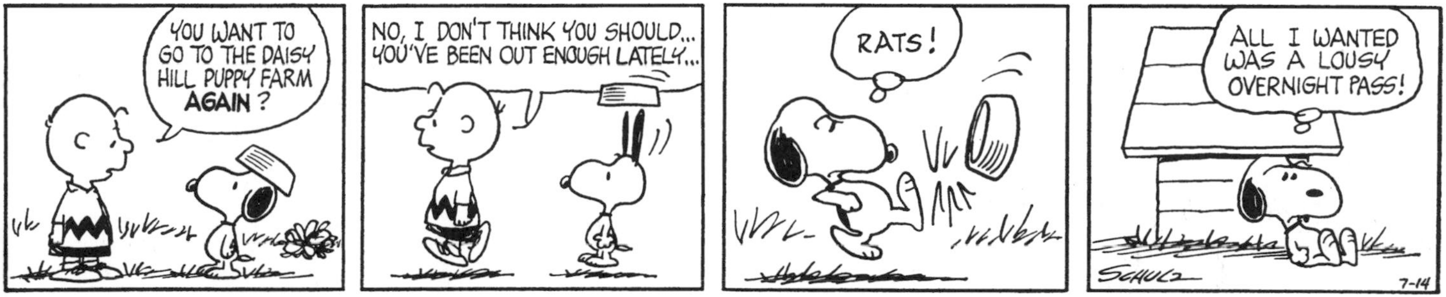
YOU WANT TO GO TO THE DAISY HILL PUPPY FARM **AGAIN** ?
NO, I DON'T THINK YOU SHOULD... YOU'VE BEEN OUT ENOUGH **LATELY**...
RATS!
ALL I WANTED WAS A LOUSY OVERNIGHT PASS!

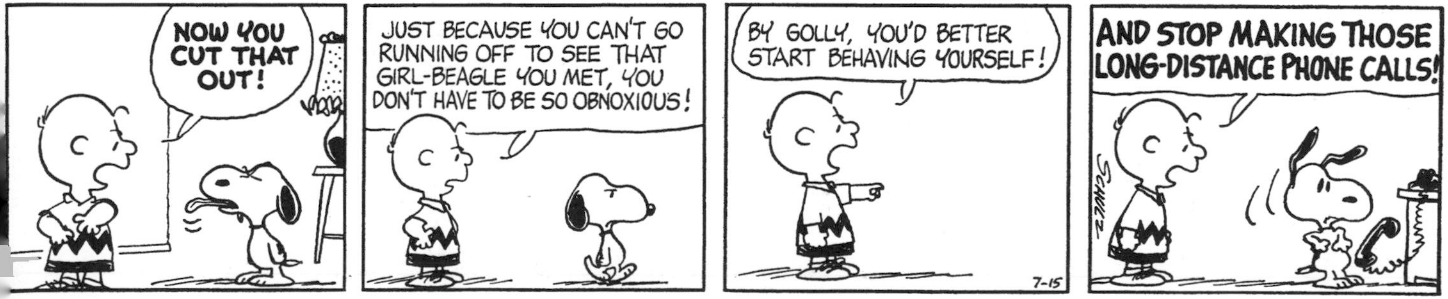
NOW YOU CUT THAT OUT!
JUST BECAUSE YOU CAN'T GO RUNNING OFF TO SEE THAT GIRL-BEAGLE YOU MET, YOU DON'T HAVE TO BE SO OBNOXIOUS!
BY GOLLY, YOU'D BETTER START BEHAVING YOURSELF!
AND STOP MAKING THOSE LONG-DISTANCE PHONE CALLS!

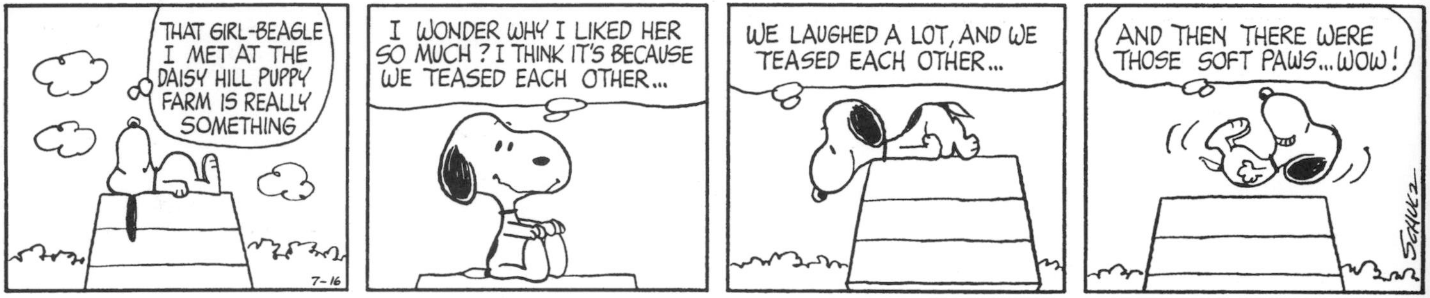
THAT GIRL-BEAGLE I MET AT THE DAISY HILL PUPPY FARM IS REALLY SOMETHING
7-16
I WONDER WHY I LIKED HER SO MUCH ? I THINK IT'S BECAUSE WE TEASED EACH OTHER...
WE LAUGHED A LOT, AND WE TEASED EACH OTHER...
AND THEN THERE WERE THOSE SOFT PAWS...WOW!
SCHULZ

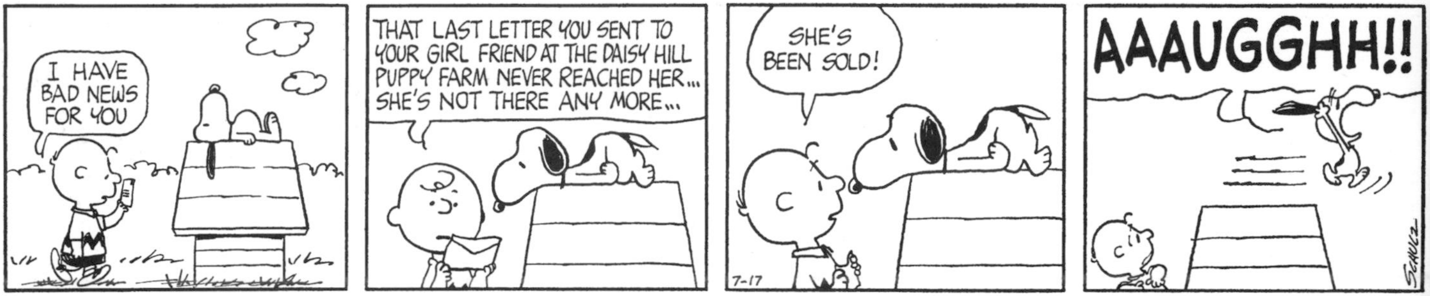
I HAVE BAD NEWS FOR YOU
THAT LAST LETTER YOU SENT TO YOUR GIRL FRIEND AT THE DAISY HILL PUPPY FARM NEVER REACHED HER... SHE'S NOT THERE ANY MORE...
SHE'S BEEN SOLD!
7-17
AAAUGGHH!!
SCHULZ

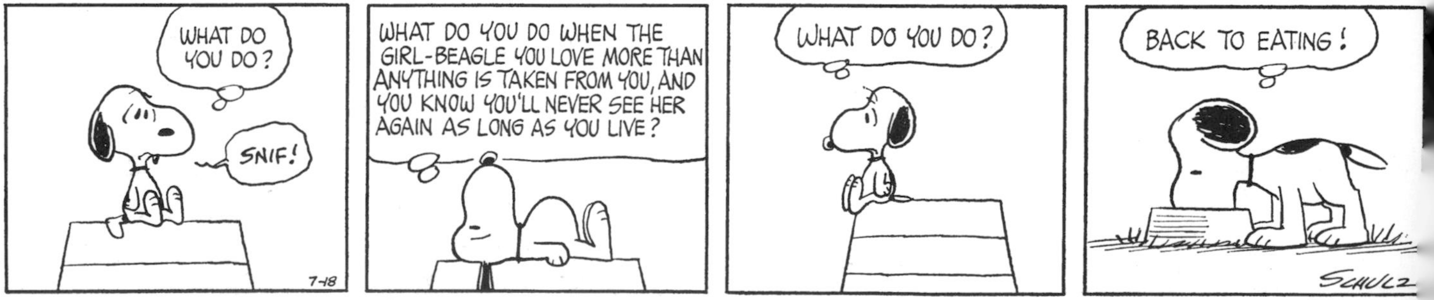
WHAT DO YOU DO?
SNIF!
7-18
WHAT DO YOU DO WHEN THE GIRL-BEAGLE YOU LOVE MORE THAN ANYTHING IS TAKEN FROM YOU, AND YOU KNOW YOU'LL NEVER SEE HER AGAIN AS LONG AS YOU LIVE?
WHAT DO YOU DO?
BACK TO EATING!
SCHULZ

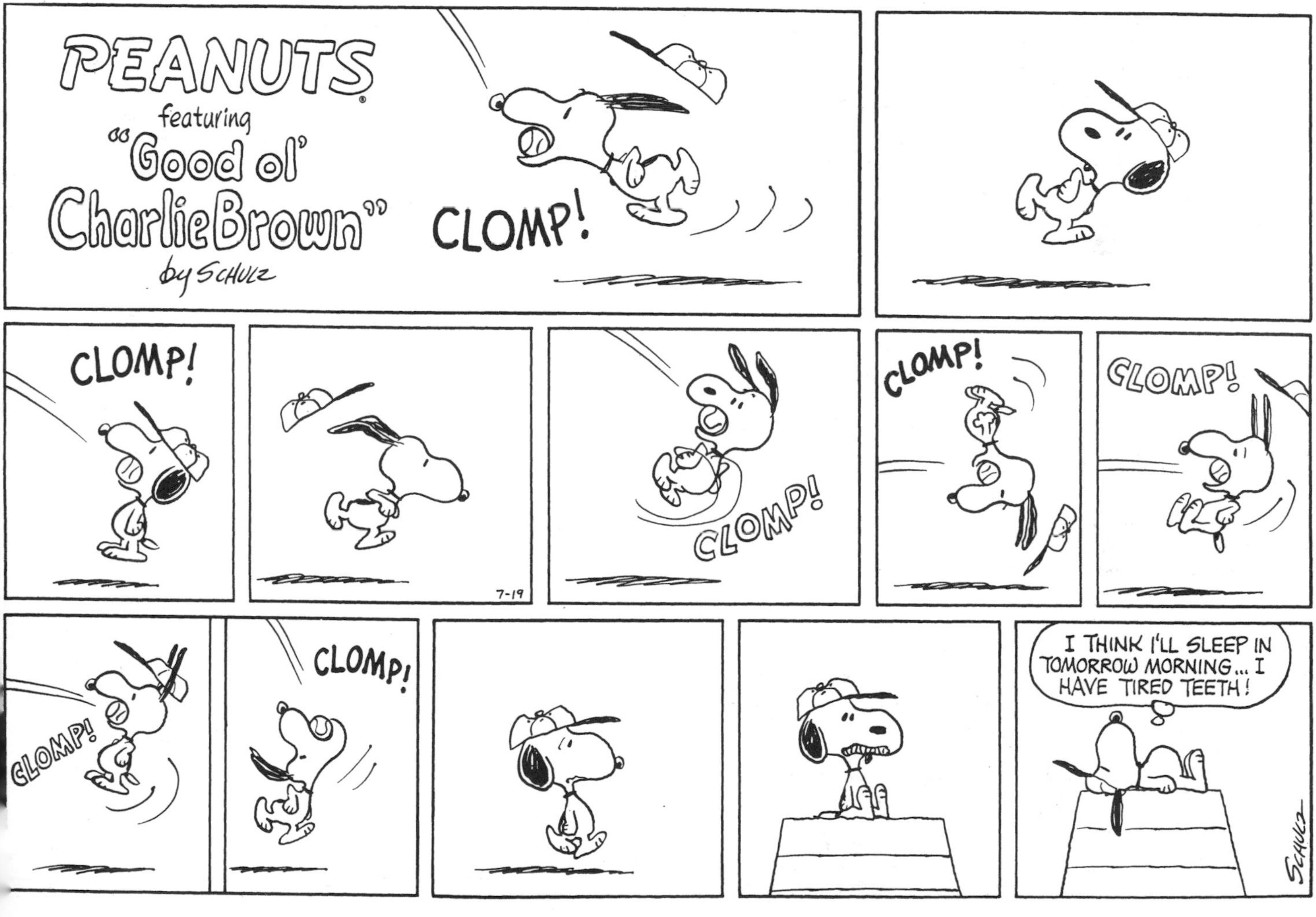
PEANUTS
featuring
"Good ol' Charlie Brown"
by SCHULZ
CLOMP!
CLOMP!
7-19
CLOMP!
CLOMP!
CLOMP!
CLOMP!
CLOMP!
I THINK I'LL SLEEP IN TOMORROW MORNING... I HAVE TIRED TEETH!
SCHULZ

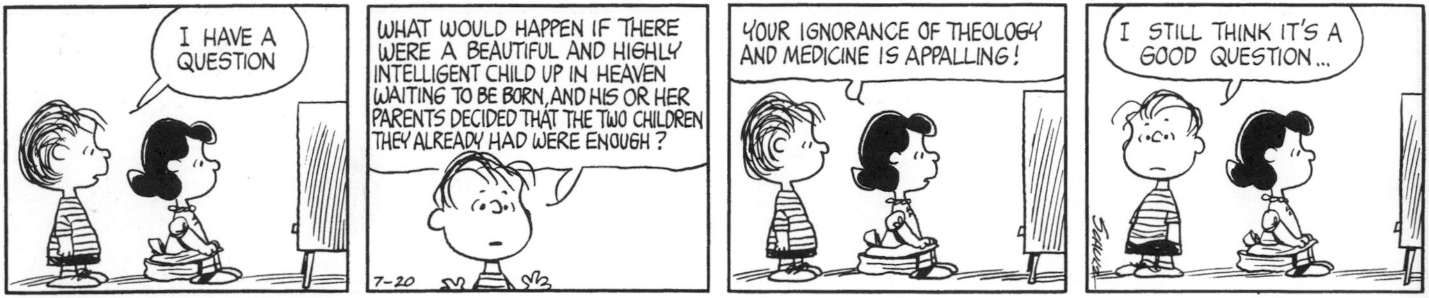
I HAVE A QUESTION
WHAT WOULD HAPPEN IF THERE WERE A BEAUTIFUL AND HIGHLY INTELLIGENT CHILD UP IN HEAVEN WAITING TO BE BORN, AND HIS OR HER PARENTS DECIDED THAT THE TWO CHILDREN THEY ALREADY HAD WERE ENOUGH?
7-20
YOUR IGNORANCE OF THEOLOGY AND MEDICINE IS APPALLING!
I STILL THINK IT'S A GOOD QUESTION...
SCHULZ

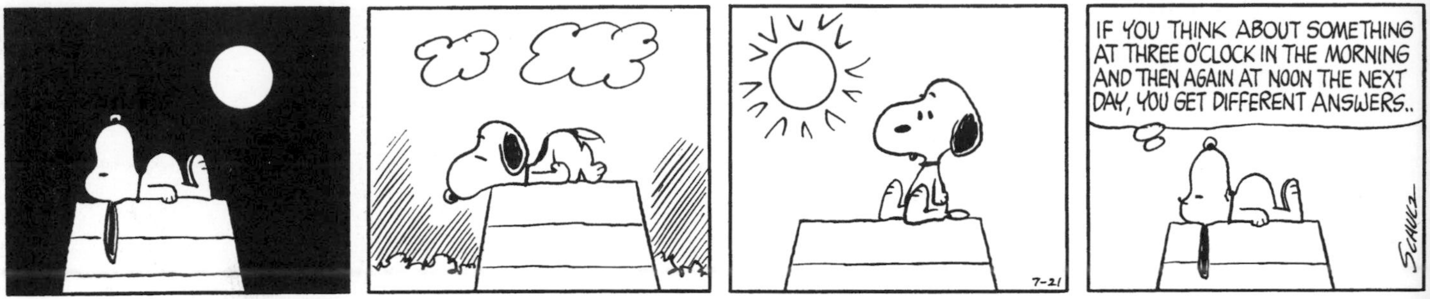
7-21
IF YOU THINK ABOUT SOMETHING AT THREE O'CLOCK IN THE MORNING AND THEN AGAIN AT NOON THE NEXT DAY, YOU GET DIFFERENT ANSWERS..
SCHULZ

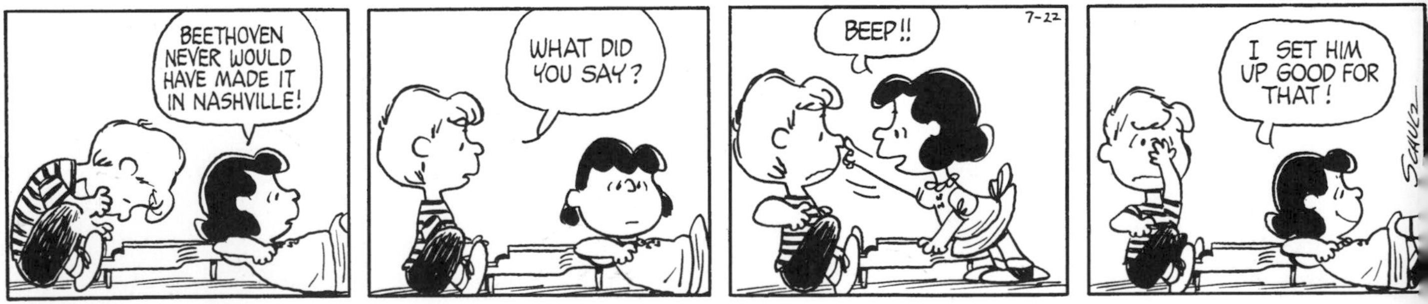
BEETHOVEN NEVER WOULD HAVE MADE IT IN NASHVILLE!
WHAT DID YOU SAY?
BEEP!!
7-22
I SET HIM UP GOOD FOR THAT!
SCHULZ

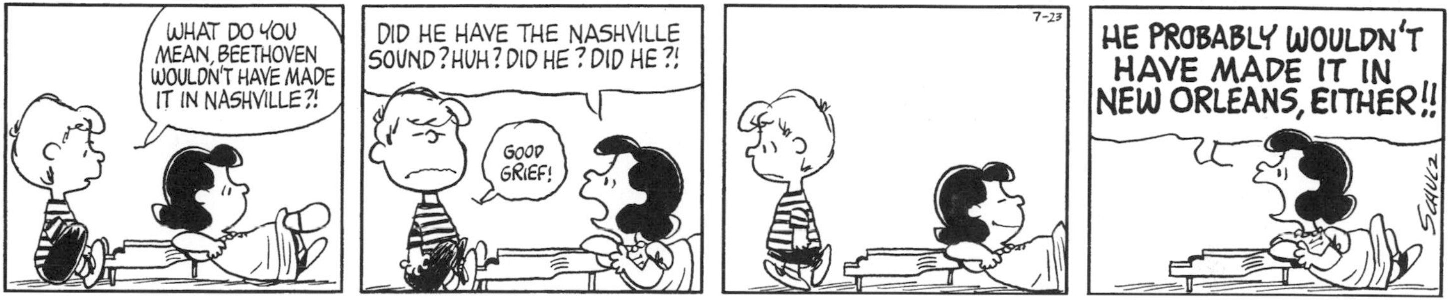
WHAT DO YOU MEAN, BEETHOVEN WOULDN'T HAVE MADE IT IN NASHVILLE?!
DID HE HAVE THE NASHVILLE SOUND? HUH? DID HE? DID HE?!
GOOD GRIEF!
7-23
HE PROBABLY WOULDN'T HAVE MADE IT IN NEW ORLEANS, EITHER!!
SCHULZ

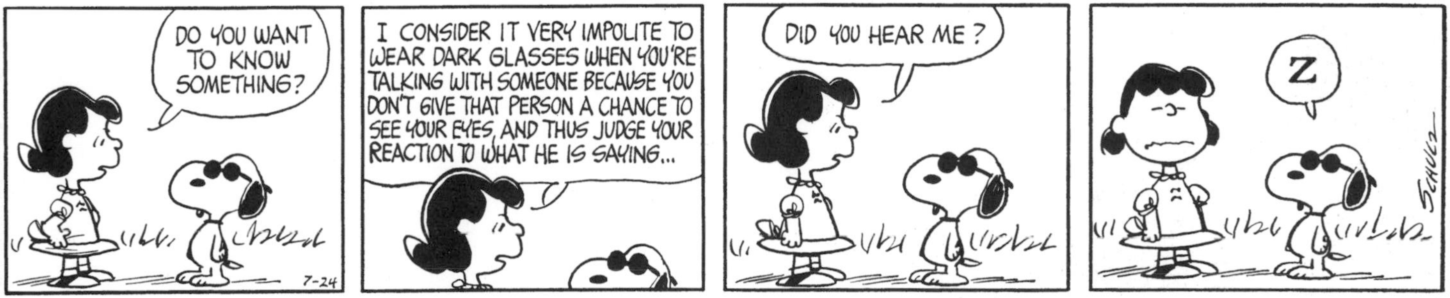
DO YOU WANT TO KNOW SOMETHING?
7-24
I CONSIDER IT VERY IMPOLITE TO WEAR DARK GLASSES WHEN YOU'RE TALKING WITH SOMEONE BECAUSE YOU DON'T GIVE THAT PERSON A CHANCE TO SEE YOUR EYES, AND THUS JUDGE YOUR REACTION TO WHAT HE IS SAYING...
DID YOU HEAR ME?
Z
SCHULZ

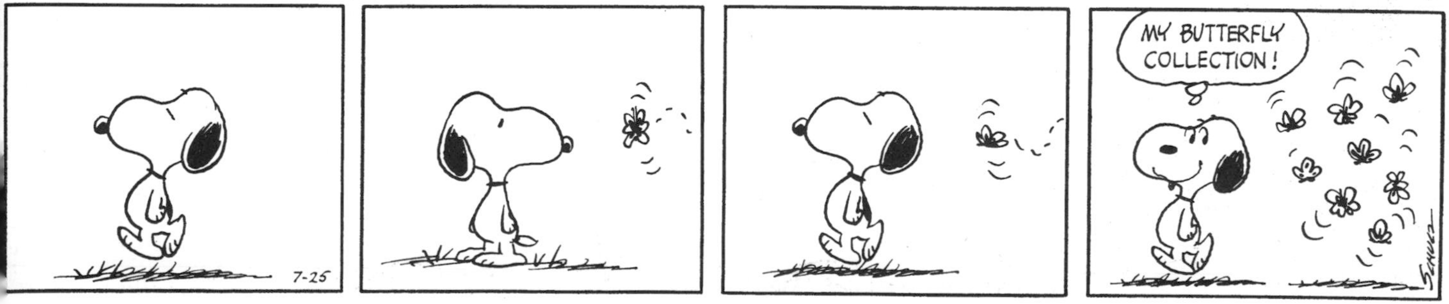
7-25
MY BUTTERFLY COLLECTION!
SCHULZ

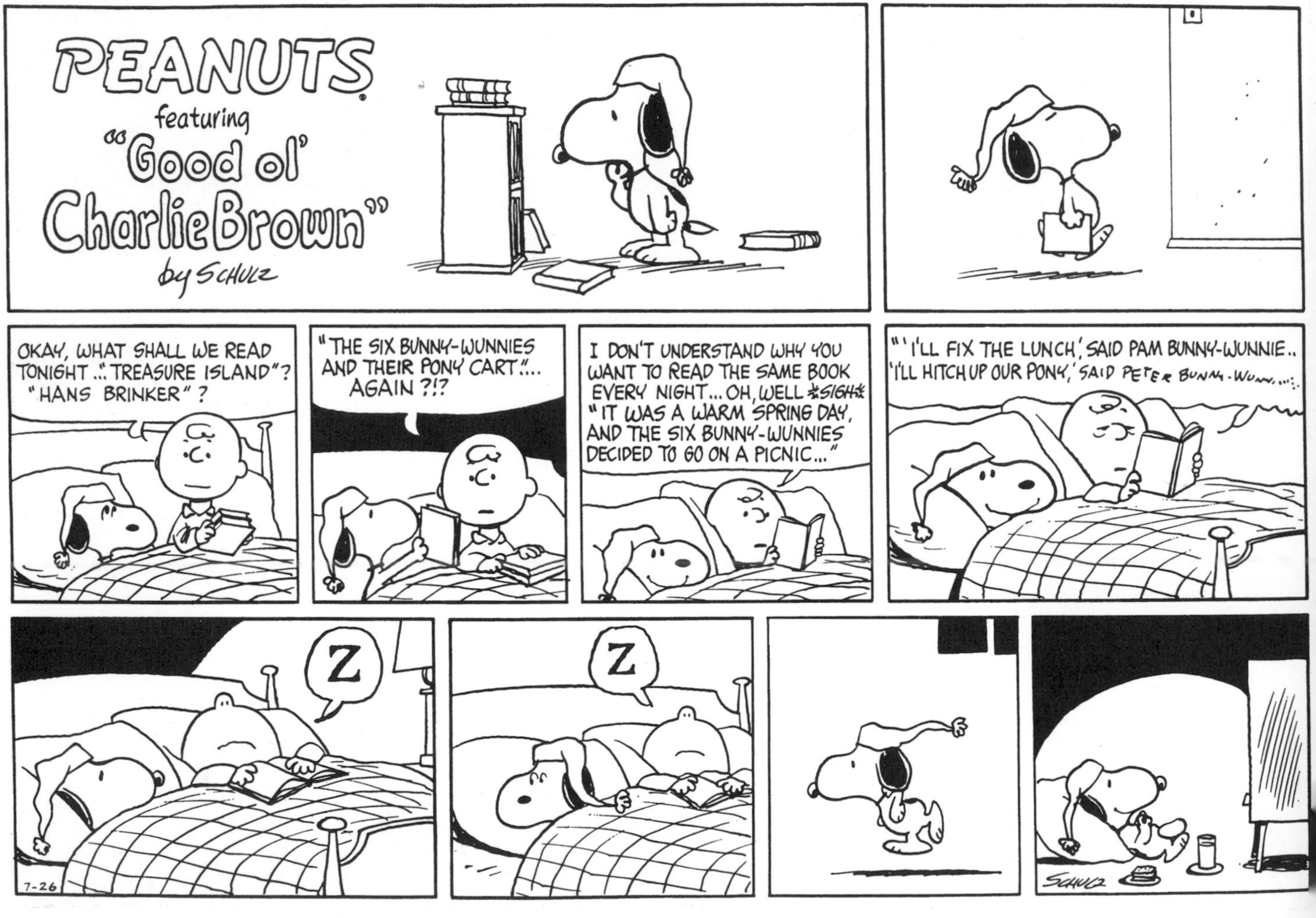
PEANUTS
featuring
"Good ol' Charlie Brown"
by SCHULZ
OKAY, WHAT SHALL WE READ TONIGHT ..."TREASURE ISLAND"? "HANS BRINKER"?
"THE SIX BUNNY-WUNNIES AND THEIR PONY CART"... AGAIN ?!?
I DON'T UNDERSTAND WHY YOU WANT TO READ THE SAME BOOK EVERY NIGHT... OH, WELL *SIGH* "IT WAS A WARM SPRING DAY, AND THE SIX BUNNY-WUNNIES DECIDED TO GO ON A PICNIC..."
"'I'LL FIX THE LUNCH,' SAID PAM BUNNY-WUNNIE.. 'I'LL HITCH UP OUR PONY,' SAID PETER BUNNY-WUNNY...
Z
Z
7-26
SCHULZ

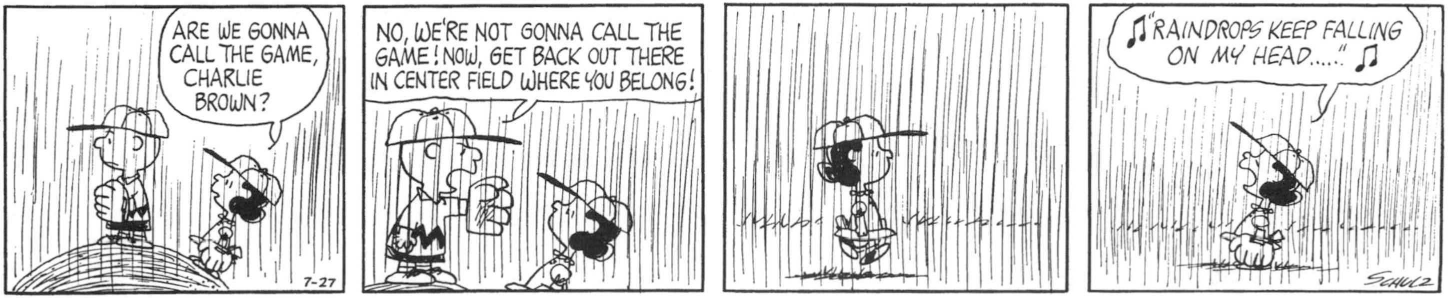

ARE WE GONNA CALL THE GAME, CHARLIE BROWN?
7-27
NO, WE'RE NOT GONNA CALL THE GAME! NOW, GET BACK OUT THERE IN CENTER FIELD WHERE YOU BELONG!
♫ "RAINDROPS KEEP FALLING ON MY HEAD....." ♫
SCHULZ

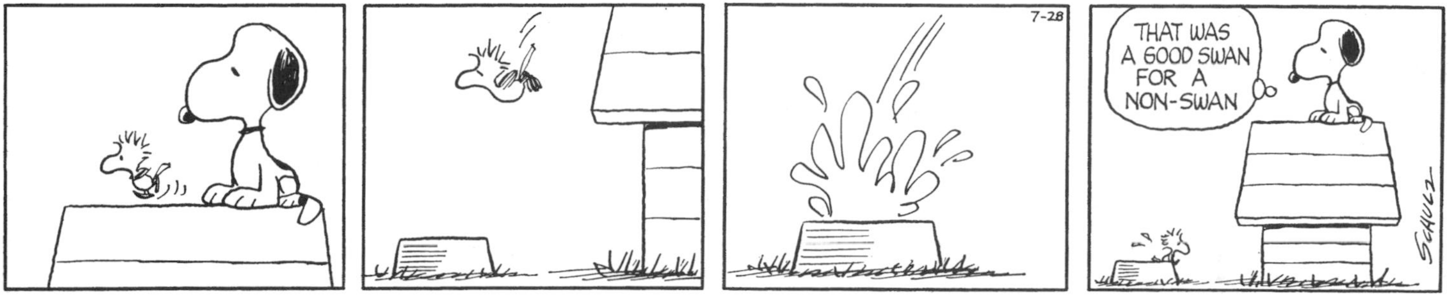

7-28
THAT WAS A GOOD SWAN FOR A NON-SWAN
SCHULZ

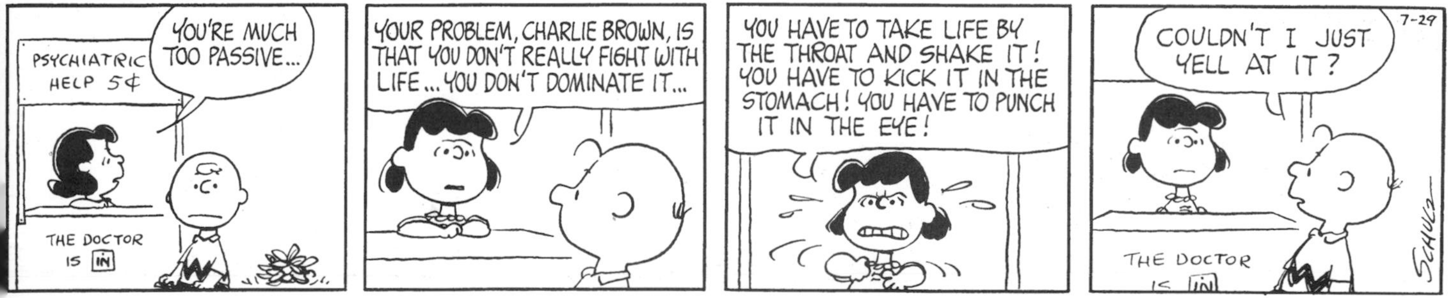

PSYCHIATRIC HELP 5¢
YOU'RE MUCH TOO PASSIVE...
THE DOCTOR IS IN
YOUR PROBLEM, CHARLIE BROWN, IS THAT YOU DON'T REALLY FIGHT WITH LIFE... YOU DON'T DOMINATE IT...
YOU HAVE TO TAKE LIFE BY THE THROAT AND SHAKE IT! YOU HAVE TO KICK IT IN THE STOMACH! YOU HAVE TO PUNCH IT IN THE EYE!
7-29
COULDN'T I JUST YELL AT IT?
THE DOCTOR
SCHULZ

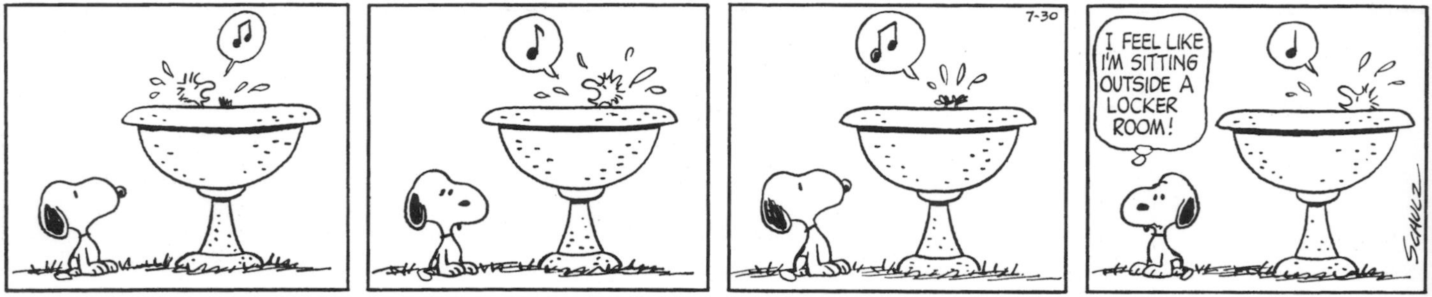
I FEEL LIKE I'M SITTING OUTSIDE A LOCKER ROOM!

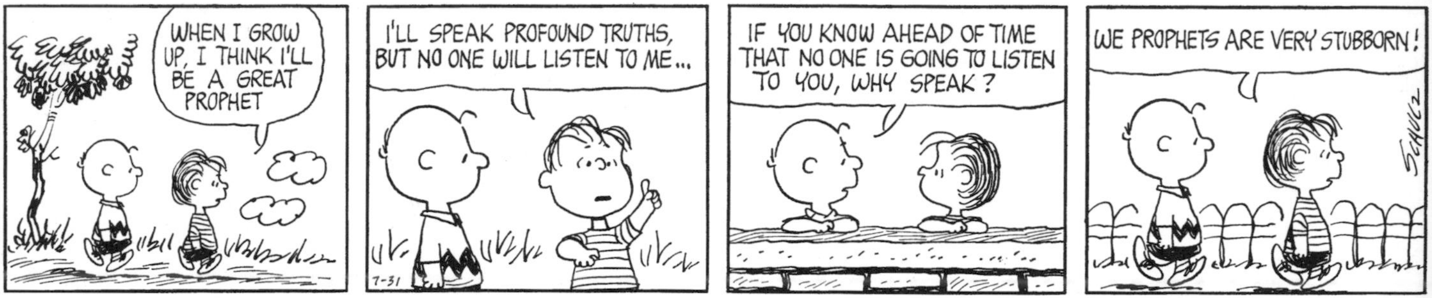
WHEN I GROW UP, I THINK I'LL BE A GREAT PROPHET
I'LL SPEAK PROFOUND TRUTHS, BUT NO ONE WILL LISTEN TO ME...
IF YOU KNOW AHEAD OF TIME THAT NO ONE IS GOING TO LISTEN TO YOU, WHY SPEAK?
WE PROPHETS ARE VERY STUBBORN!

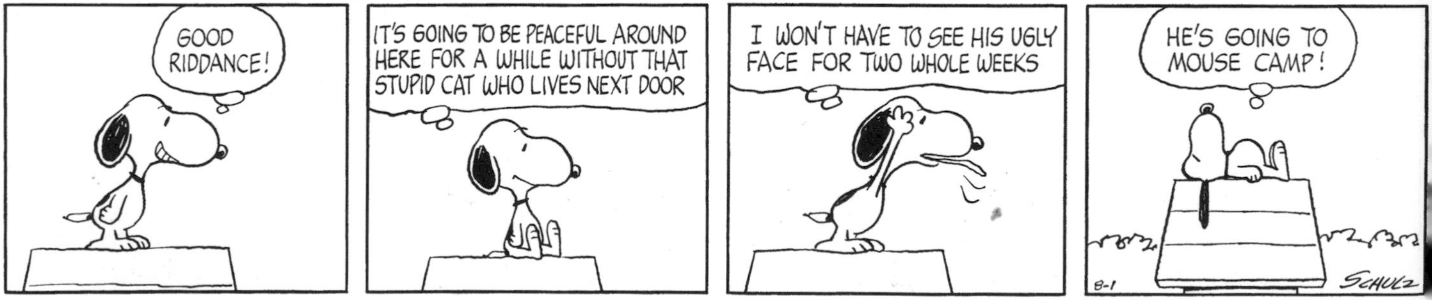
GOOD RIDDANCE!
IT'S GOING TO BE PEACEFUL AROUND HERE FOR A WHILE WITHOUT THAT STUPID CAT WHO LIVES NEXT DOOR
I WON'T HAVE TO SEE HIS UGLY FACE FOR TWO WHOLE WEEKS
HE'S GOING TO MOUSE CAMP!

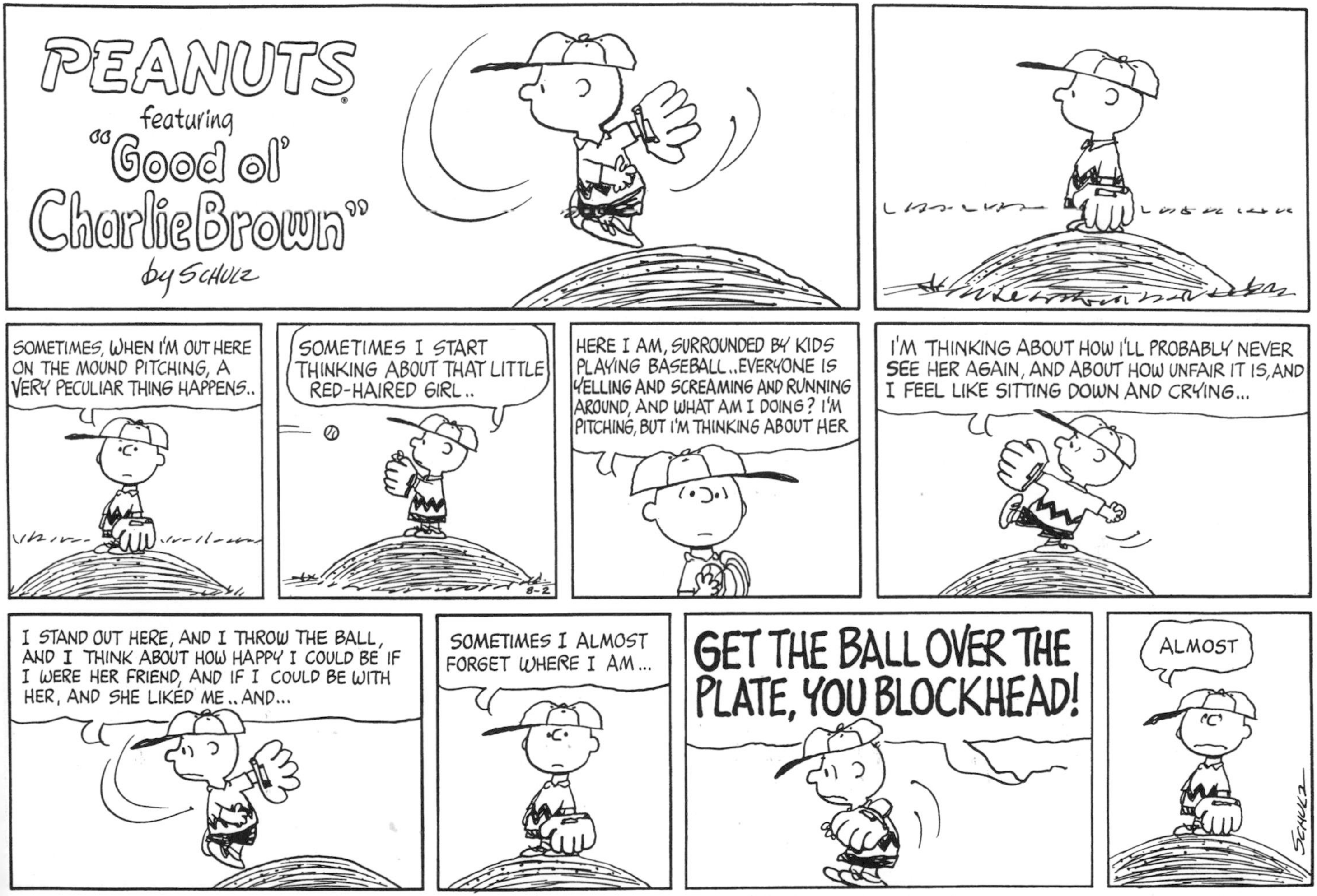
PEANUTS
featuring "Good ol' Charlie Brown"
by SCHULZ
SOMETIMES, WHEN I'M OUT HERE ON THE MOUND PITCHING, A VERY PECULIAR THING HAPPENS..
SOMETIMES I START THINKING ABOUT THAT LITTLE RED-HAIRED GIRL..
HERE I AM, SURROUNDED BY KIDS PLAYING BASEBALL..EVERYONE IS YELLING AND SCREAMING AND RUNNING AROUND, AND WHAT AM I DOING? I'M PITCHING, BUT I'M THINKING ABOUT HER
I'M THINKING ABOUT HOW I'LL PROBABLY NEVER SEE HER AGAIN, AND ABOUT HOW UNFAIR IT IS, AND I FEEL LIKE SITTING DOWN AND CRYING...
I STAND OUT HERE, AND I THROW THE BALL, AND I THINK ABOUT HOW HAPPY I COULD BE IF I WERE HER FRIEND, AND IF I COULD BE WITH HER, AND SHE LIKED ME..AND...
SOMETIMES I ALMOST FORGET WHERE I AM...
GET THE BALL OVER THE PLATE, YOU BLOCKHEAD!
ALMOST
SCHULZ

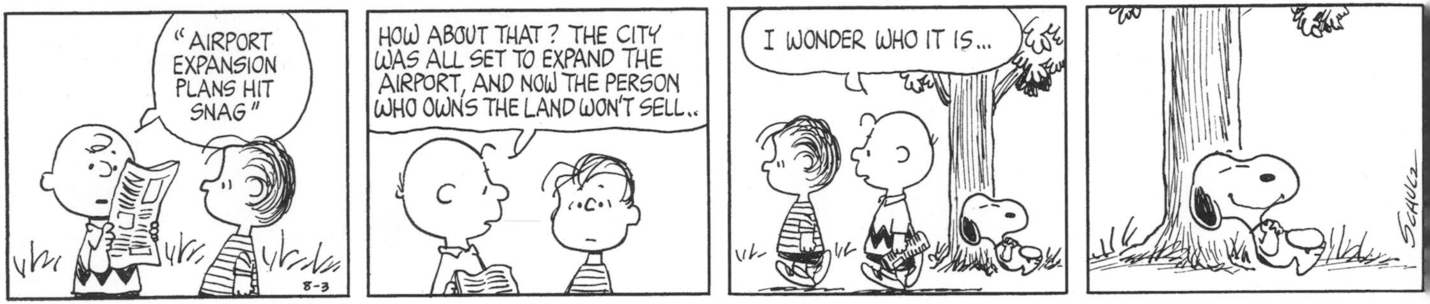
"AIRPORT EXPANSION PLANS HIT SNAG"
HOW ABOUT THAT? THE CITY WAS ALL SET TO EXPAND THE AIRPORT, AND NOW THE PERSON WHO OWNS THE LAND WON'T SELL..
I WONDER WHO IT IS...
8-3
SCHULZ

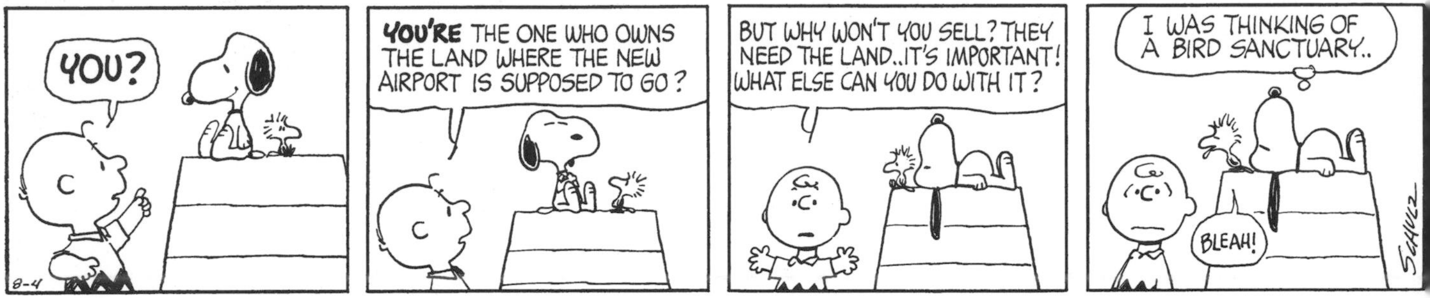
YOU?
8-4
YOU'RE THE ONE WHO OWNS THE LAND WHERE THE NEW AIRPORT IS SUPPOSED TO GO?
BUT WHY WON'T YOU SELL? THEY NEED THE LAND..IT'S IMPORTANT! WHAT ELSE CAN YOU DO WITH IT?
I WAS THINKING OF A BIRD SANCTUARY..
BLEAH!
SCHULZ

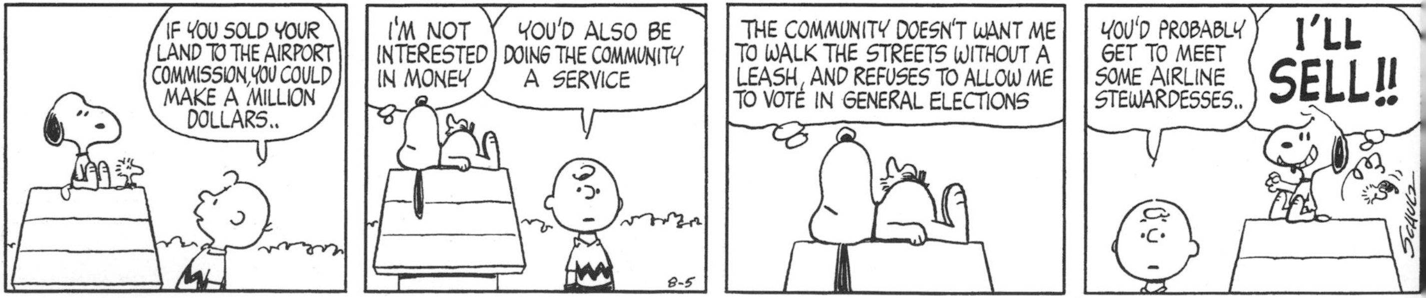
IF YOU SOLD YOUR LAND TO THE AIRPORT COMMISSION, YOU COULD MAKE A MILLION DOLLARS..
I'M NOT INTERESTED IN MONEY
YOU'D ALSO BE DOING THE COMMUNITY A SERVICE
8-5
THE COMMUNITY DOESN'T WANT ME TO WALK THE STREETS WITHOUT A LEASH, AND REFUSES TO ALLOW ME TO VOTE IN GENERAL ELECTIONS
YOU'D PROBABLY GET TO MEET SOME AIRLINE STEWARDESSES..
I'LL SELL!!
SCHULZ

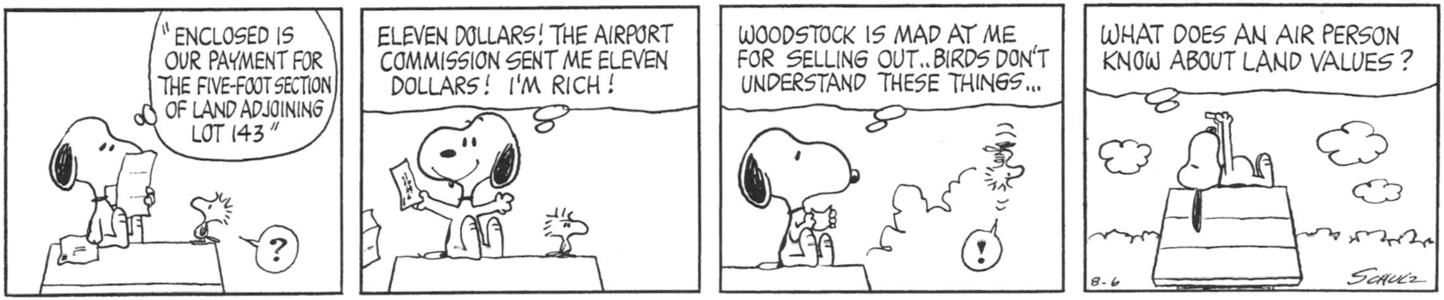
"ENCLOSED IS OUR PAYMENT FOR THE FIVE-FOOT SECTION OF LAND ADJOINING LOT 143"
?
ELEVEN DOLLARS! THE AIRPORT COMMISSION SENT ME ELEVEN DOLLARS! I'M RICH!
WOODSTOCK IS MAD AT ME FOR SELLING OUT..BIRDS DON'T UNDERSTAND THESE THINGS...
!
WHAT DOES AN AIR PERSON KNOW ABOUT LAND VALUES?
8-6
SCHULZ

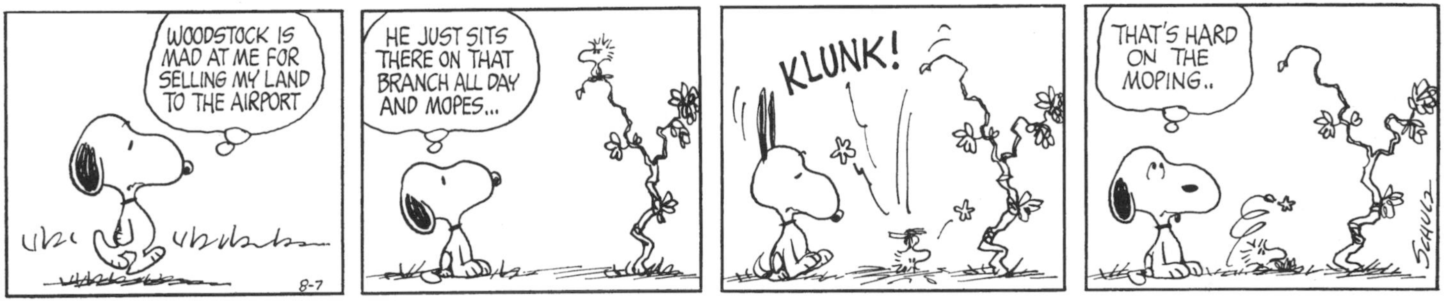
WOODSTOCK IS MAD AT ME FOR SELLING MY LAND TO THE AIRPORT
8-7
HE JUST SITS THERE ON THAT BRANCH ALL DAY AND MOPES...
KLUNK!
THAT'S HARD ON THE MOPING..
SCHULZ

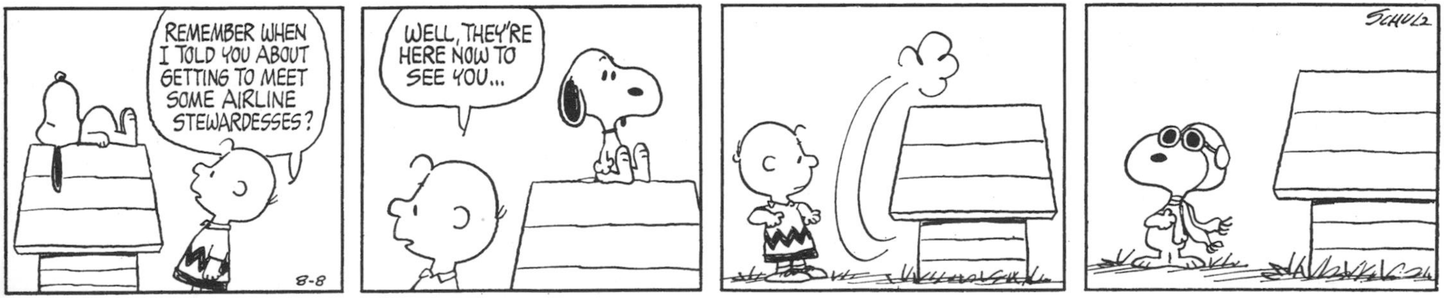
REMEMBER WHEN I TOLD YOU ABOUT GETTING TO MEET SOME AIRLINE STEWARDESSES?
8-8
WELL, THEY'RE HERE NOW TO SEE YOU...
SCHULZ

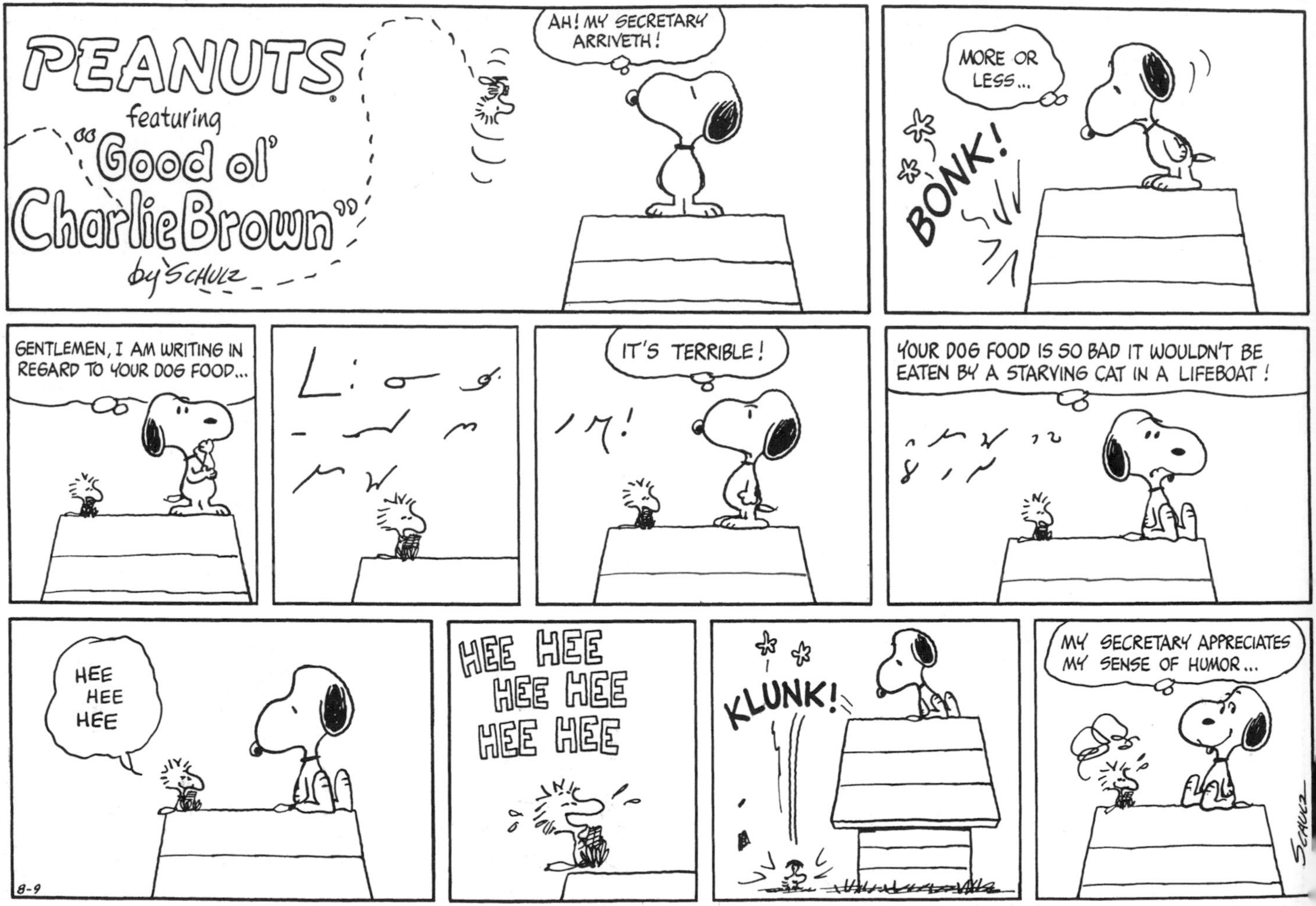
PEANUTS
featuring
"Good ol' Charlie Brown"
by SCHULZ
AH! MY SECRETARY ARRIVETH!
MORE OR LESS...
BONK!
GENTLEMEN, I AM WRITING IN REGARD TO YOUR DOG FOOD...
IT'S TERRIBLE!
YOUR DOG FOOD IS SO BAD IT WOULDN'T BE EATEN BY A STARVING CAT IN A LIFEBOAT!
HEE HEE HEE
8-9
HEE HEE HEE HEE HEE HEE
KLUNK!
MY SECRETARY APPRECIATES MY SENSE OF HUMOR...
SCHULZ

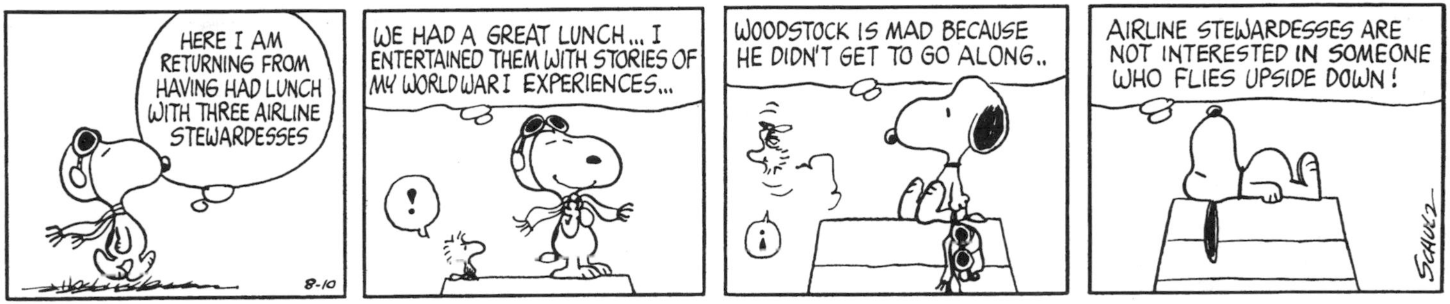
HERE I AM RETURNING FROM HAVING HAD LUNCH WITH THREE AIRLINE STEWARDESSES
8-10
WE HAD A GREAT LUNCH... I ENTERTAINED THEM WITH STORIES OF MY WORLD WAR I EXPERIENCES...
!
WOODSTOCK IS MAD BECAUSE HE DIDN'T GET TO GO ALONG..
AIRLINE STEWARDESSES ARE NOT INTERESTED IN SOMEONE WHO FLIES UPSIDE DOWN!
SCHULZ

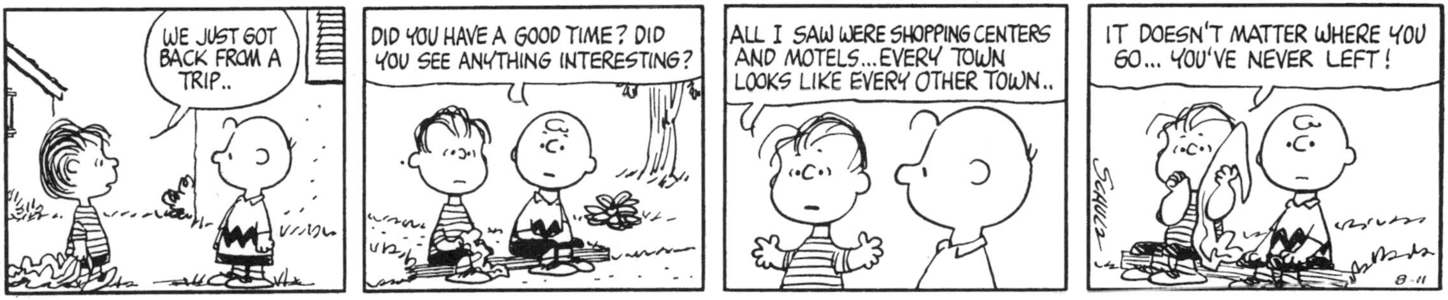
WE JUST GOT BACK FROM A TRIP..
DID YOU HAVE A GOOD TIME? DID YOU SEE ANYTHING INTERESTING?
ALL I SAW WERE SHOPPING CENTERS AND MOTELS...EVERY TOWN LOOKS LIKE EVERY OTHER TOWN..
IT DOESN'T MATTER WHERE YOU GO... YOU'VE NEVER LEFT!
SCHULZ
8-11

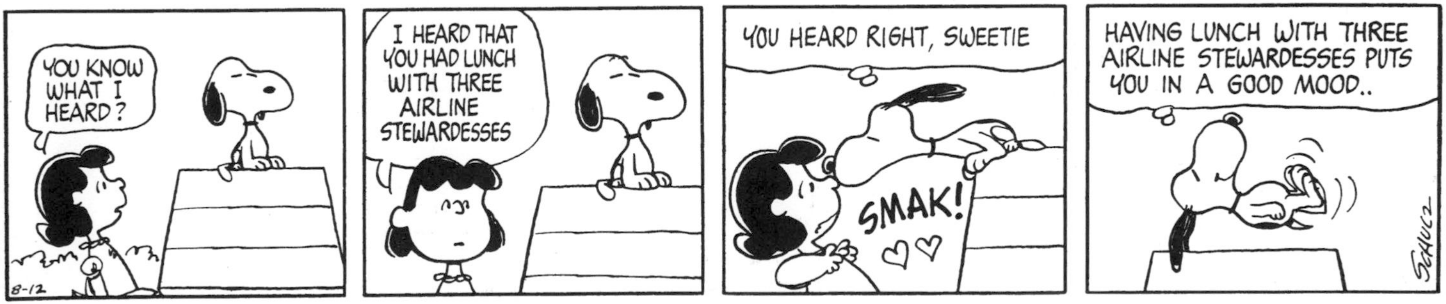
YOU KNOW WHAT I HEARD?
8-12
I HEARD THAT YOU HAD LUNCH WITH THREE AIRLINE STEWARDESSES
YOU HEARD RIGHT, SWEETIE
SMAK!
HAVING LUNCH WITH THREE AIRLINE STEWARDESSES PUTS YOU IN A GOOD MOOD..
SCHULZ

Panel 1: THEY MAKE ME SO MAD IN THAT STORE! THEY NEVER WAIT ON LITTLE KIDS!

Panel 2: I STOOD THERE FOR FORTY-FIVE MINUTES, AND THEY NEVER PAID ANY ATTENTION TO ME! 8-13

Panel 3: I HOPE YOUR ESCALATOR JAMS! I HOPE ALL THE BLACKTOP IN YOUR PARKING LOT CRACKS!

Panel 4: THE ANGRY CONSUMER   SCHULZ

Panel 5: 8-14   WOODSTOCK HAS SURE BEEN CRABBY LATELY

Panel 6: HE'S LUCKY HE'S NOT LIVING IN A CAGE..IF YOU'RE NOT LIVING IN A CAGE, ALL YOU REALLY NEED IN THIS LIFE TO BE HAPPY IS YOUR HEALTH..

Panel 7: KLUNK!!

Panel 8: SCHULZ   ..AND A SENSE OF BALANCE

Panel 9: THIS IS YOUR ROCK COLLECTION, CHARLIE BROWN?

Panel 10: YES, I'VE BEEN SAVING SOME OF THESE ROCKS FOR YEARS   THAT'S THE WORST ROCK COLLECTION I'VE EVER SEEN! 8-15

Panel 11: IT'S DRAB, DULL AND COMPLETELY BORING!

Panel 12: MY ROCK COLLECTION HAS TURNED TO STONE..   SCHULZ

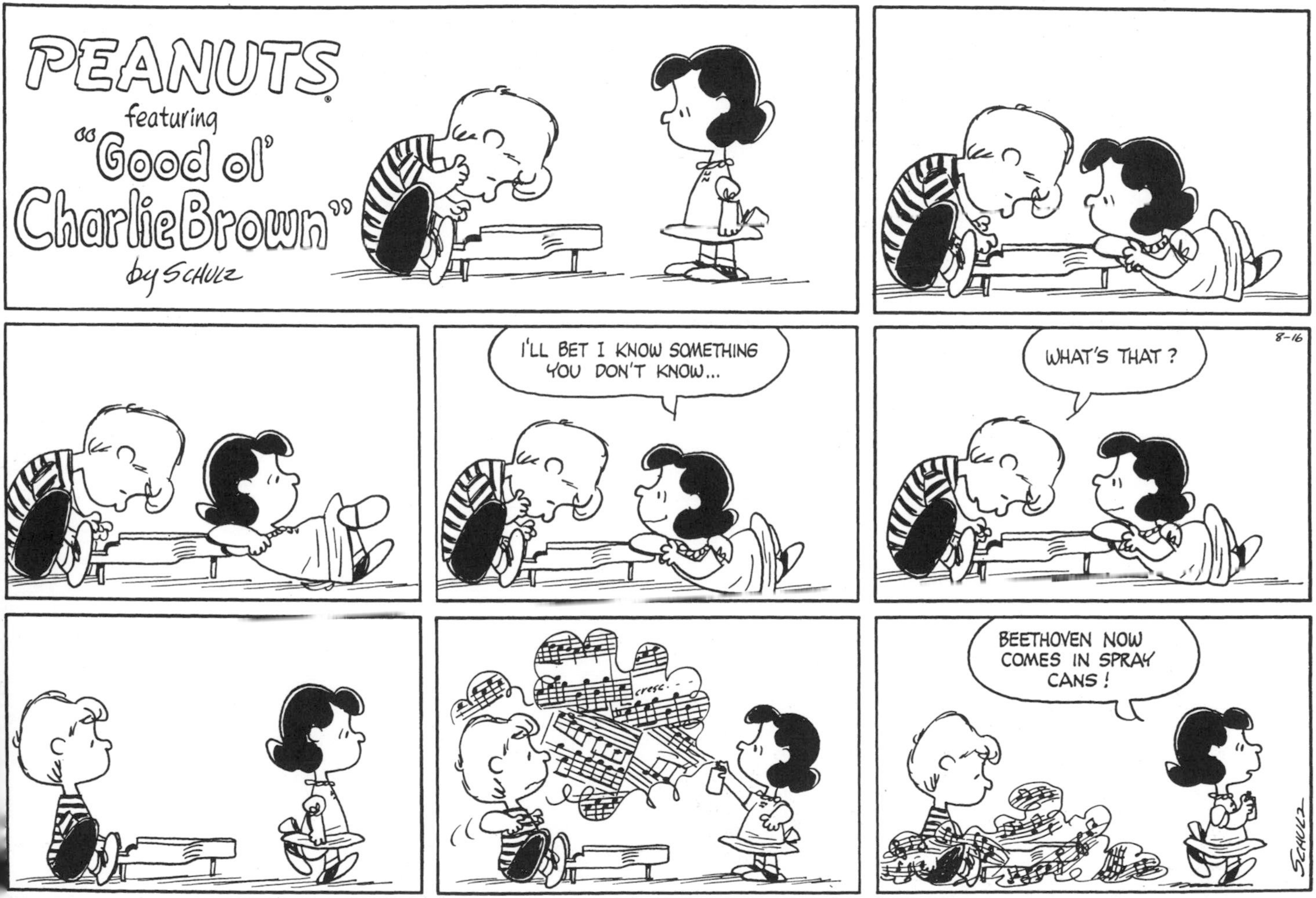
PEANUTS
featuring
"Good ol' Charlie Brown"
by SCHULZ
8-16
I'LL BET I KNOW SOMETHING YOU DON'T KNOW...
WHAT'S THAT ?
cresc.
BEETHOVEN NOW COMES IN SPRAY CANS !
SCHULZ

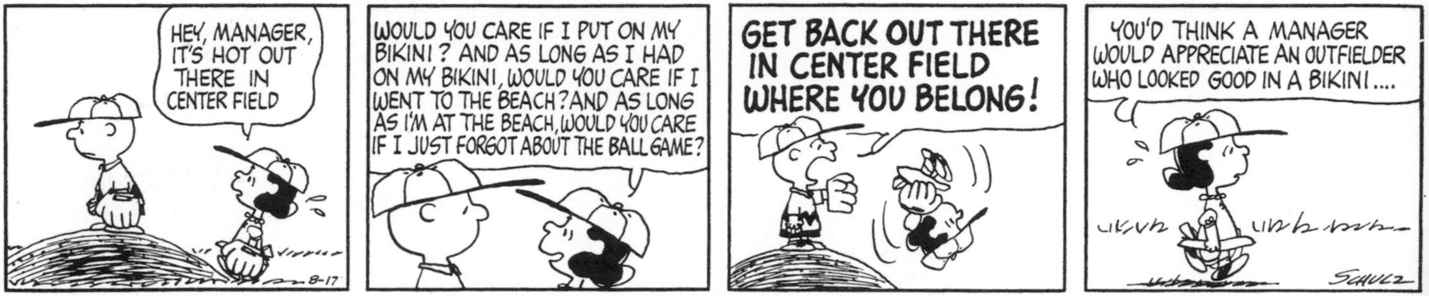
HEY, MANAGER, IT'S HOT OUT THERE IN CENTER FIELD
8-17
WOULD YOU CARE IF I PUT ON MY BIKINI? AND AS LONG AS I HAD ON MY BIKINI, WOULD YOU CARE IF I WENT TO THE BEACH? AND AS LONG AS I'M AT THE BEACH, WOULD YOU CARE IF I JUST FORGOT ABOUT THE BALL GAME?
GET BACK OUT THERE IN CENTER FIELD WHERE YOU BELONG!
YOU'D THINK A MANAGER WOULD APPRECIATE AN OUTFIELDER WHO LOOKED GOOD IN A BIKINI....
SCHULZ

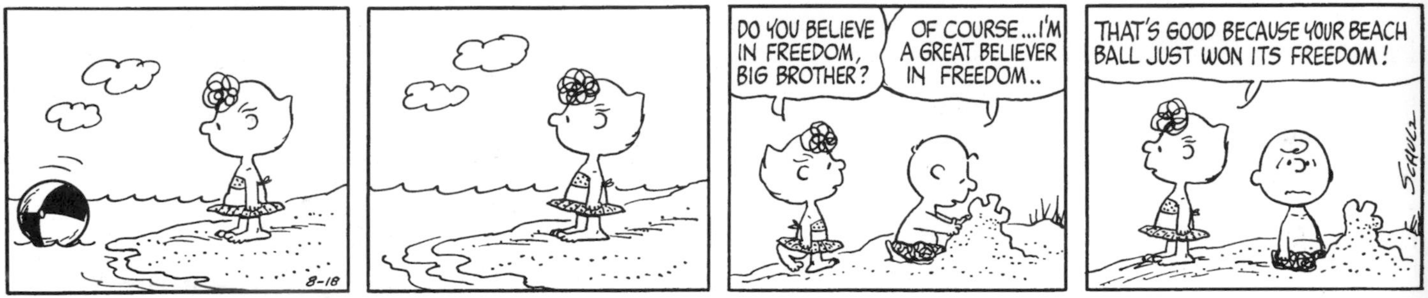
8-18
DO YOU BELIEVE IN FREEDOM, BIG BROTHER?
OF COURSE...I'M A GREAT BELIEVER IN FREEDOM..
THAT'S GOOD BECAUSE YOUR BEACH BALL JUST WON ITS FREEDOM!
SCHULZ

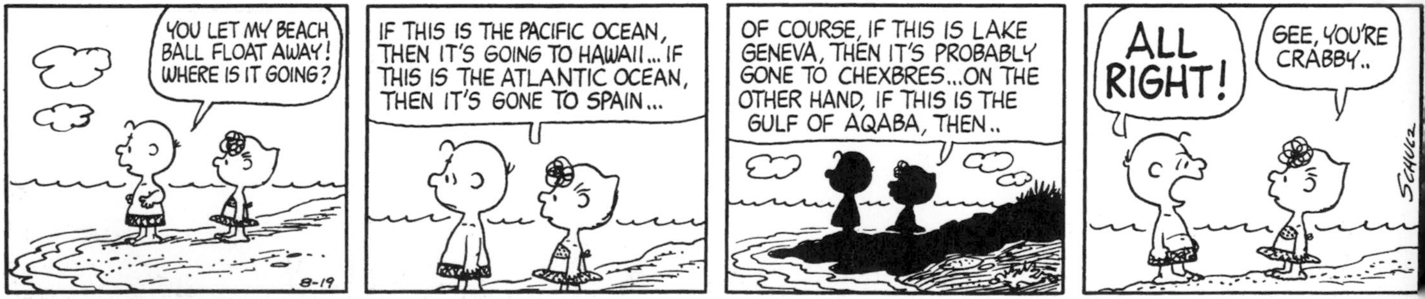
YOU LET MY BEACH BALL FLOAT AWAY! WHERE IS IT GOING?
8-19
IF THIS IS THE PACIFIC OCEAN, THEN IT'S GOING TO HAWAII... IF THIS IS THE ATLANTIC OCEAN, THEN IT'S GONE TO SPAIN...
OF COURSE, IF THIS IS LAKE GENEVA, THEN IT'S PROBABLY GONE TO CHEXBRES...ON THE OTHER HAND, IF THIS IS THE GULF OF AQABA, THEN..
ALL RIGHT!
GEE, YOU'RE CRABBY..
SCHULZ

PSYCHIATRIC HELP 5¢

ALL I WANT IS TO LEAD A NORMAL LIFE..

THE DOCTOR IS [IN]

HELP 5¢

YOU?!

THE DOCTOR IS [IN]

8-20

HELP 5

FIVE CENTS, PLEASE!

THE DOCTOR

THERE'S A GOOD PROFIT IN THOSE SHORT SESSIONS

THE DOCTOR IS [IN]

PSYCHIATRIC HELP 5¢

WHAT'S WRONG WITH WANTING TO LEAD A NORMAL LIFE?

THE DOCTOR IS [IN]

8-21

NOTHING, CHARLIE BROWN, NOTHING AT ALL ...NOTHING...

THE DOCTOR IS [IN]

IF THAT'S WHAT YOU WANT, WHY, NOTHING, I GUESS..NOTHING AT ALL...NOTHING..NOTHING AT ALL... NOTHING...NOTHING....

I HAVE A FEELING THERE'S SOMETHING WRONG WITH IT..

THE DOCTOR IS [IN]

8-22

AHCHOO!

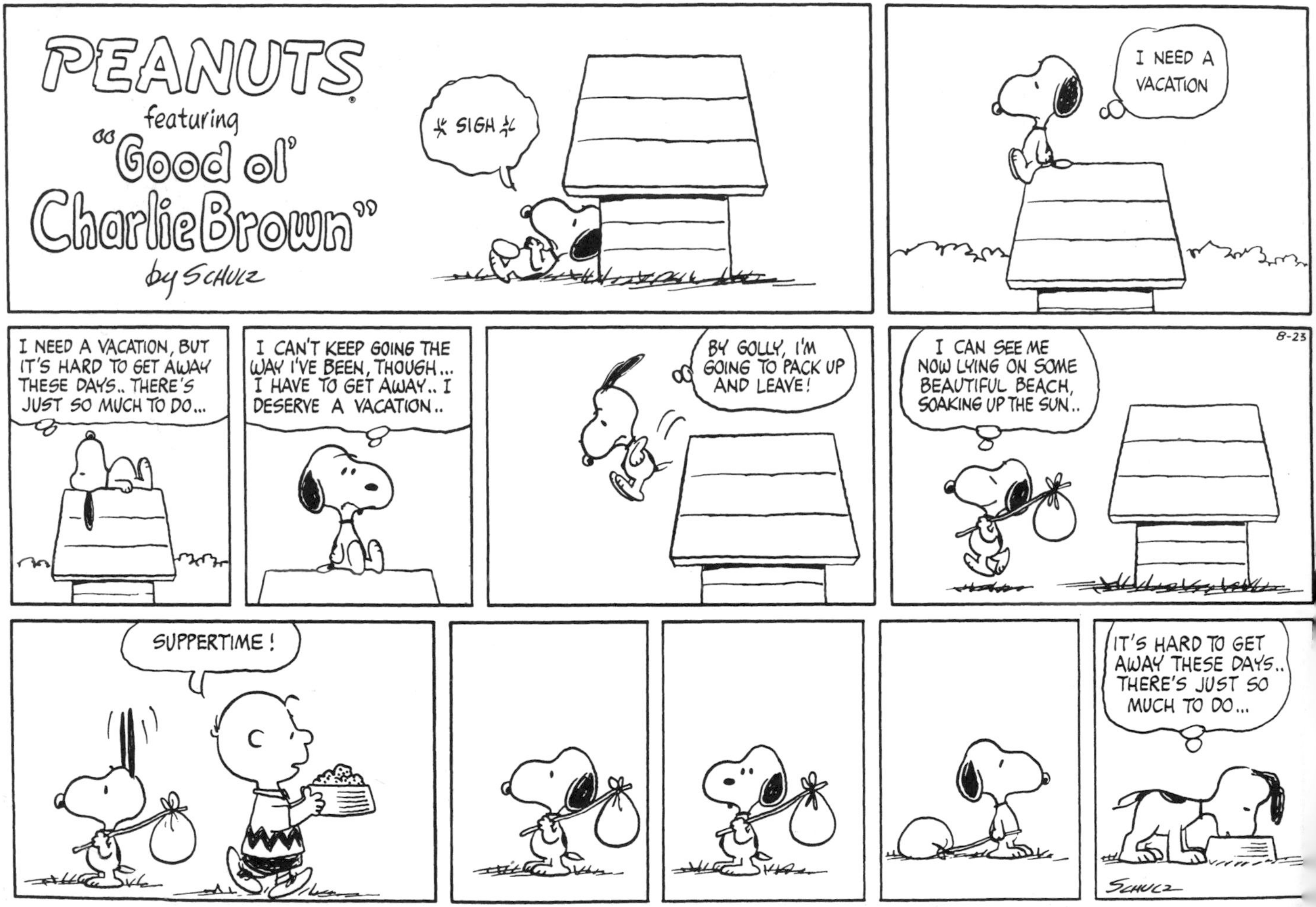
PEANUTS
featuring
"Good ol' Charlie Brown"
by SCHULZ
* SIGH *
I NEED A VACATION
I NEED A VACATION, BUT IT'S HARD TO GET AWAY THESE DAYS.. THERE'S JUST SO MUCH TO DO...
I CAN'T KEEP GOING THE WAY I'VE BEEN, THOUGH... I HAVE TO GET AWAY.. I DESERVE A VACATION..
BY GOLLY, I'M GOING TO PACK UP AND LEAVE!
8-23
I CAN SEE ME NOW LYING ON SOME BEAUTIFUL BEACH, SOAKING UP THE SUN..
SUPPERTIME!
IT'S HARD TO GET AWAY THESE DAYS.. THERE'S JUST SO MUCH TO DO...
SCHULZ

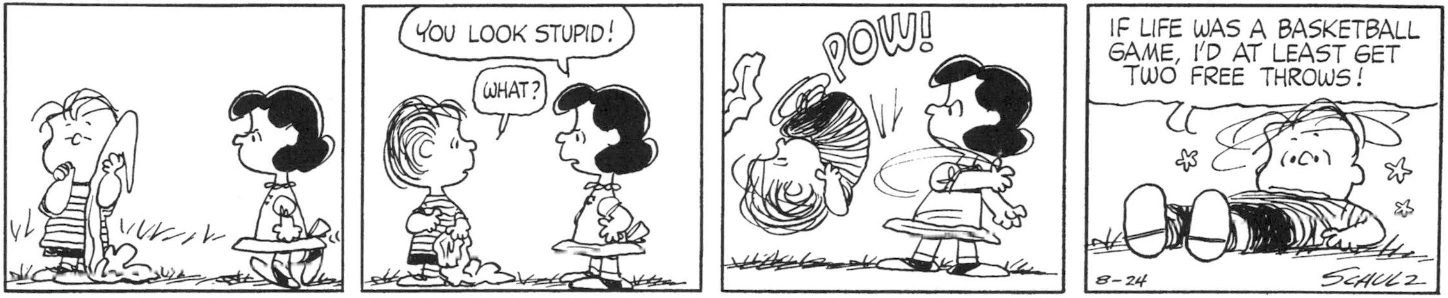
YOU LOOK STUPID!
WHAT?
POW!
IF LIFE WAS A BASKETBALL GAME, I'D AT LEAST GET TWO FREE THROWS!
8-24
SCHULZ

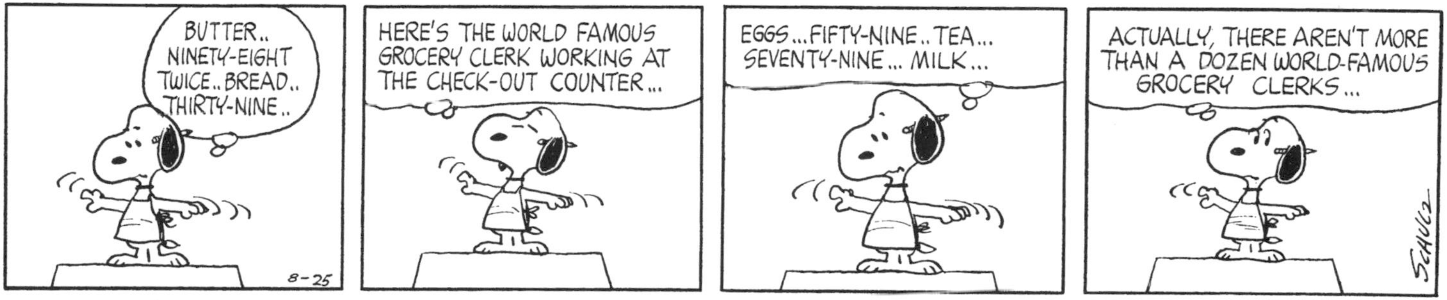
BUTTER.. NINETY-EIGHT TWICE.. BREAD.. THIRTY-NINE..
8-25
HERE'S THE WORLD FAMOUS GROCERY CLERK WORKING AT THE CHECK-OUT COUNTER...
EGGS...FIFTY-NINE.. TEA... SEVENTY-NINE... MILK...
ACTUALLY, THERE AREN'T MORE THAN A DOZEN WORLD-FAMOUS GROCERY CLERKS...
SCHULZ

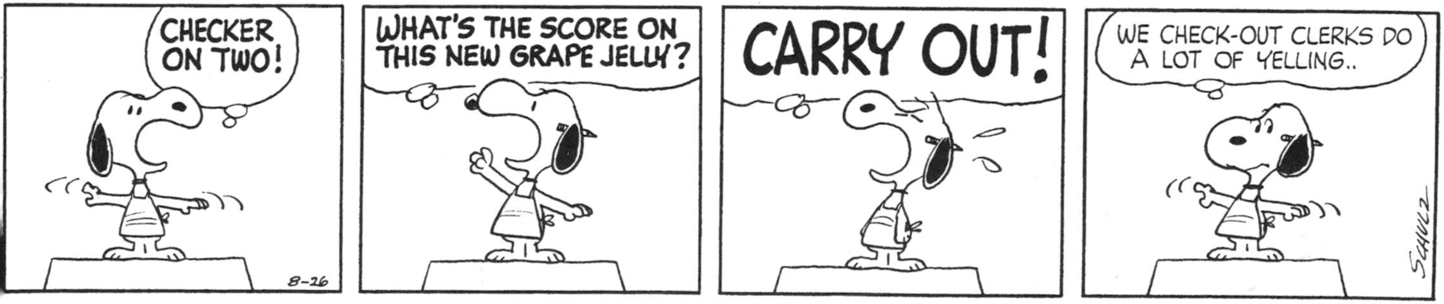
CHECKER ON TWO!
8-26
WHAT'S THE SCORE ON THIS NEW GRAPE JELLY?
CARRY OUT!
WE CHECK-OUT CLERKS DO A LOT OF YELLING..
SCHULZ

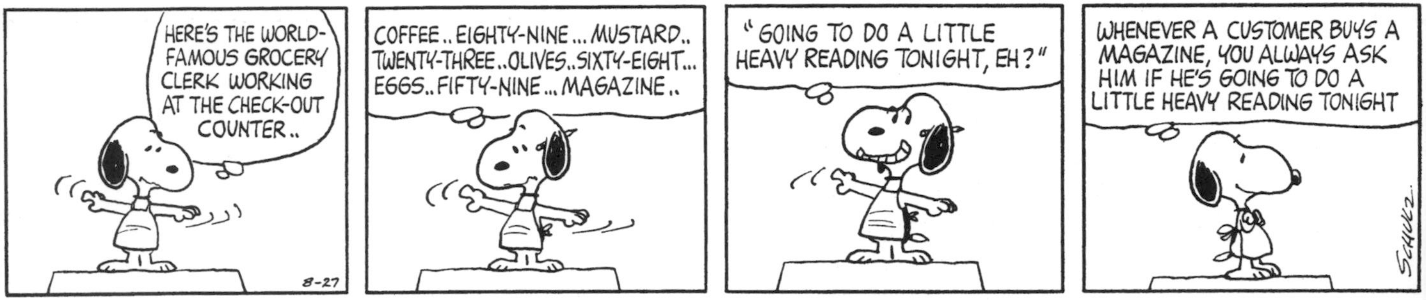
HERE'S THE WORLD-FAMOUS GROCERY CLERK WORKING AT THE CHECK-OUT COUNTER..
8-27
COFFEE..EIGHTY-NINE...MUSTARD.. TWENTY-THREE..OLIVES..SIXTY-EIGHT... EGGS..FIFTY-NINE...MAGAZINE..
"GOING TO DO A LITTLE HEAVY READING TONIGHT, EH?"
WHENEVER A CUSTOMER BUYS A MAGAZINE, YOU ALWAYS ASK HIM IF HE'S GOING TO DO A LITTLE HEAVY READING TONIGHT
SCHULZ

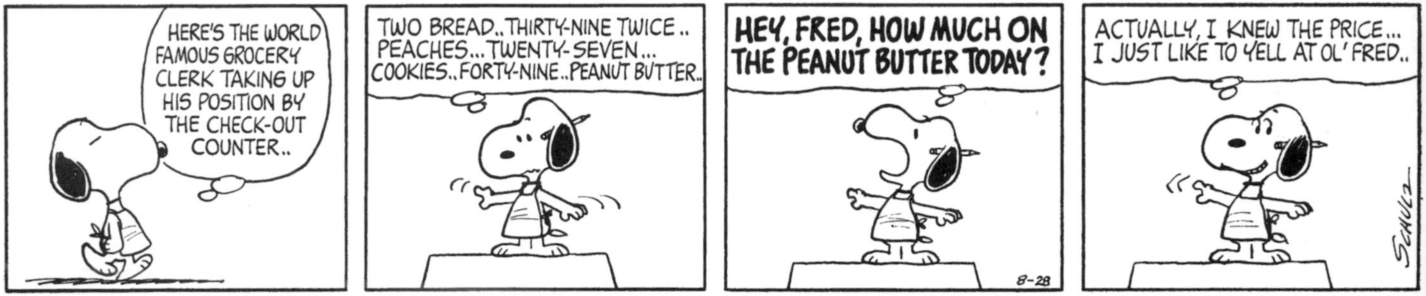
HERE'S THE WORLD FAMOUS GROCERY CLERK TAKING UP HIS POSITION BY THE CHECK-OUT COUNTER..
TWO BREAD..THIRTY-NINE TWICE.. PEACHES...TWENTY-SEVEN... COOKIES..FORTY-NINE..PEANUT BUTTER..
HEY, FRED, HOW MUCH ON THE PEANUT BUTTER TODAY?
8-28
ACTUALLY, I KNEW THE PRICE... I JUST LIKE TO YELL AT OL' FRED..
SCHULZ

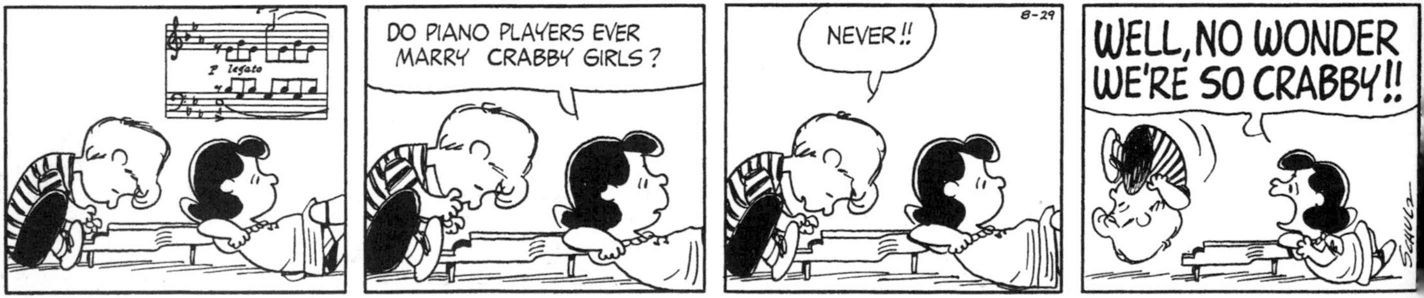
p legato
DO PIANO PLAYERS EVER MARRY CRABBY GIRLS?
NEVER!!
8-29
WELL, NO WONDER WE'RE SO CRABBY!!
SCHULZ

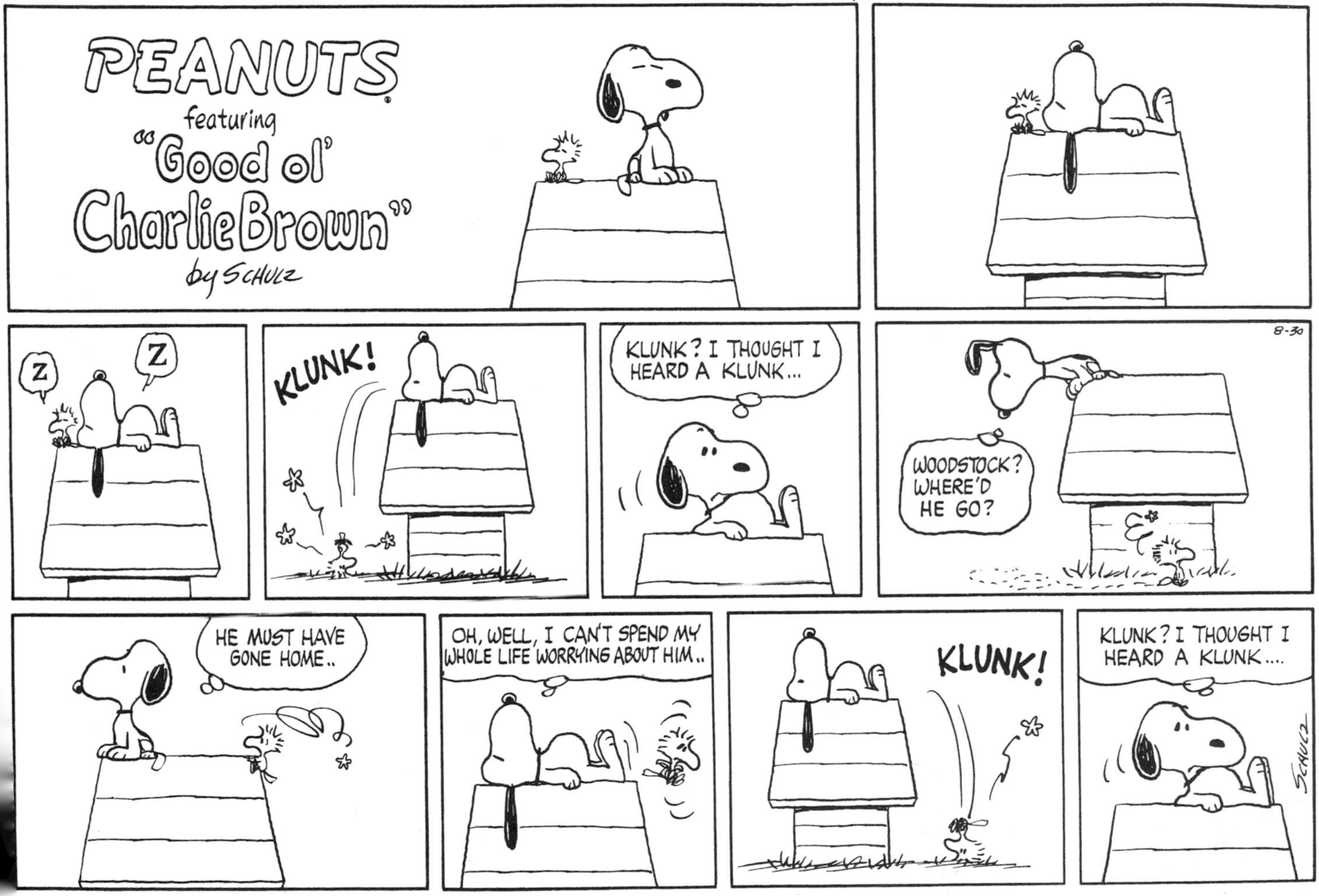
PEANUTS
featuring
"Good ol' Charlie Brown"
by SCHULZ
Z
Z
KLUNK!
KLUNK? I THOUGHT I HEARD A KLUNK...
8-30
WOODSTOCK? WHERE'D HE GO?
HE MUST HAVE GONE HOME..
OH, WELL, I CAN'T SPEND MY WHOLE LIFE WORRYING ABOUT HIM..
KLUNK!
KLUNK? I THOUGHT I HEARD A KLUNK....
SCHULZ

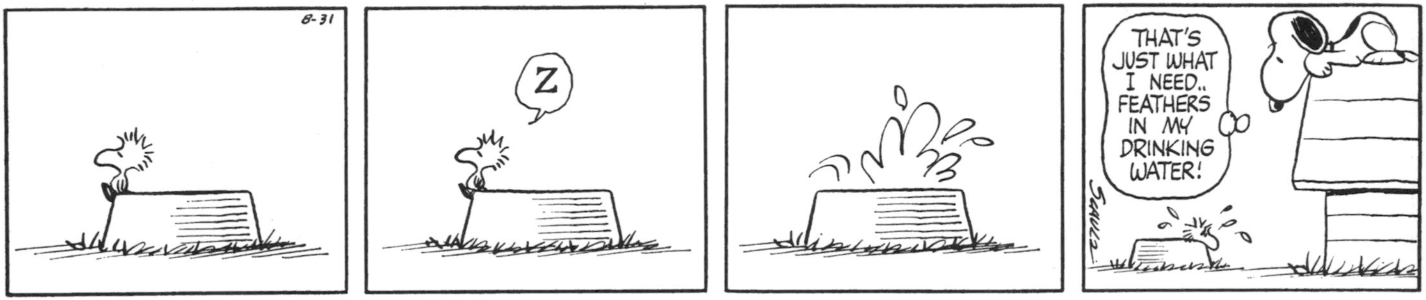
8-31
Z
THAT'S JUST WHAT I NEED.. FEATHERS IN MY DRINKING WATER!
SCHULZ

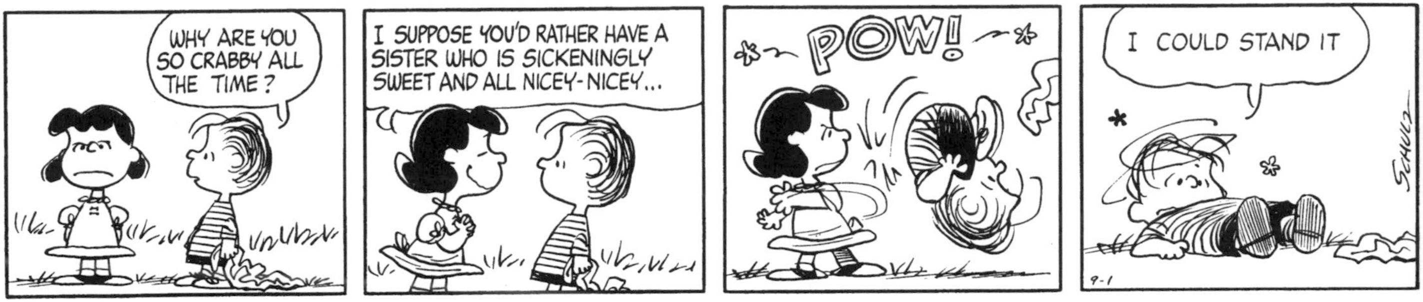
WHY ARE YOU SO CRABBY ALL THE TIME?
I SUPPOSE YOU'D RATHER HAVE A SISTER WHO IS SICKENINGLY SWEET AND ALL NICEY-NICEY...
POW!
I COULD STAND IT
SCHULZ
9-1

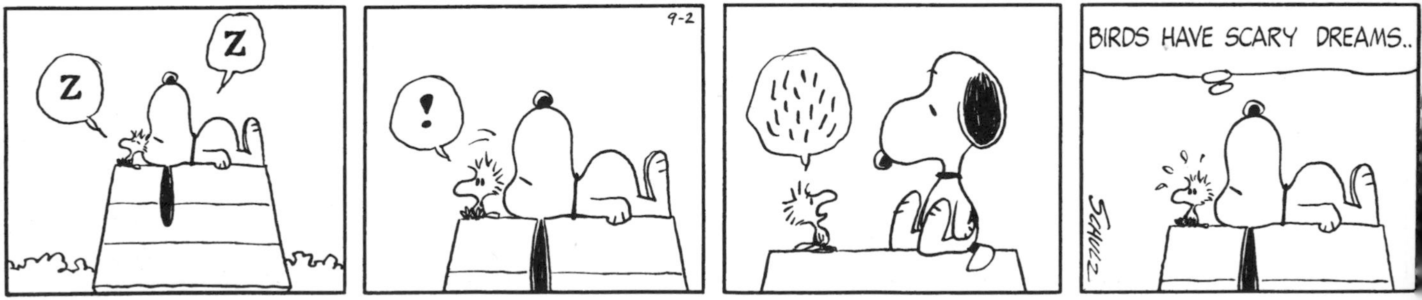
Z
Z
9-2
!
BIRDS HAVE SCARY DREAMS..
SCHULZ

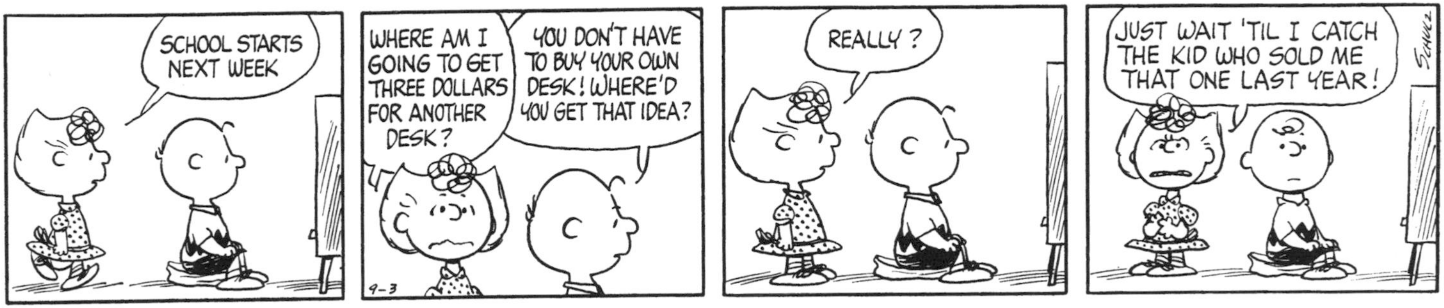
SCHOOL STARTS NEXT WEEK
WHERE AM I GOING TO GET THREE DOLLARS FOR ANOTHER DESK?
YOU DON'T HAVE TO BUY YOUR OWN DESK! WHERE'D YOU GET THAT IDEA?
9-3
REALLY?
JUST WAIT 'TIL I CATCH THE KID WHO SOLD ME THAT ONE LAST YEAR!
SCHULZ

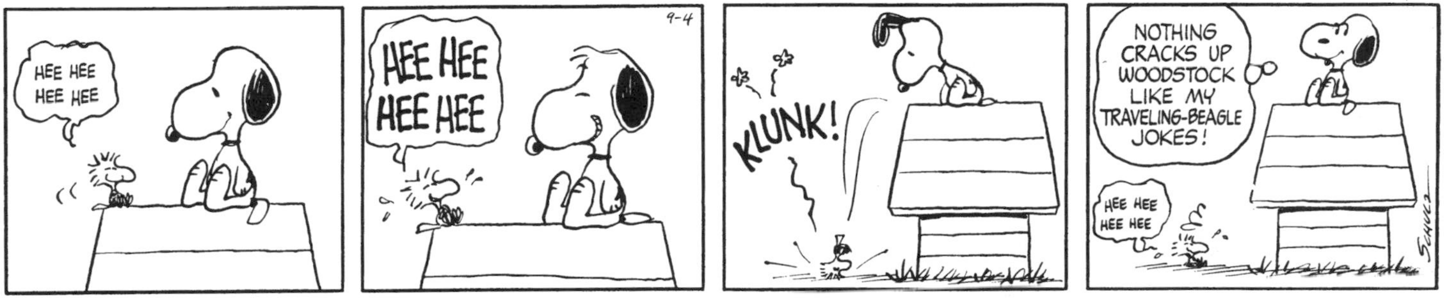
HEE HEE HEE HEE
HEE HEE HEE HEE
9-4
KLUNK!
NOTHING CRACKS UP WOODSTOCK LIKE MY TRAVELING-BEAGLE JOKES!
HEE HEE HEE HEE
SCHULZ

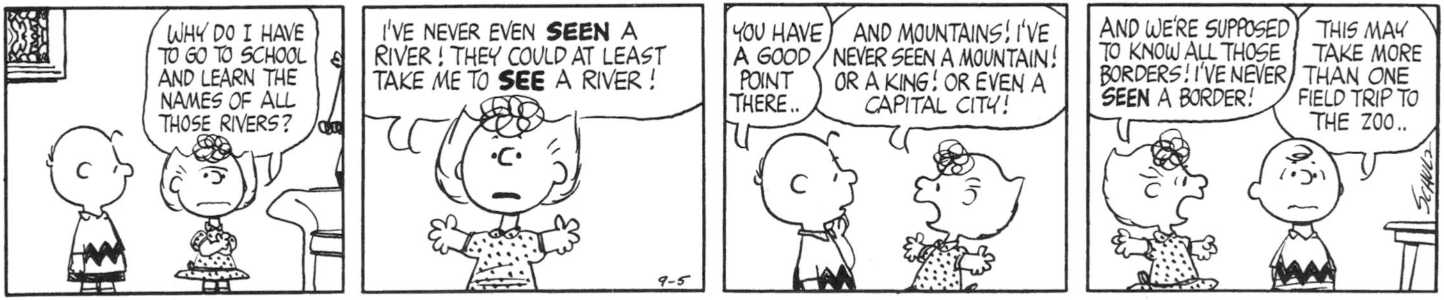
WHY DO I HAVE TO GO TO SCHOOL AND LEARN THE NAMES OF ALL THOSE RIVERS?
I'VE NEVER EVEN SEEN A RIVER! THEY COULD AT LEAST TAKE ME TO SEE A RIVER!
9-5
YOU HAVE A GOOD POINT THERE..
AND MOUNTAINS! I'VE NEVER SEEN A MOUNTAIN! OR A KING! OR EVEN A CAPITAL CITY!
AND WE'RE SUPPOSED TO KNOW ALL THOSE BORDERS! I'VE NEVER SEEN A BORDER!
THIS MAY TAKE MORE THAN ONE FIELD TRIP TO THE ZOO..
SCHULZ

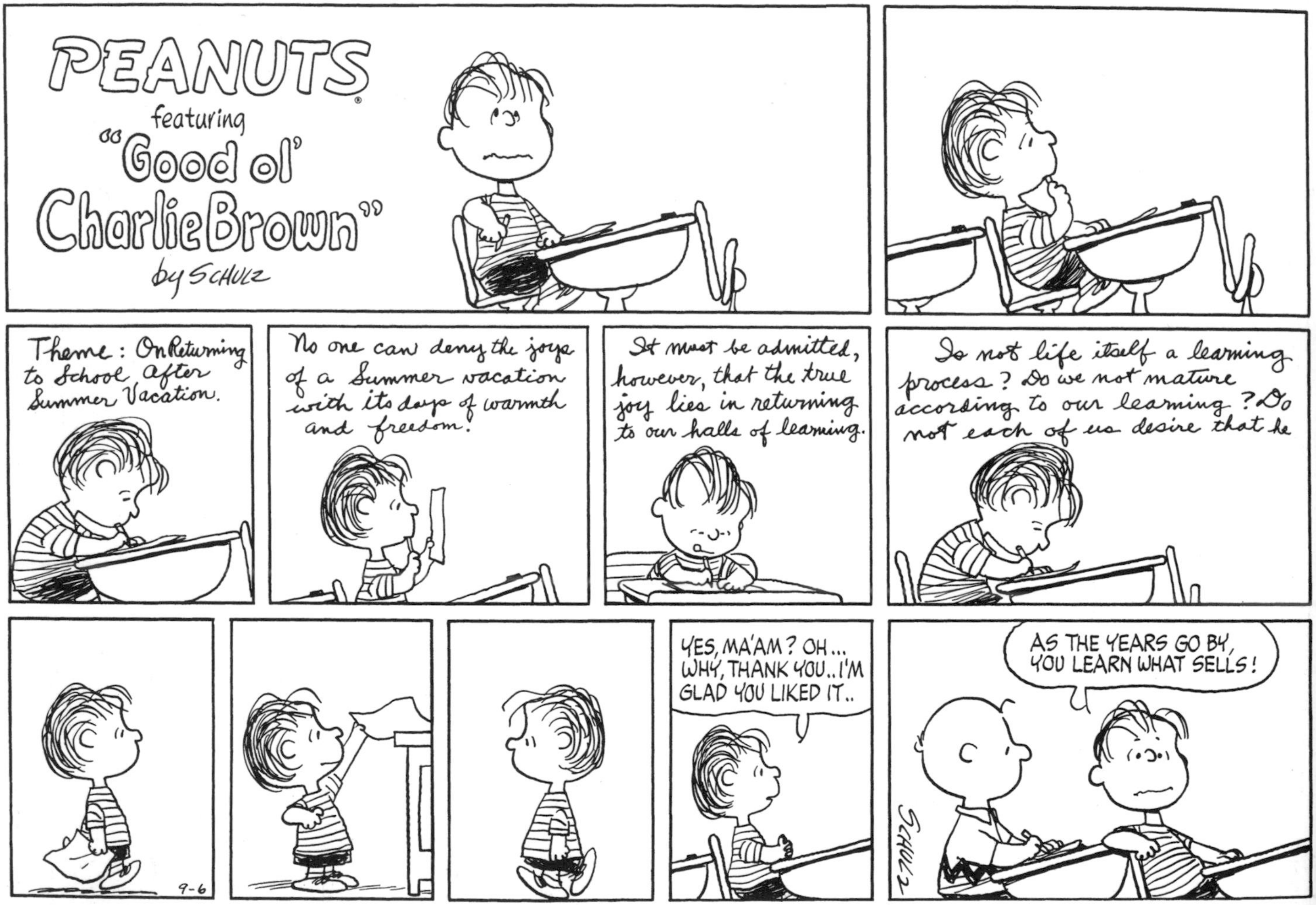
PEANUTS
featuring "Good ol' Charlie Brown"
by SCHULZ
Theme: On Returning to School after Summer Vacation.
No one can deny the joys of a Summer vacation with its days of warmth and freedom!
It must be admitted, however, that the true joy lies in returning to our halls of learning.
Is not life itself a learning process? Do we not mature according to our learning? Do not each of us desire that he
9-6
YES, MA'AM? OH... WHY, THANK YOU..I'M GLAD YOU LIKED IT..
SCHULZ
AS THE YEARS GO BY, YOU LEARN WHAT SELLS!

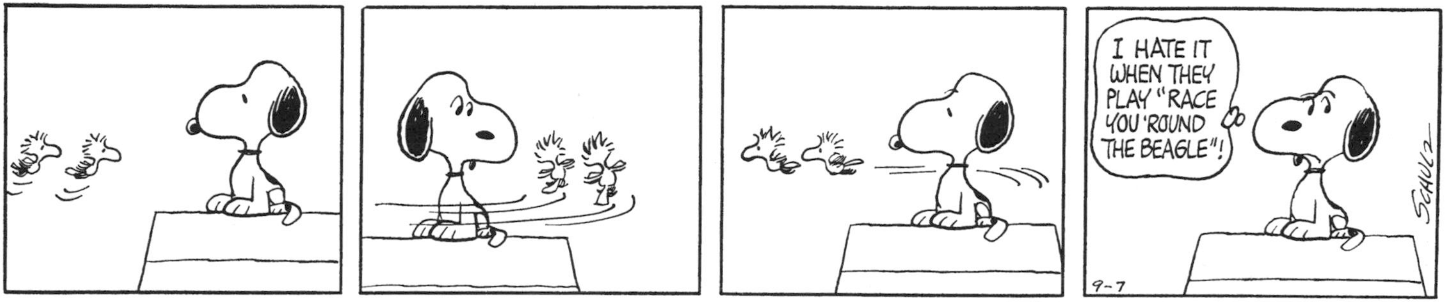
I HATE IT WHEN THEY PLAY "RACE YOU 'ROUND THE BEAGLE"!
SCHULZ
9-7

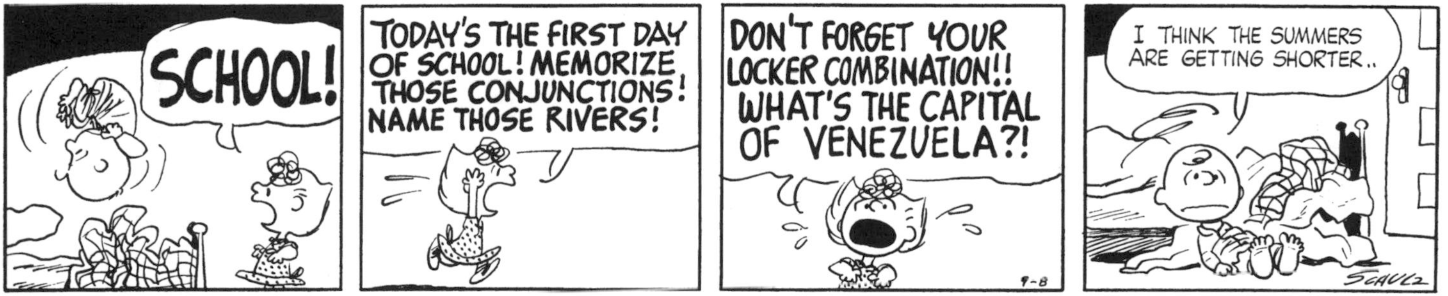
SCHOOL!
TODAY'S THE FIRST DAY OF SCHOOL! MEMORIZE THOSE CONJUNCTIONS! NAME THOSE RIVERS!
DON'T FORGET YOUR LOCKER COMBINATION!! WHAT'S THE CAPITAL OF VENEZUELA?!
9-8
I THINK THE SUMMERS ARE GETTING SHORTER..
SCHULZ

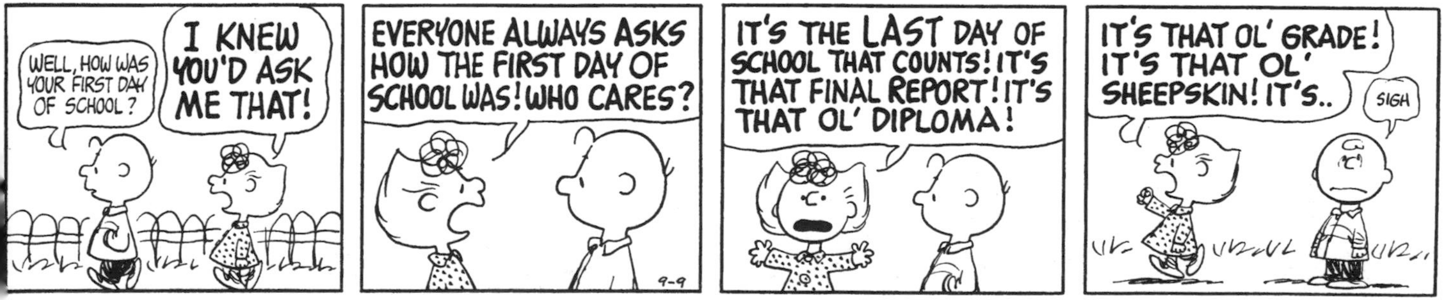
WELL, HOW WAS YOUR FIRST DAY OF SCHOOL?
I KNEW YOU'D ASK ME THAT!
EVERYONE ALWAYS ASKS HOW THE FIRST DAY OF SCHOOL WAS! WHO CARES?
9-9
IT'S THE LAST DAY OF SCHOOL THAT COUNTS! IT'S THAT FINAL REPORT! IT'S THAT OL' DIPLOMA!
IT'S THAT OL' GRADE! IT'S THAT OL' SHEEPSKIN! IT'S..
SIGH

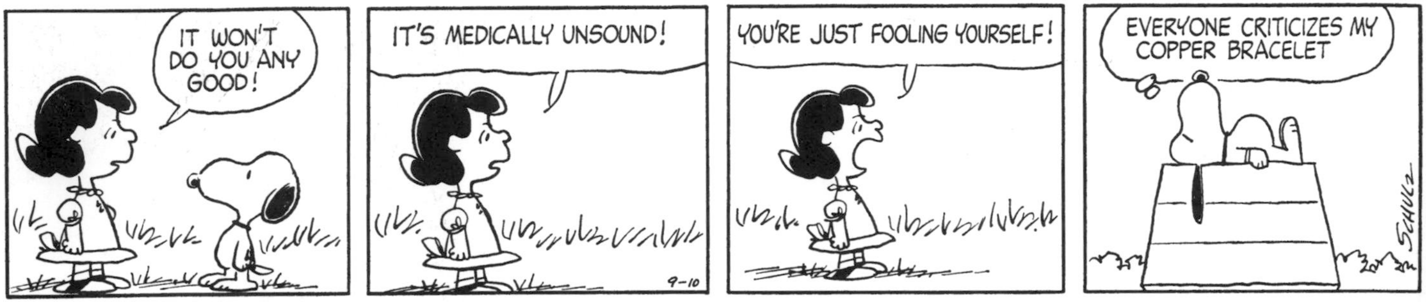
IT WON'T DO YOU ANY GOOD!
IT'S MEDICALLY UNSOUND!
9-10
YOU'RE JUST FOOLING YOURSELF!
EVERYONE CRITICIZES MY COPPER BRACELET
SCHULZ

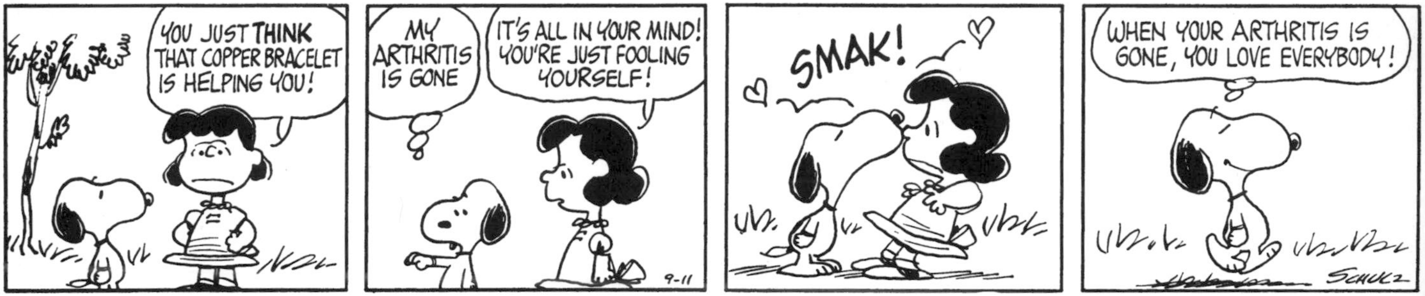
YOU JUST THINK THAT COPPER BRACELET IS HELPING YOU!
MY ARTHRITIS IS GONE
IT'S ALL IN YOUR MIND! YOU'RE JUST FOOLING YOURSELF!
9-11
SMAK!
WHEN YOUR ARTHRITIS IS GONE, YOU LOVE EVERYBODY!
SCHULZ

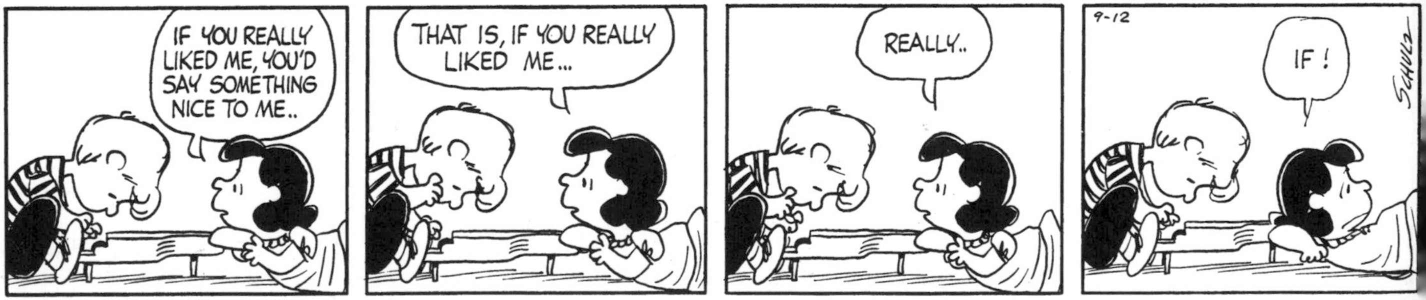
IF YOU REALLY LIKED ME, YOU'D SAY SOMETHING NICE TO ME..
THAT IS, IF YOU REALLY LIKED ME...
REALLY..
9-12
IF!
SCHULZ

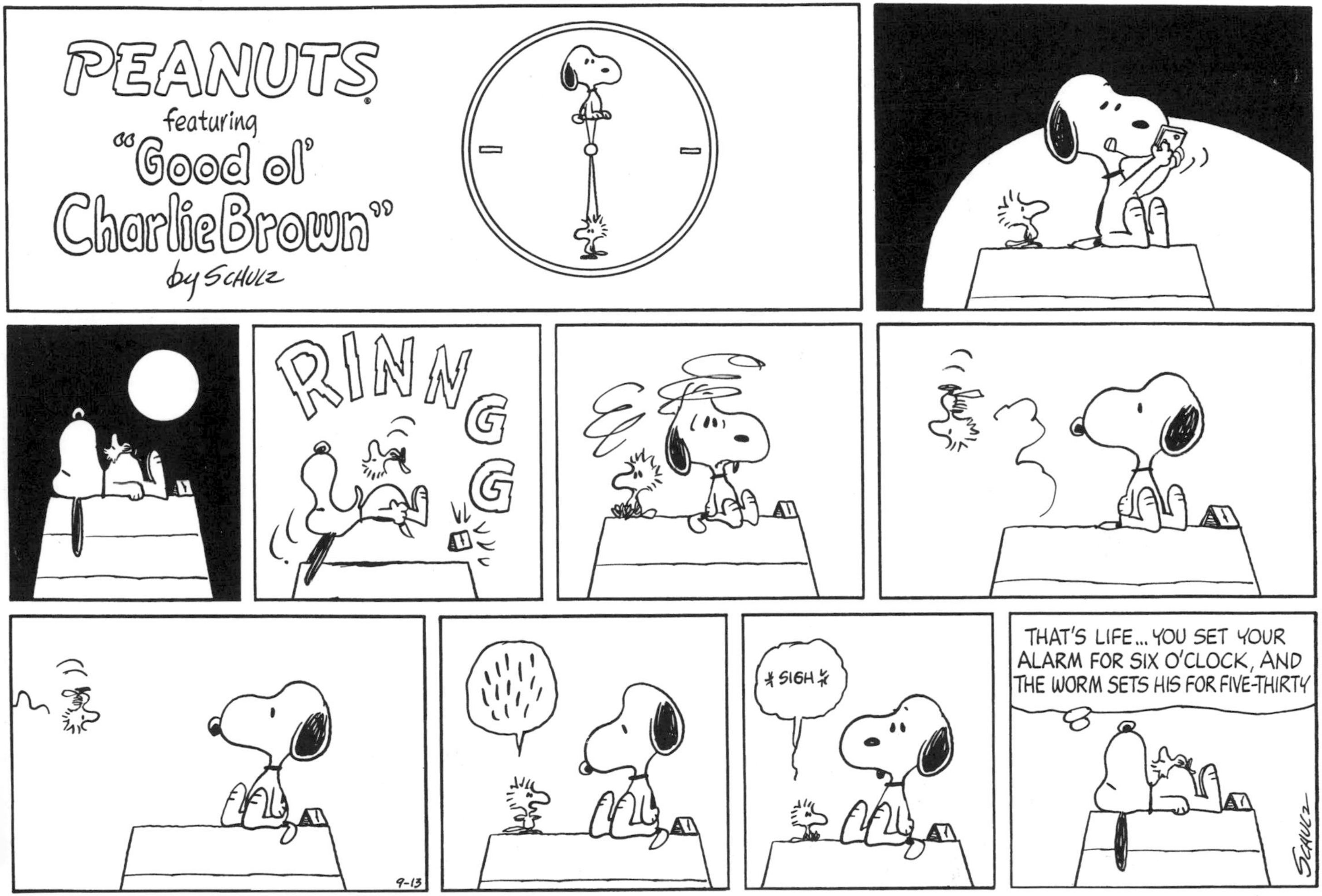
PEANUTS
featuring
"Good ol' CharlieBrown"
by SCHULZ
RINNGG
SIGH
THAT'S LIFE... YOU SET YOUR ALARM FOR SIX O'CLOCK, AND THE WORM SETS HIS FOR FIVE-THIRTY
9-13
SCHULZ

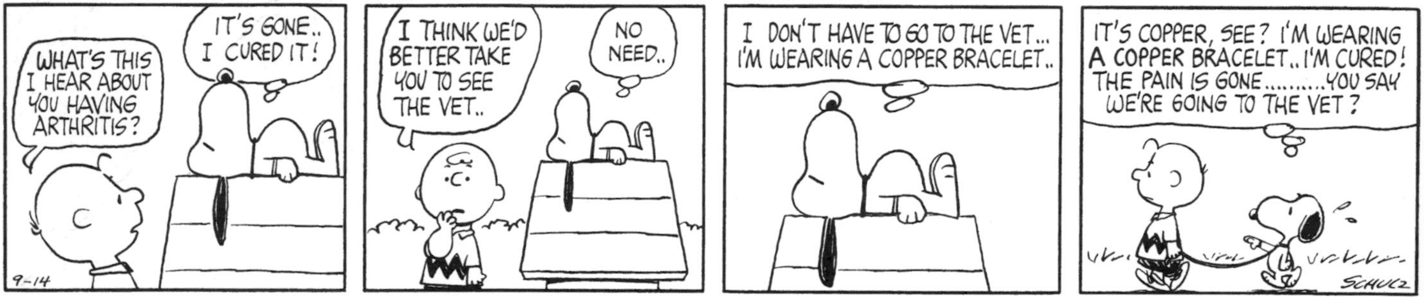
WHAT'S THIS I HEAR ABOUT YOU HAVING ARTHRITIS?
IT'S GONE.. I CURED IT!
9-14
I THINK WE'D BETTER TAKE YOU TO SEE THE VET..
NO NEED..
I DON'T HAVE TO GO TO THE VET... I'M WEARING A COPPER BRACELET..
IT'S COPPER, SEE? I'M WEARING A COPPER BRACELET.. I'M CURED! THE PAIN IS GONE.........YOU SAY WE'RE GOING TO THE VET?
SCHULZ

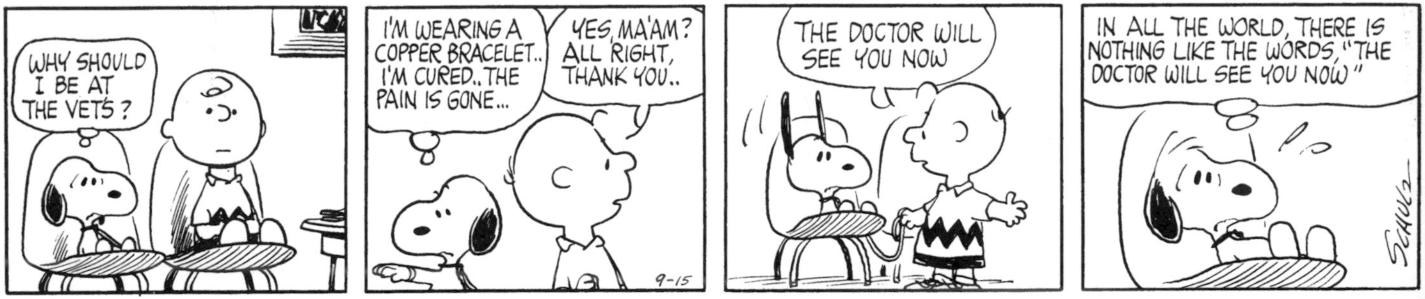
WHY SHOULD I BE AT THE VET'S?
I'M WEARING A COPPER BRACELET.. I'M CURED.. THE PAIN IS GONE...
YES, MA'AM? ALL RIGHT, THANK YOU..
9-15
THE DOCTOR WILL SEE YOU NOW
IN ALL THE WORLD, THERE IS NOTHING LIKE THE WORDS, "THE DOCTOR WILL SEE YOU NOW"
SCHULZ

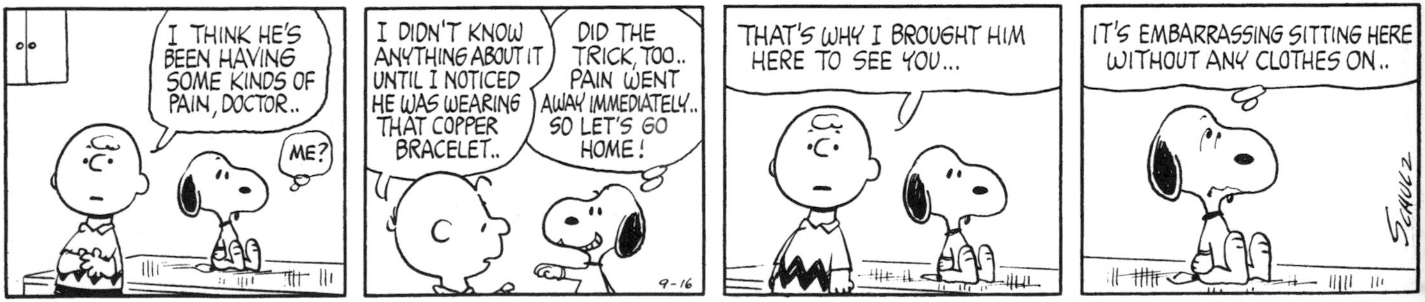
I THINK HE'S BEEN HAVING SOME KINDS OF PAIN, DOCTOR..
ME?
I DIDN'T KNOW ANYTHING ABOUT IT UNTIL I NOTICED HE WAS WEARING THAT COPPER BRACELET..
DID THE TRICK, TOO.. PAIN WENT AWAY IMMEDIATELY.. SO LET'S GO HOME!
9-16
THAT'S WHY I BROUGHT HIM HERE TO SEE YOU...
IT'S EMBARRASSING SITTING HERE WITHOUT ANY CLOTHES ON..
SCHULZ

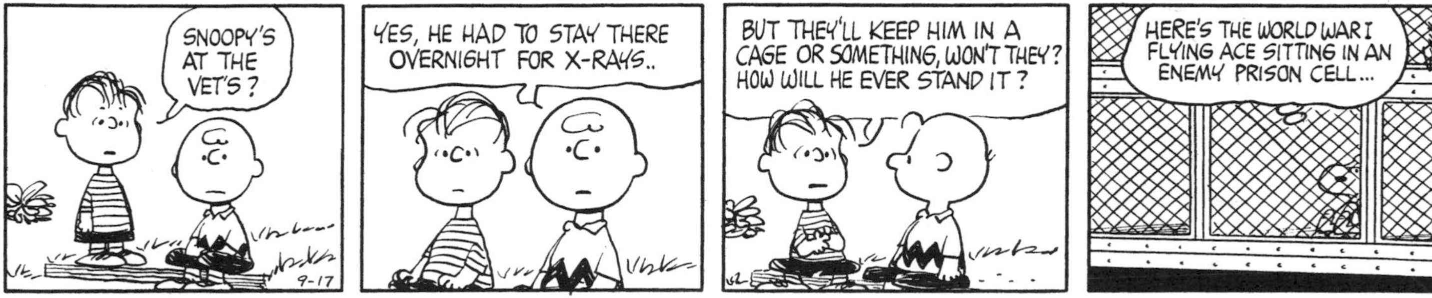
SNOOPY'S AT THE VET'S ?
YES, HE HAD TO STAY THERE OVERNIGHT FOR X-RAYS..
BUT THEY'LL KEEP HIM IN A CAGE OR SOMETHING, WON'T THEY? HOW WILL HE EVER STAND IT ?
HERE'S THE WORLD WAR I FLYING ACE SITTING IN AN ENEMY PRISON CELL...
9-17

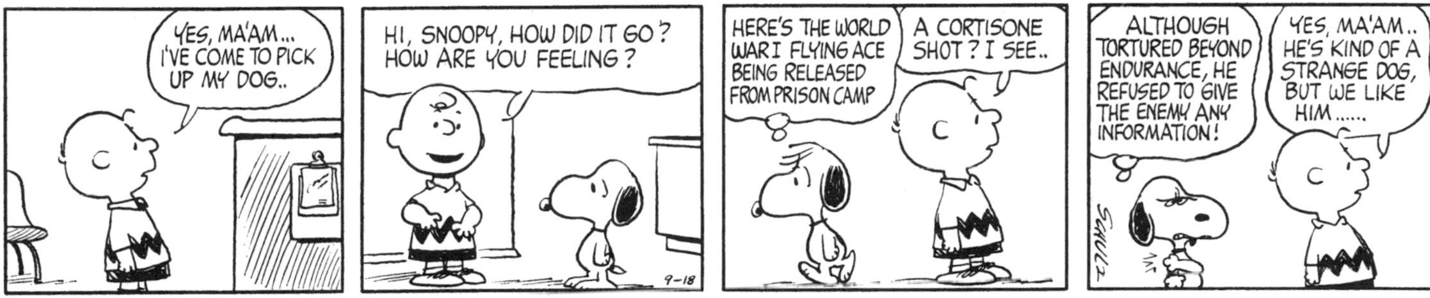
YES, MA'AM... I'VE COME TO PICK UP MY DOG..
HI, SNOOPY, HOW DID IT GO ? HOW ARE YOU FEELING ?
HERE'S THE WORLD WAR I FLYING ACE BEING RELEASED FROM PRISON CAMP
A CORTISONE SHOT ? I SEE..
ALTHOUGH TORTURED BEYOND ENDURANCE, HE REFUSED TO GIVE THE ENEMY ANY INFORMATION !
YES, MA'AM.. HE'S KIND OF A STRANGE DOG, BUT WE LIKE HIM......
9-18

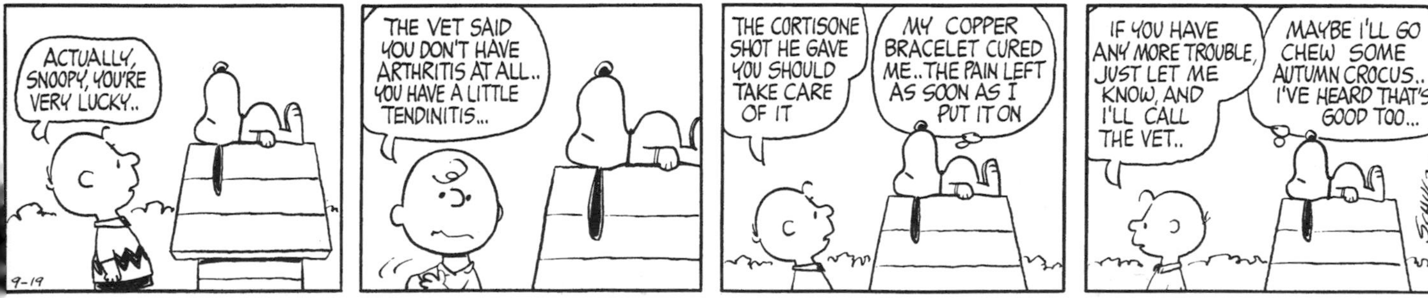
ACTUALLY, SNOOPY, YOU'RE VERY LUCKY..
THE VET SAID YOU DON'T HAVE ARTHRITIS AT ALL.. YOU HAVE A LITTLE TENDINITIS...
THE CORTISONE SHOT HE GAVE YOU SHOULD TAKE CARE OF IT
MY COPPER BRACELET CURED ME..THE PAIN LEFT AS SOON AS I PUT IT ON
IF YOU HAVE ANY MORE TROUBLE, JUST LET ME KNOW, AND I'LL CALL THE VET..
MAYBE I'LL GO CHEW SOME AUTUMN CROCUS.. I'VE HEARD THAT'S GOOD TOO...
9-19

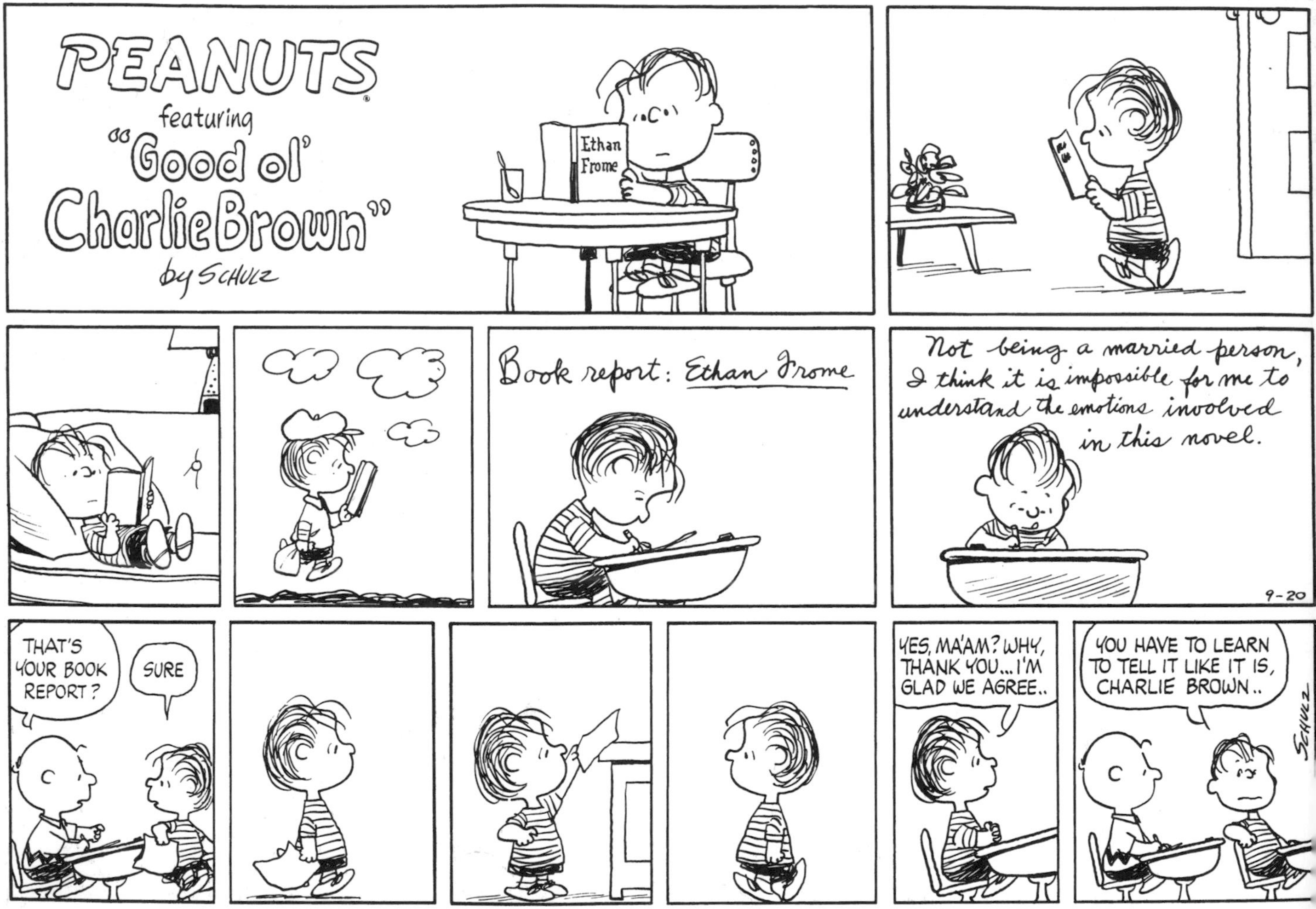
PEANUTS
featuring
"Good ol' Charlie Brown"
by SCHULZ
Ethan Frome
Book report: Ethan Frome
Not being a married person, I think it is impossible for me to understand the emotions involved in this novel.
9-20
THAT'S YOUR BOOK REPORT?
SURE
YES, MA'AM? WHY, THANK YOU... I'M GLAD WE AGREE..
YOU HAVE TO LEARN TO TELL IT LIKE IT IS, CHARLIE BROWN..
SCHULZ

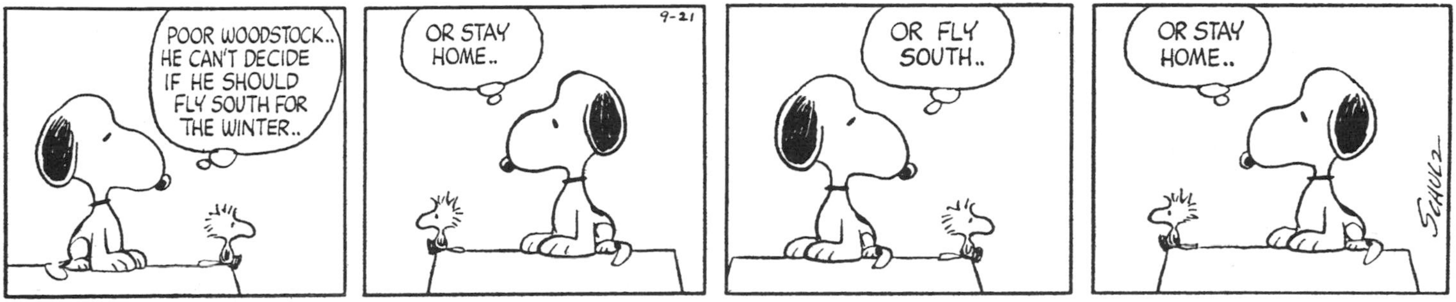

POOR WOODSTOCK.. HE CAN'T DECIDE IF HE SHOULD FLY SOUTH FOR THE WINTER..
9-21
OR STAY HOME..
OR FLY SOUTH..
OR STAY HOME..
SCHULZ

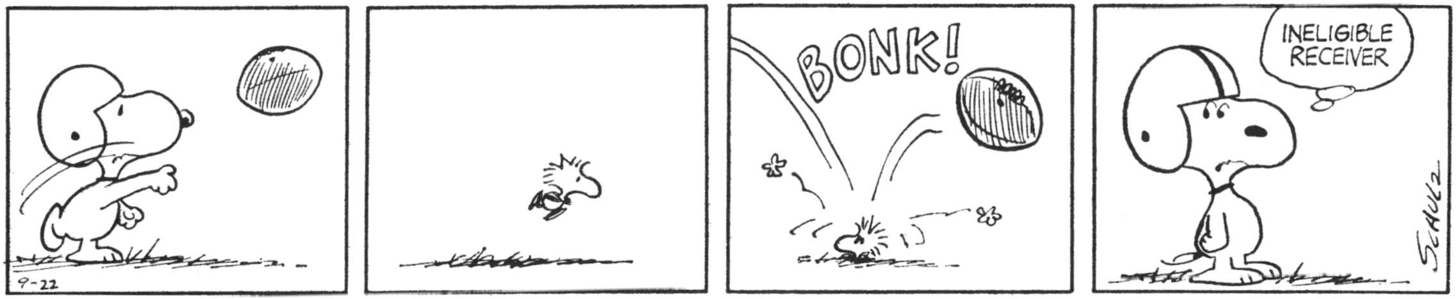

9-22
BONK!
INELIGIBLE RECEIVER
SCHULZ

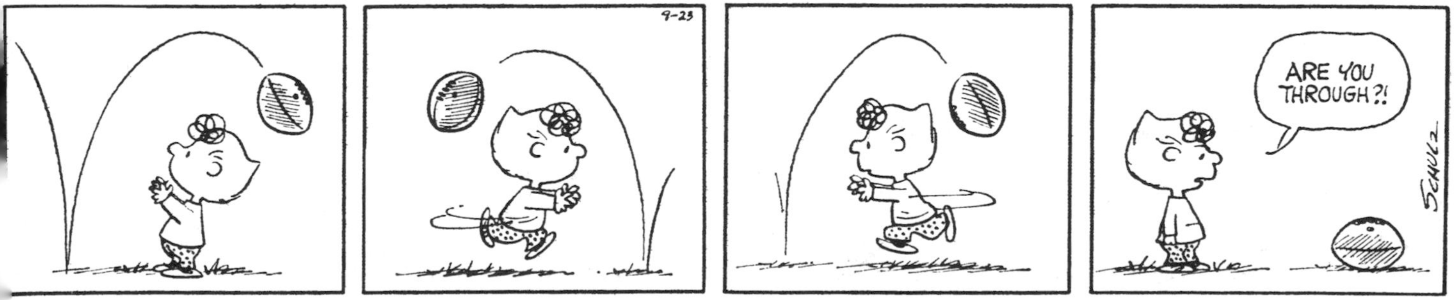

9-23
ARE YOU THROUGH?!
SCHULZ

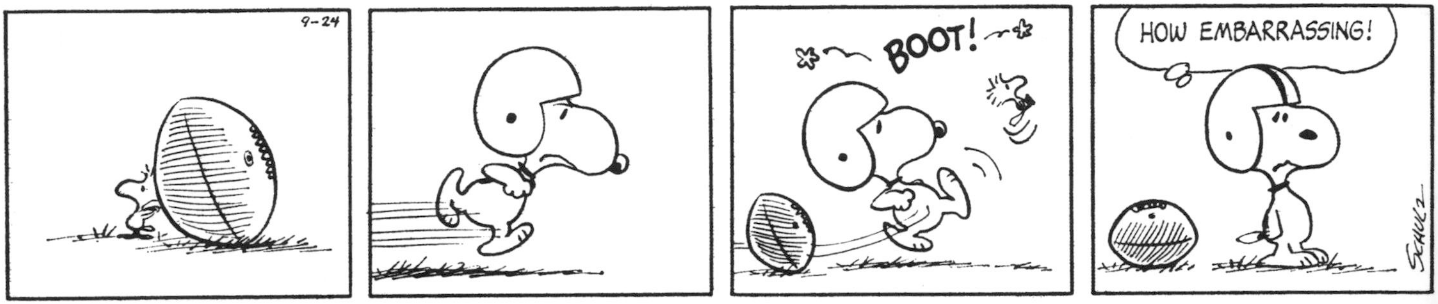
9-24
BOOT!
HOW EMBARRASSING!
SCHULZ

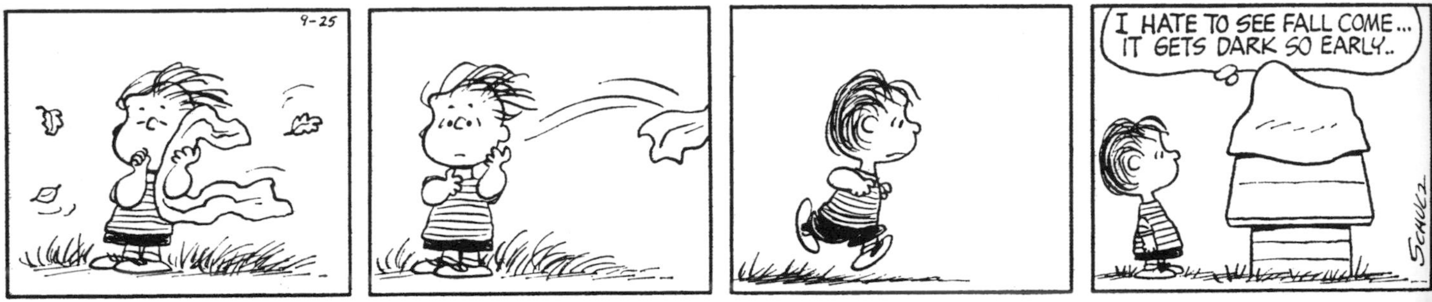
9-25
I HATE TO SEE FALL COME...
IT GETS DARK SO EARLY..
SCHULZ

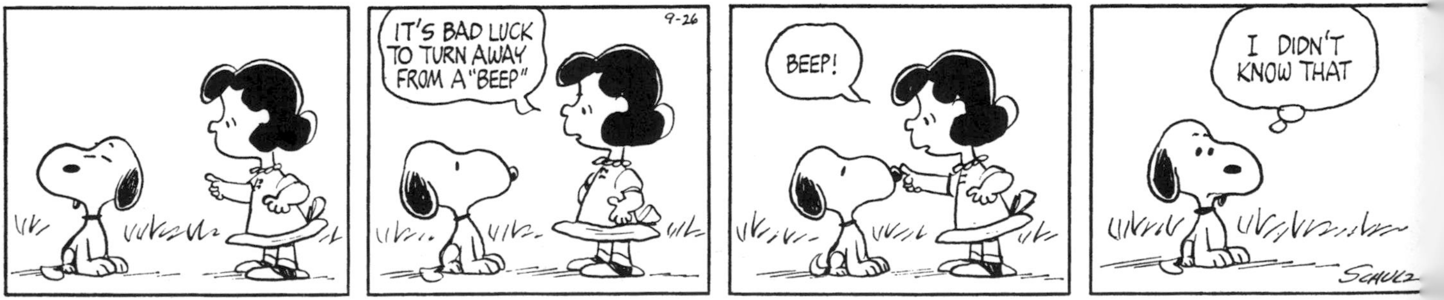
9-26
IT'S BAD LUCK TO TURN AWAY FROM A "BEEP"
BEEP!
I DIDN'T KNOW THAT
SCHULZ

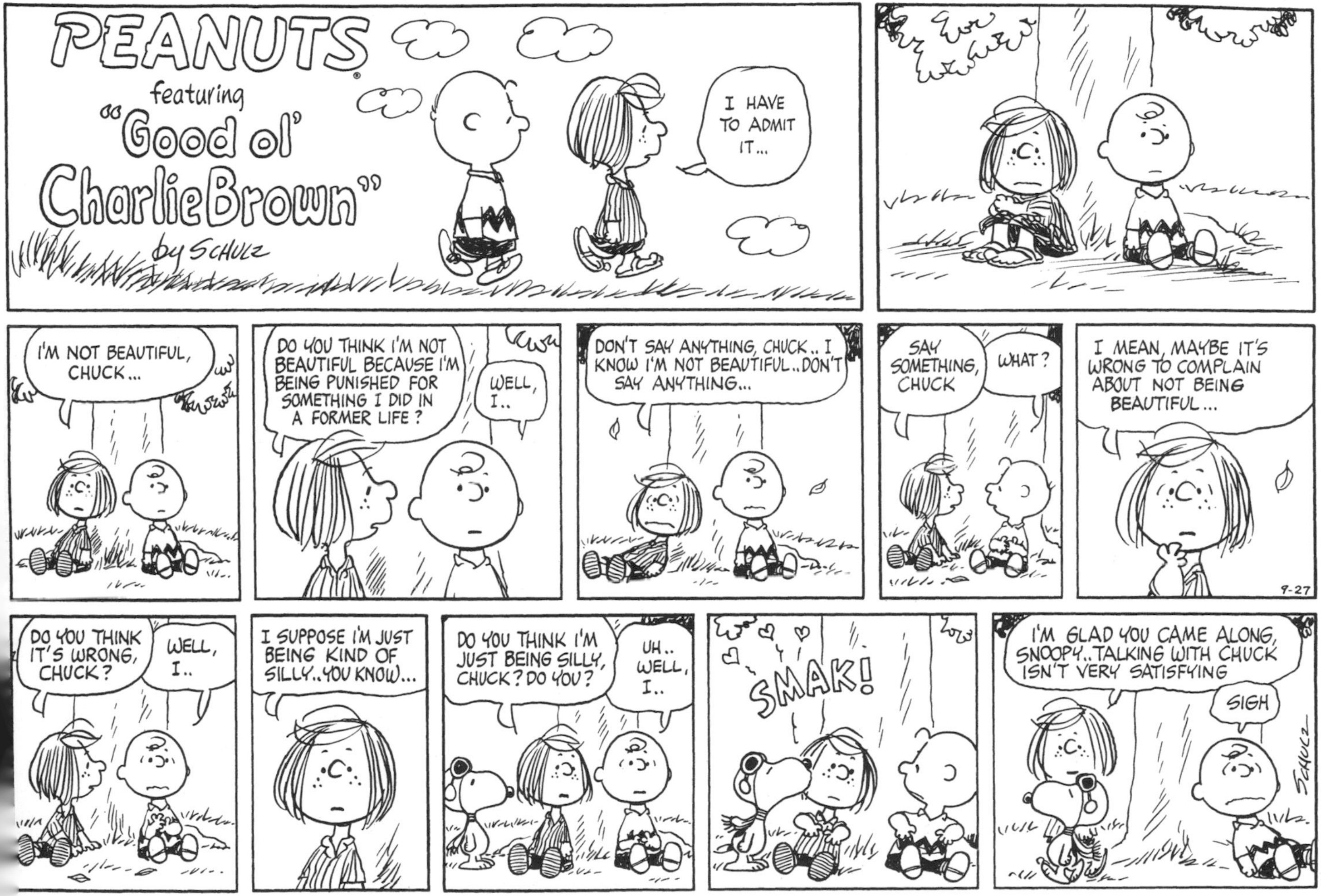
PEANUTS
featuring "Good ol' CharlieBrown"
by SCHULZ
I HAVE TO ADMIT IT...
I'M NOT BEAUTIFUL, CHUCK...
DO YOU THINK I'M NOT BEAUTIFUL BECAUSE I'M BEING PUNISHED FOR SOMETHING I DID IN A FORMER LIFE?
WELL, I..
DON'T SAY ANYTHING, CHUCK.. I KNOW I'M NOT BEAUTIFUL..DON'T SAY ANYTHING...
SAY SOMETHING, CHUCK
WHAT?
I MEAN, MAYBE IT'S WRONG TO COMPLAIN ABOUT NOT BEING BEAUTIFUL...
9-27
DO YOU THINK IT'S WRONG, CHUCK?
WELL, I..
I SUPPOSE I'M JUST BEING KIND OF SILLY..YOU KNOW...
DO YOU THINK I'M JUST BEING SILLY, CHUCK? DO YOU?
UH.. WELL, I..
SMAK!
I'M GLAD YOU CAME ALONG, SNOOPY..TALKING WITH CHUCK ISN'T VERY SATISFYING
SIGH
SCHULZ

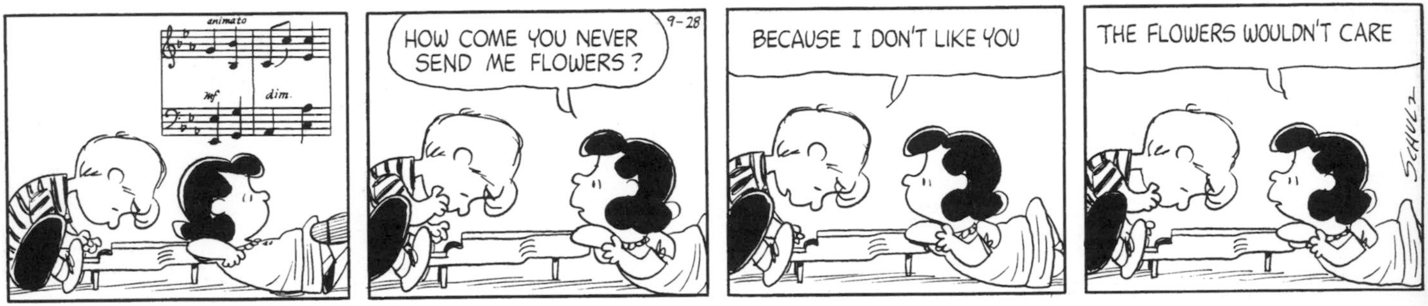
animato
mf
dim.
9-28
HOW COME YOU NEVER SEND ME FLOWERS?
BECAUSE I DON'T LIKE YOU
THE FLOWERS WOULDN'T CARE
SCHULZ

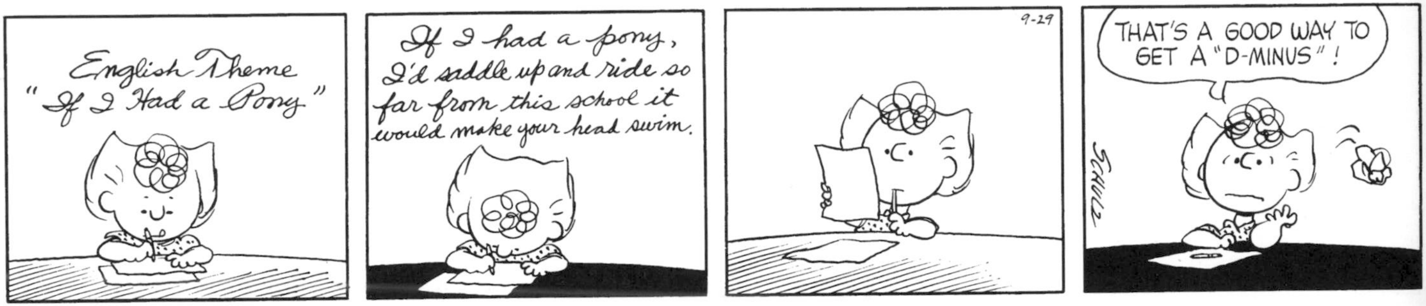
English Theme "If I Had a Pony"
If I had a pony, I'd saddle up and ride so far from this school it would make your head swim.
9-29
THAT'S A GOOD WAY TO GET A "D-MINUS"!
SCHULZ

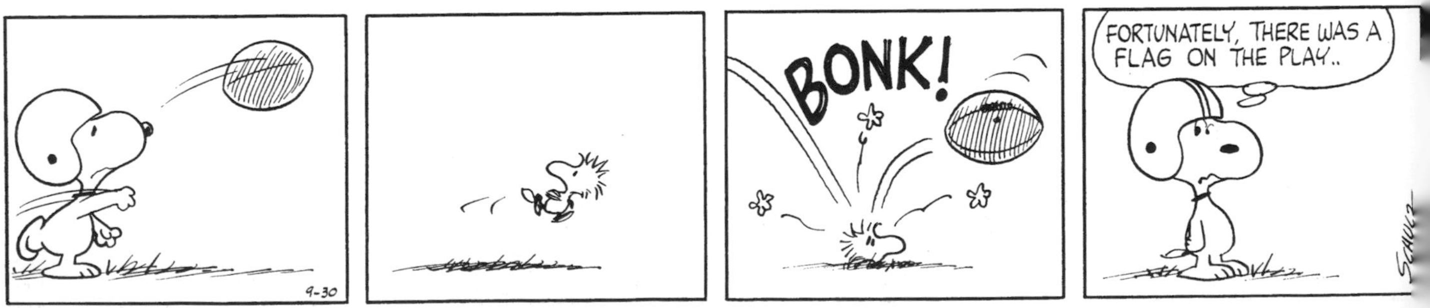
9-30
BONK!
FORTUNATELY, THERE WAS A FLAG ON THE PLAY..
SCHULZ

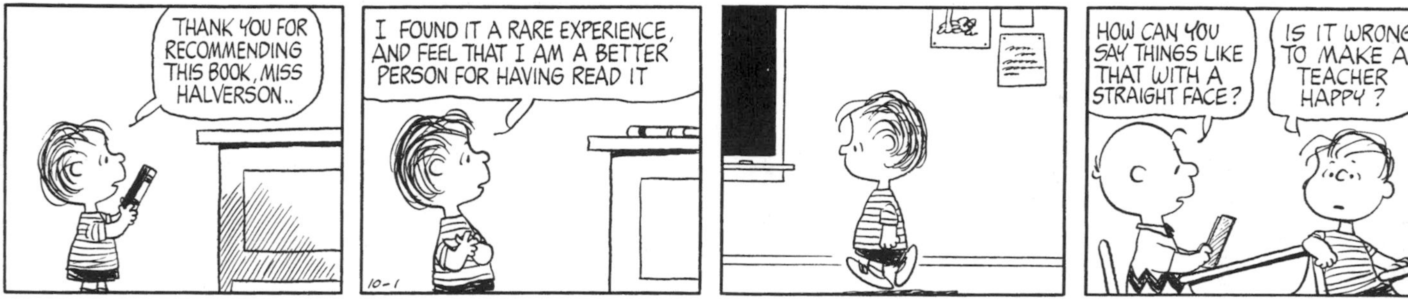
THANK YOU FOR RECOMMENDING THIS BOOK, MISS HALVERSON..
I FOUND IT A RARE EXPERIENCE, AND FEEL THAT I AM A BETTER PERSON FOR HAVING READ IT
HOW CAN YOU SAY THINGS LIKE THAT WITH A STRAIGHT FACE?
IS IT WRONG TO MAKE A TEACHER HAPPY?
SCHULZ
10-1

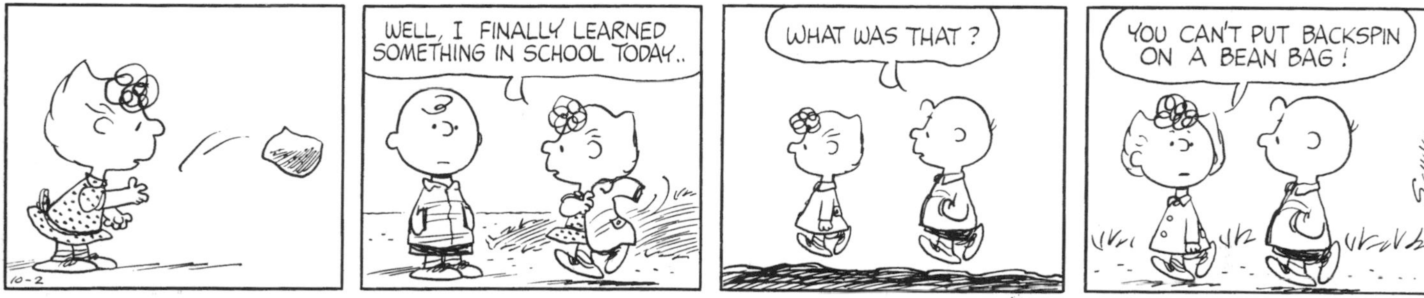
10-2
WELL, I FINALLY LEARNED SOMETHING IN SCHOOL TODAY..
WHAT WAS THAT?
YOU CAN'T PUT BACKSPIN ON A BEAN BAG!
SCHULZ

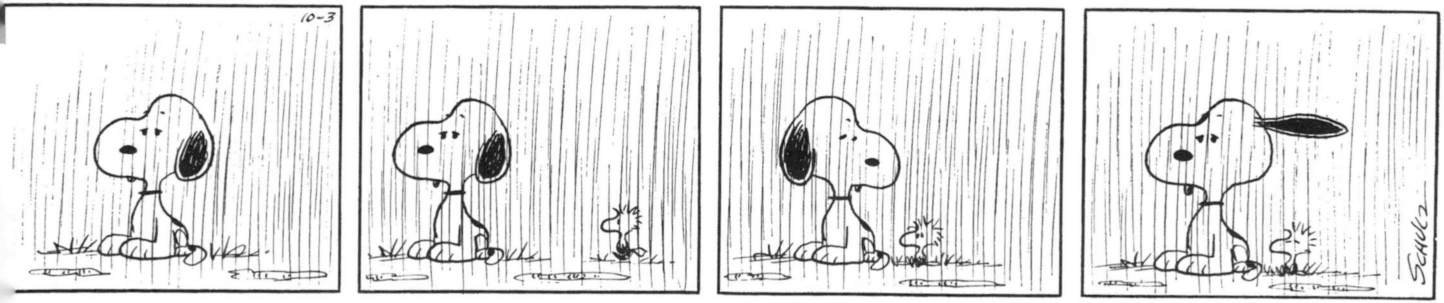
10-3
SCHULZ

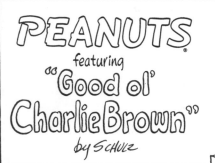

PEANUTS featuring "Good ol' Charlie Brown" by SCHULZ

!

HEY, CHUCK, COME ON OVER, AND SEE WHAT MY DAD GAVE ME FOR MY BIRTHDAY..

ROSES!

WOW!

AND YOU KNOW WHAT HE SAID?

10-4

HE SAID THAT I'M GROWING UP FAST, AND SOON I'LL BE A BEAUTIFUL YOUNG LADY, AND ALL THE BOYS WILL BE CALLING ME UP SO HE JUST WANTED TO BE THE FIRST ONE IN MY LIFE TO GIVE ME A DOZEN ROSES!

HE CALLS ME "A RARE GEM"

YOUR DAD LIKES YOU... HAPPY BIRTHDAY..

SUDDENLY, I FEEL VERY FEMININE!

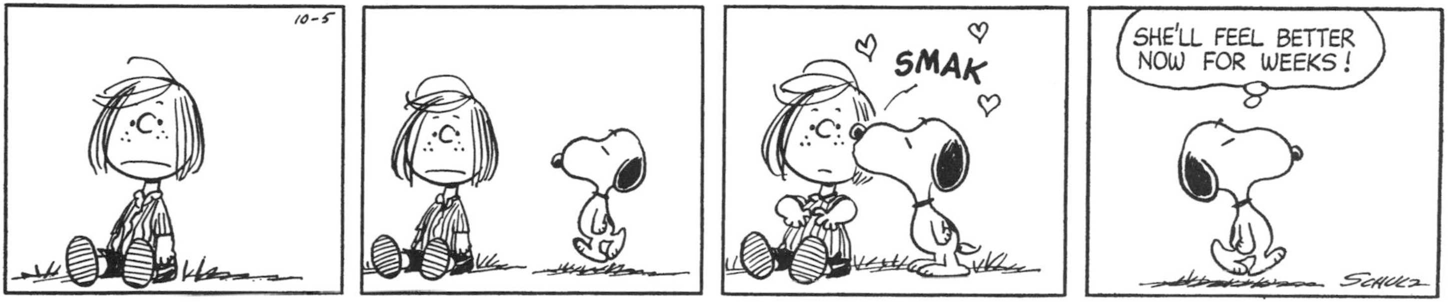
10-5
SMAK
SHE'LL FEEL BETTER NOW FOR WEEKS!
SCHULZ

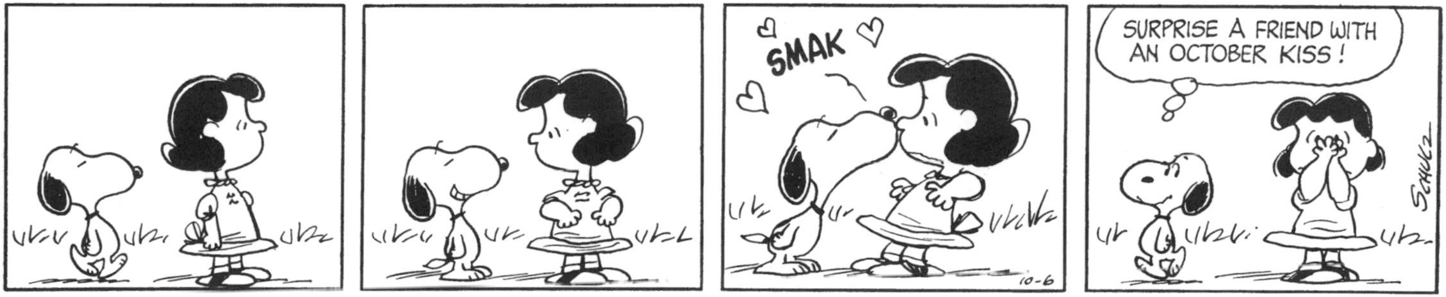
SMAK
10-6
SURPRISE A FRIEND WITH AN OCTOBER KISS!
SCHULZ

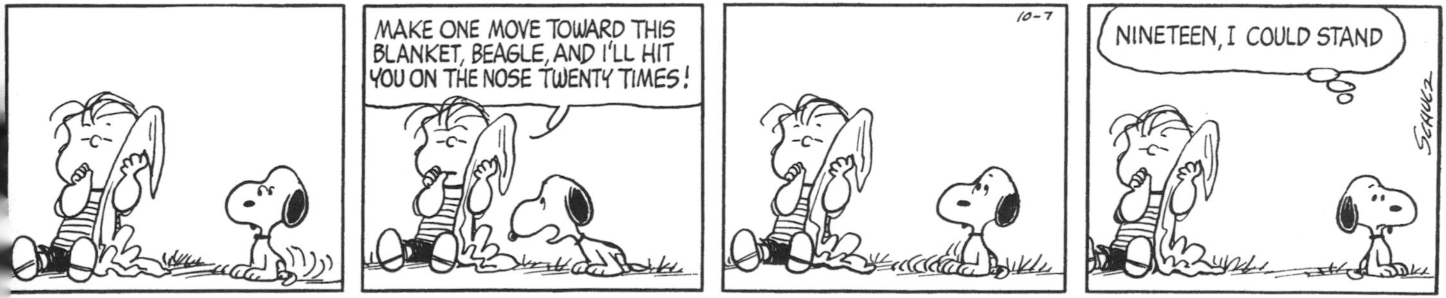
MAKE ONE MOVE TOWARD THIS BLANKET, BEAGLE, AND I'LL HIT YOU ON THE NOSE TWENTY TIMES!
10-7
NINETEEN, I COULD STAND
SCHULZ

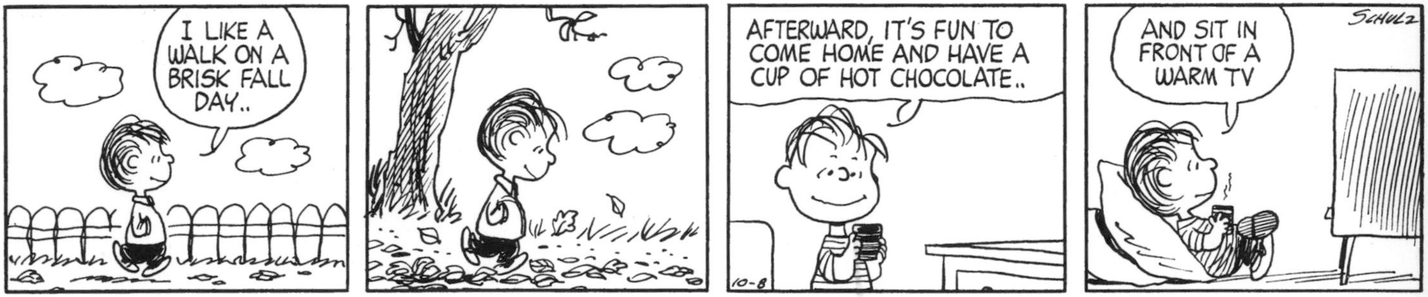
I LIKE A WALK ON A BRISK FALL DAY..
AFTERWARD, IT'S FUN TO COME HOME AND HAVE A CUP OF HOT CHOCOLATE..
AND SIT IN FRONT OF A WARM TV

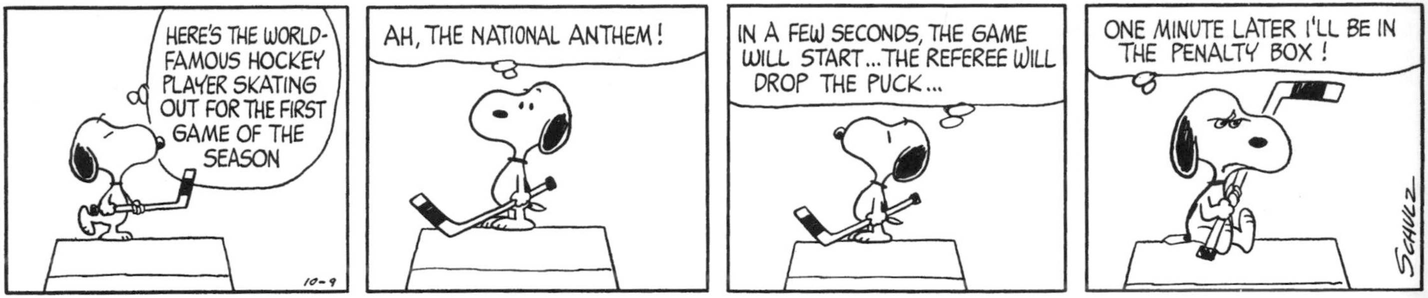
HERE'S THE WORLD-FAMOUS HOCKEY PLAYER SKATING OUT FOR THE FIRST GAME OF THE SEASON
AH, THE NATIONAL ANTHEM!
IN A FEW SECONDS, THE GAME WILL START...THE REFEREE WILL DROP THE PUCK...
ONE MINUTE LATER I'LL BE IN THE PENALTY BOX!

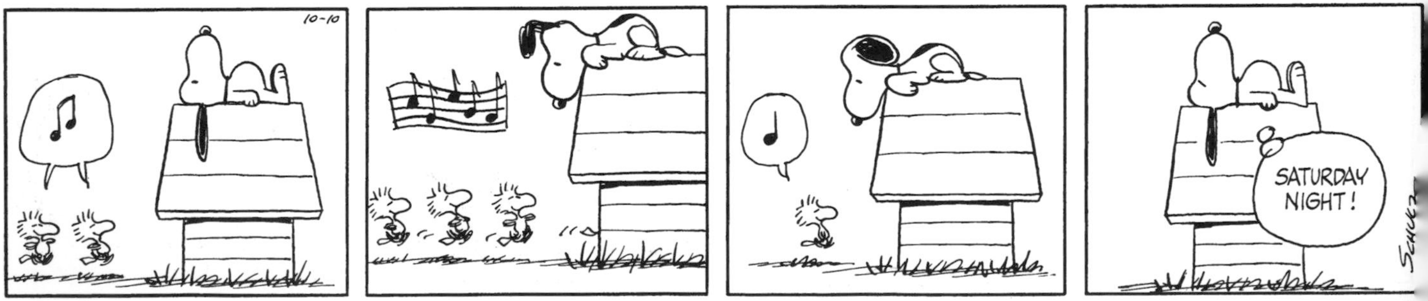
SATURDAY NIGHT!

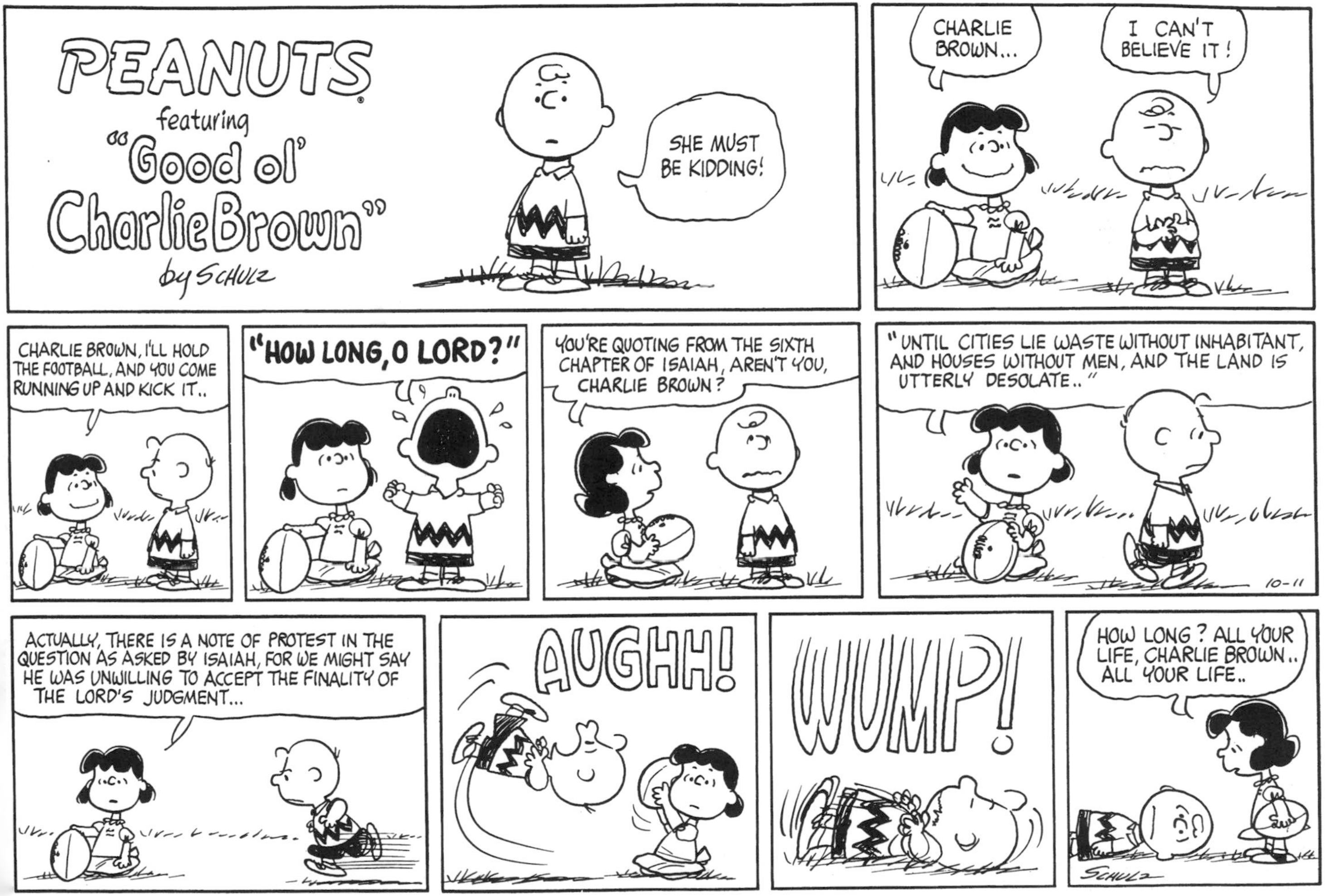
PEANUTS
featuring "Good ol' CharlieBrown"
by SCHULZ
SHE MUST BE KIDDING!
CHARLIE BROWN...
I CAN'T BELIEVE IT!
CHARLIE BROWN, I'LL HOLD THE FOOTBALL, AND YOU COME RUNNING UP AND KICK IT..
"HOW LONG, O LORD?"
YOU'RE QUOTING FROM THE SIXTH CHAPTER OF ISAIAH, AREN'T YOU, CHARLIE BROWN?
"UNTIL CITIES LIE WASTE WITHOUT INHABITANT, AND HOUSES WITHOUT MEN, AND THE LAND IS UTTERLY DESOLATE.."
10-11
ACTUALLY, THERE IS A NOTE OF PROTEST IN THE QUESTION AS ASKED BY ISAIAH, FOR WE MIGHT SAY HE WAS UNWILLING TO ACCEPT THE FINALITY OF THE LORD'S JUDGMENT...
AUGHH!
WUMP!
HOW LONG? ALL YOUR LIFE, CHARLIE BROWN.. ALL YOUR LIFE..
SCHULZ

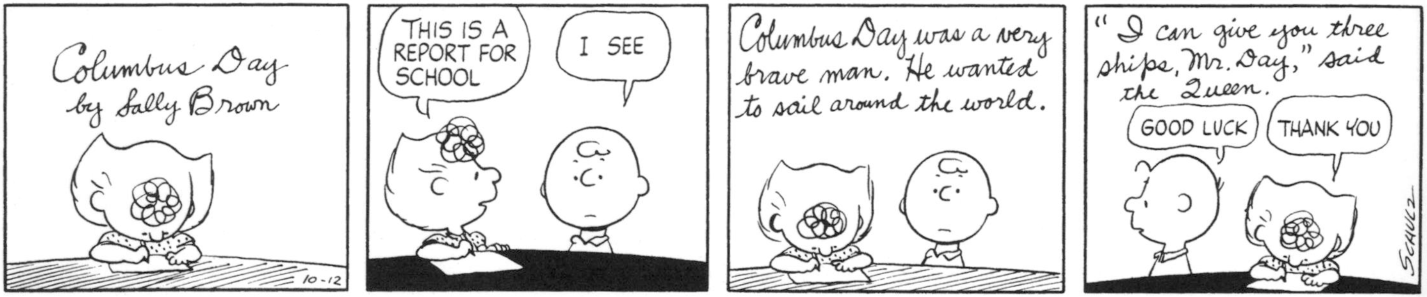
Columbus Day
by Sally Brown
10-12
THIS IS A REPORT FOR SCHOOL
I SEE
Columbus Day was a very brave man. He wanted to sail around the world.
"I can give you three ships, Mr. Day," said the Queen.
GOOD LUCK
THANK YOU
SCHULZ

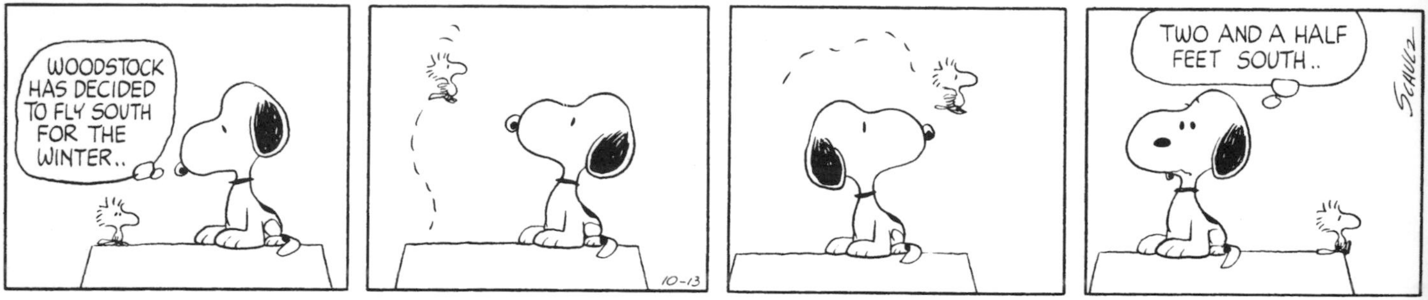
WOODSTOCK HAS DECIDED TO FLY SOUTH FOR THE WINTER..
10-13
TWO AND A HALF FEET SOUTH..
SCHULZ

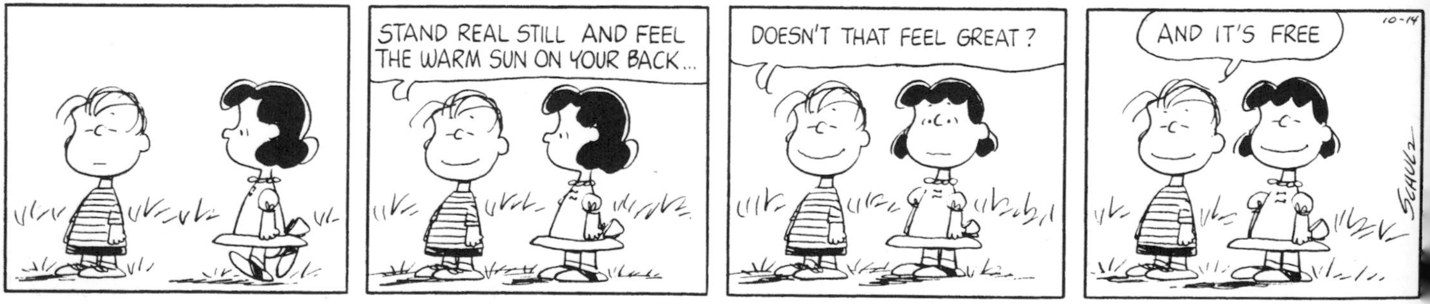
STAND REAL STILL AND FEEL THE WARM SUN ON YOUR BACK...
DOESN'T THAT FEEL GREAT ?
AND IT'S FREE
10-14
SCHULZ

Panel 2: WHAT WOULD YOU DO IF YOU DIDN'T HAVE ME TO BRING YOU YOUR TOASTED ENGLISH MUFFIN EVERY MORNING?

10-15

Panel 4: THAT'S THE SORT OF THING I'D RATHER NOT THINK ABOUT

Panel 3: I JUST SAW A FALLING LEAF! / SO?

10-16

Panel 4: IS IT SPRING ALREADY?

10-17

Panel 4: IT'S AMAZING HOW MANY FRIENDS YOU HAVE AFTER YOUR WAFFLE IRON GETS FIXED

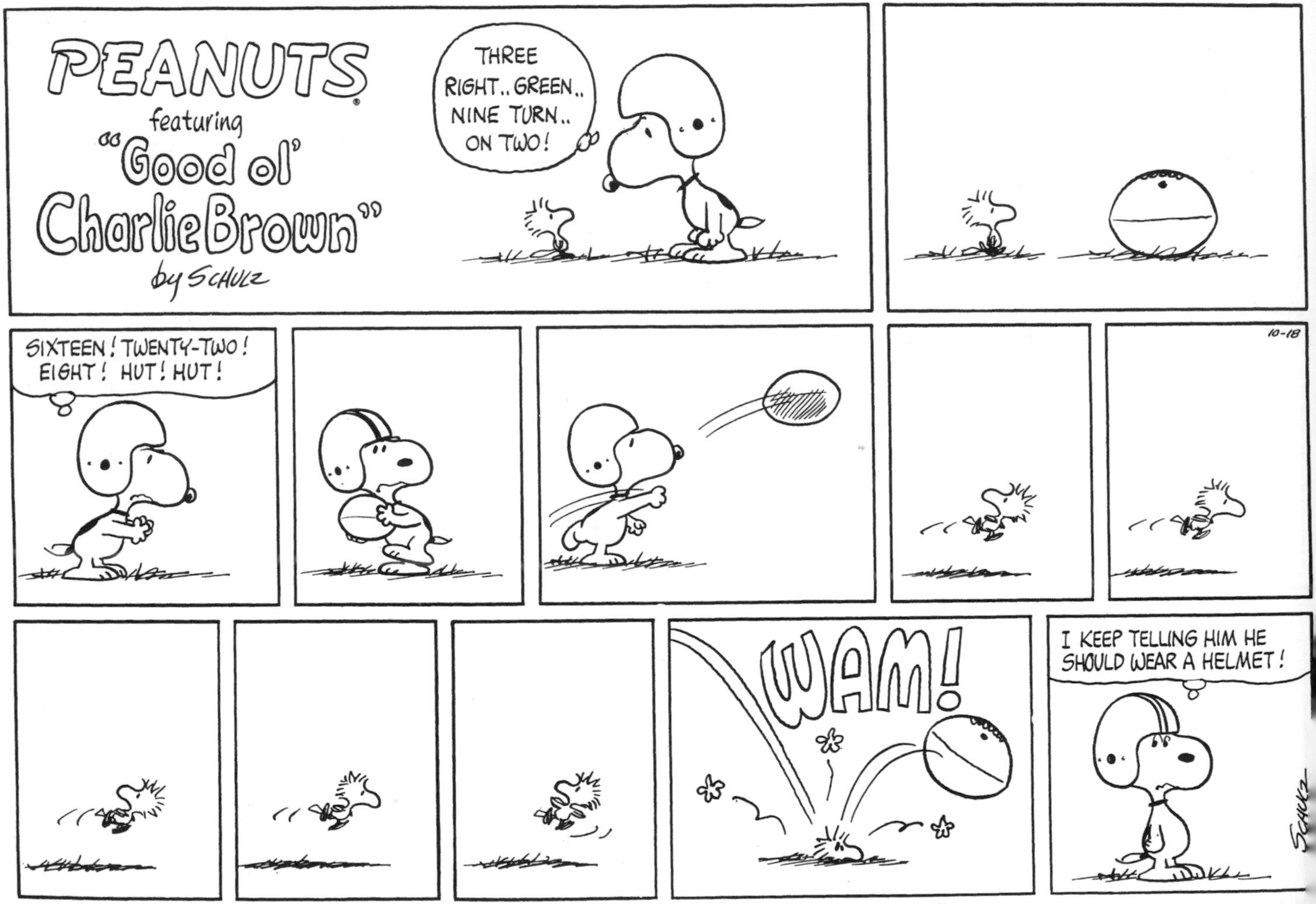
PEANUTS
featuring
"Good ol' Charlie Brown"
by SCHULZ
THREE RIGHT.. GREEN.. NINE TURN.. ON TWO!
10-18
SIXTEEN! TWENTY-TWO! EIGHT! HUT! HUT!
WAM!
I KEEP TELLING HIM HE SHOULD WEAR A HELMET!
SCHULZ

HAVE YOU EVER KNOWN ANYONE WHO WAS HAPPY?

SMAK ♡

AND WAS STILL IN HIS RIGHT MIND, I MEAN..

PSYCHIATRIC HELP 5¢

THE DOCTOR IS IN

IT'S TOO BAD YOU'RE NOT A "SELF-ACTUALIZING" PERSON, CHARLIE BROWN..

SELF-ACTUALIZING PERSONS ARE FREE FROM FEARS AND INHIBITIONS.. THEY ACCEPT THEMSELVES AND THEY ACCEPT OTHERS..... THEY HAVE SELF-ESTEEM AND CONFIDENCE..

CAN I BECOME A SELF-ACTUALIZING PERSON?

THE DOCTOR IS IN

NO WAY! FIVE CENTS, PLEASE..

SIGH

THE DOCTOR IS IN

BONK

I KNEW THAT WOULD HAPPEN... JUST THE OTHER DAY I ASKED HIM, "HOW CAN YOU FLY SOUTH WHEN THERE'S A TREE IN THE WAY?"

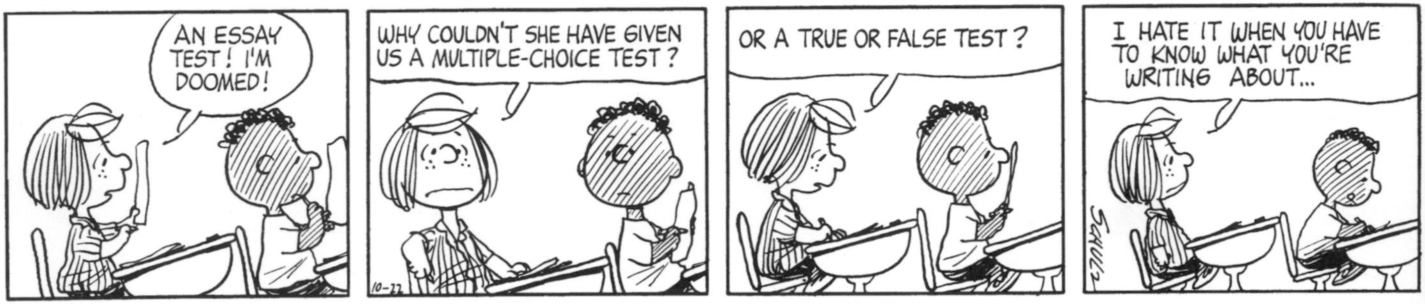
AN ESSAY TEST! I'M DOOMED!
WHY COULDN'T SHE HAVE GIVEN US A MULTIPLE-CHOICE TEST?
OR A TRUE OR FALSE TEST?
I HATE IT WHEN YOU HAVE TO KNOW WHAT YOU'RE WRITING ABOUT...
10-22
SCHULZ

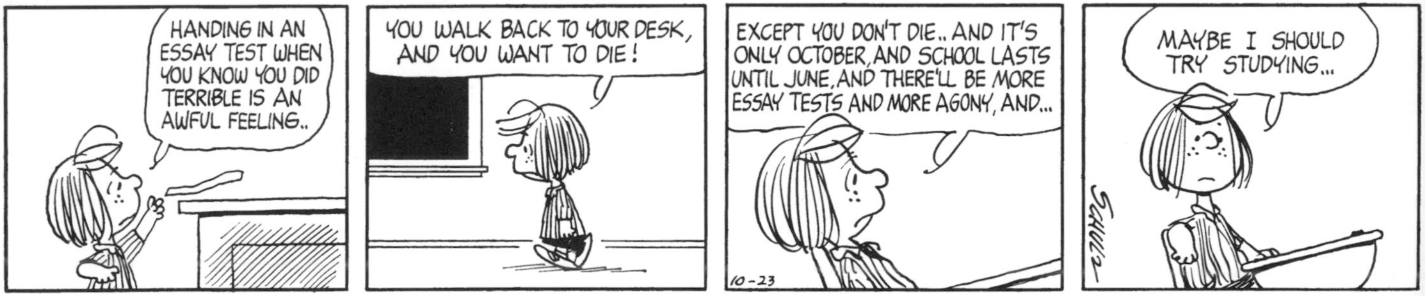
HANDING IN AN ESSAY TEST WHEN YOU KNOW YOU DID TERRIBLE IS AN AWFUL FEELING..
YOU WALK BACK TO YOUR DESK, AND YOU WANT TO DIE!
EXCEPT YOU DON'T DIE.. AND IT'S ONLY OCTOBER, AND SCHOOL LASTS UNTIL JUNE, AND THERE'LL BE MORE ESSAY TESTS AND MORE AGONY, AND...
10-23
MAYBE I SHOULD TRY STUDYING...
SCHULZ

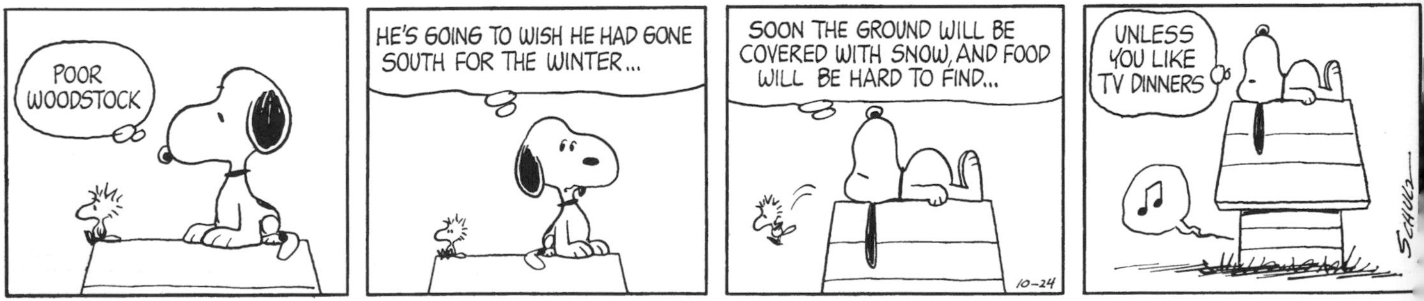
POOR WOODSTOCK
HE'S GOING TO WISH HE HAD GONE SOUTH FOR THE WINTER...
SOON THE GROUND WILL BE COVERED WITH SNOW, AND FOOD WILL BE HARD TO FIND...
10-24
UNLESS YOU LIKE TV DINNERS
SCHULZ

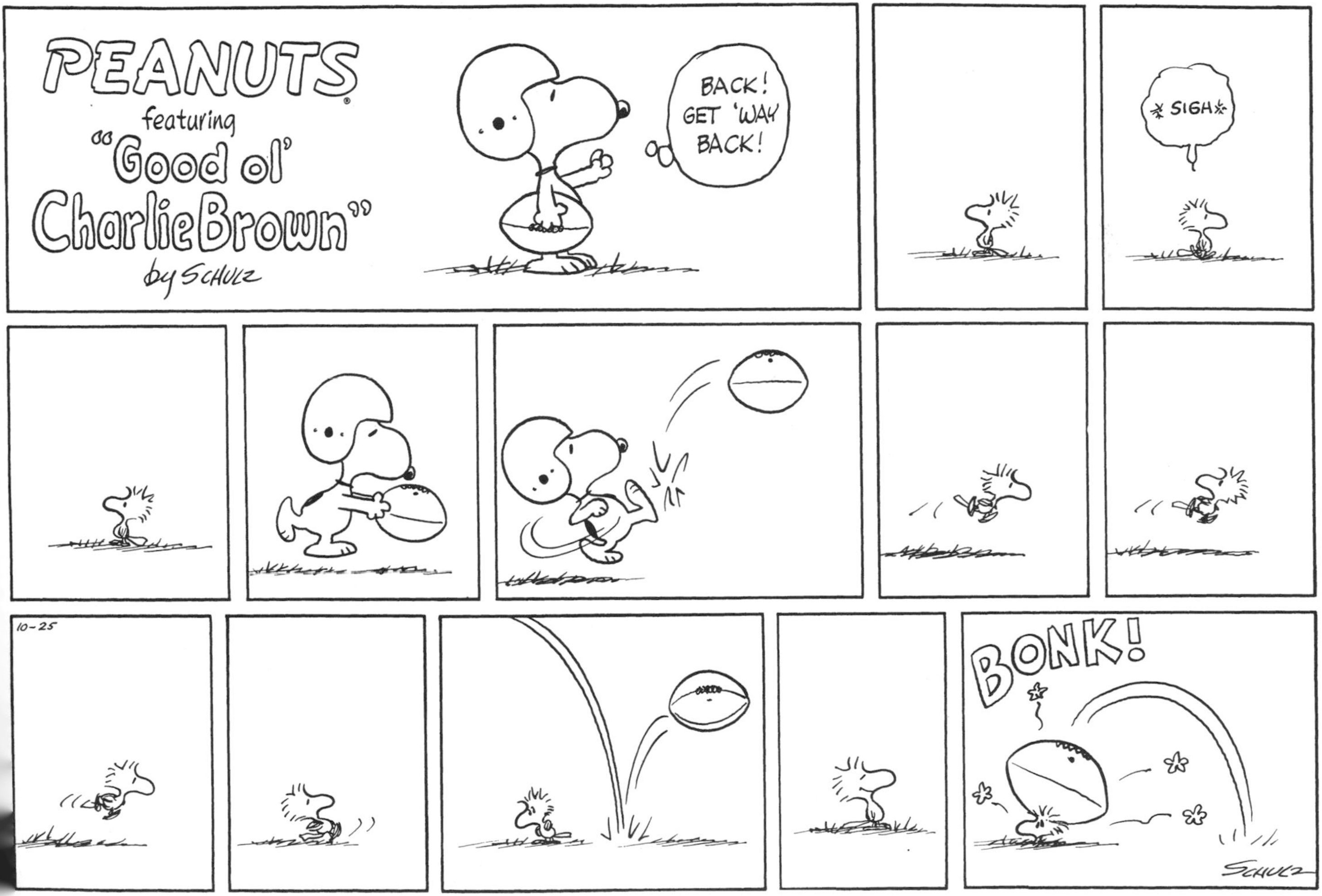
PEANUTS
featuring
"Good ol' Charlie Brown"
by SCHULZ
BACK! GET 'WAY BACK!
SIGH
10-25
BONK!
SCHULZ

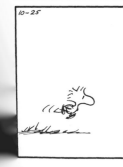

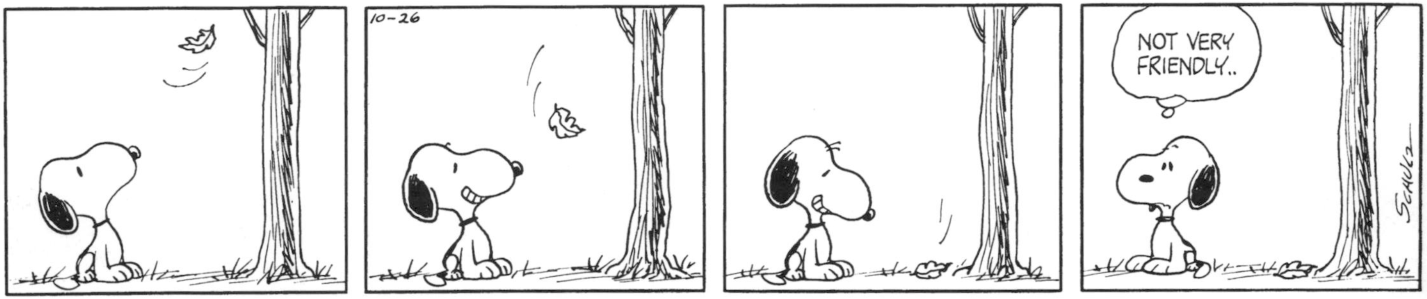
10-26
NOT VERY FRIENDLY..
SCHULZ

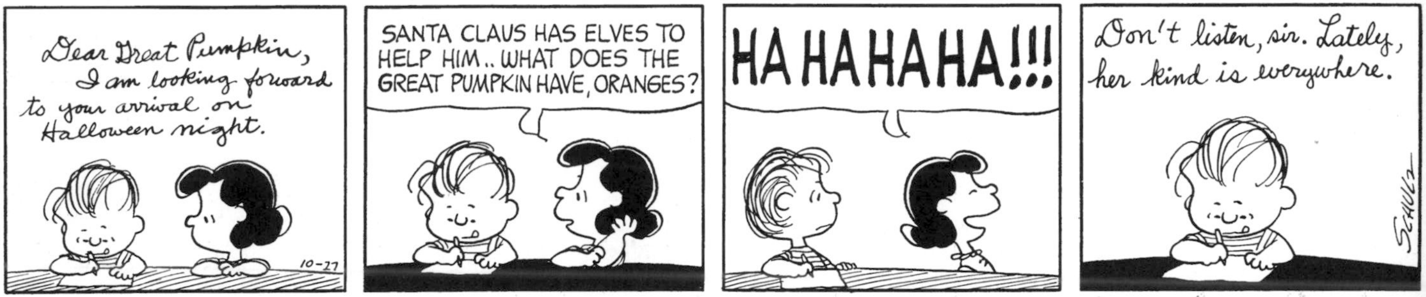
Dear Great Pumpkin,
I am looking forward to your arrival on Halloween night.
10-27
SANTA CLAUS HAS ELVES TO HELP HIM.. WHAT DOES THE GREAT PUMPKIN HAVE, ORANGES?
HA HA HA HA HA!!!
Don't listen, sir. Lately, her kind is everywhere.
SCHULZ

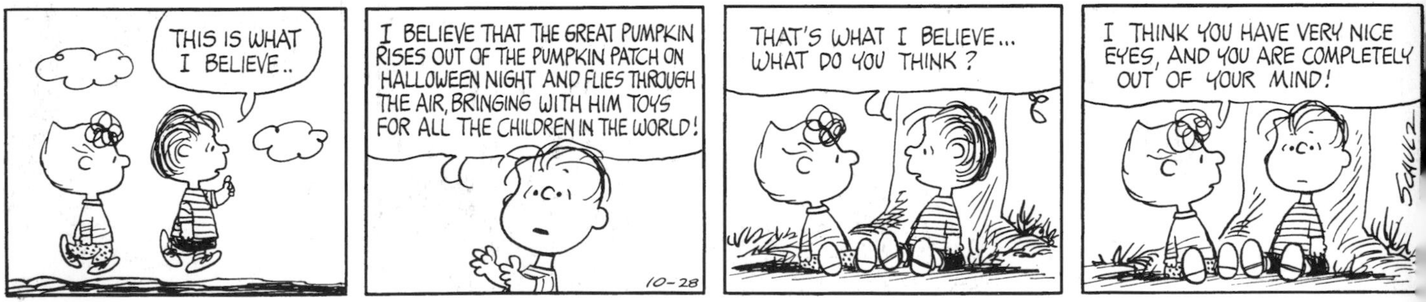
THIS IS WHAT I BELIEVE..
I BELIEVE THAT THE GREAT PUMPKIN RISES OUT OF THE PUMPKIN PATCH ON HALLOWEEN NIGHT AND FLIES THROUGH THE AIR, BRINGING WITH HIM TOYS FOR ALL THE CHILDREN IN THE WORLD!
10-28
THAT'S WHAT I BELIEVE... WHAT DO YOU THINK?
I THINK YOU HAVE VERY NICE EYES, AND YOU ARE COMPLETELY OUT OF YOUR MIND!
SCHULZ

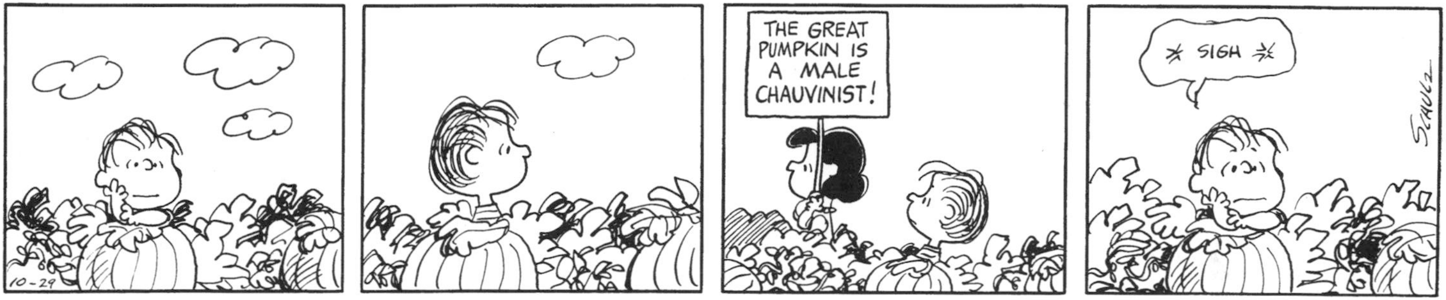
10-29
THE GREAT PUMPKIN IS A MALE CHAUVINIST!
SIGH

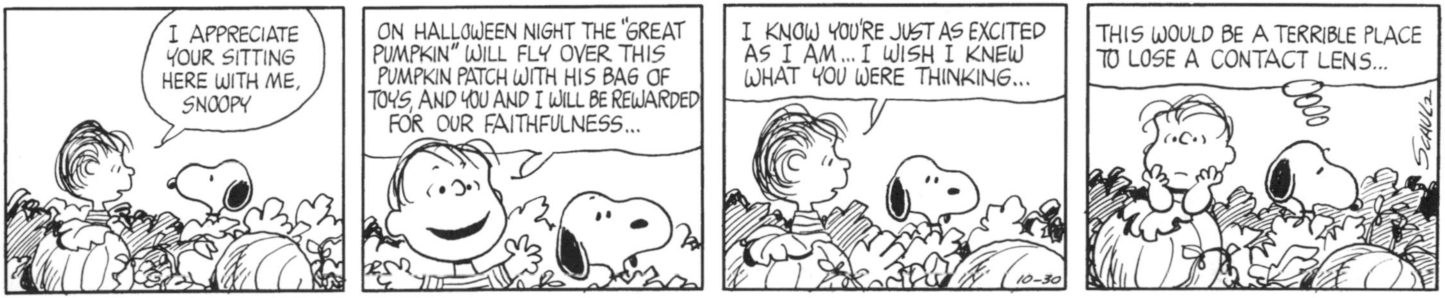
I APPRECIATE YOUR SITTING HERE WITH ME, SNOOPY
ON HALLOWEEN NIGHT THE "GREAT PUMPKIN" WILL FLY OVER THIS PUMPKIN PATCH WITH HIS BAG OF TOYS, AND YOU AND I WILL BE REWARDED FOR OUR FAITHFULNESS...
I KNOW YOU'RE JUST AS EXCITED AS I AM... I WISH I KNEW WHAT YOU WERE THINKING...
10-30
THIS WOULD BE A TERRIBLE PLACE TO LOSE A CONTACT LENS...

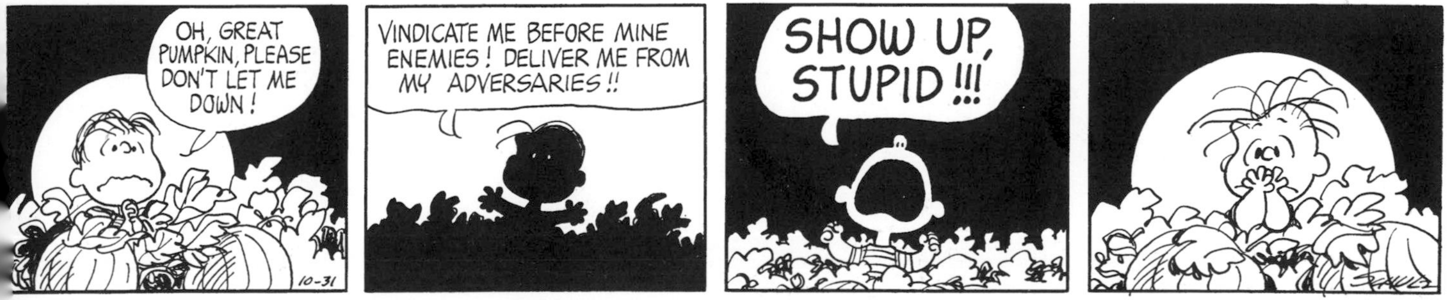
OH, GREAT PUMPKIN, PLEASE DON'T LET ME DOWN!
10-31
VINDICATE ME BEFORE MINE ENEMIES! DELIVER ME FROM MY ADVERSARIES!!
SHOW UP, STUPID!!!

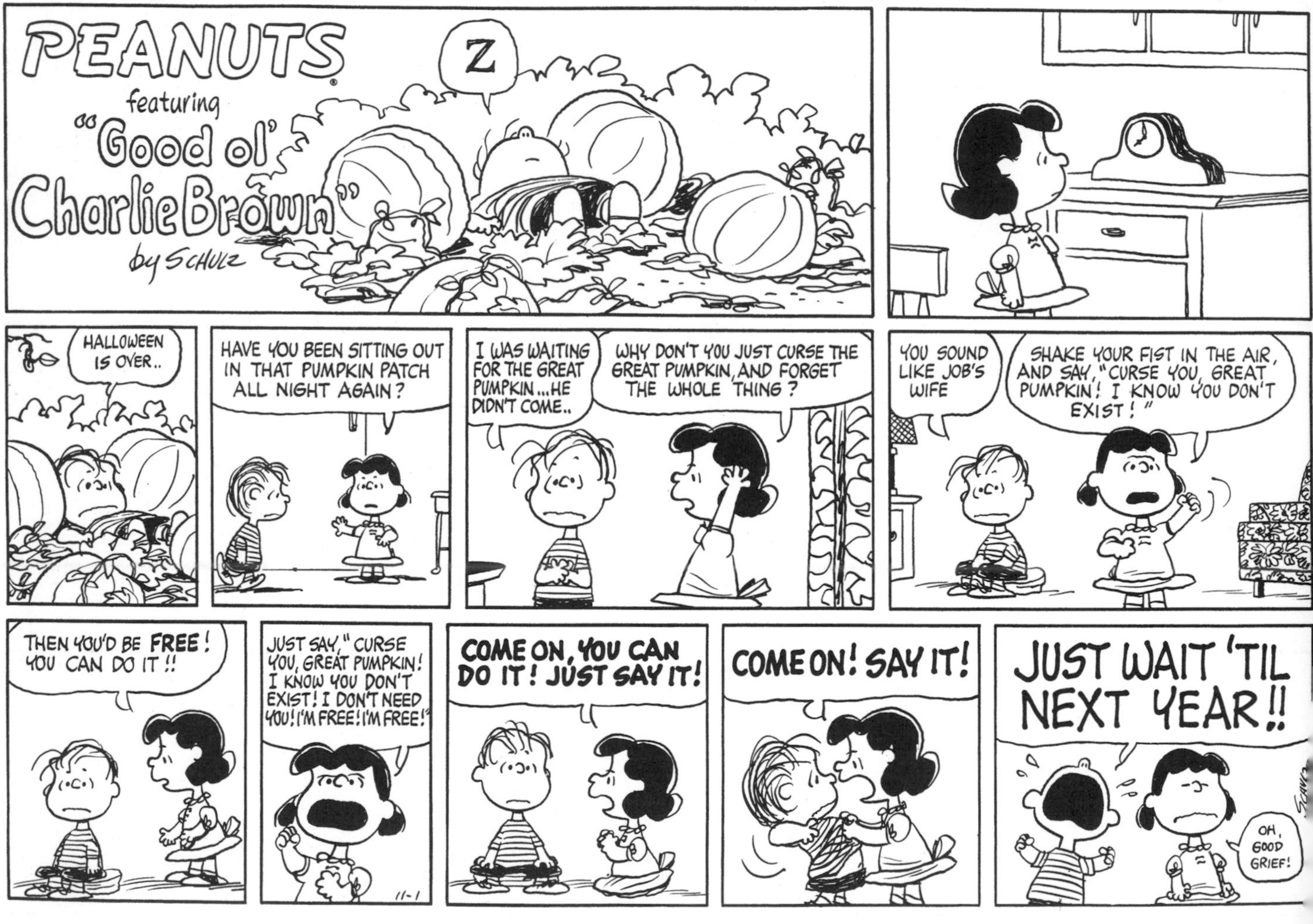
PEANUTS
featuring "Good ol' Charlie Brown"
by SCHULZ
Z
HALLOWEEN IS OVER..
HAVE YOU BEEN SITTING OUT IN THAT PUMPKIN PATCH ALL NIGHT AGAIN?
I WAS WAITING FOR THE GREAT PUMPKIN...HE DIDN'T COME..
WHY DON'T YOU JUST CURSE THE GREAT PUMPKIN, AND FORGET THE WHOLE THING?
YOU SOUND LIKE JOB'S WIFE
SHAKE YOUR FIST IN THE AIR, AND SAY, "CURSE YOU, GREAT PUMPKIN! I KNOW YOU DON'T EXIST!"
THEN YOU'D BE **FREE**! YOU CAN DO IT!!
JUST SAY, "CURSE YOU, GREAT PUMPKIN! I KNOW YOU DON'T EXIST! I DON'T NEED YOU! I'M FREE! I'M FREE!"
11-1
COME ON, YOU CAN DO IT! JUST SAY IT!
COME ON! SAY IT!
JUST WAIT 'TIL NEXT YEAR!!
OH, GOOD GRIEF!

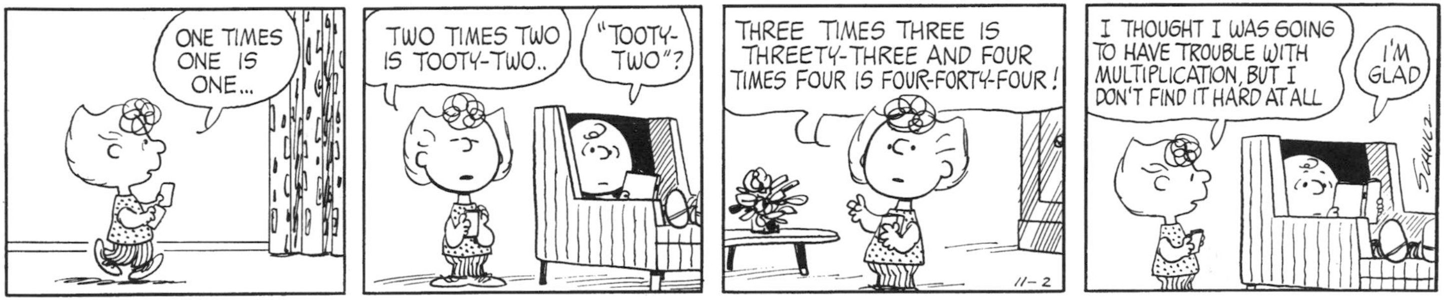
ONE TIMES ONE IS ONE...
TWO TIMES TWO IS TOOTY-TWO..
"TOOTY-TWO"?
THREE TIMES THREE IS THREETY-THREE AND FOUR TIMES FOUR IS FOUR-FORTY-FOUR!
11-2
I THOUGHT I WAS GOING TO HAVE TROUBLE WITH MULTIPLICATION, BUT I DON'T FIND IT HARD AT ALL
I'M GLAD

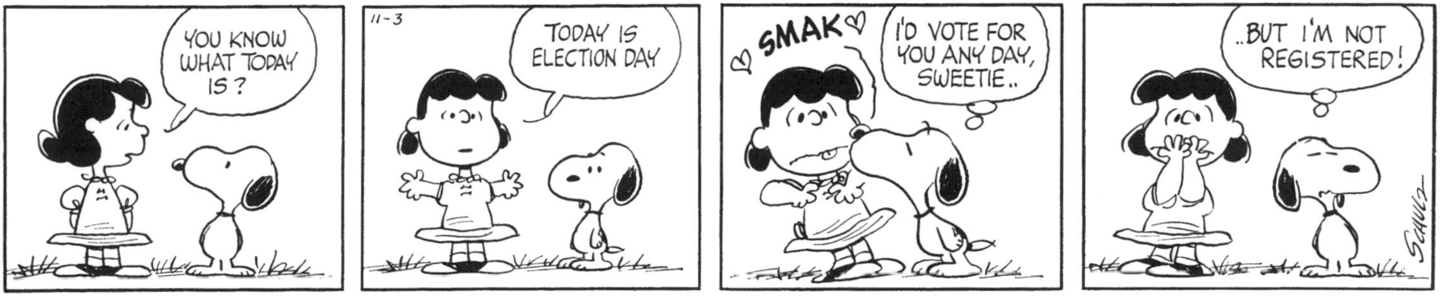
YOU KNOW WHAT TODAY IS?
11-3
TODAY IS ELECTION DAY
SMAK
I'D VOTE FOR YOU ANY DAY, SWEETIE..
..BUT I'M NOT REGISTERED!

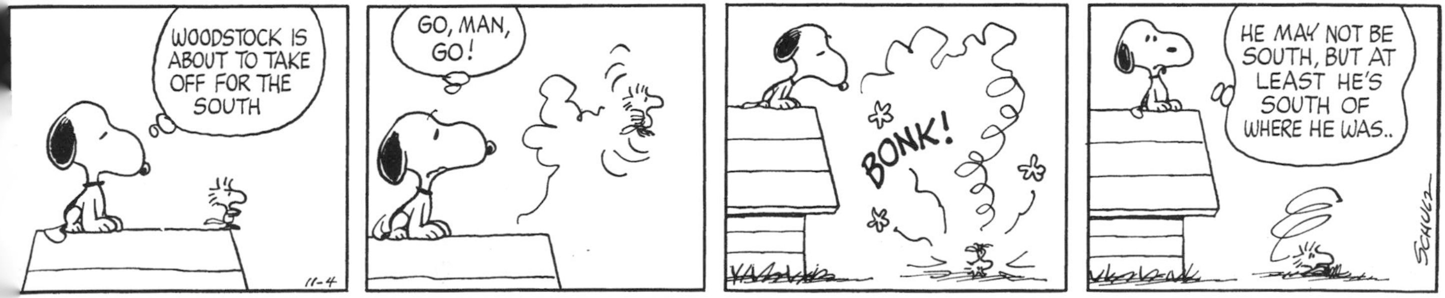
WOODSTOCK IS ABOUT TO TAKE OFF FOR THE SOUTH
11-4
GO, MAN, GO!
BONK!
HE MAY NOT BE SOUTH, BUT AT LEAST HE'S SOUTH OF WHERE HE WAS..

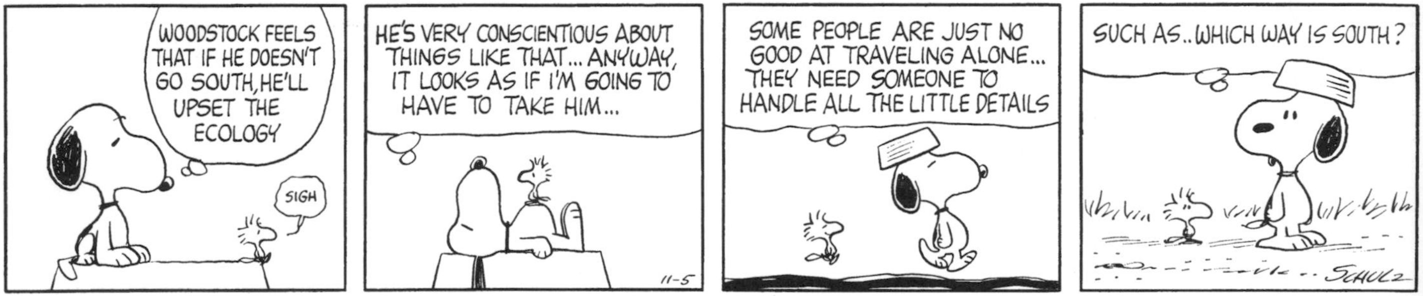
WOODSTOCK FEELS THAT IF HE DOESN'T GO SOUTH, HE'LL UPSET THE ECOLOGY
SIGH
HE'S VERY CONSCIENTIOUS ABOUT THINGS LIKE THAT... ANYWAY, IT LOOKS AS IF I'M GOING TO HAVE TO TAKE HIM...
11-5
SOME PEOPLE ARE JUST NO GOOD AT TRAVELING ALONE... THEY NEED SOMEONE TO HANDLE ALL THE LITTLE DETAILS
SUCH AS.. WHICH WAY IS SOUTH?
SCHULZ

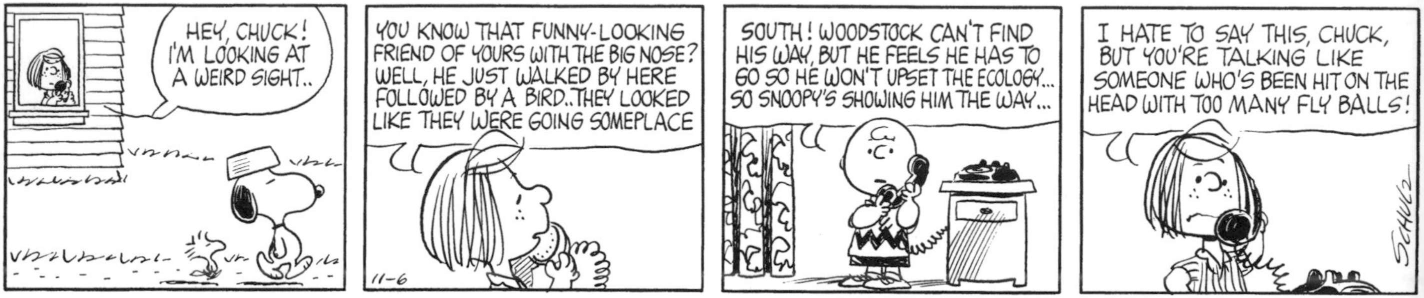
HEY, CHUCK! I'M LOOKING AT A WEIRD SIGHT..
YOU KNOW THAT FUNNY-LOOKING FRIEND OF YOURS WITH THE BIG NOSE? WELL, HE JUST WALKED BY HERE FOLLOWED BY A BIRD.. THEY LOOKED LIKE THEY WERE GOING SOMEPLACE
11-6
SOUTH! WOODSTOCK CAN'T FIND HIS WAY, BUT HE FEELS HE HAS TO GO SO HE WON'T UPSET THE ECOLOGY... SO SNOOPY'S SHOWING HIM THE WAY...
I HATE TO SAY THIS, CHUCK, BUT YOU'RE TALKING LIKE SOMEONE WHO'S BEEN HIT ON THE HEAD WITH TOO MANY FLY BALLS!
SCHULZ

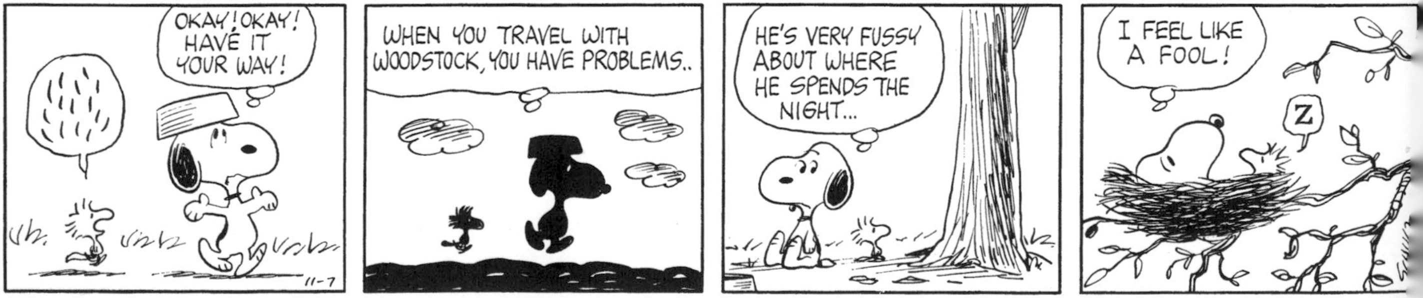
OKAY! OKAY! HAVE IT YOUR WAY!
11-7
WHEN YOU TRAVEL WITH WOODSTOCK, YOU HAVE PROBLEMS..
HE'S VERY FUSSY ABOUT WHERE HE SPENDS THE NIGHT...
I FEEL LIKE A FOOL!
Z

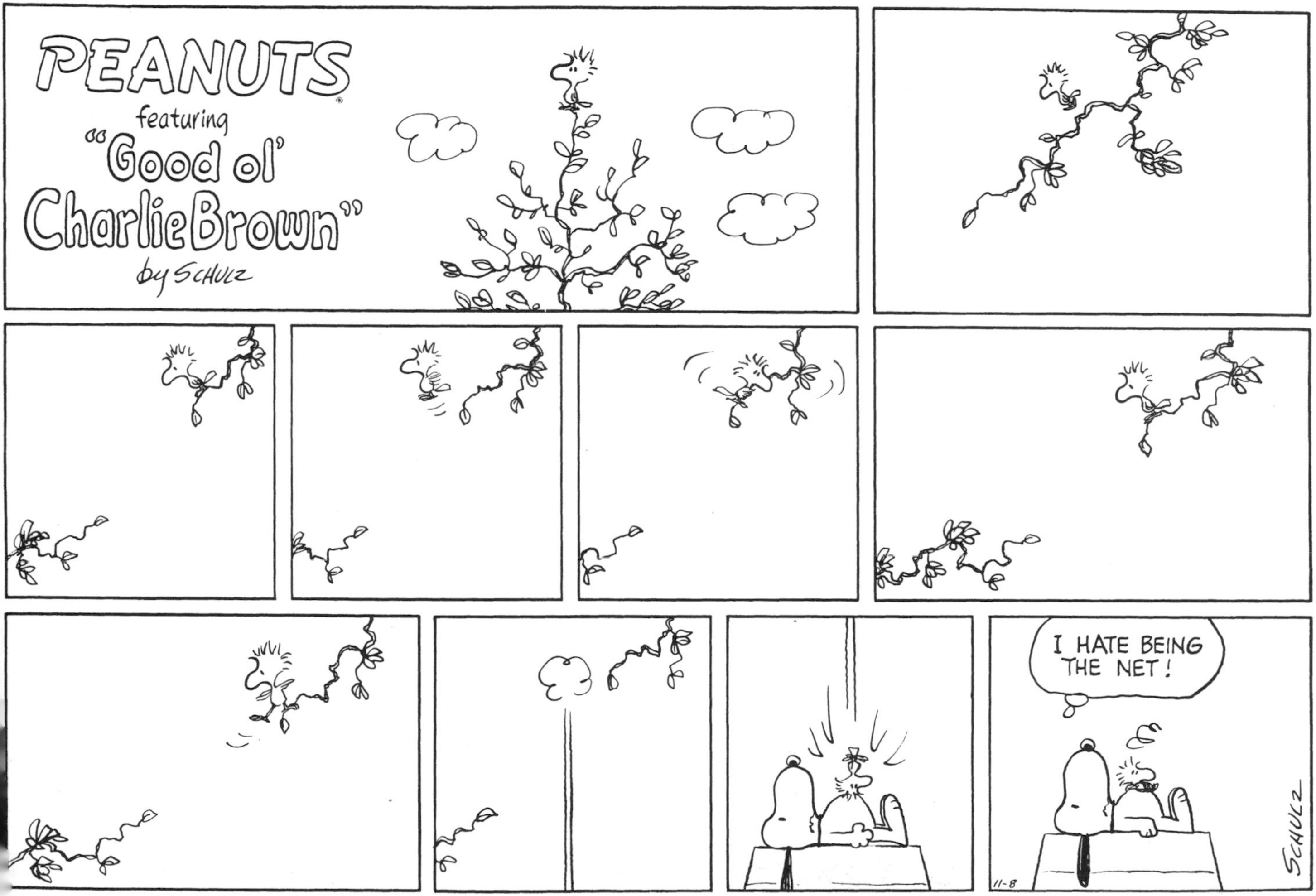
PEANUTS
featuring
"Good ol' Charlie Brown"
by SCHULZ
I HATE BEING THE NET!
11-8
SCHULZ

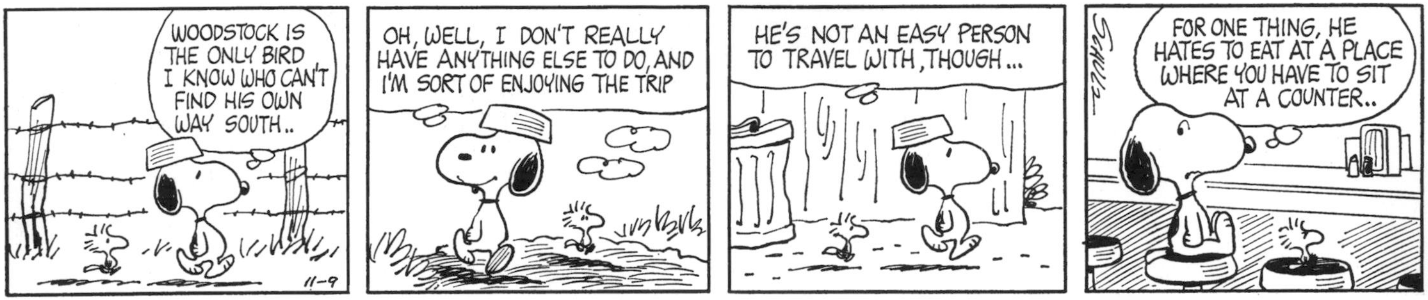
WOODSTOCK IS THE ONLY BIRD I KNOW WHO CAN'T FIND HIS OWN WAY SOUTH..
11-9
OH, WELL, I DON'T REALLY HAVE ANYTHING ELSE TO DO, AND I'M SORT OF ENJOYING THE TRIP
HE'S NOT AN EASY PERSON TO TRAVEL WITH, THOUGH...
SCHULZ
FOR ONE THING, HE HATES TO EAT AT A PLACE WHERE YOU HAVE TO SIT AT A COUNTER..

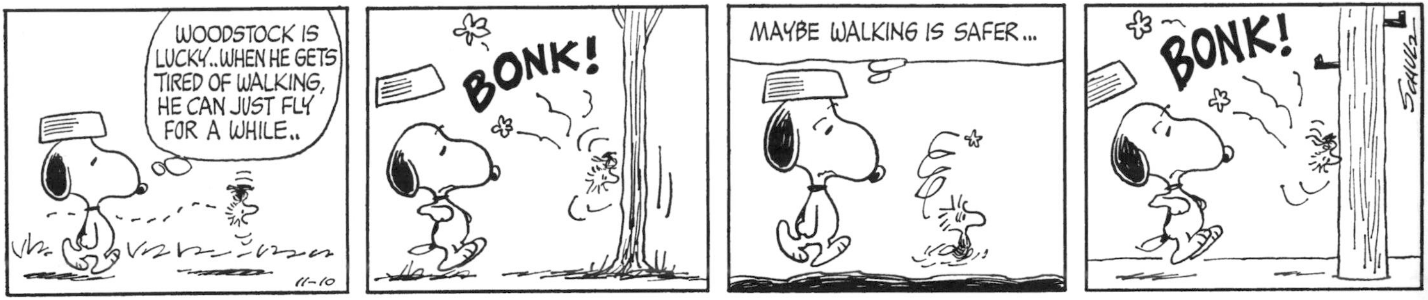
WOODSTOCK IS LUCKY..WHEN HE GETS TIRED OF WALKING, HE CAN JUST FLY FOR A WHILE..
11-10
BONK!
MAYBE WALKING IS SAFER...
BONK!
SCHULZ

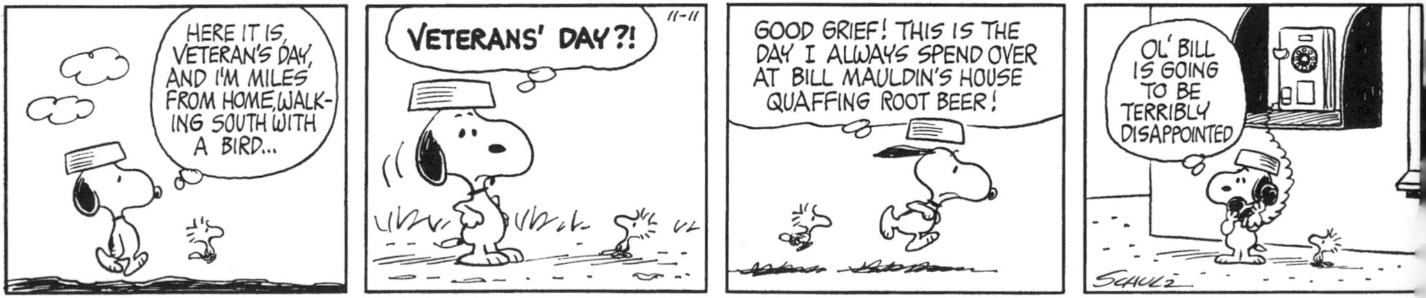
HERE IT IS, VETERAN'S DAY, AND I'M MILES FROM HOME, WALKING SOUTH WITH A BIRD...
11-11
VETERANS' DAY?!
GOOD GRIEF! THIS IS THE DAY I ALWAYS SPEND OVER AT BILL MAULDIN'S HOUSE QUAFFING ROOT BEER!
OL' BILL IS GOING TO BE TERRIBLY DISAPPOINTED
SCHULZ

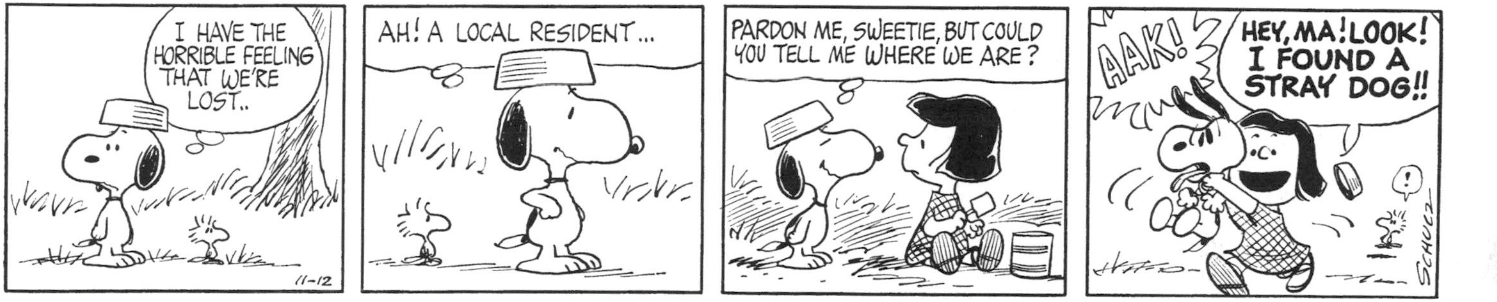
I HAVE THE HORRIBLE FEELING THAT WE'RE LOST..
11-12
AH! A LOCAL RESIDENT...
PARDON ME, SWEETIE, BUT COULD YOU TELL ME WHERE WE ARE?
AAK!
HEY, MA! LOOK! I FOUND A STRAY DOG!!
!
SCHULZ

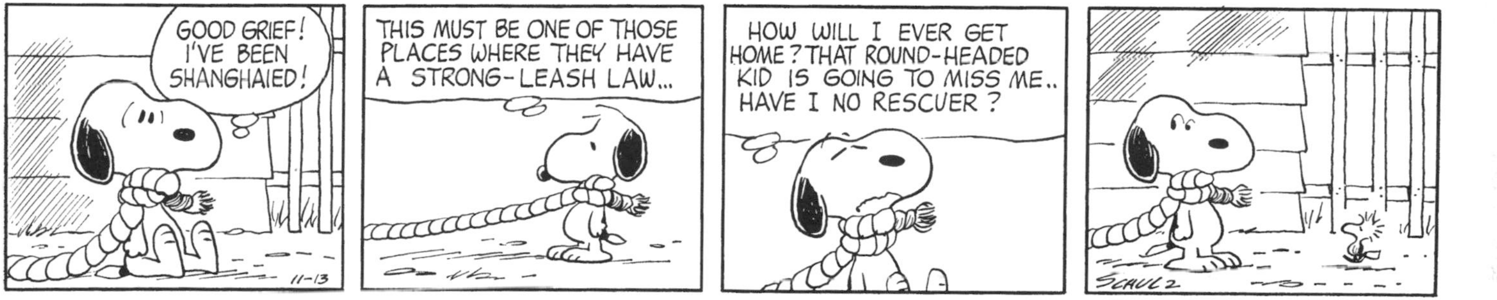
GOOD GRIEF! I'VE BEEN SHANGHAIED!
11-13
THIS MUST BE ONE OF THOSE PLACES WHERE THEY HAVE A STRONG-LEASH LAW...
HOW WILL I EVER GET HOME? THAT ROUND-HEADED KID IS GOING TO MISS ME.. HAVE I NO RESCUER?
SCHULZ

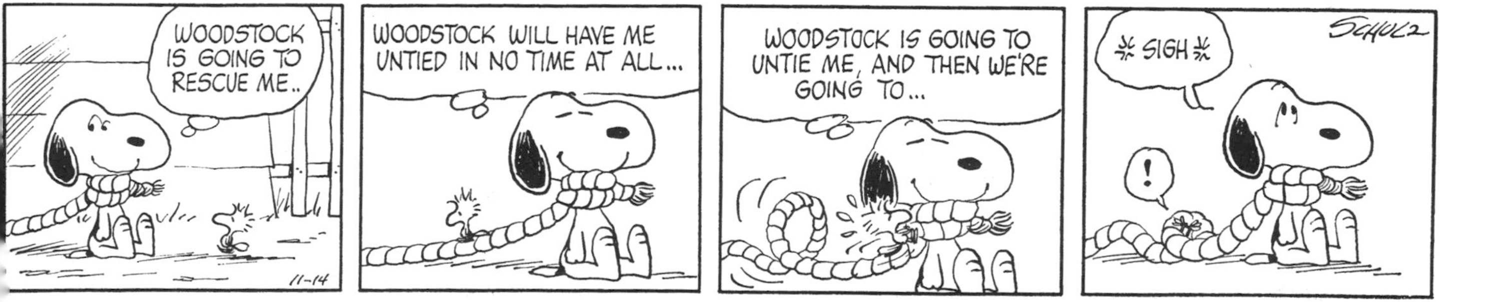
WOODSTOCK IS GOING TO RESCUE ME..
11-14
WOODSTOCK WILL HAVE ME UNTIED IN NO TIME AT ALL...
WOODSTOCK IS GOING TO UNTIE ME, AND THEN WE'RE GOING TO...
SCHULZ
SIGH
!

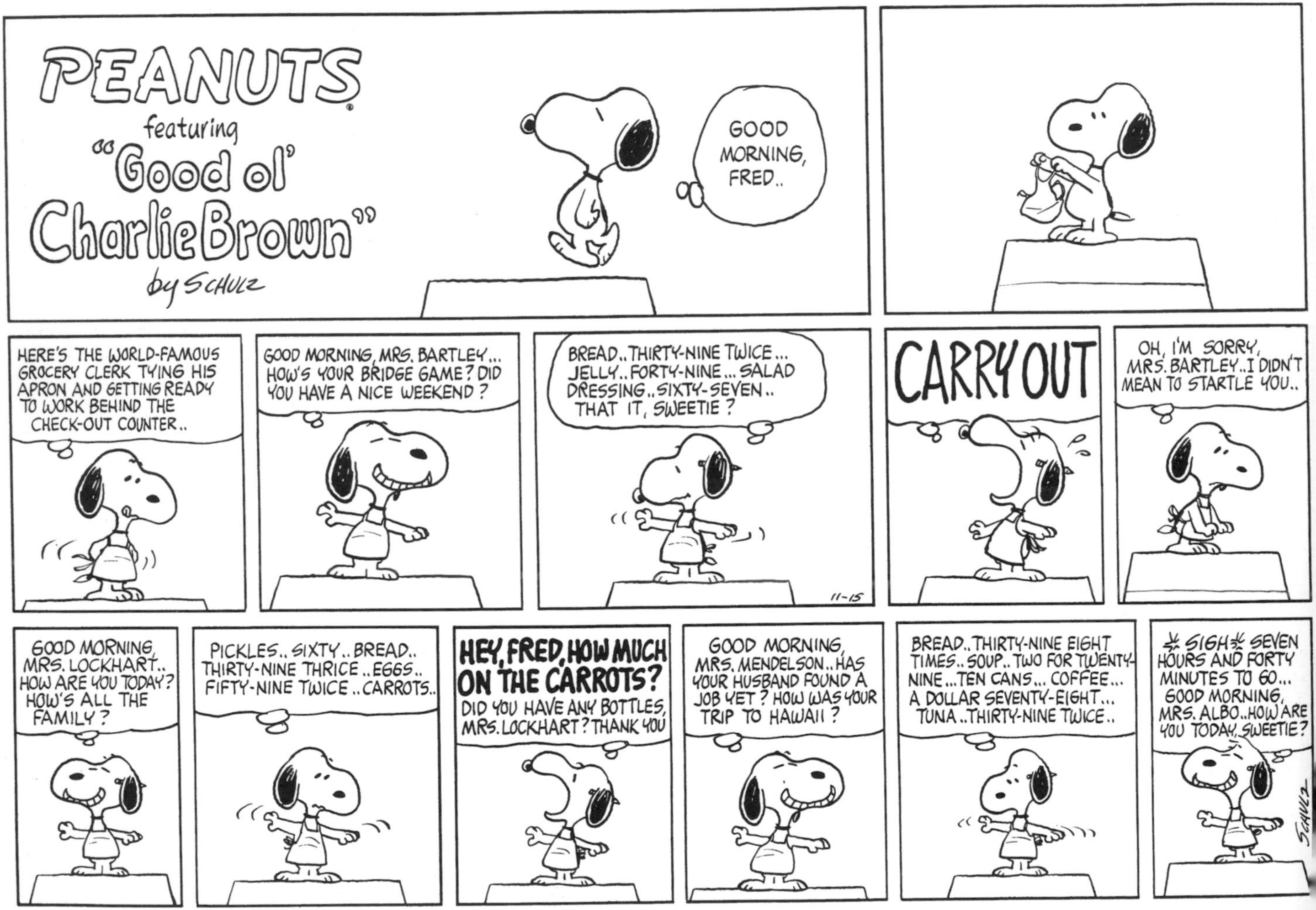
PEANUTS featuring "Good ol' CharlieBrown" by SCHULZ
GOOD MORNING, FRED..
HERE'S THE WORLD-FAMOUS GROCERY CLERK TYING HIS APRON AND GETTING READY TO WORK BEHIND THE CHECK-OUT COUNTER..
GOOD MORNING, MRS. BARTLEY... HOW'S YOUR BRIDGE GAME? DID YOU HAVE A NICE WEEKEND?
BREAD..THIRTY-NINE TWICE... JELLY..FORTY-NINE... SALAD DRESSING..SIXTY-SEVEN.. THAT IT, SWEETIE?
11-15
CARRY OUT
OH, I'M SORRY, MRS. BARTLEY..I DIDN'T MEAN TO STARTLE YOU..
GOOD MORNING, MRS. LOCKHART.. HOW ARE YOU TODAY? HOW'S ALL THE FAMILY?
PICKLES..SIXTY..BREAD.. THIRTY-NINE THRICE..EGGS.. FIFTY-NINE TWICE..CARROTS..
HEY, FRED, HOW MUCH ON THE CARROTS?
DID YOU HAVE ANY BOTTLES, MRS. LOCKHART? THANK YOU
GOOD MORNING, MRS. MENDELSON..HAS YOUR HUSBAND FOUND A JOB YET? HOW WAS YOUR TRIP TO HAWAII?
BREAD..THIRTY-NINE EIGHT TIMES..SOUP..TWO FOR TWENTY-NINE...TEN CANS... COFFEE... A DOLLAR SEVENTY-EIGHT... TUNA..THIRTY-NINE TWICE..
SIGH SEVEN HOURS AND FORTY MINUTES TO GO... GOOD MORNING, MRS. ALBO..HOW ARE YOU TODAY, SWEETIE?
SCHULZ

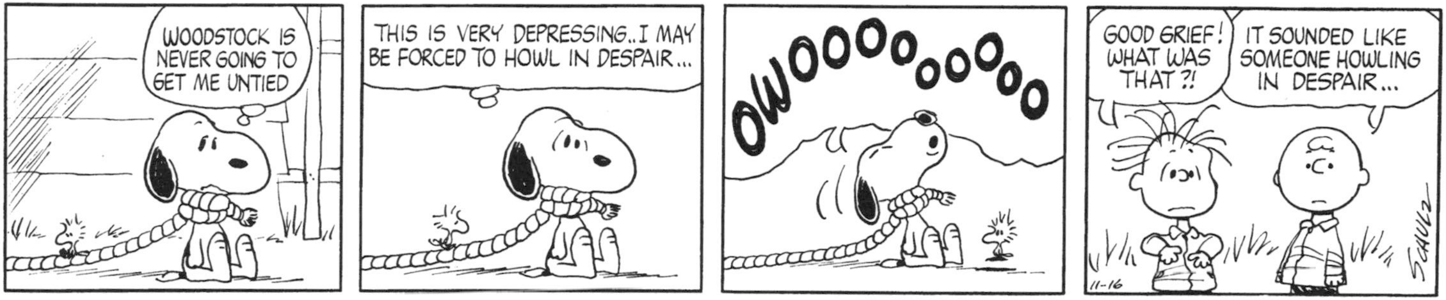
WOODSTOCK IS NEVER GOING TO GET ME UNTIED
THIS IS VERY DEPRESSING..I MAY BE FORCED TO HOWL IN DESPAIR...
OWOOOOOOOOO
GOOD GRIEF! WHAT WAS THAT?!
IT SOUNDED LIKE SOMEONE HOWLING IN DESPAIR...
11-16
SCHULZ

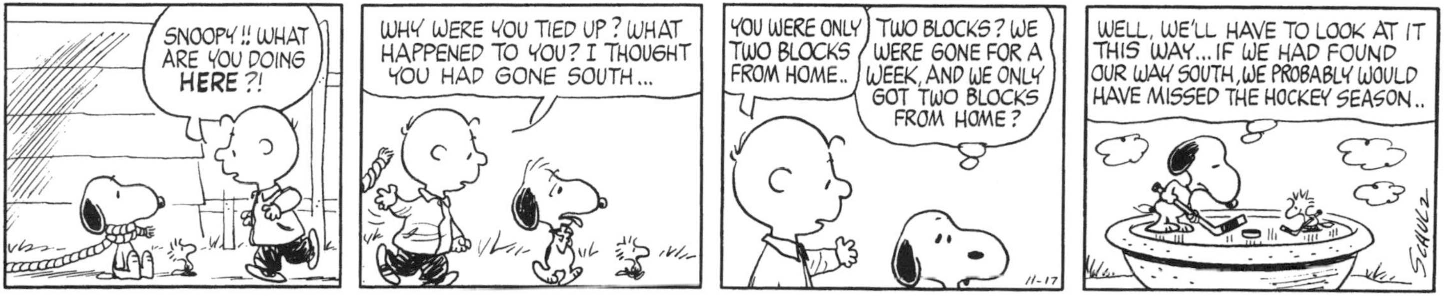
SNOOPY!! WHAT ARE YOU DOING **HERE**?!
WHY WERE YOU TIED UP? WHAT HAPPENED TO YOU? I THOUGHT YOU HAD GONE SOUTH...
YOU WERE ONLY TWO BLOCKS FROM HOME..
TWO BLOCKS? WE WERE GONE FOR A WEEK, AND WE ONLY GOT TWO BLOCKS FROM HOME?
11-17
WELL, WE'LL HAVE TO LOOK AT IT THIS WAY... IF WE HAD FOUND OUR WAY SOUTH, WE PROBABLY WOULD HAVE MISSED THE HOCKEY SEASON..
SCHULZ

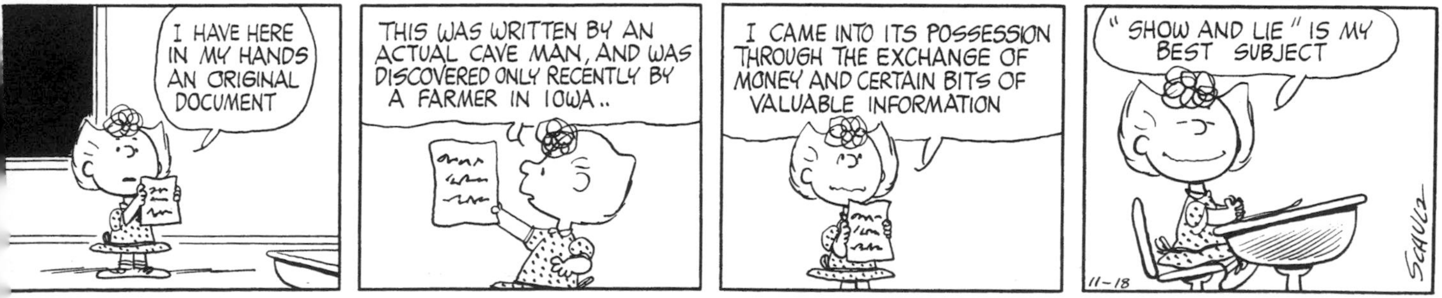
I HAVE HERE IN MY HANDS AN ORIGINAL DOCUMENT
THIS WAS WRITTEN BY AN ACTUAL CAVE MAN, AND WAS DISCOVERED ONLY RECENTLY BY A FARMER IN IOWA..
I CAME INTO ITS POSSESSION THROUGH THE EXCHANGE OF MONEY AND CERTAIN BITS OF VALUABLE INFORMATION
"SHOW AND LIE" IS MY BEST SUBJECT
11-18
SCHULZ

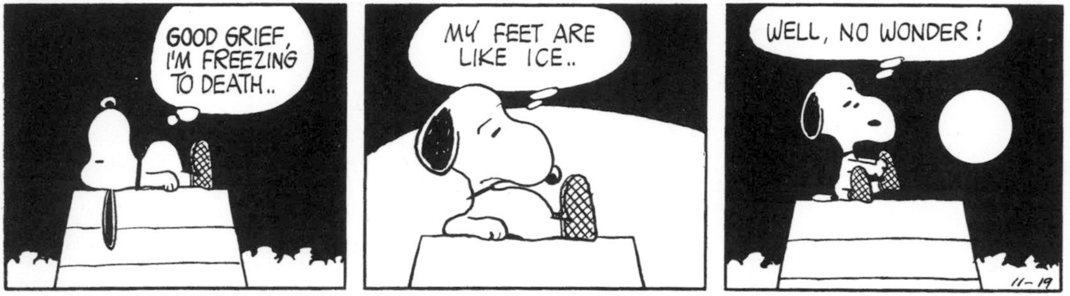
GOOD GRIEF, I'M FREEZING TO DEATH..
MY FEET ARE LIKE ICE..
WELL, NO WONDER!
11-19
THE BATTERY IN MY ELECTRIC SOCKS HAS GONE DEAD...
SCHULZ

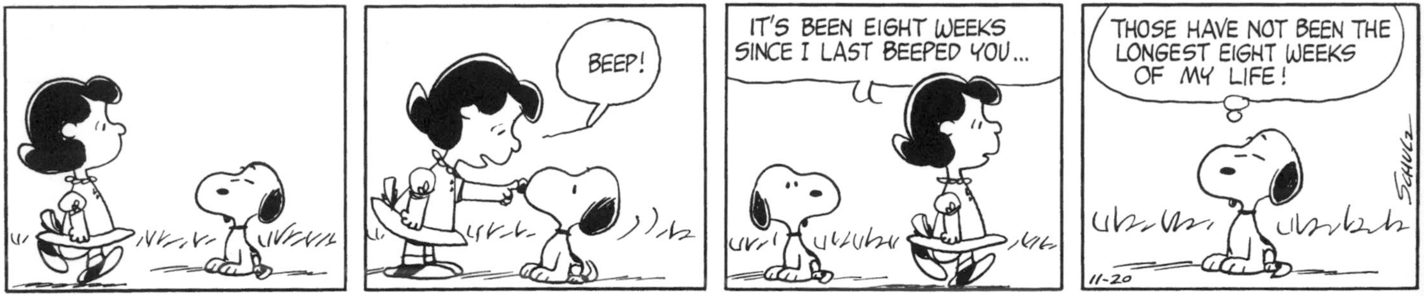
BEEP!
IT'S BEEN EIGHT WEEKS SINCE I LAST BEEPED YOU...
THOSE HAVE NOT BEEN THE LONGEST EIGHT WEEKS OF MY LIFE!
SCHULZ
11-20

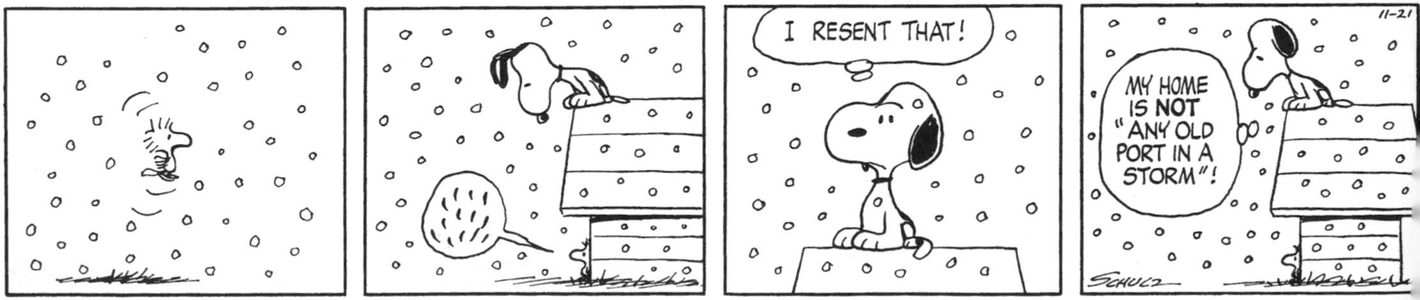
I RESENT THAT!
11-21
MY HOME IS NOT "ANY OLD PORT IN A STORM"!
SCHULZ

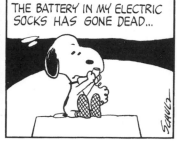

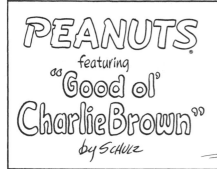

PEANUTS featuring "Good ol' CharlieBrown" *by Schulz*

I MUST BE CRAZY TO WATCH THIS..

IT'S A BEAUTY CONTEST, CHUCK, AND FOR SOMEONE LIKE ME, IT'S VERY DEPRESSING...

LOOK, THERE'S THE GIRL WHO WON... SEE HOW HAPPY SHE IS?

YOU THINK THAT'LL EVER HAPPEN TO ME, CHUCK? **NO WAY!!**

I'M NOT BEAUTIFUL, CHUCK...I'M NOT BEAUTIFUL, AND I'LL NEVER **BE** BEAUTIFUL..YOU THINK I ENJOY WATCHING BEAUTY CONTESTS? I HATE THEM!

NOW I'M ALL DEPRESSED..RATS!

SAY SOMETHING TO CHEER ME UP, CHUCK...

WELL, I..

CLICK!

SMAK

HE'S A FUNNY-LOOKING KID, BUT HE KNOWS HOW TO MAKE A GIRL HAPPY..

SIGH

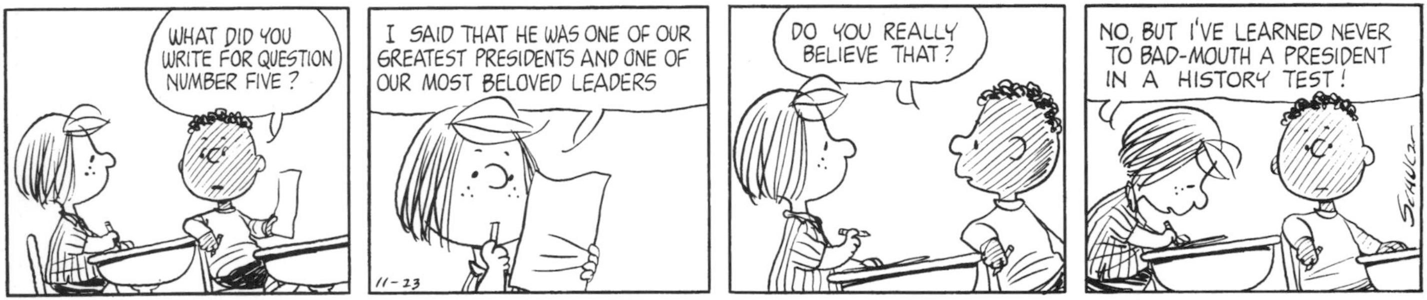
WHAT DID YOU WRITE FOR QUESTION NUMBER FIVE ?
I SAID THAT HE WAS ONE OF OUR GREATEST PRESIDENTS AND ONE OF OUR MOST BELOVED LEADERS
11-23
DO YOU REALLY BELIEVE THAT ?
NO, BUT I'VE LEARNED NEVER TO BAD-MOUTH A PRESIDENT IN A HISTORY TEST !
SCHULZ

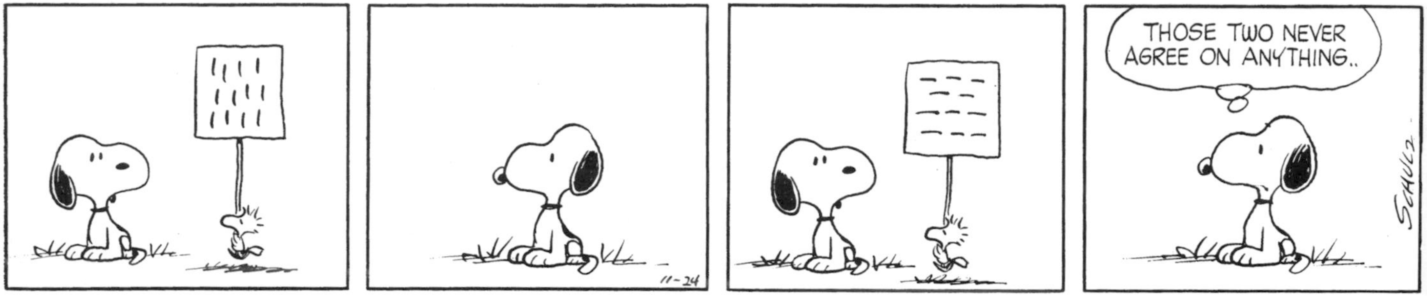
11-24
THOSE TWO NEVER AGREE ON ANYTHING..
SCHULZ

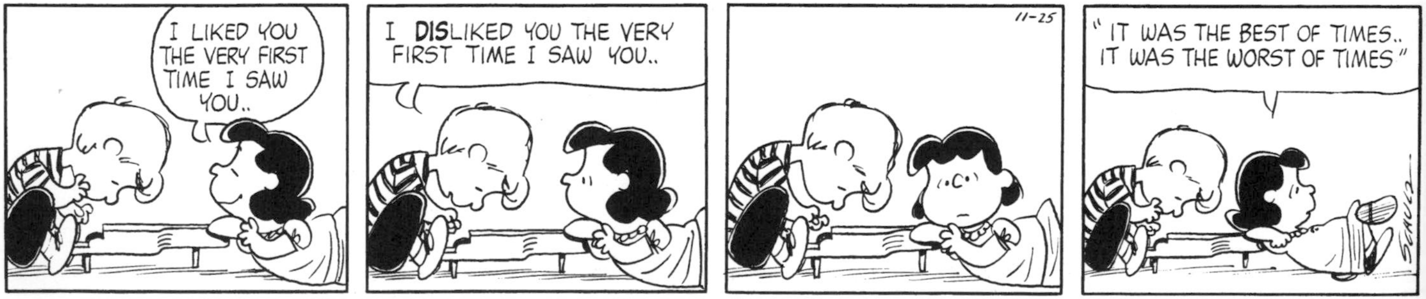
I LIKED YOU THE VERY FIRST TIME I SAW YOU..
I DISLIKED YOU THE VERY FIRST TIME I SAW YOU..
11-25
" IT WAS THE BEST OF TIMES.. IT WAS THE WORST OF TIMES "
SCHULZ

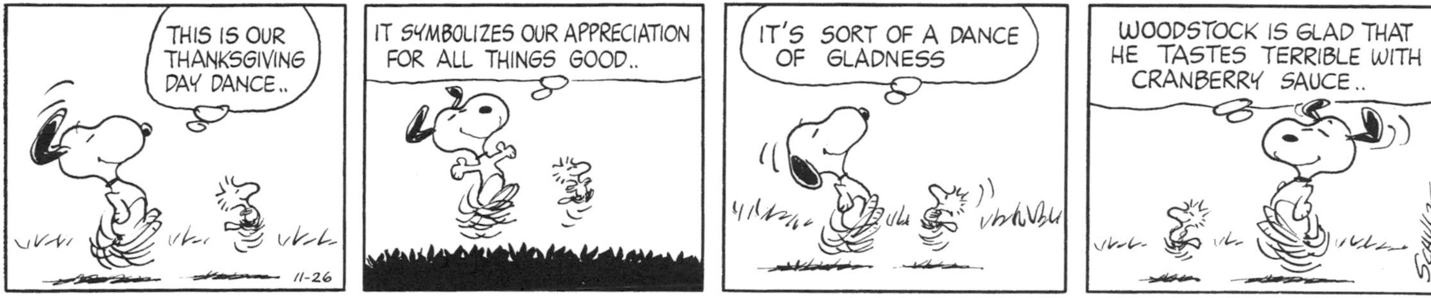
THIS IS OUR THANKSGIVING DAY DANCE..
11-26
IT SYMBOLIZES OUR APPRECIATION FOR ALL THINGS GOOD..
IT'S SORT OF A DANCE OF GLADNESS
WOODSTOCK IS GLAD THAT HE TASTES TERRIBLE WITH CRANBERRY SAUCE..
SCHULZ

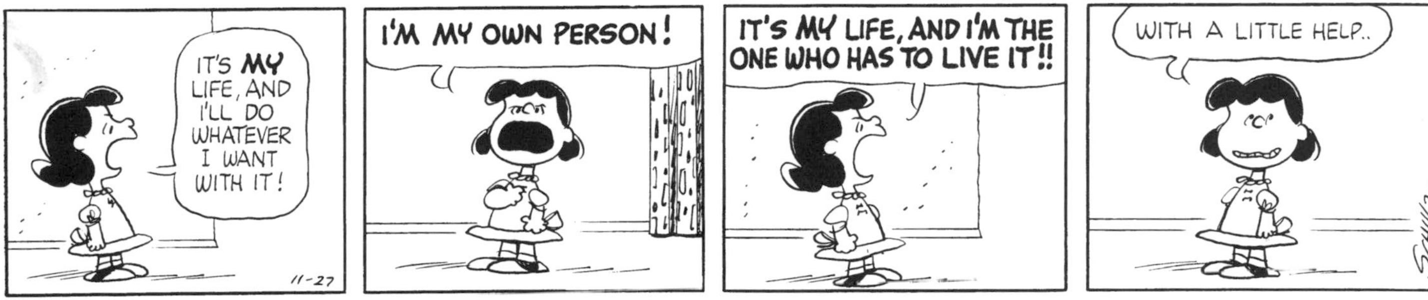
IT'S **MY** LIFE, AND I'LL DO WHATEVER I WANT WITH IT!
11-27
I'M MY OWN PERSON!
IT'S MY LIFE, AND I'M THE ONE WHO HAS TO LIVE IT!!
WITH A LITTLE HELP..
SCHULZ

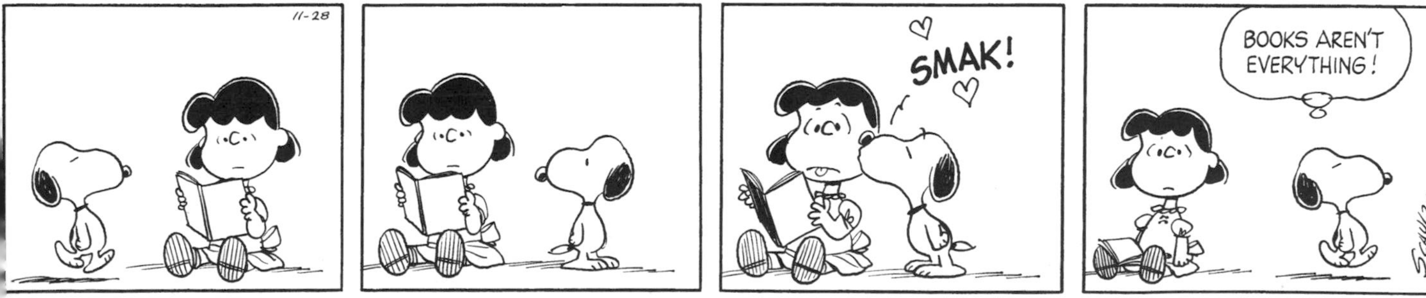
11-28
SMAK!
BOOKS AREN'T EVERYTHING!
SCHULZ

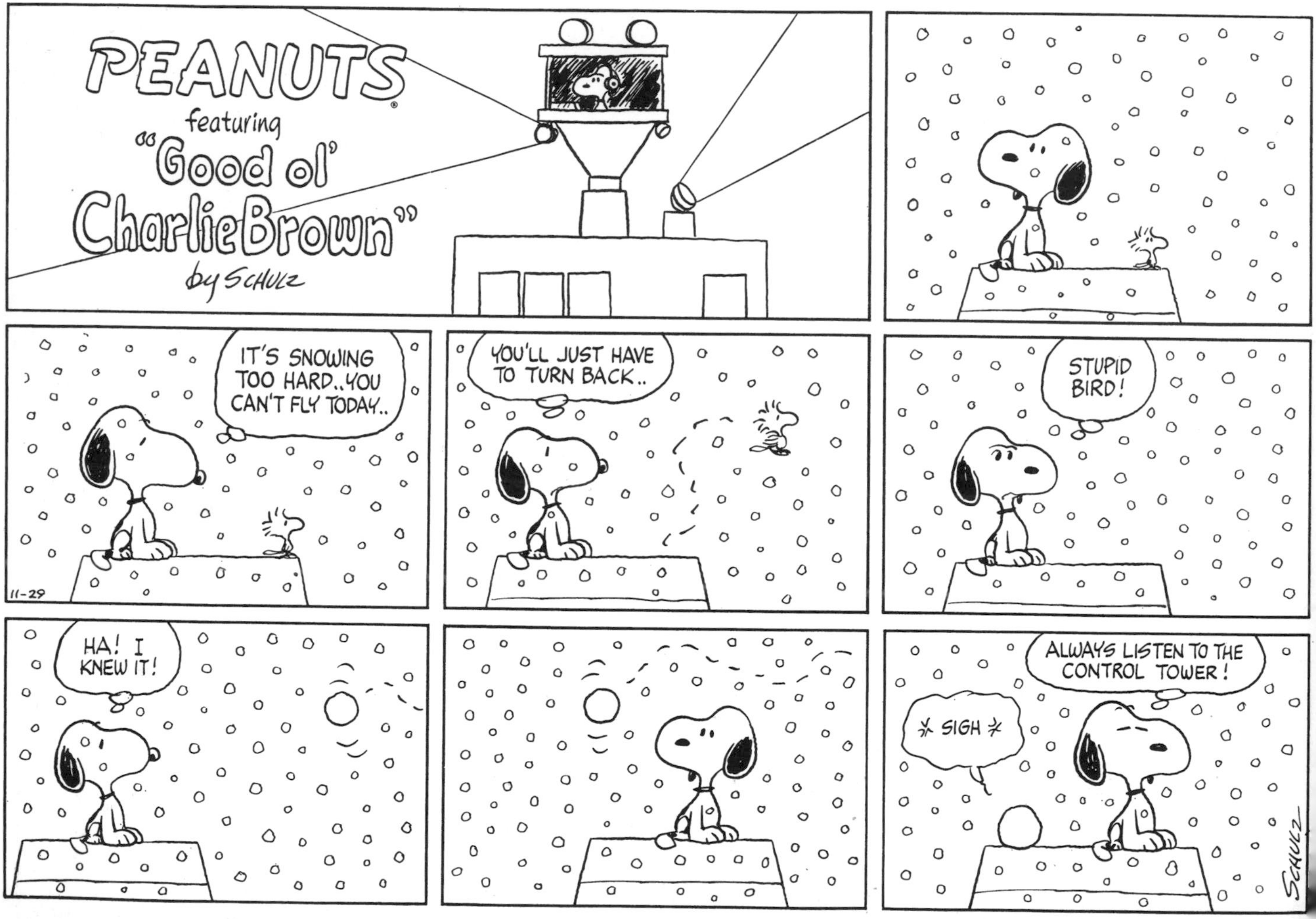
PEANUTS®
featuring
"Good ol' Charlie Brown"
by SCHULZ
11-29
IT'S SNOWING TOO HARD..YOU CAN'T FLY TODAY..
YOU'LL JUST HAVE TO TURN BACK..
STUPID BIRD!
HA! I KNEW IT!
ALWAYS LISTEN TO THE CONTROL TOWER!
* SIGH *
SCHULZ

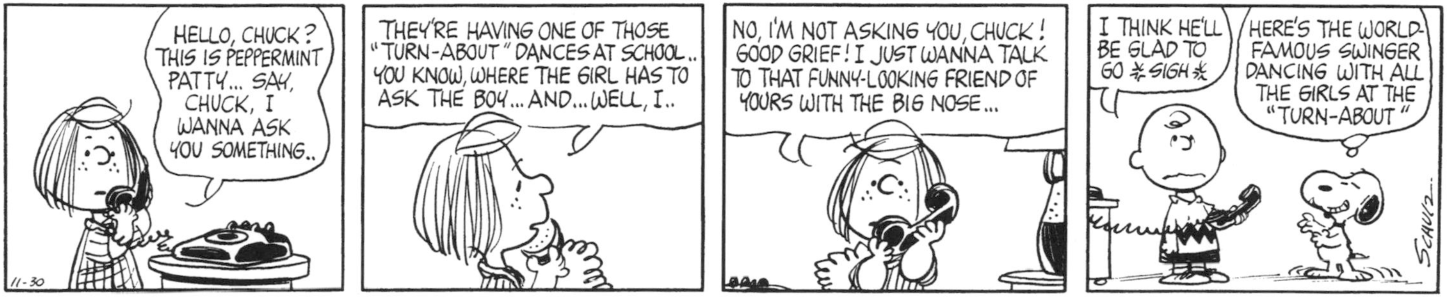
HELLO, CHUCK? THIS IS PEPPERMINT PATTY... SAY, CHUCK, I WANNA ASK YOU SOMETHING..
11-30
THEY'RE HAVING ONE OF THOSE "TURN-ABOUT" DANCES AT SCHOOL.. YOU KNOW, WHERE THE GIRL HAS TO ASK THE BOY... AND... WELL, I..
NO, I'M NOT ASKING YOU, CHUCK! GOOD GRIEF! I JUST WANNA TALK TO THAT FUNNY-LOOKING FRIEND OF YOURS WITH THE BIG NOSE...
I THINK HE'LL BE GLAD TO GO *SIGH*
HERE'S THE WORLD-FAMOUS SWINGER DANCING WITH ALL THE GIRLS AT THE "TURN-ABOUT"
SCHULZ

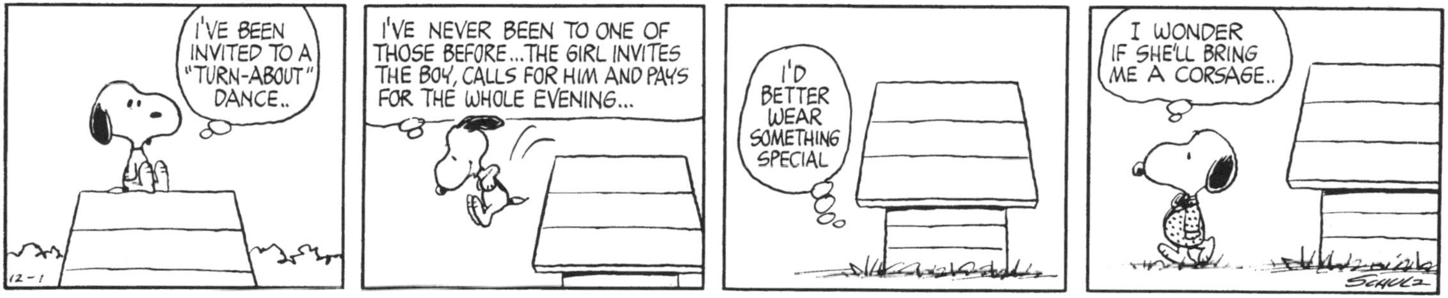
I'VE BEEN INVITED TO A "TURN-ABOUT" DANCE..
12-1
I'VE NEVER BEEN TO ONE OF THOSE BEFORE... THE GIRL INVITES THE BOY, CALLS FOR HIM AND PAYS FOR THE WHOLE EVENING...
I'D BETTER WEAR SOMETHING SPECIAL
I WONDER IF SHE'LL BRING ME A CORSAGE..
SCHULZ

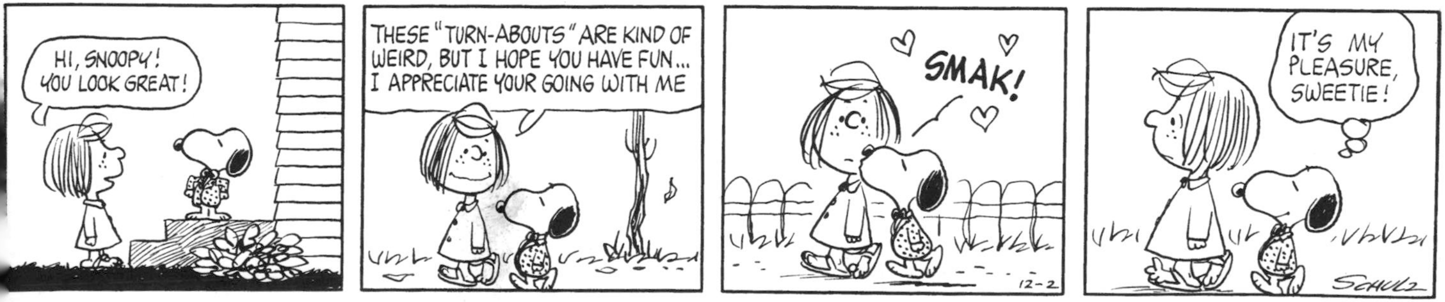
HI, SNOOPY! YOU LOOK GREAT!
THESE "TURN-ABOUTS" ARE KIND OF WEIRD, BUT I HOPE YOU HAVE FUN... I APPRECIATE YOUR GOING WITH ME
SMAK!
12-2
IT'S MY PLEASURE, SWEETIE!
SCHULZ

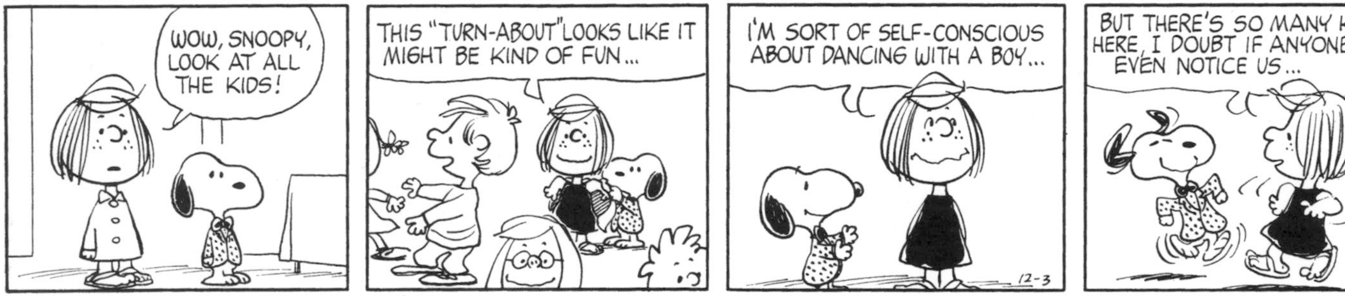
WOW, SNOOPY, LOOK AT ALL THE KIDS!
THIS "TURN-ABOUT" LOOKS LIKE IT MIGHT BE KIND OF FUN...
I'M SORT OF SELF-CONSCIOUS ABOUT DANCING WITH A BOY...
12-3
BUT THERE'S SO MANY KIDS HERE, I DOUBT IF ANYONE WILL EVEN NOTICE US...
SCHULZ

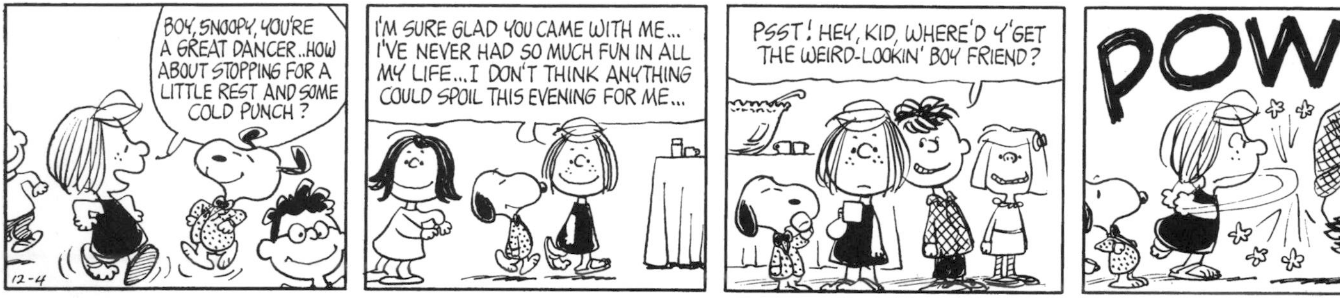
BOY, SNOOPY, YOU'RE A GREAT DANCER..HOW ABOUT STOPPING FOR A LITTLE REST AND SOME COLD PUNCH?
12-4
I'M SURE GLAD YOU CAME WITH ME... I'VE NEVER HAD SO MUCH FUN IN ALL MY LIFE...I DON'T THINK ANYTHING COULD SPOIL THIS EVENING FOR ME...
PSST! HEY, KID, WHERE'D Y'GET THE WEIRD-LOOKIN' BOY FRIEND?
POW!!
SCHULZ

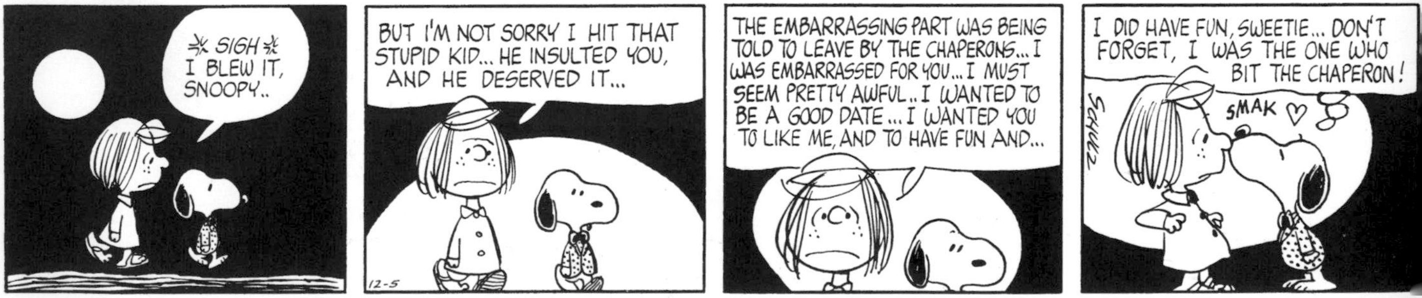
SIGH I BLEW IT, SNOOPY..
BUT I'M NOT SORRY I HIT THAT STUPID KID... HE INSULTED YOU, AND HE DESERVED IT...
12-5
THE EMBARRASSING PART WAS BEING TOLD TO LEAVE BY THE CHAPERONS... I WAS EMBARRASSED FOR YOU... I MUST SEEM PRETTY AWFUL.. I WANTED TO BE A GOOD DATE... I WANTED YOU TO LIKE ME, AND TO HAVE FUN AND...
I DID HAVE FUN, SWEETIE... DON'T FORGET, I WAS THE ONE WHO BIT THE CHAPERON!
SCHULZ
SMAK

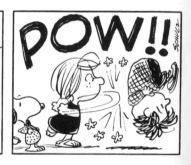

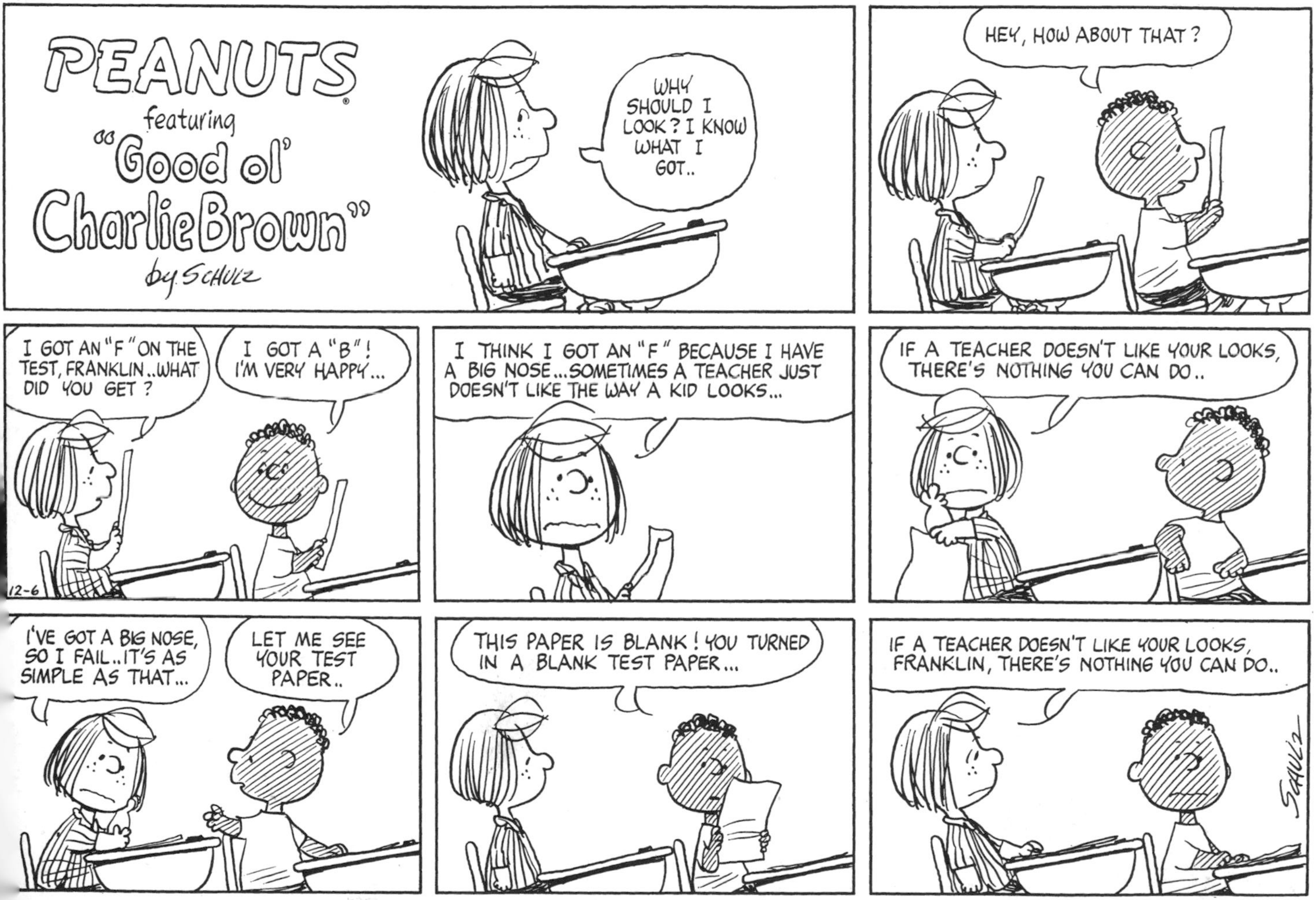
PEANUTS
featuring
"Good ol' Charlie Brown"
by SCHULZ
WHY SHOULD I LOOK? I KNOW WHAT I GOT..
HEY, HOW ABOUT THAT?
I GOT AN "F" ON THE TEST, FRANKLIN..WHAT DID YOU GET?
I GOT A "B"! I'M VERY HAPPY...
12-6
I THINK I GOT AN "F" BECAUSE I HAVE A BIG NOSE...SOMETIMES A TEACHER JUST DOESN'T LIKE THE WAY A KID LOOKS...
IF A TEACHER DOESN'T LIKE YOUR LOOKS, THERE'S NOTHING YOU CAN DO..
I'VE GOT A BIG NOSE, SO I FAIL..IT'S AS SIMPLE AS THAT...
LET ME SEE YOUR TEST PAPER..
THIS PAPER IS BLANK! YOU TURNED IN A BLANK TEST PAPER...
IF A TEACHER DOESN'T LIKE YOUR LOOKS, FRANKLIN, THERE'S NOTHING YOU CAN DO..
SCHULZ

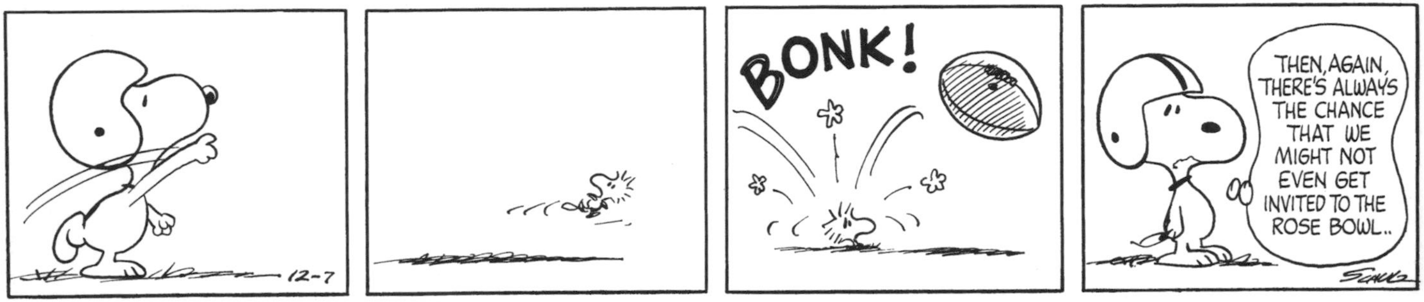
12-7
BONK!
THEN, AGAIN, THERE'S ALWAYS THE CHANCE THAT WE MIGHT NOT EVEN GET INVITED TO THE ROSE BOWL..
SCHULZ

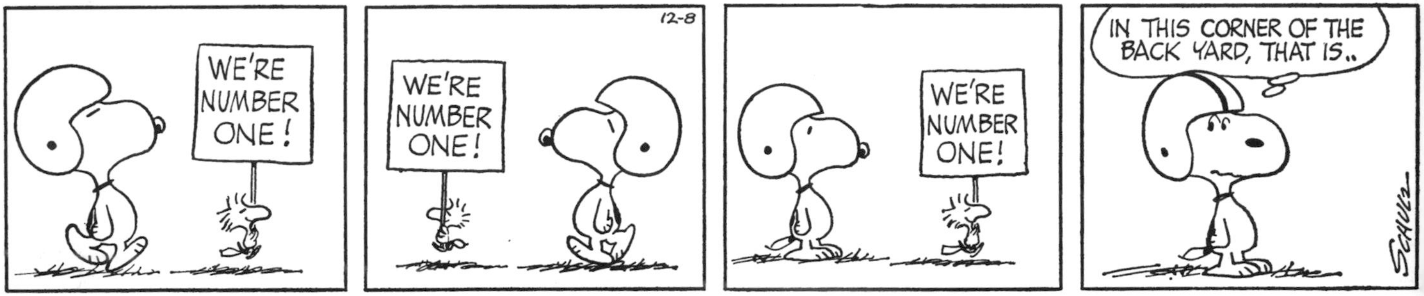
WE'RE NUMBER ONE!
12-8
WE'RE NUMBER ONE!
WE'RE NUMBER ONE!
IN THIS CORNER OF THE BACK YARD, THAT IS..
SCHULZ

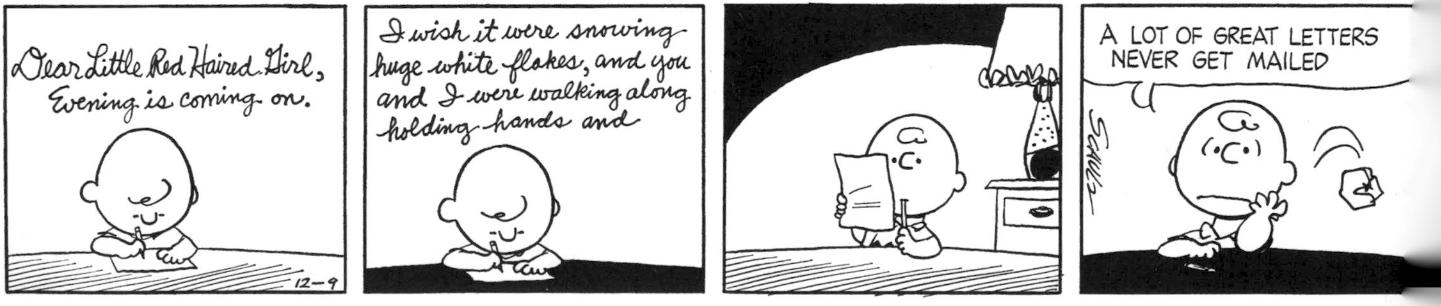
Dear Little Red Haired Girl,
Evening is coming on.
12-9
I wish it were snowing huge white flakes, and you and I were walking along holding hands and
A LOT OF GREAT LETTERS NEVER GET MAILED
SCHULZ

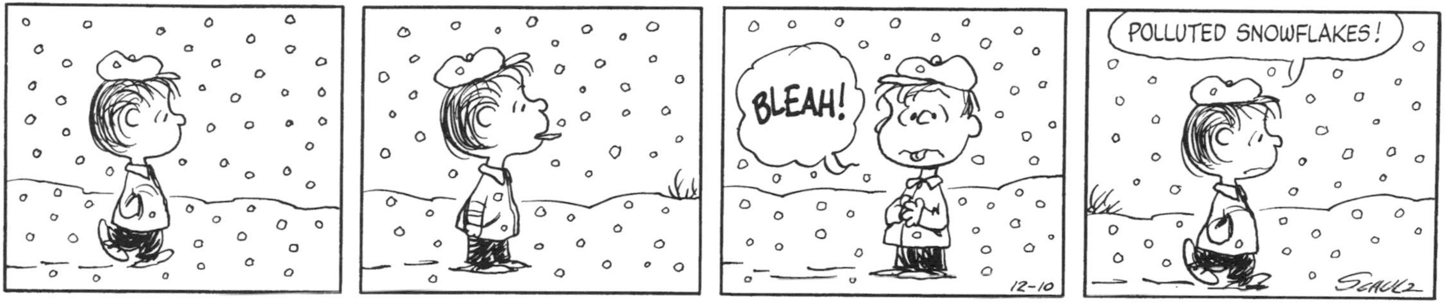
BLEAH!
POLLUTED SNOWFLAKES!
12-10
SCHULZ

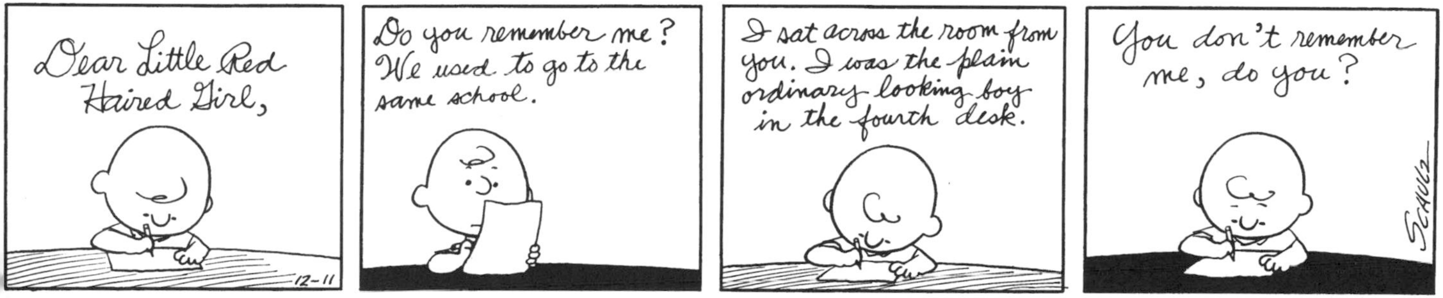
Dear Little Red Haired Girl,
12-11
Do you remember me? We used to go to the same school.
I sat across the room from you. I was the plain ordinary looking boy in the fourth desk.
You don't remember me, do you?
SCHULZ

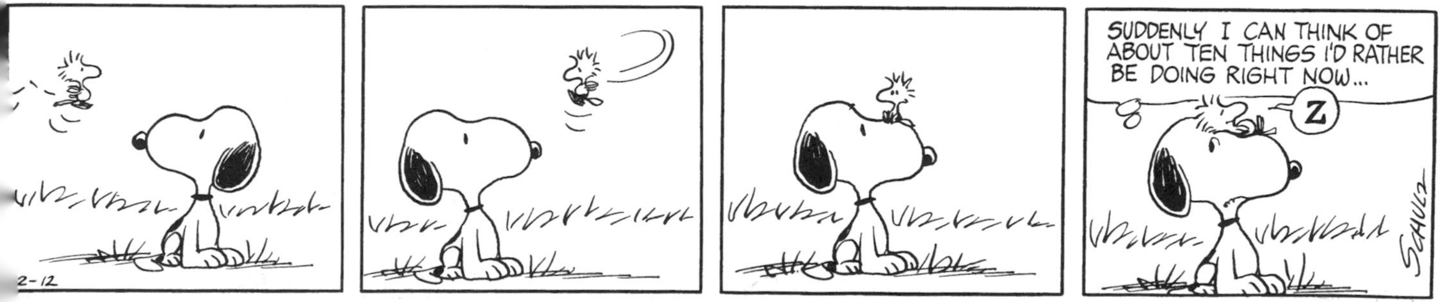
SUDDENLY I CAN THINK OF ABOUT TEN THINGS I'D RATHER BE DOING RIGHT NOW...
Z
SCHULZ

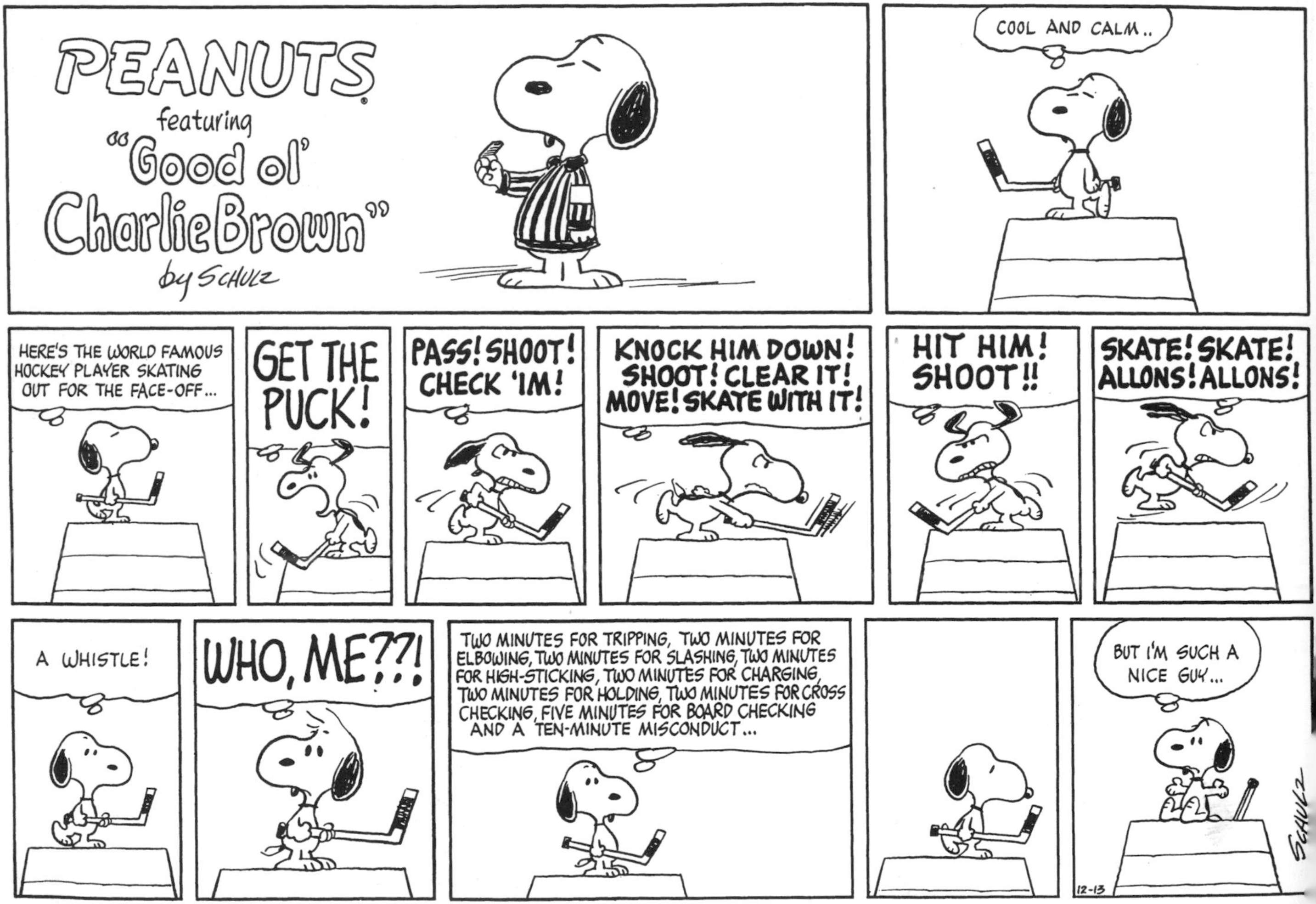
PEANUTS
featuring
"Good ol' Charlie Brown"
by SCHULZ
COOL AND CALM..
HERE'S THE WORLD FAMOUS HOCKEY PLAYER SKATING OUT FOR THE FACE-OFF...
GET THE PUCK!
PASS! SHOOT! CHECK 'IM!
KNOCK HIM DOWN! SHOOT! CLEAR IT! MOVE! SKATE WITH IT!
HIT HIM! SHOOT!!
SKATE! SKATE! ALLONS! ALLONS!
A WHISTLE!
WHO, ME??!
TWO MINUTES FOR TRIPPING, TWO MINUTES FOR ELBOWING, TWO MINUTES FOR SLASHING, TWO MINUTES FOR HIGH-STICKING, TWO MINUTES FOR CHARGING, TWO MINUTES FOR HOLDING, TWO MINUTES FOR CROSS CHECKING, FIVE MINUTES FOR BOARD CHECKING AND A TEN-MINUTE MISCONDUCT...
BUT I'M SUCH A NICE GUY...
12-13
SCHULZ

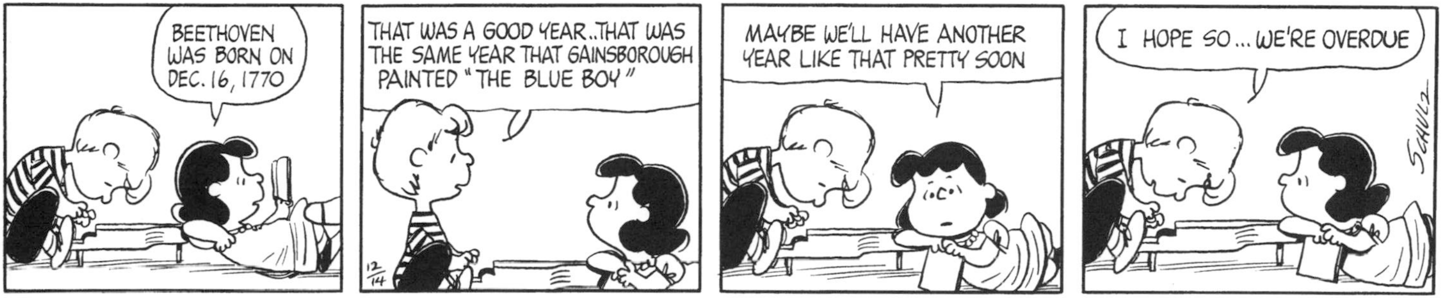
BEETHOVEN WAS BORN ON DEC. 16, 1770
THAT WAS A GOOD YEAR..THAT WAS THE SAME YEAR THAT GAINSBOROUGH PAINTED "THE BLUE BOY"
12/14
MAYBE WE'LL HAVE ANOTHER YEAR LIKE THAT PRETTY SOON
I HOPE SO... WE'RE OVERDUE
SCHULZ

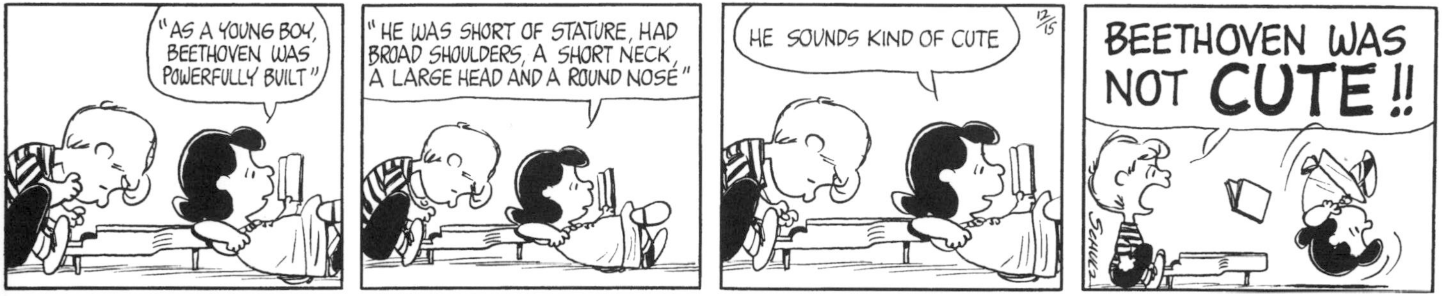
"AS A YOUNG BOY, BEETHOVEN WAS POWERFULLY BUILT"
"HE WAS SHORT OF STATURE, HAD BROAD SHOULDERS, A SHORT NECK, A LARGE HEAD AND A ROUND NOSE"
HE SOUNDS KIND OF CUTE
12/15
BEETHOVEN WAS NOT CUTE!!
SCHULZ

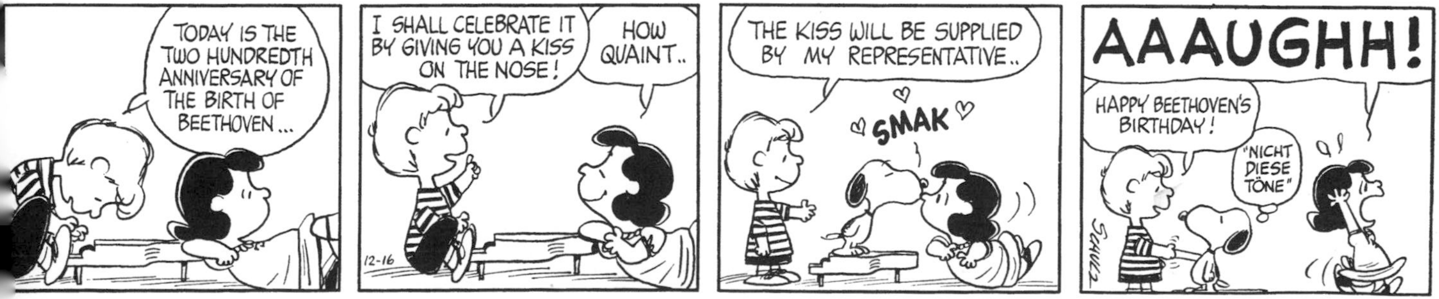
TODAY IS THE TWO HUNDREDTH ANNIVERSARY OF THE BIRTH OF BEETHOVEN...
I SHALL CELEBRATE IT BY GIVING YOU A KISS ON THE NOSE!
HOW QUAINT..
12-16
THE KISS WILL BE SUPPLIED BY MY REPRESENTATIVE..
SMAK
AAAUGHH!
HAPPY BEETHOVEN'S BIRTHDAY!
"NICHT DIESE TÖNE"
SCHULZ

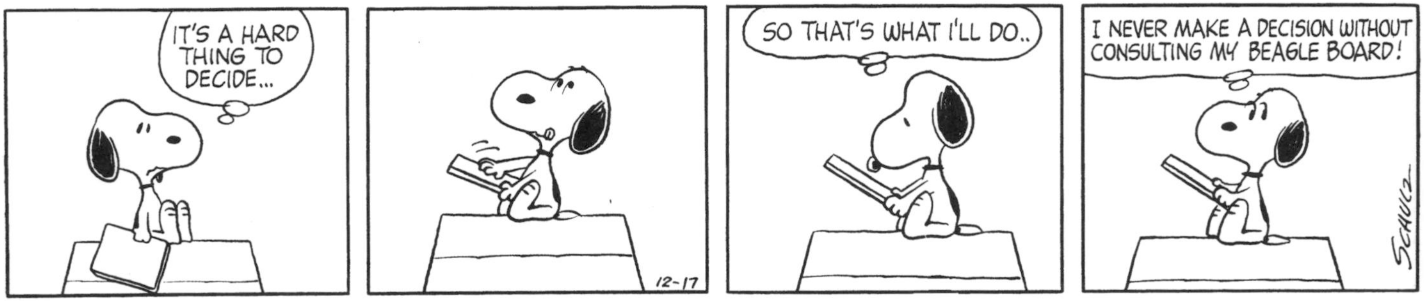
IT'S A HARD THING TO DECIDE...
12-17
SO THAT'S WHAT I'LL DO..
I NEVER MAKE A DECISION WITHOUT CONSULTING MY BEAGLE BOARD!
SCHULZ

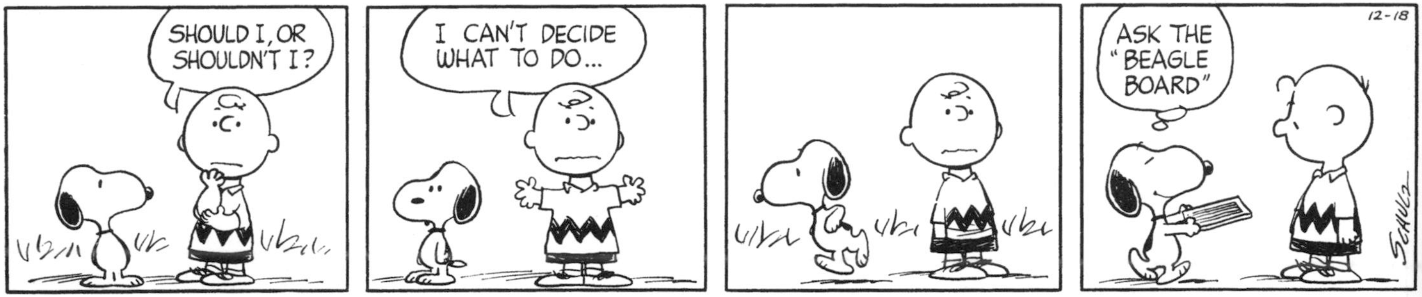
SHOULD I, OR SHOULDN'T I?
I CAN'T DECIDE WHAT TO DO...
12-18
ASK THE "BEAGLE BOARD"
SCHULZ

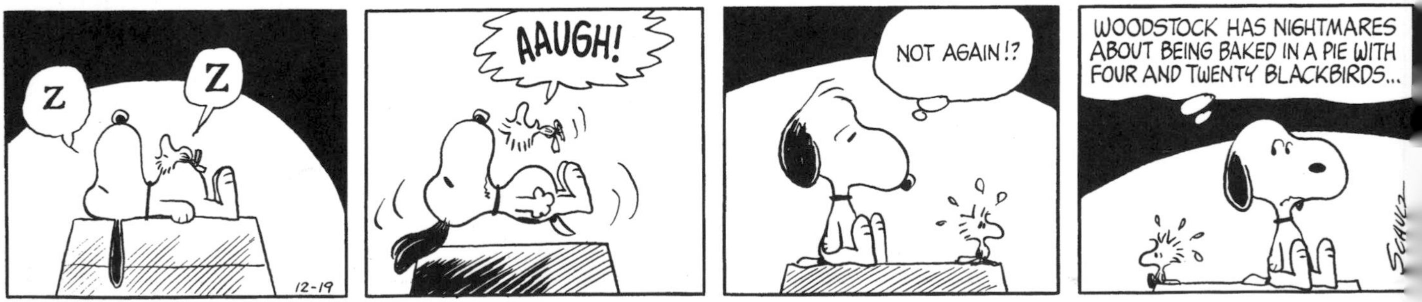
Z
Z
12-19
AAUGH!
NOT AGAIN!?
WOODSTOCK HAS NIGHTMARES ABOUT BEING BAKED IN A PIE WITH FOUR AND TWENTY BLACKBIRDS...
SCHULZ

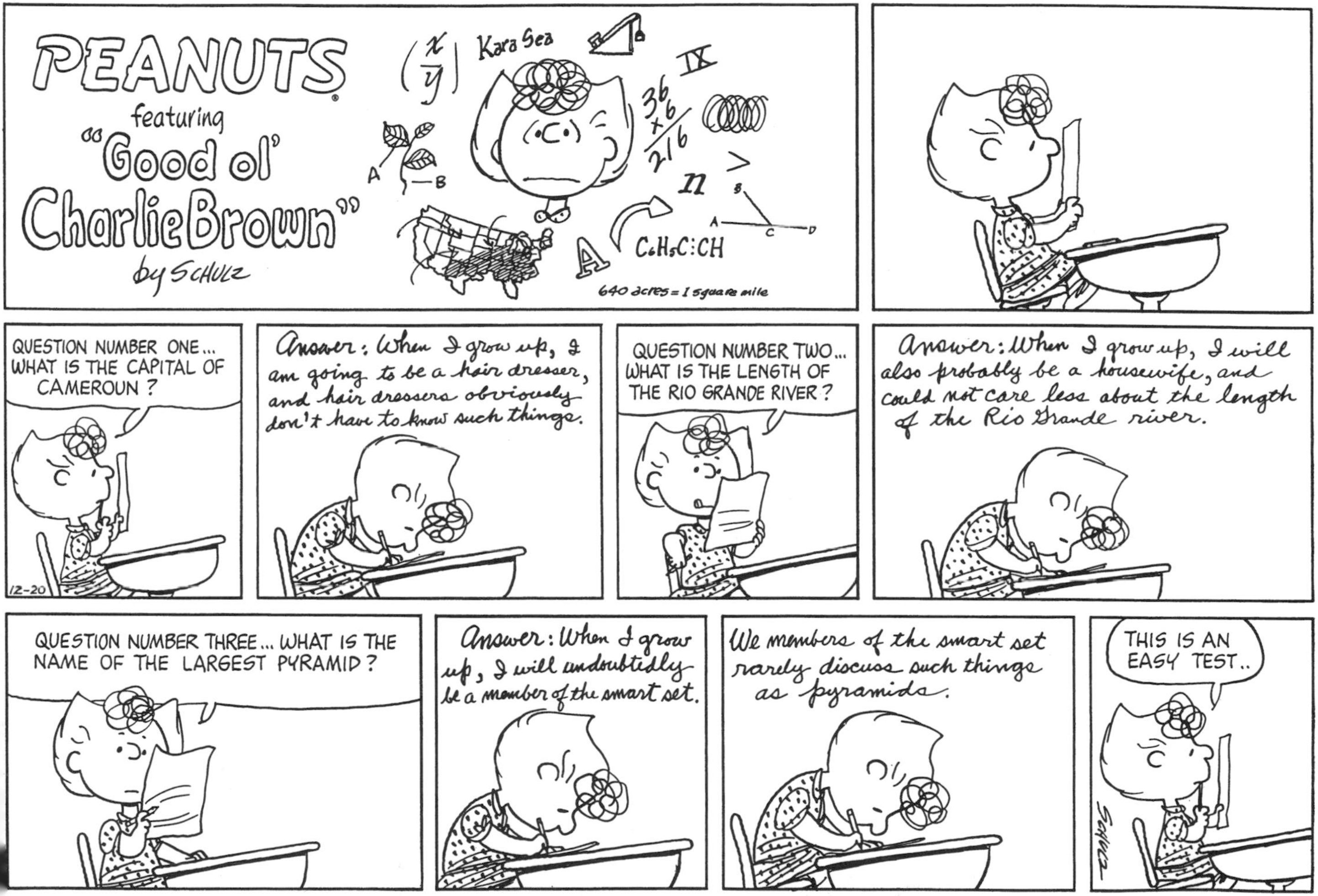
PEANUTS
featuring
"Good ol' Charlie Brown"
by SCHULZ
Kara Sea
IX
36
x6
216
C6H5C:CH
640 acres = 1 square mile
12-20
QUESTION NUMBER ONE... WHAT IS THE CAPITAL OF CAMEROUN ?
Answer: When I grow up, I am going to be a hair dresser, and hair dressers obviously don't have to know such things.
QUESTION NUMBER TWO... WHAT IS THE LENGTH OF THE RIO GRANDE RIVER ?
Answer: When I grow up, I will also probably be a housewife, and could not care less about the length of the Rio Grande river.
QUESTION NUMBER THREE... WHAT IS THE NAME OF THE LARGEST PYRAMID ?
Answer: When I grow up, I will undoubtedly be a member of the smart set.
We members of the smart set rarely discuss such things as pyramids.
THIS IS AN EASY TEST..
SCHULZ

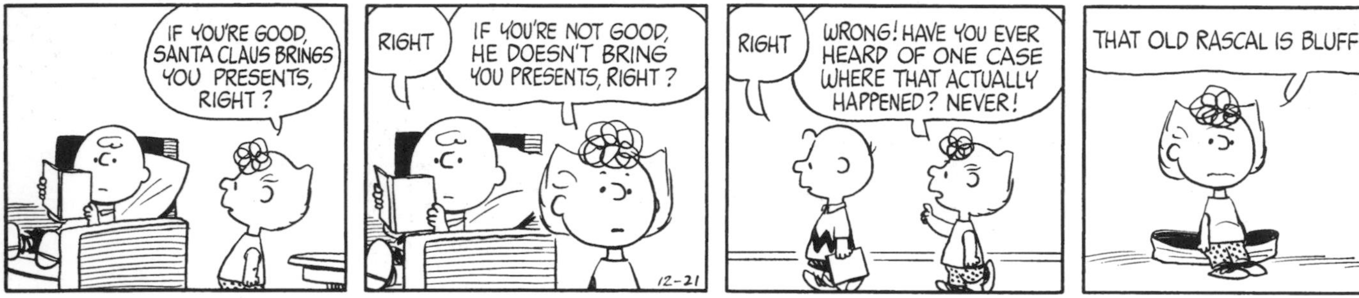
IF YOU'RE GOOD, SANTA CLAUS BRINGS YOU PRESENTS, RIGHT?
RIGHT
IF YOU'RE NOT GOOD, HE DOESN'T BRING YOU PRESENTS, RIGHT?
12-21
RIGHT
WRONG! HAVE YOU EVER HEARD OF ONE CASE WHERE THAT ACTUALLY HAPPENED? NEVER!
THAT OLD RASCAL IS BLUFFING!
SCHULZ

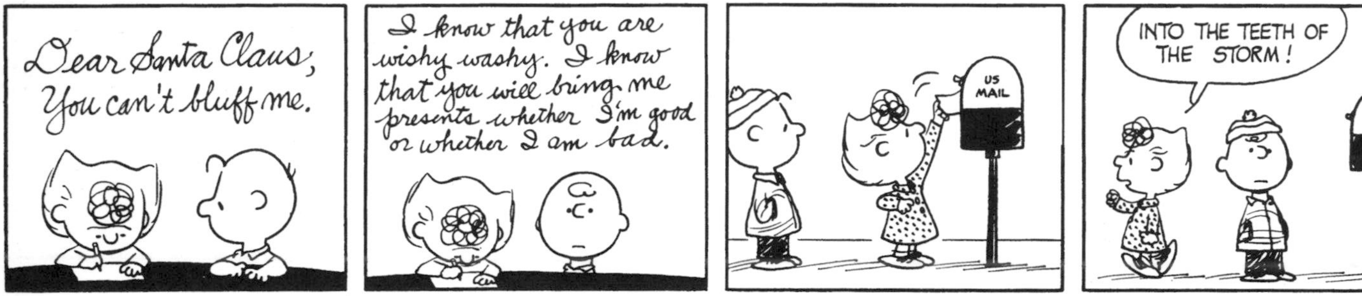
Dear Santa Claus; You can't bluff me.
I know that you are wishy washy. I know that you will bring me presents whether I'm good or whether I am bad.
US MAIL
12-22
INTO THE TEETH OF THE STORM!
US MAIL
SCHULZ

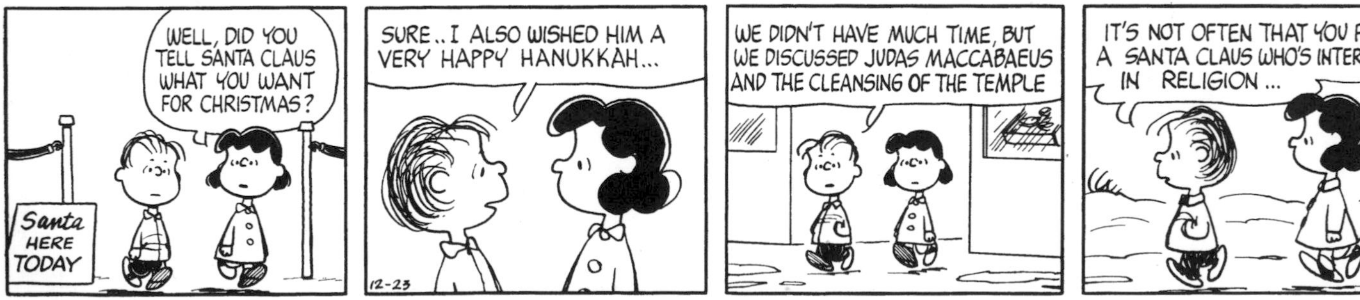
WELL, DID YOU TELL SANTA CLAUS WHAT YOU WANT FOR CHRISTMAS?
Santa HERE TODAY
SURE..I ALSO WISHED HIM A VERY HAPPY HANUKKAH...
12-23
WE DIDN'T HAVE MUCH TIME, BUT WE DISCUSSED JUDAS MACCABAEUS AND THE CLEANSING OF THE TEMPLE
IT'S NOT OFTEN THAT YOU FIND A SANTA CLAUS WHO'S INTERESTED IN RELIGION...
SCHULZ

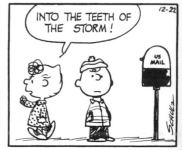

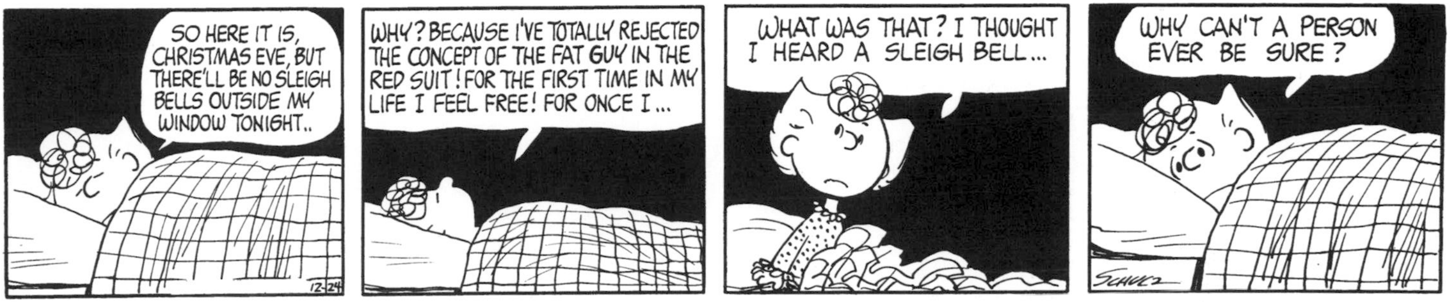
SO HERE IT IS, CHRISTMAS EVE, BUT THERE'LL BE NO SLEIGH BELLS OUTSIDE MY WINDOW TONIGHT..
12-24
WHY? BECAUSE I'VE TOTALLY REJECTED THE CONCEPT OF THE FAT GUY IN THE RED SUIT! FOR THE FIRST TIME IN MY LIFE I FEEL FREE! FOR ONCE I ...
WHAT WAS THAT? I THOUGHT I HEARD A SLEIGH BELL...
WHY CAN'T A PERSON EVER BE SURE?
SCHULZ

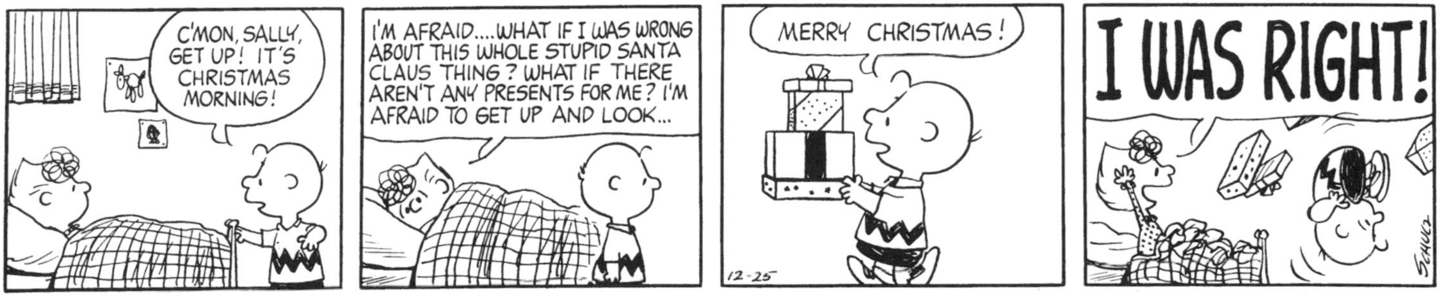
C'MON, SALLY, GET UP! IT'S CHRISTMAS MORNING!
I'M AFRAID....WHAT IF I WAS WRONG ABOUT THIS WHOLE STUPID SANTA CLAUS THING? WHAT IF THERE AREN'T ANY PRESENTS FOR ME? I'M AFRAID TO GET UP AND LOOK...
MERRY CHRISTMAS!
12-25
I WAS RIGHT!
SCHULZ

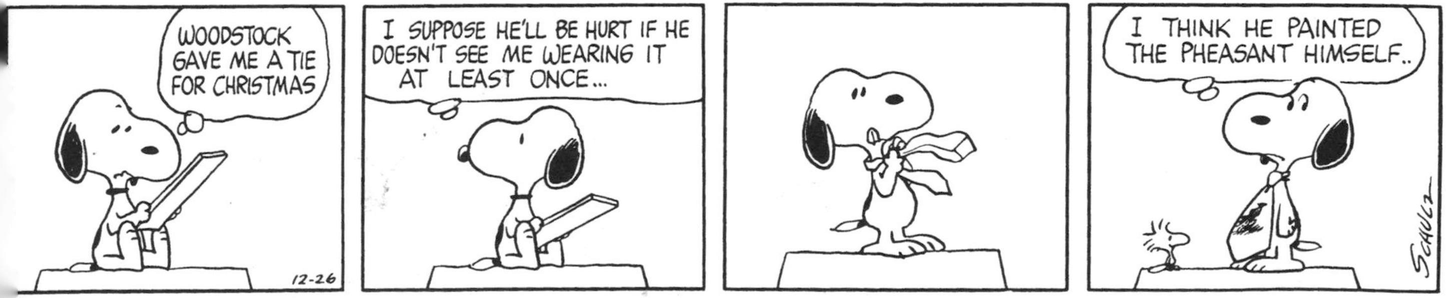
WOODSTOCK GAVE ME A TIE FOR CHRISTMAS
12-26
I SUPPOSE HE'LL BE HURT IF HE DOESN'T SEE ME WEARING IT AT LEAST ONCE...
I THINK HE PAINTED THE PHEASANT HIMSELF..
SCHULZ

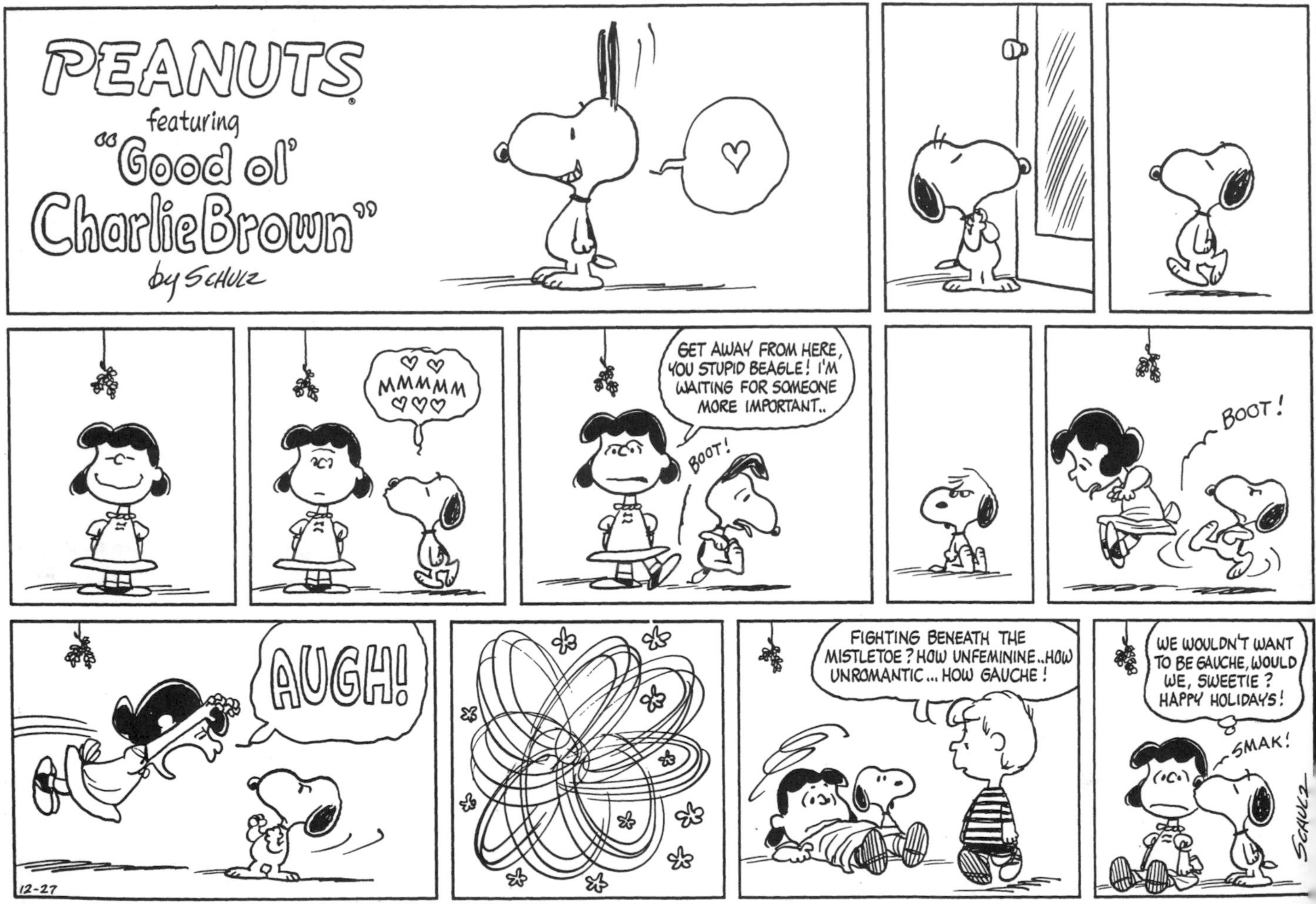
PEANUTS
featuring "Good ol' Charlie Brown"
by SCHULZ
GET AWAY FROM HERE, YOU STUPID BEAGLE! I'M WAITING FOR SOMEONE MORE IMPORTANT..
BOOT!
BOOT!
AUGH!
12-27
FIGHTING BENEATH THE MISTLETOE? HOW UNFEMININE..HOW UNROMANTIC... HOW GAUCHE!
WE WOULDN'T WANT TO BE GAUCHE, WOULD WE, SWEETIE? HAPPY HOLIDAYS!
SMAK!
SCHULZ

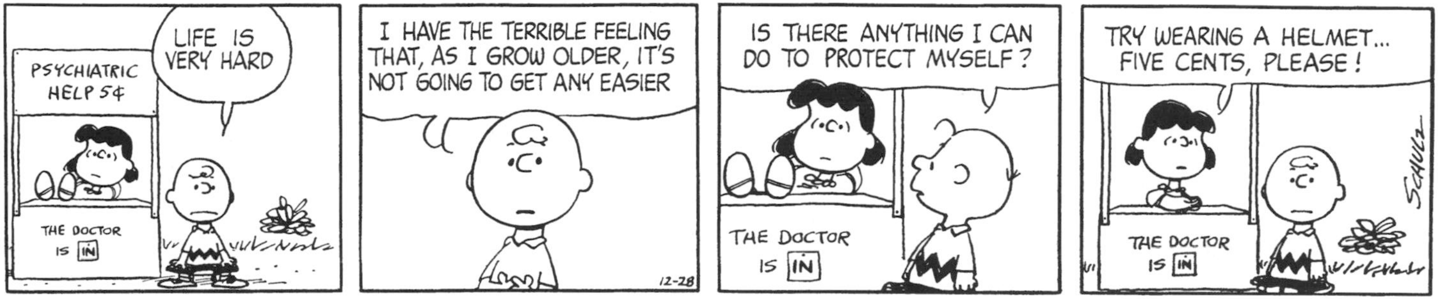
PSYCHIATRIC HELP 5¢
THE DOCTOR IS IN
LIFE IS VERY HARD
I HAVE THE TERRIBLE FEELING THAT, AS I GROW OLDER, IT'S NOT GOING TO GET ANY EASIER
12-28
IS THERE ANYTHING I CAN DO TO PROTECT MYSELF?
THE DOCTOR IS IN
TRY WEARING A HELMET... FIVE CENTS, PLEASE!
THE DOCTOR IS IN
SCHULZ

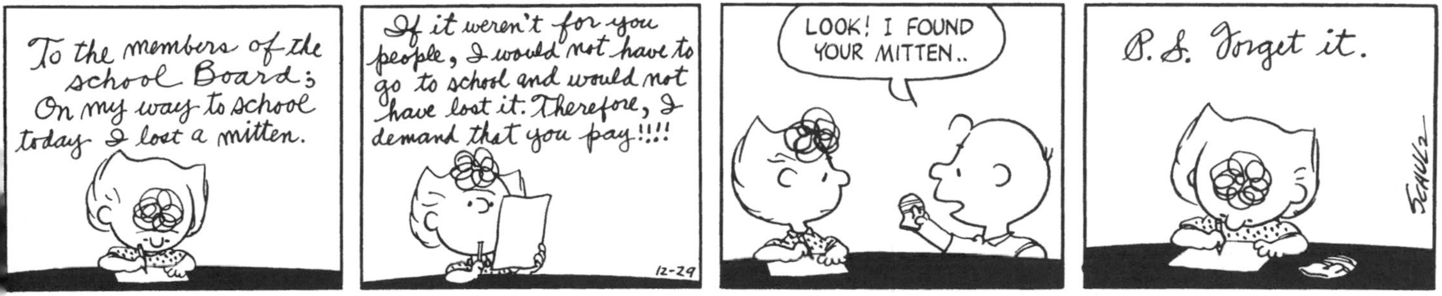
To the members of the school Board: On my way to school today I lost a mitten.
If it weren't for you people, I would not have to go to school and would not have lost it. Therefore, I demand that you pay!!!!
12-29
LOOK! I FOUND YOUR MITTEN..
P. S. Forget it.
SCHULZ

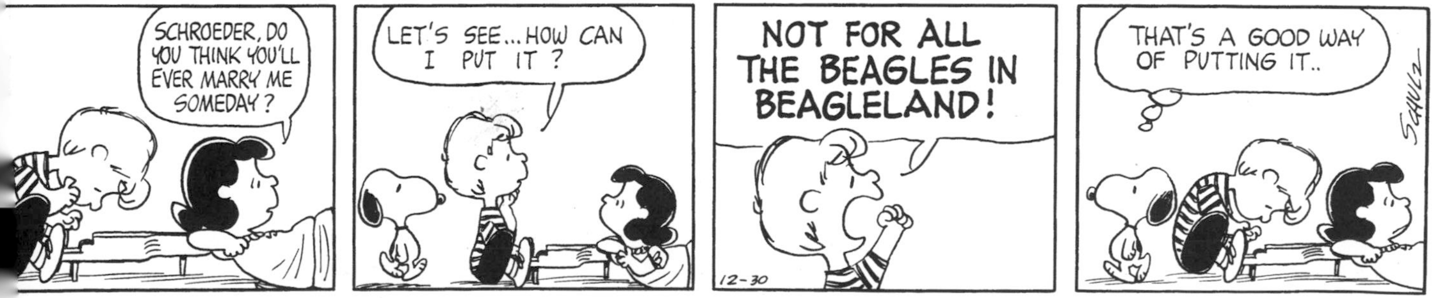
SCHROEDER, DO YOU THINK YOU'LL EVER MARRY ME SOMEDAY?
LET'S SEE...HOW CAN I PUT IT?
NOT FOR ALL THE BEAGLES IN BEAGLELAND!
12-30
THAT'S A GOOD WAY OF PUTTING IT..
SCHULZ

LAST YEAR REALLY WASN'T A VERY GOOD ONE FOR ME
I HOPE THIS NEXT YEAR WILL BE BETTER
12/31
SMAK!
THAT SHOULD GET IT OFF TO A PERFECT START!
SCHULZ

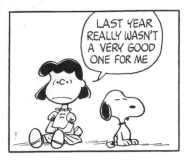

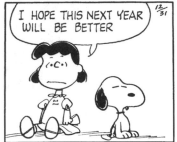

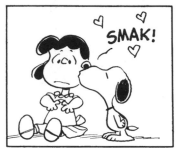

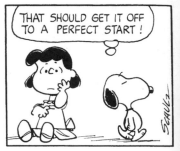

GOOD GRIEF! Our printer accidentally printed the May 1, 1967 strip twice in our last volume, booting the May 3 strip. This blockhead error will be corrected in future printings of *The Complete Peanuts*, but in the meantime, here is that missing strip.

YOU THINK YOU'RE SMART, CHARLIE BROWN...
WELL, YOU'RE **NOT**! NYAAH!
5-3
DID SHE HURT YOUR FEELINGS, CHARLIE BROWN?
NO...
SHE JUST NICKED ME WITH A "NYAAH"

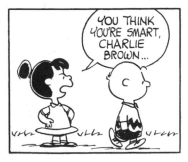

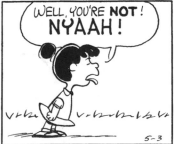

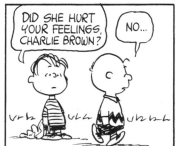

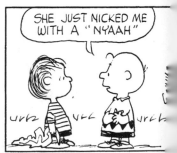

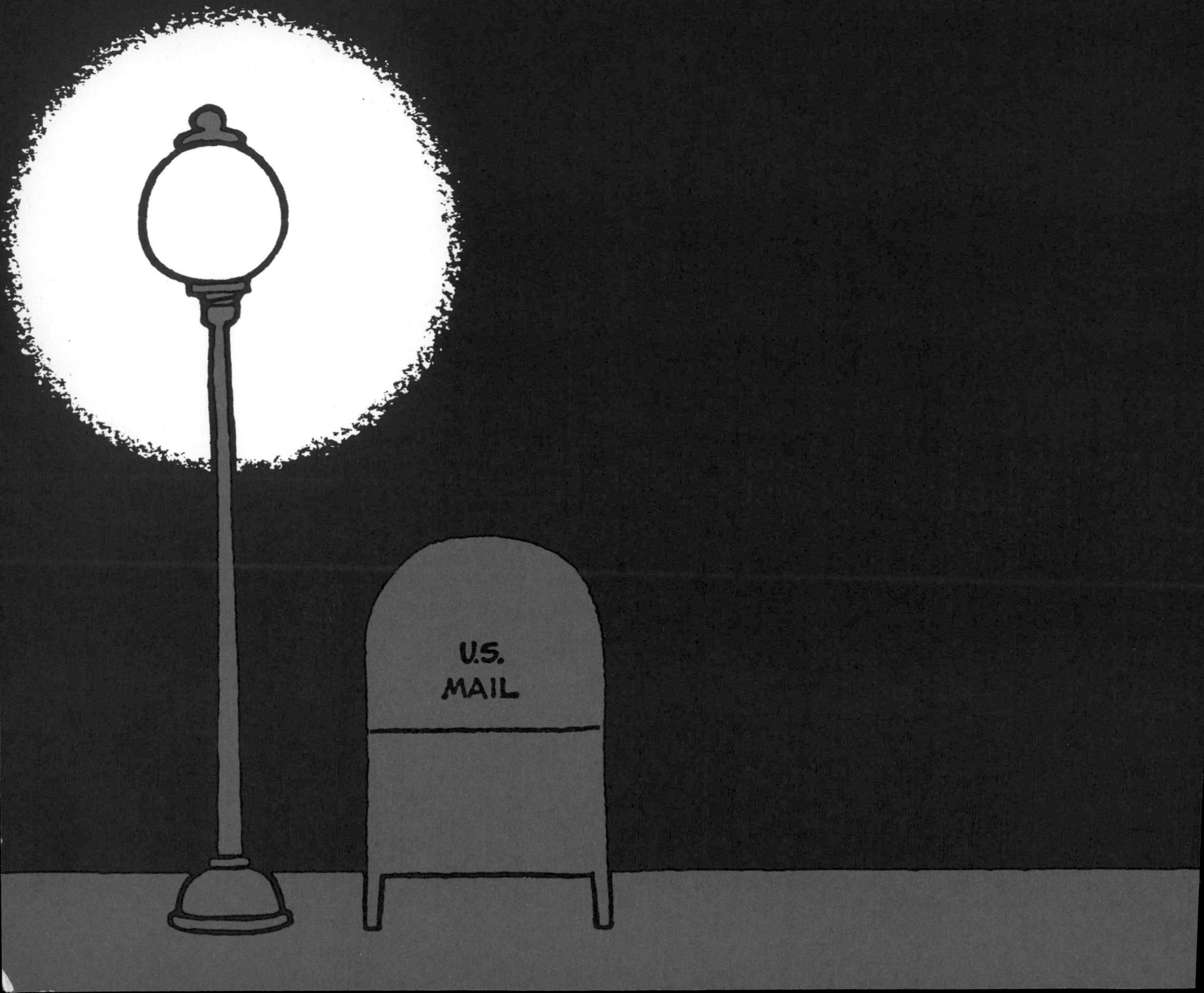
U.S.
MAIL

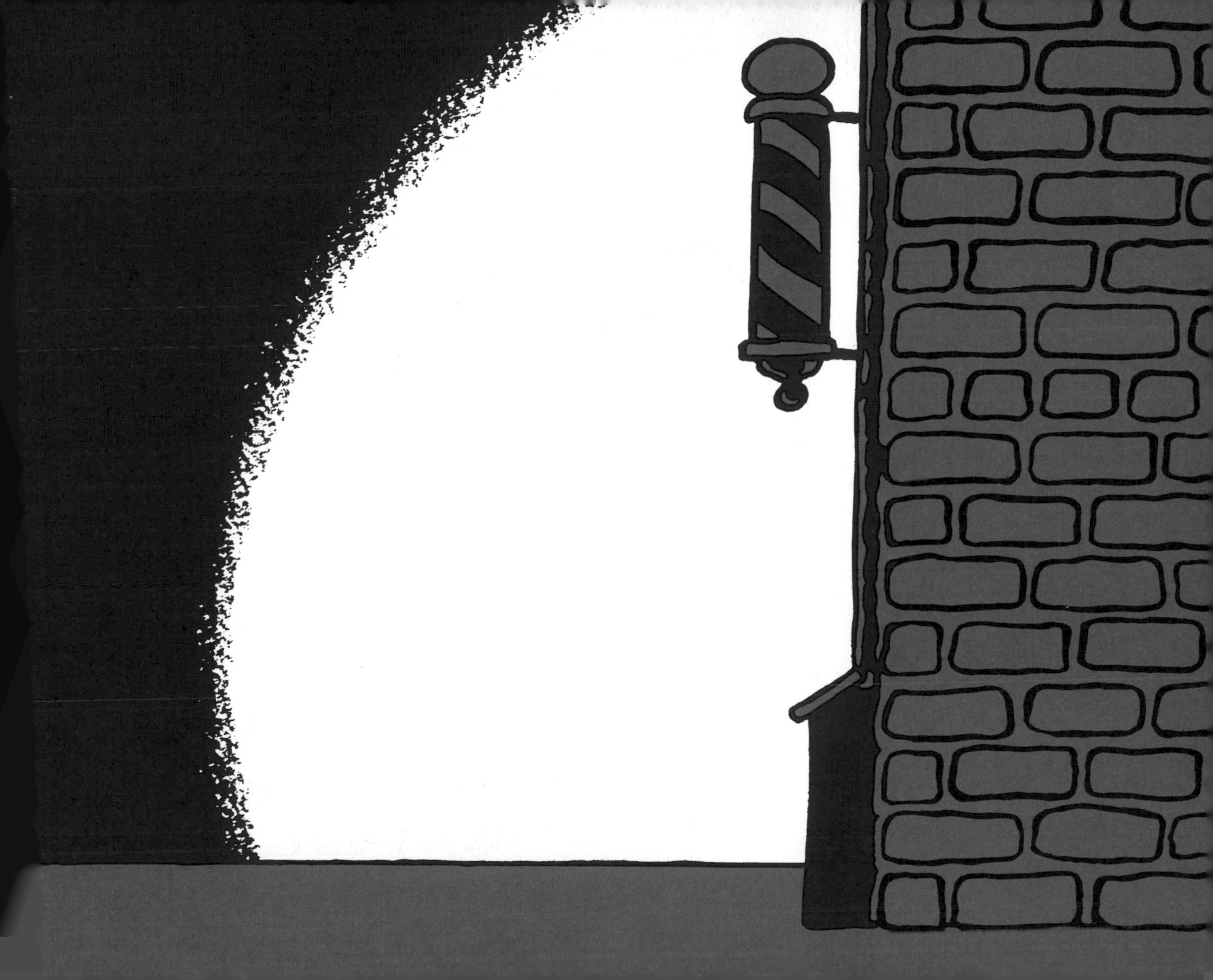

INDEX

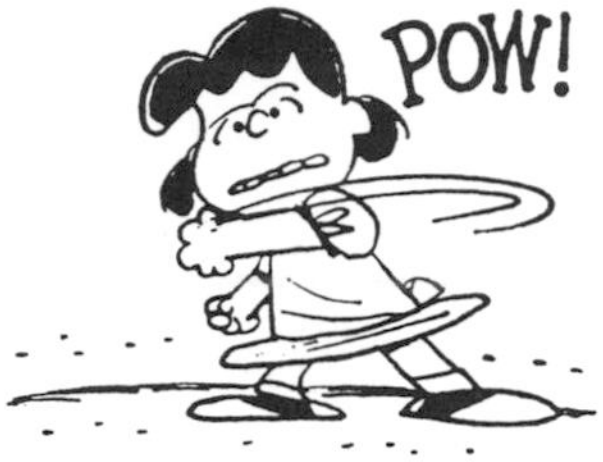
POW!

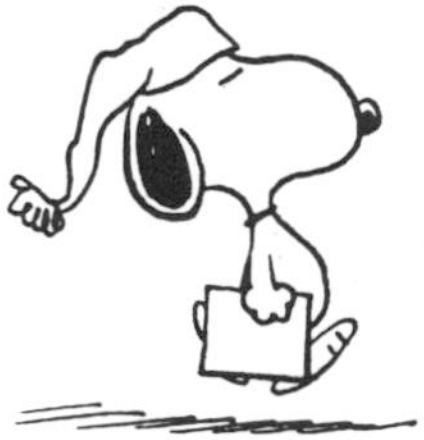

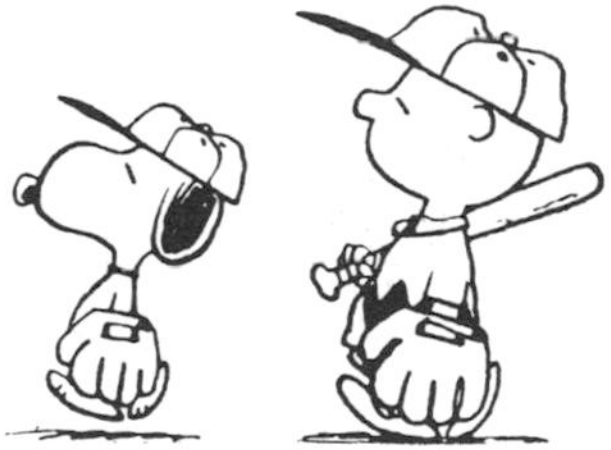

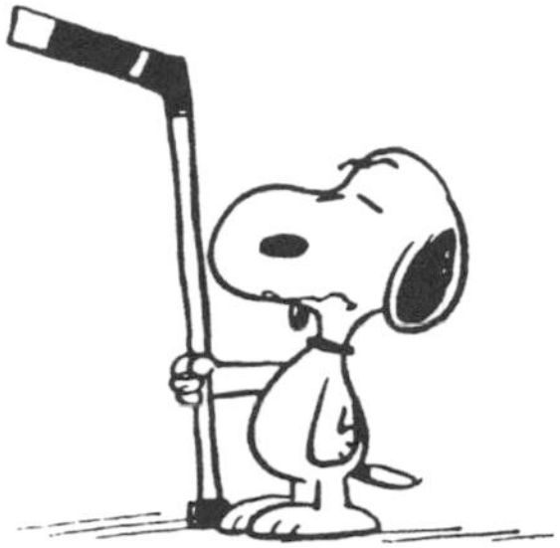

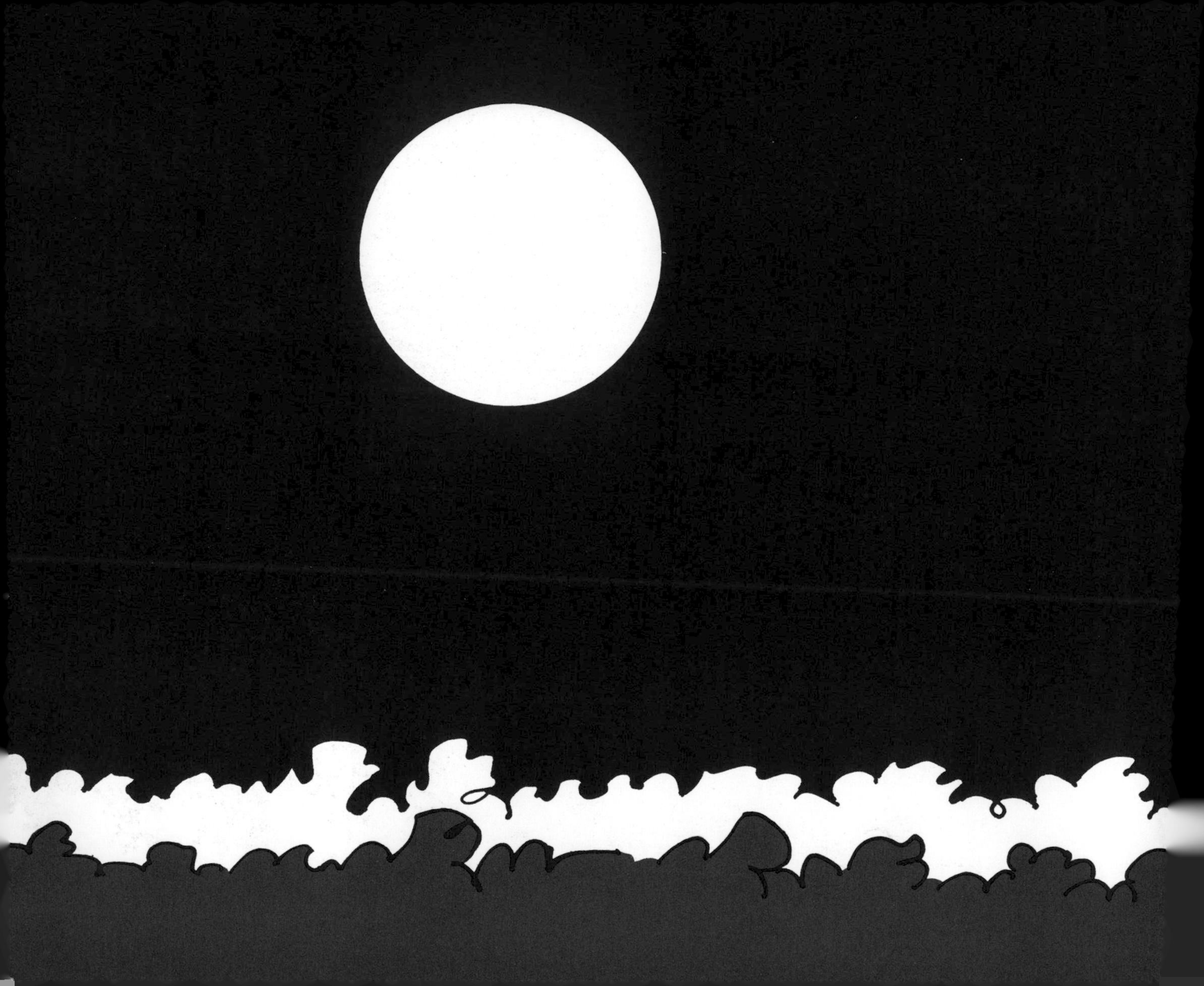

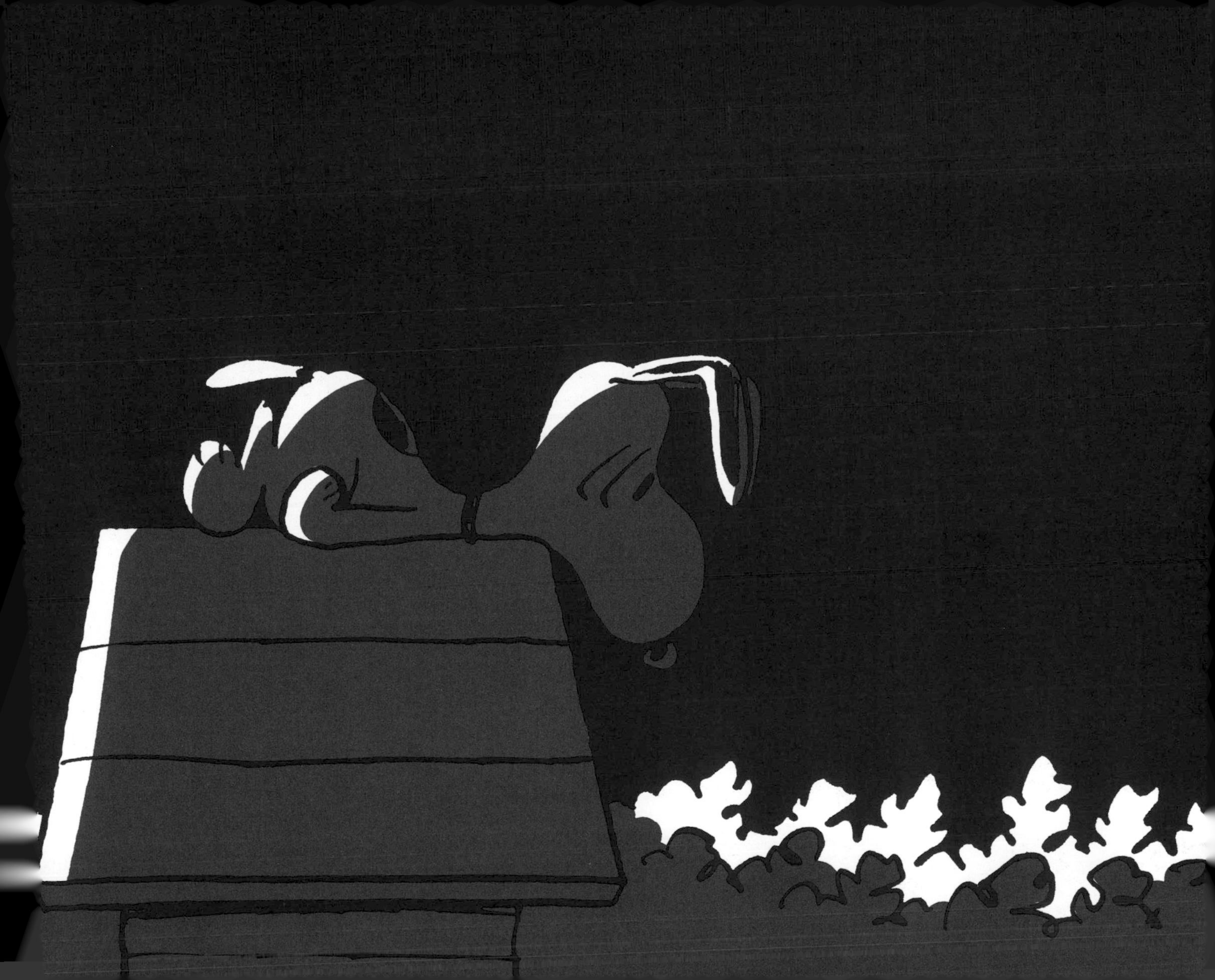

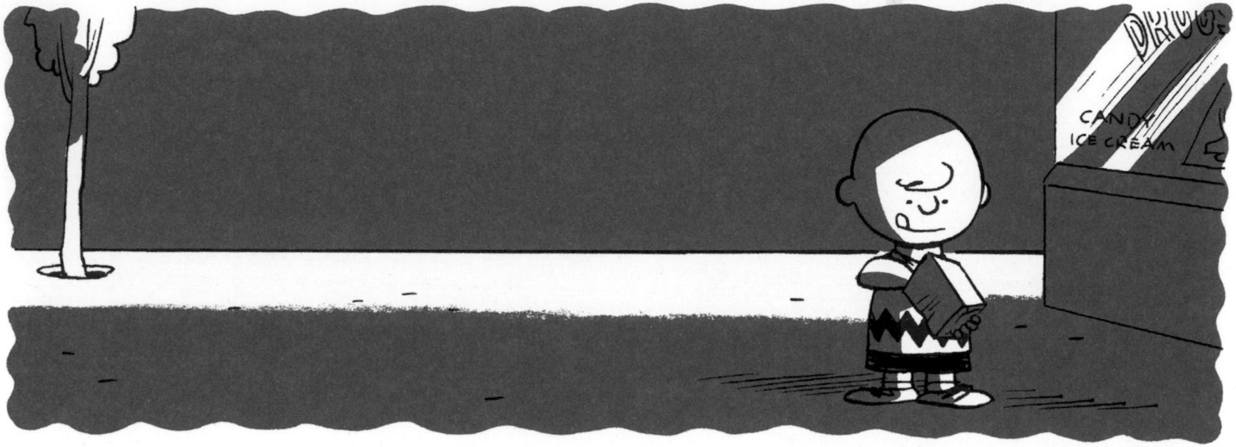

CHARLES M. SCHULZ · 1922 To 2000

Charles M. Schulz was born November 25, 1922 in Minneapolis. His destiny was foreshadowed when an uncle gave him, at the age of two days, the nickname Sparky (after the racehorse Spark Plug in the newspaper strip *Barney Google*).

Schulz grew up in St. Paul. By all accounts, he led an unremarkable, albeit sheltered, childhood. He was an only child, close to both parents, his eventual career path nurtured by his father, who bought four Sunday papers every week — just for the comics.

An outstanding student, he skipped two grades early on, but began to flounder in high school — perhaps not so coincidentally at the same time kids are going through their cruelest, most status-conscious period of socialization. The pain, bitterness, insecurity, and failures chronicled in *Peanuts* appear to have originated from this period of Schulz's life.

Although Schulz enjoyed sports, he also found refuge in solitary activities: reading, drawing, and watching movies. He bought comic books and Big Little Books, pored over the newspaper strips, and copied his favorites — *Buck Rogers*, the Walt Disney characters, *Popeye*, *Tim Tyler's Luck*. He quickly became a connoisseur; his heroes were Milton Caniff, Roy Crane, Hal Foster, and Alex Raymond.

In his senior year in high school, his mother noticed an ad in a local newspaper for a correspondence school, Federal Schools (later called Art

Instruction Schools). Schulz passed the talent test, completed the course and began trying, unsuccessfully, to sell gag cartoons to magazines. (His first published drawing was of his dog, Spike, and appeared in a 1937 *Ripley's Believe It Or Not!* installment.)

After World War II had ended and Schulz was discharged from the army, he started submitting gag cartoons to the various magazines of the time; his first breakthrough, however, came when an editor at *Timeless Topix* hired him to letter adventure comics. Soon after that, he was hired by his alma mater, Art Instruction, to correct student lessons returned by mail.

Between 1948 and 1950, he succeeded in selling 17 cartoons to the *Saturday Evening Post* — as well as, to the local *St. Paul Pioneer Press*, a weekly comic feature called *Li'l Folks*. It was run in the women's section and paid $10 a week. After writing and drawing the feature for two years, Schulz asked for a better location in the paper or for daily exposure, as well as a raise. When he was turned down on all three counts, he quit.

He started submitting strips to the newspaper syndicates. In the Spring of 1950, he received a letter from the United Feature Syndicate, announcing their interest in his submission, *Li'l Folks*. Schulz boarded a train in June for New York City; more interested in doing a strip than a panel, he also brought along the first installments of what would become *Peanuts* — and that was what sold. (The title, which Schulz loathed to his dying day, was imposed by the syndicate). The first *Peanuts* daily appeared October 2, 1950; the first Sunday, January 6, 1952.

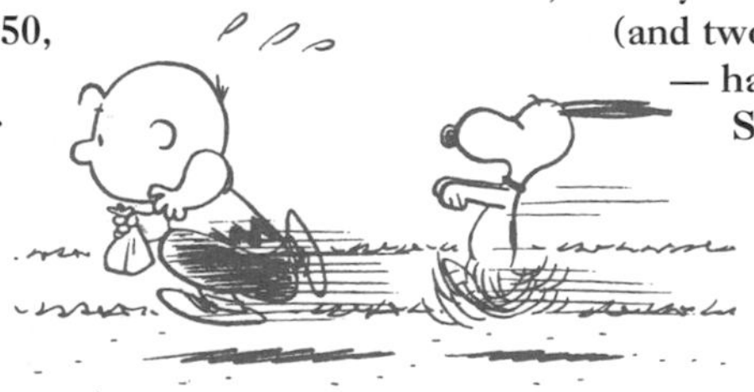

Prior to *Peanuts*, the province of the comics page had been that of gags, social and political observation, domestic comedy, soap opera, and various adventure genres. Although *Peanuts* changed, or evolved, during the 50 years Schulz wrote and drew it, it remained, as it began, an anomaly on the comics page — a comic strip about the interior crises of the cartoonist himself. After a painful divorce in 1973 from which he had not yet recovered, Schulz told a reporter, "Strangely, I've drawn better cartoons in the last six months — or as good as I've ever drawn. I don't know how the human mind works." Surely, it was this kind of humility in the face of profoundly irreducible human question that makes *Peanuts* as universally moving as it is.

Diagnosed with cancer, Schulz retired from *Peanuts* at the end of 1999. He died on February 12th 2000, the day before his last strip was published (and two days before Valentine's Day) — having completed 17,897 daily and Sunday strips, each and every one fully written, drawn, and lettered entirely by his own hand — an unmatched achievement in comics.

—Gary Groth

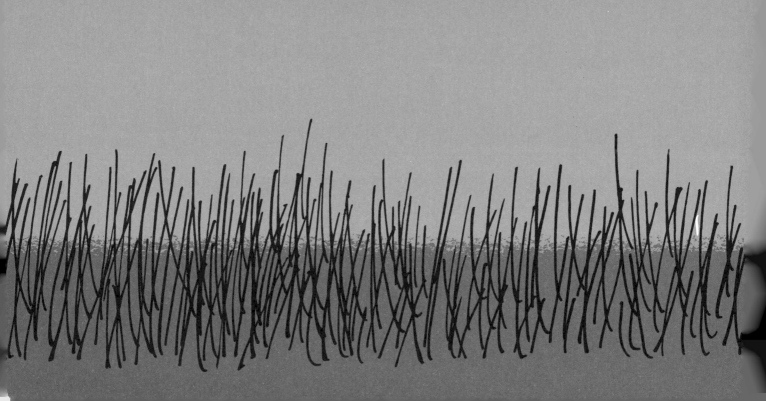

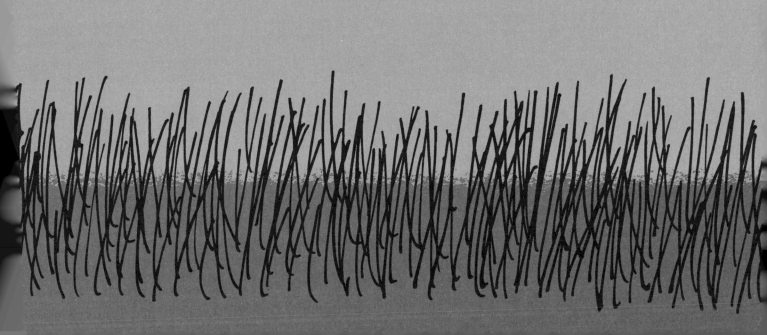

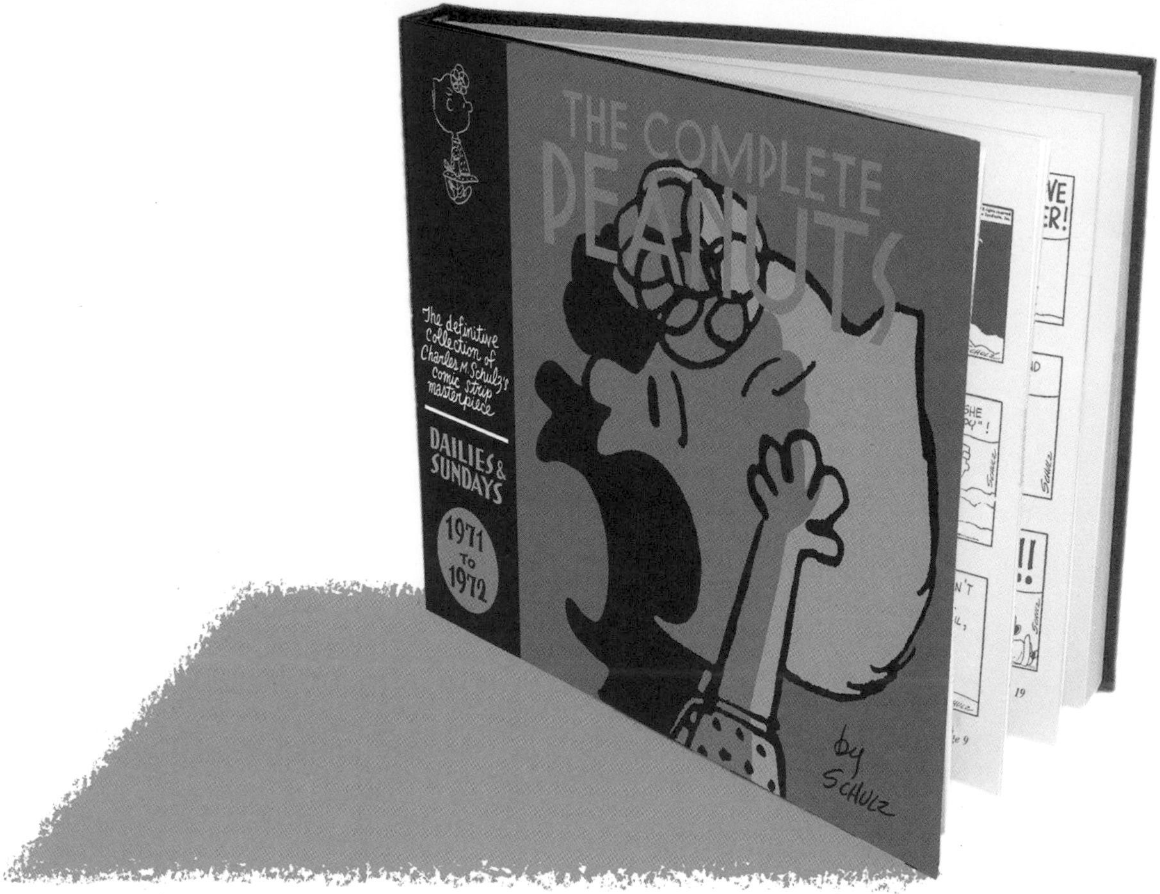

THE COMPLETE PEANUTS
The definitive collection of Charles M. Schulz's comic strip masterpiece
DAILIES & SUNDAYS
1971 TO 1972
by SCHULZ

COMING IN *THE COMPLETE PEANUTS: 1971-1972*

Snoopy turns into Joe Cool... Woodstock attends worm school and nearly gets himself eaten by the neighbor's cat... more dress-code woes for Peppermint Patty (and her new attorney isn't helping)... Peppermint Patty believes Charlie Brown's in love with her... three long stories involving Miss Helen Sweetstory of "Bunny-Wunnies" fame... the one and only Marcie ("Don't call me sir!") shows up... and the birth of Rerun Van Pelt!

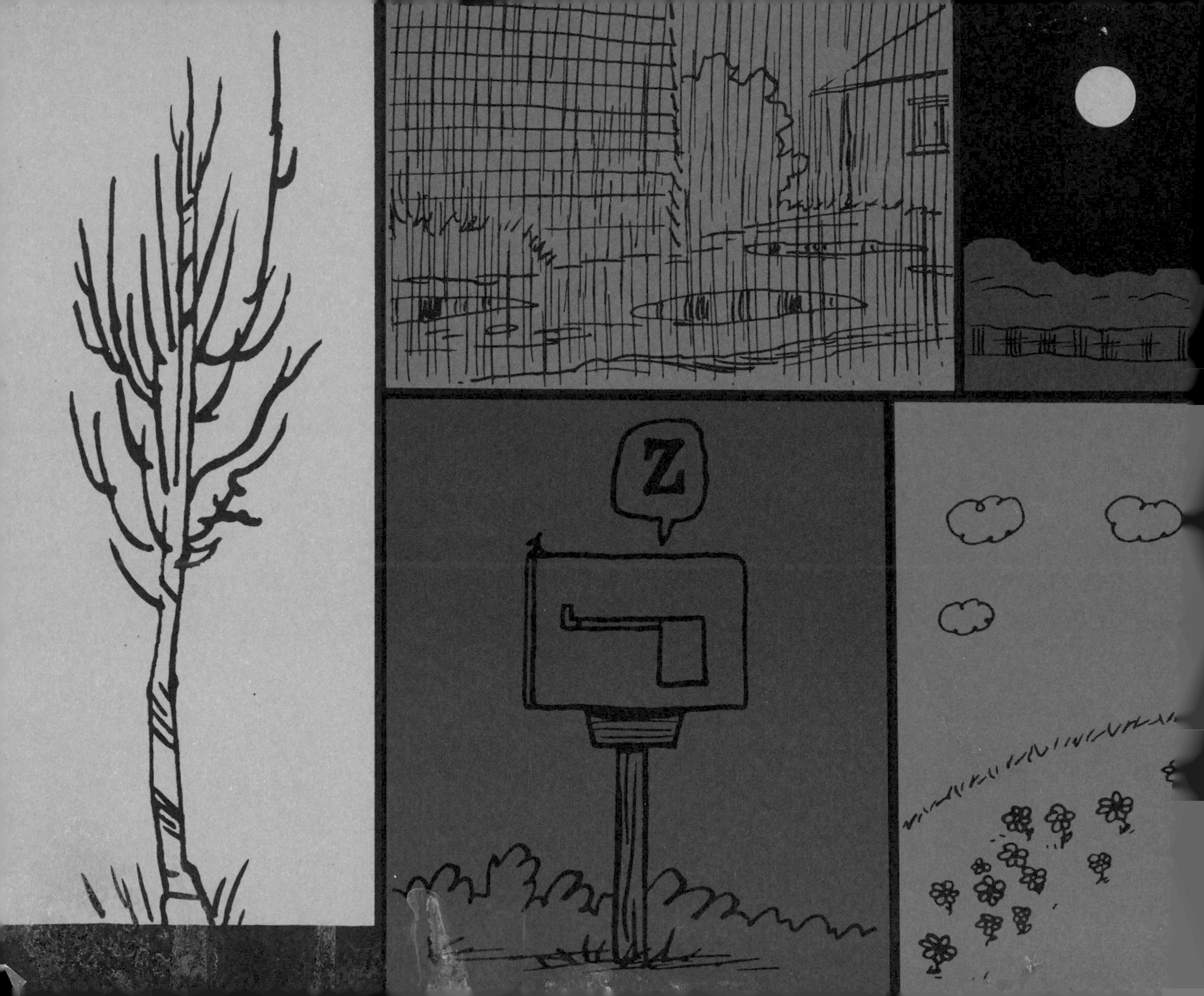
Z